LANDMARK CASES IN PUBLIC LAW

Landmark Cases in Public Law answers the need for an historical examination of the leading cases in this field, an examination which is largely absent from the standard textbooks and journal articles of the day. Adopting a contextualised historical approach, this collection of essays by leading specialists in the field provides both an explanation of the importance and impact of the chosen decisions, as well as doctrinal analysis.

This approach enables each author to throw light on the driving forces behind the judicial outcomes, and shows how the final reasoning of the court was ultimately as much dependent upon such human factors as the attitudes, conduct, and personalities of the parties, their witnesses, their counsel, and the judges, as the drive to seek legal realignment with the political developments that were widely perceived to be taking place. In this way, this form of analysis provides an expositi

REGENT LIBRARY

Library counter
T: +44 (0)203 506 9614

Library postal address
University of Westminster
Regent Library
4–12 Little Titchfield Street
London W1W 7BY

westminster.ac.uk/library

UNIVERSITY OF
WESTMINSTER♯

25 0332370 X

Landmark Cases in Public Law

Edited by
Satvinder Juss and Maurice Sunkin

·HART·
OXFORD · LONDON · NEW YORK · NEW DELHI · SYDNEY

HART PUBLISHING
Bloomsbury Publishing Plc
Kemp House, Chawley Park, Cumnor Hill, Oxford, OX2 9PH, UK

HART PUBLISHING, the Hart/Stag logo, BLOOMSBURY and the Diana logo are
trademarks of Bloomsbury Publishing Plc

First published in hardback, 2017
Paperback edition, 2018

© The Editors and Contributors 2017

The Editors and Contributors have asserted their right under the Copyright, Designs and Patents
Act 1988 to be identified as Authors of this work.

All rights reserved. No part of this publication may be reproduced or transmitted in any form
or by any means, electronic or mechanical, including photocopying, recording, or any
information storage or retrieval system, without prior permission in writing from the publishers.

While every care has been taken to ensure the accuracy of this work, no responsibility for
loss or damage occasioned to any person acting or refraining from action as a result of any
statement in it can be accepted by the authors, editors or publishers.

All UK Government legislation and other public sector information used in the work is
Crown Copyright ©. All House of Lords and House of Commons information used in the
work is Parliamentary Copyright ©. This information is reused under the terms of the Open
Government Licence v3.0 (http://www.nationalarchives.gov.uk/doc/open-government-
licence/version/3) except where otherwise stated.

All Eur-lex material used in the work is © European Union,
http://eur-lex.europa.eu/, 1998-2018.

A catalogue record for this book is available from the British Library.

Library of Congress Cataloging-in-Publication Data
Names: Juss, Satvinder S. (Satvinder Singh), editor. | Sunkin, Maurice, editor.
Title: Landmark cases in public law / Edited by Satvinder Juss and Maurice Sunkin.
Description: Portland, Oregon : Hart Publishing, 2017. | Series: Landmark cases |
Includes bibliographical references and index.
Identifiers: LCCN 2016059421 (print) | LCCN 2016059679 (ebook) | ISBN 9781849466035
(hardback : alk. paper) | ISBN 9781782255574 (Epub)
Subjects: LCSH: Constitutional law—Great Britain—Cases. | Administrative law—Great Britain—Cases.
Classification: LCC KD3930 .L36 2017 (print) | LCC KD3930 (ebook) | DDC 342.41—dc23
LC record available at https://lccn.loc.gov/2016059421

ISBN: HB: 978-1-78043-157-4
PB: 978-1-50992-583-4
ePDF: 978-1-78043-157-6
ePub: 978-1-78043-157-7

Typeset by Compuscript Ltd, Shannon

To find out more about our authors and books visit www.hartpublishing.co.uk.
Here you will find extracts, author information, details of forthcoming events and
the option to sign up for our newsletters.

FOREWORD

One purpose of a landmark is to delineate a boundary; another is to signal a significant location. Over time, a small number of cases establish themselves, or are established by others, as markers of the limits or the cardinal points of the law—in other words, as landmarks. A few—*Anisminic* for example—seem to come from almost nowhere: a well-recognised limiting principle that only errors, which vitiate the jurisdiction of subordinate bodies, are justiciable, enlarged by a kind of jurisprudential osmosis into a doctrine of universal justiciability. Others, like *GCHQ* in 1983, are links in a long chain that runs from Coke's decision in the *Case of Proclamations* in 1611, through *Ex parte Lain* in 1967, and on to *Bancoult*—for the latter, in spite of its ignoble outcome on the facts (or rather, as we now know, its supposed facts), has confirmed that prerogative acts are bounded by the principles of common law.

One case which it is pleasing to find absent from this book is *Wednesbury*. It is not so much that it took many years to acquire its canonical status (in its first decade it was referred to only twice in reported cases), for *Anisminic* too took time to bed in. It is that neither in 1948 nor since has Lord Greene's ticklist been a satisfactory account of the grounds of judicial review. The case—one of a succession of challenges to local authorities, which were misusing their new power of waiving the Sunday observance laws in order to keep cinemas closed on Sundays—was argued and decided without reference to what we now recognise as the *Padfield* principle. It is therefore appropriate that it should be the latter and not the former which features among the landmarks surveyed here. I have noted elsewhere that when Lord Diplock in 1981, in the *National Federation of the Self-Employed* case, warned that any judicial statements about public law made before 1950 were likely to be misleading, he was not just picking a conveniently tidy date: he was bringing down the curtain on *Wednesbury*, which by then was being used in the Divisional Court as if it were a complete manual of judicial review.

John W Smith, in the preface to the first edition of *Smith's Leading Cases* (1837), defined a leading case as one in which the student 'might discover those great principles of Law of which it is necessary that he should render himself thorough master, before he can trace with accuracy the numerous ramifications into which those principles are expanded in the surrounding multitude of decisions'.[1] Yet it is interesting that in the celebrated 1929 edition of *Smith's*, with Alfred Thompson

---

[1] John William Smith, Esq., *Barrister at Law*, 'A Selection of Leading Cases on Various Branches of the Law' (2nd Ed) London, Maxwell, (1841), Preface at p. v.

Denning among its editors, *Entick v Carrington* does not feature. Indeed, almost the only case in the title's two volumes which would be regarded today as a leading case is *Ashby v White*.

The present volume does not escape the telescopic effect of time. *Entick v Carrington* is the only case in it decided before the 20th century. But that is not surprising, for a landmark case is something different from a leading case: it delineates a landscape, and landscape is constantly changing. It has in fact changed while this book was in preparation. The decision of first the High Court and then the Supreme Court that ministers cannot lawfully use the treaty-making prerogative to sever the United Kingdom's statutory ties to the European Union has established no novel principle; but it has historically reasserted the primacy of parliamentary sovereignty in a constitutional upheaval, which owes at least as much to demagogy as to democracy.

Here, then, are some of the major markers of the great landscape of public law in England and Wales as it lies in the second decade of the twenty-first century.

Stephen Sedley
Oxford, September 2016

PREFACE

The contribution of the courts to the development of UK public law, which for the purposes of this volume includes constitutional and administrative law as well as human rights law, is widely recognised as having been one of the great successes of the common law.[1] Developments in public law have enabled the courts to play an increasingly central constitutional, and some would say contentious, role in the UK's still largely unwritten constitution. The overall effect has been to give greater constitutional meaning and substance to the principle of legality and the rule of law in this system.

The current volume complements previous volumes in this series, which have brought together discussions of landmark cases in areas of private law—including trusts, property law, and tort. In this book leading practitioners and academic commentators provide accounts of cases which stand out as reflecting key moments in the evolution of public law. While these cases are already well known, the authors are able to place them in their context, assess their impacts, and provide fresh insights.

Given the scale, range and dynamic nature of public law litigation, and indeed the uncertain parameters of public law itself, there can be much discussion around which cases deserve to be included in, or excluded from, a volume of landmark decisions. One problem is that there are different ways of assessing whether a case is a landmark. In his penetrating foreword to this volume, Sir Stephen Sedley offers us a sobering reminder that, '[o]ne purpose of a landmark is to delineate a boundary; another is to signal a significant location' and that, though the landmark 'delineates a landscape' the fact remains that the 'landscape is constantly changing'. In this sense, it is different from what may be designated a 'leading case'.

In the context of her discussion of *Coughlan* in chapter nine, Dr Kirsty Hughes observes that we can distinguish between 'three notions of a landmark, something that identifies the boundaries of an area, something that offers guidance or direction, and finally something that identifies a period or turning point in history'. Each of the cases discussed displays one or more of these characteristics and they justify inclusion in this volume for one or more of the following reasons. First, because they establish, illustrate, or clarify foundational principles of public law.

---

[1] Lord Diplock said that the 'rapid development in England of a rational and comprehensive system of administrative law' was 'the greatest achievement of the English courts' in his judicial career: *Racal Communications Ltd*, Re [1980] UKHL 5 at para 14. See also, *IRC v National Federation of Self-Employed and Small Businesses Ltd* [1982] AC 617 at 641, [1981] 2 All ER 93 at 104, HL.

The eighteenth-century decision in *Entick v Carrington* (discussed by Richard Gordon QC in chapter one), is a prime example, displaying the foundational requirement that public bodies must have positive legal authority if they propose to interfere with common law rights.

Second, because they mark a turning point in judicial approach, indicating a break with the past. Prime examples are the decisions of the House of Lords, led by Lord Reid, in the 1960s in *Ridge v Baldwin* (discussed by Professor S H Bailey in chapter two), *Padfield* (discussed by Professor Maurice Sunkin in chapter three), and *Anisminic* (discussed by Professor David Feldman in chapter four). These decisions are widely considered to mark a break with the past and the beginning of the modern age of public law.

Third, because they establish principles that are novel. *Anisminic*, for instance, effectively established the proposition that all errors of law go to jurisdiction. *GCHQ* (discussed by Richard Drabble QC in chapter five) established that when reviewing executive powers it does not matter that the power derives from the prerogative or from statute. *M v Home Office* (discussed by Professor Christopher Forsyth in chapter eight) showed that ministers were no longer able to claim that they were not bound to respect injunctions issued by the courts. And *Coughlan* showed the willingness of the courts to enforce substantive legitimate expectations in order to ensure fairness.

Fourth, because they help to define key constitutional relationships including those between UK legislative competence and EU law (*Factortame*, discussed by Professor John McEldowney in chapter six), courts and Parliament (*Jackson*, discussed by Professor Elizabeth Wicks in chapter ten); courts and the executive (*Bancoult*, discussed by Professor Satvinder Juss in chapter eleven, and *Evans*, discussed by Thomas Fairclough in chapter thirteen), judicial review of devolved legislative powers (*AXA*, discussed by Sir Clive Lewis in chapter twelve), and between the prerogative power of the executive and the role of Parliament (*Miller*, discussed by Professor Paul Craig in the epilogue).

This brief summary should not be taken to imply that the landmark decisions compiled in this volume can be viewed as being clear, non-controversial steps along a defined path to greater justice. As Feldman remarks 'what landmark cases decide and what they are later regarded as authority for may be very different'. This is something also recognized by Gordon, who observes that 'constitutional narratives are justificatory in nature … and … almost always fictionalise the past'. A similar point is made by Bailey, when he shows that, while *Ridge v Baldwin* is now regarded as establishing that the rules of natural justice can apply to administrative as well as judicial or quasi-judicial decisions, 'on closer inspection, the significance of the decision is more complex than that' and that this is 'not quite what it decided'. Thus, landmark decisions may only be identified as such with the benefit of hindsight.

Also, cases may be landmarks not because of the decision, but because the case provides particular insights into how judges deal with the tensions that arise when they are called upon to adjudicate on contentious public law matters. The *Padfield* case, for instance, provides an excellent opportunity to examine how judges approached the relationship between the accountability of ministers to the courts and their political accountability to Parliament. This and other cases of that period are often viewed as having stimulated the legalisation of the constitution at the expense of the political constitution. Yet here it is argued that the case shows the judges to be very much aware of the need to navigate between the legal and political spheres. The result is that they adopted an approach that shows there to be no necessary contradiction between furthering common law rights and ensuring democratic values; and that judicial review may reinforce and strengthen political accountability.

One of the obvious messages of the cases discussed in this volume is that judgments are rooted in real events and real events do not come packaged into neat distinctions such as between the legal and the political. Moreover real events are likely to be part of a dynamic process rather than static instances. For example, Feldman points out how '[t]he *Anisminic* case, in its social, political and administrative context, illustrates the interplay of social and political forces: the Commission, courts, Government departments, their legal advisers and Parliament reacting to each other within a framework which was changing in the face of profound challenges'. Drabble stresses how '[t]he professional mood in the 1960s, like the social mood, was one of decreasing deference to traditional authority, and growing willingness to question legal and social boundaries'. In this milieu, 'a major contribution of *GCHQ* was its explosion of the proposition that the scope of judicial review might vary depending on the source of the power', so that, '*GCHQ* arrived at a time when the potential for reconsideration of the position was very real'.

It would be overly simplistic to see these decisions as reflecting a single movement along a path to greater legality and justice. Nonetheless, there are clear themes running through the pages of this volume. For example, the enduring struggle to maintain and further the rule of law in circumstances where there are significant pressures in favour of its limitation. For the most part, the cases in this volume are instances of where the courts have been successful in furthering the rule of law. Thus, Forsyth stresses, when discussing *M v Home Office*, how the inclination of government officials and departments to disregard court orders and injunctions often leaves the courts powerless. In that case 'the threat to the rule of law came not only from a Minister who—on legal advice—decided not to obey a court order, but from judges who inadvertently, no doubt, fell into elementary constitutional error. The judiciary should be the reliable defender of the rule of law. In the end, with the decision of the House of Lords, it was. But before then the foundations rocked.'

The protection of personal liberty is perhaps the cardinal attribute of a system under the rule of law, and when discussing *Belmarsh* (chapter eight) Richard Clayton QC recalls that, despite the decision of the House of Lords that the nine Belmarsh prison detainees should be released, they all remained in detention—except for two who chose to leave the UK and another who had been released on bail on conditions amounting to house arrest. Nevertheless, this was a 'towering decision' which, Lord Bingham said, was the most important he had decided in his career: It was 'an arresting conclusion in a most unpromising terrain, reviewing administrative detention of aliens, where traditionally the Courts have taken a very deferential approach' and where 'the political climate in which the decision was made was intense and problematic'.

At a time when, post-Brexit, the UK faces many unprecedented challenges and anti-democratic forces are on the rise in much of the developed democratic world, the record of the courts in the cases discussed in this collection of essays will, it is hoped, serve as salutary reminder of the role of the judiciary in keeping the constitution in balance and in holding those who abuse power to account.

We would like to thank our authors for agreeing so enthusiastically to participate in this project and for providing what we trust readers will find to be fascinating and valuable accounts of the landmark cases they discuss. We also thank Elisabeth Johnston for her help with the editing and for seeing that the various chapters met the publisher's house style. We owe a huge debt of thanks to the team at Hart, and especially to Bill Asquith for his unstinting encouragement, to Chris Harrison for so expertly checking and correcting the text, and to Anne Flegel for her patience and support while seeing that the final manuscript was ready for publication. We finally thank Professor Paul Craig for letting us have his brilliantly clear and succinct account of *Miller* case (epilogue) within days of the judgment and Sir Stephen Sedley for his foreword to this volume.

Satvinder Juss and Maurice Sunkin
March 2017

CONTENTS

Foreword v
Preface vii
Notes on Contributors xv
Table of Cases xvii
Table of Legislation xxxiii

1. *Entick v Carrington* [1765]: Revisited All the King's Horses 1
   Richard Gordon
   I. Introduction 1
   II. The Facts and Issues..2
   III. Why *Entick v Carrington* is a Landmark 4

2. *Ridge v Baldwin* [1964]: 'Nuff Said'..11
   SH Bailey
   I. Introduction 11
   II. The Context: Natural Justice in the 1950s..............................11
   III. The Context: Policing...15
   IV. The Context: The Brighton Conspiracy Trial 17
   V. Reception of the Decision in *Ridge v Baldwin* 33
   VI. Conclusion..39

3. *Padfield v Ministry of Agriculture Fisheries and Food* [1968]:
   Judges and Parliamentary Democracy...43
   Maurice Sunkin
   I. Introduction 43
   II. Background 45
   III. The Issues..46
   IV. The Court Decisions 47
   V. Lord Morris's Dissent..52
   VI. The Aftermath 53
   VII. *Padfield* and the Constitutional Architecture........................54
   VIII. Conclusions 61

4. *Anisminic Ltd v Foreign Compensation Commission* [1968]:
   In Perspective 63
   David Feldman
   I. The Suez Crisis and its Consequences....................................63
   II. Sinai Mining's Dealings with the Egyptians...........................64

	III.	The UK Government Establishes the Egypt Fund 66
	IV.	Anisminic's Application to the Foreign Compensation Commission 68
	V.	Anisminic Launches a Challenge to the Determination 70
	VI.	The First-Instance Judgment of Browne J 72
	VII.	The Commission and the Foreign Office Decide Whether to Appeal 74
	VIII.	The Court of Appeal's Judgment.. 76
	IX.	Anisminic's Appeal to the House of Lords... 78
	X.	The Ratio 80
	XI.	Responses to the Judgment 1: Legislation.. 83
	XII.	Reception of the Judgment 2: The Commission re-determines Anisminic's Claim 90
	XIII.	The Demise of Anisminic Ltd.. 91
	XIV.	Anisminic's Long-term Significance 92

5. *Council of Civil Service Unions v Minister for the Civil Service* [1984]: Reviewing the Prerogative 97
   Richard Drabble
   I.   Introduction 97
   II. The Place of the GCHQ Judgment in the Development of Modern Administrative Law 100
   III. Reviewability of the Prerogative 105
   IV. GCHQ—The Prerogative in the Lords 109
   V.   Datafin 111
   VI. Conclusion... 113

6. The *Factortame* Litigation: Sovereignty in Question 115
   John McEldowney
   I.   Introduction 115
   II.   Facts of the *Factortame* Case in the Context of Britain's Maritime History... 117
   III. The Common Fisheries Policy (CFP) and the Merchant Shipping Act 1988 121
   IV.   The Litigation 127
   V.   The *Factortame* Aftermath 129
   VI.   Impact on the UK's Legal System 129
   VII. Sovereignty in Question... 131
   VIII. Conclusion... 138

7. *M v The Home Office* [1992]: Ministers and Injunctions................................ 143
   Christopher Forsyth
   I. Introduction 143
   II. A Tangled Tale: How It All Came About 144

    III. Putting the Rule of Law 'back on the rails': Part One
Proceedings for Contempt of Court 149
    IV. Putting the Rule of Law 'back on the rails': Part Two
Judicial Review and the Coercion of Ministers..................................154
    V. The Enforcement of Injunctions against Ministers:
Why Have no Ministers Been Sent to Gaol? 157
    VI. The Scottish Dimension..158
    VII. Conclusion..159

8. *A v Secretary of State for the Home Department* [2005]:
The *Belmarsh* Case 161
Richard Clayton
    I. Introduction 161
    II. The Anti-Terrorism Crime and Security Act 2001 162
    III. The Human Rights Act (HRA) 1998..166
    IV. The Issues before the House of Lords 169
    V. The House of Lords' Decision 176
    VI. The Strasbourg Decision..179

9. *R v North and East Devon Health Authority* [2001]: *Coughlan* and
the Development of Public Law..181
Kirsty Hughes
    I. Introduction 181
    II. What is a Landmark Case?...183
    III. Was *Coughlan* a Turning Point? The Law of Legitimate
Expectations prior to *Coughlan*..184
    IV. The Decision in *Coughlan*..190
    V. Limited Enforcement of Substantive Legitimate
Expectations Post-*Coughlan* 193
    VI. Setting out Guidance and Identifying the Boundaries
of a Concept—The *Coughlan* Legacy...197
    VII. Establishing the Principles of Administrative Law...........................201
    VIII. Conclusion..207

10. *R (Jackson) v Attorney-General* [2005]: Reviewing Legislation 211
Elizabeth Wicks
    I. Introduction: The Hunting Act 2004 and the
Legal Challenge in *Jackson* 211
    II. Background: The Parliament Acts..213
    III. The Judgment...220
    IV. *Jackson* in Context: The Evolution of a
Constitutional Democracy 228
    V. Parliament Limiting its own Sovereignty:
The Manner and Form Argument...232

  VI. Legal Constitutionalism: The Rule of Law as the
    Ultimate Controlling Factor 233
  VII. Conclusion..236

11. *Bancoult* and the Royal Prerogative in Colonial Constitutional Law 239
  Satvinder S Juss
  I. Introduction 239
  II. Judicial Scrutiny of Colonial Law..243
  III. The Chagos Islanders 252
  IV. Colonial Legislatures and The Rule of Law.......................................258
  V. Confusion in the House of Lords..262
  VI. Conclusion...266

12. *AXA General Insurance Ltd v HM Advocate and Others* [2012]:
  The Nature of Devolved Legislation and the Role of the Courts 271
  The Honourable Mr Justice Lewis
  I. Introduction 271
  II. The *AXA* Case..272
  III. The Structure of the Devolution Settlements....................................273
  IV. The First Issue—Determining The Scope of
    Legislative Competence...274
  V. The Second Issue—The Nature of Devolved
    Legislation and the Role of the Courts..274
  VI. Conclusion...283

13. *Evans v Attorney General* [2015]: The Underlying Normativity
  of Constitutional Disagreement...285
  Thomas Fairclough
  I. Introduction 285
  II. Entangled in a Factual Web: History of the Black
    Spider Memos Litigation 286
  III. The Justices' Judgments 289
  IV. Disagreement in the Supreme Court 292
  V. Interpreting *Evans* 295
  VI. Normative Reasoning and Doctrinal Change...................................299
  VII. Conclusion...302

Epilogue: *Miller*, the Legislature and the Executive..305
  Paul Craig
  I. Limits on Prerogative Power: The Ambiguities 306
  II. Limits on Prerogative Power: Values and
    the Resolution of Ambiguities 308
  III. Limits on Prerogative Power: The 'Legal' and the 'Political' 311

Index 315

NOTES ON CONTRIBUTORS

S H Bailey is Professor of Public Law at the University of Nottingham.

Richard Clayton QC is a barrister at Seven Bedford Row Chambers, London.

Paul Craig is Professor of English Law at the University of Oxford and Fellow of St John's College.

Richard Drabble QC is a barrister at Landmark Chambers, London.

Thomas Fairclough is AHRC PhD Candidate at Gonville and Caius College, University of Cambridge.

David Feldman is Rouse Ball Professor of English Law at the University of Cambridge and Fellow of Downing College.

Christopher F Forsyth is Emeritus Sir David Williams Professor of Public Law, Quondam Professor of Public Law and Private International Law at the University of Cambridge, and Fellow of Robinson College.

Richard Gordon QC is a barrister at Brick Court Chambers, London.

Kirsty Hughes is Fellow of Clare College, Director of Studies in Law and University Lecturer in Public Law at the University of Cambridge.

Satvinder Juss is Professor of Law at King's College London.

The Honourable Mr Justice Lewis is a Justice of the High Court of England and Wales.

John McEldowney is Professor of Law at the University of Warwick.

Maurice Sunkin is Professor of Public Law and Socio-Legal Studies at the University of Essex.

Elizabeth Wicks is Professor of Human Rights Law at the University of Leicester.

TABLE OF CASES

Australia

Kaur v Minister for Immigration and Citizenship [2012] HCA 31 208
Minister for Immigration and Multicultural Affairs, ex p Lam,
  Re [2003] HCA 6, (2003) 214 CLR 1 208
State of Victoria v Australian Building Federation [1982] 152 CLR 25 157
Union Steamship Company of Australia Pty Ltd v King [1988]
  166 CLR 1 .... 255, 264

Canada

Agraira v Canada (Minister of Public Safety and Emergency
  Preparedness) 2013 SCC 36 208
Canada (Attorney-General) v Mavi [2011] 2 SCR 504 208
Conseil des Ports Nationauxv Langlier [1969] SC 60 (Can) 150
Mount Sinai Hospital Centre v Quebec (Minister of Health
  and Social Services) [2001] 2 SCR 281 208

Hong Kong

Chiu Teng@Kallang Pted Ltd v Singapore Land Authority' [2016] Public Law 1 208
Ng Siu Tung v Director of Immigration [2002] 1 HKLRD 561 (CA (HK)) 208

New Zealand

Family First New Zealand, Re [2015] NZHC 1493 208

Singapore

Chiu Teng@Kallang Pte Ltd v Singapore Land Authority [2013] SGHC 262 208

United Kingdom

A v Secretary of State for the Home Department [2002] EWCA
  Civ 1502, [2004] QB 335, [2003] 2 WLR 564, [2003] 1 All ER 816,
  [2003] HRLR 3, [2002] UKHRR 1141, 13 BHRC 394, [2003] ACD 10,
  (2002) 99(46) LSG 33, (2002) 146 SJLB 246 (CA) 168
A v Secretary of State for the Home Department [2002] HRLR 45,
  [2002] ACD 98 (SIAC) 167

Table of Cases

A v Secretary of State for the Home Department [2004] UKHL 56, [2005] 2 AC 68, [2005] 2 WLR 87, [2005] 3 All ER 169, [2005] HRLR 1, [2005] UKHRR 175, 17 BHRC 496, [2005] Imm AR 103, (2005) 155 NLJ 23, (2005) 149 SJLB 28 (HL) 40, 161, 163, 165, 166, 167, 171, 176, 177, 179, 180

A v United Kingdom (3455/05) (2009) 49 EHRR 29, 26 BHRC 1 (ECtHR) 179

Agricultural Sector (Wales) Bill, Re. See Attorney General for England and Wales v Counsel General for Wales

Ahmed Saeed Flugreisen v Zentrale zur Bekampfung unlauteren Wettbewerbs eV (1 ZR 170/83) (No 2) [1991] ECC 261 (BG)..........................124

Amministrazione delle Finanze dello Stato v Simmenthal SpA (106/77) [1978] ECR 629, [1978] 3 CMLR 263 (ECJ).....................................131

Anisminic Ltd v Foreign Compensation Commission (Preliminary Issue: Jurisdiction)(1964) 108 SJ 541 (CA)..........................71, 72

Anisminic Ltd v Foreign Compensation Commission [1968] 2 QB 862, [1967] 3 WLR 382, [1967] 2 All ER 986, (1967) 111 SJ 374 (CA)...76, 77, 78, 91

Anisminic Ltd v Foreign Compensation Commission [1969] 2 AC 147, [1969] 2 AC 223,[1969] 2 WLR 163, [1969] 1 All ER 208, (1968) 113 SJ 55 (HL) 11, 40, 43, 49, 50, 51, 60, 63, 65, 67, 68, 70, 71, 72, 73, 74, 78, 79, 80, 81, 82, 83, 84, 85, 89, 90, 92, 93, 94, 95, 105, 179, 286

Associated Provincial Picture Houses Ltd v Wednesbury Corp [1948] 1 KB 223, [1947] 2 All ER 680, (1947) 63 TLR 623, (1948) 112 JP 55, 45 LGR 635, [1948] LJR 190, (1947) 177 LT 641, (1948) 92 SJ 26 (CA)...............................44, 103, 110, 166, 179, 182, 185, 187, 188, 189, 191, 198, 204, 207, 285, 300, 301, 302, 303

Attorney General for England and Wales v Counsel General for Wales [2014] UKSC 43, [2014] 1 WLR 2622, [2014] 4 All ER 789 (SC) 274

Attorney General of Hong Kong v Ng Yuen Shiu [1983] 2 AC 629, [1983] 2 WLR 735, [1983] 2 All ER 346, (1983) 127 SJ 188 (PC HK) 98, 102, 113, 201

Attorney General of New South Wales v Trethowan [1932] AC 526 (PC Aus)..150

Attorney General v National Assembly for Wales Commission [2012] UKSC 53, [2013] 1 AC 792, [2012] 3 WLR 1294, [2013] 1 All ER 1013 (SC)..276

AXA General Insurance Ltd, Petitioners [2011] UKSC 46, [2012] 1 AC 868, [2011] 3 WLR 871, 2012 SC (UKSC) 122, 2011 SLT 1061, [2012] HRLR 3, [2011] UKHRR 1221, (2011) 122 BMLR 149, (2011) 108(41) LSG 22 (SC) 271, 272, 274, 276, 277, 279, 280, 282, 283

Bagg's Case, Re, 77 ER 1271, (1615) 11 Co Rep 93.. 13, 23, 27, 30
Bank Mellat v HM Treasury [2013] UKSC 39, [2014] AC 700, [2013]
   3 WLR 179, [2013] 4 All ER 533, [2013] HRLR 30, [2013] Lloyd's
   Rep FC 580 (SC) 39, 204
Bates v Lord Hailsham of St Marylebone [1972] 1 WLR 1373,
   [1972] 3 All ER 1019, (1972) 116 SJ 584 (Ch D)...277
Beggs v Scottish Ministers [2005] SC 342..158
Beggs v Scottish Ministers [2007] UKHL 3, [2007] 1 WLR 455,
   2007 SLT 235, 2007 SCLR 287, (2007) 151 SJLB 258, 2007
   GWD 5-72 (HL)...158
Belgian Linguistic Case (A/6) (1979–80) 1 EHRR 252 (ECtHR) 175
Berkeley v Secretary of State for the Environment [2000] UKHL 36 (HL)............................140
BICI v Ministry of Defence [2004] EWHC 786 (QB)..7
Board of Education v Rice [1911] AC 179 (HL) 13
Boddington v British Transport Police [1999] 2 AC 143, [1998]
   2 WLR 639, [1998] 2 All ER 203, (1998) 162 JP 455, (1998)
   10 Admin LR 321, (1998) 148 NLJ 515 (HL)..93
Bradlaugh, ex p (1878) 3 QBD 509 (QBD) 73, 82
Breen v Amalgamated Engineering Union [1971] 2 QB 175, [1971]
   2 WLR 742, [1971] 1 All ER 1148, 10 KIR 120, (1971) 115 SJ 203 (CA) 43
British Broadcasting Corporation v Johns (Inspector of Taxes)
   [1965] Ch 32, [1964] 2 WLR 1071, [1964] 1 All ER 923, [1964]
   RVR 579, 10 RRC 239, 41 TC 471, (1964) 43 ATC 38, [1964] TR 45,
   (1964) 108 SJ 217 (CA)..7
British Railways Board v Pickin [1974] AC 765, [1974] 2 WLR 208,
   [1974] 1 All ER 609, (1974) 118 SJ 134 (HL) 220
Brown v Stott [2003] 1 AC 681, [2001] 2 WLR 817, [2001]
   2 All ER 97, 2001 SC (PC) 43, 2001 SLT 59, 2001 SCCR 62,
   [2001] RTR 11, [2001] HRLR 9, [2001] UKHRR 333, 11 BHRC 179,
   (2001) 3 LGLR 24, (2001) 145 SJLB 100, 2000 GWD 40-1513 (PC)................................166
Buckoke v Greater London Council [1971] Ch 655, [1971]
   2 WLR 760, [1971] 2 All ER 254, [1971] RTR 131, 69 LGR 210,
   '(1971) 115 SJ 174 (CA)..38
Burmah Oil Co (Burma Trading) Ltd v Lord Advocate [1965] AC 75,
   [1964] 2 WLR 1231, [1964] 2 All ER 348, 1964 SC (HL) 117,
   1964 SLT 218, (1964) 108 SJ 401 (HL)...43, 86
C (L) (An Infant), Re [1965] 2 QB 449, [1964] 3 WLR 1041,
   [1964] 3 All ER 483, 63 LGR 16, (1964) 108 SJ 638 (CA)..71
Calvin's Case (1608) 7 Co Rep 1a..234
Campbell v Brown [1829] 3 Wils & S 441 (HL)...82
Campbell v Hall (1774) 1 Cowp 204..256, 263
Case of Proclamations [1611] 12 Co Rep 74, 77 ER 1352 .... 4, 6, 239, 265
Case of Prohibitions [1607] EWHC J23 (KB)..6
Chagos Islanders v Attorney General [2003] EWHC 2222 (QB) (QBD)..............................241
Chagos Islanders v Attorney General [2004] EWCA Civ 997 (CA) 266
Chagos Islanders v United Kingdom (Admissibility) (35622/04)
   (2013) 56 EHRR SE15 (ECtHR) 250
Chahal v United Kingdom (22414/93) (1997) 23 EHRR 413,
   1 BHRC 405 (ECtHR) 163, 164, 165, 173

Civilian War Claimants Association Ltd v King, The [1932] AC 14 (HL) 66
Commission of the European Communities v Ireland (C-61/77 R)
    (No 2) [1977] ECR 1411 (ECJ) 124
Congreve v Home Office [1976] QB 629, [1976] 2 WLR 291,
    [1976] 1 All ER 697, (1975) 119 SJ 847 (CA) 6
Conway v Rimmer [1968] AC 910, [1968] 2 WLR 998, [1968]
    1 All ER 874, (1968) 112 SJ 191 (HL) 43
Cooper v Wandsworth Board of Works, 143 ER 414, (1863)
    14 CB NS 180 (CCP) 13, 14, 23, 27, 29
Cooper v Wilson [1937] 2 KB 309, [1937] 2 All ER 726 (CA)................................... 17, 21, 24
Costa v Ente Nazionale per l'Energia Elettrica (ENEL) (6/64)
    [1964] ECR 585, [1964] CMLR 425 (ECJ) 131
Council for Civil Service Unions v Minister for the Civil Service
    [1985] AC 374, [1984] 3 WLR 1174, [1984] 3 All ER 935,
    [1985] ICR 14, [1985] IRLR 28, (1985) 82 LSG 437, (1984)
    128 SJ 837 (HL)..6, 7, 44, 72, 97, 98, 201,
                                                                                                        257, 268, 285
Council of Civil Service Unions v Minister for the Civil
    Service [1984] UKHL 9 254
Davidson v Scottish Ministers (No 1) [2005] UKHL 74,
    2006 SC (HL) 41, 2006 SLT 110, 2006 SCLR 249, 2006 GWD 4-72 (HL) 159
Dawkins v Antrobus (1881) 17 Ch D 615 (Ch D)..27
Day v Savadge (1614) Hob 84 (KB) 234
De Freitas v Benny [1976] AC 239, [1975] 3 WLR 388, [1976]
    Crim LR 50, (1975) 119 SJ 610 (PC T&T)..106
De Verteuil v Knaggs [1918] AC 557 (PC)... 22, 27, 29
Duke v GEC Reliance Ltd [1988] AC 618, [1988] 2 WLR 359,
    [1988] 1 All ER 626, [1988] 1 CMLR 719, [1988] ICR 339,
    [1988] IRLR 118, [1988] 1 FTLR 398, (1988) 85(11) LSG 42,
    (1988) 132 SJ 226 (HL)... 120, 132
Durayappah v Fernando [1967] 2 AC 337, [1967] 3 WLR 289,
    [1967] 2 All ER 152, (1967) 111 SJ 397 (PC Cey) 30, 38
Edinburgh & Dalkeith Railway v Wauchope, 8 ER 279, (1842)
    8 Cl & F.710 (HL)..220
Edwards (Inspector of Taxes) v Bairstow [1956] AC 14, [1955]
    3 WLR 410, [1955] 3 All ER 48, 48 R & IT 534, 36 TC 207,
    (1955) 34 ATC 198, [1955] TR 209, (1955) 99 SJ 558 (HL)..103
Ellis v Earl Grey, 58 ER 574, (1833) 6 Sim. 214 (Ct of Ch) 150
Entick v Carrington [1765] 2 Wilson KB 275, 85 ER 807,
    19 Howell's State Trials 1029 ....2, 3, 4, 5, 6, 7, 8,
                                                                                                        9, 10, 55, 179
Evans v Attorney-General. See R (Evans) v Attorney General
Evans v Information Commissioner [2012] UKUT 313 (AAC)................................287, 288
Evans v McLoughlan (1861) 4 LT 31 or above 67, 73
Findlay, Re [1985] AC 318, [1984] 3 WLR 1159, [1984] 3 All ER 801,
    [1985] Crim LR 154, (1985) 82 LSG 38, (1984) 128 SJ 816 (HL) 182, 185, 186

Fisher (Louis Walter) v Keane (1878) 11 Ch D 353 (Ch D) 27, 29, 30
Fraser v Mudge [1975] 1 WLR 1132, [1975] 3 All ER 78,
    (1975) 119 SJ 508 (CA)..38
Fry, ex p [1954] 1 WLR 730, [1954] 2 All ER 118, (1954) 118 JP 313,
    52 LGR 320, (1954) 98 SJ 318 (CA) 14, 38
Furnell v Whangerei High Schools Board [1973] AC 660, [1973]
    2 WLR 92, [1973] 1 All ER 400, (1972) 117 SJ 56 (PC NZ)...37
G v Secretary of State for the Home Department S.C./2/2002,
    Bail Application SCB/10, 20 May 2004 161
G, Re (Adoption: Unmarried Couple) [2009] 1 AC 38...170
Gaiman v National Association for Mental Health [1971]
    Ch 317, [1970] 3 WLR 42, [1970] 2 All ER 362, (1970) 114 SJ 416 (Ch D)................38
Garland v British Rail Engineering Ltd (12/81) [1982]
    2 All ER 402, [1982] ECR 359, [1982] 1 CMLR 696,
    [1982] IRLR 111 (ECJ) 120, 131
Gaygusuz v Austria (17371/90) (1997) 23 EHRR 364 (ECtHR) 175
Geys v Societe Generale [2012] UKSC 63, [2013] 1 AC 523,
    [2013] 2 WLR 50, [2013] 1 All ER 1061, [2013] ICR 117,
    [2013] IRLR 122 (SC)...27
Ghaidan v Godin-Mendoza [2004] UKHL 30, [2004] 2 AC 557,
    [2004] 3 WLR 113, [2004] 3 All ER 411, [2004] 2 FLR 600,
    [2004] 2 FCR 481, [2004] HRLR 31, [2004] UKHRR 827,
    16 BHRC 671, [2004] HLR 46, [2005] 1 P & CR 18, [2005]
    L & TR 3, [2004] 2 EGLR 132, [2004] Fam Law 641, [2004]
    27 EG 128 (CS), (2004) 101(27) LSG 30, (2004) 154 NLJ 1013,
    (2004) 148 SJLB 792, [2004] NPC 100, [2004] 2 P & CR DG17 (HL)...................39, 51
Gillick v West Norfolk and Wisbech AHA [1986] AC 112, [1985]
    3 WLR 830, [1985] 3 All ER 402, [1986] Crim LR 113, (1985)
    82 LSG 3531, (1985) 135 NLJ 1055, (1985) 129 SJ 738 (HL) 102
Glynn v Keele University [1971] 1 WLR 487, [1971] 2 All ER 89,
    (1970) 115 SJ 173 (Ch D) 38
Gouriet v Union of Post Office Workers [1978] AC 435, [1977]
    3 WLR 300, [1977] 3 All ER 70, (1977) 121 SJ 543 (HL)..106
Granovski v Secretary of State for the Home Department [2015]
    EWHC 1478 (Admin) (QBD)...194
Hedley Byrne & Co Ltd v Heller & Partners Ltd [1964] AC 465,
    [1963] 3 WLR 101, [1963] 2 All ER 575, [1963] 1 Lloyd's Rep 485,
    (1963) 107 SJ 454 (HL)...39
Her Majesty's Treasury v Ahmed and Others [2010] UKSC 2, [2010]
    2 AC 534, [2010] 2 WLR 378, [2010] 4 All ER 745, [2010] HRLR 15,
    [2010] UKHRR 204, [2010] Lloyd's Rep FC 217, (2010) 154(4) SJLB 28 (SC).................7
HK (An Infant), Re [1967] 2 QB 617, [1967] 2 WLR 962, [1967]
    1 All ER 226, (1967) 111 SJ 296 (QBD)..36, 37
Hogg v Scott [1947] KB 759, [1947] 1 All ER 788, 63 TLR 320,
    (1947) 111 JP 282, 1948] LJR 666, 177 LT 32, (1947) 91 SJ 264 (KBD) 17
Hopkins v Smethwick Local Board of Health (1890) 24 QBD 712 (CA) 27, 29

Huang v Secretary of State for the Home Department [2007]
    UKHL 11, [2007] 2 AC 167, [2007] 2 WLR 581, [2007] 4 All ER 15,
    [2007] 1 FLR 2021, [2007] HRLR 22, [2007] UKHRR 759,
    24 BHRC 74, [2007] Imm AR 571, [2007] INLR 314, [2007]
    Fam Law 587, (2007) 151 SJLB 435 (HL) 172, 204, 264
Indelicato v Italy (31143/96) (2002) 35 EHRR 40 (ECtHR) 164
Internationale Handelsgesellschaft mbH v Einfuhr- und Vorratsstelle
    fur Getreide und Futtermittel (11/70) [1970] ECR 1125, [1972]
    CMLR 255 (ECJ) 131
Jackson v Attorney-General. See R (Jackson) v Attorney General
Jayawardane (Don Leonard) v VP Silva [1970] 1 WLR 1365, (1970)
    114 SJ 787 (PC Cey) 38
Julius v Lord Bishop of Oxford (1880) 5 App Cas 214 (HL) 48
Kennedy v Charity Commission [2014] UKSC 20, [2015] AC 455,
    [2014] 2 WLR 808, [2014] 2 All ER 847, [2014] EMLR 19, [2014]
    HRLR 14, (2014) 158(13) SJLB 37 (SC) 135, 203, 282, 301
Kilduff v Wilson [1939] 1 All ER 429 17
L v Birmingham City Council [2007] EWCA Civ 26, [2008] QB 1,
    [2007] 2 WLR 1097, [2007] HRLR 15, [2007] UKHRR 645, [2007]
    BLGR 241, (2007) 10 CCL Rep 7, (2007) 95 BMLR 33, [2007]
    MHLR 69, (2007) 151 SJLB 199, [2007] NPC 12 (CA) 196
L v Birmingham City Council [2007] UKHL 27, [2008] 1 AC 95,
    [2007] 3 WLR 112, [2007] 3 All ER 957, [2007] HRLR 32, [2008]
    UKHRR 346, [2007] HLR 44, [2008] BLGR 273, (2007) 10 CCL
    Rep 505,[2007] LS Law Medical 472, (2007) 96 BMLR 1, (2007)
    104(27) LSG 29, (2007) 157 NLJ 938, (2007) 151 SJLB 860, [2007]
    NPC 75 (HL) 196
Lapointe v L'Association de Bienfaisance et de Retraite de la Police
    de Montreal [1906] AC 535 (PC Canada) 27
Lee v Bude & Torrington Junction Rly Co (1870–71) LR 6 CP 576 235
Litster v Forth Dry Dock & Engineering Co Ltd [1990] 1 AC 546,
    [1989] 2 WLR 634, [1989] 1 All ER 1134, 1989 SC (HL) 96,
    1989 SLT 540, [1989] 2 CMLR 194, [1989] ICR 341, [1989] IRLR 161,
    (1989) 86(23) LSG 18, (1989) 139 NLJ 400, (1989) 133 SJ 455 (HL) 132
Liversidge v Anderson [1942] AC 206, [1941] 3 All ER 338 (HL) 28, 39, 44, 179, 262
Liyanage (Don John Francis Douglas) v Queen, The [1967]
    1 AC 259, [1966] 2 WLR 682, [1966] 1 All ER 650, [1966]
    Crim LR 102, (1966) 110 SJ 14 (PC Cey) 260, 261
M v Home Office [1992] QB 270, [1992] 2 WLR 73, [1992]
    4 All ER 97, [1992] COD 97, (1991) 141 NLJ 1663 (CA) 143, 144, 145, 146
M v Home Office [1994] 1 AC 377, [1993] 3 WLR 433, [1993]
    3 All ER 537, (1995) 7 Admin LR 113, (1993) 90(37) LSG 50,
    (1993) 143 NLJ 1099, (1993) 137 SJLB 199 (HL) 4, 129, 144, 145, 146,
                                                                                              149, 150, 151, 152, 154,
                                                                                              157, 158, 160, 240
Macarthys Ltd v Smith (Reference to ECJ) [1979] 1 WLR 1189,
    [1979] 3 All ER 325, [1979] 3 CMLR 44, [1979] 3 CMLR 381,
    [1979] ICR 785, [1979] IRLR 316, (1979) 123 SJ 603 (CA) 120, 131

Maradana Mosque (Board of Trustees) v Badiuddin Mahmud
[1967] 1 AC 13, [1966] 2 WLR 921, [1966] 1 All ER 545, (1966)
110 SJ 310 (PC Cey)...38
Marshall v Southampton and South West Hampshire AHA (152/84)
[1986] QB 401, [1986] 2 WLR 780, [1986] 2 All ER 584, [1986]
ECR 723, [1986] 1 CMLR 688, [1986] ICR 335, [1986] IRLR 140,
(1986) 83 LSG 1720, (1986) 130 SJ 340 (ECJ)..132
Matadeen v Pointu [1999] 1 AC 98, [1998] 3 WLR 18, (1998)
142 SJLB 100 (PC Maur) 175
Maxwell v Department of Trade and Industry [1974] QB 523,
[1974] 2 WLR 338, [1974] 2 All ER 122, (1974) 118 SJ 203 (CA)....................38
McCartan Turkington Breen v Times Newspapers Ltd [2001]
2 AC 277, [2000] 3 WLR.1670, [2000] 4 All ER 913, [2000] NI 410,
[2001] EMLR 1, [2001] UKHRR 184, 9 BHRC 497, (2000) 97(47)
LSG 40, (2000) 150 NLJ 1657, (2000) 144 SJLB 287 (HL)..............................166
McCarthy & Stone (Developments) Ltd v Richmond-upon-Thames
LBC [1992] 2 AC 48, [1991] 3 WLR 941, [1991] 4 All ER 897,
90 LGR 1, (1992) 4 Admin. LR 223, (1992) 63 P & CR 234, [1992]
1 PLR 131, [1992] JPL 467, [1991] EG 118 (CS), (1992) 89(3) LSG 33,
(1991) 141 NLJ 1589, (1991) 135 SJLB 206, [1991] NPC 118 (HL) 10
McDonald (James McFarlane) v Secretary of State for Scotland (No 1)
1994 SC 234, 1994 SLT 692, 1994 SCLR 318 (CSIH) 158, 159
McKerr's Application for Judicial Review, Re [2004] UKHL 12, [2004]
1 WLR 807, [2004] 2 All ER 409, [2004] NI 212, [2004] HRLR 26,
[2004] UKHRR 385, 17 BHRC 68, [2004] Lloyd's Rep Med 263,
[2004] Inquest LR 35, (2004) 101(13) LSG 33, (2004) 148 SJLB 355 (HL)....170
Merricks v Heathcoat-Amory [1955] Ch 567, [1955] 3 WLR 56, [1955]
2 All ER 453, (1955) 99 SJ 400 (Ch D)...153, 154, 160
Moohan, Petitioner [2014] UKSC 67, [2015] AC 901, [2015]
2 WLR 141, [2015] 2 All ER 361, 2015 SC (UKSC) 1, 2015 SLT 2,
2015 GWD 1-1 (SC) 280
Nakkuda Ali v MF de S Jayaratne [1951] AC 66, 66 TLR (Pt 2) 214,
(1950) 10 CR 421, (1950) 94 SJ 516 (PC) 12, 14, 22, 23, 26, 28, 29,
30, 31, 32, 35, 36, 37, 38
Noakes v Smith [1942] 107 JP 101 17
O'Reilly v Mackman [1983] 2 AC 237, [1982] 3 WLR 1096, [1982]
3 All ER 1124, (1982) 126 SJ 820 (HL) 38, 70, 94, 98, 101, 112
Osborn v Parole Board [2013] UKSC 61, [2014] AC 1115, [2013]
3 WLR 1020, [2014] 1 All ER 369, [2014] NI 154, [2014] HRLR 1,
(2013) 157(39) SJLB 37 (SC)...57, 135, 282
Osgood v Nelson (1871–72) LR 5 HL 636 (HL) 29
Padfield v Minister of Agriculture, Fisheries and Food [1968]
AC 997, [1968] 2 WLR 924, [1968] 1 All ER 694, (1968)
112 SJ 171 (HL)... 11, 40, 43, 44, 45, 46, 47, 48,
50, 51, 52, 53, 54, 55, 56, 57,
58, 59, 60, 61, 106, 150
Paponette v Attorney General of Trinidad and Tobago [2010]
UKPC 32, [2012] 1 AC 1, [2011] 3 WLR 219 (PC Trin & Tob).............193, 194

Pearlberg v Varty (Inspector of Taxes) [1972] 1 WLR 534, [1972]
   2 All ER 6, 48 TC 14, [1972] TR 5, (1972) 116 SJ 335 (HL) 38, 93
Pearlman v Keepers and Governors of Harrow School [1979]
   QB 56, [1978] 3 WLR 736, [1979] 1 All ER 365, (1979)
   38 P & CR 136, (1978) 247 EG 1173, [1978] JPL 829 (CA) 93
Pepper (Inspector of Taxes) v Hart [1993] AC 593, [1992]
   3 WLR 1032, [1993] 1 All ER 42, [1992] STC 898, [1993]
   ICR 291, [1993] IRLR 33, [1993] RVR 127, (1993) 143 NLJ 17,
   [1992] NPC 154 (HL) 179, 262
Pergamon Press, Re [1971] Ch 388, [1970] 3 WLR 792, [1970]
   3 All ER 535, (1970) 114 SJ 569 (CA) 38
Pham v Secretary of State for the Home Department [2015]
   UKSC 19, [2015] 1 WLR 1591, [2015] 3 All ER 1015, [2015]
   2 CMLR 49, [2015] Imm AR 950, [2015] INLR 593 (SC) 203, 301
Phillips v Eyre (1868–69) LR 4 QB 225 (QB) 260
Phillips v Eyre (1870–71) LR 6 QB 1 (Ct of Exch) 260, 261
Pickstone v Freemans Plc [1989] AC 66, [1988] 3 WLR 265,
   [1988] 2 All ER 803, [1988] 3 CMLR 221, [1988] ICR 697,
   [1988] IRLR 357, (1988) 138 NLJ Rep 193 (HL) 120
R (on the application of Miller) v The Secretary of State for Exiting
   the European Union [2016] EWHC 2768 (Admin) 305
R (on the application of Miller) v Secretary of State for Exiting
   the European Union [2017] UKSC 5 305
R v Aston University Senate ex p Roffey [1969] 2 QB 538,
   [1969] 2 WLR 1418, [1969] 2 All ER 964, (1969) 133 JP 463,
   (1969) 113 SJ 308 (DC) 38
R v Barnsley MBC ex p Hook [1976] 1 WLR 1052, [1976] 3 All ER 452,
   74 LGR 493, (1976) 120 SJ 182 (CA) 37, 38
R v Bolton, 113 ER 1054, (1841) 1 QB 66 (KB) 73
R v Bow Street Metropolitan Stipendiary Magistrate ex p Pinochet
   Ugarte (No 2) [2000] 1 AC 119, [1999] 2 WLR 272, [1999]
   1 All ER 577, 6 BHRC 1, (1999) 11 Admin LR 57, (1999) 96(6)
   LSG 33, (1999) 149 NLJ 88 (HL) 169
R v Brent LBC ex p Gunning, 84 LGR 168 (QBD) 191
R v Budimir (Nikolas) [2010] EWCA Crim 1486, [2011] QB 744,
   [2011] 2 WLR 396, [2011] 3 All ER 206, [2010] 2 Cr App R 29,
   [2010] 3 CMLR 50, [2010] Eu LR 778, [2011] LLR 277, [2011]
   Crim LR 142 (CA) 134
R v Cambridge University ex p Bentley, 93 ER 698, (1724) 2 Ld Raym
   1334, (1723) 8 Mod 148, (1723) 1 Str 557 .... 13, 23, 30
R v Chief Constable of North Wales ex p Evans [1982] 1 WLR 1155,
   [1982] 3 All ER 141, (1983) 147 JP 6, (1982) 79 LSG 1257, (1982)
   126 SJ 549 (HL) 56, 166
R v Commissioner of Police of the Metropolis ex p Parker [1953]
   1 WLR 1150, [1953] 2 All ER 717, (1953) 117 JP 440, (1953)
   97 SJ 590 (QBD) 14, 23, 30, 31, 32, 35, 37
R v Commissioners of Her Majesty's Woods, Forests, Land
   Revenues, Works and Buildings for the time being (ex p Budge)
   117 ER 646, (1850) 15 QB 761 (KB) 150

R v Criminal Injuries Compensation Board ex p Lain [1967]
2 QB 864, [1967] 3 WLR 348, [1967] 2 All ER 770, (1967)
111 SJ 331, QBD 98, 100, 102,106, 109, 111, 113
R v Customs and Excise Commissioners ex p Cook [1970]
1 WLR 450, [1970] 1 All ER 1068, (1969) 114 SJ 34 (DC) 150
R v Electricity Commissioners ex p London Electricity Joint
Committee Co (1920) Ltd [1924] 1 KB 171 (CA) 27, 28, 29, 30, 38, 107
R v Foreign Compensation Commission ex p Oak and Timber
Co Ltd, unreported, 11 November 1955 74
R v Gaming Board for Great Britain ex p Benaim [1970] 2 QB 417,
[1970] 2 WLR 1009, [1970] 2 All ER 528, (1970) 114 SJ 266 (CA) 37
R v Governor of Brixton Prison ex p Armah (No 1) [1968] AC 192,
[1966] 3 WLR 828, [1966] 3 All ER 177, (1967) 131 JP 43, (1966)
110 SJ 890 (HL) 79
R v Governor of Brixton Prison ex p Soblen (No 2) [1963] 2 QB 243 (CA) 37
R v Governor of Durham Prison ex p Singh [1984] 1 WLR 704,
[1984] 1 All ER 983, [1983] Imm AR 198, (1984) 128 SJ 349 (QBD) 164
R v Governor of Pentonville Prison ex p Herbage [1987] QB 872,
[1986] 3 WLR 504, [1986] 3 All ER 209, (1986) 83 LSG 2750,
(1986) 130 SJ 697 (QBD) 155
R v Hammersley (1958) 42 Cr App R 207 (CA) 17
R v Horseferry Road Magistrates' Court ex p Bennett [1994]
1 AC 42, [1993] 3 WLR 90, [1993] 3 All ER 138, (1994) 98
Cr App R 114, [1994] COD 123, (1993) 157 JPN 506, (1993)
143 NLJ 955, (1993) 137 SJLB 159 (HL) 10
R v Hull University Visitor ex p Page [1993] AC 682, [1992]
3 WLR 1112, [1993] 1 All ER 97, [1993] ICR 114, (1993) 143 NLJ 15,
(1993) 137 SJLB 45 (HL) 93
R v Hurst (Judge Sir Donald) ex p Smith [1960] 2 QB 133, [1960] 2 WLR
961, [1960] 2 All ER 385, 58 LGR 348, (1960) 104 SJ 468 (QBD) 67, 73, 82
R v IRC ex p MFK Underwriting Agents Ltd [1990] 1 WLR 1545,
[1990] 1 All ER 91, [1990] STC 873, 62 TC 607, [1990] COD 143,
(1989) 139 NLJ 1343 (QBD) 201
R v IRC ex p National Federation of Self Employed and Small
Businesses Ltd [1982] AC 617, [1981] 2 WLR 722, [1981] 2 All ER 93,
[1981] STC 260, 55 TC 133, (1981) 125 SJ 325, HL 100, 105
R v IRC ex p Preston [1985] AC 835, [1985] 2 WLR 836, [1985]
2 All ER 327, [1985] STC 282, 59 TC 1 (HL) 201
R v IRC ex p Unilever Plc [1996] STC 681, 68 TC 205, [1996]
COD 421 (CA) 202
R v Legislative Committee of the Church Assembly ex p
Haynes-Smith [1928] 1 KB 411 (KBD) 23, 29, 30
R v Leman Street Police Station Inspector ex p Venicoff [1920]
3 K.B. 72 (KBD) 13
R v Licensing Authority ex p Smith Kline & French Laboratories
Ltd (No 2) [1990] 1 QB 574, [1989] 2 WLR 378, [1989]
2 All ER 113, (1989) 133 SJ 263 (CA) 155

R v Liverpool Corp ex p Liverpool Taxi Fleet Operators
Association [1972] 2 QB 299, [1972] 2 WLR 1262, [1972]
2 All ER 589, 71 LGR 387, (1972) 116 SJ 201 (CA) 37, 38
R v Local Government Board ex p Arlidge [1915] AC 120 (HL) 12, 28
R v Lord Chancellor ex p Witham [1998] QB 575, [1998] 2 WLR 849,
[1997] 2 All ER 779, [1997] COD 291, (1997) 147 NLJ 378, (1997)
141 SJLB 82 (QBD) 55, 198
R v Mahony [1910] 2 IR 695 ....67, 73
R v Medical Appeal Tribunal ex p Gilmore [1957] 1 QB 574, [1957]
2 WLR 498, [1957] 1 All ER 796, (1957) 101 SJ 248 (CA) 67, 73, 82
R v Ministry of Agriculture, Fisheries and Food ex p Hamble
(Offshore) Fisheries Ltd [1995] 2 All ER 714, [1995] 1 CMLR 533,
(1995) 7 Admin LR 637, [1995] COD 114 (QBD) 182, 188, 189,
192, 200, 209
R v Nat Bell Liquors Ltd [1922] 2 AC 128 (PC Can) 67, 73, 79, 82
R v North and East Devon HA ex p Coughlan (1999) 2 CCL Rep 27,
(1999) 47 BMLR 27, [1999] COD 174 (QBD) 190
R v North and East Devon HA ex p Coughlan [2001] QB 213,
[2000] 2 WLR 622, [2000] 3 All ER 850, (2000) 2 LGLR 1,
[1999] BLGR 703, (1999) 2 CCL Rep 285, [1999] Lloyd's
Rep Med 306, (2000) 51 BMLR 1, [1999] COD 340, (1999)
96(31) LSG 39, (1999) 143 SJLB 213 (CA) 181, 182, 183, 184, 185,
189, 190, 191, 192, 193, 194, 195,
196, 197, 198, 199, 200, 201, 202,
203, 204, 205, 206, 207, 208, 209, 285
R v Northumberland Compensation Appeal Tribunal
ex p Shaw [1952] 1 KB 338, [1952] 1 All ER 122,
[1952] 1 TLR 161, (1952) 116 JP 54, 50 LGR 193,
(1951–52) 2 P & CR 361, (1952) 96 SJ 29 (CA) 67, 73
R v Offen (Matthew Barry) (No 2) [2001] 1 WLR 253,
[2001] 2 All ER 154, [2001] 1 Cr App R 24, [2001]
2 Cr App R (S) 10, [2000] Prison LR 283, [2001] Crim LR 63,
(2001) 98(1) LSG 23, (2000) 144 SJLB 288 (CA) 166
R v Panel on Takeovers and Mergers ex p Datafin Plc [1987]
QB 815, [1987] 2 WLR 699, [1987] 1 All ER 564, (1987)
3 BCC 10, [1987] BCLC 104, [1987] 1 FTLR 181, (1987)
131 SJ 23 (CA) 102, 109, 111, 112, 113
R v Secretary of State for Education and Employment ex p Begbie
[2000] 1 WLR 1115, [2000] Ed CR 140, [2000] ELR 445,
(1999) 96(35) LSG 39 (CA) 197, 198, 199, 200, 204
R v Secretary of State for Education and Science ex p Avon
CC (No 2) [1991] 1 QB 558, [1991] 2 WLR 702, [1991]
1 All ER 282, 89 LGR 121, (1991) 3 Admin LR 17, [1990]
COD 349, (1990) 140 NLJ 781 (CA) 146
R v Secretary of State for Employment ex p Equal Opportunities
Commission [1995] 1 AC 1, [1994] 2 WLR 409, [1994]
1 All ER 910, [1995] 1 CMLR 391, [1994] ICR 317, [1994]
IRLR 176, 92 LGR 360, [1994] COD 301, (1994) 91(18)
LSG 43, (1994) 144 NLJ 358, (1994) 138 SJLB 84 (HL) 133

R v Secretary of State for Foreign and Commonwealth Affairs
ex p World Development Movement Ltd [1995] 1 WLR 386,
[1995] 1 All ER 611, [1995] COD 211, (1995) 145 NLJ 51, DC 101
R v Secretary of State for the Home Department ex p Doody
[1994] 1 AC 531, [1993] 3 WLR 154, [1993] 3 All ER 92,
(1995) 7 Admin LR 1, (1993) 143 NLJ 991 (HL) 39
R v Secretary of State for the Home Department ex p Hargreaves
[1997] 1 WLR 906, [1997] 1 All ER 397, [1997] COD 214,
(1997) 94(5) LSG 33, (1997) 141 SJLB 6 (CA) 189, 193, 199, 200
R v Secretary of State for the Home Department ex p Pierson
[1998] AC 539, [1997] 3 WLR 492, [1997] 3 All ER 577,
(1997) 94(37) LSG 41, (1997) 147 NLJ 1238, (1997) 141 SJLB 212 (HL) 9, 285
R v Secretary of State for the Home Department ex p Ruddock
[1987] 1 WLR 1482, [1987] 2 All ER 518, (1987)
131 SJ 1550 (QBD) 182, 186, 187, 188
R v Secretary of State for the Home Department ex p Simms
[2000] 2 AC 115, [1999] 3 WLR 328, [1999] 3 All ER 400, [1999]
EMLR 689, 7 BHRC 411, (1999) 11 Admin LR 961, [1999]
Prison LR 82, [1999] COD 520, (1999) 96(30) LSG 28, (1999)
149 NLJ 1073, (1999) 143 SJLB 212 (HL)..8, 285
R v Secretary of State for Transport ex p Factortame Ltd (No 1)
[1989] 2 CMLR 353, (1989) 139 NLJ 540, (1989) 133 SJ 724 (CA) 127
R v Secretary of State for Transport ex p Factortame Ltd (No 1)
[1990] 2 AC 85, [1989] 2 WLR 997, [1989] 2 All ER 692, [1989]
3 CMLR 1, [1989] COD 531, (1989) 139 NLJ 715 (HL)......................... 115, 116, 117, 127,
130, 149, 154, 160
R v Secretary of State for Transport ex p Factortame Ltd (No 2)
[1991] 1 AC 603, [1990] 3 WLR 818, [1991] 1 All ER 70, [1991]
1 Lloyd's Rep 10, [1990] 3 CMLR 375, (1991) 3 Admin LR 333,
(1990) 140 NLJ 1457, (1990) 134 SJ 1189 (HL) 117, 118, 128,
136, 226, 279
R v Secretary of State for Transport ex p Factortame Ltd
(C-213/89) [1991] 1 All ER 70, [1990] 2 Lloyd's Rep 351,
[1990] ECR I-2433, [1990] 3 CMLR 1, (1990) 140 NLJ 927 (ECJ)................117, 128, 136
R v Secretary of State for Transport ex p Factortame Ltd
(C-221/89) [1992] QB 680, [1992] 3 WLR 288, [1991] 3 All ER 769,
[1991] 2 Lloyd's Rep 648, [1991] ECR I-3905, [1991] 3 C.MLR 589,
(1991) 141 NLJ 1107 (ECJ) 128
R v Secretary of State for Transport ex p Factortame Ltd (No 4),
The Times 7 March 1996..128
R v Secretary of State for Transport ex p Factortame Ltd (No 5)
[2000] 1 AC 524, [1999] 3 WLR 1062, [1999] 4 All ER 906, [1999]
3 CMLR 597, [2000] Eu LR 40, (1999) 96(43) LSG 32,
[1999] NPC 126 (HL)..128
R v Secretary of State for Transport ex p Richmond upon
Thames LBC (No 1) [1994] 1 WLR 74, [1994] 1 All ER 577, [1994]
Env LR 134 (QBD)..182, 187, 188
R v Smith, 114 ER 1381, (1844) 5 QB 614 (CKB) 27

R v Somerset CC ex p Fewings [1995] 1 All ER 513, 92 LGR 674, (1994)
6 Admin LR 446, [1994] COD 338, (1994) 158 LG Rev 461, [1994]
NPC 17 (QBD) 265
R (Abbasi) v Secretary of State for Foreign and Commonwealth
Affairs [2002] EWCA Civ 1598, [2003] UKHRR 76, (2002)
99(47) LSG 29 (CA) 258
R (Alansi) v Newham LBC [2013] EWHC 3722 (Admin),
[2014] PTSR 948, [2014] HLR 25, [2014] BLGR 138 (QBD) 196
R (Alconbury Developments Ltd and Others) v Secretary of
State for the Environment, Transport and the Regions [2001]
UKHL 23, [2003] 2 AC 295, [2001] 2 WLR 1389, [2001] 2 All ER 929,
[2002] Env LR 12, [2001] HRLR 45, [2001] UKHRR 728, (2001)
3 LGLR 38, (2001) 82 P & CR 40, [2001] 2 PLR 76, [2001] JPL 920,
[2001] 20 EG 228 (CS), (2001) 98(24) LSG 45, (2001) 151 NLJ 727,
(2001) 145 SJLB 140, [2001] NPC 90 (HL) 9
R (B) v Nursing and Midwifery Council [2012] EWHC 1264 (Admin) (QBD) 194
R (Bancoult) v Secretary of State for the Foreign and Commonwealth
Office [2001] QB 1067, [2001] 2 WLR 1219, [2001] ACD 18,
(2000) 97(47) LSG 39 (DC) 239, 258, 265
R (Bancoult) v Secretary of State for Foreign and Commonwealth
[2007] EWCA Civ 498, [2008] QB 365, [2007] 3 WLR 768, (2007)
104(23) LSG 31, (2007) 151 SJLB 707 (CA) 254, 255, 266, 268
R (Bancoult) v Secretary of State for Foreign and Commonwealth
Affairs [2008] UKHL 61, [2009] 1 AC 453, [2008] 3 WLR 955,
[2008] 4 All ER 1055, (2008) 105(42) LSG 20, (2008) 158 NLJ 1530,
(2008) 152(41) SJLB 29 (HL) 7, 202, 209, 239, 240, 243, 246,
252, 255, 256, 257, 258, 263, 264,
265, 266, 267, 268, 270
R (Bancoult) v Secretary of State for Foreign and
Commonwealth [2012] EWHC 2115 (Admin) (QBD) 248
R (Bancoult) v Secretary of State for Foreign and Commonwealth
Affairs [2013] EWHC 1502 (Admin), [2014] Env LR 2, [2013]
ACD 83 (QBD) 248, 253
R (Bancoult) v Secretary of State for Foreign and Commonwealth
Affairs [2016] UKSC 35, [2016] 3 WLR 157, [2017] 1 All ER 403,
[2016] HRLR 16 (SC) 241, 242, 243, 260, 268, 269
R (Bhatt Murphy (A Firm) v Independent Assessor [2008]
EWCA Civ 755, (2008) 152(29) SJLB 29 (CA) 200
R (Bibi) v Newham LBC (No.1) [2001] EWCA Civ 607,
[2002] 1 WLR 237, (2001) 33 HLR 84, (2001) 98(23) LSG 38,
[2001] NPC 83 (CA) 199, 200
R (Birks) v Commissioner of Police of the Metropolis [2014]
EWHC 3041 (Admin), [2015] ICR 204, [2014] Inquest LR 221 (QBD) 196
R (Buckinghamshire CC) v Secretary of State for Transport
[2014] UKSC 3, [2014] 1 WLR 324, [2014] 2 All ER 109,
[2014] PTSR 182 (SC) 279

R (Cart) v Upper Tribunal [2011] UKSC 28, [2012] 1 AC 663,
[2011] 3 WLR 107, [2011] 4 All ER 127, [2011] PTSR 1053,
[2011] STC 1659, [2012] 1 FLR 997, [2011] Imm AR 704,
[2011] MHLR 196, [2012] Fam Law 398, [2011] STI 1943,
(2011) 161 NLJ 916, (2011) 155(25) SJLB 35 (SC) 78
R (Cowl) v Plymouth City Council [2001] EWCA Civ 1935, [2002] 1 WLR 803,
[2002] CP Rep 18, (2002) 5 CCL Rep 42, [2002] ACD 11, [2002] Fam
Law 265, (2002) 99(8) LSG 35, (2002) 146 SJLB 27 (CA) 193
R (D) v Worcestershire CC [2013] EWHC 2490 (Admin),
[2013] BLGR 741, (2013) 16 CCL Rep 323 (QBD) 191
R (Daly) v Secretary of State for the Home Department
[2001] UKHL 26, [2001] 2 AC 532, [2001] 2 WLR 1622,
[2001] 3 All ER 433, [2001] HRLR 49, [2001] UKHRR 887,
[2001] Prison LR 322, [2001] ACD 79, (2001) 98(26) LSG 43,
(2001) 145 SJLB 156 (HL) 39
R (East Midlands Care Ltd) v Leicestershire CC [2011]
EWHC 3096 (Admin) (QBD) 191
R (EasyJet Airline Co Ltd) v Civil Aviation Authority [2009]
EWCA Civ 1361, [2010] ACD 19 (CA) 191
R (Evans) v Attorney General [2013] EWHC 1960 (Admin),
[2013] 3 WLR 1631, [2014] 1 All ER 23, [2014] 1 CMLR 8,
[2014] ACD 2, (2013) 163(7570) NLJ 18 (DC) 289, 290, 291
R (Evans) v Attorney General [2015] UKSC 21, [2015] AC 1787,
[2015] 2 WLR 813, [2015] 4 All ER 395, [2015] 2 CMLR 43,
[2015] Env LR 34, [2015] FSR 26 (SC) 5, 55, 285, 286, 289, 290,
291, 292, 293, 294, 295, 296,
297, 298, 299, 300, 301
R (Heather) v Leonard Cheshire Foundation [2002]
EWCA Civ 366, [2002] 2 All ER 936, [2002] HRLR 30,
[2002] UKHRR 883, [2002] HLR 49, (2002) 5 CCL Rep 317,
(2003) 69 BMLR 22, [2002] ACD 43 (CA) 196
R (HS2 Action Alliance Ltd) v Secretary of State for Transport
[2014] UKSC 3, [2014] 1 WLR 324, [2014] 2 All ER 109, [2014]
PTSR 182 (SC) 135, 140
R (HSMP Forum (UK) Ltd) v Secretary of State for the Home
Department [2009] EWHC 711 (Admin) (QBD) 194, 195, 196
R (Jackson) v Attorney General [2005] EWCA Civ 126, [2005]
QB 579, [2005] 2 WLR 866, (2005) 102(15) LSG 32, (2005)
155 NLJ 297, [2005] NPC 24 (CA) 212, 224
R (Jackson) v Attorney General [2005] EWHC 94 (Admin),
(2005) 102(13) LSG 27, (2005) 149 SJLB 177 (DC) 212
R (Jackson) v Attorney General [2005] UKHL 56, [2006] 1 AC 262,
[2005] 3 WLR 733, [2005] 4 All ER 1253, (2005) 155 NLJ 1600,
[2005] NPC 116 (HL) 2, 134, 211, 212, 218, 219, 220, 221,
223, 224, 226, 227, 228, 229, 230,
231, 232, 233, 235, 236, 237,
278, 279, 280, 286, 297

R (Keyu) v Secretary of State for Foreign and Commonwealth
   Affairs [2015] UKSC 69, [2016] AC 1355, [2015] 3 WLR 1665,
   [2016] 4 All ER 794, [2016] HRLR 2, 40 BHRC 228 (SC) 203, 209
R (L) v West London Mental Health NHS Trust [2014] EWCA Civ 47,
   [2014] 1 WLR 3103, (2014) 137 BMLR 76, [2014] MHLR 361,
   [2014] ACD 79, (2014) 158(6) SJLB 37 (CA) 39
R (Lamari) v Secretary of State for the Home Department
   (Post Judgment Judgment) [2012] EWHC 1895 (Admin) (QBD) 158
R (Laporte) v Chief Constable of Gloucestershire [2006]
   UKHL 55, [2007] 2 AC 105, [2007] 2 WLR 46, [2007] 2 All ER 529,
   [2007] HRLR 13, [2007] UKHRR 400, 22 BHRC 38, [2006] Po LR 309,
   [2007] Crim LR 576, [2007] ACD 25, (2007) 151 SJLB 26 (HL) 166
R (Lumba) v Secretary of State for the Home Department [2011]
   UKSC 12, [2012] 1 AC 245, [2011] 2 WLR 671, [2011] 4 All ER 1, [2011]
   UKHRR 437, (2011) 108(14) LSG 20, (2011) 155(12) SJLB 30 (SC) 93, 164
R (Moseley) v Haringey LBC [2014] UKSC 56, [2014] 1 WLR 3947, [2015]
   1 All ER 495, [2014] PTSR 1317, [2014] BLGR 823, [2015] RVR 93 (SC) 191
R (Nadarajah) v Secretary of State for the Home Department [2005]
   EWCA Civ 1363 (CA) 199, 200
R (Nicklinson) v Ministry of Justice [2014] UKSC 38, [2015] AC 657,
   [2014] 3 WLR 200, [2014] 3 All ER 843, [2014] 3 FCR 1, [2014]
   HRLR 17, 36 BHRC 465, (2014) 139 BMLR 1 (SC) 209
R (Patel) v General Medical Council [2013] EWCA Civ 327, [2013]
   1 WLR 2801, (2013) 133 BMLR 14 (CA) 195, 196
R (Rashid) v Secretary of State for the Home Department [2005]
   EWCA Civ 744, [2005] Imm AR 608, [2005] INLR 550 (CA) 202
R (Sandiford) v Secretary of State for Foreign and Commonwealth
   Affairs [2014] UKSC 44, [2014] 1 WLR 2697, [2014] 4 All ER 843,
   [2014] HRLR 21 (SC) 277
R (Simpson) v Chief Constable of Greater Manchester [2013]
   EWHC 1858 (Admin), [2014] ACD 20 (QBD) 194
R (T) v Sheffield City Council [2013] EWHC 2953 (QB), (2013)
   16 CCL Rep 580 (QBD) 191
R (Wakil (t/a Orya Textiles)) v Hammersmith and Fulham LBC
   [2012] EWHC 1411 (QB), [2013] Env LR 3, [2013] 1 P & CR 13,
   [2012] JPL 1334 (QBD) 191
R (Wray) v Darlington School Governors, 115 ER 257, (1844) 6 QB 682 27
R (Youssef) v Secretary of State for Foreign and Commonwealth
   Affairs [2016] UKSC 3, [2016] AC 1457, [2016] 2 WLR 509, [2016]
   3 All ER 261 (SC) 203, 204, 209
Racal Communications Ltd, Re [1981] AC 374, [1980] 3 WLR 181,
   [1980] 2 All ER 634 (HL) 93
Ramirez Sanchez v France (59450/00) (2007) 45 EHRR 49, [2007]
   Prison LR 169 (ECtHR) 164
Ramshay, ex p, 118 ER 65, (1852) 18 QB 173 (CKB) 27, 29
Rankin v Huskisson, 58 ER 6, (1830) 4 Sim 13 (Ct of Ch) 150
Ridge v Baldwin [1963] 1 QB 539, [1962] 2 WLR 716, [1962] 1 All ER 834,
   (1962) 126 JP 196, 60 LGR 229, (1962) 106 SJ 111 (CA) 21, 22

Ridge v Baldwin [1964] AC 40, [1963] 2 WLR 935, [1963] 2 All ER 66,
 (1963) 127 JP 295, (1963) 127 JP 251, 61 LGR 369, 37 ALJ 140,
 234 LT 423, 113 LJ 716, (1963) 107 SJ 313 (HL) 11, 15, 17, 18, 19, 20, 21,
 22, 23, 24, 25, 26, 27, 28, 29, 30,
 31, 32, 33, 34, 35, 36, 37, 38,
 39, 40, 41, 43, 184, 285
Rothwell v Chemical & Insulating Co Ltd [2007] UKHL 39, [2008]
 1 AC 281, [2007] 3 WLR 876, [2007] 4 All ER 1047, [2007] ICR 1745,
 [2008] PIQR P6, [2008] LS Law Medical 1, (2008) 99 BMLR 139,
 (2007) 104(42) LSG 34, (2007) 157 NLJ 1542, (2007)
 151 SJLB 1366 (HL) 272
Rustomjee v R (1876) 2 QBD 69 (CA) 66, 85
Rylands v Fletcher (1868) LR 3 HL 330 (HL) 39
Saadi v Italy (37201/06) (2009) 49 EHRR 30, 24 BHRC 123, [2008]
 Imm AR 519, [2008] INLR 621, [2008] Crim LR 898 (ECtHR) 163
Schmidt v Secretary of State for Home Affairs [1969] 2 Ch 149,
 [1969] 2 WLR 337, [1969] 1 All ER 904, (1969) 133 JP 274,
 (1969) 113 SJ 16 (CA) 37, 184
Secretary of State for the Home Department v F [2009] UKHL 28,
 [2010] 2 AC 269, [2009] 3 WLR 74, [2009] 3 All ER 643, [2009]
 HRLR 26, [2009] UKHRR 1177, 26 BHRC 738, (2009) 106(25) LSG 14 (HL) 165
Secretary of State for the Home Department v Rehman [2001]
 UKHL 47, [2003] 1 AC 153, [2001] 3 WLR 877, [2002] 1 All ER 122,
 11 BHRC 413, [2002] Imm AR 98, [2002] INLR 92, [2002] ACD 6,
 (2001) 98(42) LSG 37, (2001) 145 SJLB 238 (HL) 168, 171
Shareef v Commissioner for Registration of Indian and Pakistani
 Residents [1966] AC 47, [1965] 3 WLR 704, (1965) 109 SJ 679 (PC Cey) 38
Sheffield v Ratcliffe (1616) Hob 334a 234
Shergill v Khaira [2014] UKSC 33, [2015] AC 359, [2014] 3 WLR 1,
 [2014] 3 All ER 243, [2014] PTSR 907, [2014] WTLR 1729,
 17 ITELR 700 (SC) 267
Smith and others (FC) v The Ministry of Defence [2013] UKSC 41,
 [2014] AC 52, [2013] 3 WLR 69, [2013] 4 All ER 794, [2013]
 HRLR 27, 35 BHRC 711, [2014] PIQR P2, [2013] Inquest LR 135 (SC) 7
Smith v East Elloe Rural DC [1956] AC 736, [1956] 2 WLR 888,
 [1956] 1 All ER 855, (1956) 120 JP 263, 54 LGR 233, (1956)
 6 P & CR 102, (1956) 100 SJ 282 (HL) 73, 74, 79, 82
Smith v Queen, The (1878) 3 App. Cas. 614 (PC Australia) 27
South East Asia Fire Bricks Sdn Bhd v Non Metallic Mineral
 Products Manufacturing Employees Union [1981] AC 363, [1980]
 3 WLR 318, [1980] 2 All ER 689, (1980) 124 SJ 496 (PC Mal) 93
Spackman v Plumstead Board of Works (1885) 10 App Cas 229 (HL) 27
State v O'Donnell [1945] IR 126 .... 67, 73
Tamaki v Baker [1901] AC 561 (PC NZ) 150
Terrell v Secretary of State for the Colonies [1953] 2 QB 482,
 [1953] 3 WLR 331, [1953] 2 All ER 490, (1953) 97 SJ 507 (QBD) 27

Thoburn v Sunderland City Council [2002] EWHC 195 (Admin),
  [2003] QB 151, [2002] 3 WLR 247, [2002] 4 All ER 156, (2002)
  166 JP 257, [2002] 1 CMLR 50, [2002] Eu LR 253, [2002] LLR 548,
  (2002) 99(15) LSG 35, (2002) 152 NLJ 312, (2002) 146 SJLB 69 (DC) 134
United Australia Ltd v Barclays Bank Ltd [1941] AC 1, [1940]
  4 All ER 20 (HL) 268
Venicoff. See R v Leman Street Police Station Inspector ex p Venicoff
Wallwork v Fielding [1922] 2 KB 66 (CA) 16, 17, 21
Walton v Scottish Ministers [2012] UKSC 44, [2013] PTSR 51, 2013
  SC (UKSC) 67, 2012 SLT 1211, [2013] 1 CMLR 28, [2013]
  Env LR 16, [2013] JPL 323, 2012 GWD 34-689 (SC) 140
Wandsworth LBC v Winder (No 1) [1985] AC 461, [1984]
  3 WLR 1254, [1984] 3 All ER 976, (1985) 17 HLR 196, 83 LGR 143,
  (1985) 82 LSG 201, (1985) 135 NLJ 381, (1984) 128 SJ 838, HL 101
Weinberger v Inglis [1919] AC 606 (HL) 27, 29
West v Secretary of State for Scotland, 1992 SC 385, 1992 SLT 636,
  1992 SCLR 504 (CSIH) 276
Wheeler v Office of the Prime Minister [2014] EWHC 3815 (Admin),
  [2015] 1 CMLR 46, [2015] ACD 25 (QBD) 279
Wiseman v Borneman [1971] AC 297, [1969] 3 WLR 706, [1969]
  3 All ER 275, 45 TC 540, [1969] TR 279, (1969) 113 SJ 838 (HL) 38
Wood v Woad (1873–74) LR 9 Ex 190, (1873) 43 LJ Ex 153 .... 13, 27, 29, 30, 34

United States of America

Bhatnager v Minister of Employment and Immigration
  [1990] 71 DLR (4th) 84 157
Boyd v United States [1886] 116 US 616 8

TABLE OF LEGISLATION

International Instruments

European Convention on Human Rights and Fundamental Freedoms 1950 166
    Art 3 .... 163, 164, 169
    Art 5 .... 164, 169, 170, 176, 178
    Art 5(1) 179
    Art 5(4) 179
    Art 8 .... 196, 197, 206
    Art 10 166
    Art 11 166
    Art 14 .... 168, 170, 175, 176
    Art 15 .... 164, 167, 169, 170
    Art 15(1) 165, 170, 174
    Protocol 1
        Art 1 274
General Assembly Resolution 1541 (XV) of 15 December 1960 247
Geneva Convention on the High Seas 1958
    Art 5 126
Salisbury Convention 217
Treaty of Accession 124
Treaty of Amsterdam 1997
    Art 43 115
    Art 48 115
    Art 294 115
Treaty of Lisbon 2007 140
Treaty of Rome 1957
    Art 3(d) 122
    Art 7 124
    Art 38(10) 122
    Art 52 128
    Art 119 132
    Art 177 127
Treaty on European Union 1992
    Art 50 138
Treaty on the Functioning of the European Union 2007
    Art 157 133
    Art 198 249
UN Charter 1945 248

Ch XI 248, 252, 266
Art 73 ....246, 247, 252
Art 73e 247
Art 103 7
UN Convention on the law of the Sea 1982 ....245, 246, 249
Art 92 126
Vienna Convention on Diplomatic Relations 1961 249

Council Directive 75/117/EEC of 10 February 1975 on the approximation
  of the laws of the Member States relating to the application of the
  principle of equal pay for men and women 133
Council Directive 76/207/EEC of 9 February 1976 on the implementation
  of the principle of equal treatment for men and women as regards access
  to employment, vocational training and promotion,
  and working conditions 132, 133
Council Directive 83/189/EEC of 28 March 1983 laying down a
  procedure for the provision of information in the field of technical
  standards and regulations 134
Council Directive 2011/92/EU on the assessment of the effects of
  certain public and private projects on the environment 135
Council Regulation 101/76/EEC of 19 January 1976 laying down
  a common structural policy for the fishing industry
  Art 2(1) 124

Australia

Constitution Act 1902 (NSW)
  s 5 255

Hong Kong

Immigration Ordinance 1971 ....265, 266

Sri Lanka

Criminal Procedure Code
  s 440A 261
Penal Code
  Pt IV 261

United Kingdom

Act of Settlement 1701 ....6, 140
  s 3 4
Act of Union 1707 ....4, 140
Agricultural Marketing Act 1931 153
  s 1 153
Agricultural Marketing Act 1933 153
Agricultural Marketing Act 1949 153

Agricultural Marketing Act 1958 46
   s 19 47
   s 19(3) 46, 49, 50, 51
   s 19(6) 46, 52
Anti-Terrorism Crime and Security Act 2001 .... 162, 163, 167, 180
   Pt 1 163
   Pt 2 163
   Pt 4 .... 163, 164, 170, 173, 174, 175, 178
   Pt 5 163
   Pt 6 163
   Pt 7 163
   Pt 8 163
   s 21 174
   ss 21–23 .... 173, 174
   s 23 176
   s 25(2), (3) 165
   s 26(5) 165
   s 30(1) 164
Bill of Rights 1689 .... 6, 140
British Indian Ocean Territory Order 1965 265
British Indian Ocean Territory (Immigration) Order 2004 254
British Indian Ocean Territory (Constitution) Order 2004
   s 9 .... 255, 261, 264, 266
   s 15 254
   s 17 261
Civil Procedure Rules 1998, SI 1998/3132
   Sch 1 RSC
      Ord 53 156
      Ord 53 r 1(2) 155
      Ord 53 r 3(10) 157
      Ord 53 r 3(10)(b) 155
Civil Service Order in Council 1982
   art 4 .... 97, 104
Claim of Rights Act 1689 140
Colonial Boundaries Act 1895 .... 254, 265
Colonial Laws Validity Act 1865 .... 256, 257, 258, 259
   s 1 256
   s 2 256
   s 3 256
Constitutional Reform Act 2005 .... 90, 140
County and Borough Police Act 1919 .... 16, 21, 24
   ss 1–4 16
County and Borough Police Act 1856 15
   s 26 16
County and Borough Police Act 1859 15
County Police Act 1839
   s 4 .... 16, 34

Crown Proceedings Act 1947 158
  s 21 .... 151, 152, 156, 158
  s 21(1) 151, 160
  s 21(2) 151, 152, 153, 154, 155, 157, 159, 160
  s 23 154
  s 23(2)(b) 155
  s 38 154
  s 38(2) 154, 159
  s 42 158
Damages (Asbestos-related Conditions) (Scotland) Act 2009 272
Employment Protection (Consolidation) Act 1978 133
Equal Pay Act 1970 132
European Communities Act 1972 ....116, 117, 133, 135, 136, 140,
                                                                                                                141, 153, 227, 235, 237
  Pt II 154
  s 2(2) 134
  s 2(4) 115, 131, 137
  s 3(1) 131
European Parliamentary Elections Act 1999 220
European Union Act 2011 137
  s 18 ....135, 137
Foreign Compensation Act 1950 ....66, 77
  s 4(4) 66, 67, 70, 71, 72, 75, 76, 77, 78, 79,
                                                                                      82, 83, 84, 86, 89, 90, 93
  s 7 75
Foreign Compensation Act 1962 ....75, 92
Foreign Compensation Act 1969 ....84, 90
  s 3 ....86, 90
Foreign Compensation (Egypt) (Determination and Registration
  of Claims) Order 1959, SI 1959/625 67
Foreign Compensation (Egypt) (Determination and Registration
  of Claims) Order 1962, SI 1962/2187 68
  Ord 4 81
  Ord 4(1) 68
  Ord 4(1)(b) 79
  Ord 4(1)(b)(ii) 68, 69
Freedom of Information Act 2000 ....67, 286
  s 1(1) 288
  s 2(1)(b) 288
  s 53 ....289, 290, 291, 294
  s 53(2) 289
Government of Wales Act 1998 273
Government of Wales Act 2006
  s 107 277
  s 107(1) 273
  s 108(2) 273
  Sch 7 ....273, 274

Table of Legislation

House of Lords Act 1999 215
Human Rights Act 1998 .... 39, 99, 140, 161, 166, 173, 177, 179,
180, 205, 206, 226, 227, 235,
237, 273, 282, 283, 300
    s 1 170
    s 2 174
    s 3 .... 51, 166, 174
    s 4 .... 166, 168, 176
    s 4(5) 166
    s 4(6) 174
    s 6 173
    s 10 174
    s 23 173
    Sch 1 170
    Sch 3 178
Human Rights Act 1998 (Amendment No 2) Order 2001 SI 2001/4032 165
Human Rights Act 1998 (Amendment) Order 2005 SI 2005/1071 ....165, 178
Human Rights Act 1998 (Designated Derogation) Order 2001 SI 2001/3644 165
Hunting Act 2004 .... 134, 211, 212, 220, 221, 223, 236
Immigration Act 1971 164
Merchant Shipping Act 1894 .... 115, 117, 125
Merchant Shipping Act 1988 .... 115, 117, 118, 119, 121, 125,
126, 127, 128, 134, 139
    ss 3–5 126
    s 14 ....126, 128
Merchant Shipping Act 1995 139
Merchant Shipping Act 1998 (Amendment) Order 1989, SI 1989/2006 128
Merchant Shipping (Registration of Ships) Regulations 1993, SI 1993/3138............126, 128
    reg 14 128
Merchant Shipping (Registration etc.) Act 1993 134
    s 3 128
Metropolitan Police Act 1829
    s 5 16
Municipal Corporation Act 1882 ....21, 33
    s 191(4) 16, 18, 20, 21, 22, 23, 24, 26, 31
Northern Ireland Act 1998
    s 5 273
    s 5(5) 277
    s 6 273
Obscene Publications Act 1857 73
Parliament Act 1911 .... 212, 213, 215, 216, 217, 218, 219, 220,
221, 222, 223, 224, 225, 226, 228,
229, 230, 232, 236, 278
    s 2(1) 220, 224, 225
Parliament Act 1949 .... 134, 211, 212, 217, 219, 220,
221, 223, 232, 237
Parliament (No 2) Bill 1969 89

Petition of Rights 1628 140
Police Act 1964 33
Police (Appeals) Act 1927 ....20, 21
   s 2(3) 25, 30
Police (Discipline) (Deputy Chief Constables, Assistant Chief
   Constables and Chief Constables) Regulations 1952, SI 1952/1706 ....16, 17
   reg 15 18
Police (Discipline) Regulations 1952, SI 1952/1705 ....16, 17, 20, 21, 34
Police Pensions (Scotland) Regulations 1955, SI 1955/485
   reg 52 24
Police Regulations 1920, SR & O 1920/1484 16
Police (Scotland) Regulations 1952, SI 1952/1355 16
Prevention of Terrorism Act 2005 178
Prison Rules 1999
   r 5(2) 102
Reform Act 1832 ....9, 228, 229
Rules of the Supreme Court (Amendment No 3) Order 1977, SI 1977/1955
   Ord 53 11
Scotland Act 1998 ....226, 227, 237, 274, 276, 277, 278
   s 28 ....273, 277
   s 28(1) 273
   s 29(2) 273
   s 29(2)(b) 273
   s 29(2)(c) 273
   s 29(2)(d) 272
Sea Fisheries (Conservation and Rational Exploitation)
   Order 1977, SI 1977/38 123
Senior Courts Act 1981
   s 31 ....156, 157, 160
   s 31(2) 155
Sexual Offences (Amendment) Act 2000 220
Special Immigration Appeals Act 1997 165
Terrorism Act 2000 163
Tribunals and Inquiries Act 1958 ....67, 78, 88, 90
Video Recording Act 1984 134
Video Recording Act 2010 134
War Crimes Act 1991 220
War Damage Act 1965 86
Weights and Measures Act 1985 134

1

Entick v Carrington [1765] Revisited: All the King's Horse

RICHARD GORDON

I. Introduction

Constitutional narrative, like most other forms of narrative, works backwards. It explains the present by referring to the past. But the explanations offered by constitutional narratives are justificatory in nature. By being justificatory they almost always fictionalise the past.

In this fashion outcomes become rooted in origins. With a constitutional settlement we are (however precarious the foundations) taken back to some primal moment that is said to condition where we are now.[1] In this sense, at least, such narratives differ from myths[2] which make no attempt at proof but describe fantastic events without linking past to present or requiring belief in the detail of that which is symbolic as opposed to presented fact.

Memory is a vital component of factual narrative since, without the claims of memory, the legitimacy of narrative falls away or else dissolves into myth. Yet collective memory is, at best, a treacherous guide and, in the constitutional context, a guide with a compelling vested interest; that of promoting and maintaining belief (in order to retain power) in the existing institutional and social order. Nor does collective memory reflect a single stab of ostensible recall; it is, rather, an extended series of assertions over time with nuanced differences in the telling.[3]

We see this process at work in our own constitutional arrangements. The narrative of continuous and unlimited Parliamentary sovereignty (Parliament's capacity to make and unmake any law at will) and, its close cousin, a deliberately

---

[1] See, further, P Brooks The Rhetoric of Constitutional Narratives: A Response to Elaine Scarry *Yale Journal of the Humanities* vol 2 Issue 1 Art 10.

[2] The focus here is on narrative. However, there are, necessarily, distinctions of degree between myth, narrative and, indeed, legend (a popular history but one that is not claimed to be authenticated).

[3] Explanations of myth may also engender a process of assertions and disputations over time. Consider, for example, the myth of Romulus and Remus and its different versions over the centuries: see M Beard (2015) *SPQR—A History of Ancient Rome* Profile Books pp 53–89.

crafted unwritten constitution, as our prevailing political axioms have neither an historical starting point nor any doctrinal inevitability about them.

Parliamentary sovereignty as currently understood only came in with Dicey in the late nineteenth century.[4] Like the dogma of papal infallibility (another ambitious late nineteenth-century construct)[5] it was an assertion rather than a fact, which is, no doubt, why scholars continue to debate its provenance[6] and why some judges lay claim to common law over constitutional supremacy.[7] Similarly, as the historian Linda Colley has pointed out, hardly anyone at Westminster talked about an unwritten Constitution before 1850 and the idea of an unwritten British Constitution as a framework for political analysis remained rare at Westminster and in the media until the 1870s.[8]

Of course, facts can become law so that the fact of an assertion (however historically unjustified) repeated, without contradiction, sufficiently often can, over time, morph into a constitutional doctrine. This is what has happened with the power-doctrine of Parliamentary sovereignty and also with its potentially competing judicial power-doctrine the rule of law.

The decision in *Entick v Carrington*[9] is a landmark ruling precisely because it is the most visible early stepping stone in the development of the doctrine of the rule of law. As I suggest that case shows, although nothing in the court's judgment can, sensibly, be viewed as a statement of a priori principle it has paved the way for a system of judicial review that adds substance as well as process to the rule of law. Moreover, it is the foundation for the assertion (repeated in different guises many times since) of a demarcated power relationship between judicial and executive power.

II. The Facts and Issues

The essential facts of *Entick v Carrington* are in short compass. They involved the issuing by the Earl of Halifax, one of the King's principal Secretaries of State, of a specific warrant directed to the Defendants authorising and requiring them with the assistance of a constable to search for John Entick, the plaintiff, apprehend him and bring him together with his books and papers in safe custody before the

---

[4] See A Dicey *Introduction to the Study of the Law of the Constitution* (London, Macmillan, 1855).
[5] Papal infallibility was defined in the first Vatican Council of 1869–70.
[6] See, generally, J Goldsworthy *Parliamentary Sovereignty* (Cambridge, 2010).
[7] See, most notably, *Jackson v Attorney-General* [2005] UKHL 56 per Lord Steyn at para 102; Lord Hope at para 126; Lady Hale at para 159 and Lord Carswell at para 168.
[8] See Professor Colley's evidence on 12 January 2012 to the Political and Constitutional Reform Committee of the House of Commons (response to Q 154).
[9] [1765] 2 Wilson KB 275, 85 ER 807; 19 Howell's State Trials 1029.

Secretary of State to be examined concerning his authorship of *The Monitor or British Freeholder* which was alleged to constitute a seditious libel containing 'gross and scandalous reflections and invectives upon his majesty's government and upon both Houses of Parliament'.

The plaintiff alleged, and the jury found, that the defendants had, as the plaintiff contended, broken and entered his dwelling-house, remained on the premises for four hours without his consent and against his will and broken open the doors to the rooms as well as boxes, chests and drawers examining all his private papers and books and taking away many of them. The jury awarded a sum of damages contingent on the prior question (which they asked the court to decide) of whether the search and seizure were lawful. Notwithstanding the jury's factual findings, therefore, the case raised, in acute form, the relationship between the Crown and the courts. The defendants maintained the plea of justification on the footing that they were simply acting under a lawful warrant issued by the Secretary of State.

It was apparent by the time that *Entick v Carrington* was decided that the Secretary of State had power to issue warrants for arrest and committal for both high treason and seditious libel. The court, with some reluctance, was unwilling to depart from the various precedents to that effect. So, the plaintiff could not maintain a claim for false imprisonment. Despite that, however, the full Court of Common Pleas refused to permit warrants to be issued for search and seizure.

The reasoning underpinning that conclusion together with the approach taken to the scope of the court's jurisdiction is what marks *Entick v Carrington* as exceptional. As Lord Camden explained:

> If this is law it would be found in our books, but no such law ever existed in this country; our law holds the property of every man so sacred that no man can set his foot upon his neighbour's close without his leave … if there was [such a law] it would destroy all the comforts of society; for papers are often the dearest property a man can have.

In concluding thus, the court did not accept that the mere practice of search warrants of this kind being issued without prior legal challenge meant that they were lawful:

> … this is the first instance of an attempt to prove a modern practice of a private office to make and execute warrants to enter a man's house, search for and take away all his books and papers in the first instance, to be law, which is not to be found in our books. It must have been the guilt or poverty of those upon whom such warrants have been executed, that deterred or hindered them from contending against the power of a Secretary of State and the Solicitor of the Treasury, or such warrants could never have passed for lawful till this time.

Nor did it avail the defendants that the practice had existed since the Revolution of 1688:

> [T]he usage of these warrants since the Revolution, if it began then, is too modern to be law; the common law did not begin with the Revolution; the ancient Constitution which had been almost overthrown and destroyed was then repaired and revived; the Revolution added a new buttress to the ancient venerable edifice.

The basis on which *Entick v Carrington* was decided was formal more than substantive. It lay in the absence of legal authority to do that which the Crown claimed to be necessary and (with an elision on the Crown's part somewhat lacking logical coherence) to be justified. It was substantive only in the sense that power to interfere with 'dearest property' had to be established. The formal requirement might have been less has the substance of the 'right' been less.

Lord Camden's judgment strictly adheres to the law irrespective of its content. Although the court appeared to cast doubt on the coherence of earlier legal precedents it was unwilling to depart from them because they were, in their turn, law recorded in 'the books'.

Nevertheless, the judgment represents a significant assertion of judicial power because the political (including legislative) context was somewhat different then from now. *Entick v Carrington* was decided less than a century after the Glorious Revolution and at a time when the independence of the judiciary itself had only been statutorily guaranteed since 1701 by Section 3 of the Act of Settlement.

Certainly the power of the Crown had been curtailed by the Bill of Rights in 1688 and even before that by the *Case of Proclamations* in 1611.[10] But the constitutional relationship between the courts, the Crown and Parliament was still being conducted on uncertain constitutional terrain with the King as an extremely powerful participant. The country was only just emerging from the fear of a Stuart restoration bringing with it a Roman Catholic monarchical succession under the influence of France; it was, as it happens, the same fear that had acted as a spur to the 1707 Act of Union. Only a century or so later would Bagehot be in a position to refer to the Crown as exercising a largely symbolic power as the 'dignified' part of our Constitution in contrast to the 'efficient' role of Parliament.[11]

III. Why *Entick v Carrington* is a Landmark

When viewed from an historical perspective *Entick v Carrington* is the first case after the Glorious Revolution to claim primacy for law over executive fiat and at a time when there was (and as some critics of the Grayling approach to judicial review claim still is) a real prospect of the executive seeking to diminish the power of the judges. In this sense, it was not only a brave ruling but also one that created a precedent for much more recent claims to a certain kind of judicial supremacy. In *M v Home Office*,[12] for example, Lord Templeman criticised 'the proposition that the executive obey the law as a matter of grace and not as a matter of necessity [as] a proposition which would reverse the result of the Civil War'.

---

[10] [1611] 12 Co Rep 74.
[11] W Bagehot (eds) *The English Constitution* (Oxford Paperbacks New, 2001).
[12] [1994] 1 AC 377, 395: See Ch 7 *Leading Administrative Law Cases: M v The Home Office*.

Even more recently, in *Evans v Attorney-General*[13] (a case about the legality of the Attorney-General's overruling of a decision of the Upper Tribunal to require the disclosure of royal correspondence with ministers) Lord Neuberger said this:

> A statutory provision which entitles a member of the executive (whether a Government Minister or the Attorney-General) to overrule a decision of the judiciary merely because he does not agree with it would not merely be unique in the laws of the United Kingdom. It would cut across two constitutional principles, which are also fundamental components of the rule of law.

He then articulated the two principles:

> First, subject to being overruled by a higher court or (given Parliamentary supremacy) a statute, it is a basic principle that a decision of a court is binding as between the parties, and cannot be ignored or set aside by anyone, including (indeed it may fairly be said, least of all) the executive. Secondly, it is also fundamental to the rule of law that decisions and actions of the executive are, subject to necessary well-established exceptions (such as declarations of war), and jealously scrutinised statutory exceptions, reviewable by the court at the suit of an interested citizen. Section 53, as interpreted by the Attorney-General's argument in this case, flouts the first principle and stands the second principle on its head. It involves saying that a final decision of a court can be set aside by a member of the executive (normally the minister in charge of the very department against whom the decision has been given) because he does not agree with it. And the fact that the member of the executive can put forward cogent and/or strongly held reasons for disagreeing with the court is, in this context, nothing to the point: many court decisions are on points of controversy where opinions (even individual judicial opinions) may reasonably differ, but that does not affect the applicability of these principles.

Each of these principles may be derived from *Entick v Carrington* making it, in this sense, one of the earliest judicial review decisions. The first principle comes straight from the *Entick v Carrington* lexicon in that courts apply the law; so if the executive may not ignore a court ruling, no more may it ignore the law. The second principle is a corollary of the first. If the executive may neither ignore court rulings nor the law itself there must be a route of challenge to allegedly unlawful executive decisions since, otherwise, the executive could, indeed, ignore the law with impunity.

The rule of law is, of course, an imprecise concept. It has once only appeared in statutory form and, even then, without attempt at definition. Nor, in *Entick v Carrington* was Lord Camden purporting to articulate that concept as such. He was dealing with a case of trespass in which there was no law justifying that which had occurred. Yet it is, as implicitly foreshadowed earlier, in narrative that constitutional doctrines are forged. The rule of law is as much of a constitutional or political doctrine as is that of the sovereignty of Parliament and the development of these doctrines has come about, incrementally, through narrative.

We can see how early judicial pronouncements in *Entick v Carrington* have been able to be used to create the narrative of a rather more substantial rule of law

---

[13] [2015] UKSC 21 at paras 51–52.

principle. Without dwelling on the detail, narrative makes links between unconnected events to create a design or pattern stemming from a *fons et origo*. Just as the Whig narrative of history looks to disconnected past events as an ever-increasing march to greater liberty so, too, can the rule of law be viewed as a linear progression towards the embedding of rule of law values (whatever they might consist of) into our unwritten Constitution.

On this linear map we might, perhaps, start with Magna Carta (access to justice and no penalty without breach of the law). Travelling through the *Prohibitions del Roy*[14] (the separation of courts from the executive) and the *Case of Proclamations*[15] (law through Acts of Parliament and not through Royal Proclamations) we would linger at the Bill of Rights 1689 (no executive power to suspend or dispense with law), the Act of Settlement in 1701 (independence of the judiciary) and, of course, at *Entick v Carrington* before completing our journey in modern times with recent cases such as *Congreve v Home Office*[16] (no taxation without Parliamentary consent), *Council for Civil Service Unions v Minister for the Civil Service*[17] (subjection of most executive power to judicial review), and all the cases on the common law principle of legality that I will consider separately.

The difficulty with a trajectory of this kind is that it is a journey to nowhere unless the self-deceiving but ultimately necessary role of narrative is understood and encompassed in our analysis of constitutional doctrine. With the various cases and statutes I have referred to as a possible constitutional travelogue (and others could have been included) we are starting to enter into a world of apples and oranges and not comparing like with like. For the purpose of a concept supposed to be unchanging this is a manifestly impossible position. For example, Magna Carta was a response to a political situation; most of its provisions have little or nothing to do with any incarnation of a rule of law notion and it has gone through so many different readings (as well as, for a time, neglect) as to be virtually meaningless for the purpose of analytic description.

But the position changes once it is borne in mind that the very process of narrative adjusts the concept in the telling. The scientific parallel is, perhaps, the so-called *observer effect* where the viewer changes the nature of that which is being viewed.

Both Parliamentary sovereignty and the rule of law have been strengthened by narrative. As mentioned earlier, the Victorian jurist AV Dicey gave sovereignty a scope that had previously been lacking by claiming for Parliament unlimited power to make and unmake laws at any time. The breadth of the concept has also created some challenges as, for example, the conundrum faced by an omnipotent god in any divestment of power. In similar vein, it is the very imprecision of the rule of law as a substantive concept that has enabled courts in subsequent case

---

[14] [1607] 12 Co Rep 6.
[15] ibid.
[16] [1976] QB 629.
[17] [1985] AC 374.

law to refer directly to Lord Camden's judgment in *Entick v Carrington* to create a principle designed to curtail the powers of the executive.

Thus, in the context of the royal prerogative, in *R (Bancoult) v Secretary of State for Foreign and Commonwealth Affairs*[18] Lord Bingham observed:

> It is for the courts to inquire into whether a particular prerogative power exists or not, and, if it does exist, into its extent: Council of Civil Service Unions v Minister for the Civil Service [1985] AC 374, 398E. Over the centuries the scope of the royal prerogative has been steadily eroded, and it cannot today be enlarged (British Broadcasting Corporation v Johns (Inspector of Taxes) [1965] Chapter 32, 79E). As an exercise of legislative power by the executive without the authority of Parliament, the royal prerogative to legislate by order in council is indeed an anachronistic survival. When the existence or effect of the royal prerogative is in question the courts must conduct an historical inquiry to ascertain whether there is any precedent for the exercise of the power in the given circumstances. "If it is law, it will be found in our books. If it is not to be found there, it is not law": Entick v Carrington (1765) 19 St Tr 1030, 1066.

Entick v Carrington has also been used to support the proposition that combat immunity in the armed forces ought not to be extended beyond the situations to which the immunity thus far had been applied. In *Smith and others (FC) v The Ministry of Defence*[19] Lord Hope giving the majority judgment said this:

> Such an extension would also go beyond the situations to which the immunity has so far been applied. In Biciv Ministry of Defence [2004] EWHC 786 (QB), para 90, Elias J noted that combat immunity was exceptionally a defence to the government, and to individuals too, who take action in the course of actual or imminent armed conflict and cause damage to property or death or injury to fellow soldiers or civilians. It was an exception to the principle that was established in [1765] Entick v Carrington 19 State Tr 1029 that the executive cannot simply rely on the interests of the state as a justification for the commission of wrongs. In his opinion the scope of the immunity should be construed narrowly. That approach seems to me to be amply justified by the authorities.

Here, *Entick v Carrington* is being relied on to justify limiting the extension of existing law. But it has also been used to support the common law principle of legality, which is a principle of statutory interpretation requiring the use of clear and unequivocal language before a court will rule that fundamental rights have been intentionally abrogated by Parliament.

Thus in an early case to come before the Supreme Court *Her Majesty's Treasury v Ahmed and Others*[20] Lord Hope stated that:

> ... Two fundamental rights were in issue in G's case, and as they were to be found in domestic law his right to invoke them was not affected by article 103 of the UN Charter. One was the right to peaceful enjoyment of his property, which could only be interfered with by clear legislative words: [1765] Entick v Carrington 19 Howell's State Trials 1029, 1066 ... .

---

[18] [2008] UKHL 61 at para 68: further see Ch 11.
[19] [2013] UKSC 41 at para 90.
[20] [2010] UKSC 2 at para 75.

In a recent lecture Lady Hale also suggested that the principle of legality 'dates back at least as far as the famous 18th century case of *Entick v Carrington*'.[21] On any view, *Entick v Carrington* was concerned with property rights but it has been cited by Lord Neuberger as authority for a far wider constitutional proposition:[22]

> the flow of legal ideas and concepts between Britain and mainland Europe has been and is a two-way process. Since the 17th century, England and Wales have been in the forefront of liberty. We executed our king more than 140 years before the French. The famous 18th century case of Entick v Carrington, decided before Louis XVI had even come to the throne, provided the basis for the right to liberty, security and property …

The US Supreme Court has also referred to *Entick v Carrington* as the foundation of modern ideas of liberty and privacy. In *Boyd v United States*[23] the Supreme Court observed that:

> The principles laid down in [Lord Camden's] opinion affect the very essence of constitutional liberty and security. They reach farther than the concrete form of the case then before the court, with its adventitious circumstances; they apply to all invasions on the part of the government and its employees of the sanctity of a man's home and the privacies of life.

All this reflects the behind-the-scenes power of embellishment of narrative rather than straightforward application of the ruling in *Entick v Carrington*. When ruling on the invalidity of the specific warrant Lord Camden was careful to distinguish warrants of search and seizure from warrants of committal because the latter were endorsed by binding authority. It is, therefore, not immediately obvious that the case was in any discrete substantive sense concerned in terms of statements of principle with the protection of any fundamental rights as such and certainly not the fundamental right to either liberty or privacy. Neither was Lord Camden obviously concerned with the royal prerogative; nor with limiting the extension of existing law in an appropriate case.

As for the common law principle of legality, it is by no means obvious that the court was, in *Entick v Carrington*, laying down any principle of statutory interpretation let alone one that would compel the legislature to use clear words in order to limit fundamental rights. The principle of legality is, at heart, a democratic principle. This appears from Lord Hoffmann's observation in *R v Secretary of State for the Home Department,* ex parte *Simms*[24] that in terms of statutory interpretation where fundamental rights are engaged 'the principle of legality means that Parliament must squarely confront what it is doing and accept the political cost'. In *Entick v Carrington* the context was entirely different. Eighteenth century Britain was not noted for adherence to democratic principles and it would be another

---

[21] '*Magna Carta—Did she die in vain?*' Gray's Inn 19 October 2015.
[22] Cambridge Freshfields Annual Law Lecture 12 February 2014: '*The British and Europe*' at paragraph 53.
[23] [1886] 116 US 616, 630.
[24] [2000] 2 AC 115, 131.

60 years or so before the enactment of the first Reform Act in 1832 even then granting only a limited form of suffrage.

In any case, the notion that a court was in 1765 using techniques of statutory interpretation to ensure greater protection of fundamental rights assumes that the protection of fundamental rights, as opposed to the straightforward application of private law (in *Entick v Carrington* the private law of trespass) was on the judicial radar. Certainly nothing in either the 'adventitious circumstances' or the judicial observations in Lord Camden's judgment comes close to justifying such an assumption. None of this diminishes the real significance of *Entick v Carrington*. The common law process is, almost by definition, one of incremental accretion of principle built upon applying older statements of principle to new situations.

But *Entick v Carrington* is rather more than a foundational stepping-stone for forensic narrative. Its ultimate importance lies in the fact that it is one of the earliest instances in which a court was prepared to inquire into the public law jurisdiction of the executive. It is, in fact, the first such case following the Glorious Revolution and the growing ascendancy of Parliament in which a court looked at the scope of executive power and determined that the executive was subject to the ordinary law of the land unless expressly exempted. In that sense it is the first case of judicial review in which we understand those words today.

Judicial review has, in its turn, grown hugely since *Entick v Carrington*. Modern judicial review now encompasses the rule of law at its centre. Notwithstanding the imprecision of that expression it is generally recognised as having two potential component elements: a 'thin' and a 'thick' version. Under a 'thin' or formalist version, the rule of law requires law to comply with certain formal rules irrespective of content. In its 'thick' or substantive version, the rule of law mandates the recognition of substantive rights.[25]

The following observations demonstrate that judicial review now encompasses each of these elements:

> There is however another relevant principle which must exist in a democratic society. That is the rule of law ... The principles of judicial review give effect to the rule of law. They ensure that administrative decisions will be taken rationally, in accordance with a fair procedure and within the powers conferred by Parliament ...[26]

> ... the rule of law enforces minimum standards of fairness, both substantive and procedural.[27]

> Ministers and public officers at all levels must exercise the powers conferred on them in good faith, fairly, for the purpose for which the powers were conferred, without exceeding the limits of such powers and not unreasonably.[28]

---

[25] See T Bingham *The Rule of Law* (Allen Lane, 2010) pp 66–67. The three citations that follow are from A Street *Judicial Review and the Rule of Law: Who is in Control* (the Constitution Society, 2013) at p 14.
[26] *R (Alconbury Developments Ltd and Others) v Secretary of State for the Environment, Transport and the Regions*. [2003] 2 AC 295, para 73 per Hoffmann.
[27] *R v Secretary of State for the Home Department, ex p. Pierson* [1998] AC 539, 591F per Lord Steyn.
[28] T Bingham, *op cit* at p. 60.

Although *Entick v Carrington* applied the law of trespass to the particular set of facts before it, the court applied it to what would now be treated as an exercise of public law power amenable to judicial review. In public law terms, Lord Camden's ruling was in substance to the effect that the rule of law compelled the conclusion that a *public body* was only empowered to act within the law and could not, without legal authority, claim power merely because it was desirable to have that power or even because the executive considered it necessary to have the power in the national interest.

This is the foundational principle of judicial review deriving from the rule of law. For example, absence of power invalidates executive action even if the executive is not behaving unfairly. As Lord Griffiths observed in *R v Horseferry Road Magistrates' Court, ex parte Bennett*:

> ... In the present case there is no suggestion that the appellant cannot have a fair trial, nor could it have been suggested that it would have been unfair to try him if he had been returned to this country through extradition procedures. If the court is to have the power to interfere with the prosecution in the present circumstances it must be because the judiciary accept a responsibility for the maintenance of the rule of law that embraces a willingness to oversee executive action and to refuse to countenance behaviour that threatens either basic human rights or the rule of law.

'My lords, I have no doubt that the judiciary should accept this responsibility in the field of criminal law ... '.[29]

The notion that public law power may be implied without proper legal authority in the name of some supervening consideration was also scotched in *Entick v Carrington*. We see echoes of similar arguments and their rejection today. In *McCarthy & Stone (Developments) Ltd v Richmond-upon-Thames London Borough Council*[30] Lord Lowry there observed (in the context of a power to charge conferred in part of the statute but not, relevantly, in another):

> ... The rule is that a charge cannot be made unless the power to charge is given by express words or by necessary implication. These last words impose a rigorous test going far beyond the proposition that it would be reasonable or even conducive or incidental to charge for the provision of a service.

It is these aspects of the ruling in *Entick v Carrington* that are timeless. They are at least as timeless as judicial review itself. They will live as long as the rule of law. And it is, ultimately, for the rule of law that *Entick v Carrington* may legitimately claim its legacy to history.

---

[29] [1994] 1 AC 42, 62.
[30] [1992] 2 AC 48, 70–71.

2

Ridge v Baldwin [1964]: 'Nuff Said'

SH BAILEY

I. Introduction

The decision of the House of Lords in *Ridge v Baldwin*[1] that the dismissal of a chief constable was void is widely celebrated as one of the trio of cases in the 1960s[2] that helped set the principles of judicial review of administrative action on a modern footing. In particular, it is regarded as having decided that the *audi alteram partem* rule of natural justice (the right to a fair hearing: 'hear both sides') can apply to administrative as well as judicial or quasi-judicial decisions. On closer inspection, the significance of the decision is more complex than that. First, we shall see that, while the proposition just stated reflects how *Ridge v Baldwin* was subsequently treated, it is not quite what it decided. Second, as regards the applicability of the *audi alteram partem* rule, it corrected what was already seen by contemporary critics as a deviation from established principles. Third, it addressed some other important points of law concerning judicial review beyond the requirements of natural justice. Fourth, the case was litigated well before the procedural unification of the application (now claim) for judicial review effected by the new RSC Order 53 in 1977.[3] The proceedings took the form of an action for a declaration and damages. Finally, the case addressed some interesting issues of statutory interpretation.

II. The Context: Natural Justice in the 1950s

The state of the law as it was in the 1950s concerning the extent to which public bodies were subject to implied requirements to observe natural justice in the course of their decision-making is best understood from two works: the first

---

[1] [1964] AC 40, HL.
[2] With *Padfield* (see Ch 3) and *Anisminic* (see Ch 4).
[3] See Rules of the Supreme Court (Amendment No 3), SI 1977/1955.

edition of Stanley de Smith's *Judicial Review of Administrative Action* published in 1959[4] and the first edition of William Wade's *Administrative Law* published in 1961.[5] De Smith's book was 'the first of its kind to have been written by an English author',[6] and was aimed at academics and practitioners. Never before had there been a systematic analysis of the principles (so far as they could be discerned) and remedies governing the role of the English courts in 'passing upon' the acts of ministers, local authorities and other public bodies.[7] As regards to the principles, separate treatment was given to 'vires, jurisdiction, law and fact', 'natural justice: the right to a hearing', 'natural justice: interest and bias', and the 'review of discretionary powers'. Overall, de Smith's views as to the efficacy of judicial review were sombre.[8] 'Complicated problems' were caused by the significance attached by the courts to the classification of functions as judicial, administrative, legislative or ministerial; judicial review 'lacked breadth and depth'; review of the acts and decisions of bodies other than statutory tribunals 'tends to be perfunctory and ineffective'; and while the statutory powers of central government directly affecting the interests of members of the public had strikingly increased in the twentieth century, 'the relative efficacy of judicial controls have declined'.

In some instances the judges had been 'too ready to disclaim power to review the exercise of discretions in which the policy element has been comparatively small'. This 'excess of caution' was no doubt influenced by the experience of two world wars and their immediate aftermaths, during which time restrictive interpretation of executive powers might have proved contrary to the public interest; however, precedent in wartime and emergency cases 'continued to colour juridical attitudes in normal times'. It had also been influenced by 'narrow conceptions of the judicial function' entertained by many judges in recent years, which de Smith saw as a fear of seeming to follow the path taken by the US Supreme Court in the 1930s, so prejudicing the constitutional status of the judiciary.[9] The practical effect had been to create a widespread impression that there was no point in attacking the validity of powers exercised by ministers unless a purely technical flaw could be discovered. It appeared that this impression extended to powers exercised by local authorities.

Turning to the right to a hearing,[10] notwithstanding doubts expressed from time to time as to the usefulness of the expression 'natural justice',[11] the *audi*

---

[4] London, Stevens & Sons Ltd pp 486. De Smith was then Reader in Public Law in the University of London (at LSE).

[5] Oxford, Clarendon Press. Wade had just moved from Cambridge to Oxford, where he was Professor of English Law.

[6] de Smith (1959) p v. It was based on his PhD thesis.

[7] ibid.

[8] de Smith (1959) pp 17–25.

[9] de Smith referred to 'extra-judicial utterances' and cited Patrick Devlin's address, 'The Common Law, Public Policy and the Executive' 9 CLP 1.

[10] de Smith (1959) Ch 4. This had previously appeared in print in [1958] 68 *Harv LR* 569. De Smith had previously expressed similar views in a series of notes and articles: See [1948] 11 *MLR* 306 ('The Limits of Judicial Review'); [1951] 14 *MLR* 71 (note on *Nakkuda Ali v Jayaratne*).

[11] de Smith (1959) p 101 citing Lord Shaw's comment in *Local Government Board v Arlidge* [1915] AC 120 (HL), 138 ('vacuous').

alteram partem rule was firmly recognised by the common law in such contexts as summary proceedings before justices; the deprivation of office and other dignities where removal could only be for cause;[12] arbitrators; and professional bodies and voluntary associations exercising disciplinary functions.[13] Where a statute authorised interference with property or civil rights but was silent on the question of notice and hearing the courts invoked 'the justice of the common law' to 'supply the omission of the legislature'.[14] In a famous dictum in *Board of Education v Rice*[15] Lord Loreburn LC noted that comparatively recent statutes had extended the practice of imposing on departments or officers of state the duty of deciding or determining questions of various kinds: 'In such cases ... they must act in good faith and fairly listen to both sides, for that is a duty lying upon everyone who decides anything.' This did not, however, mean that the procedure appropriate for a trial necessarily had to be followed.

On the other hand, de Smith noted eight factors that led the courts to hold the rule to be impliedly excluded.[16] He was particularly critical of some of these.[17] First, as to the ground that the function in question was 'administrative' not 'judicial',[18] the cases or certiorari and prohibition showed that almost any act or decision of a statutory body that imposed obligations or affected rights might be held to be judicial, and in the older cases the courts seldom troubled themselves with questions of characterisation.[19] Second, the 'hotchpotch' of cases where existence of a wide discretionary power was treated as a significant factor in exclusion did 'not yield any general principles'.[20] Indeed, where the width of the discretion made challenge on other grounds almost impossible, there was all the more reason

---

[12] *Bagg's Case* (1628) 11 Co Rep 93 (removal of chief burgess without notice or hearing); (1723) *R v Chancellor of the University of Cambridge* 1 Str 557 (Bentley's Case) (deprivation of degrees without a summons). These principles 'seem to have been largely forgotten': de Smith (1959) at p 104.

[13] *Wood v Woad* (1874) LR 9 Ex 190 (expulsion of the plaintiff from mutual insurance society without giving him an opportunity of being heard held to be void). At p 196 it was said by Kelly CB that the rule applied to 'every tribunal or body of persons invested with authority to adjudicate upon matters involving civil consequences to individuals'.

[14] *Cooper v Wandsworth Board of Works* (1863) 14 CB (NS) 180, 194 per Byles J. Here, the Board had demolished the plaintiff's house without prior warning and was held liable for trespass.

[15] [1911] AC 179 (HL), p 182.

[16] de Smith (1959) pp 114–122.

[17] He expressed some or no concern about such matters as non-disclosure of information where that would be prejudicial to the public interest and the need not to obstruct prompt preventive or remedial action.

[18] Usually, 'a rationalisation of a conclusion already reached on other grounds': de Smith (1959) at pp 115–116. (This observation draws attention to the circularity inherent in some of the judicial analysis in this area: was the true question: 'Is the function administrative? If so natural justice need not be observed'; or 'Is there a duty to act judicially? If so the function is not administrative.)

[19] ibid p 116.

[20] ibid pp 116–118. The main authority was *Ex p Venicoff* [1920] 3 KB 72 (DC), holding that the Home Secretary is deporting an alien where he deemed it 'conducive to the public good' was acting in a purely executive capacity, the alien having no right to notice or a hearing (although in practice the Home Secretary said he was willing to listen to representations).

why the authority should hear representations before it acted. The third factor was where the action taken constituted denial of a privilege rather than interference with a right.[21] No such distinction appeared to have been drawn in the early English cases but the distinction had assumed considerable importance in recent years.

De Smith went on to say that the *audi alteram partem* rule had 'lately shown signs of debility'.[22] He analysed[23] the extensive case law on statutory procedure for the compulsory acquisition of land, and argued[24] that the approach in these cases was misapplied in other contexts, leading the courts wrongly to assume that functions could only be characterised as judicial (or quasi-judicial), requiring observation of natural justice, where there was a *lis inter partes* or an express statutory requirement to hold an inquiry. The older cases where the nature of the impact of a decision on a person's rights or interest had been sufficient for application of *audi alteram partem* had been forgotten. The most prominent example was *Nakkuda Ali v Jayaratne*.[25] Here the Controller of Textiles in Ceylon exercised a statutory power to revoke a textile dealer's licence where he had reasonable grounds for believing him to be unfit to continue as a dealer. The Privy Council held that his decision was not amenable to certiorari, and natural justice did not have to be observed, first, as there was no requirement to follow a judicial procedure and, second, as he was not determining a question affecting the rights of subjects but simply 'taking executive action to withdraw a privilege'.

De Smith noted that the first assertion was contradicted in many cases in the scope of certiorari and the second served to demonstrate the limitations of the conceptual approach to administrative law. Demolition of an uninhabitable house might be for the owner a supportable misfortune,[26] but loss of a licence to trade could lead to a 'calamitous loss of livelihood', the decision in *Nakkuda Ali* being contrary to the general attitude of the English courts towards the licensing and regulation of trades and professions.[27] De Smith concluded by saying[28] that 'the ancient presumption that the validity of the exercise of powers directly operating upon individual rights is conditional upon observance of the *audi alteram partem* principle should be restored to its former status'.

---

[21] ibid pp 118–119.
[22] ibid p 122.
[23] ibid pp 125–129.
[24] At pp 122–133.
[25] [1951] AC 55 (PC). The opinion was given by Lord Radcliffe. For criticism, see HWR Wade, 'The Twilight of Natural Justice?' (1951) 67 *LQR* 103. Other cases where a similar approach was adopted include *R v Metropolitan Police Commissioner, ex p Parker* [1953] 1 WLR 1150 (DC) (revocation of taxi driver's licence for misconduct not a judicial act), criticised by A Goodhart, (1954) 70 *LQR* 203, and *Ex parte Fry* [1954] 1 WLR 730 (DC) (holding that chief officer disciplining a fireman was not acting judicially or quasi-judicially) (the correctness of this was left open by the Court of Appeal: [1954] 1 WLR 730 (CA)).
[26] cf *Cooper v Wandsworth Board of Works* (n 14).
[27] de Smith (1959) p 132.
[28] At p 136.

This reasoning is set out at some length because, as we shall see, it is in essence the reasoning adopted by Lord Reid in *Ridge v Baldwin*. It is also important to note that similar points had since the late 1940s been made by H.W.R. Wade.[29]

It is also interesting to note the review of the first edition of *de Smith* by the leading American scholar, Kenneth Culp Davis.[30] Davis was highly complimentary of de Smith's work, subject to the point that he could have said more in terms of proposing solutions to the many problems he had cogently identified and analysed. However, Davis was coruscating in his criticism of the narrow approach to the judicial function by English judges. He identified a:

> prevailing belief ... that the task of the judges is limited to the application of previously existing law and does not extend either to a re-examination of case law with a view to improving it or to the making of policy choices in giving meaning to silent or unclear statutes ... the attitude runs very deep that judges should have no concern for policy.[31]

De Smith was to some extent a victim of this tradition: while he disapproved of recent decisions sustaining the denial of a hearing 'he makes no effort to work out an affirmative principle'.[32]

III. The Context: Policing

Arrangements whereby there were police forces covering the whole of England and Wales were a product of the nineteenth century.[33] By the mid-1950s there were four main types of police force in England and Wales.[34] These were county police forces controlled by the Chief Constable, subject to the authority of the Standing Joint Committee, which comprised representatives in equal numbers of the justices in quarter sessions and the county council. Borough police forces, also

---

[29] See '"Quasi-judicial" and its background' (1949) 10 *CLJ* 216 (criticising *Franklin*); 'The Twilight of Natural Justice?' (1951) 67 *LQR* 102 (criticising *Nakkuda Ali*); 'Administrative' Law and the Right of Self-Defence' in *The Law in Action* (London, Stevens & Sons Ltd, 1954), 79–90; 'The Future of Certiorari' (1958) *CLJ* 218. See also, Wade (1961), Ch 5.

[30] 'The Future of Judge-Made Public Law in England: A Problem of Practical Jurisprudence' (1961) 61 *Col LR* 201. Wade's view ('Law, Opinion and Administration' (1962) 78 *LQR* 188, 200) was that Davis' criticisms were clearly aimed at the right target but overstated, Wade having reservations about 'overt judicial policy-making'. Davis' view was that 'the judicial task should be largely creative': (1961) 61 *Col LR* 201, 210.

[31] (1961) 61 *Col LR* 201, 202.

[32] (1961) 61 *Col LR* 201, 204. There was, however, here and there a tendency to break out of the intellectual climate of the English legal profession: (1961) 61 *Col LR* 201, 205 n10.

[33] See in particular the County and Borough Police Acts 1856 and 1859. On the history of policing in England and Wales see T Critchley (1978), *A History of Police in England and Wales* London, Constable, Revised edn; K. Smith (2010) in *The Oxford History of the Laws of England* Vol XIII Oxford, OUP, Pt 1, Ch 2.

[34] C Moriarty (1955), *Police Procedure and Administration* London, Butterworth & Co. Publishers Ltd. 6th edn, pp 12–14.

led by a Chief Constable, were subject to the authority of the Watch Committee of the relevant borough council. The Metropolitan Police Force was overseen by the Home Secretary and the City of London Police by the Common Council of the City of London. Outside London, there were many more separate police forces than today.[35]

The law relating to the police was complicated, although standard terms and conditions were introduced for all police forces in England and Wales by the Police Act 1919,[36] which authorised the Secretary of State to make regulations as to, inter alia, the 'government' and 'conditions of service' of members of police forces.[37] The relationship of the new power to make regulations to existing statutory provisions allowing for the suspension or dismissal of a chief officer[38] received very little attention.[39]

The relationship between the old statutory provisions and the new disciplinary regulations was, however, subsequently discussed in a small number of cases. In *Wallwork v Fielding*[40] the Court of Appeal rejected an argument that the power of suspension under the Municipal Corporation Act 1882 Section 191(4) had been impliedly repealed by the provisions of the Police Act 1919 and the regulations made thereunder by the Secretary of State.[41] Implied repeal could not arise where

---

[35] By 1955 there were 52 county and 73 city and borough forces: Moriarty, *op cit* n 34, pp 14–15.

[36] The 1919 Act ss 1–3 established a new Police Federation, prohibited members of a police force from membership of a trade union, and established new offence governing incitement of a member of a police force to disaffection. This Act was passed in response to the police strike of that year: see G Reynolds and A Judge (1962), *The Night the Police Went on Strike* London, Weidenfeld & Nicolson.

[37] 1919 Act Section 4. This was regarded as including discipline. The 1919 Act implemented the recommendations of the Desborough Report, [1920] Reports of the Committee on the Police Service Cmd 574 and Cmd 874, See further the Police Regulations 1920, SR & O 1920/1484, as amended. In 1948 the Oaksey Committee (Reports of the Committee on Police Conditions of Service, Cmd 7674 and Cmd 7831) made further recommendations for the improvement of pay and other matters, which were given effect in the new consolidated Police Regulations 1952, SI 1952/1704, Police (Discipline) Regs 1952, SI 1952/1705 and Police (Discipline) (Deputy Chief Constables, Assistant Chief Constables and Chief Constables) Regulations 1952, SI 1952/1706, as amended.

[38] Metropolitan Police Act 1829 s 5; County Police Act 1839 s 4; County and Borough Police Act 1856 s 26; Municipal Corporations Act 1882 s 191(4). The 1839 Act s 4 provided that a county chief constable held office until dismissed by the police authority. The 1882 Act s 191(4) provided: 'The Watch Committee ... may at any time suspend, and ... may at any time dismiss, any borough constable whom they think negligent in the discharge of his duty, or otherwise unfit for the same.' (This applied to dismissal of a borough chief constable.) Borough chief constables tended to be appointed from less exalted social backgrounds than county chief constables; while the grounds for dismissal of the former were narrower than those applicable to the latter, in practice borough chief constables were more likely to be subjected to dismissal: see D Wall (1998), *The Chief Constables of England and Wales* Aldershot, Ashgate pp 260–263 and Ch 9.

[39] Objections at Third Reading in the Commons (HC Deb 1 August 1919 vol 118 cc 2441–74) that inclusion of the word 'government' in Clause 4 would enable the Home Secretary to exercise 'executive powers' and so 'supersede entirely the watch committees' (E Shortt MP at c 2469) were denied by the Home Secretary (E Shortt MP, c 2469), who said that the provision merely gave power to make regulations to standardise conditions and did not take executive power from the watch committee. See to the same effect comments in the House of Lords (HL Deb 08 August 1919 vol 36 cc 633–7).

[40] [1922] 2 KB 66 (CA).

[41] The regulations at that time made no provision for suspension.

the subsequent Act does not deal with the subject matter of the previous Act.[42] This was confirmed, obiter, by Greer LJ in *Cooper v Wilson*.[43] His Lordship also expressed the view[44] that 'the regulations … must be read as applying to the way in which the Watch Committee are to exercise their powers in a borough'.[45]

All this meant that the Watch Committee in Brighton in dealing with difficulties presented to them in the case of their Chief Constable, Charles Ridge, was in an uncertain legal position. Clear guidance as to the relationship between the statutory powers of dismissal and the discipline regulations was not to be found in court decisions, the 1952 Regulations themselves, or indeed in Home Office guidance on the Regulations.[46]

IV. The Context: The Brighton Conspiracy Trial

In the 1950s the Brighton police force was a borough force of 260 officers serving a population of 156,900.[47] According to James Morton,[48] Scotland Yard officers had had suspicions about the Brighton Police Force for some years. However, there was no hard evidence until one Alan Bennett[49] approached them with evidence that he had given money to Detective Sergeant Heath and Detective Inspector Hammersley (Deputy Head of Brighton CID) in exchange for information. This led to an investigation by Scotland Yard officers and the arrests on 25 October 1957 of Heath and Hammersley, the Chief Constable of Brighton, Charles Feild Williams Ridge,[50] Anthony John Lyons, the proprietor of Sherry's Bar in Brighton

---

[42] Lord Sterndale MR at p 71.
[43] [1937] 2 KB 309 (CA), at p 316.
[44] ibid. This view was cited to but not expressly addressed by Cassels J in *Hogg v Scott* [1947] 1 KB 759, which concerned the powers of dismissal exercisable by the Metropolitan Police Commissioner.
[45] There were also cases where non-compliance with particular regulations had been held to be breaches of requirements that were directory only and not mandatory, and so not fatal to the lawfulness of the decision: *Kilduff v Wilson* [1939] 1 All ER 429; *Noakes v Smith* [1942] 107 JP 101.
[46] See HO Circular No 209/1952, Police (Discipline) Regulations, 1952, and Police (Discipline) (Deputy Chief Constables, Assistant Chief Constables and Chief Constables) Regulations, 1952. The Circular did mention (at p 11) the distinction between *suspension from duty* now provided for under the Regulations and *suspension* under the statutory powers, referring to *Cooper v Wilson* and *Wallwork v Fielding* (see n 40), and noting that suspension under the latter did, but the former did not, include suspension of a constable's right to resign. This clearly contemplated co-existence of the two regimes.
[47] See Moriarty (n 34 above), para 328.
[48] J Morton (1994), *Bent Coppers: A Survey of Police Corruption* London, Warner Books, pp 95–101. The following account is mostly based on Morton's book.
[49] Bennett ran the Astor Club in Brighton, known as the 'Bucket of Blood' because of the claret spilt during fights there.
[50] Ridge joined the Burnley Police Force in 1924, transferred to Brighton in 1925, and was promoted to Sergeant in 1936, Detective Inspector in 1948, Detective Chief Inspector in 1949, Detective Superintendent in 1950 and Deputy Chief Constable in 1954. He received a number of commendations. This information comes from the Cases and Appendices for *Ridge v Baldwin* in the Parliamentary Archives at HL/PO/JU/4/3/1111. When it came to his appointment as Chief Constable in 1956, Ridge was interviewed alongside a number of external candidates. The Home Office was assured by HM Inspector of

and Samuel Bellson, owner of the Burlesque Club. They were charged with conspiracy to solicit and obtain rewards for Heath, Hammersley and Ridge for showing or promising favours contrary to their duty as police officers. Ridge was also charged with a separate offence of corruptly receiving £20 from Bennett. They were all remanded in custody on that day.[51] Ridge was suspended from duty by the Watch Committee under the powers conferred by the Regulations;[52] he was released on bail on 30 October on the order of Diplock J.[53] After extensive committal proceedings,[54] they were committed for trial at the Old Bailey.

The conspiracy trial was a cause célèbre and received extensive newspaper coverage.[55] The trial judge was Donovan J.[56] Ridge was defended by Geoffrey Lawrence QC.[57] There were two episodes concerning Ridge. The first, in December 1954, concerned an investigation by Heath and Hammersley of one John Leach for theft. There was evidence that Bellson told John Leach and John's father, Harry, that he thought he could get the prosecution washed out and that Harry gave him £100 with that end in view. There was evidence by two police officers that Bellson had told them that he had been sent along by Ridge to Harry Leach

---

Constabulary William Johnson that the best candidate would be chosen on merit by the Watch Committee. While the Watch Committee would do better to appoint an outsider, Ridge was 'very well liked locally', and there was no reason not to approve the appointment. The Home Office decided to ignore an anonymous letter from 'A Brother West Indian (Trinidad)' that said that Ridge was 'not a popular man except with the local business men who put him there for their own purpose. It is not considered policy to appoint a local man for very obvious reasons. Nuff said.' The relevant documents are in the National Archives, HO 287/328.

[51] *The Times*, October 26, 1957. When Ridge was charged by Detective Superintendent I Forbes-Leith, he said: 'I would like to say it is absolutely preposterous': *Police Review* 1 November 1957, p 775.

[52] ie the Police (Discipline) (Deputy Chief Constables, Assistant Chief Constables and Chief Constables) Regulations 1952, SI 1952/1706 reg 15. When Ridge was suspended from duty the Watch Committee wished to appoint the Chief Constable of Exeter, Albert Rowsell, as acting Chief Constable of Brighton. This led to consideration by the Home Office of complex legal issues. Suspension under the Regulations (as distinct from under the power in the 1882 Act s 191(4) simply 'to suspend') did not mean there was a vacancy in the office of Chief Constable of Brighton; Rowsell said he would return to Exeter if he was appointed as a Deputy, to exercise the Chief Constable's powers in Ridge's absence. In the event the Home Office decided to risk a legal challenge to the acts of Rowsell as Chief Constable and simply approved his appointment 'to act as Chief Constable'. The relevant documents are in the National Archives, HO 287/328. On his appointment by the Watch Committee on 28 October 1958, Rowsell was described by Baldwin as recommended by the Home Office as a 'strong man with great detective experience': *Daily Express*, 29 October 1957.

[53] *The Times* 31 October 1957.

[54] Documented in D Rowland (2007), *Bent Cops: The Brighton Police conspiracy trial* Peacehaven, Finsbury Books.

[55] See *The Times* passim for February 1958. The proceedings were summarised in H Palmer, 'The Brighton Conspiracy Case' [1958] *Crim LR* 422. While there was a single count of conspiracy, there were nine separate groups of overt acts relied on as evidence. Only two concerned Ridge; one of these was the only one that concerned Lyons.

[56] See ODNB Obituary by Bob Hepple. He was regarded as a 'conscientious and effective trial judge', being selected by the Lord Chief Justice to sit on the 'highly publicized and arduous trial' of Ridge and the others. His handling of the trial was commended by the Court of Criminal Appeal: *R v Hammersley*, *The Times*, May 13, 1958.

[57] See ODNB Obituary by GR Rubin.

'to do some business for him'.⁵⁸ There was also evidence that Ridge went to see Harry privately, after being told that Harry had tried to bribe the police, although not that anything improper was said. The second episode, dating back to 1955, involved evidence by Bennett that Lyons had been involved in arrangements to pay Ridge to ensure that late night drinking could proceed at the Astor Club without being bothered.⁵⁹

At the end of the trial, on 28 February 1958, Heath, Hammersley and Bellson were convicted but Ridge and Lyons acquitted.⁶⁰ In passing sentence on Heath and Hammersley, Donovan J said that the facts admitted in the course of the trial 'establish that neither of you had that professional and moral leadership which both of you should have had and were entitled to expect from the Chief Constable'. Donovan J referred here to Ridge's visit to a suspected briber in private and alone, and Ridge's meeting in his private room with 'a much convicted and hectoring bookmaker' (one Page), as setting a bad example. The same day, Ridge applied through his solicitors for reinstatement.⁶¹

On 6 March 1958, Ridge returned to court to face the charge alleging corruption, but no evidence was offered. On this occasion, Donovan J referred to the Brighton police force and the need for a leader for it. He said it was not difficult to foresee how the incidents found in the case would be used to discredit officers on the force as witnesses in future prosecutions and the results might be unfortunate. This risk would remain:

> until a leader is given to that force who will be a new influence, and who will set a different example from that which has lately occurred. I realise that this is a matter which is about to engage the attention of those persons whose responsibility it is, and I have no desire to trespass upon their domain, but since the matter will also affect the administration of justice in the courts I felt it right to make these observations.⁶²

According to the account of Neville Faulks⁶³ (who was leading counsel for the Watch Committee in the ensuing litigation), that night, the junior counsel on

---

⁵⁸ Bellson denied this in evidence at the trial. Donovan directed the jury that what was alleged to have been said by Bellson to the police officers in 1957 was no evidence in law against Ridge and in any event they might take the view, having seen Bellson in the witness box, that 'they would not hang a cat on his evidence, let alone a Chief Constable': Palmer, [1958] *Crim LR* 422, 425–426. It was also alleged that Heath and Hammersley asked John Leach directly for money to get rid of the evidence.

⁵⁹ Donovan J directed the jury to bear in mind that Bennett had a criminal record to 1948 and that, if his story was true, he was an accomplice upon whose evidence it was dangerous to convict without corroboration: Palmer, [1958] *Crim LR* 422, 427.

⁶⁰ The following facts are taken from the Law Report of *Ridge v Baldwin* [1964] AC 40.

⁶¹ JC Bosley, Ridge's solicitor, gave evidence at the subsequent trial in *Ridge v Baldwin* that the letter was dictated on the morning of the 28th and sent to the Town Clerk's office before he heard of Donovan's remarks. Nevertheless, it was subsequently conceded that the application was premature: Case for the Appellant on the appeal to the House of Lords para 5 (viii).

⁶² [1964] AC 40, 45. The obituary of Lord Donovan (as he subsequently became) in *The Guardian* December 14, 1971, states that 'the Bar looked askance at the homily delivered by the judge after the Chief Constable had been acquitted.' There was also criticism in the *Police Review*: 7 March 1958, at 167.

⁶³ N Faulks 1978, *A Law Unto Myself*, London, William Kimber pp 80–87.

whom the Watch Committee normally relied was rung up at home and asked what they should do in the circumstances. 'It was a tricky one and it is impossible not to have sympathy with him, but he did not bring the Police Discipline Regulations 1952 to the attention of the Watch Committee.'[64]

The next day, 7 March, the Watch Committee met and considered the length of Ridge's service, the trial, Donovan J's statements, the statements made by Ridge in evidence at the trial and 'certain statements made today by members of the Committee and the Town Clerk'. Ridge was not present and had not been notified of any specific charges. The Committee concluded that he had been negligent in the discharge of his duty and was unfit for the same, and dismissed him under Section 191(4) of the Municipal Corporation Act 1882. After some correspondence, Ridge's solicitor, Mr Bosley,[65] was allowed to address the Watch Committee on 18 March 1958, but specific charges were not mentioned. The Committee adhered to its previous decision, this time with three in dissent.

Ridge then appealed against dismissal to the Home Secretary under the Police Appeals Act 1927, the notice of appeal stating this was 'without prejudice to Mr Ridge's rights to contend that the purported notice of dismissal is bad in law'. The Home Secretary rejected the appeal, holding that there was sufficient material before the Committee to justify the dismissal.[66]

A civil action for damages for breach of contract was commenced by Ridge against the members of the Watch Committee, of which Councillor GB Baldwin was the chairman. After amendment, the claim subsequently became one for (A) a declaration that the purported dismissal was illegal, ultra vires and void and that Ridge was and at all material times had been the Chief Constable of Brighton; (B) payment of salary of £1,990 pa from 7 March 1958; (C) alternatively, a declaration that Ridge was entitled to a pension of £1,070 per annum from 7 March 1958; (D) payment of such pension; (E) alternatively, damages; and (F) interest.[67]

The Watch Committee first sought advice from Gerald Gardiner QC, but as he could not guarantee to do the case because of the pressure of his extensive practice, the brief passed to Neville Faulks QC.[68] Gardiner's view was that 'we had "had it" as the Regulations obviously applied, and we hadn't followed them'.[69] However,

---

[64] Faulks, n 63, p 81. (This is of course odd in that the Watch Committee should have been aware of them as they had relied on them to *suspend* Ridge.)

[65] A 'terrier of a solicitor ... a very able man': Faulks n 63, p 82. John Cyril Bosley's firm, Bosley & Co, was founded by him in 1929. The firm is still in existence: www.bosley.co.uk.

[66] At this point, on 11 July 1958, Mr Rowsell was appointed as Chief Constable of Brighton: 'The 'strong man' stays' *Daily Express*, July 12, 1958. The post was not advertised: HO 287/328.

[67] Pleadings in *Ridge v Baldwin* in the Parliamentary Archives at HL/PO/JU/4/3/1111.

[68] Faulks appeared with Anthony Harmsworth. Leading counsel for Ridge at trial was Stanley Rees QC, who appeared with John MacManus.

[69] Faulks, n 63, p 83.

Faulks developed an argument, which subsequently prevailed at the trial of the action before Streatfeild J.[70]

A. *Ridge v Baldwin*: The Decisions of the High Court and the Court of Appeal

Streatfeild J[71] held (i) that the power to dismiss had to be exercised fairly and in accordance with natural justice; (ii) that Ridge's appointment had been on terms and conditions that incorporated the Police Acts and Regulations and the term 'Police Acts' included the relevant provisions of the 1882 Act; (iii) that Section 191(4) of the 1882 Act had not been impliedly repealed by the Police Act 1919 and the regulations, made thereunder, there being 'peaceful coexistence' between them, and had not been excluded by the terms of the contract;[72] (iv) that the concerns about Ridge could be regarded as concerning 'discreditable conduct', under the 1952 Regulations; but (v) the Regulations did not apply as the Committee had not acted on a 'report or allegation' received by them but had simply concluded under Section 191(4) that Ridge had been negligent and was unfit for office on the basis of matters admitted at the trial;[73] (vi) that there had been no breach of natural justice on the facts as 'out of his own mouth at the Old Bailey' Ridge had 'convicted himself of unfitness to hold the office of Chief Constable';[74] and (vii) that in any event he had waived his right to go to the courts by appealing to the Home Secretary, whose decision under the Police Act 1927 was 'final and binding'. The action was dismissed. Faulks was 'surprised and very pleased'; there was 'jubilation' among his clients.[75]

When the case went to the Court of Appeal,[76] Stanley Rees was replaced by Neil Lawson, but he 'found an unsympathetic Bench',[77] which comprised Holroyd Pearce, Harman and (Arthian) DaviesL JJ. The defendants conceded that, had the dismissal been effected under the regulations, the rules of natural justice would apply, but dismissal under the 1882 Act Section 191(4) was an 'administrative act',

---

[70] In 1958, the Town Clerk of Brighton also sought advice from the Home Office, but the view was taken that where a suit was pending the Home Office should 'normally be very chary' of supplying advice beyond drawing attention to decided cases that might be relevant. The Home Office followed the course of the litigation with interest, but did not wish to appear 'too interested' (HO 287/92).
[71] [1963] 1 QB 539. See G Ganz [1961] *Public Law* 341.
[72] His Lordship considered *Wallwork v Fielding* [1922] 2 KB 66 and *Cooper v Wilson* [1937] 2 KB 309, 316 per Greer LJ.
[73] Heath and Hammersley had been dismissed following their convictions. Ridge conceded in evidence that had he been convicted he could not have complained about dismissal outside the Regulations: see Streatfeild J. [1963] 1 QB 539, at p 552.
[74] Streatfeild J at p 556.
[75] Faulks, n 63, p 84.
[76] [1963] 1 QB 539. De Smith [1962] 25 *MLR* 455 was generally critical of the Court of Appeal's decision.
[77] Faulks, n 63, p 84.

contrary to the view of Streatfeild J.[78] The only case relied on for this proposition was *Nakkuda Ali v Jayaratne*.[79] In reply, the plaintiff relied only on *De Verteuil v Knaggs*,[80] as a case where 'the power was administrative but the principles of natural justice were applied'.[81] Most of the argument centered on the relevance of the Police (Discipline) Regulations.[82]

The Court of Appeal agreed with Streatfeild J on the points concerning the applicability of the statutory provisions, but disagreed on the points concerning natural justice. On the latter, the Court held, first, that dismissal under the 1882 Act Section 191(4) was 'administrative' not 'quasi-judicial'.[83] Harman LJ noted[84] that 'the defendants were not deciding a question between two opposing parties. There was no lis and nothing to decide'. However, if the power *had* been quasi-judicial, then there would have been a breach of natural justice in that there was a real issue to be considered, indeed the 'real point' of this case,[85] namely whether Ridge should be permitted to resign, thus preserving his pension.[86] A further point made was that had the dismissal been unlawful it would have been voidable not void.[87]

B. *Ridge v Baldwin* in the House of Lords

The House of Lords gave leave to appeal, and in due course allowed the appeal by four to one.[88] In the meantime there was a further change of counsel. As Neil Lawson was committed in a case in the Court of Appeal, he was replaced by Desmond Ackner QC.[89] Ackner consulted William Wade before and during the hearing in the House of Lords,[90] and came armed with additional cases and arguments on the

---

[78] N Faulks QC at p 561.
[79] [1951] AC 66 (PC) see above n 25.
[80] [1918] AC 557 (PC). Here, the power of the Governor of Trinidad 'on sufficient ground shown to his satisfaction' to transfer the indentures of immigrants from one employer to another was held to require compliance with *audi alteram partem*.
[81] N Lawson, [1963] 1 QB 539 at p 562.
[82] N Lawson at p 562.
[83] Relying on *Nakkuda Ali v Jayaratne*. *De Verteuil v Knaggs* was to be distinguished: the words 'on sufficient ground shown to his satisfaction' implied that an inquiry was to be made and these were very different from the words 'may dismiss any constable whom they think negligent': Holroyd Pear LJ [1963] 1 QB 539 at 569.
[84] [1963] 1 QB 539, 577.
[85] Holroyd Pearce LJ [1963] 1 QB 539 at 570.
[86] Harman LJ felt 'great doubt' whether natural justice had been satisfied: [1963] 1 QB 539, 578. Davies LJ (at para 582) 'inclined' to this view.
[87] Holroyd Pearce LJ [1963] 1 QB 539 at 572: 'there was jurisdiction even if wrongly exercised'. See to the same effect Harman LJ at 579.
[88] [1964] AC 40 (HL). Lords Reid, Hodson, Morris of Borth-y-Gest and Devlin, Lord Evershed dissenting. Borth-y-Gest lies one mile from Portmadoc (now Portmadhog), Ridge's birthplace.
[89] Faulks, n 63, p 86.
[90] According to the ODNB obituary by Christopher Forsyth, when approached by Ackner during the hearing, Wade sacrificed an evening at the theatre with his wife, analysed the issues, and provided the necessary authorities for Ackner early the following morning. Ackner cited Wade's writings in his Reply in the House of Lords: see n 97. The story was amplified in an interview of Lord Ackner (as he

natural justice points. Faulks' view was that the Court of Appeal had 'had the facts of the matter very firmly in mind' while in the House of Lords 'the facts seemed to be secondary, and we were dealing with abstract questions of law'.[91] He recounted that 'Lord Evershed was with me from the start, but there were four other stony faces turned towards me when I rose to answer my opponent's argument'.

At this stage, Ackner did not seek to argue that the power under the 1882 Act Section 191(4) had been impliedly repealed; instead, he argued that the regulations were 'grafted onto it'. There had indeed been a 'report or allegation', the regulations had not been followed and the dismissal was accordingly void.[92] Apart from that, natural justice had to be observed anyway.[93] The breach of natural justice itself rendered the decision void and of no effect, not voidable.[94] In response Faulks[95] defended the position taken by the Court of Appeal.[96] In reply,[97] Ackner adduced further cases and on *Nakkuda Ali* cited two articles by Wade and, on the alleged finality of the appeal to the Home Secretary, Wade's book on *Administrative Law*.[98]

The Appellate Committee of the House of Lords was presided over by Lord Reid,[99] who had become senior Law Lord in succession to Viscount Simmonds in 1962. According to Lord Reid's note of the initial positions taken by the members of the House after the hearing,[100] most of the key points made at this stage related to the position as regards the regulations. It is interesting to note that Lord Devlin at this point mentioned 'de Smith Judicial Review' in relation to the void/voidable distinction; de Smith's writings were, however, not mentioned in the reported summary of counsel's arguments or in any of the opinions.

Moving to the opinions subsequently delivered, Lords Reid, Morris of Borth-y-Gest and Hodson held that the dismissal was void for both non-compliance

---

then was) by A. Paterson for the thesis on which A Paterson (1982), *The Law Lords* Palgrave Macmillan, was based. During argument, Lord Morris (to Lord Reid's irritation) mentioned four cases on dismissal that he thought the respondents might find of assistance; by the next day, Ackner was able to cite six cases in response (see [1964] AC 40 (HL) at 59–60, 62) (Paterson, 'A sociological investigation of the creative role performance of English appellate court judges in hard cases' DPhil Thesis, p 5.89). I am grateful to Alan Paterson for drawing this to my attention.

[91] Faulks, n. 63, pp 84–85.
[92] [1964] AC 40 (HL), paras 49–50.
[93] On this, he cited a long line of authorities going back to the case of *Bagg* and *Dr Bentley*, and including *Cooper v Wandsworth Board of Works*: see above nn 12–14. *Nakkuda Ali* [1951] AC 66 (PC) was out of line with the old cases. Where the rights of citizens were involved, the courts would readily assume the necessity of an inquiry; there might be administrative functions which by their very nature required application of the principle of natural justice: [1964] AC 40 (HL), 52–53.
[94] A further series of cases was cited that had not been mentioned in the courts below.
[95] [1940] AC 40 (HL), pp 55–60.
[96] This included reliance on *Nakkuda Ali, R v Metropolitan Police Commissioner,* ex parte *Parker* (see above n 25) and *R v Legislative Committee of Church Assembly, ex p Haynes-Smith* [1928] 1 KB 411 (DC) for the point that was here 'no determination between two people'.
[97] [1940] AC 40 (HL), pp 60–63.
[98] (1951) 67 *LQR* 103, 106 and (1962) 78 *LQR* 188, n199; *Administrative Law* (1961) p 112.
[99] For biographical information see ODNB obituary by T Smith.
[100] I am grateful to A. Paterson for drawing this to my attention. Lord Reid's Notebooks are kept in the Parliamentary Archives at REI.

with the regulations and breach of natural justice. Lord Devlin held the dismissal void for non-compliance with the regulations. Lord Evershed dissented. Lord Reid's opinion dealt mainly with natural justice and Lord Morris's mainly with the regulations.

C. Non-compliance with the Police Discipline Regulations

Lord Morris provided a detailed account of the issues concerning applicability of the regulations,[101] which itself constituted a *tour de force* whose significance has perhaps been under-appreciated in comparison with Lord Reid's landmark opinion on natural justice. Lord Morris agreed with the Court of Appeal that the effect of the Police Act 1919 was that the powers given by the 1882 Act Section 191(4) had to be exercised in accordance with any regulations made under the 1919 Act 'which are applicable'.[102] He was not prepared to say that *every* power under Section 191(4) was controlled by the regulations: the regulations did not appear to cover dismissal of a constable thought to be unfit for the discharge of his duties. However, the regulations would be applicable wherever a constable was thought to be negligent in the discharge of his duties and so guilty of an offence under Section 4 of the Discipline Code, or to be guilty of some other offence under the Code. The Watch Committee had rested the summary dismissal on both negligence and unfitness; had there been unfitness without negligence 'it would seem to be inherently unlikely that they would have exercised a power of summary dismissal'.[103]

Ridge was nearing the date when he could retire on his pension; the Committee had power under the Police Pensions Regulations 1955[104] to require him to retire on the grounds that his retention with the force would not be in the general interest of efficiency. But the Committee had found Ridge to be negligent and so had made a finding of misconduct without a charge or hearing. It could not be doubted that a finding of 'negligence' under Section 191(4) also constituted 'neglect of duty' under the regulations. The suggestion that the Committee had not received any report or allegation was 'most surprising'.[105] Indeed it was difficult to understand how the Committee could ever act in a disciplinary matter without first having some report or some allegation that an offence may have been committed. Here, in so far as they considered evidence that emerged at trial[106] they would be treating that material as a report or allegation; in so far as they considered

---

[101] [1964] AC 40 (HL), pp 102–121.
[102] [1964] AC 40 (HL), p 110. His Lordship cited Greer LJ's dictum in *Cooper v Wilson* [1937] 2 KB 309, 316, see above n 44.
[103] [1964] AC 40 (HL), p 110.
[104] SI 1955/480 reg 52.
[105] [1964] AC 40 (HL), p 111.
[106] They did not on March 7 have a transcript of evidence but it was to be expected that they were following proceedings.

(as they said they did) Donovan J's statements and 'certain statements made by members of the Committee and the Town Clerk'[107] they must have received 'reports or allegations'. The Regulations were applicable, the Committee had not begun to comply with them and their decision could have no validity[108] unless subsequent events had made it valid. Compliance with at least the essentials of the regulations was a condition precedent to any dismissal based on a finding of guilt. These essentials included and incorporated the principles of natural justice: 'here is something, which is basic to our system: the importance of upholding it far transcends the significance of any particular case'.[109]

Lord Morris pointed out that while Ridge had not been on trial for negligence in the discharge of duty, if facts had emerged at the trial suggesting that it would have been simple for the Watch Committee to state them. Furthermore, Ridge denied any impropriety in the Leach and Page matters but had had no opportunity to deal with them in front of the Committee before the decision to dismiss was made. As to the subsequent events, neither the meeting on 18 March, at which the solicitor was 'received with courtesy but in silence' and was given no further particulars of the case against Ridge, nor the appeal to the Home Secretary, could give validity to what was done on 7 March. The provision of the Police (Appeals) Act 1927 Section 2(3) that the decision of the Secretary of State was 'final and binding on all parties' could not give validity to a nullity.

Lords Reid[110] and Hodson[111] expressly agreed with Lord Morris's views on the Regulations. Lord Devlin adopted a different analysis leading to the same outcome.[112] Lord Evershed[113] dissented on the applicability of the Regulations.[114]

Overall, the views of the majority are easily more persuasive than those in dissent although neither side really deals with the 'absurdity' argument presented by the other. However, it cannot be said that the answer was obvious.[115] The Police

---

[107] Lord Morris inferred that these included conclusions that Ridge had given false evidence at the trial to the effect that he had reported one matter to the Deputy Town Clerk and the Chairman of the Watch Committee and another to the then Chief Constable. The Committee had mentioned this in their statements on the appeal to the Home Secretary dated 18 April: [1964] AC 40 (HL), pp 47, 113.

[108] They had acted 'without jurisdiction' and their decision was a 'nullity' [1964] AC 40 (HL) p 118 and 'void' [1964] AC 40 (HL), p 119.

[109] [1964] AC 40 (HL) p 114.

[110] [1964] AC 40 (HL), p 80. He noted that Neville Faulks QC had accepted that if 'some busybody' had formally reported Donovan J's observations to the Committee then the Regulations would have applied. It would be absurd if Ridge's rights were to depend on whether a formal report or allegation had been made to the Committee before they proceeded to deal with the case.

[111] [1964] AC 40 (HL), pp 133–136.

[112] [1964] AC 40, (HL) pp 136–142.

[113] [1964] AC 40 (HL), pp 82–85.

[114] Ridge's 'shortcomings' as described by Donovan J did not constitute 'discreditable conduct' or 'neglect of duty' under Sections 1 and 4 of the Discipline Code. In addition there had not been a 'report or allegation' as contemplated by the regulations. This expression would apply to an 'accusation' rather than a judicial conclusion reached after a protracted trial. Otherwise it would have been necessary to follow the procedure in the Regulations before lawfully dismissing Heath and Hammersley, and this was 'manifestly absurd'.

[115] Pace Gerald Gardiner: see n 69.

Regulations seemed to have been drafted without consideration of the exact relationship between them and power of dismissal under the 1882 Act Section 191(4) or their application to Chief Constables. Without saying so in terms,[116] the majority adopted a purposive rather than literal interpretation of the Regulations. The view that dismissal without any compliance with the Regulations was void was an orthodox application of existing principle, it being accepted that minor deviations from particular requirements would not invalidate the outcome.[117]

D. Natural Justice

Ridge v Baldwin is best known for Lord Reid's speech, which was focussed largely on *audi alteram partem*. The general structure of his analysis echoes the position previously espoused by de Smith and Wade, and adopted by Ackner.[118] Accordingly, one key objective achieved by the opinion was the rescue of long established principles from a relatively recent misunderstanding, which had led to aberrant cases now held to have been wrongly reasoned, although not necessarily wrongly decided. The academic commentary provided plenty of firepower for the demolition of *Nakkuda Ali*. But how far would Lord Reid go further and establish principles that would guide future courts and the development of the law?

Important contextual points made early in the opinion were that the *audi alteram partem* principle goes back many centuries and appears in a multitude of judgments. Modern opinions that 'natural justice' was so vague as to be practically meaningless[119] were 'tainted by the perennial fallacy that because something cannot be cut and dried or nicely weighed or measured therefore it does not exist'.[120] What a reasonable person would regard as fair procedure in particular circumstances and what they would regard as negligence, were equally capable of serving as tests in law. Furthermore, 'insufficient attention has been paid to the great difference between various kinds of cases in which it has been sought to apply the [*audi alteram partem*] principle'. Cases concerning ministerial approval of schemes might be very different from the dismissal of a Chief Constable.[121]

There is here articulation probably for the first time in the courts of two key features of the principles of judicial review as they are now understood: First, that these are broad principles rather than precise rules; and, secondly, that their application depends on the context. The price to be paid is the fact that the law is less certain and predictable is a price worth paying.

---

[116] The nearest to doing so was Lord Devlin at p 138 referring to the 'object' of Article 2 of the Code in the Regulations.

[117] See Lord Morris at p 113. Although the term was not used, in common contemporary terminology these requirements would be 'directory' only.

[118] See above, text accompanying nn 4–29.

[119] cf de Smith (1959) pp 101–102.

[120] [1964] AC 40 (HL), p 65.

[121] [1964] AC 40 (HL), p 65.

Lord Reid's opinion turned next to dismissal cases.[122] In the case of master and servant (not applicable here as the Chief Constable was not the servant of the Watch Committee or anyone else), whether observation of natural justice was necessary for the dismissal not to be a breach of contract turned on the terms of the contract. However, the courts would not grant an order of specific performance.[123] In the cases of offices terminable 'at pleasure', there was no right to be heard before dismissal.[124] However, there was such a right where (as here) the office-holder could only be dismissed for cause.[125] Accordingly, the authorities seemed wholly to be in Ridge's favour. Indeed, the authorities relied upon by the Watch Committee dealt with different subject-matter—decisions by ministers, officials and other bodies adversely affecting property rights. It was necessary to examine these cases as Ridge's real interest was not to secure reinstatement but to save his pension rights. Given this, the respondent's argument that nothing Ridge could have said could have made any difference failed on the facts (and was at least very doubtful anyway); permitting resignation could not have been regarded as a wrongful act or wholly unreasonable.

Lord Reid then considered the cases starting with *Cooper v Wandsworth Board of Works*[126] that established that no person could be deprived of their property without having the opportunity to be heard. Ordering a house to be pulled down 'from the nature of the thing done it must be a judicial act'.[127] The same principle applied in cases of deprivation of membership of a professional or social body.[128] Had the present case arisen thirty or forty years previously, the courts would have had no difficulty in finding for Ridge. However, the Court of Appeal had relied on more recent authorities to reject his claim. Lord Reid thought there were three reasons for how this had come about. First, cases concerning the limited application of natural justice to the decisions of ministers had been reflected in other decisions on matters to which in principle they did not appear to Lord Reid to apply. Secondly, the same was true of certain wartime decisions. Thirdly there had, he thought, been a misunderstanding of the judgment of Atkin LJ in *R v Electricity Commissioners*.[129]

---

[122] [1964] AC 40 (HL), pp 65–68.

[123] It should be noted that the Supreme Court has recently decided that, contrary to the understanding at the time of *Ridge v Baldwin*, repudiation of a contract of employment does not take effect unless accepted: *Geys v Société Générale, London Branch* [2012] UKSC 63, [2013] 1 AC 523 (SC).

[124] Reid cited, inter alia, *Terrell v Secretary of States for the Colonies* [1953] 2 QB 482 (QBD); *R v Darlington School Governors* (1844) 6 QB 682.

[125] Reid cited, inter alia, *Bagg's Case*; *R v Smith* (1844) 5 QB 614; *Ex p Ramshay* (1852) 18 QB 173.

[126] Other cases mentioned were *Hopkins v Smethwick Local Board of Health* (1880) 24 QBD 712 (CA); *Smith v The Queen* LR (1878) 3 App Cas 614 (PC); *De Verteuil v Knaggs* [1918] AC 557 (PC); *Spackman v Plumstead District Board of Works*(1885) 10 App Cas 229.

[127] Wills J in *Hopkins* at pp 714–715.

[128] *Wood v Woad* (1874) LR 9 Ex 190 approved in *Lapointe v L'Association de Bienfaisance et de Retraite de la Police de Montréal* [1906] AC 535 (PC); *Fisher v Keane* (1878) 11 ChD 353; *Dawkins v Antrobus* (1879) 17 ChD 615 (CA);] *Weinberger v Inglis* [1919] AC 606 (HL). All were cases cited by de Smith (1959) 105.

[129] [1924] 1 KB 171 (CA).

As to cases concerning ministers and departments, their functions often concerned schemes such as for a major new road rather than the individual cases of the kind dealt with by the Board of Works or a club committee. The minister would have to consider all manner of questions of public interest and could not be prevented from attaching more importance to the fulfilment of the minister's policy than to the fate of individual objectors. As explained in *Local Government Board v Arlidge*[130] a minister could not do everything himself.

> His officers will have to gather and sift all the facts, including objections by individuals, and no individual can complain if the ordinary accepted methods of carrying on public business do not give him as good protection as would be given by the principles of natural justice in a different kind of case.[131]

We do not have a developed system of administrative law[132]—perhaps because until fairly recently we did not need it. So it is not surprising that in dealing with new types of cases the courts have had to grope for solutions, and have found that old powers, rules and procedures are largely inapplicable to cases which they were never designed or intended to deal with.[133]

That did not, however, justify a view that the old methods were any less applicable to the older kind of case. As to the wartime cases, it was reasonable to infer from the circumstances and subject matter of the Defence Regulations that the intention must have been to exclude the principles of natural justice. It was not to be expected that this would be stated openly as that 'would have been almost calculated to create the alarm and despondency against which one of the regulations was specifically directed'.[134]

Furthermore, in many regulations there was an alternative safeguard in the requirement of an objective test[135] that the officers have reasonable cause. (He added:[136] 'I leave out of account the very peculiar decision of this House in *Liversidge v Anderson*.[137] Accordingly, wartime decisions should not be regarded as of any great weight in dealing with cases of the older type, such as the present one.

A further complication had been a misunderstanding of the much cited dictum of Atkin LJ in *R v Electricity Commissioners, ex parte London Electricity Joint Committee Co*, that the writs of certiorari and prohibition were available 'wherever any body of persons having legal authority to determine questions affecting the rights

---

[130] [1915] AC 120 (HL).
[131] This is presumably an implicit reference to the contemporary position, endorsed in *Arlidge*, that the report of an inspector after a public inquiry did not have to be disclosed.
[132] This is one of the first references in the courts to the concept of 'administrative law'.
[133] [1964] AC 40 (HL), pp 72–73.
[134] [1964] AC 40 (HL) p 73. This is presumably a reference to Defence Reg 39(B)(A), made in June 1940, forbidding the publication of 'any report or statement relating to matters connected with the war which is likely to cause alarm or despondency'.
[135] ie presumably there would have to be sufficient evidence on the point put before the court for it to be satisfied that there were reasonable grounds: the approach adopted by the Privy Council in *Nakkuda Ali v Jayaratne* [1951] AC 66 (PC).
[136] [1964] AC 40, (HL) p 73. An observation invariably cited by critics of *Liversidge*.
[137] [1942] AC 206 (HL).

of subjects, act in excess of their legal authority'.[138] In *R v Legislative Assembly of the Church of England, ex p Haynes-Smith*[139] the Divisional Court had held that the Assembly was a deliberative or legislative body not a judicial one. However, Lord Hewart[140] had interpreted Atkin LJ's judgment as requiring both 'legal authority to determine questions affecting the rights of subjects' and a 'superadded' duty to act judicially. Lord Reid said that this was typical of what had been said in subsequent cases, but was wrong, being inconsistent with many earlier authorities.[141]

Indeed, in *R v Electricity Commissioners* itself, Atkin and Bankes LJJ had 'inferred the judicial element from the nature of the power', and that in a case concerning the exercise of power on a large scale.[142] This brought Lord Reid to consideration of *Nakkuda Ali v Jayaratne*,[143] on which the Court of Appeal had relied. He was prepared to agree that in this case, like other Defence Regulation cases, the legislature had substituted an obligation not to act without reasonable grounds for the ordinary obligation to afford to the person affected an opportunity to submit his defence. However, the Privy Council in *Nakkuda Ali* had held that certiorari would not lie because there was no 'superadded' duty to act judicially, citing *Ex p Haynes-Smith*. Lord Reid noted that no case before 1911 had been cited in *Nakkuda Ali* and that 'it was given under a serious misapprehension of the effect of the older authorities and therefore cannot be regarded as authoritative'. Accordingly, the old cases still applied, and the Watch Committee should have informed Ridge of the grounds on which they proposed to proceed and have given him a proper opportunity to present his case.[144]

Lord Reid dealt succinctly with the remaining points. If what had been done on 18 March had been a full reconsideration of the matter afresh, after affording Ridge a proper opportunity to present his case, then the latter decisions would have been valid. However, what was actually done was a very inadequate substitute for a full rehearing. Indeed, three members of the Committee had changed their minds and it was impossible to say what the decision could have been had there been a full rehearing.[145] Next, the outcome of a breach of natural justice was to render the decision void not voidable.[146] Finally, the claim was not barred by exercise of the right of appeal to the Home Secretary.[147]

It will be noted that Lord Reid's natural justice analysis was cautious, perhaps more cautious than usually thought. Essentially, the outcome was based on old

---

[138] [1924] 1 KB 171 (CA), p 205.
[139] [1928] 1 KB 411 (DC).
[140] [1928] 1 KB 411 (DC), p 415.
[141] Reid cited *R v Smith; ex parte Ramshay; Osgood v Nelson; Cooper v Wandsworth Board of Works; Hopkins v Smethwick Local Board; De Verteuil v Knaggs; Wood v Woad; Fisher v Keane; Weinberger v Inglis*: see nn 125–128, above.
[142] [1964] AC 40 (HL) p 76.
[143] [1951] AC 66 (PC).
[144] [1964] AC 40 (HL), p 79.
[145] [1964] AC 40 (HL), pp 79–80.
[146] [1964] AC 40 (HL), p 80. Reid simply cited *Wood v Woad*, n 13 above.
[147] There was no express waiver as Ridge had expressly preserved his rights. The Secretary of State's decision was not an independent decision that Ridge should be dismissed. Accordingly, the only

cases concerning offices from which the holder could only be dismissed for cause. Lord Reid showed that these cases had never been doubted, were not shaken by recent cases in other contexts, and had not been cited to the Court of Appeal. Furthermore this was a context in which a 'judicial element' was to be inferred from the nature of the power exercised. The opinion is particularly helpful in disposing of Lord Hewart's unnecessary gloss on *R v Electricity Commissioners*.[148] Strictly speaking, this gloss had been rarely cited apart from in *Nakkuda Ali*,[149] and it is notable that *Nakkuda Ali* was disapproved by Lord Reid solely on the question whether certiorari was available and not whether on its facts natural justice should have been observed. He did, however, regard it as a 'wartime' case. Lord Reid did not mention ex parte *Parker*. Neither did he cast any doubt on the correctness of the decisions concerning ministers and those arising in wartime in their respective contexts; his language suggested that he regarded them as rightly decided rather than that he did not need to establish that they were wrong, only distinguishable.

How did the other judges deal with the natural justice issues? Lord Morris dealt briefly with them.[150] The dismissal could not be regarded as an executive or administrative act if based upon a suggestion of neglect of duty.[151] Dismissal from an office where this could only be done for cause was a 'quasi-judicial' function demanding observance of natural justice. The rules of natural justice were not observed, the Watch Committee's decision 'must be regarded as of no effect and invalid, and so can be declared by the court to be void'.[152] The decision was only 'voidable' in the sense that it would stand as a matter of practicality unless Ridge took action to challenge it; should the Court ultimately decide that Ridge's argument was right, then it would hold the dismissal to be void.[153] Ridge's claim was not barred by the appeal, where he had reserved his rights. Accordingly, like Lord Reid, Lord Morris was cautious on natural justice, holding that a decision to dismiss involved exercise of a quasi-judicial function.

---

operative decision was that of the Watch Committee, which was a nullity. Ridge left open the question whether an independent decision would have been protected by the Police (Appeals) Act 1927 s 2(3), but he did not see how the Secretary of State's statement on the appeal 'that there was sufficient material on which the watch committee could properly exercise their power of dismissal' could make a nullity valid.

[148] See above nn 139–142.
[149] *Nakkuda Ali* was the first case in which *Haynes-Smith* was relied on to hold that certiorari was *not* available. *Haynes-Smith* is only cited in de Smith (1959), (p 276) for the proposition that the rules of natural justice do not apply to deliberative bodies. However the *Haynes-Smith* dictum echoes the '*lis inter partes*' formula of cases concerning ministerial orders.
[150] [1964] AC 40 (HL) pp 121–127.
[151] [1964] AC 40 (HL) p 121. Lord Morris cited *Bentley's* case and many of the cases cited by Lord Reid.
[152] On this point Lord Morris was more expansive than Lord Reid, citing *Bagg, Bentley, Wood v Woad* and *Fisher v Keane*.
[153] The Privy Council in *Durayappah v Fernando* [1967] 2 AC 337, 354, subsequently regarded Lord Morris as endorsing the 'voidable' school of thought. This is unconvincing.

In terms of general propositions about the applicability of natural justice, Lord Hodson's speech[154] was the most illuminating. For him, propositions that clearly emerged from the authorities included, first, that the absence of a *lis inter partes* was not a decisive feature although the presence of a *lis* would involve the necessity for the observation of natural justice; and, secondly, that the answer in a given case was not provided by the statement that the decision-maker was acting in an executive or administrative capacity. The cases seemed to Lord Hodson 'to show that persons acting in a capacity which is not on the face of it judicial but rather executive or administrative have been held by the courts to be subject to the principles of natural justice'.[155] Furthermore, the expression 'natural justice' was not so vague as to be inapplicable: no one disputed that three features stood out, the right to be heard by an unbiased tribunal, the right to have notice of charges of misconduct and the right to be heard in answer to those charges. He was aware that what he had said might not be thought to be in line with cases where wide words had been held sufficient to cover the exercise of arbitrary power, 'as in the issue and withdrawal of licences where no question of punishment arises'[156] but ultimately each case depended on its own facts.[157]

Lord Devlin found it unnecessary to deal separately with the question of natural justice, as the Regulations applied and themselves prescribed the rules of justice that were to be followed: However, he expressed no dissent from the view that, if the 1882 Act Section 191(4) stood alone, the decision to be made was not 'purely administrative', although had there been a 'miscarriage of justice' apart from the regulations (which he thought on the whole there was) the decision would have been voidable only.[158]

Lord Evershed dissented as to the overall outcome. On the application of natural justice, he was content to assume that the rules were not limited to cases where the body concerned was 'exercising judicial or quasi-judicial functions strictly so called' but their invocation 'may also be had in cases where the body concerned can properly be described as administrative' so long as it can be said that the invocation is required 'in order to conform to the ultimate principle of fitness with regards to the nature of man as a rational and social being'.[159] Provided the body in question had jurisdiction to make the kind of decision in question, breach of natural justice would only, however, render the decision voidable, other than in cases where the decision-maker acted on 'frivolous or futile grounds' in which case the court would treat the whole proceeding and not merely the (ultimate) decision as a nullity.[160] As to the application of natural justice in the present case, had the

---

[154] [1964] AC 40 (HL), pp 130–133.
[155] [1964] AC 40 (HL), p 130.
[156] Lord Hodson referred to *Nakkuda Ali* and *Ex p Parker*.
[157] [1964] AC 40 (HL), p 133.
[158] [1964] AC 40 (HL), pp 141–142, Lord Devlin agreeing with Lord Evershed on this last point.
[159] [1964] AC 40 (HL) p 86, using the definition of natural justice in the words of F Pollock (1961), *Jurisprudence and Legal Essays* London, Macmillan p 124.
[160] [1964] AC 40 (HL), pp 86–94.

only question been whether Ridge should have ceased to be the Chief Constable then there would be no need to observe the *audi alteram partem* rule: the Watch Committee were under a duty to give effect to what Donovan J had in effect determined. However, given the real issue was whether Ridge should have been allowed to retire, he expressed no concluded view on whether observing *audi alteram partem* was required. He was prepared to assume it was, but on that basis there had been no real substantial miscarriage of justice as the relevant points had been put at the 18 March meeting by Ridge's solicitor.[161] Furthermore the claim was barred by the fact that the Secretary of State's decision was 'final and binding'.[162] One other point of particular interest was Lord Evershed's comment in passing, in respect of the distinction supported by ex parte *Parker* between withdrawal of a licence or privilege and interference with vested rights or proprietary interest, that withdrawal of a licence 'may in fact mean the destruction of his means of livelihood'.[163]

Overall the clear view emerges from the majority that Ridge had been treated unfairly in not being given notice of the grounds for his dismissal or a proper opportunity to make representations. Lord Evershed's view that the 18 March meeting was sufficient is unpersuasive.

What guidance did the House give for future cases as to the general approach to be adopted? How, if at all, would the classification of the function in question as judicial, quasi-judicial or administrative be relevant? Two judges, Lords Morris and Devlin appear to take the view that natural justice would not apply to the exercise of administrative or executive functions, and Lord Morris expressly characterised the present case as involving a quasi-judicial function. However, their position seems to be that if there is good reason to observe natural justice then the decision is to be labelled 'quasi-judicial'. Lords Hodson and Evershed seem to take the view that in the case of some administrative functions, there will be a duty to observe natural justice. Lord Reid is slightly more opaque on this point, simply noting that a 'judicial element' can be inferred from the nature of the power in an appropriate case. All seem agreed that natural justice is not to be confined to cases involving a *lis inter partes*.[164]

---

[161] [1964] AC 40 (HL), pp 94–99.
[162] [1964] AC 40 (HL), pp 99–101.
[163] [1964] AC 40 (HL), p 95. This suggests that Lord Evershed had some doubts about *Ex p Parker* although he dissented from the view that he understood some of his colleagues to be taking that *Nakkuda Ali* ought not to be followed ([1964] AC40, 94) as there the enactment in question 'in truth conferred upon the Governor an unfettered discretion'. In the event, none of his colleagues suggested that *Nakkuda Ali* was wrong on the natural justice point and Evershed's comment does not seem to relate to the certiorari analysis. Benjafield and Whitmore (n 170), at pp 143–144, expressed concern that this point had been left 'clouded with doubt'.
[164] Lord Evershed is least clear on this. But note his implied criticism of ex parte *Parker* and that he was undecided whether there was a requirement to observe natural justice or the facts of the present case.

E. The Aftermath

The House of Lords remitted the case to the High Court to determine the appropriate consequential relief.[165] Immediately after judgment was given Ridge gave notice of resignation. Leave was given to amend the statement of claim by adding a claim for a declaration that in the event of the plaintiff resigning he would be entitled to a pension-based on his salary at the date of resignation, and for an order that all further proceedings be stayed on agreed terms.[166]

The position as regards police discipline had also moved on. Also in 1958, Glyn Davies, Chief Constable of the Worcester City Police, was convicted for misappropriating £1,147 of the Police Club Funds, and subsequently dismissed, the Watch Committee following the Police Discipline Regulations procedure.[167] The Brighton and Worcester cases were among a number of controversial incidents involving disagreements between Chief Constable and police authority or allegations of police misbehaviour that led to the appointment of a Royal Commission on the Police, chaired by Sir Henry Willink.[168] This led to a range of reforms, including a common legislative structure for county and borough forces, repeal of the 1882 Act provisions and new disciplinary regulations.[169]

V. Reception of the Decision in *Ridge v Baldwin*

A. Academics

Curiously for a 'landmark case' the academic reception was mixed. Bradley[170] noted that the decision ultimately turned on the interpretation of the legislation

---

[165] *Ridge v Baldwin*, The Times, July 30 1963, [1963] *Crim LR* 705, Mocatta J.

[166] These included payment by the Watch Committee of £6,424 6s 8d by way of compromise of the claim for arrears of salary to 31 July 1963 and an undertaking to pay as from 1 August 1963, pension at such a rate as would have been applicable had Ridge been compulsorily retired on 7 March 1958. Following his suspension, Ridge had moved away from Brighton to live in Shrewsbury and later Cheam. He had found employment for seven months as a display manager and then as a property negotiator, earning substantially less than he had as Chief Constable (Further and better particulars set out in the Appendix to the Case for the hearing in the House of Lords (Parliamentary Archives)). By the time the case came to the House of Lords, he was legally aided. He died, aged 79, in Newtown, Powys (Record of deaths).

[167] See National Archives, HO287/345. The Town Clerk of Worcester wrote to the Home Office for advice, noting that Brighton went under the 1882 Act but that he felt doubtful about that 'as it seems to me that the discipline regulations were provided for this particular purpose' at least in the case of an acquittal. He asked whether the same should apply in the case of a conviction. The Home Office advised off the record (Ridge's appeal was then before the Home Secretary) that 'use of the 1882 Act raised a number of difficulties' and 'they would be well advised not to take risks'.

[168] Report of the Royal Commission on the Police (Cmnd 1728, 1962).

[169] Police Act 1964. See generally G Marshall (1965), *Police and Government* London, Methuen & Co Ltd.

[170] 'A failure of justice and defect of police' [1964] *CLJ* 83. Compare A Goodhart, '*Ridge v Baldwin*: Administration and Natural Justice' (1964) 80 *LQR* 105, who seemed concerned that the case had

governing dismissal of a borough Chief Constable. Dismissal of a county Chief Constable was governed by a different provision,[171] which provided simply that he held office until dismissed. Had Ridge been a county Chief Constable, while the Police Discipline Regulations would have applied, 'the rules of natural justice would almost certainly have helped him but little ... A lasting structure of administrative law can hardly be built on such a brittle foundation'.[172]

Bradley acknowledged that, assuming that the rejection by Lords Reid,[173] Morris and Hodson of the view that there was only 'duty to act judicially' where there was an express statutory requirement to give a hearing was applied to other statutory contexts, then the result would 'at the least be a return to the position expressed in many earlier authorities'.[174] However, his preference would be for the two-stage approach then adopted by the courts (asking (i) is there a duty to observe natural justice in this situation?; and (ii) if so, has either of the two rules of natural justice been broken?), to be replaced by a single, more flexible and realistic question: 'Is it a reasonable interpretation of the instrument conferring this power to infer that certain unwritten requirements of fair procedure should be observed?' The two stage approach was unhelpful in that stage one led in practice to the many difficulties inherent in the attempt to locate the 'duty to act judicially' The flexible approach would recognise that the court would have a discretion in interpretation, 'guided but not fettered by earlier decisions on comparable powers'. While the decision in *Ridge v Baldwin* was not inconsistent with this, it was 'difficult to find anything more in the speeches than a return to the older authorities and a disallowance of recent errors'.[175] As to the consequence of the errors made by the Watch Committee, Bradley's view was that it was not difficult to agree with the proposition that the failure to apply the Police Regulations made the decision void. However, as to the question of the effect of a breach of natural justice, the correct position was that 'it must depend on the particular circumstances' and not necessarily lead to a declaration that the original decision was void. The dicta of Lords Reid, Morris and Hodson were wider than justified by *Wood v Woad*.[176] The authorities indeed suggested that breach of the *nemo judex* rule rendered the decision voidable. In any event the 'void'/'voidable' distinction should not be decisive in administrative law, given that it 'does not sufficiently reveal the variety of the

---

gone too far. See also D Benjafield and H. Whitmore, 'The House of Lords' and 'Natural Justice' [1963] 37 *ALJ* 140, 147 ('it will clearly have a very important effect on the future development of natural justice in administrative law'). For a later evaluation see K. Keith, '*Ridge v Baldwin*—twenty years on' [1983] 13 *VUWLR* 239.

[171] County Police Act 1839 s 4.
[172] [1964] *CLJ* 83.
[173] It was noted that Reid had 'lent authority' to the views of many academic commentators, Bradley citing de Smith, Wade and Gordon: [1964] *CLJ* 83, 94, n 67.
[174] [1964] *CLJ* 83, 95.
[175] [1964] *CLJ* 83, 93, pp 95–96.
[176] n 13 above.

"degrees of validity" with which an administrative act may be clothed'.[177] Bradley's conclusions were (i) that the residual powers of dismissal exercisable by police authorities should be the subject of legislation; (ii) it might be 'somewhat-easier' to challenge administrative action for failure to give a prior hearing; but (iii) the approach of the House of Lords was essentially looking to the past. Coherent principles of public law, effective procedure and new institutions could not be brought about by judicial decisions alone.[178]

Bradley's caution is entirely understandable given the speeches of the majority. However, it must be remembered that at the time the House was only at the start of a move away from the formalism of the 1950s. On the face of it, *Ridge v Baldwin* can be seen as something of a hybrid, relying on old precedents (thus demonstrating consistency with old law rather than a voyage into uncharted waters) for the actual decision, but also laying the groundwork for future developments. The trouble with the latter dimension of any case is that a judge today can lay foundations but the judge tomorrow can choose to build elsewhere. Bradley was clearly concerned that there was insufficient direction for the future. We shall see shortly how matters developed.

As might be expected, de Smith and Wade were more welcoming. De Smith commented:[179] 'Leading cases are more easily recognised by hindsight than contemporary identification. But even the most myopic observer could hardly fail to place the decision of the majority of the House of Lords in *Ridge v Baldwin* on a prominent pedestal.' He welcomed the recognition that a 'duty to act judicially' might arise by implication but noted that 'it would be imprudent to assume that we have suddenly leapt from twilight to a new dawn, that our familiar judicial-administrative dichotomy has been scrapped and that green pastures lie ahead'.[180] Indeed it was not clear that any previously reported case would have been decided any differently. No case was overruled or disapproved.[181] The impact on cases concerning administrative powers affecting individual rights might not be striking as the vast majority of these were subject to express procedural safeguards imposed by legislation. The least satisfactory aspect was the ruling that any decision in breach of the *audi alteram partem* rule would be void (subject only to a discretionary refusal of relief), particularly as the authorities on breach of the *nemo judex* rule were that this rendered the decision voidable. It would be better for the outcome to turn on whether a 'substantial injustice' had been done, the question posed by Lord Evershed.

Wade's reaction[182] was more effusive. The 'alarm and despondency' he had felt for years had now been 'alleviated by a striking decision of the House of Lords'.

---

[177] [1964] *CLJ* 83, pp 98–104.
[178] [1964] *CLJ* 83, pp 105–107.
[179] (1963) 26 MLR 543.
[180] (1963) 26 MLR 543, p 545.
[181] Even *Nakkuda Ali* and *Parker* preserved a 'meagre vestige of authority'.
[182] 'The Due Process of Law', *The Listener*, 8 August 1963. See also comments in the Second Edition of *Administrative Law* (Oxford, Clarendon Press, 1967), p 124 (a case of 'outstanding importance' on the scope of certiorari) and 185 (an 'important landmark' on natural justice).

This was a 'broad and far-reaching decision' that should protect due process of law for many people whose rights or livelihoods were at the mercy of the powers of government.

B. The Courts

It is self-evident that Wade's view of the implications of *Ridge v Baldwin* was distinctly optimistic given the specific context of the decision and the wording of the opinions. Nevertheless, as a prediction, it turned out to be accurate. That is because of how both the opinions of the majority and the spirit that could be detected as lying behind them were used and reflected in subsequent decisions of the courts. There are a number of threads here, including the positions taken in the Privy Council and the House of Lords in *audi alteram partem* cases; decisions in the Court of Appeal, led by Lord Denning MR; and the development of a 'duty to act fairly' whose original impulse was a decision in the Divisional Court. It is convenient to take these in reverse order.

A key case in the Divisional Court was *Re HK (An Infant)*.[183] This concerned a rule that a person who 'satisfied an immigration officer' that he or she was 'a child under 16' had, in the circumstances, a right of entry. It was argued that natural justice had to be observed when the officer was determining whether he was so satisfied, this being a judicial or quasi-judicial decision. In response, it was accepted that the immigration officer was under a statutory duty to carry out an 'examination' but argued that 'a summary and expeditious examination was all that was contemplated' and that on the facts, HK and his father had been given a fair opportunity to satisfy the immigration officer of the relevant facts.[184] Lord Parker CJ[185] doubted that the officer was acting in a judicial or quasi-judicial capacity but thought that even if he was not, he had to give the immigrant the opportunity of satisfying him of the relevant matters and let the immigrant know what his immediate impression was so that the immigrant could disabuse him: 'That is not, as I see it, a question of acting or being required to act judicially, but of being required to act fairly ... [O]nly to that limited extent do the so-called rules of natural justice apply.'

Lord Parker recognised that this might be going further than permitted on the decided cases, referring to *Nakkuda Ali v Jayuratne*,[186] but he interpreted this case as going no further than saying that 'there is no duty to invoke judicial process unless there is a duty to act judicially'. It did not mean that if there was no duty to act judicially 'then there is no duty even to be fair'.[187] However, the immigration

---

[183] [1967] 2 QB 617 (DC). Decided on 7 December 1966.
[184] Nigel Bridge, counsel for the Chief Immigration Officer, [1967] 1 QB 617 (DC), p 622.
[185] [1967] 2 QB 617 (DC), pp 630–631.
[186] [1951] AC 66 (PC), above n 25.
[187] [1967] 2 QB 617 (DC) p 631. It is curious that *Ridge v Baldwin* is not mentioned by counsel or the court. Judgment was not reserved.

officer had been fair on the facts. Salmon LJ and Blain J agreed.[188] This goes well beyond the speeches in *Ridge v Baldwin*, and that in a sensitive area of central government decision-making. But the limits should be noted. It is *not* said that there is a requirement to observe natural justice in respect of *every* administrative decision; the duty to act fairly here is firmly based on the statutory context and the implications of the decision for the applicant; the relevance of analytical labels is downplayed but not denied altogether. What is particularly important is that the approach of Lord Parker was subsequently endorsed by Lord Denning in a series of cases in the Court of Appeal.[189]

This leads on to the point that Lord Denning's consistent approach in cases concerning natural justice was to examine whether observation was needed in the particular circumstances of the case rather than to be driven by analytical labels.[190] In *Schmidt v Secretary of State for Home Affairs*[191] Lord Denning MR held[192] that natural justice need not be observed where an alien was refused an extension of stay in the UK as there was no 'right, interest, or I would add, some legitimate expectation, of which it would not be fair to deprive him without hearing what he had to say'.[193] Previous judgments had held that the Home Secretary did not have to observe natural justice in decisions concerning aliens on the ground that the Home Secretary was exercising an administrative power and not doing a judicial act. After *Ridge v Baldwin* 'that distinction is no longer valid.'[194] Many subsequent cases followed this line, making it clear that natural justice had to be observed by statutory bodies, for example, where a licence was revoked, interfering with livelihood;[195] where inspectors were investigating the affairs of a company in a way that

---

[188] [1967] 2 QB 617 (DC), pp 632, 635. Salmon LJ said that where a person was making a decision affecting basic rights and in the circumstances the law impliedly imposed a duty to act fairly, then that would be 'quasi-judicial'. Here, the decision was of vital importance to the immigrant and natural justice had to be observed. Blain J said that here there was a duty to act fairly whether the decision be administrative, quasi-judicial or judicial.

[189] See in particular *R v Gaming Board for Great Britain, ex parte Benaim and Khaida* [1970] 2 QB 417 (CA), 431. *Re HK* was referred to without any reservation by the majority of the Privy Council in *Furnell v Whangerei High Schools Board* [1973] AC 660, 680 per Lord Morris of Borth-y-Gest.

[190] Before *Ridge v Baldwin*, see *R v Governor of Brixton Prison, ex parte Soblen* [1963] 2 QB 243 (CA), which concerned a deportation order. Lord Denning MR stated (at p 298) that where a public officer had power to deprive a person of liberty or property the general principle was that there should first be an opportunity to make representations; but, as here, this could be ruled out by the statutory context.

[191] [1969] 2 Ch 149 (CA).

[192] [1969] 2 Ch 149 (CA), p 170.

[193] From this dictum grew the modern mountain of case law on 'legitimate expectations'. In the present context, where an existing permission was revoked there would be interference with a legitimate expectation. Non-renewal was different.

[194] [1969] 2 Ch 149 (CA), p 170 Lord Denning also referred without any reservation to Lord Parker CJ's judgment in *Re HK (An Infant)*, above n 183.

[195] See *R v Gaming Board, ex parte Benain and Khaida* [1970] 2 QB 417 (revocation of a gaming licence). Lord Denning said (at p 430–431): 'At one time it was said that the principles only apply to judicial proceedings and not administrative proceedings. That heresy was scotched in *Ridge v Baldwin*.' The proposition that they did not apply to the grant or revocation of licences (ex parte *Parker*; *Nakkuda Ali*) was also wrong, following *Ridge v Baldwin*. *Re HK* was also expressly approved. See also *R v Liverpool Corporation* [1972] 2 QB 299 (CA) (taxi licences); *R v Barnsley MBC, ex p Hook* [1976] 1 WLR 1052 (CA) (revocation of market trader's licence).

affected reputation;[196] and by disciplinary bodies.[197] These were all cases going beyond *Ridge v Baldwin* in terms of the principles; but most of the cases failed on the facts; the two of these in this period that did not[198] were not taken to the House of Lords.

Some opinions in the House of Lords and Privy Council remained wedded to the old language for longer. Some were in cases where it was conceded that the decision-maker was acting in a quasi-judicial capacity and so natural justice had to be observed.[199] Matters were taken a little further in *Durayappah v Fernando*[200] where the Privy Council held that the *audi alteram partem* rule did have to be observed in the exercise of a Minister's statutory power to dissolve a council. Lord Upjohn stated[201] that outside the well-established areas such as dismissal from office, deprivation of property and expulsion from clubs, it was necessary when deciding whether natural justice had to be observed to bear in mind the nature of the property held, status employed or services to be performed by the complainant, the circumstances in which the power to intervene arose and the nature of the sanctions that might be imposed. This seems entirely sensible but has rarely been cited.[202] However, he went out of his way to say that it should not be assumed that their Lordships necessarily agreed with Lord Reid's analysis of *R v Electricity Commissioners* or *Nakkuda Ali*. This reservation has sunk without a trace (at least in English courts). By 1982, Lord Diplock for an unanimous House of Lords in *O'Reilly v Mackman*[203] affirmed the proposition that wherever any person or body of persons has authority to make decisions affecting the common law or statutory rights or obligations of other persons as individuals, it is amenable to being

---

[196] *Re Pergamon Press Ltd* [1971] Ch 388 (CA); *Maxwell v Department of Trade and Industry* [1972] QB 523 (CA).
[197] *Buckoke v Greater London Council* [1971] Ch 655; rejecting ex parte *Fry* [1954] 1 WLR 730 (DC) (above n 27). (Lord Denning noted that this case had not been canvassed before them although it had in the Divisional Court.) See also *Fraser v Mudge* [1975] 1 WLR 1132 (CA) (prison discipline).
[198] *Liverpool Corporation; Hook*.
[199] *Maradana Mosque Trustees v Mahmud* [1967] 1 AC 13 (PC) (decision of minister to take over a school where he was satisfied it was being administered in contravention of the relevant Act); *MKS Seyed Mohamed Shareef v Commissioner for Registration of Indian and Pakistani Residents* [1966] AC 47 (PC) (inquiry by Commissioners 'semi-judicial').
[200] [1967] 2 AC 337 (PC) (Viscount Dilhome and Lords Guest, Devlin, Upjohn and Pearson). Another echo of the old approach was the decision of the Privy Council (Lords Hodson, Guest, Donovan and Pearson) in holding that a preliminary decision of the Collector of Customs was not judicial or quasi-judicial and so not amenable to certiorari: *Jayawardane v Silva* [1970] 1 WLR 1365 (PC).
[201] [1967] 2 AC 337 (PC), p 349.
[202] Examples are the Divisional Court in *R v Aston University, ex p Roffey* [1969] 2 QB n 538, 552, Megarry J in *Gaiman v National Association for Mental Health* [1971] Ch 317 (ChD), 333; Pennycuick VC in *Glynn v Keele University* [1971] 1 WLR 487 (ChD).
[203] [1983] 2 AC 237, 279. In the meantime there had been dicta that natural justice had to be observed by those acting judicially (see *Wiseman v Borneman* [1971] AC 297 (HL), 308 (Lord Reid), 308–309 (Lord Morris). But this case concerned a statutory tribunal whose proceedings were conceded to be judicial: see Lord Donovan at 317. In *Pearlburg v Varty* [1972] 1 WLR 534 (HL), Lord Pearson suggested that natural justice might apply to judicial or quasi-judicial functions and the duty of fairness to administrative. This analysis has not found favour.

quashed if it fails to observe the requirements of natural justice or fairness. The relevance of arguments based on subtle distinctions between decisions that were administrative and those that were quasi-judicial had been 'destroyed' by *Ridge v Baldwin*. Even broader was the statement in 1994 by Lord Mustill for the House of Lords in *R v Secretary of State for the Home Department*, ex parte *Doody*[204] that where an Act of Parliament confers an administrative power there is a presumption that it will be exercised in a fair manner, and that fairness very often requires that a person who may be adversely affected by a decision will have an opportunity to make representations and be informed of the gist of the case to be answered. This was said in the politically sensitive context of the rights of mandatory life sentence prisoners, and the applications were at least partially successful.

Apart from issues as to the applicability of natural justice, *Ridge v Baldwin* has been regularly cited on such issues as invalidity and voidness; the status of *Liversidge v Anderson*;[205] the argument that a hearing need not be given where that would make no difference; the effect of an appeal against a decision where natural justice should have, but has not been, observed; the effect of a hearing held after the decision in question; offices and employments; the scope of certiorari; and the effect of 'finality' clauses.[206] In most of these areas, the learning of *Ridge v Baldwin* has not been seriously challenged[207] although in some cases it has been developed.

VI. Conclusion

Cases may be 'landmark cases' for different reasons. They may establish discrete branches of the common law,[208] or introduce new principles of liability,[209] or provide authoritative statements as to how landmark statutes are to be interpreted,[210] or provide a legal structure affecting government decision-making in a broad area

---

[204] [1994] 1 AC 531 (HL), p 560. For modern broad statements see *Bank Mellat v HM Treasury (No2)* [2013] UKSC 39, [2013] 4 All ER 533, at paras [29] (Lord Sumption, with whom Lady Hale and Lords Dyson, Kerr, Clarke agreed); para [146] (Lord Hope with whom Lords Reid and Carnwath agreed; paras [178]–[179] (Lord Neuberger). For a modern nuanced analysis of how determining the requirements of procedural fairness should be approached, see Beatson LJ in *R (on the application of L) v West London Mental Health NHS Trust* [2014] EWCA Civ 47.

[205] [1942] AC 206 (HL).

[206] See C Forsyth (2014), Wade and Forsyth, *Administrative Law* Oxford, OUP, 11th edn, pp 247–255; 367; 424–426; 446–448; 449–450; 465–466, 468–469; 515–516; and 609–610.

[207] An exception is the issue of the effect of invalidity: see D Feldman, 'Error of law and flawed administrative Acts' [2014] *CLJ* 275. cf Bradley, n 177.

[208] *Rylands v Fletcher* (1868) LR 3 HL 330 (HL).

[209] eg *Hedley Byrne & Co Ltd v Heller and Partners Ltd* [1964] AC 465 (HL) (duty of care can arise in respect of negligent misstatements that cause pure economic loss).

[210] *R (on the application of Daly) v Secretary of State for the Home Department* [2001] 2 AC 532 (HL); *Ghaidan v Godin-Mendoza* [2004] 2 AC 557 (HL) (the Human Rights Act 1998).

of public policy,[211] or establish particular principles of public law that are novel.[212] The focus here is on the law laid down. There are other landmark cases where the novelty lies in a change of approach in the application of existing principles to particular kinds of factual situation or policy area.[213] Yet others, such as *Ridge v Baldwin*, can be leading cases not so much because of the ratio decidendi or the precise content of the opinions as for the general approach or tone which can then be picked up and developed by subsequent courts. Lord Reid's opinion in *Ridge v Baldwin* stands out among public law decisions of the House of Lords on judicial review as the first to involve extended analysis of a broad sweep of cases (founded on the work of Wade (certainly) and de Smith (probably)) and to recognise that there was a need to develop a systematic approach to administrative law, while emphasising the importance of context. His opinion was also a landmark in a new approach to the judicial function in the House of Lords, moving away from an emphasis on formalism to recognition that judges inevitably, but within limits, 'make law' and need to engage more openly with arguments of policy.[214] The move from (convoluted and inconsistent) analysis of whether bodies or functions were 'judicial', 'quasi-judicial' or 'administrative' to consideration of what precise procedural standards it is appropriate to impose in a particular statutory context well illustrates the shift in approach.

Why did the lower courts find it so easy to take the law beyond the cautious statements in *Ridge v Baldwin*? A key point here is that the new approach had the twin advantages for a generally cautious judiciary of finding principles that were intellectually more satisfying but did not lead to a radical shift as regards the outcomes of decided cases. In what kinds of cases have claimants most clearly benefited from *Ridge v Baldwin*? Most obviously, they are the licensing and discipline cases concerning livelihood and reputation, for which *Ridge v Baldwin* is an indirect rather than direct authority. Of more general significance in *Ridge v Baldwin* itself is the recognition that the principles of natural justice are of particular importance where the claimant might be seen undeserving of sympathy (here a Chief Constable publicly censured by a High Court judge). Some of the arguments in the lower courts seem skewed by an obvious lack of sympathy for

---

[211] *A v Secretary of State for the Home Department; X v Secretary of State for the Home Department* [2005] 2 AC 68 (HL) (anti-terrorism measures). See Ch 8 of this volume.

[212] *Anisminic Ltd v The Foreign Compensation Commission* [1969] 2 AC 147 (HL) (in effect, the proposition that all errors of law go to jurisdiction). See Ch 4 of this volume.

[213] Examples here might include the general trend of the courts to become less deferential to the discretionary decision-making of ministers eg *Padfield v Minister of Agriculture, Fisheries and Food* [1968] AC 997 (HL). See Ch 3 of this volume.

[214] See Lord Reid, 'The Judge as Law Maker' [1972] XII JSPTL (NS) 22; R Stevens (1979) *Law and Politics* London, Weidenfeld and Nicolson, Chs 12–14; A Paterson (1982), *The Law Lords* London, Macmillan Ch 6; L Blom-Cooper, B Dickson and G Drewry (2009) (eds) *The Judicial House of Lords 1876–2009* Oxford, OUP, Chapter 14); A Paterson (2013), *Final Judgment* Oxford and Portland, Oregon, Hart Publishing Ch 7.

Ridge. The more probing analysis in the House of Lords demonstrated that there had indeed been a risk of injustice.

According to Marcel Berlins,[215] Lord Reid himself regarded *Ridge v Baldwin* as the case of which he was proudest. According to Berlins, 'Lord Reid's judgment went on to suggest that natural justice should be an essential element of the relationship between the individual and "authority"'. It is rather difficult to extract that proposition from the words Lord Reid actually used; no doubt his pride extended to the changes they helped set in train.

---

[215] Article by Marcel Berlins on Reid's retirement (when he was 84) from sitting in the House of Lords: *The Times*, 14 January 1975. Lord Morris of Borth-y-Gest also expressed pride in the courts' development of the principles of natural justice: 'Natural Justice' (1973) 26 CLP 1, 16.

3

Padfield v Ministry of Agriculture Fisheries and Food [1968]: Judges and Parliamentary Democracy[1]

MAURICE SUNKIN

I. Introduction

Padfield v Ministry of Agriculture Fisheries and Food is 'a landmark in modern administrative law'[2] which provides a classic case study of the contested nature of judicial review in the UK's constitutional system. It was one of five judgments delivered by the Appellate Committee of the House of Lords under the leadership of Lord Reid[3] during the 1960s which are widely acclaimed as having 'inaugurated a new era of public law decision-making ... ' and judicial creativity.[4] HWR Wade tells us that during this period: 'the judicial mood completely changed. It began to be understood how much ground had been lost and what damage had been done to the only defences against abuse of power which still remained.'[5] Even those who may not share Wade's enthusiasm for, and faith in, the judiciary saw these decisions as marking a significant constitutional change.[6]

In what was an exceptional decision for the period the court held that a government minister had unlawfully exercised discretionary power conferred upon him by Parliament and in effect forced the minister to do something he had decided

---

[1] [1968] AC 997. I am grateful to Mark Elliot, Andrew Le Sueur and Satvinder Juss for their helpful comments on an earlier draft.

[2] Per Lord Denning MR *Breen v Amalgamated Engineering Union* [1971] 2 QB 175, at 190. De Smith refers to *Padfield* as an 'important landmark', *De Smith's Judicial Review*, Harry Woolf, Jeffrey Jowell, Andrew Le Sueur (eds) Sweet & Maxwell, 7th. edn. 2013, para 5-018, p 249.

[3] *The Judicial House of Lords 1876–2009*, L Cooper, B Dickson and G Drewry eds. (OUP 2009) p 218 'Lord Reid was, beyond question, the pre eminent actor ... of the period- an actor who was to dictate the courts role for the rest of the twentieth century ... '.

[4] ibid. The other decisions were: *Ridge v Baldwin* [1964] AC 40, See Ch 2 of this volume; *Burmah Oil v Lord Advocate* [1965] AC 75; *Conway v Rimmer* [1968] AC 910; *Anismimic Ltd v Foreign Compensation Commission* [1969] 2 AC 147, see Ch 4 of this volume.

[5] This is reiterated in HWR Wade & CF Forsyth, *Administrative Law* (OUP) 10th edn. p 14.

[6] C Harlow and R. Rawlings say that these decisions constituted a shift 'in the constitutional tectonics': C Harlow and R. Rawlings, 'Administrative Law in Context: Restoring a Lost Connection' (2014) *Public Law*, 28, p 39

against doing. This was a radical outcome, especially given the deference previously shown by the courts to those exercising public powers.[7] It showed the courts willing to be involved in politically important matters and not content to play a purely passive role in the political and constitutional system.[8] Some may consider aspects of the court's approach, such as the focus on powers and processes rather than rights, to be somewhat formalistic when viewed against the backcloth of more recent developments.[9] Such criticisms, however, are made largely with the benefit of hindsight and do not detract from the *Padfield's* continuing significance in providing fascinating insights into how the courts of the period sought to resolve tensions, including those between the interests of justice and the legitimate ability of the executive to make decisions based on policy, which remain pertinent to our public law.

Unsurprisingly, the decision has attracted both praise and critical comment over the years. Certainly, there has been fierce criticism of the judges in the majority for having 'strayed outside the traditional boundaries of their constitutional function', for having 'substituted their subjective views' for those of the minister, and for adopting an approach that 'did not ... measure up to the standards of rational decision making' they sought to impose on others.[10] Such criticisms may reinforce the claim of that judicial review is at best: 'an ambiguous check on the arbitrary power of executives given that judges may also deliver arbitrary judgements'.[11] As we shall see later, even amongst those broadly enthusiastic about having robust legal scrutiny of executive powers there are those who regard *Padfield* and its aftermath as an example of the inherent limitations of judicial review.

There is undoubtedly room for criticism, but it is also clear that the decision established, or more accurately re-established, common law principles which underpin judicial review of executive power. It showed that when parliament by statute confers discretion on the executive such discretion is always confined by what the judges understand to be the objects and policy of the statute. This key principle implies that executive power, at least when conferred by parliament, is necessarily subject to legal limits.[12] Application of this principle requires the judiciary to be an active player in the constitutional system, both in relation to constraining executive discretion and in relation to identifying and furthering

---

[7] The classic examples being: *Liversidge v Anderson* [1942] AC 206 and *Associated Provincial Picture Houses v Wednesbury Corporation* [1948] 1KB 223.

[8] See, eg, D Nicol, 'Law and politics after the Human Rights Act' (2006) *Public Law* 722 and T Hickman, 'The courts and politics after the Human Rights Act: a comment', (2008) *Public Law* 84.

[9] T Poole refers to the 'ghosts' of cases such as *Padfield*, which were, he says, at core concerned with an essentially formalistic concern with the examination of powers and procedures: T Poole, 'The reformation of English administrative law' (2009) vol 68 Cambridge Law Journal pp 142–168; cf Jason. NE Varuhas, The reformation of English administrative law? 'Rights', rhetoric and reality (2013) *Cambridge Law Journal*, (vol 72) pp 369–413

[10] C Harlow and R Rawlings, *Law and Administration* 3rd ed. (Cambridge University Press) p 102.

[11] R Bellamy (2007), *Political Constitutionalism* Cambridge University Press p 247.

[12] The ability to review prerogative powers was not to be explicit until *Council for Civil service Unions v Minister for the Civil Service* [1985] AC 374. See further Ch 5 in this volume.

parliamentary intentions. Most broadly, as will be argued later, *Padfield* illustrates how robust application of common law principles may reinforce the rule of law while at the same time further the political Constitution. The overall effect of the decision was to show that government ministers are both legally and politically accountable for their decisions and that there is no inevitable conflict between legal and political constitutionalism. Before saying more about these matters we need to consider the background to *Padfield*, the judgments, and the aftermath to the litigation.

II. Background

The case arose out of the operation of the milk marketing scheme which was introduced in 1933 to ensure stability in the supply of milk for the benefit of farmers and consumers. Milk is important nutritionally but gives rise to a number of problems for farmers largely because it has a short shelf life and therefore must be quickly transported to consumers. For this reason farmers risk losing money if their milk is not sold, while consumers could find the cost of milk varying considerably depending on factors such as their distance from farms. The milk marketing scheme was intended to remove these uncertainties and to ensure that milk was available across the country at a consistent price that did not vary according to the costs of production and transportation. At the same time dairy farmers received a predictable sum for their milk and in this way were protected from the vagaries of the market.[13]

Under the scheme dairy farmers were required to sell their milk to the Milk Marketing Board for a price set by the Board. The Board sold the milk to consumers and the sums received by Board went into a pool of money out of which the farmers were paid. England and Wales was divided into 11 regions and the price paid to farmers varied between the regions, reflecting variations including in the costs of transporting milk to centres of consumption. Each region was represented on the Board and decisions on how much was to be paid to farmers in each region were taken by majority voting. Since payments were made out of a finite pool of money, an increase in payments to farmers in one region would leave less money for farmers in the other regions. Majority voting meant that farmers in one region would receive additional money only if the majority of the Board agreed that this was in the general interest. If a majority of the Board were not persuaded that it was in the general interest to pay more to farmers in a particular region these

---

[13] For background see J Heptonstall A dissertation upon the economic organisation of the fluid milk industry in England and wales 1900–1954, Durham Theses, Durham University. Available at E Durham thesis on line: http://etheses.dur.ac.uk/10454/. The milk industry continues to be affected by the sort of problems with which the Milk Marketing Scheme was intended to deal.

farmers would normally be expected to abide by the majority decision. In this way the scheme was intended to allow the dairy industry, through the Board, to regulate the day-to-day operations of the scheme, subject to overall ministerial control in relation to broader policy issues.

Unsurprisingly on occasion disappointed farmers were unwilling to accept majority decisions. Anticipating that there would be disputes the legislation established machinery for dealing with complaints. How complaints were to be handled was central to the *Padfield* case.

III. The Issues

Farmers in the South-East of England are close to London. In normal market conditions these farmers would have been able to charge more for their milk than dairy farmers in regions in which there were lower levels of demand. On the other hand costs, including of transporting milk, were higher in part because farmers in the South-East tended to be further from the main areas of milk consumption (compared with more rural areas in which most farms were relatively distant from where most people actually lived). The Milk Marketing Scheme recognised this by paying the South-Eastern farmers an additional sum, a 'differential'. This differential had not been increased since the Second World War despite repeated complaints by the South-Eastern farmers that the differential no longer reflected their costs and should be increased. Although committees which had looked into the scheme had accepted the need to increase the differential,[14] calls by the South-Eastern farmers for an increase had been repeatedly rejected by the Milk Marketing Board and it was evident that a majority of the Board could not be persuaded to pay extra sums to these farmers.

The Agricultural Marketing Act 1958 (the Act) enabled the establishment of a committee of investigation to look into complaints and to make recommendations to the Minister. Section 19(3) of the Act provided that:

> A committee of investigation shall ... be charged with the duty, *if the Minister in any case so directs*, of considering, and reporting to the Minister on ... any complaint made to the Minister as to the operation of the scheme. (emphasis added)

Section 19(6) said that if a committee of investigation reported to the Minister that:

> any provision of a scheme or any act or omission of a board administering a scheme is contrary to the interests ... of any persons affected by the scheme and is not in the public interest, the Minister, if he thinks fit so to do after considering the report—*(a) may*

---

[14] The Cutforth Committee, set up by the then Minister, reported in 1936 and the David Committee, set up by the Milk Marketing Board, reported in 1963.

*by order make such amendments in the scheme as he considers necessary or expedient ... ;
(b) may by order revoke the scheme; ...* (emphasis added)

The South-Eastern farmers asked the minister to refer their complaint to a committee of investigation, but the minister refused to do so. Through his officials he gave various reasons. First, he said that the complaint was not suitable for consideration by a committee because it:

> ... raises wide issues going beyond the immediate concern of [the farmers in this region] ... It would also affect the interests of other regions and involve the regional price structure as a whole.

Second, he said that the complaint should be 'resolved through the arrangements available to producers and the board within the scheme itself' and that the minister owed no duties to those in any particular region. Third, he said that if the complaint were referred and then upheld by the committee he 'would be expected to make a statutory Order to give effect to the committee's recommendation'. This was something he was not willing to do as a matter of policy.

Faced with this decision, representatives of the South-Eastern farmers decided to challenge the minister in the courts. They argued that the minister's decision was unlawful and sought an order of mandamus to compel him to act in accordance with the law and refer their complaint to a committee of investigation. The minister responded by arguing that Section 19 of the Act gave him complete or unfettered discretion and that his decision could not be challenged. Alternatively, if his decision could be challenged, he argued the challenge could not be based on reasons he had voluntarily chosen to provide.

IV. The Court Decisions

A Divisional Court (Lord Parker CJ, Sachs LJ and Nield LJ) granted mandamus, essentially on the ground that the farmers had a bona fide complaint which if investigated would show the board to have acted contrary to the public interest. This decision was set aside by the Court of Appeal, which by a majority (Diplock LJ and Russell LJ) stressed that parliament had entrusted the decision whether or not a complaint should be investigated to the minister and that his decision was a matter of policy with which the courts would not interfere and Lord Justice Diplock said:

> Subject to his accountability to Parliament, it is for him and no one else to decide ... whether he will permit a complainant to set in motion the statutory [complaints] machinery ...[15]

Diplock also said that the minister 'need give no reasons for his refusal to refer a complaint'[16] and that if any reasons were given as a courtesy they should not be

---

[15] [1968] AC 997, at 1012 G.
[16] ibid 1011 E-F.

'meticulously examined for some mistake or omission which might lend colour to a suggestion that [the minister] had erred in law'.[17] If the court were to examine reasons in this way 'the High Court would only discourage such courtesy and so would stultify its own function as guardian of the rule of law ... '.[18]

Lord Denning dissented from this deferential approach taking a typically more robust position. In his view the farmers had a genuine complaint. He said that:

> every genuine complaint which is worthy of investigation by the committee of investigation should be referred to the committee. The Minister is not at liberty to refuse it on grounds which are arbitrary or capricious. Nor because he has personal antipathy to the complaint or does not like his political views. Nor on any other irrelevant ground.[19]

Not only did he disagree with Diplock's view that the courts could not examine the minister's reasons, he went on to find that the reasons given showed the minister to have acted unlawfully.

Pausing here, the difference between majority and minority judgments in the Court of Appeal reflects the classic distinction between a court unwilling to interfere with executive decisions on matters of policy, possibly out of deference to the minister or respect for the broader aims of the parliamentary scheme, on the one hand, and on the other a court concerned to vigorously protect what it considers to be the interests of justice; here the interests of the farmers in having their complaint fully investigated. The farmers appealed to the House of Lords which, by a majority of four to one (Lords Reid, Hodson, Pearce and Upjohn; with Lord Morris of Borth-Y-Gest dissenting), overturned the Court of Appeal and reinstated the decision of the Divisional Court.

As in the other key decisions of the period, Lord Reid delivered the leading judgment and his reasoning displays features typical of the new judicial confidence of the period and in particular the court's ability to maximise its freedom to reconcile the competing constitutional pressures in order to achieve what the court considers to be a just outcome. His primary motivation was to protect what he considered to be the interests of justice, that is to say, the interest of the farmers in having their complaint fully investigated. To achieve this: he worked from general principle rather from specific legal authority;[20] he took a purposive approach to statutory interpretation which enabled him to act in the name of parliament's intentions while feeling able to depart from the actual wording of the statute;[21] he was not deterred from reviewing ministerial discretion by claims that the matter was one of policy with which the courts should not interfere; and he approached

---

[17] ibid.
[18] ibid.
[19] [1968] AC 997, 1006 E.
[20] The sole authority referred to by Reid was the 19th century decision *Julius v Lord Bishop of Oxford* 5 App. Cas 214 *which appears to have little to do with the exercise of statutory power by members of the executive in a modern industrial and policy setting.*
[21] See also Reid's extra judicial writing, Reid (1972) 'The Judge as Law Maker' 12 *Journal of the Society Public Teachers of Law*, at p 22. Also M Elliott, *The Constitutional Foundations of Judicial Review*, Hart, 2001 pp 121–123.

review of ministerial discretion on the basis that the onus was upon the minister to justify the legality of his decision by providing lawful reasons. It is important to recognise that, while in all these respects his approach elevated the judicial role, the ultimate effect of his reasoning and that of the other judges in the majority, was to reinforce the degree to which the executive had to account to parliament. In other words, this decision exemplifies how principle and pragmatism can combine in modern public law to maximise the ability of the court to protect common law interests (that is to say, interests which judges consider it important for the law to protect) within a constitutional system that is ultimately rooted in parliamentary democracy.

Lord Reid rejected the farmers' argument that the minister had a duty to refer every genuine and substantial complaint and he also rejected the Minister's argument that Section 19(3) of the Act gave him an unfettered and therefore unreviewable discretion. Lord Reid accepted that the minister had discretion. However, in what has become one of the core statements of legal principle in public law, he explained that even when statute provides no express limits to discretionary power the scope of such power is limited:

> [...] Parliament must have conferred the discretion with the intention that it should be used to promote the policy and objects of the Act, the policy and objects of the Act must be determined by construing the Act as a whole and construction is always a matter of law for the court. ... if the Minister, by reason of his having misconstrued the Act or for any other reason, so uses his discretion as to thwart or run counter to the policy and objects of the Act, then our law would be very defective if persons aggrieved were not entitled to the protection of the court.

Lord Upjohn took this point further to suggest that the courts would impose limits on discretionary powers even in circumstances where the legislation expressly said that the discretion was 'unfettered'. In reasoning similar to that later employed by the majority of the House of Lords in *Anisminic v Foreign Compensation Commission*[22] decided a year or so later, Lord Upjohn said that if legislation had said that discretion was unfettered that would mean that it would only be unfettered if lawfully exercised. By this he means that discretion is inevitably fettered in the sense that it can only lawfully be used within the limits that are expressly or implicitly set by the legislation that confers the discretion:

> My Lords, ... even if the Section did contain ... [the adjective "unfettered"] ... I doubt if it would make any difference in law to his powers, save to emphasise ... that acting lawfully he has a power of decision which cannot be controlled by the courts; it is unfettered. But the use of that adjective, even in an Act of Parliament can do nothing to unfetter the control which the judiciary have over the executive, namely that in exercising their powers the latter must act lawfully and that is a matter to be determined by looking at the Act and its scope and object ...[23]

---

[22] [1969] 2 AC 147.
[23] [1968] AC 997, at 1060 G.

A. Discovering the Objects and Policy of the Act

Having explained that the minister would be acting unlawfully if he failed to exercise his discretion to further the objects and policy of the Act, the majority judges went on to consider what were the objects and policy of the Act. As we have seen these were to be identified by construction of the Act as a whole rather than by focusing on the specific wording of Section 19(3).

Two factors were of particular significance for the majority. One was the importance of protecting the interests of farmers who had been compelled by the scheme to sell their milk to the Board for a price fixed by a majority of the Board. The other was the ability of the majority of Board to make decisions adversely affecting minority interests. As Lord Reid put it:

> it was obvious that ... [the majority of the Board] might use their power to the detriment of consumers, distributors or a minority of the producers.

Lord Reid said that this was why parliament had established the complaints procedure to enable an investigation into whether the Board had acted contrary to the public interest. He reasoned that if the minister exercised his discretion so as to prevent an investigation into whether the Board has acted contrary to the public interest he would be overriding a safeguard imposed by Parliament.

> ... if a complaint relevantly alleges that the board has [acted contrary to the public interest] ... as this complaint does, then it appears to me that the Act does impose a duty on the Minister to have it investigated. If he does not do that he is rendering nugatory a safeguard provided by the Act and depriving complainers of a remedy which I am satisfied that Parliament intended them to have. ...

This is a striking example of judicial confidence to depart from the literal wording of legislation. While recognising the constitutional need to give effect to parliament's intention Lord Reid clearly does not consider the courts to be constrained by wording of specific statutory provisions which would enable the minister to prevent what amounts to access to justice. Unlike *Anisminic*, the issues in *Padfield* were not about parliament's ability to prevent access to courts, but they did concern parliament's ability to allow the minister to prevent the pursuit of justice. In the view of the majority parliament had intended that genuine complaints that the Milk Marketing Board had acted contrary to the public interest would be fully investigated. Section 19(3) had to be read so as to give effect to this intention. And this meant that the minister could not have complete discretion to prevent an investigation. On the contrary, Lord Reid took the view that the section should be understood, not as conferring a discretion, but as imposing a duty on the minister to refer a complaint that 'relevantly alleges that the board has ... [acted contrary to the public interest]'.[24]

---

[24] Morris of Borth-y-Gest also dissented in *Anisminic*.

In his dissenting judgment Lord Morris was not convinced by Lord Reid's approach. He observed:

> If parliament had intended to impose a duty on the Minister to refer any ... complaint of a particular nature, it would have been so easy to impose a duty in plain terms.[25]

Academic commentary has also been critical. Rodney Austin, for example, said in a close and critical assessment of the reasoning of the majority in *Padfleld* that:

> [Lord Reid's] ... reasoning is inconsistent. If the Minister has a duty to refer complaints, he cannot at the same time possess a discretion not to refer ... Lord Reid's implication of a duty is based on no authority other than his *ipse dixit*.[26]

Arguably there is nothing new in courts liberally interpreting legislation in order to protect interests which are important to the common law. This has now been explicitly acknowledged by parliament, albeit in the specific context of legislative compliance with Convention Rights.[27] Nonetheless it is interesting that Lord Reid and his colleagues felt able in effect to revise the wording of Section 19(3) in order to ensure that a complaint was fully investigated and to further what we might now refer to as administrative justice, bearing in mind the complaint did not concern legal rights as such, or access to a court.[28] We shall return to this below.

However, Lord Reid is perhaps more circumspect than the above may suggest. While he indicates that the discretion should be treated as if it were a duty, his reasoning is not quite so emphatic. If the minister had been under a duty to refer the complaint arguably there would have been no need to examine why that duty had not been exercised: failure to refer the complaint would be an unlawful failure to perform a duty and that would be that.[29] But, Lord Reid does not go that far. Rather, like Lord Denning in the Court of Appeal, he approaches the issue by indicating that the legislation creates a presumption that genuine complaints should be referred to a committee for investigation and that such a presumption could only be rebutted if the minister had good reasons for not referring them. In other words, while the minister had discretion, given the nature of the complaint, he had a duty to refer unless there were good reasons to justify not doing so.[30] That the burden falls upon public

---

[25] [1968] AC 997, 1038.
[26] R Austin (1975), 'Judicial Review of subjective Discretion—At the Rubicon; Whither Now?' *Current Legal Problems*, 150, pp 169–170 (emphasis in original).
[27] S 3 Human Rights Act 1998 as explained by Nicholls in *Ghaidan v Godin-Mendoza* [2004] UKHL 30.
[28] A similar approach was taken by the majority of House of Lords in *Anisminic* in relation to the wording of the Foreign Compensation Act, which on its face appeared to exclude judicial review. For discussion of whether this indicates the clash of two constitutional imperatives, one being to respect Parliament's intentions and the other to ensure access to justice, see Mark Elliott, *The Constitutional Foundations of Judicial Review*, Hart Publishing at p 31; see also T Allan (1993), *Law. Liberty and Justice*, Clarendon Press Oxford, pp 65–78.
[29] Given that they were seeking Mandamus, there may have been a question as to whether the duty was owed to the farmers.
[30] See also T Allan (1988), 'Pragmatism and theory in public law', *Law Quarterly Review*, 422, at p 434: 'Since, however, the Minister's discretion must be exercised so as to promote the policies

bodies to justify the legality of their action is now recognised as a key principle of judicial review and may be less radical than it was fifty years ago when the dominant judicial approach was to presume that public bodies act within their powers and to impose a heavy burden upon those who sought to challenge them.

B. Reasons

Given his approach Lord Reid, and the other judges in the majority, naturally rejected the view that the giving of reasons was purely a matter of courtesy and that the minister could not be challenged on the basis of reasons he had volunteered. On this point, Lord Upjohn said that:

> [... I]f [the minister] does not give any reason for his decision ... a court may be at liberty to come to the conclusion that he had no good reason for reaching that conclusion and order a prerogative writ to issue accordingly.[31]

Lord Reid and the other judges in the majority agreed with the Divisional Court and Lord Denning that the reasons given by the minister for not referring the complaint were bad in law. In response to the Minister's reason that the complaint was unsuitable for investigation because it raised 'wide issues', Lord Reid said:

> Here it appears to me that the Minister has clearly misdirected himself. Section 19(6) contemplates the raising of issues so wide that it may be necessary for the Minister to amend a scheme or even to revoke it. [...][32]

In response to the Minister's concerns that if the complaint were upheld he 'would be expected to make a statutory Order to give effect to the committee's recommendations'. Lord Reid said:

> If this means that he is entitled to refuse to refer a complaint because, if he did so, he might later find himself in an embarrassing situation, that would plainly be a bad reason.[33]

V. Lord Morris's Dissent

In his dissenting judgment Lord Morris broadly agreed with the majority in the Court of Appeal. Whereas his fellow Law Lords had emphasised the need to protect

and objects of the Act, he could only refuse to refer a complaint on limited grounds. The producers aggrieved by the operation of the marketing scheme had, therefore, the more limited rights that the Minister's discretion be properly exercised.'

[31] [1968] AC 997, at paras 1061–1062.
[32] [1968] AC 997, at para 1031 E-F.
[33] [1968] AC 997, at p 1032 D-E.

the interests of the farmers Lord Morris stressed the broader goals of the milk marketing scheme, including the Milk Marketing Board's role in providing for government of the industry. Under the scheme, the board, he said, was intended to be the final decision maker in relation to 'such matters as terms of sale and price fixation'.[34] Given that the board decided pricing by majority decision-making, it was inevitable that farmers in some regions would gain while others would lose. If those who lost were always able to have their complaints examined by a committee of investigation this would undermine the role of the board as final arbiter on matters such as pricing. He said that the farmers:

> ... are asking that the determination of prices should be made by the committee. The committee could only recommend that the appellants should receive a higher price on the basis that other producers should receive a lower price. The position of all those others would be affected. The committee would be acting as an appellate body from the decision of the board.[35]

The minister's discretion was therefore central to the scheme and it was a matter of policy whether the committee of investigation should become involved. This was not something the courts could decide. In short, the minister's decision against referring the farmers' complaint for investigation furthered rather than deviated from the objects and policy of the legislation. Lord Morris agreed that the minister had to exercise his discretion lawfully and could not base his decision on irrelevant or improper considerations, but he allowed the minister much more leeway to decide what was improper than did the majority and was not prepared to place a justificatory burden upon the minister. In these respects his approach was in accord with the dominant cautious attitude, which had previously prevailed.

VI. The Aftermath[36]

Faced with the mandamus the minister probably had little choice but to refer the complaint to a committee of investigation. As the minister had feared and the judges had perhaps expected, the committee upheld the complaint and decided that the payments the South-Eastern farmers had received for their milk from the Board 'were contrary to the reasonable interests of the complainants and were not in the public interest'.[37]

---

[34] [1968] AC 997, at p 1035 G.
[35] Above at p 1038, B.
[36] See further *Bailey, Jones & Mowbray, Cases, Materials & Commentary on Administrative law* 4th edn Sweet & Maxwell. S Bailey, pp 533–534.
[37] Report on Agricultural Marketing Schemes for 1967–68, p 12 (1968–69 HCP 445).

The farmers' success, however, was short-lived. The saga ended when the minister announced in a written answer in the House of Commons that:

> ... having carefully considered the Committee's findings, he was satisfied that the committee's recommendations ... would have a profound effect on the incomes of milk producers in different parts of the country. Many of them ... would suffer significant losses. Moreover, if the principle that ... every producer should be paid according to his proximity to a ... market were pursued to its logical conclusion, it would bring to an end the present system for the organised marketing of milk which has been so successful ... I have concluded that it would not be in the public interest for me to direct the Board to implement the Committee's conclusions.[38]

VII. *Padfield* and the Constitutional Architecture

The core message of Lord Reid's judgment, with which his colleagues in the majority agreed, is that in order to protect what they consider the requirements of justice, the judiciary is willing to be an active player in the constitutional system. The case illustrates AV Dicey's comment that: 'powers, however extraordinary, which are conferred or sanctioned by statute, are never really unlimited, for they are confined by the words of the Act itself, *and what is more, by the interpretation put upon the statute by the judges*'.[39] *Padfield* illustrates the significance of the words to which emphasis has been given and shows the court willing both to discern the objects and policy of the statute and then to invalidate a ministerial policy decision which it considers to be incompatible with what it considers to be the objects and policy of the statute.

By the early 1960s the prevailing judicial view favoured judicial restraint in relation to policy decisions with courts only willing to get involved where it could be established that decision makers had exceeded their powers or had acted irrationally. The justifications for such deference are well known. They are rooted in a view of the UK's parliamentary democracy which stresses: (i) that the executive's authority to make policy in the public interest derives from its support in, and accountability to, parliament and ultimately the electorate; (ii) that the judges are not democratically accountable and therefore have no legitimate authority to intervene in policy; and (iii) that courts lack competence in relation to policy since they have neither the knowledge nor the ability to make decisions in the wider public interest, especially when such decisions involve weighing factors which are not of a legal or justiciable character, and may affect those who are not involved in the litigation. Whether and how to regulate the milk industry and decisions about how much farmers should be paid for their milk in a regulated market are

---

[38] 780 HC Deb.cols n 46–47 (Mr Cledwyn Hughes) (31 March 1969).
[39] A Dicey, Law of the Constitution, pp 413–414 (emphasis added).

examples of matters which at first sight fall beyond the judicial terrain for the reasons mentioned above. The majority decision of the Court of Appeal and Lord Morris's dissenting judgment in the House of Lords were very much in accord with the then prevailing attitudes to review of matters of policy.

A. Policy is Not Necessarily a 'no go' Area for the Courts

However, the approach of the majority in *Padfield* showed that policy decisions may have legal dimensions that justify judicial intervention. First, the minister's power to decide was conferred by an Act of Parliament and the power was therefore delineated by the law, and more particularly by how the legislation was construed and applied by the courts. Second, the minister's decision invited judicial scrutiny because the court considered that it directly affected interests which the common law was willing to protect. In particular, the minister's decision was considered to interfere with the farmers' pursuit of justice: a matter falling within the province of the courts and rather than that of the executive. On the basis of established common law principles the executive could only interfere with such interests if this was justified by positive legal authority.[40] Here the minister could not establish that he had authority to prevent the complaint being fully investigated. As was noted earlier, the case indicates the importance attached by the majority to what might today be referred to as the needs of administrative justice. Whatever the label *Padfield* shows that interests of justice fall within the judicial, rather than the executive, terrain even when policy is involved. In passing it may be observed that *Padfield* is a precursor to later decisions which show the courts willing to protect access to justice from threats by parliament[41] and the executive, including *R v Lord Chancellor* ex parte *Witham*,[42] and more recently *R (Evans) v Attorney-General*.[43]

B. Checking Executive Power while Increasing Accountability to Parliament

Padfield, along with the other decisions of the period, is of undoubted constitutional significance, not least because it helped lay the foundations for the development of legal constitutionalism and the growing importance of judicial review. Of

---

[40] *Entick v Carrington* [1765] 19 St Tr 1030.
[41] The language used *Anisminic*, a decision directly concerned with ability to access courts, was not couched in terms of access to justice either.
[42] [1998] QB 575.
[43] [2015] UKSC 21, [2015] 2 WLR 813. See M Elliott (2015), 'A tangled constitutional web: The black-spider memos and the British Constitution's relational architecture' *Public Law* p 539.

course, such developments have been contentious and have led to considerable debate around the appropriate place of the judiciary in a system such as the UK's. While enthusiasts for judicial activism draw on *Padfield* to show its value, others are more sceptical. For present purposes two forms of scepticism about judicial review can be identified, one is specific and the other general.

The specific form of scepticism focuses on what the *Padfield* saga, including its aftermath, reveals about the limits of judicial review as a remedy. The farmers may have obtained a landmark victory in the courts and the judgment may have been strong on principle, but what was actually achieved? Certainly the farmers appeared to achieve little if any substantive benefit. As Carol Harlow says:

> … [the case] … was hailed by the judiciary and academics alike as a milestone in English administrative law and a sign of great things to come … .Yet what resulted? The complaint having been duly investigated, the Minister refused to follow the advice of the committee. The remedy proved illusory; the same decision could be reached with only nominal deference to the court, and the waste of time and money entailed is a deterrent to future complainants.[44]

This being so, even at its most vigorous judicial review may be ' … seen as a tedious … detour on a previously mapped out route'.[45]

The broader form of scepticism argues that decisions such as *Padfield* illustrate the dangers that arise when judges trespass into the territory of politics, which should be occupied not by courts but by processes that are able to reflect wider interests and ensure proper democratic accountability.

C. *Padfield*: Illustrates the Failings of Judicial Review?

The eventual outcome of the *Padfield* saga certainly warns against assuming that when claimants win in court in judicial review proceedings they necessarily achieve tangible benefits.[46] There are several considerations here. It is elementary that judicial review litigation, especially as it was understood in the 1960s, tends to concentrate on matters of process rather than substance.[47] Judicial review is not an appeal on the merits and the courts will only rarely replace a decision of a public authority with their own. In some ways *Padfield* provides a classic example of the process-oriented focus of traditional judicial review litigation in the UK.[48] While

---

[44] C Harlow, 'Administrative Reaction to Judicial Review', above cited at p 117.
[45] C Harlow, 'Administrative Reaction to Judicial Review', above cited at p 117
[46] See further V Bondy, L Platt, M Sunkin (2015) 'The Value and Effects of Judicial Review' Public Law Project; also M. Sunkin and V Bondy 'The Use and Effects of Judicial Review: assumptions and the empirical evidence' in J Bell, M Elliott, JNE Varuhas and P Murray (eds) *Public Law Adjudication in Common Law Systems: Process and Substance*, (2016, Hart Publishing)
[47] In *R v Chief Constable of the North Wales Police, ex p Evans* [1982] 1 WLR 1155, at 1173–4, Lord Brightman summarised this approach by saying that 'Judicial review is concerned, not with the decision, but with the decision-making process.' Lines between process and substance, however, are often by no means clear: see generally, Bell *et al* cited above.
[48] See also Poole, fn 9 above.

the farmers wanted to obtain more money the litigation was not immediately concerned with securing additional funding. Rather the legal arguments were about how their complaint had been handled, or more accurately about their ability to have their complaint properly and independently investigated. The majority clearly considered the complaints to be genuine and to raise serious issues, however, their task was not to decide whether the complaints should be upheld and whether the differential payments to cover transport costs should be increased. The judges knew, and one assumes the farmers also knew, that if the grievance were referred to, and upheld by, the committee of investigation the Act gave the minister final power to decide whether or not the farmers should get any extra money. The case, in other words, only focused on process, and then only on one stage of the process. The farmers were driven to litigate because their case for an increase in payments had been repeatedly blocked by a majority of members of the Milk Marketing Board and had now been blocked by the minister, from whom there was no appeal. Against this background it seems reasonable to assume that having the grievance considered by the committee of investigation was important to the farmers, irrespective of the ultimate outcome.

There is much literature on why issues of process matter.[49] In the context of *Padfield* two particular considerations may have been relevant. First, as is often stressed, process matters because there is an intrinsic link between being able to participate in a process that is fair and having confidence in the legitimacy of the system. In short the farmers felt that justice had not been done. Second, being able to participate may contribute to the quality of the decision being made or the quality of the process. The farmers, for instance, may have felt that a full investigation could lead to a change in the decision. Or, they may have hoped that bringing the case would lead to a wider reconsideration of the policy behind the minister's decision. Their motivation may have been to attract attention to their cause and to keep the matter politically alive by forcing it out of the department and into a more public domain, and ultimately into parliament.

With these process aims in mind the farmers may well have achieved success despite their ultimate failure to obtain a substantive benefit. This leads us to the broader concerns of those who are sceptical about the value of judicial review.

D. Padfield: Does the Case Show Judicial Review Undermining Parliamentary Democracy?

The most fundamental challenge to judicial review in the UK context is that mounted by those who argue that it detracts from the political constitution and

---

[49] See, eg, G Richardson, *Law, Process and Custody: Prisoners and Patients* (London, 1993); TR Tyler, *Why People Obey the Law*, 2nd edn (Princetown University Press, 2006). See also *Osborn & Others v Parole Board* [2013] UKSC 61, per Lord Reed at paras 67–71 regarding the importance of procedural justice when Parole Board make decisions affecting prisoners.

undermines parliamentary democracy, without contributing wider democratic benefits.[50] From this perspective *Padfield* may be criticised along the following lines.[51] It is fundamentally undemocratic for unelected judges to strike down a decision taken by an elected and politically accountable minister. This is especially so when the minister is exercising discretion expressly conferred on him by parliament to further a scheme which is intended to correct the shortcomings of the market for the wider social good. In such situations the minister is to be held politically accountable to parliament rather than accountable to judges who are not competent to judge matters of wider social worth. Only parliament is in a position to weigh the competing public interests and judges should not trespass into the parliamentary domain at the behest of those with particular and self-serving interests. Most specifically it may be argued that the case illustrates how the judges can undermine parliamentary legislation intended to achieve wider social goals in order to protect the property and commercial interests of claimants who have the resources enabling them to exploit the advantages offered by litigation.[52] These are certainly telling criticisms, but to what extent are they justified in relation to the *Padfield saga*?

E. The Protection of Minorities

Those who argue that judicial review undermines democracy accept that judicial review may be justified on democratic grounds when it protects minorities from the tyranny of majorities. As we have seen this is a factor that was also important to the judges in the majority in *Padfield,* who sought to ensure that the parliamentary scheme was not undermined by a majority of the Milk Marketing Board.

We earlier saw that Lord Reid stressed the importance of the complaints procedure as a safeguard to protect the minority interests of the South-Eastern farmers from the majoritarian decisions of the Board. Lord Pearce paid particular attention to these aspects. His starting position was typically libertarian and rooted in concerns about the potential power of the majority. Lord Pearce emphasised that the scheme created a monopoly and imposed severe restrictions on the farmers' liberty of action, and he noted that:

> With the aim of general betterment Parliament was interfering with the individual farmer's method of earning a livelihood and subjecting him to the mercies of the majority of the board[53]

---

[50] See, eg, R Bellamy (2007), *Political Constitutionalism* Cambridge University Press.
[51] This brief summary does not claim to do justice to the fuller case against judicial review presented by writers like Bellamy.
[52] J Griffith, *Politics of the Judiciary* 5th ed. p 105, p 339.
[53] [1968] AC 997, at 1051 D.

Like Lord Reid, Pearce stressed that the complaints procedure was intended to safeguard minority interests from the unfairness that flows from majority decision-making:

> If justice to a minority is to be imposed at the expense of a majority, it is probably more convenient that it should be imposed ... [by judges][54]

Such statements resonate with the idea that judicial review plays a legitimate democratic role when protecting minorities from the tyranny of the majority. However, they may not persuade critics of judicial review that *Padfield* is a decision that fundamentally supports parliamentary democracy. For one thing, it was parliament that decided that the Milk Marketing Board should use majority voting. And in any case it is not always in the interests of democracy to protect minorities from majorities. As Bellamy puts it:

> ... the test of whether minority rights are being unfairly overridden cannot be that all the rights a given group ... [claims] ... are not ... legally acknowledged.[55]

There are situations, and decisions of the Milk Marketing Board may be an example, when minorities simply lose out because the majority decide against them. Moreover, when the court interferes to protect some minority interests the effect is to frustrate rather than further democracy. As Mark Tushnet observes:[56]

> we have to distinguish between mere losers and minorities that lose because they can't protect themselves in politics.[57]

So, it is not in the interests of democracy always to protect minorities from majorities. In relation to *Padfield* critics of judicial review are likely to argue that protection of the minority interests of the South-Eastern farmers does not justify the court overturning the minister and meddling with the scheme established by parliament because the farmers did not need protection. On the contrary, they appeared to be a well-resourced group who chose to litigate to protect their own commercial interests. As such they were exactly the sort of claimant Bellamy seems to have in mind when he refers to litigants able to use judicial review in order to ensure that their voice is given particular weight thereby distorting the political agenda in their favour.[58]

F. Padfield and Judicial Review's Contribution to the Political Process

Critics of judicial review, then, are unlikely to be persuaded that the decision in *Padfield* can be justified on the grounds that the farmers were a minority which

---

[54] Above at 1051 C.
[55] Bellamy above cited at p 255.
[56] cited by Bellamy, above cited at p 255.
[57] Tushnet, *Taking the Constitution Away from the Courts*, p 159.
[58] Bellamy, above cited at p 245.

needed judicial protection from the majority. There is, however, another aspect of the case that critics of judicial review may have more sympathy with.

As was suggested earlier, it can be plausibly argued that a key motivation for the claim was to force matters out of the minister's office and into an arena that would allow full consideration of the grievance and ultimately require the minister to justify his decision in relation to these farmers to parliament. While *Padfield* can be presented as being about judicial interference with a minister's decision, it can also be seen as an example of the judges using judicial review to ensure that a minister is fully accountable both to the courts and to parliament, which has the last word.

Certainly the judges in the majority were well aware that their decision would increase parliament's role. As Lord Pearce explained:

> Parliament ... wished to have the published views of an independent committee of investigation ... It also wished that committee to consider and weigh the public interest—a fact that makes it clear that the question of public interest was not at that stage being left to the Minister. When the report is published then the Minister may and must make up his own mind on the subject. He has power to do what he thinks best and decide whether or not to implement the report. He is then answerable only to Parliament, which will have the advantage of being able to understand the pros and cons of the matter from the published report of an independent committee ...[59]

Lord Upjohn echoed this, adding that the minister 'must be prepared to face the music in Parliament'[60] and cannot use his discretion to avoid political embarrassment or to insulate himself from parliamentary criticism.

These observations show the judges to be very much aware of how their decision would affect the relationship between the executive and parliament. They knew that the ultimate effect of their judgment would be to force the minister to revisit the matter in a more public and political arena, and ultimately to face parliament. In short, the decision in *Padfield* did much of what the political constitutionalists say judicial review does not do. Far from undermining and detracting from the parliamentary process the decision enabled parliament to have a say when but for the litigation the matter is unlikely to have moved beyond the minister's, or an official's, desk. As Lord Pearce commented, it was precisely because the complaint raised wide matters that they needed to be fully ventilated by means of a process that would ultimately lead to consideration in parliament.

That the legal process gave particular voice to the South-Eastern farmers does not alter the fact that the overall effect of the litigation was to enhance both the legal and political accountability of the executive. While in this instance the courts forced the minister to account to parliament in accordance with the particular statutory scheme that applied to the case there are many instances of judicial review stimulating parliamentary activity more generally: *Anisminic v Compensation*

---

[59] [1968] AC 997, at 1054 C-E.
[60] Above at para 1061 F.

Commission decided a year or so after *Padfield* is one such example where the court decision led Parliament to amend the legislation.[61]

VIII. Conclusions

The decision in *Padfield* is of enduring relevance and deserves to be revisited. As well as being of historical importance as a landmark at the dawn of the modern era of judicial review, the decision enunciated legal principles that continue to be of central relevance to our public law. In particular *Padfield* crystallised what is arguably the single most important principle of modern judicial review, namely that when an Act of Parliament confers discretionary power on public bodies, including government ministers, however broadly expressed the power is always circumscribed by the law and must be exercised in conformity with what the courts construe to be the objects and policy of the Act.

The judgment is an example of judicial activism, in the sense that it shows the judiciary to be an active constitutional player willing to use the common law to protect what are considered to be interests in justice against encroachment by parliament and the executive. *Padfield* inevitably raises questions about the legitimacy of judicial review in a democratic age. Some will see the decision as an example of the courts usurping the power of the democratic branches of government in order to further the narrow interests of a well-resourced minority. This chapter, however, has argued that the majority judges in the House of Lords were well aware of the political environment in which they were working. While intent to expand their jurisdictional domain into areas of policy and legislation in order to protect what we might now call the needs of administrative justice the judges were alive to fundamental requirements of the UK's political constitution. In particular, they knew that by increasing judicial scrutiny they would force the minister and his officials into an arena that would ultimately be more public and more political: the ultimate effect of their decision would be, as Lord Upjohn put it, to compel the minister to face the music in parliament.[62] In this sense the particular decision supports, rather detracts from, the political constitution and shows that there is no necessary contradiction between furthering common law rights and ensuring democratic values. In short, the saga provides an important illustration of how robust judicial review can reinforce and sustain our parliamentary democracy.

---

[61] The possibility of parliamentary amendments to the ministerial override provisions in the Freedom of Information Act following the decision in *Evans* (above cited) is a further example: I am grateful to M. Elliott for this point.

[62] Above at 1061 F.

4

Anisminic Ltd v Foreign Compensation Commission [1968]: In Perspective

DAVID FELDMAN

I. The Suez Crisis and its Consequences

On 26 July 1956, Gamal Abdel Nasser, President of the United Arab Republic (a short-lived union of Egypt and Syria), nationalised the Suez Canal, owned by a British-controlled company and of immense strategic and commercial importance. The UK's Conservative Prime Minister, Anthony Eden, equated Nasser's move with Hitler's aggression in the 1930s, and argued for military intervention. The Labour Opposition would not support military intervention without the authority of a United Nations Security Council resolution. The Government, however, secretly negotiated with the French and Israeli governments for Israel to attack Egypt, whereupon Britain and France would deploy troops, ostensibly as peace-keepers but actually to wrest back control of the Canal from Egyptian forces.

On 29 October 1956, Israel invaded the Sinai Peninsula. British and French aircraft more or less wiped out the Egyptian air force, and allied ground troops landed on Egyptian soil. On 1 November, the Egyptian Government retaliated by appointing a sequestrator to take control of the property of British and French nationals in Egypt.[1] These included Sinai Mining Co Ltd,[2] an English-registered company later to become Anisminic Ltd, which operated 16 mining leases in the Sinai Peninsula. Without support from the US, and with opposition to the campaign mounting in the UK, Eden declared a ceasefire on 6 November.

---

[1] Proclamation No 5 of 1956 (translation in TNA FO 1004/386 Folder 1 ff 1–18).
[2] The company was incorporated in England on 3 April 1913, and moved its management to Egypt in 1952 after which its articles prohibited meetings of directors and general meetings from taking place in the UK: anon., 'Presidium Board for Sinai Mining', *The Times*, 21 January 1957, p 11; TNA FO 1004/385/1.

By then Israeli forces had reached the part of the Sinai Peninsula where Sinai Mining operated. On 23 November, Dennis Day, the company's General Resident Manager, met Shimon Peres, the Director General of the Israeli Ministry of Defence. Peres told him that Israeli forces would pursue a 'scorched earth' policy in Sinai, but undertook to try to protect the company's property while they were in occupation. In the event, Israeli forces damaged or removed plant, machinery and equipment valued at £532,773.[3] Although the UK's Ambassador to Israel had agreed to tell the Israeli Government that they would be held responsible for any damage or losses that Israeli forces inflicted, the company was later advised that state immunity precluded any claim against the Israeli Government.[4]

II. Sinai Mining's Dealings with the Egyptians

On 29 April 1957, shortly after Israeli forces withdrew from Sinai, the Egyptian Government authorised the sequestrator to sell and liquidate British-owned property.[5] On 29 April, the sequestrator made a contract for the sale of Sinai Mining's assets in Egypt (which the company alleged to be worth £4.5 million sterling) to the chairman of The Economic Development Organisation (TEDO), a government-owned body, as representative of a new company, the Sinai Manganese Co. SAE, then in the process of formation, for a price of £E487,500.[6] That money did not reach Sinai Mining. It was held by the sequestrator until 1961, when it was transferred back to TEDO.[7] Sinai Manganese came into existence by Presidential Decision of 18 May 1957. On 4 September the Minister of Industry in Egypt retroactively cancelled Sinai Mining's sixteen mining leases with effect from 29 April;[8] leases were then granted to Sinai Manganese.

Sinai Mining, unable to mine or trade and without access to its plant and equipment, established a Presidium Board, based in Zurich, to take steps to protect the interests of shareholders.[9] In order to mark its claim to share in any compensation scheme the UK Government might establish, on 11 June 1957 it registered a claim with the Foreign Office in London. At the same time, it tried to bring commercial pressure to bear on Sinai Manganese and TEDO to provide compensation directly. On 9 July Sinai Mining's worldwide agents told customers that the sequestration and sale of the company's assets contravened international law and

---

[3] Statutory declaration by Sidney Dennis Day, 10 May 1961, TNA FO 1004/385, unnumbered ff near back of file.
[4] Advice by E Lauterpacht of counsel, TNA FO 1004/385 f 15D.
[5] Proclamation No. 387 of 1957. (Translations of the Egyptian legislation are in TNA FO 1004/386 Folder 1.)
[6] £1 Egyptian was worth 16s. 0d. sterling (or 80p. in decimal currency).
[7] Decree No. 14 of 1961.
[8] Proclamation No. 426 of 1957.
[9] Anon., 'Presidium Board for Sinai Mining', *The Times*, 21 January 1957, p 11.

had no legal effect, and that the company would regard any transaction relating to 'its' assets as a violation of their legal rights and would take whatever action was required to protect those rights. Sinai Manganese threatened to sue Sinai Mining, but commercial pressure eventually induced TEDO to reach a negotiated settlement on 23 November 1957.[10] This took the form of a contract whereby Sinai Mining agreed to sell its whole business in Egypt to TEDO, with the consent of the sequestrators, for £500,000, payable in instalments out of Sinai Manganese's receipts from the sale of manganese.[11] The sale included Sinai Mining's assets and liabilities in Egypt, but did not include any claim which it 'might be entitled to assert against any Government authority other than the Egyptian Government, as a result of loss suffered by, or of damage to or reduction in the value of' the company's business or assets resulting from the events of 1956.[12] According to Egyptian law, the business had already been sold by TEDO on 29 April, so the contract was, as Browne J was to find, 'purporting to sell something the [company] had not got to someone who had bought it already ... with the consent of the person who had sold it before ... [I]n substance this agreement was a device by which [Sinai Mining] successfully used their nuisance value to extract from the Egyptian Government some measure of compensation for the loss of their business and assets in Egypt'.[13] As part of the deal, Sinai Mining agreed to change its name to avoid confusion with Sinai Manganese.[14]

At Sinai Mining's AGM on 30 January 1958 Sinai Mining's shareholders ratified the agreement. The Chairman reported the Presidium Board's view that little could be expected from the UK Government, and said that:

> [t]he Agreement with the Egyptian authorities direct, was in the best interests of shareholders ... The Agreement represents to us the realism of the situation with a larger measure of control in the channeling of the payments than would have been the case if we had been one of a large number of claimants under a Governmental omnibus Agreement.[15]

The AGM also approved a change of name to Anisminic Ltd. 'Anisminic' had been the company's telex address;[16] it was made up of the first four letters of Sinai (reversed), the first four letters of Mining, and 'c' for Company. From this point, Anisminic gave up any hope of resuming mining operations. The company had investments in Switzerland of about £200,000, interest from which met its

---

[10] TNA FO 1004/385 f 7(a).
[11] Anisminic was to receive all proceeds of sale up to £100,000, 20% until the next £100,000 had been paid, and then 10% until the full £500,000 had been paid: Clause 3.
[12] Clause 1 of the Agreement.
[13] Note: *Anisminic Ltd v Foreign Compensation Commission* [1969] 2 AC 223 at 227, adopting the description by counsel for Anisminic.
[14] Clause 9 of the Agreement.
[15] Minutes of the meeting are at FO 1004/386 Folder 4 ff 206–207, and the Chairman's speech to the meeting is at ff 208–211. Board of Trade approval for the change of name had been obtained: *The Times*, 24 February 1958, p 14.
[16] FO 1004/386 Folder 4 f 211.

administrative costs, and no liabilities.[17] By January 1959 its shares had fallen to less than one-third of their pre-Suez value.[18] William Baird & Co bought a majority of its shares, and Anisminic became part of the investment division in its group of companies.

III. The UK Government Establishes the Egypt Fund

After long negotiations, the UK Government on 28 February 1959 concluded an agreement with the Egyptian Government for compensation for British nationals whose property had been nationalised (or Egyptianised), sequestrated (or, later, re-sequestrated), or marooned in Egypt. Egypt agreed to pay £27.5 million to the UK Government in full and final settlement in respect of all claims by UK nationals. The two Governments were aware that Sinai Mining had entered into a special arrangement with TEDO, and that was noted in Annex E to the agreement. They had no objection to it, but expressed no opinion as to its validity. The payment to the UK Government 'was not directly based on a calculation of separate amounts relating to the value of the various properties belonging to U.K. nationals whose names appeared in Annex E of the Agreement; it was founded rather on a general consideration of all the claims under discussion'.[19]

The sum paid by Egypt to the UK was received by the Crown under the royal prerogative, and, in the absence of legislation, the Crown would not have owed any legal duty to anyone in respect of the money; it was not an agent or trustee for claimants, and would have had an unfettered discretion as to its distribution.[20] In 1950, however, the Foreign Compensation Act 1950 had replaced decision-making by the Foreign and Commonwealth Office (taking account of external advice) with an independent decision-making tribunal, the Foreign Compensation Commission (the Commission). The Commission was composed of eminent lawyers, assisted by a secretariat and a Legal Officer who took legal points concerning the eligibility of applications and, during hearings, represented the Fund.

Section 4(4) of the 1950 Act provided: 'The determination by the commission of any application made to them under this Act shall not be called in question in any court of law.' Such provisions had been increasingly common in legislation since the nineteenth century, and it had been well established for a century or more that they excluded the courts' jurisdiction if a decision was within the jurisdiction of an

---

[17] *The Times*, 8 January 1958, p 13.
[18] *The Times*, 13 January 1959, p 11.
[19] Letter from A Mackay, Foreign Office, to Linklaters & Paines, Anisminic's solicitors, 21 September 1962, TNA FO 1004/385 f 78.
[20] *Rustomjee v The Queen* (1876) 2 QBD 69, CA; *Civilian War Claimants Association Ltd v The King* [1932] AC 14, HL.

Anisminic Ltd v Foreign Compensation Commission 67

inferior body, but not if it was outside it.[21] The Tribunals and Inquiries Act 1958 repealed most such provisions relating to judicial and administrative tribunals, conferred a right to appeal to the courts against their decisions on points of law, and imposed a duty on most of them to give reasons for their decisions. The Commission, however, had been treated as a special case, because it was thought not to affect the liberty or property rights of subjects in respect of property in the UK, and was regarded as an administrative, rather than judicial, body.[22] The Act therefore expressly preserved Section 4(4) of the Foreign Compensation Act 1950, and gave no right of appeal from the Commission's determinations. By an Order in Council made under the 1950 Act, the Government made the Commission responsible for assessing claims for eligibility to receive compensation from the fund in accordance with criteria set out in the Order, and making provisional and final determinations of entitlement.[23]

Meanwhile *Anisminic* found that getting money under its November 1957 Agreement with TEDO was a slow business. The international market in manganiferous iron ore was unfavourable, and the agreement was postponed for some time.[24] Shareholders became concerned that they might have done better to participate in the fund established as a result of the Anglo-Egyptian Agreement rather than pursue a separate agreement.[25]

Money did eventually start to flow: Anisminic received £279,042. 14s 8d by 31 December 1961,[26] and by 1966 the whole £500,000 had been paid.[27] In the meantime, however, Anisminic, which in April 1959 had no intention of participating in the Egypt compensation fund, changed its mind, and lodged an application with the Commission on 15 September 1959,[28] although the company

---

[21] In the first instance judgment Browne J. referred to *Evans v McLoughlan* (1861) 4 LT 31 at 33, 34, 35, HL; *R. v Mahony* [1910] 2 I.R. 695 at 738, 743, 750; *R. v Nat Bell Liquors* [1922] 2 AC 128, PC, at 152; *The State v O'Donnell* [1945] I.R. 126 at 161; *R. v Northumberland Compensation Appeal Tribunal*, ex parte *Shaw* [1952] 1 K.B. 338, CA, at 716 *per* Goddard C.J.; *R. v Medical Appeal Tribunal*, ex parte *Gilmore* [1957] 1 QB 574 at 586, 588; *R. v Hurst*, ex parte *Smith* [1960] 2 QB 133, DC: Note: *Anisminic Ltd v Foreign Compensation Commission* [1969] 2 AC 223 at 234. See too H Wade, 'Anglo-American Administrative Law' (1966) 82 L.Q.R. 226.

[22] Copy of letter dated 31 January 1958 from G. Fitzmaurice, then the Foreign Office Legal Adviser, to C. Hayes at the Treasury, attached to a note from A. Morley, Claims Department, Foreign and Commonwealth Office, to Franklin Berman, then a young Foreign Office lawyer, 23 December 1968, TNA FCO 64/131 f 4.

[23] Foreign Compensation (Egypt) (Determination and Registration of Claims) Order 1959 (SI 1959/625).

[24] In May 1958 the Presidium Board reported that there had been no sales of ore so far, and the Board could not forecast when payments might begin: *The Times*, 30 May 1958, p 23.

[25] Letter from Anisminic's representative to managing director of Sinai Manganese, TNA FO 1004/386 Folder 4, ff 237–238 at f 238, 9 April 1959, and see reply at ff 241–242, 30 April 1959.

[26] TNA FO 1004/386 Folder 4, f 297, a certificate made by the Chairman of Anisminic for the purpose of making its claim on the Egypt Fund for compensation.

[27] Note: *Anisminic Ltd v Foreign Compensation Commission* [1969] 2 AC 223 at 227A *per* Browne J.

[28] The application, and copies of the correspondence and pleadings together with other material, are in TNA FO 1004/385 and 386. These files were originally to be closed until 2045, but The National Archives, after consulting the Foreign Office and other interested parties, agreed to open them in 2015 following a request under the Freedom of Information Act 2000. I am grateful to all those who participated in the process.

considered that it would not be fair and equitable to seek compensation in respect of assets covered by the agreement, unless the Government had advanced a claim to the Egyptians on the company's behalf.[29] Information from the Foreign Office indicated that the Government, while aware of the company's position, had not advanced any specific individuals' claims to the Egyptian Government,[30] but Browne J later decided that it was more probable than not that the Government had not intended to exclude Anisminic's claim from the fund.[31]

IV. Anisminic's Application to the Foreign Compensation Commission

During more than three years of correspondence with Anisminic's solicitors,[32] the Commission's Legal Officer raised a number of questions about Anisminic's claim, and the company abandoned parts of it. Further issues ceased to be contentious when the Foreign Compensation (Egypt) (Determination and Registration of Claims) Order 1962 (SI 1962/2187) relaxed the eligibility criteria for compensation. By 1963, the main remaining point of contention between the company and the Legal Officer was whether the agreement of November 1957 made TEDO, which was not a UK national, the company's successor in title within the meaning of Order 4(1)(b)(ii) of the 1962 Order, and excluded the company's claim. Article 4 (1) provided:

> The commission shall treat a claim under this Part of the Order as established if the applicant satisfies them of the following matters:
>
> (a) that his application relates to property in Egypt which is referred to in Annex E;
> (b) if the property is referred to in paragraph (1)(a) or paragraph (2) of Annex E—
>   (i) that the applicant is the person referred to in paragraph (1)(a) or in paragraph (2), as the case may be, as the owner of the property or is the successor in title of such person; and
>   (ii) that the person referred to as aforesaid and any person who became successor in title of such person on or before February 28, 1959, were British nationals on October 31, 1956, and February 28, 1959;
> (c) if the property is referred to in paragraph (1)(b) of Annex E—

---

[29] Linklaters & Paines to the Commission, 17 July 1962, TNA FO 1004/385 f 68, para 4.
[30] A. Mackay (1962), Foreign Office, to Linklaters & Paines, TNA FO 1004/385 f 78.
[31] *Note: Anisminic v Foreign Compensation Commission and another* (1966) [1969] 2 AC 223, 227. This view was shared by a senior official in the Foreign Office Claims Department, E Brooks: Confidential note of a meeting on 10 August 1966, TNA FO 950/807, para 1.
[32] In a letter of 25 July 1961 to the Legal Officer, Linklaters & Paines wrote that their clients 'are very disturbed at the continued delays which have extended over many months now in giving us any indication of when their claim, which is a substantial one, is likely to be dealt with by the Commission'. The Directors had a duty to inform shareholders, as well as to recover compensation as soon as possible: TNA FO 1004/386 f 29.

(i) that the applicant was the owner on October 31, 1956, or, at the option of the applicant, on the date of the sale of the property at any time before February 28, 1959, by the Government of the United Arab Republic under the provisions of Egyptian Proclamation No. 5 of November 1, 1956, or is the successor in title of such owner; and

(ii) that the owner on October 31, 1956, or on the date of such sale, as the case may be, and any person who became successor in title of such owner on or before February 28, 1959, were British nationals on October 31, 1956 and February 28, 1959.

The Legal Officer contended that Anisminic's claim failed because of Article 4(1)(b)(ii), because Anisminic, by the November 1957 agreement, had 'sold' a claim against the Egyptian Government, and made TEDO the company's successor in title to that claim. Anisminic denied that the agreement was a sale of anything, since (after the forced sale under Proclamation No 5 of 1956) it had nothing left to sell, and further denied that the agreement 'constituted [TEDO] its successor in title in any material meaning or has any relevant effect upon its claim other than by way of the deduction of monies received under such sale as admitted'.[33]

An initial oral hearing of the claim took place on 27 March 1962. It was decided that a resumed hearing would deal only with whether a claim could be established and should be registered, not with valuing the claim; later the subject of the hearing was further narrowed to the 'successor in title' point only.[34] This hearing took place on 1–4 April 1963 before a panel of three commissioners.[35] On 8 May 1963 the Commission provisionally determined that Anisminic had failed to establish a claim in respect of the assets 'sold' to TEDO in November 1957.[36] At a further session without oral hearing, the Commission provisionally determined that Anisminic's claim in respect of damage caused by Israeli military action should be registered; the Commission did not contest Anisminic's valuation of the loss at £532,773, but, despite being registered, it was unlikely that this loss would be compensated from the Egypt Fund, as the Egyptian Government had not been responsible for it.[37]

---

[33] The reply is TNA FO 1004/385 f 72.

[34] T Brown (for Secretary) to Linkaters & Paines, 27 July 1962, TNA FO 1004/385 f 69; H. Morgan, Legal Officer, to Linklaters & Paines, 5 March 1963, TNA FO 1004/385 f 90.

[35] The panel was C Montgomery White (Chairman of the Commission), R Mullarkey (the Vice-Chairman), and William Temple. The company was represented by R Parker QC and E Lauterpacht, and the Fund by the Legal Officer, H. Morgan.

[36] TNA FO 1004/385 f 103. Someone has written across it in red ink, 'Declared a Nullity by House of Lords Decision dated 17 December 1968'.

[37] Provisional determinations of 8 May 1963 and 21 June 1963, TNA FO 1004/385 ff 103 and 145A, and letters to Linklaters & Paines of 17 June and 3 and 4 July 1963, FO 1004/385 ff 102, 104 and 105, letter from F Bayliss, Foreign Office Claims Department, to W Fletcher in Cairo, 5 March 1963, TNA FO 1004/385 f 91, and Foreign Office to the Commission, 12 June 1963, TNA FO 1004/385 f 144A.

Neither the formal record of the first determination nor the letter by which it was communicated contained reasons.[38] Anisminic's advisers thought that TEDO must have been regarded as the company's successors in title, and wrote to the Secretary of the Commission to ask whether they were correct so to advise their clients.[39] The Legal Officer did not want to answer the question,[40] but the Chairman decided that the Commission could be slightly more forthcoming, so its Secretary informed the solicitors that, while their general rule was not to give reasons for dismissing applications, 'in this case I am to confirm that you have rightly advised your clients'.[41]

V. Anisminic Launches a Challenge to the Determination

Anisminic decided to challenge the provisional determinations in an action in the High Court seeking various declarations to the effect that they were erroneous in law and nullities. Unlike an application for certiorari, this did not require the court's leave, which would almost certainly have been refused because Anisminic was unable to point to any evidence that the Commission had erred in law. The action compelled the Commission to plead its defence, which eventually disclosed an error of law.

There were disadvantages to Anisminic in pursuing a declaration rather than certiorari. First, there was no precedent for using a declaration as a remedy in such a case; the Commission argued that allowing declarations to be used in that way might make certiorari redundant. (This argument failed at the time, but it is essentially the argument that succeeded less than 20 years later in *O'Reilly v Mackman*.)[42] Secondly, it forced Anisminic to argue that any unlawfulness the company could assert made the determination void, not merely voidable, as a voidable determination would be effective unless quashed by certiorari (although the Commission might take its earlier error into consideration if it reviewed its determination). But the effect of Section 4(4) of the Foreign Compensation Act 1950 was to require that in any case, in order to take the Commission outside the protection of the sub-Section. The company took on these challenges because, despite risking a huge bill for costs, the company had nothing to lose. It was unable to mine, and had been reduced to a rump which survived on its investment income alone and

---

[38] TNA FO 1004/385 f 98.
[39] Letter of 16 May 1963, TNA FO 1004/385 f 99.
[40] Minute 138 by H.G.M[organ] at front of TNA FO 1004/385, 24 May 1963.
[41] Minute 142 at front of TNA FO 1004/385, 17 June 1963, C M[ontgomery] W[hite]; letter to Linklaters & Paines, TNA FO 1004/385 f 101.
[42] [1983] 2 AC 237, HL.

was being steadily wound down by reductions in share capital. For William Baird & Co., Anisminic's parent company, the main hope of a return seemed to rest on the claim on the Egypt Fund.

In an attempt to head off the action, the Commission pleaded that Section 4(4) of the Foreign Compensation Act 1950 deprived the High Court of jurisdiction to hear the case. The Commission also pleaded that the question of Anisminic's eligibility to claim was *res judicata*, so Anisminic was estopped from seeking any relief inconsistent with the determinations of the Commission. In its further and better particulars, the Commission explained that the adjudication said to give rise to *res judicata* was its own determination of questions of fact and law listed in a confidential Minute of Adjudication, a copy of which was provided. This was a tactical mistake, because Browne J later held that in these circumstances the Commission could not deny that the Minute formed part of its determination, opening up the reasoning therein to judicial scrutiny.[43]

Procedural wrangling continued into 1964 as the Commission sought an order to have the issue of the High Court's jurisdiction tried as a preliminary issue. Successful at first instance, the Commission lost on appeal. Lord Denning, with whom Harman LJ concurred, said that as a general rule it would be undesirable to order a point of law to be tried as a preliminary issue unless the court was satisfied that determining the point of law would dispose of all the issues in the case. In *Anisminic*, the issue of the court's jurisdiction was bound up with interpretation of the Order, so it would be better for one judge to try the whole case.[44] Diplock LJ, dissenting, thought that it would be wrong to interfere with the judge's discretion in a case where the preliminary point went to the very jurisdiction of the court to entertain the claim.[45] Nigel Bridge, Junior Treasury Counsel representing the Commission, advised against appealing to the Lords, but Montgomery White pressed the point 'in view of the importance of the principle involved'.[46] At an oral hearing by the House of Lords Appeals Committee of the Commission's application for leave to appeal,[47] Lord Radcliffe, for the Committee (sitting with Lord Cohen and Lord Upjohn), rejected the Attorney-General's argument that there were issues of principle involved. It would be very unusual for the House to hear an appeal on procedure in the absence of a question of principle. The House would not grant the petition, 'but were not to be understood as endorsing all that could be found in or read into the judgments of the Court of Appeal'.[48]

---

[43] [1969] AC at 232D.
[44] In debate on the Foreign Compensation Bill in the House of Lords in 1969, Denning was to recall this with evident satisfaction: HL Deb 11 March 1969 vol 300 cols 395–396.
[45] (1964) 108 SJ 541, CA.
[46] Minutes 187 (J Gordon to the Chairman, 9 July 1964) and 188 (Chairman to Legal Officer, 9 July 1964) at front of TNA FO 1004/385.
[47] Sir John Hobson, the Attorney General, appeared for the Commission, and Roger Parker QC and R (Patrick) Neill appeared for Anisminic.
[48] (1964) 108 SJ 638; *Times Law Report*, 29 July 1964 (p 15), HL.

VI. The First-Instance Judgment of Browne J

Nearly two years later, Browne J conducted a trial of all the issues. His judgment contains both a valuable analysis of the proper interpretation of the Order and a wide-ranging analysis of earlier case-law on the effect of errors of law on decisions and on the effect of statutory clauses restricting the jurisdiction of the courts to remedy errors of law.[49] He rejected Roger Parker QC's argument for Anisminic that Section 4(4) of the 1950 Act protected only to final, not provisional, determinations. He also rejected the argument of Nigel Bridge, for the Commission, that a declaration would do the plaintiffs no good because certiorari was needed to quash a determination. Browne J thought that the court had power to make a declaration at least in cases where it would be open to the original decision-maker to take the declaration into account when reviewing its decision prior to making a final determination. But in any case a declaration would be sufficient if the determination was a complete nullity, and if it were not a nullity it would be protected by Section 4(4).[50] Bridge argued that the Commission, having been established by the 1950 Act to exercise a function previously exercised solely under the (then unreviewable) royal prerogative,[51] should not itself be subject to the High Court's supervisory jurisdiction, especially since the importance of finality when dealing with a limited fund, for which all applications had to be provisionally determined before any final determination would be possible, made it unlikely that Parliament would have intended the Commission's determinations to be judicially reviewable. But Browne J considered that 'whenever Parliament creates a new inferior tribunal the High Court has an inherent jurisdiction to supervise and control it, and any person aggrieved by a decision of the tribunal has an inherent right to ask the court to exercise those powers'.[52]

The questions for the judge, therefore, were (i) whether the Commission had made an error of law in interpreting and applying the Order, and, if it had done so, (ii) whether the error was of a type which was protected by the ouster provision in Section 4(4) of the Act. Browne J thus considered that he had to decide whether there was an error of law before applying Section 4(4), which was not treated as excluding the court's supervisory jurisdiction from the outset.

---

[49] Note: *Anisminic Ltd v Foreign Compensation Commission* [1969] 2 AC 223, Browne J. It was referred to extensively in the later judgments of the Court of Appeal and House of Lords, and officially reported, very unusually, as a Note following the report of the House of Lords' decision in the *Appeal Cases*, not having first been published in Vol 2 or 3 of the *Weekly Law Reports*. The stimulus for this seems to have come from Professor William Wade, then of the University of Oxford: HWR Wade, 'Constitutional and administrative aspects of the Anisminic case' (1969) 85 LQR 198–212 at 198 n 3, and 'Mr Justice Browne's judgment in the *Anisminic* case' [1969] CLJ 230–250 at 230–231.

[50] [1969] 2 AC 223 at 233.

[51] Judicial supervision of prerogative powers was first recognised in the judgment of the House of Lords in *Council of Civil Service Unions v Minister for the Civil Service* [1985] AC 374, HL.

[52] [1969] 2 AC 223 at 234.

Browne J examined earlier decisions on the application of statutory provisions excluding the jurisdiction of the High Court. It was clear that such provisions normally had no effect where the inferior tribunal has made an error of such a kind that the tribunal's decision was outside its jurisdiction, so that it was a nullity, 'because there is in truth no order or decision of the tribunal at all'.[53] He thought that the nineteenth and twentieth-century authorities supported the view that the High Court's exercise of its supervisory power could be divided into four classes.

Class 1 consisted of cases where the tribunal had no power to embark on an inquiry at all. In this class, there is in law no decision for the preclusive provision to protect.

Class 2 consisted of cases where a tribunal has power to embark on its inquiry, but makes an order, which it has no power to make. Here, too, any purported order is a nullity; but it was hard to decide the limits. Browne J thought that it included only cases where the order was different in kind from any order that the tribunal was empowered to make, such as passing sentence of imprisonment for a non-imprisonable offence. Another example was ex parte *Bradlaugh*, where a magistrate made an order for destruction of books under the Obscene Publications Act 1857. The Act allowed such an order where in the magistrate's judgment (i) the books were obscene and (ii) it amounted to a misdemeanour proper to be prosecuted. The magistrate expressed himself satisfied as to (i), but made no finding as to (ii).[54] In other words, a tribunal's failure to show that legal preconditions to making an order had been met during a hearing deprived it of jurisdiction to make the order. Errors could make a decision a nullity even if they did not prevent the tribunal from entering lawfully on its inquiry.

Class 3 consisted of cases where the error was within the tribunal's jurisdiction. 'In the end, I think the question whether error is error within jurisdiction or amounts to acting without or in excess of jurisdiction will usually depend on the construction of the particular statutory provision in question.' This was different from cases like *R v Bolton*,[55] where the issue was 'whether evidence of facts was admissible beyond what appeared on the face of the record'.[56]

Class 4 contained cases relating to tribunals that had been biased, or acted in bad faith, or disregarded the principles of natural justice. In *Smith v East Elloe Rural District Council*,[57] four Law Lords (Lord Reid dissenting) had distinguished

---

[53] [1969] 2 AC at 234. His Lordship referred to *Evans v McLoughlan* (1861) 4 L.T. 31 at 33, 34, 35, HL; *R. v Mahony* [1910] 2 I.R. 695 at 738, 743, 750; *R. v Nat Bell Liquors* [1922] 2 AC 128, PC, at 152; *The State v O'Donnell* [1945] I.R. 126 at 161; *R. v Northumberland Compensation Appeal Tribunal*, ex parte *Shaw* [1952] 1 K.B. 338, CA, at 716 per Goddard C.J.; *R. v Medical Appeal Tribunal*, ex parte *Gilmore* [1957] 1 QB 574 at 586, 588; *R. v Hurst*, ex parte *Smith* [1960] 2 QB 133, DC; and, on the distinction between errors of law on the face of the record and other errors of law, ex parte *Bradlaugh* (1878) 3 QBD. 509, and the *Northumberland* case, above.

[54] (1878) 3 QBD. 509 at 511–513 per Cockburn CJ, 513 per Mellor.

[55] (1841) 1 QB 66.

[56] [1969] 2 AC at 243, and see Philip Murray, 'Escaping the wilderness: *R v Bolton* and judicial review for error of law' [2016] CLJ 333–365.

[57] [1956] AC 736, HL.

between the effect of the provision on an order bad on its face, which would not be protected by a time-limit clause, and one good on its face which was challenged on a ground which would require the court to go behind the face of the order which could be challenged only within the statutory time-limit. Browne J was inclined to think that the latter class of errors did not make a decision a nullity, and this allowed him to distinguish *Smith*'s case from one in which a determination was a nullity.[58]

Had the Commission made an error of law? The Commission argued that 'successor in title' meant the person who had acquired the business or was the successor to beneficial ownership following sale. But had this been accepted, nobody whose property had been Egyptianised in 1956 would have had a claim, because TEDO or the Egyptian Government would have been successor in title to all of them. For Anisminic, it was argued that 'successor in title' meant a person who had succeeded to property on the death of a person. The problem with this was that it was hard to envisage circumstances in which that could apply to corporations, as the Order contemplated that it would.

In the end, Browne J decided that the anomalies flowing from *Anisminic*'s interpretation were easier to bear than those flowing from the Commission's interpretation.[59] That being so, Anisminic could have no successor in title, so the Commission had committed a legal error in inquiring into whether the Anisminic's successor in title was a British national. Its determination was one it was not entitled to make: its determination was founded on Anisminic's failure to satisfy it of something which the Order did not make a requirement. The Commission had effectively added an extra requirement to those set out in the Order, and so had embarked on an inquiry for which it had no jurisdiction (a Class 2 error). Browne therefore declared that the Commission's decision was a nullity, and not protected by the statutory exclusion of the High Court's jurisdiction. As it was common ground that Anisminic had met the other relevant requirements of the Order, Browne J further declared that the Commission was legally obliged to determine that Anisminic's claim had been established.[60]

VII. The Commission and the Foreign Office Decide Whether to Appeal

The judgment caused deep concern in the Commission and the Foreign Office. It meant that the Commission could not be safely used in any future distribution

---

[58] [1969] 2 AC at 245–246. He also treated the unreported judgment of the Divisional Court in *R. v Foreign Compensation Commission,* ex parte *Oak and Timber Co Ltd.*, unreported, 11 November 1955, as one where no question as to the Commission's jurisdiction had been raised.
[59] [1969] 2 AC at 248–252.
[60] [1969] 2 AC at 254–256.

in which the money in the fund was insufficient to pay all claims in full. Montgomery White, the Commission's Chairman, wanted to appeal both against the judge's interpretation of the Order and against his decision concerning the effect of Section 4(4) of the 1950 Act,[61] and thought that the case might have to go to the House of Lords. Noel Charlton, of the Treasury Solicitor's Department, said that he would find it difficult to recommend a further appeal if the Court of Appeal should rule unanimously against them, in view of the costs involved: the case already had involved several thousands of pounds (a figure above £9,000 and a brief fee of 1,000 guineas for leading Counsel were mentioned), and the cost of taking the case to the Lords would be very heavy indeed. It was not even clear where the money for the litigation would come from. It would probably have to come out of the Foreign Office vote, if not directly from the Treasury, as there was no authority to deduct it from the Egypt Fund unless it was regarded as 'an expense attributable to the discharge by the Commission of their functions in relation to the distribution of those sums' within Section 7 of the 1950 Act.[62] On the other hand, if Anisminic succeeded the fund might have to pay out an extra £1.25 million or more in compensation, and the Foreign Office would need to seek a supplementary vote so that it could top-up the fund (a possibility authorised by the Foreign Compensation Act 1962). That might not be possible, as economic difficulties might lead the Government to limit its commitment.[63] Everyone agreed that, if an appeal were unsuccessful, urgent legislation would be needed to recover the Commission's usefulness.[64]

Immediately a further problem emerged. Anisminic had joined the Commission's new Legal Officer, Cecil Cooper, as a defendant.[65] The Commission thought it would look as if the defendants lacked confidence in their case if their Legal Officer did not appeal, but Cooper was worried about personal liability to pay costs if he did. He refused to instruct the Treasury Solicitor to give notice of appeal on his own behalf without a written indemnity against costs.[66] As the deadline for lodging notice of appeal approached, there were increasingly urgent communications between Cooper, the Foreign and Commonwealth Office, and the Treasury. The Treasury reluctantly agreed to a guarantee of payment of costs in the Court of Appeal out of public funds, but Cooper wanted indemnity against costs in the House of Lords as well. Eventually Eric Brooks of the Foreign and Commonwealth Office was able to write to Cooper informing him of the Treasury's agreement that 'any costs in the above action which may be awarded against you personally, either by the Court of Appeal or the House of Lords, will, if not paid by the

---

[61] Confidential note of a meeting held on 10 August 1966 between Messrs Charlton, Peacock and Roberts from TSD, Messrs Batstone and Brooks from the FO, and Mr Montgomery White and Harold Willan (respectively Chairman and a Commissioner of the FCC) and Mr Cooper (the Legal Officer, succeeding Mr Morgan, who had died on 22 May): FO 950/807, para 1.
[62] ibid paras 4, 5, and Batstone's manuscript note on the back of the final page.
[63] ibid para 7(b).
[64] ibid para 2.
[65] Cooper replaced H Morgan, who had died on 22 May 1966.
[66] Letter from Treasury Solicitor to Brooks at the Foreign Office, 19 August 1966, TNA FO 950/806.

Foreign Compensation Commission, be paid out of Public Funds, and you will be indemnified against all liability in respect thereof'. Work clearly remained to be done to identify the source of funds to cover the costs should they be awarded, for Brooks added, 'You will notice that I have not mentioned payment by the Foreign Office because it has not yet been decided which Vote would bear any costs, but it will almost certainly be a charge on the Foreign Office Vote.'[67] Notice of appeal was accordingly given.

VIII. The Court of Appeal's Judgment

The Court of Appeal heard 13 days of argument between 16 January and 1 February 1967. Sellers LJ presided, sitting with Diplock and Russell LJJ. Sellers LJ told counsel that the Court wanted argument first on whether Section 4(4) of the 1950 Act excluded the High Court's jurisdiction to entertain the claim. Sydney Templeman QC, leading Bridge and Cochrane, argued that it did. Roger Parker QC and Patrick Neill QC[68] argued that it did not. The Court then decided to hear argument on the interpretation of the Order. On 22 March the Court delivered judgment.[69] They unanimously reversed Browne J's judgment on the effect of Section 4(4), and did not need to decide how the Order should be interpreted. All three judges accepted that Section 4(4) would not protect a purported determination that was in law a nullity because beyond the Commission's jurisdiction, but considered that the interpretation of the Order was a matter that the Order had remitted to the Commission for determination.

Diplock LJ, with whom Sellers and Russell LJJ agreed, said that the concept of 'jurisdiction' had been used in different senses in earlier cases, but in his view a determination would be made without jurisdiction only if it was made by an unqualified person, or was not preceded by an inquiry in accordance with the statute and, usually, the rules of natural justice, or if the determination related to a person or type of dispute which is not described in the statute, or if the determination did not state whether the required situation exists (essentially Browne J's Class1). As these matters involved deciding whether the statute's requirements were met, and construction of a statute was always a question of law, tribunals

---

[67] See TNA FO 950/806: minute by Bayliss to Smithers (Finance Department, FCO), 31 August 1966; Bayliss to Lucas, 1 September 1969 (dispatched 2 September); Cooper to Bayliss, 14 September 1969; Whitbread to Bayliss, 14 September 1969 ('We agree with the view of the Treasury Solicitor that the Legal Officer is being quite unnecessarily cautious in this respect but, in the somewhat unusual circumstances and in the light of the advice given by the Treasury Solicitor's Department, we agree that the Foreign Office should give the Legal Officer an assurance that public funds would bear any costs made against him by the Court of Appeal in the event of an appeal being unsuccessful'); minute by Bayliss to Brooks, 16 September 1966; letter from Brooks to Cooper, 16 September 1966.
[68] Patrick Neill had taken Silk soon after the first instance decision in 1966.
[69] [1968] 2 QB 862, CA.

always had jurisdiction to decide some questions of law. Only if the tribunal wrongly decided that the situation described in the statute as a condition for the exercise of its functions existed would there be an error going to jurisdiction, and the determination would be a nullity.[70] In *Anisminic*, the court was concerned not only with the jurisdiction of the Commission but also with the jurisdiction of the High Court, itself a statutory tribunal. Parliament was always presumed to expect the High Court to exercise supervisory jurisdiction in relation to errors within an inferior tribunal's jurisdiction unless a statute expressly deprived it of that kind of jurisdiction. Section 4(4) was a provision of that kind, which Diplock LJ called a 'no certiorari clause'. But such a clause did not make an inferior tribunal the final judge of whether the state of affairs exists which was required for the tribunal to exercise jurisdiction to affect legally enforceable rights and liabilities of individuals, because if the situation did not exist the decision was a nullity:

> neither an express provision conferring jurisdiction on an inferior tribunal to make such a determination nor a "no certiorari clause" will deprive the High Court of its jurisdiction to correct a purported determination of the inferior tribunal for "error going to the jurisdiction" of the inferior tribunal and to decide whether the statement of the inferior tribunal, which purports to be a determination, is a nullity or not.[71]

The Commission, when reaching its determination, had been properly constituted, and had conducted an inquiry in accordance with its rules. *Anisminic*'s application was of the kind described in the 1950 Act and the Order in Council. Terms in the Order such as 'property in Egypt' and 'successor in title' raised questions of law, but they:

> are but illustrations of the many "questions of law" about which the commission must form an opinion as to the answer, in order to arrive at a decision whether the applicant has satisfied them that a situation [in which they are eligible to receive compensation from the Fund] exists ... To answer such "questions of law" is a necessary incident of their jurisdiction to determine whether a claim made in an application is established or not. The High Court has no jurisdiction to substitute its own opinion as to the answer to any of these "questions of law" for the opinion of the commission, so as to lead to a different determination as to whether the claim is established or not. Even if the High Court thought that the commissioners' answers were erroneous the error would be an "error within jurisdiction".[72]

The plaintiffs' primary argument confused 'the description in the statute of the kind of case into which an inferior tribunal has jurisdiction to inquire' with 'the description ... of the kind of situation the existence or non-existence of which that tribunal has jurisdiction to determine'. An error in relation to the former matter would prevent the tribunal from having jurisdiction; in the latter case, any error

---

[70] [1968] 2 QB at 887, 889.
[71] [1968] 2 QB at 894.
[72] [1968] 2 QB at 901.

(including asking themselves a wrong question, or misinterpreting the terms of the Order) would be within its jurisdiction. If the Minute of Adjudication disclosed any error, it was one within the Commission's jurisdiction, and Browne J had had no jurisdiction to inquire into it.[73]

Russell LJ added a comment similar to those made in the Supreme Court in *Cart v Upper Tribunal*[74] to the effect that the use of judicial resources must be proportionate to the importance of the issue involved in a case:

> ... in all mundane matters requiring decision or adjudication there must as a practical matter be an appropriate level at which a question must be finally resolved. In the particular field now under review it does not seem to me in any way inappropriate that the commission should be at that level: and that was the view of the legislature when the Tribunals and Inquiries Act, 1958, was enacted. In substance the executive is dealing broadly with matters not strictly matters of right, and the time-consuming precision of the ordinary judicial processes may well be out of place.

Despite its unanimity, the Court of Appeal took the unusual step of giving leave to Anisminic to appeal to the House of Lords.

IX. Anisminic's Appeal to the House of Lords

Nineteen months later, in October 1968, the Appellate Committee heard 12 days of argument. Roger Parker QC and Patrick Neill QC once again appeared for Anisminic. For the Commission, Sydney Templeman QC was joined by the new Treasury Devil, Gordon Slynn, as Nigel Bridge had been appointed to the High Court bench earlier that year. Parker distinguished between decisions which are good while they stand and those, which are complete nullities, and acknowledged that Anisminic must fail if the decision was not a complete nullity,[75] but then attacked Diplock LJ's analysis of the case-law. Templeman's argument for the Commission in the Lords was broadly similar to that advanced below, except that at a late stage he resurrected a point concerning the appropriateness of the making of a declaration, an argument rejected by a majority of their Lordships as it had been by Browne J.[76]

The House delivered judgment on 17 December 1968. All five of their Lordships (Lords Reid, Morris, Pearce, Wilberforce and Pearson) agreed that Section 4(4), like every other example in the long history of statutory provisions limiting recourse to courts to challenge decisions of inferior tribunals, protected every determination which was not a nullity, but did not protect any purported

---

[73] [1968] 2 QB at pp 904–909.
[74] *R (Cart) v Upper Tribunal (Public Law Project and another intervening)* [2011] UKSC 28, [2012] 1 AC 663, SC, *per* Lady Hale at [59], Lord Phillips at [92]–[95] and Lord Dyson at [123]–[125].
[75] [1969] 2 AC 147 at 152.
[76] [1969] 2 AC at 169 *per* Lord Reid, 206 *per* Lord Pearce, 214 *per* Lords Wilberforce. Morris and Pearson would have rejected *Anisminic*'s substantive arguments, so did not need to consider remedies.

determination which was a nullity. It would not prevent a court from deciding whether a purported determination was a forgery, and, said Lord Reid, 'I do not see how it could be said that such a provision protects some kinds of nullity but not others: if that were intended it would be easy to say so'.[77] All agreed that an error in Browne J's Class 1, resulting in the decision-maker having no authority to enter on the inquiry, meant that a purported decision was in truth no decision. Beyond that, however, there was disagreement.

Lord Morris essentially agreed with the Court of Appeal that only an error in Class 1 would fall outside the protection of Section 4(4) of the Act. It was 'abundantly clear that questions of law as well as of fact could be remitted for the determination of a tribunal'. Any error in relation to a matter remitted to the Commission for determination, whether of law or of fact, was within its jurisdiction, and 'cannot be asserted to be wrong if Parliament has enacted that the determination is not to be called in question in any court of law'.[78] When considering Anisminic's application, the Commission had been acting within its remit and conditions precedent to its functions were fulfilled.[79]

> When they were hearing argument as to the meaning of those relevant parts they were not acting without jurisdiction. They were at the very heart of their duty, their task and their jurisdiction. It cannot be that their necessary duty of deciding as to the meaning would be or could be followed by the result that if they took one view they would be within jurisdiction and if they took another view that they would be without. If at the moment of decision they were inevitably within their jurisdiction because they were doing what they had to do, I cannot think that a later view of someone else, if it differed from theirs, could involve that they trespassed from within their jurisdiction at the moment of decision.[80]

As Lord Reid had said in an earlier case, 'If he has jurisdiction to go right he has jurisdiction to go wrong. Neither an error in fact nor an error in law will destroy his jurisdiction.'[81] By questioning a determination on grounds that had nothing to do with a Class 1 question, Browne J had exceeded his own jurisdiction.[82]

The other Law Lords, by contrast, considered that if the Commission had misconstrued Article 4(1)(b) of the Order they acted outside their jurisdiction. Lord Pearson thought that the Commission's interpretation had been correct, so

---

[77] [1969] 2 AC at 170 *per* Lord Reid. See to the same effect Lord Morris at 181, Lord Pearce at 194–195, Lord Wilberforce at 207–208, and Lord Pearson at n 215.
[78] [1969] 2 AC at 182.
[79] [1969] 2 AC at 183–184.
[80] [1969] 2 AC at 189 and 194.
[81] [1968] *R. v Governor of Brixton Prison,* ex parte *Armah* AC 192 at 234.
[82] [1969] 2 AC at 183, citing *R v Nat Bell Liquors* [1922] 2 AC 128 at 156 *per* Lord Sumner. Lord Morris left open the possibility that an error in Class 4 (fraud, bad faith, or breach of natural justice) in the course of an inquiry might make the ultimate decision a nullity, although so to hold would, he thought, involve reconsidering *Smith v East Elloe Rural District Council* [1956] AC 736, HL, where a majority of the House had held that a preclusive provision protected an allegedly fraudulent decision.

there had been no error.[83] But Lords Reid, Pearce and Wilberforce, like Browne J,[84] thought that the Commission had erred in considering whether TEDO were Anisminic's successors in title.

X. The Ratio

Lord Reid expressed his *ratio decidendi* narrowly. The question was whether, under the Order, the plaintiffs had to prove anything concerning successors in title.

> If the commission were entitled to enter on the inquiry whether the applicants had a successor in title, then their decision as to whether TEDO was their successor in title would I think be unassailable whether it was right or wrong: it would be a matter remitted to them for their decision. The question I have to consider is not whether they made a wrong decision but whether they inquired into and decided a matter which they had no right to consider.

He had 'great difficulty in seeing how in the circumstances there could be a successor in title of a person who is still in existence'.[85] As Anisminic had not needed to satisfy the Commission of anything relating to a successor in title, the Commission had had no right to consider the matter. This made their determination null, not simply because they had made an error of law but because of the particular kind of error they had made.

> It was argued that the whole matter of construing the Order was something remitted to the commission for their decision. I cannot accept that argument. I find nothing in the Order to support it. The Order requires the commission to consider whether they are satisfied with regard to the prescribed matters. That is all they have to do. It cannot be for the commission to determine the limits of its powers. Of course if one party submits to a tribunal that its powers are wider than in fact they are, then the tribunal must deal with that submission. But if they reach a wrong conclusion as to the width of their powers, the court must be able to correct that—not because the tribunal has made an error of law, but because as a result of making an error of law they have dealt with and based their decision on a matter with which, on a true construction of their powers, they had no right to deal. If they base their decision on some matter which is not prescribed for their adjudication, they are doing something which they have no right to do and, if the view which I expressed earlier is right, their decision is a nullity.[86]

It followed that 'the commission rejected the appellants' claim on a ground which they had no right to take into account and that their decision was a nullity'.[87]

---

[83] [1969] 2 AC at 215 *et seq.*
[84] [1969] 2 AC at 208.
[85] [1969] 2 AC at 174.
[86] [1969] 2 AC at 174. As we shall see, parliamentary counsel later regarded the first five sentences of the passage as the crux of the decision, and drafted legislation to reverse its effect accordingly.
[87] [1969] 2 AC at 175.

Lord Wilberforce, like the Court of Appeal, accepted that the Order conferred power on the Commission to decide some questions of law, but, endorsing Browne J's reasoning, considered that it also limited that power. Article 4 of the Order spoke of 'successor in title' to a person, not to property. The drafting of the article was unfortunately 'telescopic'; the draftsman ought to have dealt separately with cases where the claimant was the original owner and cases where the claimant was successor in title to the original owner. There was no obvious reason why a British national who had disposed of property should be allowed to claim on the Fund in respect of that property if the assignee was another British national, but not otherwise. It followed that that TEDO could not be the plaintiff's successor in title for the purpose of Article 4.[88] The scope of a decision-maker's power to make final decisions on questions of law depended on the legislation, which in this regard had to be interpreted in the light of the type of decision-maker and decision. Where the decision in question involved a degree of policy-making rather than fact-finding, especially when the decision-maker was a Government Department:

> I think that we have reached a stage in our administrative law when we can view this question quite objectively, without any necessary predisposition towards one that questions of law, or questions of construction, are necessarily for the courts.

In other cases,

> it may be apparent that Parliament is itself directly and closely concerned with the definition and delimitation of certain matters of comparative detail and has marked by its language the intention that these shall accurately be observed ... The present case, ... as examination of the relevant Order in Council will show, is clearly of the latter category.

In some cases it had been held that a tribunal could go outside its proper limits even after having properly entered on its designated inquiry, falling into an error which made its decision not merely erroneous but a nullity. These included cases where a tribunal could be said to have asked the wrong question or applied the wrong test in a way that made the decision invalid.[89] The Order required the Commission to admit a claim by an original owner of the property (rather than by a successor in title) if three, and only three, conditions were satisfied: (i) that the application related to property in Egypt referred to in Annex E to the treaty between the Egyptian and UK Governments; (ii) that the claimant was the person referred to in Annex E as the owner of the property; and (iii) that the claimant was a British national at the specified dates. All these conditions were fulfilled. By adding a fourth condition of its own, namely that the claimant's successor in title to property be a British national, the Commission was failing to comply with its statutory obligation to admit the claim, by continuing to look for reasons to reject the claim despite being satisfied that all the statutory conditions for admitting it had been fulfilled.[90]

---

[88] [1969] 2 AC at 212–214. See to the same effect Lord Reid at para 173.
[89] [1969] 2 AC at 209–210.
[90] [1969] 2 AC at 214.

As Lord Pearce said: 'This is simply an enforcement of Parliament's mandate to the tribunal.'[91] It would be wrong to interpret 'determination' in Section 4(4) of the 1950 Act as including a forged determination, or one which did not accurately record what the Commission had decided. Interpreting it as meaning a real, not purported, determination would be in accordance with the long line of cases, which had interpreted preclusive provisions in that way.[92] By misconstruing the Order which gave them jurisdiction and laid down the precise limit of their duty, the Commission had exceeded or departed from their mandate, so their determination was made without jurisdiction and was not protected by Section 4(4) of the 1950 Act.[93]

What, then, did the case decide? Cutting through differences of terminology and leaving obiter dicta aside, it established the following.

First, it unanimously reaffirmed a long line of cases holding that statutory provisions excluding the Court's supervisory function over inferior tribunals are not to be interpreted as excluding the Court's jurisdiction to check any attempt by an inferior tribunal to extend its remit by failing to comply with statutory limits on its functions.

Second, by a majority of four to one (Lord Morris dissenting) it held that an inferior tribunal could go outside its jurisdiction having properly embarked on the inquiry remitted to it if it adds an additional condition for action over and above those described in empowering legislation.

Third, unanimously, it established that, in order to decide whether an error makes a decision null, one has to construe the empowering legislation to determine whether the legislation remitted to the decision-maker power to decide the matter in relation to which the error occurred as one of its own functions.

Fourth, unanimously, a decision resulting from an error of law or of fact on a matter which had been remitted to the decision-maker by legislation would not be null, so it could be set aside only by certiorari, and not at all if protected by a statutory provision excluding certiorari.

Fifth, by a majority of three to one (Lord Pearson dissenting and Lord Morris expressing no opinion), it was held that the identity of a claimant's 'successor in title' was relevant under the Order only where the claimant was successor in title to an original claimant who no longer existed.

---

[91] [1969] 2 AC at 194–195. The reference to [1922] *Nat Bell Liquors* is to 2 AC 128 at 156.

[92] [1969] 2 AC at 199–200. The cases on which Lord Pearce relied were *Campbell v Brown* (1829) 3 Wils. & S. 441, HL, In re *Bradlaugh* (1878) 3 QBD. 509, *R. v Hurst*, ex parte *Smith* [1960] 2 QB 133 at 142 *per* Lord Parker CJ. On absence of jurisdiction, and *R. v Medical Appeal Tribunal*, ex parte *Gilmore* [1957] 1 QB 574, CA, at 586 *per* Denning LJ on excess of jurisdiction. He would have been prepared to reconsider *Smith v East Elloe Rural District Council* in the light of the powerful dissenting opinions of Lord Reid and Somervell had he thought that it compelled a different conclusion.

[93] [1969] 2 AC at 201.

XI. Responses to the Judgment 1: Legislation

On Thursday 19 December 1968, two days after the House of Lords delivered its judgment, Montgomery White, Chairman of the Commission, wrote to Vincent Evans, who had recently become Legal Adviser to the Foreign and Commonwealth Office.[94]

> We think that if this decision is allowed to stand it would have very serious effects on the usefulness of the Commission. It is not of great consequence as regards the Egyptian Fund since distributions under the Egypt Order are made according to a set scale and the original Fund is now being supplemented by the Exchequer. The situation would be much more serious as regards any fund which consisted solely of moneys received from a foreign country which are limited in amount and have to be distributed rateably amongst all successful applicants. As regards any such Fund it would appear that the Commission could not carry out its duty of making a rateable distribution so long as it was open to any applicant to question a determination of the Commission on grounds such as succeeded in Anisminic's case. The result would be that distribution might be held up almost indefinitely if an action or actions were on their way to the House of Lords.

White therefore suggested that a new clause might be introduced by way of a Foreign Compensation Bill that was then fortuitously before the House of Commons. This should allow a future Order to provide that:

> the Commission may determine any question as to the construction or meaning or interpretation of such Order and any other matter incidental to the determination of claims or distribution of compensation under that Order and any determination of the Commission made under any such provision shall for the purposes of Section 4(4) of the Foreign Compensation Act 1950 be deemed to be a determination of an application.

The next day, representatives of the Lord Chancellor's Office, Treasury Solicitor and Treasury agreed to 'work towards an amendment to Section 4(4) of the Foreign Compensation Act 1950 which was "safe but unprovocative".[95] Terena Skemp, parliamentary counsel then seconded to the Law Commission, was asked to consider how 'to exclude actions such as that in the *Anisminic* case (excess of jurisdiction by misinterpretation of an Order), and restore the position to that which Parliament really intended in 1950'.[96] Skemp took the key point in the *Anisminic* case to be Lord Reid's conclusion that nothing in the Egypt Order indicated that the interpretation of the Order had been remitted to the Commission for decision.[97] Skemp therefore drafted a clause which would have amended the 1950 Act to

---

[94] FCO 64/131 f 1.
[95] Anderson (FCO) to Skemp, 20 December 1968, FCO 64/131 f 3.
[96] ibid.
[97] [1969] 2 AC 147 at 174.

permit the making of an Order to confer on the Commission power to make any determination and relating to the interpretation of the Orders, and to bring such determinations expressly within the protection of Section 4(4) of the 1950 Act. The amendment would have allowed such an Order to apply the provisions retrospectively to the Egypt Order itself, at least in relation to claimants whose claims had not yet been determined.

A number of civil servants were worried about the retrospective potential of Skemp's draft clause. Wilfrid Bourne, of the Lord Chancellor's Office, wrote to Sir Alexander Morley that whether to extend the amendment to the Egypt Order was a matter of policy to be decided in the light of the practical importance of doing so, and observing that, if confined to future Orders, nobody could object on the ground of retrospection.[98] Ronald Watts of the Foreign and Commonwealth Office wrote to Charlton at the Treasury Solicitor's Department:

> In the Foreign Office view it would be unthinkable to try to frustrate the House of Lords decision by taking action affecting the rights of claimants under the Egypt Order, whether their particular claims have already been determined or not ... I do not think it could be said that it is the fault of the claimants that their claims have remained pending for so long, and to change the rules of the game so near to its end would be most unfair.[99]

Two days later, Watts wrote again, making it clear that the FCO would regard it as unfair to change the rules retrospectively, because it would create two classes of claimant, those who had received determinations before the amendment and those who were still waiting.[100] At the Commission, Montgomery White thought that the *Anisminic* judgment produced too little practical inconvenience for the Commission to justify allowing retrospective legislation. The only cases under the Egypt Order likely to be affected by the House of Lords' decision in *Anisminic* on the 'successor in title' point related to certain shareholdings in Tractor and Engineering Co SAE, and the Commission hoped to be able to deal with those on the basis of the *Anisminic* ruling without litigation. The Commission 'would not contemplate the making of an amending Order in Council to defeat claims which should succeed on the construction of the existing Order approved by the House of Lords'.[101]

These representations were effective, and the clause was redrafted to apply only to claims under Orders made after the coming into force of the 1969 Act. In the course of a few days, the proposal to introduce the amending clause to the Bill was agreed by the Lord Chancellor, who did not think it necessary to consult the Cabinet Home Affairs or Legislation Committee, and by the Foreign Secretary (Michael Stewart MP) and Dick Taverne MP, then a Treasury Minister.[102]

---

[98] FCO 64/131 f 13, 7 January 1969.
[99] FCO 64/131 f 18, 8 January 1969, paras 3 and 4.
[100] FCO 64/131 ff 17–18, 10 January 1969.
[101] FCO 64/131 f 16, 8 January 1969.
[102] Gardiner to Michael Stewart, Foreign Secretary, 10 January 1969, FO 64/131 f 20; Dick Taverne to Gardiner, 13 January 1969, FO 64/131 f 22.

Skemp himself had reservations about another aspect of his draft clause.

> In your letter to me of 20th December you expressed the hope that the amendment would be safe and unprovocative. My own view is that to be unprovocative the solution ought to confer some sort of right of appeal against the FCC's decisions on law. I appreciate that you do not want claims to be outstanding for a number of years, but would it not be possible to provide for an appeal on law if brought within say three months of the FCC's decision? Presumably it would go straight to the Court of Appeal. If you object that one appeal would prevent a distribution to claimants, my answer is that at the end of a given period the FCC would know the size of the claims still outstanding and they could make a distribution to claimants, in the form of a payment on accounts of the balance. If the outstanding claims then failed, they could follow this up with a final payment.[103]

But the advice seems to have fallen on deaf ears. Official policy was to protect the Commission's determinations entirely from the courts. The judgments in *Anisminic*:

> did not cast doubt on the principle laid down in Rustomjee v The Queen and Civilian War Claimants Association v The King that the Crown, in receiving such compensation, is in no sense an agent or trustee for individual claimants. In other words, until an Order under the Foreign Compensation Act is made, no individual claimant has any legal rights to share in such compensation. It will be seen, therefore, that the Foreign Compensation Commission operates on a somewhat different plane from Tribunals, which are constituted to decide questions affecting the rights and liberties of subjects of the Crown.[104]

In addition:

> ... In most cases in which the Foreign Compensation Commission has been used or will be used in the future, the amount available for compensation is a finite "lump sum". Accordingly, it cannot be judged with any degree of certainty what the rateable share attributable to each claimant will be until all applications of any magnitude have been disposed of. It will be clear, therefore, that if appeal to or review by the courts were to be possible to the extent permitted by the Anisminic case, the possibility of applications to the courts by dissatisfied claimants would have a very serious delaying effect on the payment of the final (or even a substantial interim) dividend to the remaining claimants ... .
>
> ... The costs and incidental expenses of defending proceedings before the courts would have to come out of the Compensation Fund and thereby reduce the dividend paid to the successful claimants.[105]

On 22 January 1969 in the House of Commons, William Whitlock, Labour's Parliamentary Under-Secretary of State at the Foreign and Commonwealth Office,

---

[103] Skemp to Anderson, 31 December 1968, FCO 64/131 f 8.
[104] *The Jurisdiction of the Courts to review determinations of the Foreign Compensation Commission*, a briefing paper for ministers, probably by Sir Alexander Morley, attached to TNA FCO 64/131 f 5, para 4(i), 23 December 1968. Morley was a very distinguished and long-serving member of the Foreign Service. Aged nearly 61, he had retired from his diplomatic position and been re-employed in the FCO's Claims Department.
[105] ibid para 4(ii) and (iii).

during the Report Stage on the Bill, moved an amendment to add a new sub-Clause (4) in Clause 2 of the Bill, as follows:

> An Order in Council under the said Section 3 [of the 1950 Act] may confer power on the Foreign Compensation Commission to determine any question as to the construction or interpretation of any provision with respect to claims falling to be determined by them which is included in any Order made under that section after the passing of this Act; and any determination of the Commission by virtue of this subsection shall be included among the determinations to which Section 4(4) of the Foreign Compensation Act, 1950 (determinations of the Commission not to be questions in courts of law) applies.[106]

He explained that this would give effect to what, in the Government's opinion, had been the intention of Parliament in passing Section 4(4) of the 1950 Act, and would allow compensation to be distributed more expeditiously than would be possible if it were necessary to wait until the possibility of litigation had passed before finally determining the share attributable to each successful claimant. Whitlock asserted that the amendment was not retrospective; it would apply only to distributions begun after the passing of the Bill, and would not affect reconsideration of Anisminic's claim in the light of the House of Lords' judgment. Nor, he said, would it prevent judicial review of 'an alleged failure to observe the rules of natural justice, or a complaint … of some fundamental error of procedure', though it was hard to conceive of lawyers as distinguished as members of the Commission being challenged on such grounds.[107] (It is not clear, however, where in the amendment this was guaranteed.) He drew attention to the special character of the work of the Commission, making distributions of funds to which no individual claimant has any right unless such right is granted by the Crown, and authorising pro rata payments from cash-limited funds.

For the Opposition, Conservative MP Richard Wood (later Lord Holderness) reserved judgment on the merits of the amendment, as to which he hoped that it would be possible to achieve a balance between preserving the substance of the Commission's determinations from the danger of appeal and safeguarding the right of claimants to challenge decisions which are nullities.[108] Sir John Foster MP, the distinguished Conservative lawyer, went further,[109] drawing a parallel between the amendment and the passage of the War Damage Act 1965 which had retrospectively reversed the judgment against the Crown in the great case of *Burmah Oil v Lord Advocate*.[110] He was supported by Robin Maxwell-Hyslop MP.[111] In

---

[106] HC Deb 22 January 1969, vol 776 cols 568–572. Morley had prepared a draft of the speech on the afternoon of 13 January and sent it to D Anderson and V Evans, commenting, 'I think this says about as much as is wise in the moving speech.' Anderson commented, 'It would be prudent to copy the draft to Bourne (LCD) and Hetherington (LOD), at the time it goes to Whitlock, for their comments (not their masters').' FCO 64/131 f 21, with Anderson's manuscript note on it.

[107] ibid at col 571.

[108] ibid at col 573.

[109] ibid at col 577.

[110] [1965] AC 75, HL. See A. Goodhart, 'The Burmah Oil case and the War Damage Act 1965' (1966) 82 LQR 97–114.

[111] HC Deb 22 January 1969, vol 776 cols 578–580.

reply, Mr Whitlock quoted from the judgment of Russell LJ in the Court of Appeal: to seek excessive precision in cases of this kind would be supererogatory. The House agreed to the amendment, and the Bill was read a third time and approved by 161 votes to 115.[112]

Before the Bill was considered in the Lords, a campaign against the clause built up among lawyers outside Parliament. Professor H.W.R Wade, already responsible for ensuring that Browne J's judgment was published, led the way with a letter to *The Times*.[113] 'The law's delay, like its uncertainty and expense, is a tempting reason for sacrificing justice to speed. But if the courts are prevented from protecting legal rights, the remedy is much worse than the disease.' There could be good reasons for restricting on judicial scrutiny of administrative decisions.

> But drastic restrictions have become a matter of common form, in unsuitable as well as suitable cases … . The technicality of these enactments disguises their insidious character. If legal rights cannot be brought before the courts, the rule of law collapses. The judges, well understanding this, have for 300 years firmly set their faces against such provisions and have, to put it bluntly, refused to apply them. What is now needed is a thorough study of the problem from all angles, with a view to making exceptions where they are justifiable, but not elsewhere. Meanwhile, the Government should respect the wise decision of the House of Lords, which puts justice first.

Wade's point was quickly supported. The Bar Council condemned the clause as giving the Commission 'an absolutely unacceptable power to construe and misconstrue the statutory provisions which confer upon it its own jurisdiction', which was particularly wrong given that the Commission had to determine very difficult questions and did not give reasons.[114] In a joint letter to *The Times*, published on the day on which the Bill was to receive its second reading in the Lords, the Chairman of the General Council of the Bar, Desmond Ackner, and the President of the Law Society, Edmund Sargant, described the clause as 'a serious encroachment on the Rule of Law and in our view should not be made part of the law of this country save after full and thorough debate and then only for compelling reasons'. If necessary, limitations on the right of recourse to courts:

> should be kept to the minimum. The protection would surely be adequate if proceedings to challenge a determination had to be brought within a comparatively short period, say six months, or if a right of appeal to a judge on points of law were given and the decision of the judge were made final with no further right of appeal … . In any event, … we consider that it is an undesirable development of the law to make the Commission sole and final judges of the limits of their own jurisdiction and to take away from the Courts the power, which they have always possessed and which is a vital facet of the Rule of Law, of ensuring that an inferior tribunal keeps within the four corners of whatever limited jurisdiction the legislature has entrusted to it.[115]

---

[112] HC Deb 22 January 1969, vol 776, cols 614–615.
[113] *The Times*, 1 February 1969, p 11.
[114] 'Our Legal Correspondent', 'Claims Bill amendment attacked', *The Times*, 4 February 1969, p 2.
[115] *The Times*, 4 February 1949, para 9.

On the same day, a *Times* leader attacked the clause on similar grounds, pointed out that an unfettered power to construe an Order in Council in any way the Commission wishes 'would make a nonsense of the Order in Council', and urged the Lords to strike out the amendment in Committee if the Government made no attempt to overcome the difficulties it presented.[116]

Introducing the Bill to the Lords later that day, Lord Chalfont, Minister of State, Foreign and Commonwealth Office, explained that its main purpose was to allow assets in the UK belonging to people who had previously been resident in the Baltic States (and other territories ceded to the USSR by Finland, Poland, Czechoslovakia and Rumania during and after World War II) to be sold and the proceeds used to pay compensation to British people who suffered losses in those regions.[117] A secondary purpose was to protect the Commission's determinations from legal challenge by way of Clause 2(4) of the Bill as inserted on Report in the Commons. Lord Chalfont suggested that press comment on the clause betrayed misunderstanding of its true import, and advanced the same arguments in support of it as Mr Whitlock had developed in the Commons.[118] For the Opposition, the Marquess of Lansdowne attacked the main purpose of the Bill on its merits,[119] but while waiting to hear what 'legal luminaries' would say during the debate, also drew attention to Professor Wade's concerns about sacrificing justice to speed.[120]

Viscount Dilhorne, a Law Lord and former Conservative Lord Chancellor, complained that Clause 2(4) would put the Commission 'in complete control of its own jurisdiction'. On difficult matters of construction, the Commission might itself welcome a judicial ruling. The problem, he said, was 'to devise a way in which that ruling could be secured and finally secured without such a delay as would be intolerable … I am wondering … whether it would not be possible to provide that there should be an appeal to a court.' As Skemp had previously suggested privately, Viscount Dilhorne thought that this might be the Court of Appeal, and it might be provided that its decision should be final and that there should be a short time allowed to start litigation after a determination. It need not cause great delay, because the courts could hold an expedited hearing if other claims were being held up.[121]

For the Government, the Lord Chancellor, Lord Gardiner, pointed out that claimants wanted a degree of finality, and did not want to wait for six or more years for compensation while another claimant litigated his own case. The Commission was a special case, which was why it had not been included in the general repeal of provisions ousting the courts' jurisdiction by the Tribunals and Inquiries Act 1958.[122] But Lord Denning, then Master of the Rolls, spoke in support of retaining

---

[116] Anon., 'Government above the law', *The Times*, 4 February 1969, p 9.
[117] HL Deb 4 February 1969, vol 299, cols 11–15. This was a highly contentious and politically contested goal, for reasons which are not relevant to this chapter.
[118] ibid cols 15–18.
[119] ibid cols 20–27.
[120] ibid cols 27–28.
[121] ibid cols 39–40.
[122] HL Deb 4 February 1969, vol 299, cols 40–45.

recourse to a court,[123] as did Lord Wilberforce, who had been in the majority in *Anisminic*, and thought that concern about delay might be exaggerated when it had taken the Commission about four years to make a provisional determination of Anisminic's application before it reached a court.[124]

There was no division on second reading, but before the Committee Stage Viscount Dilhorne and Lord Lansdowne tabled an amendment[125] for consideration in Committee to replace Clause 2(4) of the Bill with the following: '(4) There shall be inserted at the commencement of Section 4(4) of the Foreign Compensation Act 1950 "An appeal shall lie by way of case stated to the Court of Appeal whose decision shall be final, on a question of law relating to the jurisdiction of the Commission but save as aforesaid".'[126] On 13 February at 6.20pm Viscount Dilhorne rose to move his amendment. He accepted that it was defective; for example, it did not specify whether the appeal would lie from a provisional or only from a final determination, and it did not set a time limit for appealing to the Court of Appeal.[127] Nevertheless, supported by Lord Denning (in absentia) and Lord Wilberforce,[128] he pressed his amendment to a division, on which it was approved by 55 votes to 32, a majority against the Government of 23.[129]

On 19 February, a meeting of Government Ministers took place in the Lord Chancellor's room in the House of Lords to discuss how to respond. Parliamentary Counsel had drafted some improvements to Viscount Dilhorne's clause, for possible introduction at Report Stage. But the Government remained unwilling to accept the principle that the Commission's decisions should be subject to any appeal. That being so, it was decided not to try to improve Viscount Dilhorne's clause in the Lords, but to have the original clause reinstated when the Bill returned to the Commons.[130] But by the day of Report Stage on 11 March, the Government had changed its mind. The Lord Chancellor moved an amendment to replace Viscount Dilhorne's clause with one which first conferred power on the Commission to determine any question of construction or interpretation of the Orders (instead of leaving it to a later Order to confer that power), and then permitted a person aggrieved by a determination to require the Commission to state a case for the opinion of the Court of Appeal, not only in relation to matters of jurisdiction but

---

[123] ibid cols 53–55.
[124] ibid cols 55–59.
[125] *The Times*, 8 February 1969, p 3. Lord Wilberforce, another Law Lord, had helped Viscount Dilhorne to draft the amendment: see Dilhorne at Report Stage, HL Deb 11 March 1969 vol 300 col 395.
[126] HL Deb 13 February 1969 vol 299 col 640.
[127] ibid cols 640–643.
[128] ibid cols 648–650
[129] Lord Wilberforce went so far as to vote for Viscount Dilhorne's amendment, an action which was later criticised in the House of Commons during consideration of the Parliament (No. 2) Bill of 1969, on the ground that it breached the separation of powers for the House of Lords to sit as a court of appeal, and that it was improper for a judge, having given judgment in a case, then to vote in the House of Lords on legislation intended to alter the effect of that judgment: HC Deb 2 April 1969 vol 781 cols 447–448 (Michael English MP).
[130] CAB 165/361 f 11.

also (since the construction of the Orders would now be within the Commission's jurisdiction) in relation to the construction or interpretation of the Orders.[131] 'It is not ... intended to interfere with the power—which was recognised as existing before the decision in the Anisminic case—to impeach a decision of the Commission on the ground that it was given in breach of the rules of natural justice ... '.[132]

The new clause was far more complex than Viscount Dilhorne's, extending to twelve sub-Sections. It was generally welcomed, approved without a division,[133] and accepted by the House of Commons, becoming Section 3 of the Foreign Compensation Act 1969.[134] The provision was the result of what might today be described as 'dialogue' between judges and Parliament on an important issue of constitutional principle. Parliament, in 1950 and again when considering the Tribunals and Inquiries Act 1958, had decided to prevent aggrieved applicants from challenging determinations of the Commission in the courts. The judges had their say on the matter in *Anisminic*. When the effect of the judgment in *Anisminic* proved politically and administratively unacceptable, two Lords of Appeal in Ordinary (Viscount Dilhorne and Lord Wilberforce) and the Master of the Rolls (Lord Denning), who could then speak and vote in the House of Lords, were able to exert influence in the course of the House's scrutiny of the Bill to bring about a compromise, which the Government accepted reluctantly, in part at least because it had little, if anything, to lose by doing so. This would be more difficult following the Constitutional Reform Act 2005, as Supreme Court justices no longer sit in the House of Lords.

The compromise involved extending the Commission's jurisdiction in sub-Section 1, thus reversing for the future the effect of *Anisminic* as regards the scope of the Commission's jurisdiction, leaving its jurisdiction and Section 4(4) of the 1950 Act (as interpreted by the House of Lords in *Anisminic*) in place in respect of determinations made before the 1969 Act came into force, and, for the future, introducing an appeal by case stated to the Court of Appeal (but not onward to the House of Lords) against the Commission's construction of an Order, a jurisdictional question, while allowing certiorari or declaration to continue to lie in respect of breach of natural justice.

XII. Reception of the Judgment 2: The Commission re-determines Anisminic's Claim

In 1969 the Commission re-determined Anisminic's claim on the Fund. It was clear that the claim had to be registered, and the remaining task was to assess the

---

[131] HL Deb 11 March 1969 vol 300 cols 391–392.
[132] ibid at col 393.
[133] ibid at col 397.
[134] HC Deb 1 May 1979 vol 782 cols 1735–1740.

value of Anisminic's loss. The Legal Officer, after a long negotiation with Linklaters & Paines, Anisminic's solicitors, in the first half of 1969, worked on the basis of a ten-year capitalisation of a rough average of company profits from the mines between 1951 and 1955, suggesting figures between £2.7 million and £2.9 million. He thought it unlikely that it would be possible to reduce the company's figures below £2.5 million. 'Having regard to all the uncertainties and the desirability of disposing of this large, long outstanding and troublesome application with the least possible delay, I would strongly recommend a settlement at or about a figure of £2½ million.'[135] The Commissioners agreed.[136]

A settlement of £2,500,000 was finally agreed, having taken into account the company's recoupment of £500,000 from the November 1957 agreement,[137] and a provisional determination was accordingly made on 17 July 1969.[138] On the basis of the scale of rates of compensation in the Final Distribution Order, this meant that a sum of £765,000 was payable to the company out of the fund. The size of the sum led to a delay in having the payment authorised,[139] but a cheque was finally sent to Linklaters & Paines on 16 September, closing an application that had dragged on for ten years, including six years in the courts.[140]

XIII. The Demise of Anisminic Ltd

By the time Anisminic received the money, it was a shell. It had not mined since 1956. By January 1964, in its list of share prices, *The Times* had moved its from the mining section to 'Miscellaneous', and the share price had fallen from its pre-Suez level of 4s 9d to 1s 3d. In 1966, shortly before the hearing before Browne J, and after years of reductions in the share capital, the company entered into a scheme of arrangement with its minority shareholders (ie those other than William Baird & Co). Judging by the fact that Anisminic then drops out of the list, it seems that the minority shareholders were bought out, and the company was fully absorbed into the William Baird group, maintaining an independent existence only to pursue its claim on the Egypt Fund. The payment, when it came, benefited not the company itself or its original shareholders but William Baird & Co.

What should we make of the merits of Anisminic's claim? The Commission, and Russell LJ in the Court of Appeal,[141] seem to have regarded it as opportunistic,

---

[135] Legal Officer to Montgomery White and R. Windham, TNA FO 1004/385, minute 191 at front of file, 9 June 1969.
[136] TNA FO 1005/385, minutes 192 and 193 respectively, 13 June 1969.
[137] TNA FO 1004/385 f 198B, 25 June 1969, and minute 201, 16 July 1969.
[138] TNA FO 1004/385 f 202D, 17 July 1969.
[139] The facts are recorded in minute 201 at the front of TNA 1004/385, 22 August 1969.
[140] Letter from Commission to Linklaters & Paines, TNA 1004/385 f 213a, 16 September 1969, acknowledged by letter from Linklaters & Paines, TNA 1004/385 f 215A, 23 September 1969.
[141] [1968] 2 QB 862 at 913.

unprincipled and unmeritorious. The company had made a separate agreement with the Egyptians, and had not expected to obtain more than the £500,000 due under that agreement. Why should the company obtain an additional windfall at the expense of others?

On the other hand, in the words of Lord Pearce, the company had 'just so much merits as a person has when, through no fault of his own, he has been deprived of property worth £4,000,000 and has received by his own efforts £500,000 in compensation'.[142] Anisminic's behaviour was not entirely self-interested. The company had scruples about making a claim on the fund unless the Government had made a claim on its behalf to the Egyptians. In the event, that could not be established, but it was at least clear that the Government had known of the company's agreement with the Egyptians and it was probable that the Government had not intended to exclude the company from the fund. In any case, once the Government agreed to top-up the fund under the Foreign Compensation Act 1962, the additional cost of Anisminic's claim would be spread among British taxpayers at large, and would not be borne by the other claimants. And, as Browne J said, if the company had not made its separate agreement they would have had an unanswerable claim on the fund for the whole of their loss (payable at the appropriate scale). The other claimants and taxpayers benefited from the company reducing the value of its claim by £500,000.[143]

XIV. Anisminic's Long-term Significance

Despite its demise, Anisminic has enjoyed an afterlife, not as a company but as an idea or ideal. The ratio of the House of Lords decision was relatively narrow, as noted above, but what landmark cases decide and what they are later regarded as authority for may be very different. Obiter dicta from Lords Reid and Pearce subsequently became the basis for extending the theory and practice of judicial review well beyond anything justified by the ratio. A passage from Lord Reid's speech, often taken out of context, has been particularly influential. He preferred to confine the word 'jurisdiction to 'the narrow and original sense of the tribunal being entitled to enter on the inquiry in question'. But, he continued:

> ... there are many cases where, although the tribunal had jurisdiction to enter on the inquiry, it has done or failed to do something in the course of the inquiry which is of such a nature that its decision is a nullity. *It may have given its decision in bad faith. It may have made a decision which it had no power to make. It may have failed in the course of the inquiry to comply with the requirements of natural justice.* It may in perfect good faith

---

[142] [1969] 2 AC 147 at 206.
[143] [1969] 2 AC 223 at 227–228.

have misconstrued the provisions giving it power to act so that it failed to deal with the question remitted to it and decided some question which was not remitted to it. *It may have refused to take into account something which it was required to take into account. Or it may have based its decision on some matter which, under the provisions setting it up, it had no right to take into account. I do not intend this list to be exhaustive.* if it decides a question remitted to it for decision *without committing any of these errors* it is as much entitled to decide that question wrongly as it is to decide it rightly.[144] (emphasis added)

This is obiter dictum it was unnecessary for, and irrelevant to, the narrow issue that the House of Lords had to decide. Lord Reid was not even articulating background principles on which his reasoning on the point at issue was founded. To say that the various forms of procedural mistake he mentioned could justify the High Court in quashing a decision by certiorari was trite law, and needed no authority; but the issue was different, deeper, and narrower: did the specific type of error of law established in the *Anisminic* case render the determination null? Lord Reid leapt, apparently without noticing, from uncontroversial general propositions about circumstances in which certiorari would be available to quash a decision in the absence of any provision excluding the court's jurisdiction, to a judgment about the effect of a very particular sort of error (denying eligibility for compensation for failing to comply with a condition which the legislation had not imposed) in a case where, because a declaration rather than certiorari was sought and, because of the effect of Section 4(4) of the 1950 Act, it was essential to show that the challenged determination was not merely erroneous but null.

Despite the weaknesses of that passage, the decision has subsequently been treated as authority for the proposition that any error of law makes a decision a nullity,[145] and the category of 'error of law' has been extended to a point where it is hard to find an error, which cannot be dressed up as an error of law. Some of the most extensive judicial assertions about the propositions regarding the effect of error of law for which *Anisminic* is authority appear in judgments which do not concern declarations of preclusive clauses in statutes, and in cases where judges have found and applied exceptions to the supposed rule.[146] It has never been clear whether the proposition that any error of law makes a decision a nullity is a rule

---

[144] [1969] 2 AC at 171.

[145] See particularly *Pearlman v Keepers and Governors of Harrow School* [1979] QB 56, CA, a case concerned with rights of appeal rather than review, in which Lord Denning MR and Eveleigh LJ formed the majority. The dissenting judgment of Geoffrey Lane was later approved by a majority of the Appellate Committee of the House of Lords in *In re Racal* [1981] AC 374, HL, and by the Judicial Committee of the Privy Council in *South East Asia Fire Bricks Sdn Bhd v Non-Metallic Mineral Products Manufacturing Employees Union* [1981] AC 363, PC. For discussion of *Pearlman* see H. Rawlings, 'Jurisdictional review after Pearlman' [1979] P.L. 404–419. See also *Boddington v British Transport Police* [1999] 2 AC 143, HL, at 144 *per* Lord Irvine of Lairg LC, and *R (Lumba) v Secretary of State for the Home Department (JUSTICE and others intervening)* [2011] UKSC 12, 2012 1 AC 245, SC, at para. [66] *per* Lord Dyson.

[146] See, eg *In re Racal Ltd* [1981] AC 374, HL, and *R. v Hull University Visitor, ex parte Page* [1993] AC 682, HL.

subject to exceptions or a principle (or perhaps policy) to be weighed against other principles (or policies).[147]

Those who adopt the extended interpretation of the decision tend not to analyse the case-law fully, elide the difference between a reduction in the field of errors within jurisdiction and their total elimination, and argue that the 'virtual end of error of law on the face of the record and its replacement by an all-embracing category of jurisdictional error' was 'required by principle', provided a coherent theory of jurisdiction and, by pressing declarations into service, an all-embracing remedy.[148] Lord Diplock, having initially treated the judgment as merely extending the category of errors of law which 'go to jurisdiction', and argued that this required judges to exercise self-restraint in the use of their new power,[149] later adopted a more expansive view.

> ... [T]he concept of errors of law which go to "jurisdiction" has been expanded to include errors of law which previously could only have been reviewed if they appeared on the face of the record ... .[In *Anisminic* the] House of Lords, reversing a timorous Court of Appeal, held that in asking itself the wrong question in the case before it, *as every tribunal must inevitably do it if makes any mistake as to the law applicable to the facts*, the Foreign Compensation Commission acted outside its jurisdiction. Ouster clauses, to-day, are rare, but the wider significance of this decision is that *it renders obsolete the technical distinction between errors of law which go to "jurisdiction" and errors of law which do not*. In doing so it enlarges the material that can be made available to the court on *certiorari* to found an inference that those responsible for an administrative decision have erred in law. *So technicalities as to what constitutes the "record" for the purposes of review no longer matter*.[150] (emphasis added)

Lord Diplock was indulging his predilection for conceptual categorisation, driven by what biographers have called 'a panoptic knowledge and comprehension of the law and a scientist's desire to rationalize it'.[151] Be that as it may, in the decades after the decision successive Junior Treasury Counsel set the tone for arguments advanced to courts on behalf of Government Departments in the light of *Anisminic*. They seem to have felt that the law was developing in a direction, which

---

[147] For a useful account, see H Wade and C Forsyth, *Administrative Law* 11th edn Oxford: Oxford University Press, 2014, pp 218–223.

[148] See, eg B Gould, 'Anisminic and jurisdictional error' [1970] PL 358–271 at 360, 361.

[149] 'Judicial control of the administrative process' (1971) 24 CLP 1–17. In this article he also opposed the idea of a specialist administrative law tribunal, partly on the ground that it would lead to conflicts between courts' jurisdictions and cause intolerable delays. He later turned the Crown Office List into just such a specialist tribunal and caused the problems he had foreseen: *O'Reilly v Mackman* [1983] 2 AC 237, HL.

[150] Diplock, 'Administrative law: judicial review reviewed' [1974] CLJ pp 233–245 at 242–243. Diplock was speaking at an event in Cambridge to pay tribute to the recently deceased Downing Professor of the Laws of England, Stanley de Smith. Diplock's view of the case had initially been more moderate.

[151] S Sedley and G Le Quesne, 'Diplock, (William John) Kenneth, Diplock (1907–1985), judge', *Oxford Dictionary of National Biography* Oxford: Oxford University Press, 2004; online edition, May 2015, accessed 31 August 2015.

made it pointless to rely on the actual ratio of the decision.[152] Sometimes a change of mood in the profession produces changes of law without the need for formal authority. Professor Sir John Baker has shown that the common law exists in the day-to-day understandings and practices of the profession, not in the pages of law reports;[153] the profession assimilates a decision to the professional and social temper of the times, and its view is, if anything, even more important than the ratio *decidendi* in determining what a decision will be taken to stand for.

The professional mood in the 1960s, like the social mood, was one of decreasing deference to traditional authority, and growing willingness to question legal and social boundaries. The Suez expedition had provoked a loss of trust in government. Legislation, often arising from private Members' Bills rather than Government Bills, together with a judiciary led by the legal reformer Lord Gardiner as Lord Chancellor, reformed law reform itself, as well as the treatment of racial minorities, unwillingly pregnant women, homosexual men, and the arts, the public's expectations of decision-makers, and treatment of deserted wives. The *Anisminic* case, in its social, political and administrative context, illustrates the interplay of social and political forces: the Commission, courts, Government departments, their legal advisers and Parliament reacting to each other within a framework which was changing in the face of profound challenges. The accommodation eventually achieved was, like all such constitutional accommodations, temporary. In terms of common law theory, it allowed a new orthodoxy to arise, but one which is unusual in that it is not consistently reflected in judicial decisions; it is probably better seen as a professional principle or aspiration than as a rule.[154] The continuing, lively debate about the significance of *Anisminic* after nearly 50 years shows both that it can properly be regarded as a landmark case and that the upheavals that surrounded it continue.

---

[152] S Sedley, 'The Lion Beneath the Throne: Law as History' the 2016 D Williams Lecture, University of Cambridge, accessible at www.cpl.law.cam.ac.uk/sir-david-williams-lectures/sir-stephen-sedley-lion-beneath-throne-law-history; personal conversation with Lord Brown of Eaton-under-Heywood, former Treasury Devil, 10 May 2016.
[153] J Baker, *The Law's Two Bodies* Oxford: Oxford University Press, 2001, *passim*.
[154] See D Feldman, 'Error of law and flawed administrative acts' [2014] CLJ 275–314, and Veena Srirangam Nadhamuni, 'Suspending invalidity while keeping faith with nullity: an analysis of the suspension order cases and their impact on our understanding of the doctrine of nullity' [2015] PL 596–613.

5

Council of Civil Service Unions v Minister for the Civil Service [1984]: Reviewing the Prerogative

RICHARD DRABBLE

I. Introduction

On 22 December 1983, the Minister for the Civil service gave an instruction purporting to vary the conditions of service of the staff employed at *GCHQ* in order to prohibit them from being members of trade unions. The Minister for the Civil Service was the Prime Minister, Margaret Thatcher. The power she (personally) exercised to effect the variation arose under Article 4 of the Civil Service Order in Council 1982.[1] The Order in Council was not made under any statutory authority but was said to be made under prerogative powers to control the conditions of service of officers of the Crown. The instruction was not preceded by any consultation with the unions and took immediate effect. The ban on union membership was announced by the Foreign Secretary in Parliament on 25 January 1984.

There followed a dramatic piece of ligation. The instruction was challenged in judicial review proceedings by the Council of Civil Service Unions (a trade union), and by six individual trade union members. The primary argument was that in making the instruction Thatcher had acted unlawfully because of the absence of consultation. The application succeeded at first instance, when Glidewell J made a declaration that the instruction was invalid and of no legal effect. He made the declaration on 16 July 1984. This was followed, at speed, by a hearing in the Court of Appeal on 6 August 1984. The Court of Appeal allowed the appeal, not because of any error in Glidewell J's judgment, but on the basis of an argument not put to him concerning national security, and in turn based on a single paragraph in the affidavit of Robert Armstrong, a senior civil servant who was Secretary to the

---

[1] This brief account glosses over an issue, which was politically controversial at the time, namely the exact circumstances in which the power came to be exercised. The government's case was that the Prime Minister gave an oral instruction on 22 December 1983, which was followed by the announcement in Parliament. The unions submitted that whatever happened in December did not amount to a 'instruction' under the order; a submission rejected under heading 'Minor matters' by Fraser at [1985] AC 374 at 403H.

Cabinet. There followed a hearing before the House of Lords in early October. The drama inherent in the case was enhanced by the fact that the full House of Lords was not sitting at the time, so the judicial committee hearing took place in the chamber itself rather than a committee room, as would otherwise have been the case. Accordingly, arguments about the reviewability of the prerogative were put by leading counsel in full bottomed wigs at the bar of the house itself to the five Law Lords spaced around the chamber. It was a striking spectacle.[2]

The headnote of the law report ([1985] AC 374) divides the central reasoning of the Lords into three 'holdings'. First, a ruling that 'executive action was not immune from judicial review merely because it was carried out in pursuance of a power derived from a common law, or a prerogative, source'. The case of *Reg v Criminal Injuries Compensation Board*, ex parte *Lain*[3] was applied. It will be seen that ex parte *Lain* does indeed form a very important part of the historical context into which the *GCHQ* litigation has to be fitted, leading directly on to the full strength of modern administrative law on the range of matters that can be subject to judicial review.

The second ruling is recorded as being that 'the applicants would, apart from considerations of national security, have had a legitimate expectation that unions and employees would have been consulted before the minister issued her instruction ...', applying *O'Reilly v Mackman*.[4] Although *O'Reilly* is cited in the judgments as the principal basis for the ruling on legitimate expectation, it will be suggested below that the modern, and fertile, doctrine of legitimate expectation was cemented by a trio of cases, namely *O'Reilly*, the Privy Council case of *N'g Yuen Shiu*[5] and *GCHQ* itself. The doctrine does have its difficulties, not least in its relationship with another powerful tenet of public law, namely the proposition that a decision-maker cannot fetter his or her discretion in relation to the future exercise of discretion. The problem can be seen to be at its greatest in cases concerning 'substantive' expectations.[6] The doctrine has not been universally followed in other common law jurisdictions, particularly in Australia, precisely because of the conceptual problems. However, there can be no doubting its vigour in the English jurisdiction.

The third ruling described in the headnote concerns national security. It is expressed as follows:

> That, however, it was for the executive and not the courts to decide whether, in any particular case, the requirements of national security outweighed those of fairness; and that

---

[2] I was the most junior member of the team of three counsel representing the unions—Louis Blom-Cooper QC (now Sir Louis Blom–Cooper); P Elias (now Lord Justice Elias) and myself. My own memories of the case are vivid; but consist of a combination of a sense of the constitutional (and political) importance of the issues and a struggle to cope with logistical issues such as typing and photocopying in the very different technical circumstances of the 1980s.
[3] [1967] 2 QB 864.
[4] [1983] 2 AC 237 HL(E).
[5] [1983] 2 AC 629.
[6] See Ch 9 of this volume.

the evidence established that the minister had considered, with reason, that prior consultation about her instruction would have involved a risk of precipitating disruption at GCHQ and exposing vulnerable areas of operation ....

The headnote refers to no particular case law in connection with this, crucial, finding.

To a junior advocate involved in the course of the litigation itself, one of the most fraught aspects of the case was this last, national security, aspect. At the hearing before Glidewell the government was represented by the then treasury counsel, Simon Brown (later Lord Brown of Eaton Under Heywood), but no submission was made that the very act of consultation would raise national security considerations. The point was taken for the first time in the Court of Appeal, and was dubbed by advocates for the unions as the 'Brown point'. It was based solely on paragraph 16 of Robert Armstrong's affidavit, which read:

> To have entered such consultations would have served to bring out the vulnerability of areas of operation to those who had shown themselves ready to organise disruption, and consultation with individual members of staff would have been impossible without involving the national unions. Ministers also were aware of the view that the importance of the decision was such as to warrant its first being announced in Parliament.

This paragraph was used in the two higher courts to support the proposition that, as it was put in the respondent's printed case, prior consultation 'would involve a real risk that it would occasion the very kind of disruption which was a threat to national security and which it was intended to avoid'.[7] Much forensic effort was devoted to argument about whether this was the true meaning of paragraph 16, particularly in the Lords, and the actual result in the case in the end turned on this, short, issue. The government won. Lord Fraser,[8] accepted that the affidavit did not in terms support the exact proposition in the respondent's case; but said that the proposition was borne out by the affidavit read as a whole.[9]

At this distance in time, the true meaning of paragraph 16 is of little importance to an understanding of the general development of public law, however important it was to those directly involved and indeed to the politics of 1984. As noted in *De Smith's Judicial Review*, 'the court will no longer unquestioningly accept the say-so of the executive or other experts, and will properly intervene if the decision is based on a material mistake of fact, is incompatible with Convention rights contrary to the Human Rights Act 1998, or is otherwise illegal or irrational, or is affected by procedural impropriety'.[10] Seen against a now contemporary background of the Human Rights Act (HRA) 1998 and statutory creations such as the

---

[7] See p 401 (H-402 B).

[8] At p 403B/E.

[9] For a discussion of the interpretation of para 16 in the context of earlier consultations on 'polygraph security' see '*GCHQ revisited*' Louis Blom-Cooper and Richard Drabble 2010 Public Law 18 esp at p 21.

[10] 7th edition at paras 1-041.

Special Immigration Appeals Commission (SIAC) aimed at enabling Convention compliant examination of issues involving national security, the debate about paragraph 16 has a very dated feel. It is unlikely that it would take place on the same terms now; or that the executive would feel able to submit (as it did) that the somewhat ambiguous wording was explicable by a desire not to further offend employees by being too explicit and that the courts should use their own judgment to make good the ambiguity in favour of the administration.

II. The Place of the GCHQ Judgment in the Development of Modern Administrative Law

The wider significance of the case for the development of public law has three aspects. In no particular order, they are the much quoted adumbration of general principles of administrative law set out by Lord Diplock; the categorical ruling that powers and discretions derived from the prerogative could be the subject of judicial review; and the application of the doctrine of legitimate expectation.

All three aspects need to be viewed as part of a self-conscious attempt by the higher courts to establish a principled body of administrative law primarily taking place in the 1980s and early 1990s. The *GCHQ* judgment is a key component of this body of law. In terms of the issues it itself decided, it is that relating to the prerogative—the source of the power for the decision that is reviewed—that constitutes its own contribution. The legal principles behind its application of legitimate expectation had already been strongly foreshadowed or actually decided. Lord Diplock's classic *dicta* were not themselves a central part of the reasoning that led to the result, either in relation to national security or to legitimate expectation.

Looking at the position of the *GCHQ* judgment in this body of case-law, the following cases and dates should be noted.

First, and as something of a chronological outlier, is the heavily influential Divisional Court judgment in *R v Criminal Injuries Compensation Board* ex parte *Lain*, judgment given on 20 April 1967.[11] Although a chronological outlier, the judgment is a reaction to a novel constitutional position and evidences the determination of the courts to set out the boundaries of judicial review by reference to principle rather than by narrow distinctions imposed by earlier case-law. It is relevant to note that one of the members of the Divisional Court was Diplock J (as he then was).

Second in time is the House of Lord's decision on standing, *IRC v National Federation of the Self-Employed*.[12] Coherent rules on standing are an integral part

---

[11] *Supra.*
[12] [1982] AC 617; date of judgment 9 April 1981.

of modern public law, but will not otherwise surface in the discussion below. It is accordingly worthwhile at this stage to set out the comments of Lord Diplock (as he had by now become) on the topic:

> It would, in my view, be a grave lacuna in our system of public law if a pressure group, like the federation, or even a single public-spirited taxpayer, were prevented by outdated technical rules of locus standi from bringing the matter to the attention of the court to vindicate the rule of law and get the unlawful conduct stopped. The Attorney-General, although he occasionally applies for prerogative orders against public authorities that do not form part of central government, in practice never does so against government departments. It is not, in my view, a sufficient answer to say that judicial review of the actions of officers or departments of central government is unnecessary because they are accountable to Parliament for the way in which they carry out their functions. They are accountable to Parliament for what they do so far as regards efficiency and policy, and of that Parliament is the only judge; they are responsible to a court of justice for the lawfulness of what they do, and of that the court is the only judge.[13]

Lord Diplock's determination that the proper reach of judicial review should not be defeated by 'outdated technical rules of *locus standi*' and to make a clear distinction between the role of the courts in supervising legality and of Parliament in holding ministers accountable for 'policy' and 'efficiency' is very evident from the passage. It will be seen again when the approach in *GCHQ* itself to the reviewability of the prerogative is examined. This concern, and the passage itself, were heavily influential in later cases such as *R v Secretary of State for Foreign Affairs*, ex parte *World Development Movement* ('the Pergau dam case').[14]

Next comes *O'Reilly v Mackman*.[15] Judgment was delivered on 25 November 1982. The principal thrust of the case concerned the need to bring public law challenges (for example, as in the case, to decisions of prison boards of visitors) by way of judicial review rather than proceedings in the Chancery Division claiming declaratory relief. This principle has had something of a chequered history. The case of *Wandsworth v Winder (No 1)*[16] immediately revealed that it was subject to limitations because it could not prevent collateral challenge in a context where the validity of a public law act was an essential ingredient in a private law action. However, and relevantly for present purposes, the public law/private law distinction was explained in *O'Reilly* in a way which was directly taken forward into the legitimate expectation analysis in later cases, including *GCHQ* itself. Lord Diplock (again) explained:

> It is not, and it could not be, contended that the decision of the board awarding him forfeiture of remission had infringed or threatened to infringe any right of the appellant derived from private law, whether a common law right or one created by a statute. Under the Prison Rules remission of sentence is not a matter of right but of indulgence. So far as private

---

[13] At p 644 E/G.
[14] [1995] 1 WLR 386.
[15] [1983] 2 AC 237.
[16] [1985] AC 461.

law is concerned all that each appellant had was a legitimate expectation, based upon his knowledge of what is the general practice, that he would be granted the maximum remission, permitted by rule 5 (2) of the Prison Rules, of one third of his sentence if by that time no disciplinary award of forfeiture of remission had been made against him. So the second thing to be noted is that none of the appellants had any remedy in private law.

In public law, as distinguished from private law, however, such legitimate expectation gave to each appellant a sufficient interest to challenge the legality of the adverse disciplinary award made against him by the board on the ground that in one way or another the board in reaching its decision had acted outwith the powers conferred upon it by the legislation under which it was acting; and such grounds would include the board's failure to observe the rules of natural justice: which means no more than to act fairly towards him in carrying out their decision-making process, and I prefer so to put it.

The type of legitimate expectation described by Lord Diplock in this passage played directly into the next case in the sequence, *N'gu Yuen Shiu*.[17] Judgment of the Privy Council was delivered on 21 February 1983. *GCHQ* itself followed, with judgment on 22 November 1984. It was followed by an important decision on the reviewability of guidance issued by a government department, even in the absence of any statutory basis—*Gillick v West Norfolk and Wisbech AHA*.[18] Judgment was delivered on 17 October 1985. Finally, there is another seminal decision, which flows logically and in legal policy terms from the decisions on the scope of judicial review in ex parte *Lain* and *GCHQ* itself. It is *Datafin*,[19] judgment delivered on 5 December 1986.

Whilst acknowledging, as already stated, that ex parte *Lain* is more removed in time, it remains a remarkable fact that less than six years divides the judgment in ex parte *IRC* from that in *Datafin*. A very substantial part of the foundations of modern public law were laid in this period in respect of the removal of technical limitations on the scope of judicial review and, in parallel, with the doctrine of legitimate expectation.

It is also a remarkable fact that almost all of this was most coherently articulated by a single judge, Lord Diplock. His judgment in ex parte *Lain* was referred to by Lord Donaldson in *Datafin* with the introductory comment that 'he was to make administrative law almost his own ... '. In *GCHQ*, his much quoted adumbration of the basic principles of administrative law was referred to by Lord Scarman as a 'vivid sketch' of the modern law. Shorn of its references to the source of the power which is being exercised (discussed below), the passage is plainly consciously written in the recognition of the fact that there had been a major development of the general public law in the period leading up to *GCHQ* itself. It was this development that made Lord Diplock think it appropriate to summarise the main principles

[17] [1983] 2 AC 629.
[18] [1986] AC 112.
[19] [1987] QB 815.

of what he now wanted to be seen as a coherent and, one suspects, academically respectable branch of the law. Thus:

> Judicial review has I think developed to a stage today when without reiterating any analysis of the steps by which the development has come about, one can conveniently classify under three heads the grounds upon which administrative action is subject to control by judicial review. The first ground I would call "illegality", the second "irrationality" and the third "procedural impropriety".

He went onto recognise that further grounds might be added as time passed, specifically referring to the possible adoption of the 'principle of proportionality' 'which is recognised in the administrative law of several of our fellow members of the European Economic Community'.

The passage that immediately follows contains pithy descriptions of each of his three basic heads. They are descriptions, which, for better or for worse, are probably the aspects of the *GCHQ* judgments most frequently quoted in present day skeleton arguments. But seen in the then contemporary context it is notable that Lord Diplock goes out of his way to explain that the grounds are important precisely because they are justiciable; the subject matter of each of the grounds falls within the role of the courts. He is explaining why and how public law is the task of judges not politicians. Consideration of the explanations, and the stress on the role of the courts, shows a shared theme with his classic exposition of the law on standing in ex parte *National Federation of the Self-Employed*, set out above.

He explains that by the concept of 'illegality' he refers to a requirement that the decision-maker must understand correctly the law that regulates his decision-making power and give effect to it, and immediately states: 'Whether [the decision-maker] has or not [understood the law] is par excellence a justiciable question to be decided, in the event of dispute, by those persons, the judges, by whom the judicial power of the state is exerciseable.'

In the case of irrationality, he uses the label of '*Wednesbury unreasonableness*', (referring of course to *Associated Provincial Picture Houses v Wednesbury Corporation*)[20] and further describes it as applying to a 'decision which is so outrageous in its defiance of logic or of accepted moral standards that no sensible person who has applied his mind to the question to be decided could have arrived at it'. This formulation has come to seem unnecessarily complicated and onerous with the passage of time; but, once again, the context is one of explaining that this sort of unreasonableness is a justiciable issue. 'Whether a decision falls within this category is a question that judges by their training and experience should be well equipped to answer, or else there would be something badly wrong with our judicial system.' There is, he says, no need to resort to the explanation of the fact that the courts could interfere on the grounds of unreasonableness to the effect that the lack of reason showed that there must have been some inferred but unidentifiable

---

[20] [1948] 1 KB 223.

mistake of law (see Lord Radcliffe in *Edwards v Bairstow*).[21] He explained: '"Irrationality" by now can stand upon its own feet as an accepted ground on which a decision may be attacked by judicial review.'

Accordingly, *GCHQ* must be viewed in its proper place in the development of judicial review. It is no accident that the line of cases referred to above was followed by the publication, in 1987, of the first edition of the guide drawn up by Treasury Solicitors called '*The Judge Over Your Shoulder*'. This became affectionately known in civil service circles as JOYS. Its opening words were striking:

> You are sitting at your desk granting licences on behalf of your Minister. Your enabling statutory powers are in the widest possible terms: 'The Secretary of State may grant licences on such conditions as he thinks fit.' With power like that you might think that there could be no possible ground for challenge in the courts whatever you do. But you would be wrong.

The first edition of JOYS created quite a stir at the time of its publication. And there can be no doubt that the dramatic *GCHQ* litigation was one of the catalysts causing the higher reaches of government, and government lawyers, to think hard about the risk of legal challenge in contexts where there might previously have been something of a sense of immunity, a sense that problems in relation to controversial issues might well arise in the political sphere but were unlikely to give rise to dangerous litigation—dangerous, that is, from the point of view of government. The power that was exercised by Mrs Thatcher to give her instruction was indeed cast in very wide terms. The mechanism on which she relied to alter the terms and conditions of service at *GCHQ* was an 'instruction' issued by her under the Order in Council of 1982, Article 4. That article so far as relevant provided as follows:

> As regards Her Majesty's Home Civil Service—(a) the Minister for the Civil Service may from time to time make regulations or give instructions— ... (ii) for controlling the conduct of the service, and providing for the classification of all persons employed therein and ... the conditions of service of all such persons;

But neither the width of the power, or the fact that the Order in Council was made under the prerogative, had prevented defeat at first instance. Glidewell J's judgment caused an immediate political storm. The timing in relation to the summer recess meant that the appeal had to be lodged very rapidly. The government was prevailed upon to delay the lodging of the appeal until the afternoon of the day after the judgment so that the Prime Minister could make a statement in the House of Commons. Something of the atmosphere of the time can be gleaned from the remarks of Neil Kinnock (then Labour MP for Islwyn and Leader of the Opposition) immediately after the short statement:

> ... the Government have been found guilty of breaking the law. Will the Prime Minister now admit that the judgment of the High Court makes it clear that responsibility for this major breach of natural justice and offence against civil rights rests with her and her alone? Was it not she alone who issued in instructions—[interruption]

[21] [1956] AC 14.

Mr Speaker: Order

For the compulsory removal of trade union membership rights without consultation with the trade unions? .... Why has she spurned the opportunity afforded her by Mr Justice Glidewell for a period of reflection and, instead, rushed off to appeal and thus prevent further consideration by this forum of Parliament?[22]

From the perspective of 2016, the Commons proceedings of 17 July 1984 reads as a lively reminder of the politics of the time. Thatcher responded to Kinnock in part by reminding him of defeats the previous Labour administration had suffered in the courts. Tom Dalyell could not resist a reference to instructions issued by her to sink the Belgrano some two years earlier, during the Falklands War. Dr David Owen described Mrs Thatcher's oral instruction as damaging national security and besmirching the office of Prime Minister. However, the important point for present purposes is that the explosive political content of the litigation, including the first instance defeat, propelled the power of the new public law into the consciousness of those responsible for government.

III. Reviewability of the Prerogative

In that new public law, and separately from the political drama of the subject-matter, a major contribution of *GCHQ* was its explosion of the proposition that the scope of judicial review might vary depending on the source of the power.

Before examining the way in which this was done, it is worth examining the way the issue was seen in legal academic circles before the litigation began. *De Smith's Judicial Review of Administrative Action*,[23] contained a passage headed 'Are There Unreviewable Discretionary Powers?' It stated that there was no short answer to this question.

The passage referred to three specific matters relevant to the potential existence of reviewability. The first was the attempted use of ouster clauses such as that in *Anisminic*. The second arose out of the limitation imposed by the fact that, as it was put, 'no discretionary power is reviewable unless somebody has *locus standi* to impugn the validity of its exercise' a proposition advanced, of course, before Lord Diplock's comments in the *National Federation of the Self Employed* case, and well before more modern developments such as the Pergau dam litigation brought by the World Development Movement. But it is the third proposition that is directly relevant. The third proposition was put in these terms:

> If it is claimed that the authority for the exercise of discretion derives from the royal prerogative, the courts have traditionally limited review to questions of vires in the narrowest sense of the term. They can determine whether the prerogative power exists, what is its extent,

---

[22] Hansard HC Deb 17 July 1984 vol 64 cols 171–86.
[23] Fifth edition (1980).

whether it has been exercised in the appropriate form and how far it has been superseded by statute; they have not normally been prepared to examine the appropriateness or adequacy of the grounds for exercising the power, or the fairness of the procedure followed before the power is exercised, and they would not allow bad faith to be attributed to the Crown.

On its face, this passage rules out the reviewability of the instruction in play in *GCHQ*. It is an exercise of a prerogative power; and the ground that succeeded in front of Glidewell was precisely an attack on the fairness of the procedure because of the failure to consult the unions. The authority for the proposition that there could be no such attack was given as *de Freitas v Benny*,[24] concerning the prerogative of mercy.

However, de Smith goes on to set out reasons why this statement of the classic position might be crumbling; and reading the passage as a whole it can be seen that *GCHQ* arrived at a time when the potential for reconsideration of the position was very real. The authors point out that most of the case-law in which the courts have expressed a reluctance to intervene were decided at a time when the courts were cautious about reviewing the exercise of any *statutory* discretion. They point to *Padfield*[25] as marking 'the emergence of the interventionist judicial attitude that has characterised many recent judgments'. They state that to 'draw so sharp a distinction between the exercise of different governmental powers solely on the basis of whether the historical origin of the discretion is to be found in the common law or statute is difficult to justify as a matter of principle' thus, as will be seen, foreshadowing the approach of Lord Diplock in particular in *GCHQ* itself. The passage proceeds on the basis that although the weight of authority supports only a narrow basis for review, there are counter signs—for example Lord Denning's judgment in *Laker Airways* and the fact that the court's explanation for the unreviewability of the Attorney-General's discretion in *Gouriet v Union of Post Office Workers*[26] had been the political nature of that discretion rather than its prerogative origin. Importantly, attention is also drawn to ex parte *Lain*.

Ex parte *Lain*[27] is an important case in its own right. It concerned the scheme for paying compensation for criminal injuries. The scheme had its origins in a White Paper[28] in which the government set out proposals for compensating victims of violence and persons injured whilst assisting the police. The scheme was described as experimental and non-statutory. It was promulgated under the prerogative by way of written answer to a parliamentary question by the Home Secretary, together with various amendments made in the same way. The judgment of Lord Parker set out the principal features of the scheme.[29] The scheme was administered by a body known as the Criminal Injuries Compensation Board, appointed by the Home and Scottish Secretaries after consultation with the Lord Chancellor.

---

[24] [1976] AC 239.
[25] [1968] AC 997. See Ch 3 of this volume.
[26] [1978] AC 435.
[27] [1967] 2 QB 864.
[28] Cmnd 2323.
[29] At paras 876–7.

The chairman was a person 'of wide legal experience'; and the other members of the Board were legally qualified (Paragraph 1). The Board was provided with money to meet the awards out of the votes under the Appropriation Acts of the Home Office and the Scottish Home and Health Department (Paragraph 2).

Paragraph 4 provided:

> The board will be entirely responsible for deciding what compensation should be paid in individual cases and their decisions will not be subject to appeal or to ministerial review. The general working of the scheme will, however, be kept under review by the Government, and the board will submit annually to the Home Secretary and the Secretary of State for Scotland a full report on the operation of the scheme, together with their accounts. The report and accounts will be open to debate in Parliament. ... (emphasis added)

There was provision within the scheme for decisions by a single member and subsequent review by a panel of three other members.

Mrs Lain was the widow of a police officer who had died as the result of injuries sustained when shot. She claimed compensation under the scheme. An interim award (of £300) had been made by a single member of the Board at a stage when Mr Lain was alive but had suffered sudden blindness in one eye. About a week later he was found dead in his home of gunshot wounds, in circumstances where it was accepted that his death at his own hands was attributable to the original injury. Mrs Lain then applied in her own right under the scheme and was awarded a further final award of £300. She appealed against the amount of the award to a panel of three, who dismissed the appeal and indeed went on to reduce the further award to nil. She applied for an order of certiorari aimed at quashing the panel decision, alleging errors of law on the face of the panel's decision. The contentious legal issues concerned the relationship between compensation under the scheme and payments under police pension provisions—the sort of 'overlapping benefit' argument that will be familiar to social security lawyers.

The Board was represented in the Divisional Court by Nigel Bridge, Treasury Counsel and later Lord Bridge. He began by accepting that 'It is of public importance to know whether or not the board is amenable to the prerogative order' and set out his basic proposition that the board was subject to control by the Crown by whom it has been set up and not by the Court. In terms of analysis his argument resembled that set out in *de Smith* to the effect that the exercise of powers derived from the prerogative was not judicially reviewable. His fundamental thesis was based on *Rex v Electricity Commissioners* ex parte *London Electricity Joint Committee Co*,[30] from which he derived four requirements for reviewability—legal authority; determining questions affecting the rights of subjects; a duty to act judicially and acting in excess of legal authority. Here the reviewability analysis broke down because the board did not determine the *rights* of subjects. As he put it, the 'great majority of [decided] cases [had been] concerned with whether or not there is a duty to act judicially, but in this case, a duty to act judicially is not reached'. Just

---

[30] *(1920) Ltd* [1924] 1 KB 171.

before he reached this point in the argument, he had set out his principal description of the constitutional role of the board:

> As regards the scheme, the proper view is that [it] combines the two functions of informing the board of the principles under which the Crown expects it to act in the distribution of the Crown's bounty and of informing the public, as prospective claimants, of the principles and procedure on which the board will act. None of the instruments whereby the board is constituted nor the Crown's instructions to the board as set out are of any legislative force whatever. [Reference was made to Halsbury's Laws of England, 3rd ed, vol 7 (1954) p 237.] There is no prerogative power to legislate, except in the case of new territories annexed by the Crown.
>
> Although the Constitution of the board and its instructions are by way of the exercise of the prerogative, in the ordinary exercise of prerogative the Crown cannot invest any body of persons employed by them with any independent authority at law so as to impose on them duties enforceable by law. The board only has authority to carry out the Crown's instructions and its duty is to the Crown alone.

Shortly after this passage, the law report records a typical intervention from Diplock—'*This is a new constitutional situation*'.[31]

The case for Mrs Lain had been argued by Geoffrey Howe, Margaret Thatcher's Chancellor of the Exchequer immediately following the 1979 General Election and indeed the Foreign Secretary who was to announce the ban on trade union membership at *GCHQ* on 25 January 1984. His line, unsurprisingly, foreshadowed that taken in the judgments of the Court itself. He submitted that the board was a body determining questions affecting the rights of subjects, which, even if they might not enforceable by mandamus could be protected by certiorari.

The three members of the Divisional Court (Lord Parker; Diplock LJ and Ashworth J) each gave powerful concurring judgments agreeing that the board was amenable to control by *certiorari* but rejecting Mrs Lain's case that there had been any error of law. An obvious theme discernible in the judgments is a determination not to allow new constitutional developments to escape the reach of the developing modern administrative law. There may be no right, as such, to the compensation, and, indeed the scheme providing for the board might be capable of alteration or even abolition by the executive in a way that could not be controlled by the courts, but it did not follow that those deciding issues under the scheme could not be held to their task of correctly applying the law by those courts.[32] This concept of the court holding the board members to the terms of their mandate even though that mandate had its origins in the prerogative was an important way of looking at the issue in the context of the *GCHQ* litigation. There, the unions argued that even if the prerogative was generally unreviewable, the Prime Minister could be held to the terms—express and implied—of the Order in Council under which she ordered the ban on trade union membership.

---

[31] [1967] 2 QB 872 G (emphasis added).
[32] See, especially Lord Parker CJ at paras 885E to 886D.

Council of Civil Service Unions v Minister for the Civil Service   109

In ex parte *Lain* Diplock LJ expressed these themes in the following way:

> In the present case we are concerned with an inferior tribunal lawfully constituted in time of peace by an act of government. It may be a novel development in constitutional practice to govern by public statement of intention made by the executive government instead of by legislation. But this is no more than a reversion to the ancient practice of government by Royal Proclamation, although it is now subject to the limitations imposed upon that practice by the development of constitutional law in the 17th century.

And:

> But it [the executive] chose to adopt the method of appointing a board upon which it conferred two distinct functions, one judicial in character, the other administrative. The judicial function was to determine in accordance with specified principles whether any particular applicant should be offered any money payment and, if so, how much. The administrative function was to make payments to applicants in accordance with such determinations. "The scheme" not only constituted and defined the authority of the board to make such payments but as published to applicants, was a lawful proclamation stating the conditions required to be satisfied by subjects seeking payment of compensation and requiring them as a condition precedent to the receipt of any payment to submit their claims to adjudication by the board in the exercise of its judicial functions. It was on the faith of the proclamation that the application to the board with which the present case is concerned was made.

In this context, Lord Parker rejected Mr Bridge's description of the compensation as 'the bounty of the Crown with its nostalgic echoes of Maundy Thursday', stating that the public had an interest in the proper administration of the scheme, whose 'money the board distributes to the tune of nearly a million pounds a year'. He had earlier made it clear that in his view:

> the exact limits of the ancient remedy of certiorari have never been and ought not to be specifically defined. They have varied from time to time being extended to meet changing conditions .... The only constant limits throughout were that [the body] was performing a public duty ... we have ... reached the position when the ambit of certiorari can be said to cover every case in which a body of persons of a public as opposed to a purely private or domestic character has to determine matters affecting subjects provided always that it has a duty to act judicially.

One can see in these words the basic thinking that takes us through *GCHQ* itself to *Datafin* and beyond. It is, to repeat, a firm statement of a determination to fashion a modern administrative law that looked at the substance rather than the form of governmental machinery and fashioned the remedy accordingly.

IV. GCHQ—The Prerogative in the Lords

Despite the fact that the determinative issue in the Court of Appeal had in fact been that concerning national security, and in particular the correct interpretation of Paragraph 16 of Robert Armstrong's affidavit, the parties prepared for the hearing in the Lords to argue about the prerogative in ways foreshadowed by *Lain*. The government, now represented by Robert Alexander, made it clear that its essential submission was that the Prime Minister was entitled to issue the instruction, without consultation, in the interest of national security. However, he said, the nature of the applicant's case required the Court to address the issue of the reviewability of the prerogative, and to answer three questions—is the prerogative in general reviewable? If it is, is it reviewable in the field of national security? And, thirdly, if it would otherwise be unreviewable, is the position different if it is exercised by someone to whom the power has been delegated by Order in Council?[33]

He gave traditional answers to these questions in line with contemporary academic thinking, including a reference to the passages from *de Smith* set out above. The courts could inquire into the existence scope and form of the prerogative but could not review its exercise on *Wednesbury* grounds; and argued that the fact of delegation of the prerogative under an order in council did not allow the Court to read restrictions into its exercise that it would not read into its personal exercise by the sovereign.[34]

The appellant unions placed at the forefront of their analysis an argument structured around the 'terms of the mandate' debate in ex parte *Lain*. Thus the law report records the submissions:

> where the Crown's instructions to an individual minister or public body are set out in the form of precise (or defined) instructions, and one individual minister or public body derives his or her authority from those instructions, the courts will keep the individual minister or public body within the terms of those instructions. (In this case, the Sovereign was giving instructions to one specific minister.) In so doing, the courts will construe the instructions and imply any duties, such as the duty to act fairly, that should be implied as a matter of ordinary principles of administrative law, including the duty to consult in appropriate circumstances. (There are no circumstances in which there is not a duty to hear the other party.) In an exercise of power by a minister or public body, even when receiving instructions from the Sovereign, there is a duty to act fairly.[35]

When the individual members of the judicial committee came to be involved, there was something of a divergence of views about the utility of the sort of distinctions that the arguments of both sides implied. Lord Diplock was suffering badly from breathing difficulties at the time, and was sitting in the chamber of the House of Lords with two bottles of oxygen next to him. After about two days of argument from the bar of the House, he managed to get enough breath together to wheeze out the words 'Of course the prerogative is reviewable'—thus indicating a strong view of the apparent pointlessness of the debate, a view which he had presumably held since his judgment in ex parte *Lain* some 17 years earlier.[36]

---

[33] See [1985] 1 AC at 388 F/G.
[34] See 390B/C.
[35] P383C/D.
[36] This intervention was not his only sign of irascibility. When the judgments came out, they recorded his comment that 'I should put on record that after reading and rereading Devlin's speech in

None of the judges held that the instruction issued by Mrs Thatcher could not be judicially reviewed on ordinary public law principles, national security apart. Indeed, none of them showed any sign of doubt or difficulty in reaching this central conclusion. However, there was a difference of emphasis. Lords Fraser and Brightman adopted the 'terms of the mandate' analysis derived from ex parte *Lain*, but thought it better to leave any question of the wider reviewability until it actually arose for decision[37]—Lord Fraser cited Lord Parker's judgment in ex parte *Lain* and stated that whatever there source powers, which are defined, and whether the definition is expressed or implied, are subject to judicial control.[38]

Lords Scarman, Diplock and Roskill on the other hand took the opportunity to state that administrative law had reached the stage where the source of the power was irrelevant. Lord Diplock's speech can stand as the exemplar. He just about managed to hide his impatience with the analysis when he said:

> My Lords, I intend no discourtesy to counsel when I say that, intellectual interest apart, in answering the question of law raised in this appeal, I have derived little practical assistance from learned and esoteric analyses of the precise legal nature, boundaries and historical origin of "the prerogative", or of what powers exercisable by executive officers acting on behalf of central government that are not shared by private citizens qualify for inclusion under this particular label.

He went on to preface his exposition of the three bases of review—illegality, irrationality, and procedural propriety—by commenting 'I see no reason why simply because a decision-making power is derived from a common law and not a statutory source it should *for that reason only* be immune from judicial review' [Emphasis in original].

The issue that Lords Fraser and Brightman left open was never returned to. As we shall see, *Datafin* carried the proposition that the source of a public power did not oust the potential for judicial review a stage further.

V. Datafin

The full logic of the development concerning the scope of judicial review and its relationship to the source of the power for the impugned decision was revealed shortly after *GCHQ* in the decision of the Court of Appeal in *R v Takeover Panel*, ex parte *Datafin Plc*.[39] This was an attempt to judicially review a decision of the Panel

---

Chandler v DPP ... I have gained no help from it, for I find some of his observations that are peripheral to what I understand to be the ratio decidendi difficult to reconcile with the actual decision that he felt able to reach and also with one another' (p 408B).

[37] See p 398H and 424A/B.
[38] At 399E.
[39] [1987] 1 QB 815.

on Take-overs and Mergers. The nature of this body was graphically described by the Master of the Rolls at the beginning of his judgment in the following terms:

> The Panel on Take-overs and Mergers is a truly remarkable body. Perched on the 20th floor of the Stock Exchange building in the City of London, both literally and metaphorically it oversees and regulates a very important part of the United Kingdom financial market. Yet it performs this function without visible means of legal support.[40]

He went on to explain that the body had 'no statutory, prerogative or common law powers and is not in contractual relationship with the financial market or with those who deal in that market'.[41] Unsurprisingly, counsel for the Panel argued that a body with these characteristics was simply not subject to control by the courts. As he put it—'The source of the power remains of critical importance to any determination as to whether a body was subject to judicial review'.[42] *GCHQ* had established, he accepted, that the exercise of prerogative power under a statutory instrument was amenable to review, but what was in play here was not a public duty but a 'private duty, because Parliament in its wisdom had decided to leave this area subject to self-regulation'.[43]

Lord Donaldson rejected this perspective. The description of the Panel as an example of self-regulation had to be approached on the basis that the concept was ambiguous—and in the context of the Panel the exercise of its powers had large consequences:

> The panel is a self-regulating body in the latter sense. Lacking any authority de jure, it exercises immense power de facto by devising, promulgating, amending and interpreting the City Code on Take-overs and Mergers, by waiving or modifying the application of the code in particular circumstances, by investigating and reporting upon alleged breaches of the code and by the application or threat of sanctions. These sanctions are no less effective because they are applied indirectly and lack a legally enforceable base.[44]

Accordingly he put forward an analysis very firmly based on the evolution of the case-law from ex parte *Lain* through *O'Reilly v Mackman* and *GCHQ* itself. The upshot of this process was that the only essential elements to give rise to jurisdiction were a 'public element' and the absence of a contractual relationship.[45] The Court looked at the reality of the position, which included the fact that in the absence of a body such as the Panel, the requirements of good government would have necessitated some form of legislative intervention.

---

[40] ibid para 824 H.
[41] ibid para 825 C.
[42] ibid para 821 C.
[43] ibid para 821 G.
[44] ibid para 826 C/D.
[45] ibid para 838 E. The Court had tested whether any private law remedy might be available by asking the parties to draft a writ setting out a cause of action, and found the result 'wholly unconvincing'. Counsel for the Panel did not accept that there would be a private law remedy—see para 839 B.

VI. Conclusion

At this stage, it is worth taking stock of the position travelled since it was argued that there was no available remedy against the Criminal Injuries Compensation Board in ex parte *Lain*. On this journey, the *GCHQ* judgments occupy a central place. They established that the exercise of prerogative power was in principle judicially reviewable.[46] The reservation expressed by some members of the Court about the boundaries of this breakthrough, and in particular whether it was limited to situations where a Minister was acting under powers given to her by an Order in Council, were firmly relegated to history by *Datafin* shortly afterwards.

It is this aspect of the case—the removal of the need to concentrate on the source of the power being exercised to establish jurisdiction—which can now be seen to be its central contribution to the development of public law. However, other aspects of the case, including in particular Lord Diplock's famous summary of the basic grounds for judicial review; and the application of the principle of legitimate expectation established by the earlier case-law including *N' Yuen Shiu* a little over a year before firmly locate it in the hugely fertile period of the development of administrative law in the 1980s.

---

[46] See also Ch 11 of this volume.

6

The *Factortame* Litigation: Sovereignty in Question

JOHN McELDOWNEY

I. Introduction

> If we are to be good Europeans, we must surely offer some security against undermining the European legal order ourselves. It would be quite unreasonable to leave it to our judiciary to refuse to apply future Acts of Parliament, when in conflict with Community law, by some spontaneous constitutional volte-face of their own.[1]

Few legal cases in public law are as constitutionally significant as the *Factortame* litigation on the UK's sovereignty and its compatibility with membership of the European Community.[2] The outcome of the litigation resulted in the constitutional doctrine that the courts would give effect to EU law even when it conflicts with Acts of the UK Parliament. The *Factortame* litigation refers to a series of cases that first arose when the applicants challenged the validity of the Merchant Shipping Act 1988 (the 1988 Act) and its compatibility with Articles 52, 58 and 221 of the Treaty.[3] The applicants were companies incorporated under UK law but the majority of directors and shareholders were Spanish and the companies had been registered under the registration procedures of the Merchant Shipping Act 1894. New registration arrangements were introduced under the 1988 Act that resulted in 95 vessels failing to meet the new requirements. The House of Lords unequivocally held that Community law applied in preference to the 1988 Act in circumstances where it is impossible to construe the legislation in conformity with Community law. The legality of the UK system of registration under the Merchant Shipping Act 1988 had been found to be incompatible with Community law. The decision was expressly based on Section 2(4) of the European Communities Act 1972 leading to much speculation about the impact on UK sovereignty and

---

[1] H Wade, 'Sovereignty and the European Communities' (1972) 88 Law Quarterly Review 1–5 p 4.
[2] Now European Union.
[3] The Treaty numbering has been changed after the Treaty of Amsterdam thus the relevant Articles are Articles 43, 48 and 294.

Community law, perhaps altering the sovereignty of Parliament or even rendering it redundant in EU matters. William Wade famously described the litigation as a 'constitutional revolution',[4] though many commentators expressed differing opinions.[5] It remains a fertile ground for discussion today.[6] This is a landmark case in public law that has few rivals, if only because of the litigation that made up the entire *Factortame* saga including interim relief relating to Community law, the validity of parts of an Act of Parliament and the compensation payable to the Spanish fishermen. The *Factortame* litigation has also had a transformative effect on the interpretation of European Community law in the UK and more generally in Member States providing an important conceptual approach to European Community law. At the time of writing the consequences of the UK referendum on 23 June 2016 when 51.9% voted to leave and 48.9% voted to remain in the EU with a turnout of 71%, on the relationship between the UK and EU is unclear.[7, 8] The argument, however, that the UK had lost 'control' over its own affairs because of the primacy of European Union law was an important issue in the referendum debate.[9]

The *Factortame litigation* uncovers the contrasting style of English common law legislative drafting and the more teleological interpretation of civil law systems found in Community law that is more purposive and gives effect to the policies underpinning the law. A teleological construction is a method of reasoning by a court allowing it to reach a conclusion that is believed to be intended by the specific Treaty obligation. The Parliament when passing the Merchant Shipping Act 1988 assumed that the British courts would be able to interpret the legislation in a way that was compatible with Community law on the basis that Parliament's intention should be respected. This, however, proved not to be possible.

More revealing is the policy vacuum on fisheries. In the accession negotiations prior to 1972 fishing policy was considered right at the end of negotiation with little satisfaction for the UK or Ireland.[10] The Common Fisheries Policy has proved to be unsuccessful and unpopular and highly criticised in the UK and has been

---

[4] W Wade (1991) *Law Quarterly Review* 1 and (1996) *Law Quarterly Review* 568.

[5] See P Craig, [1991] 11 YBL 221, N Gravels *Public Law* [1989] 568 and *Public Law* [1991] 180.

[6] Lord Justice Laws has ascribed to the European Community Act 1972, the status of a 'constitutional statute' which may give a special status in respect of its repeal or amendment only by 'unambiguous words on the face of the latter statute'.

[7] J O'Reilly (1991), 'Judicial review and the Common Fisheries Policy' in D Curtin and D O'Keefe eds., *Constitutional Adjudication in European Community and National Law* Dublin, Butterworths. pp 51–65. See: House of Commons Library Briefing Paper, Number 7213 *Existing the EU: impact in key UK policy areas* (4th June 2015).

[8] See: House of Lords, Library Note LLN 2014/15 *The European Union* (23 April 2014).

[9] House of Lords Library Note: Leaving the EU: Parliament's role in the Process LLN 2016/034 (4 July 2016).

[10] A useful analysis and background is provided in C Jensen, *A Critical review of the Common Fisheries Policy* (November, 1999) Working paper of the Department of Environmental and Business Economics University of Southern Denmark no 6. M. Shackelton, 'Fishing for a Policy? The Common Fisheries Policy of the Community' in H. Wallace and W. Wallace and C. Webb, *Policy-making in the European Community* (New York, Wiley 1998) pp 349–71. Also see: House of Commons Library, *The 1974–75 UK renegotiation of EEC Membership and Referendum* Briefing Paper 7253 (13 July 2015).

one of the grounds for dissatisfaction with the EU.[11] An indirect impact of the litigation is that it made it possible for the registration of fishing fleets from another Member State in the UK. This allows the fishing fleet owner to benefit from the Member State's fishing quota and to operate out of the Member State's fishing ports under the Community rights of free movement one of the fundamental principles of EU law underlined in the case law of the ECJ and confirmed by the litigation.[12] This has significant consequences for the regulation of fishing quotas within the European Union.[13] Underlining all of these issues is the political and economic complexity that surrounds EU membership, which is often articulated in terms of legal disputes through normative rules. The expectation of supporters of leaving the EU is that the UK should be able to take control of its own marine resources and manage them more effectively.[14]

It is first necessary to explain the background to the case in the context of Britain's maritime past and the legislative history leading to the Merchant Shipping Act 1988. This explains how the UK's approach to legislative drafting lacked the codification of principles and the clarity of Maritime Codes commonly found in civilian legal systems. It is also relevant to consider the development of EU law and the creation of the Common Fisheries Policy. This reveals poor policy making on the British side and a marked reluctance to engage with politically difficult issues surrounding fishing policy for fear of further delays or possible rejection of the UK's application to join the European Community. Finally, discussion of UK sovereignty *post Factortame* is considered. The result of the referendum on 23 June 2016 in favour of leaving the EU has still to be implemented.[15] In the short term, until the repeal of the European Communities Act 1972 and the UK actually leaves the EU, it is still the case that EU law will have effect in the UK.

II. Facts of the *Factortame* Case in the Context of Britain's Maritime History

R. v Secretary of State for Transport ex parte *Factortame*[16] arose from an application by Spanish Fishing boat owners that Regulations made under the terms of the

---

[11] House of Commons Library, Briefing Paper Number 7213, *Exiting the EU policy areas* (4 June 2015).
[12] See: House of Commons Library: *EU Bibliographies: proposed reform of the Common Agricultural Policy* SN/1A/6554 (21 May 2014).
[13] See: House of Lords European Union Committee, The Progress of the Common Fisheries Policy 22 July 2008 HL 146-i. Also more recently see: Common Fisheries Policy, *Politics.co.uk* 27 May 2015.
[14] See Seminar at All Souls Oxford: Agriculture and Fisheries Brexit Seminar Series 6 November 2015.
[15] House of Commons Library, Briefing Paper Number 7213, *Exiting the EU policy areas* (4 June 2015) pps 52–7 House of Commons Library Research Paper Numner 07632 Brexit: what happens next? (29th June 2016), House of Lords, Library Note: Leaving the EU: Parliament's Role in the Process LLN 2016/034 (4 July 2016).
[16] Case C-213/89 [1990] ECR 2433; [1990] 3 C.M.L.R. 1; [1990] 2 AC 85, [1991] 1 AC 603.

Merchant Shipping Act 1988 governing the registration of fishing vessels should be disapplied because it was argued they conflicted with the EEC Treaty and also Community law. In a land mark decision the House of Lords held after receiving the preliminary ruling of the European Court of Justice in *Factortame (No.2)*[17] that Community law must take precedence over national law of the Member State and accepted that the registration provisions under the Merchant Shipping Act 1988 were in direct conflict with rights under Community law. The background and history of the legislation may be briefly outlined as an explanation of the legislation.

Despite its strong maritime tradition and island status, the UK had little primary consolidating legislation covering the maritime coastal waters that surround the British Isles until the Merchant Shipping Act 1894. This is surprising given Britain's reliance on trade and the rapidly expanding export of cotton in the early sixteenth century. There was a strong tradition of 'corporations' being granted legal status and various *Fellowships of Merchant Adventurers* provided a limited form of self-regulation.[18] The fishing waters off the coast of the British Isles were relatively under exploited until the late nineteenth century.[19]

Various small fishing companies were set up but their life expectancy was limited, in many cases because of the fragility of the economics of fishing and variations in catches and market prices. The position did not radically change in the eighteenth century with small coastal towns developing limited fishing capacity in the trade for pilchards. Many local fisheries served their communities but offered limited alternatives when weather conditions prevailed or catches proved unsuccessful. Mechanised steam vessels in the second half of the nineteenth century as well as the development of trawling techniques increased the range of vessels and the potential for increased trade. Hull, Grimsby and Lowestoft became important commercial fishing centres and by the late 1890s there were over 300 trawlers operating out of those ports.

The first attempt at detailed and technical consolidation of an assortment of miscellaneous legislative enactments came with the Merchant Shipping Act 1894. The Act proved a disappointment if consolidation was to be the precursor of codification of principles. The 1894 Act had limited use as a consolidation of the law if it is compared to the equivalent Maritime Codes of many continental countries frequently adopted in the civil law tradition of codified principles. The Act established a general pattern for later legislation in that it contained a miscellaneous number of sections covering registration of vessels, registration of the owners of wrecks and general provisions on maritime safety. Since then the 1894 Act was incrementally amended several times before the passage of the 1988 Act discussed

---

[17] *R. v Secretary of State for Transport* ex parte *Factortame Ltd., (No.2)*. [1991] 1 AC 603.
[18] See House of Commons Library: *Shipping: UK Policy* SN/BT/595 (23 February 2010). Generally see: R Hope, *A New History of British Shipping* (London, 1960).
[19] J Baker, 'England in the Seventeenth Century' in H Darby eds., *An Historical Geography of England before AD 1800* (Cambridge, Cambridge University Press, 1936) p 435.

in more detail below. Given this legislative history, it is not surprising that the law was complex to find and often contained many inconsistencies as well as omissions. Interpretation was often left open to conjecture and doubts prevailed as to how common practices conformed to the legislation leaving loose arrangements with uncertain legality in place.

Prior to the UK joining the European Community, *the Rochdale Report on Shipping* (1970) was confident about the future of the shipping industry[20] in general, but the report was later proved to be over-optimistic. The period leading up to Britain's entry into the European Community in 1972 coincided with a general decline in the merchant fleet and also considerable political protest about the vulnerability of local fishing to foreign fishing vessels. The Government of the day was fairly stoical and justified many of the changes as beyond their control and as a consequence of market forces and competition. Many fishing fleet owners feared for their livelihood. This issue remained high on the political agenda for much of the decade after the UK's entry into the European Community in 1972. Many MPs had constituencies with maritime boundaries and this made policy making politically sensitive. The UK's membership of the European Community did not make it easy for the Government to offer assistance to the fishing industry as it was claimed that the Community's rules on state aids prevented government intervention.

Although the Merchant Shipping Act 1988 had a long gestation period, containing many miscellaneous technical regulations it was speedily passed and like previous legislation lacked general coherence. The Falklands conflict in 1982 revealed systemic problems with the size and condition of the merchant fleet, these were considered by The House of Commons Transport Committee which undertook an inquiry in July 1986 into the general decline of the merchant fleet. Unfortunately this inquiry was cut short by the General Election in June 1987. In 1988 the Government produced a White Paper that led to the Merchant Shipping Act 1988. The miscellaneous provisions of the Act had also to address some updating and there were limited *ad hoc* revisions. Its miscellaneous content did not help as many distinct areas required specialist treatment including responses to the Zebrugge disaster[21] in 1987. The legislation was a patchwork without any common thread.[22] The 1988 Act disappointed the demand for a long overdue statutory consolidation of the law and regulation of merchant shipping. Buried within the complex mix of miscellaneous provisions is the registration of fishing vessels that proved to be the main issue of contention in the *Factortame* litigation. It should be remembered that at that time the parliamentary procedure for pre-legislative scrutiny that would have enabled the Bill to be scrutinised in some detail and commented

---

[20] *Committee of Inquiry into Shipping: Report* Cmnd. 4337 May, 1970. para 1.
[21] See: The Sheen Report: *The Zeebrugge Disaster: the Herald of Free Enterprise* (24 July 1987).
[22] See: N Gaskell, 'The Interpretation of Maritime Conventions at Common Law' in J Gardner ed., *United Kingdom in the 1990s* London: British Institute of International and Comparative Law, 1990 pp 218–40.

upon before presentation to Parliament did not exist. The time-table for the passage of the Merchant Shipping Bill gave limited time for debate over the key issue of vessel registration and its compatibility with Community law. In the limited time Parliament did not doubt the compatibility with Community law.

The Bill was introduced into the House of Lords in November 1987, and received all party support ensuring its speedy passage through various stages to becoming law.[23] Many government amendments were introduced and some parts of the Bill were forced though late at night and just before the Easter recess. It received the Royal Assent on 3 May 1988. Technical changes on vessel registration were noted but received only limited debate. In contrast only four provisions applying to maritime disaster attracted particular public attention especially the concern to prevent recurrence of the Zebrugge disaster. This left most of the remaining 54 sections and eight schedules covering technical matters, including registration, without much public attention or comment. The point being that no consideration was given to the issues that were subsequently the subject of the litigation.

Only cursory consideration was given in Parliament to the question of the compatibility between European community law and the UK's legislation. Perhaps the most likely reason for this is a certain naive assumption that UK legislation was always likely to be interpreted by the UK courts in a constructivist way that would ensure that the Community law was compatible without having to redefine traditional approaches to sovereignty. As Lord Bingham, however, pointed out that historically, 'there is no recorded case in which the courts, without the authority of Parliament, have invalidated or struck down a statute'.[24] In *Macarthy's Ltd, v Smith*[25] Lord Denning suggested that the UK courts would attempt through statutory interpretation to give effect to a statute if it was intended to override Community law. Cases decided in the UK since the UK joined the European Community[26] are remarkable for their reluctance[27] to consider the full implications of membership and UK sovereignty. Lord Diplock in *Garland v British Rail Engineering Ltd.*,[28] went further by observing that a Community measure on the same subject matter might be interpreted as part of the UK's obligation to carry out its legal obligations under Community law and the statute and Community law read to be consistent with one another. This might include directly effective provisions of Community law that could take priority over earlier statutory provisions.

---

[23] The Labour Party was originally opposed to membership but at the March 1966 election accepted that membership was an aim provided British and Commonwealth interests are safeguarded. Michael Franklin, Joining the CAP, The Agricultural Negotiations for British Accession to the European Economic Community 1961.

[24] T Bingham, *The Rule of Law* London: Allen Lane, 2010 p 163.

[25] Denning suggested that the UK courts would give effect to a statute if it was intended to override Community law in *Macarthy's Ltd v Smith* [1979] 3 All ER 325.

[26] See: *Garland v British Rail Engineering Ltd.* [1982] 2 All ER 402 and also in 1988 two cases: *Duke v GEC Reliance Ltd.*, [1988] 1 All ER 626 and *Pickstone v Freemans* [1988] 2 All ER 803.

[27] Denning in *Macarthy's Ltd., v Smith* [1979] 3 All ER 325.

[28] *Garland v British Rail Engineering Ltd.* [1982] 2 All ER 402.

In construing an Act of Parliament a reasonable interpretation might be adopted to avoid any conflict. These views assumed that conflicts between Community and UK law would be resolved without having to disapply or overturn an Act of Parliament. However, the interpretation of the Common Fisheries Policy proved to be impossible to reconcile with UK law arising from the *Factortame* litigation.

III. The Common Fisheries Policy (CFP) and the Merchant Shipping Act 1988

The development of the Common Agriculture Policy was a cause of bitter disagreement amongst Member States and a major stumbling block for Britain's failed attempt to join the European Community in 1967. At the time of the UK's second application in 1970, the Community's Common Fisheries Policy (CFP) had only been concluded a few hours before negotiations had begun with the UK, Denmark and Ireland. The new applicant countries had to agree to a new policy which they had a direct interest in, but they had not been party to the negotiations that had just been concluded. This left them at a considerable disadvantage. The UK also had concerns over the Common Agricultural Policy beyond fishing alone. Commonwealth interests especially the New Zealand dairy industry as well as more general financial conditions of entry had also taken a considerable time to resolve.[29]

At the time of entry fishing contributed a negligible 0.1% to the UK's GDP at Factor Cost in 1970. Despite its relative insignificance to the economy overall, fishing policy and the rights of local fishing communities attracted detailed and almost daily media attention and publicity. Public support for British fishermen increased amidst a combination of jingoistic national pride and political pressure from constituency MPs. Amateur fishing is one of the largest participant sports. It has strong romantic connotations that are often synonymous with national pride, community interests and territorial loyalty. Underlying public interest in fishing is the question of the medium to long-term sustainability of the fishing industry. It is particularly at risk from overfishing and vulnerable to over-capitalisation in the fishing fleet giving rise to market distortion and potential abuse. This potent mixture of national pride, territorial sensitivities and self-interest has long historical rivalries between maritime nations and past battles for supremacy. The European Commission considered that Community law conflicted with the view that states had rights over their fisheries and could exclude foreign fishing in their territories.

---

[29] C O'Neill (2000), *Report on Britain's entry into the European Community* (edited with a foreword by David Hannay) London: Frank Cass. Con O'Neill 1912–1988 was the main negotiator on the British side and his report provides a fascinating glimpse of the strategy for entry.

Fishing rights were viewed as state property allowing fishermen from all Member States equal access to the fishing waters of each Member State. The establishment of a CFP highlighted the difficulties of ensuring that a single policy could address important policy disagreements over fishing resources and the sovereignty of Member States who wished to protect national interests.

Con O'Neill,[30] the senior civil servant, who led the UK's delegation on the negotiation of Britain's entry into the European Community in 1972, in his published account of the negotiation, devoted over thirty pages to the CFP. He notes how the Government had miscalculated public support that the British trawler fleet would receive. The Government was aware that the CFP would allow many foreign fleets to enter British waters and while the consequences of this were understood, there was little appreciation of how to stop foreign vessels entering territorial waters. The Common Fisheries Policy, shortly established before the UK's negotiations on entry began, became 'one of the most important as well as one of the most difficult questions in the whole negotiation; and it was the last to be solved'.[31] The reasons for this were not hard to discern:

> ... a good reason for the bitterness felt by all the candidate countries about the Community's Common Fisheries Policy was the way in which and the time at which it came into existence. It did so late in the afternoon of 30th June 1970 about eight hours only after the Community had opened its negotiations with the four candidates. The popular view was that these two events were not unconnected and I have no doubt whatever that the popular view was right.[32]

The legal basis of the CFP is to be found under Article 3(d) of the Treaty of Rome[33] and Article 38(10) defines agricultural products to include 'fisheries' making this an exclusive Community competence. The CFP provided a structural policy for the fishing industry consisting of the size of the fleet and the number of boats that comprised each fleet. Many Member States shared the same fishing grounds namely the North Sea, the North Atlantic and the English Channel. A fundamental principle of open access to all Member States was established with the exception of historic fishing areas comprising small coastal strips. This was to become an important aspect of the CFP later when Spain and Portugal, countries with long coastlines and advanced fishing fleets, entered the Community in 1986.

Significantly the entry of Britain, Denmark and Ireland in 1973 brought even greater attention to the sensitivity of fishing policy, as the three new Member

---

[30] C O'Neill (1912–1988) Educated Eton and Balliol College, Oxford called to the Bar in 1936, Fellow of All Souls College Oxford. Foreign Office Diplomat, and from 1965 Deputy Under Secretary of State.

[31] Report by Con O'Neill, *Britain's Entry into the European Community* (London, Frank Cass, 2000) p 245.

[32] ibid p 250.

[33] R Churchill and D. Owen, *The EC Common Fisheries Policy* (Oxford, Oxford University Press, 2010).

States had fishing catches double those of the existing six Member States.[34] Con O'Neil argued that had the CFP been in existence:

> ... a year before negotiations began, we should no doubt have had time for much more thorough considerations between Whitehall Departments; for more far-reaching consultation with the fishing industry and for more thorough contacts and exploration with our fellow-candidates. These might not have resolved all difficulties. There were inherent difficulties in the situation greater than in most others-the clash of interests between our inshore and distant-water fishermen, and the potential clash of interests between the candidate countries.[35]

Once the negotiations began, there was a year between the adoption of the agreed CFP in 30 June 1970 and its implementation announced at the Conference on Fisheries on 1 June 1971. That time between adoption and implementation was more than adequate to have engaged in negotiation with the new applicant countries. Instead postponing the debate about fisheries to the end of accession negotiations resulted in a hurried negotiation and the failure of policy making on the British side to catch up with what had already been agreed. What was decided was not a re-negotiation of the CFP policy itself but a deferment for the UK in the form of a ten-year derogation from the 1970 CFP.[36] These temporary arrangements had to be revisited in 1983. The result was that after intense negotiations lasting over seven years the CFP had to be considered further.

The timing of the entry of the UK, Ireland and Denmark coincided with a fishing policy aimed at market growth, increasing the supply of fish to the Common Market and encouraging competition. Expansion of the fishing industry was encouraged though grants and investment very much similar to the business model of incentives. The *Third UN Convention on the Law of the Sea*[37] had been agreed expanding the area of Exclusive Economic Zones (EEZ) from national coastlines to 200 nautical miles. Depletion in fish stocks and over-fishing had also emerged as fishing fleets improved and technological innovation increased catches. This set up policy conflicts in need of resolution—conserving fish stocks and recognising territorial jurisdiction by Member States over their rights. The European Community reacted to both through competing policies that were not easy to reconcile with each other. This proved difficult as Member States had different interests to protect as the size of the fishing fleets varied a great deal and there were different pressures from their own fishermen and demands for some protection against other Member States. This was particularly the case from the standpoint of British fishermen and their organisations.

One example of the problem came early on. Ireland felt its fisheries vulnerable and reacted strongly by introducing a Sea Fisheries (Conservation and Rational Exploitation) Order 1977. This imposed restrictions on the size and engine capacity of vessels and a prohibition against entering Irish fishery zones. The

---

[34] C O'Neill *op cit* p 347.
[35] ibid p 350.
[36] See: www.wurove.org.uk index, The EU's Common Fisheries Policy.
[37] The Third Convention on the Law of the Sea.

justification for such radical steps came from scientific research and the analysis that larger vessels made the largest impact on fish stocks. In practice only two Irish vessels fell into the category set by the restrictions whereas all Dutch and French vessels were included. The conservation rationale was seen by French and Dutch governments as a pretext to exclude foreign fishing vessels. The Dutch government successfully applied to the European Court of Justice[38] that held that the Irish regulations contravened Articles 7 of the Treaty of Rome and Article 2(1) of Regulation 101/76 because of the unequal treatment in the Irish Regulations. The Court did concede that Member States were competent to impose conservation regulations. The Irish experience underlined the highly sensitive political and legal issues that surrounded fishing policy. This has strong echoes of past conflicts over fishing rights as shown in the late nineteenth and twentieth centuries. Historically there have been 'Cod wars' over fishing rights and this had been an indication of the patriotic and sovereign issues at stake in a highly politicised area of policy.[39]

Eventually a modified CFP[40] emerged in 1983 that attempted to fudge competing demands namely a conservation and sustainable fishing strategy mixed with a market strategy based largely around various structural and control policies set by the European Community.[41] The control aspects included inspection of vessels and landed fishing catches at ports but these responsibilities were delegated to Member States to implement. This proved a weakness of the procedures. Four aspects of the 1983 CFP in particular are important. First, a general policy acceptance of market led strategies that would take account of the interests of consumers and fishing fleets. Second, Community funds and structural investment to provide Community support in setting limitations on fishing fleets. Third, a Community conservation policy to protect fish stocks including the concept of the principles of a quota-based system around the concept of Total Allowable Catches (TAC) for each fish species. This had been negotiated on the basis of scientific evidence that fish stocks were in decline because of over-fishing. Finally, acceptance of an additional ten years of the UK derogation agreed earlier in 1973 over coastal waters.

Three years after the revised CFP was agreed, Portugal and Spain gained admission to the European Community in 1986. This was to prove significant as both countries had large fishing fleets and argued that the distribution of quotas was unfair particularly over fishing rights in Greenland. Both Portugal and Spain made unsuccessful challenges to the European Court of Justice that their accession arrangements were not fair in the allocation of quotas.[42] It is against this background of political compromise, and differences in policy between Member States that CFP decisions were being taken. There was also a split in policy making

---

[38] Case 61/77 *European Court Reports* 1978 p 417.

[39] C Lequesne, *The Politics of Fisheries in the European Union* (Manchester, Manchester University Press; 2004).

[40] M Holden, *The Common Fisheries Policy: Origin, Evaluation and Future* (Oxford, Fishing News Books 1996).

[41] 170/83 and structural policy 2908/83. Control policy2057/82.

[42] 1986 OJL 302 Treaty of Accession.

with France and Netherlands preferring equal access amongst Member States and the UK and Ireland preferring to protect fishing resources.

In this context the UK's approach to fishing regulation in the Merchant Shipping Act 1988 concentrated on shipping registration including fishing vessel registration and also measures on marine safety. This was an attempt to protect its own fishing fleet but registration was also seen as a way of regulating fishing quotas, which would assist in setting and enforcing quotas. More generally UK fishing policy and negotiation left a lot to be desired. At the very outset the UK had got off to a bad start. The late, Hugo Young describes the 'disastrous' efforts on policy making on the British side illustrating miscalculation on the part of negotiators

On fish, however, Con O'Neil enters only a modest defence. This is the great exception. It was a complex and disastrous story. The Community concluded its own Common Fisheries Policy within hours of the enlargement process commencing which looked like an amazing piece of chicanery. Having hung fire for years, the issue of access to coastal waters was resolved between the six to the extreme disadvantage of the four candidate members, who would bring to the Community far longer coast-lines and double the fish-catch. Of all the matters on the agenda fish was therefore the least prepared by the British.[43]

The Department of Transport's consultation papers in 1981, 1984 and the White Paper in 1987[44] were oddly silent on the full extent of the problem posed by the CFP in terms of any direct conflict with national sovereignty. The White Paper identified only 'foreign-owned fishing vessels' being registered in the UK and fishing against quotas allocated to the UK under the EEC Common Fisheries Policy.

The Government's intention was to tighten up the law on registration of British fishing vessels so that any company wishing to register a fishing vessel in the UK would have to be largely owned and managed by British citizens resident in this country. To achieve this end it was necessary to set up a new system for registering fishing vessels and to set new eligibility requirements for registration for the first time. This sounded simpler than it was in reality as the 1894 Act had not clearly defined registration; the general nationality law had been changed in the British Nationality Act 1981 in order to control immigration and the existing Commonwealth registration system as a result of the Commonwealth Shipping Agreement 1931 had ended in 1977. Flags of convenience had also been shown to be open to abuse. The British Government estimated that there were approximately 129 flags of convenience of fishing vessels on the UK register. Previous attempts to set and impose licence conditions on fishing had failed including attempts to define

---

[43] Hugo Young, *This Blessed Plot Britain and Europe from Churchill to Blair* (Macmillan, London 1998) p 232. See also the National Archives Legal Department Kew Gardens collection MAF Division 27.

[44] ibid. National Archives, Kew Gardens MA Division 27, Department of Transport, *Merchant Shipping Legislative Proposals* Cm 239 October 1987. See also: Government Observations on the First Report of the Transport Committee Session 1987–1988 (Second Special Report of 1987–88) HC 681 26 October 1988.

the proportion of crew on a fishing vessel to be British. This was claimed to be in breach of Community law and litigation before the European Court of Justice had effectively prevented this form of regulation[45] after a compromise agreement was reached not to proceed with this regulation.

The White Paper was vague on the potential problems that might arise from direct competition from other Member States, notably Spain whose large and advanced fishing fleets were a real threat to British fishing at the time. In reality the main purpose of the Merchant Shipping Act 1988 was to try to prevent 'quota hopping' by fishing boats owned abroad mainly from Spain. Curiously the general question of how some form of registration might be a means of ensuring that the CFP was properly administered was also absent from the White Paper.[46] The general terms of registration were spelt out in the White Paper and the nature of registration was settled on a 'qualified person' who must be a British national resident and domiciled in the United Kingdom. The implications of defining a 'qualified person' in this way on the UK's Community membership was not mentioned in the White Paper despite this being an obvious issue. However, international law, under Article 5 of the Geneva Convention on the High Seas and Article 92 of the UN Convention on the law of the Sea 1982 had generally accepted that there should be a 'genuine link' between the ship and the state of registry. Sections 3–5 and 14 of the Merchant Shipping Act 1988 contained requirements relating to the identity of the ship-owner and the nature of their presence in the UK and circumstances where it would be appropriate to appoint a representative person in the UK which is regarded as consistent with international law.[47]

More problematic was the nature of Section 14 of the 1988 Act imposing strict eligibility requirements for ownership of British Fishing vessels. Three elements were required. First vessels had to be British owned; second they had to be effectively run from the UK including details on the requirements of direction and control of fishing operations; and finally that the charterer, operator or manager must also be qualified under the Act. Taken together the three elements required a substantial British connection that is more than a 'shell company' and a degree of day-to-day control by British citizens. In the debates on the Bill, Lord Brabazon commented that it was hoped that the Bill would address the fact that there were '… 50 or so Spanish fishing boats which managed to register at British ports and were taking part in fishing under the United Kingdom quotas'.[48]

---

[45] See N Gaskell, 'The Merchant Shipping Act 1988' *Current Law Statutes* (London, Sweet and Maxwell, 1988). Paras 12-31-32.

[46] Ironically, but largely unnoticed in the same Merchant Shipping Bill clauses were proposed that made it easier for UK owned merchant vessels, but not fishing vessels, with an open registry scheme in the Bahamas to be made available to the British Government at time of war.

[47] See the 1993 Registration Regulations.

[48] HL Deb 24 November 1987 vol 490 paras 570–573.

IV. The Litigation

The problem of quota-hopping and the Spanish fishing vessels[49] became the subject of litigation when Spanish fishermen found that regulations made under the Merchant Shipping Act that brought the new registration scheme into operation resulted in 95 fishing vessels not being qualified for registration. They had been previously registered under the previous arrangements and they sought judicial review challenging the legality of the legislation as being incompatible with Community law. The UK Government argued that the Merchant Shipping Act 1988 was compatible with Community law and that national governments were entitled to define their own nationality consistent with membership of the Community.

The Divisional Court sought a preliminary ruling from the European Court of Justice under Article 177 EEC[50] asking whether the relevant provisions of Community law had direct effect on UK law. Pending the decision of the European Court, the Divisional Court granted interim relief which had the effect of disapplying the provisions until their legality could be established. The European Court of Justice eventually ruled that the provisions relating to registration under the Merchant Shipping Act 1988 contravened Community law on the ground that it discriminated against nationals of other Member States. In the meantime, first the Court of Appeal[51] and then the House of Lords[52] were asked to consider the legality of making an interim order which would result in suspending the Merchant Shipping Act 1988. Lord Bridge regarded this outcome as 'contrary to Parliament's sovereign will'. They held that the Divisional Court had no power to make such an order and that there was no power to grant an interim injunction against the Crown. However it was agreed to refer to the European Court of Justice the question of whether or not a question of Community law was involved in providing interim protection for a party whose rights were to be adjudicated. The European Commission also questioned the legality of the Merchant Shipping Act claiming that the UK had failed in its obligations under Community Law. The immediate outcome was that the Court of Justice concluded, pending the outcome of its final decision, that an interim order could be made to suspend the operation of the nationality requirements under the Act regarding other Member State nationals.[53] In general terms a national court was obliged to set aside domestic law which might prevent Community law from having its full force and impact including the necessity to put in place interim arrangements. The House of Lords returned to

---

[49] See: M Geary, *The Third Enlargement: Spain and Portugal's Access to the EEC: Report on the Council of Ministers Archival Material* Brussels 30 June 2009 EU Council of European Union.
[50] A Arnull, 'The Use and Abuse of Article 177 EEC' (1989) 52 *Modern Law Review* 622 and also A Arnull, 'References to the European Court' (1990) 15 *European Law Review* 375.
[51] *R v Secretary of State for Transport ex p Factortame Ltd.* [1989] 2 CMLR 353.
[52] *R v Secretary of State for Transport ex p Factortame Ltd.* [1990] 2 AC 85.
[53] Case 246/89R *Commission v United Kingdom* [1989] ECR 3125.

this matter and for the first time in legal history granted an injunction against the Secretary of State requiring the suspension of provisions of primary legislation, here the application of the British residence and domicile requirements under the Merchant Shipping Act 1988[54] to nationals of other Member States. The UK complied with the ruling of the European Court of Justice by introducing a new Order amending the previous Regulations.[55]

The European Court of Justice made its ruling on the preliminary reference made by the Divisional Court. In upholding Article 52 of the EC Treaty on freedom of establishment, the European Court held that the domicile and residential requirements under the Merchant Shipping Act 1988 were contrary to Community law and this was later taken into effect by the Divisional Court.[56] Various amendments were made to bring the Act into conformity with Community law.[57] The European Court later considered[58] the issue of damages and held that the UK Government were liable for their actions and compensation was payable to the Spanish Fishing Fleet.[59] The House of Lords accepted this ruling and compensation was paid.[60]

As Gaskell has pointed out[61] the European Court of Justice did not outlaw all the provisions of Section 14 of the Merchant Shipping Act 1988 leaving the provisions about managing and controlling operations to be directed and controlled from within the UK, and part of these requirements are remodelled and contained in Regulation 14 of the 1993 Registration Regulations. This may be of little comfort to the view that the UK had made a reasonable attempt to come up with a registration formula that would avoid Member States 'quota hopping'. There are lessons about the way fishing policy within the CFP had been handled on accession and the consequences of complex legislation and technical reforms introduced in the way in which the Merchant Shipping Act 1988 had been drafted and debated. Policy makers had failed to address the problems of fishing quotas, sustainable fishing and the protection of fishing stocks. It was highly likely that the Merchant Shipping Act 1988 would be challenged in the courts and viewed differently by the European Court of Justice than by the UK courts.

---

[54] *R v Secretary of State for Transport ex p Factortame Ltd.*(No 2) [1991] 1 AC 603. (ECJ and HL).
[55] See The Merchant Shipping Act 1998 (Amendment) Order [1989] SI 1989/2006.
[56] *R v Secretary of State for Transport ex p Factortame Ltd.*(No 3) [1992] QB 680.
[57] See: The Merchant Shipping (Registration etc.,) Act 1993, Section 3 and also the Merhcant Shipping (Registration of Ships) Regulations 1993 SI 1993/3138.
[58] *R v Secretary of State for Transport ex p Factortame Ltd. (No 4) The Times* 7 March 1996.
[59] Compensation of £55 million was accepted by the Spanish Fishermen in March 2000 Guernsey Press.
[60] *R v Secretary of State for Transport ex p Factortame Ltd. (No.5)* [2000] 1 AC 524.
[61] N Gaskell, 'The Merchant Shipping Act 1995' (1995) *Current Law Statutes* (London: Sweet and Maxwell, 1995) paras 21-29-30.

V. The *Factortame* Aftermath

The aftermath of the litigation in *Factortame* continues to have consequences for the CFP. It is clear that Member States are unable to use strict registration mechanisms to discriminate against other Member States. The CFP, however, continues to struggle to be effective. Quotas and their enforcement still remains a weakness as the rules are largely dependent on Member States. The combination of overfishing, poor enforcement and high stakes politics has left major problems for the sustainability of fishing stocks within the EU. This legacy remains today[62] with plans to create an Integrated Maritime Policy (IMP) and a more focused approach to sustainable development and environmental protection. Reforming the CFP has been a continuous process. In 1992 reforms were introduced to limit the size of fishing fleets and in 2002 there were further reforms including the setting up of an enforcement agency and since 2007 there is a Common Fisheries Control Agency, aimed to provide, enforcement regulation and oversight of the CFP. A further Green Paper was published in 2009 that acknowledged the failures of reforms to date. The reform of the EU CFP was agreed in May 2012 and continues to excite debate and analysis[63] with doubts and uncertainties surrounding its overall effectiveness.[64] There is expected to be a six billion Euro European Maritime and Fisheries Fund to achieve sustainable fisheries. On the CAP more generally there is greater flexibility in implementation and strategy at national and devolved levels of government.[65]

VI. Impact on the UK's Legal System

The decision has also had a general impact on the UK's legal system. The decision of the European Court of Justice that a national court was obliged to set aside domestic law which might prevent Community law from having its full force and impact including the necessity to put in place interim arrangements had significant consequences. The principle of interim relief including injunctions against the Crown in particular was considered to have wider implications. In *M v Home Office*,[66] Lord Woolf disagreed with the previous interpretation on the

---

[62] See J Wakefield, 'Sustainability and socio-economic need in the common fisheries policy' (2010) *European Law Review* pp 476–96.
[63] See: House of Commons 12th Report if the Environment Food and Rural Affairs Committee: EU Proposals for reform of the CAP (21 February 2012).
[64] House of Commons Library: *EU bibliographies: Proposed reform of the Common Fisheries Policy* SN/1A/6551 (21 May 2014).
[65] House of Commons Library: *Subject: CAP Reforms 2014–2020 Implementation Decisions in the UK* SN0629 (3 July 2014).
[66] *M v Home Office* [1994] 1 AC 377. See Ch 7 of this volume.

use of interim injunctions against a Minister of the Crown that had been rejected in the House of Lords in the *Factortame*[67] case earlier. The result is that interim relief including injunctions against Ministers are available in judicial review proceedings.

The need for UK courts to give primacy to Community law has broad implications. The method of interpretation and the reasoning of UK courts have to take account of the European Court of Justice. Damian Chalmers has noted how the implications of Community law in the UK have had a transformative effect that is potentially redistributive in terms of decision-making and hierarchy. According to Chalmers four elements of that transformation are worthy of further consideration.

First is a reversal of the 'hierarchy between the British Judiciary and the other arms of government'.[68] National courts having the power to disapply legislative or administrative acts which conflict with community law allows courts to intervene in a way that in the UK had not been possible in the past. The second transformative effect is that Community law required UK courts to 'mediate different relationship between the individual and the State'. Driven by economic freedoms and liberal market thinking much more emphasis is given to subjective rights with consequences for interpretation that extends beyond traditional common law norms. Chalmers also calculates a third transformative effect of Community law through the undermining of existing internal judicial hierarchies. The point is that Community law provides opportunities for lower courts to apply and determine community rights that would never have been possible in the past. Finally, Community law has brought many more administrative interventions into legal institutions and civil society. Competition law is one example but wide ranging environmental rules and regulations have transformed administrative decisions that have led to economic policies having to be recalibrated to take account of these legal rules and obligations. Chalmers concludes by arguing:

> The heavy normativity of EU law is likely to be a pan-European feature and offers explanations for governmental acceptance of the EC legal order and also suggests a re-evaluation of how EC law should be critiqued by legal academics.[69]

The implications for the nature of the EU's judicial system is over the debate about the constitutional norms that inform the question of European constitutionalism. There are also questions about the use of preliminary references to the European Court and whether the application of EU law should be driven by domestic courts rather than the attitudes of the Court of Justice.

---

[67] *Factortame Ltd., v Secretary of State for Transport* [1990] 2 AC 85.
[68] See: Damian Chalmers, 'The Much Ado about Judicial Politics in the United Kingdom: A Statistical Analysis of reported decisions of United Kingdom Courts Involving EU Law 1973–1998' *Harvard Jean Monnet Working Paper 1/00* (2000).
[69] ibid p 33.

VII. Sovereignty in Question

Parliamentary authority in the UK remains a major influence over how many substantial areas of law are interpreted. This has often influenced the way policy is made and the potential for judge-made law. The question arises as to whether the submission to Community law, now European Union law, has altered the sovereignty of Parliament or even rendered it redundant in EU matters.

Initially the UK courts showed remarkable reluctance to provide an unequivocal answer even though it was inevitable that the UK's membership of the European Community would raise issues about the supremacy of Community law. Much of the case law before the *Factortame* litigation focused on the interpretation of Parliament's intention and giving effect to Section 2(4) of the European Communities Act 1972 which provides:

> ... any enactment passed or to be passed, other than one contained in this Part of this Act shall be construed and have effect subject to the foregoing provisions of this section ...

Interpretation of this section engages with Section 3(1) of the 1972 Act which requires the UK courts to determine the effects of a provision of Community law 'in accordance with the principles laid down by and relevant decision of the European Court'.

It was clear, however, that the European Court of Justice (ECJ) had interpreted its own powers and jurisdiction including the primacy of Community law. In its decision in 1964, in *Costa v ENEL*[70] its rulings created 'a body of law which binds both their nationals and themselves'. In the *Simmenthal Case*[71] the principle of supremacy of Community law was defined to mean that every national court must 'apply Community law in its entirety and protect rights which the latter confers in individuals and must accordingly set aside any provision of national law which may conflict with it, whether prior or subsequent to the Community rule'.[72] In the *Internationale Handelsgesellschaft*[73] case, the Court of Justice established that national courts had the responsibility for rights derived from Community law to be effectively protected. It has already been mentioned that Lord Denning in *Macarthy's Ltd. v Smith*[74] had accepted that English courts would give effect to Community law unless Parliament wished to override inconsistencies in Community law. This was hardly a clear indication of what the courts would do when asked to decide on any inconsistent UK Act of Parliament and Community Law. Lord Diplock was also more circumspect in his approach in *Garland v British Rail Engineering Ltd*[75] believing that the statutory words should be given their ordinary

---

[70] Case 6/64 [1964] ECR 585.
[71] Case 106/77 *Amministrazione delle Finannze dello Stato v Simmenthal Spa* [1978] ECR 629.
[72] ibid para 21.
[73] [1970] ECR 1125.
[74] [1979] 3 All R 325.
[75] [1982] 2 All ER 402.

meaning of interpretation. Both cases were unhelpful in settling how English law would have to make a choice between Community law and a UK statute indicating a circumspect approach to the discussion of sovereignty.

It was also clear that a sharp distinction could be drawn between the English common law approach to the interpretation of Community law and the approach of the European Court of Justice. In a case involving the interpretation of the Equal Treatment Directive Council Directive 76/207, *Marshall v Southampton and South West Hampshire*,[76] the European Court of Justice ruled that the Equal Treatment Directive was directly effective between private parties as well as the state and that Member State courts were obliged to follow this ruling.

Further clarification was sought in two cases: *Duke v GEC reliance Ltd* and *Pickstone v Freemans plc*.[77] In *Duke*, a case concerning the retirement ages of male and female employees, Lord Templeman was reluctant to concede that a British court could 'distort the meaning of a British statute in order to enforce against an individual a Community Directive which has no direct effect between individuals'. The House of Lords had arguably failed in its duty to interpret all national legislation in the appropriate way to give effect to the provisions of Community law. In *Pickstone*, the question of equal pay amongst men and women over the interpretation of the Equal Pay Act 1970 as amended by 1983 regulations was raised. The latter had to be interpreted under Article 119 of the EEC Treaty and the Equal Pay Directive. The courts were able to side step any constitutional conflict and found a way to read the Regulations as compatible with Community law. In *Lister*, also decided before *Factortame*, Lord Oliver accepted that a 'purposive construction to legislation designed to give effect to the UK's treaty obligations to the Community enables the court, where necessary, to supply by implication words appropriate to comply with those obligations'.[78] Even here the courts had side stepped the issue of what to do when a British Act of Parliament was inconsistent with Community law.

As Bradley[79] noted giving Community law the same status as a UK statute was not the same as deciding which was superior and which should prevail. Paul Craig observes that there is a contrast between competing views of UK sovereignty that is at the centre of the debate over Community law and UK law. The debate over sovereignty has been characterised as a contest between the traditionalists, represented by Dicey and Wade and upholders of the New View, represented by Jennings, Heuston and Marshall.

Political opinion and academic scholarship[80] remains in conflict over the effects of membership of the Community on UK sovereignty[81] not least because of the

---

[76] *Marshall v Southampton and South West Hampshire* [1986] 2 All ER 584.
[77] *Duke v GEC Reliance Ltd.* [1988] 1 All ER 626 at p 636.
[78] See *Litster v Forth Dry Dock and Engineering Co Ltd* [1989] 1 All ER 1134 at p 1153.
[79] See Anthony Bradley, 'The Sovereignty of Parliament—Form or Substance?' in Jowell and Oliver eds *The Changing Constitution* Oxford: Oxford University Press, 2007, pp 25–58 p 55.
[80] J Allison, *The English Historical Constitution* Cambridge: Cambridge University Press, 2007 pp 120–3.
[81] See A Bradley, 'The Sovereignty of Parliament-Form or Substance?' in Jowell and Oliver eds *The Changing Constitution* Oxford: Oxford University Press, 2007, pp 25–58.

political and economic policy making implications of membership. William Wade, adopts a practical approach to how a sovereign Parliament is not bound by the Acts of its predecessors and it cannot bind its successors to apply this analysis to Community membership. His perspective is that the common law is the authority and that it is on this basis that the authority of the courts to obey Acts of Parliament is found. Wade's arguments rest on parliamentary sovereignty depending on the interpretation given to it by the courts. Trevor Allan[82] advances Wade's analysis further by suggesting a twin track of legal certainty and democratic principle as influential in judicial reasoning.

We have already seen that the *Factortame* litigation settled the question of the primacy of European law. For example in *R v Secretary of State for Employment* ex parte *Equal Opportunities Commission*,[83] the House of Lords granted declarations at the request of the Equal Opportunities Commission that some of the provisions of the Employment Protection (Consolidation) Act 1978 were incompatible with the Equal Pay and Equal Treatment Directives under the Article 157 of the TFEU. The technique was to interpret the legislation in a way that was compatible with the Directive.

These cases leave many unanswered questions even when many subsequent cases have accepted the principle of primacy. An assessment is required of the implications both conceptually and substantively on the orthodoxy of UK sovereignty. Craig raises the question of the effect on the doctrine of implied repeal or the implied disapplication of a statute whereby a later Act of Parliament applies over an earlier Act, when it is accepted after the *Factortame* litigation that this is no longer generally applicable in the context of EU law. There is the possibility that in the future if Parliament wishes to derogate from EU law it has to do so in a manner that is express and unequivocal. This leaves a heavy burden on the UK courts if faced with a conflict that is directly at odds with EU obligations where these obligations are expressly forbidden by the UK Parliament. This in turn raises a question of competing competences between national courts and the European Court of Justice. The resolution of competing competences is not easy to solve as the European Court of Justice has markedly expanded its interpretation of the Treaties and there are some concerns within national jurisdictions, particularly Germany and France, that fear this expansion of the European Court of Justice might go beyond what is necessary or required.

It is arguable that the UK courts are able to retain some degree of autonomy by assuming that the will of the UK Parliament is retained as the consent to interpret EU law is expressly given authority to the courts under the European Communities Act 1972. If Parliament were to withdraw that consent on a specified matter

---

[82] T Allan, 'Parliamentary sovereignty: law, politics and revolution' [1997] 113 LQR 443. Also see: T Allan, *The Sovereignty of Law: Freedom, Constitution and Common Law* Oxford: Oxford University Press, 2013. Stuart Lakin, 'Defending and Contesting the Sovereignty of Law: The Public Lawyer as Interpretivist' (2015) 78(3) MLR 549–70.

[83] *R v Secretary of State for Employment* ex parte *Equal Opportunities Commission* [1995] 1 AC 1.

with direct and unequivocal words then the UK courts may consider that it is within their jurisdiction to give effect to the will of Parliament. Indeed there may be circumstances where it is inappropriate to adopt the *Factortame* principle of disapplication of an Act of Parliament. This is seen in 2010 in *R v Budimir*.[84] The Video Recording Act 1984 had been regarded as being in breach of the Technical Standards Directive 83/189/EEC and a company convicted under the 1984 Act sought to have the convictions set aside. The breach of the Directive had only been discovered in 2009 after many convictions had been obtained. The UK Parliament adopted the Video Recordings Act 2010 but in much the same terms as the 1984 Act. The Court regarded the company's activities as criminal and rejected the submission that the legislation was a nullity. In such circumstances the effectiveness of EU law had not been jeopardised and Parliament's authority should still be considered and the technique was to ensure that EU law was being applied within the margin of discretion left to the UK courts.

It is clear that political processes and parliamentary procedures may generate acts of Parliament that are considered by courts to be 'constitutional statutes'. The dispute in *Factortame* was confined to substantive differences between a UK statute, the Merchant Shipping Act 1988 and EU law. The case was not about the process by which legislation is enacted in Parliament. In *Jackson v Attorney-General*,[85] a case unconnected with EU law but arising from a challenge to the validity of the Hunting Act 2004 and the Parliament Act 1949, the judges recognised the changing nature of sovereignty as Lord Hope acknowledged:

> Our Constitution is dominated by the sovereignty of Parliament. But parliamentary sovereignty is no longer, if it ever was, absolute. Step by step, gradually but surely, the English principle of the absolute sovereignty of Parliament which Dicey derived from Coke and Blackstone is being qualified ... The rule of law enforced by the courts is the ultimate controlling factor on which our Constitution is based.

Some guidance as to what might be involved in defining the future role of the courts came in *Thoburn v Sunderland City Council*.[86] In this case street traders were prosecuted for selling goods using imperial measures rather than metric measures. The UK Government's obligations to apply metric measurement arose from Directives and Section 2(2) of the European Communities Act 1972. Lord Justice Laws found that there was no inconsistency between the Directive and the Weights and Measures Act 1985 and therefore no implied repeal of the European Communities Act 1972 arose. Lord Justice Laws recognised the changes in UK sovereignty and this had modified the doctrine of implied repeal when it came to EU law. The basis of the UK's relationship was a matter of the common law and the common law was the basis of any resolution. Consequently he reasoned that while ordinary statutes were subject to the implied repeal doctrine what he called 'constitutional statutes' were not. Defining a constitutional statute was one which

---

[84] [2010] EWCA Crim. 1486, [2011] 3 All ER 206.
[85] *Jackson v Attorney General* [2005] UKHL 56 [2006] 1 AC 262. See Ch 10 of this volume.
[86] *Thoburn v Sunderland City Council* [2003] QB 151.

dealt with fundamental constitutional rights, including the European Communities Act 1972, and the only conditions where such a repeal might be possible arose from express words in the later statute.

Further elaboration is forthcoming in *R(HS2 Action Alliance Ltd.,) and others v Secretary of State for Transport*[87] where the applicants argued that the adoption of a hybrid Bill procedure was not compatible with the requirements of the Environmental Impact Assessment Directive (Directive 2011/92/EU) requiring effective opportunities for objectors to participate in environmental decision-making procedures. The Government was pushing forward a plan to create a fast train link between London and Birmingham and the objectors to the proposed link claimed that there was a serious impact on the environment. The adoption of a hybrid Bill was subject to government whipping procedures in the House of Commons, meaning that there would be inadequate time to debate the detailed and complex nature of environmental issues; and that the alternatives to the proposal would not be considered until the relevant elect committee after second reading. The Supreme Court had rejected the view that the issues raised by the applicants should be referred to the European Court of Justice. Lord Reed made clear that where EU law is in direct conflict with UK domestic constitutional law, it was a matter to be resolved by the UK Supreme Court. The Supreme Court accepted that there is no *acte Claire* and that the *Factortame* principle of a disapplication of a statute was not pertinent to a constitutional principle such as settled in the Bill of Rights.

The emergence of constitutional fundamentals that are unalterable by EU law and defined by the national court creates potential limitations on the general expansionist direction of the European Court of Justice. It is in line with other cases recently decided by the Supreme Court[88] and rests on the re-assertion of domestic supremacy to be found in Section 18 of the European Union Act 2011. It remains unclear what the reaction of the European Court of Justice might be. The European Court of Justice may, as it has done in the past, subscribe to the view that it has the competence to settle any competing competence between EU law and domestic law of the Member States and that the national courts are obliged to follow its opinions. The European Court of Justice is increasingly of the view that in matters of EU law, national courts are behaving as European courts integral to the requirements of the Treaty obligations. Conceptually this view fits very well within the analysis that EU law is not determined within the boundaries of national states but within the conceptual framework of the jurisprudence of the EU.

Resolving competing competences between national courts and the European Court of Justice is likely to be a matter for some speculation over the next decade as economic and political frictions within the EU between Member States have

---

[87] *R (HS2 Action Alliance Ltd) and others v Secretary of State for Transport* [2014] UKSC 3. See also: Ben Gaston, 'Laying the Tracks' (2014) *New Law Journal* pp 14–15 (4th July 2014). P Craig 'Constitutionalizing Constitutional Law HS' (2014) *Public Law* p 373.

[88] See *Osborn v The Parole Board* [2013] UKSC 61 and *Kennedy v Charity Commission* [2014] UKSC n 20.

increased in recent years. More specifically there are also the conceptual questions of the reasoning and approach adopted by courts in reaching their decisions and to what extent has the European Court of Justice's teleological approach to interpretation become accepted by British courts. William Wade acknowledged in his *Constitutional Fundamentals* in 1989 that in matters of sovereignty 'shifts' in judicial loyalty are possible and that this occurred in the seventeenth century in England, in the attitudes of the courts in eighteenth century America and in the general dissolution of the British Empire. It is possible that new 'generations of judges' would have a different attitude to a new constitutional settlement.[89] Lord Bridge in *Factortame* when discussing the European Communities Act 1972 explained how it should be interpreted on the basis that '… whatever the limitation of its sovereignty Parliament accepted when it enacted the European Communities Act 1972 was entirely voluntary. Under the terms of the 1972 Act it has always been clear that it was the duty of a UK court, when delivering final judgement to override any rule of national law found to be in conflict with any directly enforceable rule of Community law'.[90] Lord Bingham in his book on the *Rule of Law*[91] commented that:

> This (the Factortame decision) is the best example from the critics' point of view, since the process does involve the invalidation of statutes by the courts. But the courts act in that way only because Parliament, exercising its legislative authority, has told them to. If Parliament, exercising the same authority, told them not to do so, they would obey that injunction also.[92]

The argument that statutory interpretation provides a satisfactory explanation of the *Factortame* decision on how to construct EU law as part of the national legal system, has some limitations. The construction approach does not fully explain the application of the doctrine of implied repeal or the disapplication of an earlier statute. The modification of this doctrine is a radical break with the past and one that is not simply explained by construing a statute. Wade accepts this by arguing that the way in which EU law is construed operates outside the traditional role of the courts and is not explicable by the construction of a statute. Even the express words of a statute could be overridden by EU law. This may be regarded as a 'revolution' or simply a shift in legal reasoning and doctrine.

Craig[93] supported by Allan[94] suggests another approach beyond the construction argument and also different than Wade:

> There is however a third way in which to regard the courts' jurisprudence. This is to regard decisions about supremacy as being based on normative arguments of legal principle the content of which can and will vary across time.[95]

---

[89] W Wade, '*Constitutional Fundamentals*' (Oxford, Oxford University Press, 1989) p 17.
[90] *Factortame* [1990] ECR-I -2433, [1991] 1AC 603 paras 658–9.
[91] Tom Bingham, '*The Rule of Law*' (London, Allen Lane, 2010) p 164.
[92] ibid p 164.
[93] P Craig 'Public Law, Political Theory and legal Theory' (2000) *Public Law* p 211.
[94] T Allan, 'Parliamentary Sovereignty: Law, Politics and Revolution' (1997) 113 Law Quarterly Review p 443.
[95] P Craig, *op cit.* p 120–1.

This is a welcome and refreshing approach that is subtle and nuanced in the politics of the time and the underpinnings of legal doctrine. It also reaffirms that the UK's relationship with the EU is not fixed in any one point in time but continues to evolve. This is well illustrated by the passage of the European Union Act 2011 predicated on the principle that power resides with Parliament with the addition of a referendum as a 'double lock' against any erosion of that power.[96] There is, however, nothing in the European Union Act 2011 that seeks to entrench the referendum requirement and this may be modified or repealed by a future Act of Parliament. Section 18 of the Act contains a declaratory statement on the status of EU law continuing on a statutory basis. This extends the long-standing rule that Treaty obligations require an Act of Parliament for their enforcement but there is the interesting prospect of such a change being rejected by a referendum even if approved by an Act of Parliament. Craig admits that:

> The United Kingdom's relationship with the EU, and the conception of sovereignty that shapes and is shaped by it, will continue to occupy the political terrain.[97w]

Dawn Oliver also identifies[98] some of the main reasons for British courts accepting the authority of European law and the doctrine that European law will be given effect even if it conflicts with an Act of the UK Parliament. The most obvious reason is that the doctrine was well developed by the European Court of Justice long before the UK joined; that the courts in other Member States have accepted the role of the European Court and the principle of giving direct effect and primacy to EU law is well established. Section 2(4) of the European Communities Act is also relevant as it provides instructions to British courts to accept the express intention of Parliament and this is an obligation in UK law as well as in EU law. The last point is that Section 18 of the European Union Act 2011 confirms that UK membership under the European Communities Act 1972 Act is the basis for EU law to be 'recognised and available' in law in the UK, and together the two Acts have altered the doctrine of implied repeal. Perhaps the underlying basis for the acceptance of European law is also partly contractual—it was part of the package agreed on accession and the terms of the agreement set out in the European Communities Act 1972 have to be followed.

More broadly there are associated issues connected with democracy and its links to sovereignty. Oliver's argument is that parliamentary sovereignty as it developed in the eighteenth century in England was recognised by the courts as placing parliamentary authority as superior to Royal power. The underlying features of this are that, 'the courts should recognise and give effect to Acts as law and as the highest form of law because they are produced by a formal legislative procedure

---

[96] P Craig, 'The United Kingdom, the European Union and Sovereignty' in R Rawlings and P Leyland, A Young, eds, *Sovereignty and the Law* (Oxford, Oxford University Press, 2013) pp 165–185.
[97] ibid p 185.
[98] See D Oliver, 'Parliament and the Courts' in A Horne, G Drewry and D Oliver eds *Parliament and the Law* (Oxford, Hart, 2013) pp 309–337 p 313.

(and thus mere resolutions of Parliament are not law in which elected representatives determine the content of laws'.[99]

The importance of the democratic principle is as Oliver[100] admits unconvincing as a rationale for sovereignty. Sovereignty may allow Parliament to pass legislation that is unrepresentative and unfair or discriminatory. In the context of the EU this raises a euro sceptical concern that the courts giving way to the primacy of EU law may enable policy and laws passed within the EU to have sway when their democratic credentials are in doubt. Future directions are difficult to predict. The relationship between the government of the day, Parliament and the courts is always evolving through elements of pragmatism and some degree of self-limitation that has avoided outright conflict. Writing in 1971, de Smith, was rather cautious in his prediction and measured in his judgement of the potential impact of membership of the European Community on the UK and cautioned against rash prediction or hasty conclusions. In this well-known analysis de Smith explains the timeless quality of sovereignty as it is defined and re-defined by each generation, often underpinning the overall political realities of where economic and legal powers actually reside:

> If, however, with the passage of time, the Community develops characteristics of a political federation, and if the incongruity of the orthodox doctrine of parliamentary sovereignty becomes increasingly apparent in a context of expanding Community law, then a climate of opinion will doubtless develop in which heterodoxy will thrive and eventually prevail. The legal concept of parliamentary sovereignty may then drift away into the shadowy background from which it emerged.[101]

Jacob in his Hamlyn Lectures, *The Sovereignty of Parliament: The European Way*[102] in 2006 admitted that sovereignty was not always compatible 'both internationally and internally, with another concept which also has a lengthy history, but which today is widely regarded as a paramount value: the rule of law'.[103]

VIII. Conclusion

The *Factortame* litigation has to be set in the broader context of the UK's membership of the European Union and most recently the referendum held in June 2016 and the vote to leave the EU. The referendum leaves many uncertainties. Once Article 50 of TEU is activated there is a period of up to two years for negotiations

---

[99] ibid p 314.
[100] ibid pp 335–6.
[101] de Smith (1971) 34 *Modern law Review* 597 at p 614 Also quoted by C. Turpin, *British Government and the Constitution* London: Butterworths: 1995 p 310.
[102] F Jacob, *The Sovereignty of Parliament: The European Way: The Hamlyn Lectures* (Cambridge, Cambridge University Press, 2006) p 5.
[103] ibid.

to take place.[104] EU membership remains a highly divisive issue. Scotland and N. Ireland voted to remain and it is highly likely that this will trigger further debate about Scotland's independence. EU membership for some is inextricably interwoven with the ultimate ideal of a Federal state.[105] For others membership has become the twenty-first century prophets warning against Leviathan and reaching for the exit cannot come soon enough.[106] Measuring the impact of leaving the EU and the status of the legislation[107] that comes from Europe will be the subject of much analysis over the coming years.

The full implications of the *Factortame* litigation are still being assessed today often better informed with the benefits of hindsight and a greater understanding of the history of accession and the CFP. The failure of CFP is clear from the need for more effective and robust policy making especially in consideration of environmental sustainability and fish stocks. Quota-hopping remains a general problem along with the challenges of managing limited fish stocks. It is arguable that if the UK withdrew from the EU fisheries management might become more effective, although the merits of the arguments are under active consideration in the negotiations in the run up to the referendum on EU membership in 2016/ 2017.[108] The dominance of Scottish vessels in the fishing sector should not be underestimated. Currently, Scottish vessels make up over 60% of UK fish landings and Scotland might benefit most from the elimination of EU vessels after Brexit. Joint stocks are shared with Norway and the Faroes, and also Denmark. This would put Scotland at the heart of the debate about what to do about fishing. A major question to be resolved is whether or not the UK would allow foreign ships access to the Exclusive Economic Zones defined as 200 miles off the coast. If this was agreed then the UK[109] would have to establish a very close relationship with the EU. If foreign ships were excluded this would leave the UK with the potential for the loss of fishing rights outside the UK.

The Merchant Shipping Act 1988 holds lessons for the way UK legislation is drafted and the development of policy making. The law was eventually consolidated but not codified under the Merchant Shipping Act 1995 after support from the Law Commission, but it remains technical and in need of a more comprehensive review. Since 1989 the approach to analysing and adapting EU law has measurably improved. The European Scrutiny Committee (ESC) provides an

---

[104] House of Commons Library: *The Economic impact of EU membership on the UK* SN/EP/6730 (17 September 2013).
[105] ibid.
[106] J McLean, *Searching for the State in British Legal Thought* (Cambridge, Cambridge University Press, 2012) p 310.
[107] House of Commons Library: *How much legislation comes from Europe?* Research paper 10/62 (13 October 2010).
[108] House of Commons Library, Briefing Paper Number 7213, *Exiting the EU policy areas* (4 June 2015).
[109] House of Commons: Briefing Paper Number 07213 *Exiting the EU: impact in key UK policy areas* (12 February 2016).

assessment of the legal and political importance of EU documents and keeps the law, procedures and institutional developments under review.[110] Pre-legislative scrutiny and post-legislative scrutiny is used regularly to assess and analyse the drafting of Bills and the implications of legislation.[111] Experience of European Directives and regulations has improved and the Treaty of Lisbon provides an opportunity for national parliaments to be engaged in much needed consultation.

On judicial power and approaches to interpretation the *Factortame* litigation has dramatically empowered judicial discretion. The British Constitution, throughout its history has been forced to change, even when least expected and often as a result of societal pressure and territorial loyalty.[112] The *Factortame* litigation certainly clarified the view that unequivocally UK law had to be read in a way that is consistent with EU law, even if this means disregarding part of an Act of Parliament.[113] It has given rise to the disapplication principle of domestic law when it is impossible to resolve any conflict with EU law. Member States have a general duty under the Treaty to ensure the proper application of EU law and this obligation applied to the UK courts when a breach of EU law was involved leaving the courts a 'very narrow' discretion not to quash a decision that was inconsistent with EU law. The boundaries of that discretion are always going to be a matter of dispute and interpretation as Lord Carnwath noted in the Supreme Court in *Walton v The Scottish Ministers*[114] it is a matter for judicial oversight. The direction and discretion that would be taken is hard to predict. The UK Supreme Court's approach is that the surrender to EU law is derived from Parliament, that this may be altered and that fundamental constitutional principles retain authority embedded in the common law and cover many constitutional 'instruments'.[115]

On constitutional change in general, since *Factortame*, the UK has experience of the devolution settlements of Scotland, Wales and Northern Ireland and London within the on-going debate about being 'British' in the UK. This is currently in the context of an on-going debate and referendum on Scotland's independence in September 2014. The Human Rights Act 1998, incorporating the European Convention on Human Rights, has markedly changed perceptions about rights and citizenship. Regional and local issues filter their way to the surface and the relevance of the sovereignty and ambit of the Westminster Parliament appears distant and irrelevant for many.

---

[110] The Department of the Clerk of the House of Commons, *The European Scrutiny System of the House of Commons* April 2010.
[111] House of Commons Library, *Pre-legislative scrutiny under the Coalition Government* SN/PC/5859 (4 June 2013).
[112] S Jenkins, *A Short History of England* (London: Profile Books, 2011).
[113] *Berkeley v Secretary of State for the Environment* [2000] UKHL 36 [200] Env LR.1.
[114] *Walton v The Scottish Ministers* [2012] UKSC 44 (17 October 2012).
[115] Neuberger and Mance in *R (HS2 Action Alliance Ltd.,) and others v Secretary of State for Transport* [2014] UKSC 3 para 207: The constitutional instruments include: 'Magna Carta, the Petition of Rights 1628, the Bill of Rights and in (Scotland) the Claim of Rights Act 1689, the Act of Settlement 1701, the Act of union 1707, the European Communities Act 1972, the Human Rights Act (HRA) 1998 and the Constitutional Reform Act 2005'.

On relations with Europe and issues of sovereignty the *Factortame* litigation provides a clear acceptance by the UK courts of the primacy of European law. Debates remain about the implications for the UK Parliament and the ultimate power to terminate the application of the European Communities Act 1972. The courts have embraced their role by following the jurisprudence of the European Court of Justice and in so doing are bound by the case law of the Court on the primacy of European law. Looking to the future Con O'Neill observed in the Summer of 1969 before negotiations on accession in 1972 had begun:

> The European game has become professional. Its adepts are not impressed by players who keep their head in the air instead of their eyes on the ball.[116]

The legacy of the *Factortame* litigation will live on within the EU itself long after the UK has exited. Once the UK has withdrawn from the EU it would very much depend on what has been negotiated as to future relations. The UK would have to consider how best to adjust to the consequences of exit and how much of the rights and obligations deriving from the Treaties would remain in place. Exercising management control over fishing is likely to set many difficult challenges for the negotiations over the precise meaning of Brexit.

---

[116] C O'Neill, (1969) 'Reality and illusion' *European Review* XIX, n 3 pp 4–5.

7

M v The Home Office [1992]: Ministers and Injunctions

CHRISTOPHER FORSYTH[1]

I. Introduction

One noteworthy aspect of the administration of justice in England[2] is how little coercion is used, especially in litigation against public authorities. If a judge decides in favour of the claimant then it is taken for granted that that finding will take effect (subject to any appeal) and the authorities would obey the law as found by the judge. Every day in the Administrative Court one can thus see public authorities in all their multitudinous forms—Ministers of the Crown, local authorities, police forces, regulatory bodies, etc—accepting without complaint or hesitation the discipline of the rule of law.[3] Here one sees in operation Dicey's principle that with us '… every official, from the Prime Minister down to a constable or a collector of taxes, is under the same responsibility for every act done without legal justification as any other citizen … ',[4] but without any coercion.

This ingrained fidelity to the rule of law partly explains the shock that struck the legal profession when it was held at first instance in *M v The Home Office*[5] that Ministers of the Crown could not be coerced into obeying the law.[6] The first instance judge[7] said this:

> reluctant though any court must be to proclaim the Crown beyond the reach of its ultimate coercive power … [the court recognises] that when it comes to the enforcement of

---

[1] I would like to thank my sometime student, Benjamin Mak, who rendered exemplary service as a research assistant in the writing of this chapter.
[2] And indeed in many other jurisdictions where the rule of law flourishes.
[3] One should not overlook the criticism that it has been alleged that officials sometimes contrive events to make legal challenges more difficult. See C. Harlow (1994) 'Accidental Loss of an Asylum Seeker' 57 MLR 620.
[4] AV Dicey, *Law of the Constitution* London: MacMillan, 9th ed 1950, p 194.
[5] The first instance judgment is reported in [1992] 4 All ER 97 and see [1992] COD 11; *The Times*, 5 August 1991; *The Independent*, 6 August 1991.
[6] Not all were shocked. D Wheately considered that 'the previously accepted wisdom as that Ministers of the Crown represented the Crown and like it, were immune from the orders of judges whose own appointments were derived from the Monarch. … .Judges like bishops should keep away from politics and leave it to those who have been elected' Law Society Gazette Number 8, 26 February 1994, p 2.
[7] Simon Brown J (as he then was); the words cited come from p 114 of the All ER report.

its decisions the relationship between the executive and the judiciary must, in the end, be one of trust. [If the Crown fails to be true to its obligations] it will be answerable to Parliament. It is not, then, given to the courts to exercise the power of punishment.

Could this be right: a Minister of the Crown could disobey the law and the only possible sanction he would face would be criticism in Parliament, the effectiveness of which would depend not upon law but on the vagaries of politics?

It would indeed have been 'a black day for the rule of law' if this first instance judgment had stood. But in fact it did not. The Court of Appeal (with one Lord Justice dissenting)[8] found that 'ministers of the Crown and civil servants are liable to be proceeded against for contempt of court in respect of acts or omissions by them personally and that it is no defence that what would otherwise constitute a contempt of court was committed in the discharge or purported discharge of their official duties'.[9] And when the matter went on appeal to the House of Lords, their Lordships unanimously upheld the majority of the Court of Appeal and held that the courts had power to enforce the law by injunction or contempt proceedings against a Minister of the Crown in his official capacity. Anything else, said Lord Templeman, would mean that the executive obeyed the law only 'as a matter of grace and not as a matter of necessity'.[10] Lord Woolf in a *tour de force* supplied the detailed technical reasoning. In the words of Professor Wade the rule of law was put 'back on the rails'.[11]

II. A Tangled Tale: How It All Came About

While a collective sigh of relief may be breathed by students of administrative law that the rule of law was set back on the rails much remains to be said about the case.[12] The rule of law has long been a fundamental principle of the Constitution; how did it come to be so threatened as late as May 1991 when, as we shall see, a Minister disobeyed a High Court order? What were the errors that were made by some very eminent jurists that led to that threat? And what conceptual confusion remains, even after *M*, that needs to be sorted out? Could similar confusion return?

---

[8] The lead judgment was delivered by the Master of the Rolls (Lord Donaldson MR), Nolan LJ concurring and McCowan LJ dissenting. The Master of the Rolls's judgment contains the phrase 'a black day for the rule of law'.
[9] *M. v The Home Office* [1992] 2 WLR 73 (CA), 97H (Lord Donaldson MR).
[10] *M. v The Home Office* [1993] 3 WLR 433, 437H (Lord Templeman).
[11] *The Times* 17 August 1993.
[12] The case is much commented upon. Here is an incomplete list of case notes: T Allan, (1994) 53 Cambridge 1; I Ward, (1994) 6 International Journal of Refugee Law 194; Adam Tomkins, (1994–1995) p 5 KCLJ 150. See in addition *The Nature of the Crown: A Legal and Political Analysis* Oxford University Press, 1999, eds M Sunkin and S. Payne in particular the contrasting chapters by W Wade (Ch 2) and M Loughlin (Ch 3) and the Overview by Sunkin and Payne (Ch 3).

Before we turn to these questions the facts of the case should be explained. These are complicated. There were two applications for judicial review involved (the first of which was appealed to the Court of Appeal) and, subsequently, an application to commit the Home Secretary for contempt of court. It was only the contempt of court application that went to the House of Lords. But, as will be explained, *M v The Home Office* is about much more than contempt of court. In particular it has much wider application particularly to judicial review.

A. The Refusal of Asylum and the Judicial Review of that Decision

The story started this way:[13] M was a 24 year-old school teacher from Zaire who arrived in the UK on 23 September 1990 and immediately claimed asylum. After several interviews he was informed on 11 March 1991 in a letter from the Immigration and Nationality Department of the Home Office that he was refused asylum. M based his claim for asylum on his role in Zaire in organising 'anti-government strike action amongst his fellow teachers' which had led to his arrest and imprisonment and ill-treatment while imprisoned. With the assistance of a sympathetic prison guard he escaped from the prison in Kinshasa and fled (as a stowaway on a cargo plane) to Nigeria where he obtained a fake Nigerian passport and an air-ticket to the UK. But the Home Secretary found his claim incredible pointing to the absence of documentary evidence to corroborate what M said and internal inconsistencies. So his credibility was doubted.

It was this refusal of asylum that *M* sought to challenge in his first judicial review proceedings. He applied for leave (as permission was then known) but his application was refused by the first instance judge after an oral hearing on 25 March 1991. Meanwhile his supporters arranged for him to be 'examined by an organisation called the Medical Foundation for the Care of Victims of Torture' which reported on 12 April 1991 that *M*'s tale of his experiences in prison was confirmed 'innumerable times'[14] by others imprisoned in Zaire (later the Democratic Republic of the Congo (DRC)) and that scars that *M* bore on his body confirmed part of his tale of his ill-treatment. And he suffered from several other medical problems, physical and psychological. This report was disclosed to the Home Office on 30 April just 24 hours before *M* was due to be removed to Zaire namely at 6pm on 1 May. So on the morning of 1 May a renewed application for leave to appeal was launched before the Court of Appeal now aware for the first time of the urgency of the matter.

The Court of Appeal interrupted its usual work and heard the renewed application on the afternoon of 1 May. But having heard argument and given full

---

[13] This account is based on that given by Lord Donaldson MR in the Court of Appeal and that of Lord Woolf in the House of Lords. The quoted passages come from Lord Donaldson MR's judgment.
[14] Report of V Tonge quoted by Lord Donaldson MR.

consideration to the application the Court gave judgment refusing the application. This was the end of the first application for judicial review.

B. The Second Application for Judicial Review and the Removal of M

M, still held in Pentonville, now changed his solicitors;[15] and the new solicitors launched the second application for leave to apply for judicial review (on different grounds). Since it was by now outside usual court hours the application was made to the duty judge in Chambers.[16] This second application for leave to apply for judicial review was made at 5.30pm on 1 May. In retrospect it can be seen that the case on the different grounds was weak.[17] But the judge (Garland J) faced with the impending removal of M had no time to study the documents thoroughly. And he was only able to order a stay of the proceedings if he had granted leave.[18] In these circumstances 'Garland J. did what any judge would have done': he sought an undertaking from counsel for the Home Office that M. would not be removed until he had decided whether to grant leave. He thought that he had obtained such an undertaking and 'on that basis' did not grant leave but adjourned the application. But it is clear that counsel had no instructions to give such an undertaking and did not think that he had done so. This seems to have been a genuine misunderstanding, but as will be seen Garland J thought that an undertaking had been given and acted accordingly. But the Home Office thought that the judge had only requested that M not be removed.

After Garland J rose (at 5.50pm) the Home Office made an effort to disembark M but its efforts were marred by error—Terminal 3 was phoned but the plane on which M was by now embarked was at Terminal 4. This error was criticised in the Court of Appeal.[19] In any event, the message did not get through and the plane with M aboard took off at 6.47pm for Paris; later that evening he changed planes in Paris and flew on to Kinshasa. Strenuous representations made to the Home

---

[15] This seems to have been instigated by Medical Foundation for the Care of Victims of Torture. The new solicitors were Messrs Winstanley-Burgess.

[16] Lord Donaldson MR subsequently remarked in the Court of Appeal that 'if further grounds were to be urged, [the application] should have been to this court and not to the judge in chambers. The further ... application to Garland J. was in law an abuse of the process of the court, but in saying this I am seeking to make the position clear for the future rather than criticising those who were making "agony of the moment" decisions'.

[17] It seems to have been based on the fact that, if returned to Nigeria, M would not be dealt with in a convention compliant way; but M was being removed to Zaire.

[18] See *R v Secretary of State for Education and Science ex parte Avon CC* [1991] 1 QB 558 (CA); W Wade and C Forsyth, *Administrative Law* (11th ed) p 558.

[19] 'I do not regard what occurred as reflecting any credit whatsoever upon the Home Office. There should have been established lines of communication enabling the Home Office to cancel the departure of would-be immigrants in their custody at the shortest possible notice before take-off. It is a disgrace if there were not. If there were it is a disgrace that they were not used' (Lord Donaldson MR).

Office by *M*'s solicitor and also to a Minister of State by an MP to bring *M* back from Paris were to no avail. This failure was also the subject of criticism in the Court of Appeal.

C. Garland J Orders the Return of M

Learning of *M*'s removal and the subsequent onward transfer from Paris, Mr Burgess (*M*'s new solicitor) approached Garland J and secured from him (first over the telephone) and then in writing (written in manuscript by the judge from his home at 1.15am on the morning of 2 May) a mandatory order in these terms:

> Whereas at 1755 hours on Wednesday 1st May 1991, on an application to the Judge in Chambers for leave to move for judicial review of the determination that [M.] was not entitled to the status of refugee, Counsel for the Home Office (Mr. Richard Gordon) on instructions undertook to the court that [M.] would not be removed from the United Kingdom to Zaire pending an adjourned application for leave to move for judicial review so soon as possible on Thursday 2nd May 1991;
>
> And whereas the said undertaking was embodied in the order of the Court adjourning the said application; and whereas it appears to the court that the said undertaking has been breached by the removal of [M.];
>
> Upon hearing Mr. David Burgess, Solicitor, on behalf of the said [M.]
>
> It is ordered that the Secretary of State for the Home Department by himself, his servants or agents do forthwith procure that
>
> 1. The said [M.] be returned within the jurisdiction of this court, and further that:
> 2. Pending the return of the said [M.] he be kept in the care of the servants or agents of the Secretary of State and/or of the servants or agents of Her Majesty's Government in Zaire: until further order herein.
> 3. That the Secretary of State be at liberty to apply to vary or discharge this order at 10.30 a.m. on Thursday 2nd May 1991.
> 4. Costs reserved. 2nd May 1991. (Mr. Justice Garland).

This order was faxed to the Home Office at 1.40am. The Home Office duty officer asked the FCO duty officer to arrange for the return of *M* from Zaire on the next available flight and to protect him in the interim. Although there were further delays in communicating with the Embassy in Zaire, the upshot was that once the message got through to the Embassy, *M* was booked on a flight returning at 9.00pm on the evening of 2 May. The Zairian authorities displayed no 'hostility towards or indeed interest in' him.

D. The Home Secretary Agrees to Disobey Garland J's Order

Meanwhile there were developments in London. The Home Office could not make an application to vary or discharge the order at 10.30am on 2 May (they struggled to contact their lawyers in the middle of the night) but they sent a message to the judge saying that they wished to make such an application and would do so as soon as possible. The instructions of the Home Secretary were sought but this was not possible until late in the afternoon. But until then 'it could have been said that officials and [the junior minister] had done everything possible to remedy the situation, once the Home Office had appreciated ... .[that the judge] believed that he had received an undertaking not to remove M from the jurisdiction and had subsequently issued an order for M's return and safe custody meanwhile'. But at a meeting held at 4pm that afternoon with the Home Secretary, the junior minister (Minister for Immigration), senior civil servants and a lawyer from the Home Office's legal department as well as others, the lawyer advised that Garland J 'had exceeded his powers in making an order that [M] should be returned directly from Zaire'. There was concern that if M was returned 'it would be extremely difficult to remove him if, as expected, [the Home Office] won the case'. 'The Home Secretary fully supported the action taken and, subject to Treasury Solicitor's advice, agreed in the present circumstances that [M] should not be returned to Britain.' The Home Secretary later explained[20] that he was influenced by the assurance he received that the underlying decision that M's asylum claim was ill founded was right and the 'legal advice (subsequently confirmed by Treasury Counsel) was to the effect that the order of Mr Justice Garland J was made without jurisdiction'.

Although the Home Secretary stressed that it was never suggested to him that he was in contempt of court (and he apologised to the court if he was) what is undeniable is that here Ministers and officials agreed not to obey a court order of which they were fully made aware by the High Court, a court of unlimited jurisdiction. This was the crucial point in the whole saga; this was the point at which the rule of law was clearly breached by the Minister. The point is worth stressing: because the High Court is a court of unlimited jurisdiction, it can never act outside its powers. An order of the High Court, be it ever so unreasonable or even contrary to law is never invalid. It is valid (and has to be obeyed) until it is set aside or overturned on appeal. We may call this failure to recognise the status of an Order of the High Court, 'Error One'.

A word should be added about the advice of Treasury Counsel that took the rare form of Counsel (Mr John Laws, afterwards Lord Justice Laws) advising the Minister directly in conference (at 5.15pm on 2 May). This was to the effect the Home Office should take the opportunity at the 'earliest practicable time' to challenge Garland's J order but 'in the meantime the Home Office might reasonably hold its hand'. M's flight back to the UK was cancelled. M was informed in Kinshasa that he was no longer required to attend court proceedings in London and he left the airport. And his subsequent fate is lost to history.[21]

---

[20] In an affidavit made for the Court of Appeal proceedings.
[21] The Embassy was unable to contact him on the phone numbers he had left with them. He subsequently contacted his solicitors from Nigeria but has not been heard from since. If still alive he would (in 2016) be 50 years old.

E. The Order is Set Aside

At 9.00am on 3 May Mr Laws for the Home Office duly applied for the order made at 1.15am on 2 May to be set aside. The basis of the application was that Garland J had erred in law in that he had overlooked the holding by the House of Lords in *R v Secretary of State for Transport,* ex parte *Factortame Ltd (No. 1)*[22] that interim relief (such as that provided for in Garland's J order) was not available against Ministers of the Crown. Once this was drawn to his attention the judge was persuaded that he should not have granted interim relief against the Minister and set the order aside.

F. Proceedings for Contempt of Court Against the Home Secretary Commence

And so *M* remained in Africa and the second judicial review was abandoned. But the drama had not ended; indeed it had barely begun. On 7 May 1991 proceedings for contempt of court were begun in the High Court on behalf of *M*. The alleged contempt consisted both of a failure to comply with Garland's J order and breach of the undertaking given to the court. The alleged contemnors consisted of the Home Secretary, the Minister for Immigration and three Home Office officials but at first instance 'the only charges which were maintained were those against the Home Office and the Home Secretary'. This then was the context in which Simon Brown held that 'he had no power to find either the Home Office or the Home Secretary to be in contempt'.

III. Putting the Rule of Law 'back on the rails': Part One Proceedings for Contempt of Court

M v The Home Office was not directly concerned with any application for judicial review. It concerned instead proceedings for contempt and the simple question posed was whether ministers could be liable for contempt of court when they disobeyed court orders. The argument that ministers could not be answerable for such conduct can been seen to be based upon a simple but crucial conceptual error: the conflation of Ministers of the Crown with the Crown itself.

---

[22] [1989] UKHL 1 and [1990] 2 AC 85.

A. The Simple Solution

The Crown is indeed immune from proceedings in its own courts,[23] so an injunction cannot be issued nor can a finding of contempt be made against the Crown. But the vast majority of statutory powers and duties are conferred upon designated ministers not upon the Crown; and Ministers have, or should have, no immunity. Once this is recognised and set right the difficulties of *M v The Home Office* largely disappear. Servants of the Crown, as opposed to the Crown itself, ought to be liable to injunctions as much as to other legal remedies. Questions remain over the immunity of the Crown itself. We may call the failure to recognise the distinction between Ministers of the Crown (who enjoy no immunity) and the Crown (which is immune), 'Error Two'.

This distinction between the Crown and its Ministers was recognised in the past. And it was not unprecedented for coercive relief in the form of an interim injunction to be issued against a Minister. For instance in *Ellis v Earl Grey*[24] an interim injunction was in fact made against the Prime Minister. And there are other decisions to like effect.[25] While there might be difficulties with some of the reasoning in *Ellis v Earl Grey*[26] (regarding injunctions) the position is much better established as far as mandamus and prohibition were concerned. There are many examples where the duty in question was owed to the public and is vested in the Minister 'then orders of prohibition and mandamus were granted regularly against the Minister'. In *R. v The Commissioners of Customs and Excise, ex parte Cook*[27] Lord Parker said:

> It is sometimes said as a general proposition that mandamus will not lie against the Crown or an officer or servant of the Crown. I think we all know in this day and age that that as a general proposition is quite untrue. There have been many cases, of which the most recent is *Padfield v Minister of Agriculture, Fisheries and Food* [1968] AC 997 in which a mandamus was issued to a Minister. Indeed, that has always been the case, as can be seen since as long ago as 1850 when in *Reg v Commissioners of Woods, Forests, Land, Works and Buildings, ex parte Budge* (1850) 15 QB 761, Frederick Thesiger expressed the proposition in argument in this form, at p 768: 'Whenever a person, whether filling an office under the Crown or not, has a statutory duty towards another person, a mandamus will lie to compel him to perform it.

Once then it is recognised that there is a distinction to be drawn between a Minister of the Crown and his statutory duties and the Crown itself, the position

---

[23] 'No suit or action can be brought against the king, even in civil matters, because no court can have jurisdiction over him': Bl. Comm. i. 242.
[24] [1833] 6 Sim n 214.
[25] For instance, *Rankin v Huskisson* [1830] 4 Sim p 13; [1901] *Tamaki v Baker* AC p 561; *A-G of New South Wales v Trethowan* [1932] AC 526; *Conseil des Ports Nationaux v Langlier* [1969] SC 60 (Can).
[26] See 450H (Lord Woolf's speech).
[27] [1970] 1 WLR 450 at n 455.

becomes clear. The Crown itself is immune but Ministers of the Crown are not. There are important questions about the survival of Crown Immunity. The personal immunity of Her Majesty—so that the Queen could drive her Rolls Royce at 100mph down the Mall without being called to account before the Horseferry Road Justices—is probably tolerable. But if the immunity of the Crown extends to what may broadly be terms 'the government', ie decisions taken generally and not just by ministers in the exercise of their legal powers then the question is more problematical.

The simple distinction between the Crown (which enjoys immunity) and Ministers (who do not) was somewhat befuddled at the time *M* was decided. First there is the confusion wrought by misunderstanding the Crown Proceedings Act 1947, Section 21.

B. The Crown Proceedings Act 1947, Section 21

At first sight Section 21(2) appears to provide that Ministers do in fact shelter under the Crown's immunity. But close regard must be had to Section 21 which, omitting irrelevant words, is in these terms:

(1) In any civil proceedings by or against the Crown the court shall, subject to the provisions of this Act, have power to make all such orders as it has power to make in proceedings between subjects, and otherwise to give such appropriate relief as the case may require:

Provided that:

(a) where in any proceedings against the Crown any such relief is sought as might in proceedings between subjects be granted by way of injunction or specific performance, the court shall not grant an injunction or make an order for specific performance, but may in lieu thereof make an order declaratory of the rights of the parties; and

(b) in any proceedings against the Crown for the recovery of land or other property the court shall not make an order for the recovery of the land or the delivery of the property, but may in lieu thereof make an order declaring that the plaintiff is entitled as against the Crown to the land or property or to the possession thereof.

(2) The court shall not in any civil proceedings grant any injunction or make any order against an officer of the Crown if the effect of granting the injunction or making the order would be to give any relief against the Crown which could not have been obtained in proceedings against the Crown.

It is undeniable that Section 21(2) appears to prohibit the making of orders against an officer of the Crown (such as a Minister) if the effect of that order would be to give relief against the Crown 'which could not have been obtained in proceedings against the Crown'. This appears to make it clear that coercive relief was not available against Ministers. If this apparent reading of Section 21(2) is right the Crown Proceedings Act 1947 does indeed place Ministers above the law.

The central argument here is that the law in this area has been 'bedevilled for many years by misunderstanding'[28] of Section 21(2). Correctly understood, it applies only to protect the Crown's own immunity, and does not alter the personal liability of a minister or official who commits a wrong or who misuses a power conferred upon him in his own name. The supposition that Section 21(2) should be interpreted so as to prevent injunctions or other coercive relief issuing against a Minister when she was exercising powers entrusted by law to her may be called 'Error Three'.

C. 'Error Three' Corrected in the House of Lords

In the crucial part of his speech in *M v The Home Office*, Lord Woolf said this:

> There appears to be no reason in principle why, if a statute places a duty on a specified minister or other official which creates a cause of action, an action cannot be brought for breach of statutory duty claiming damages or for an injunction, in the limited circumstances where injunctive relief would be appropriate, against the specified minister personally by any person entitled to the benefit of the cause of action. If, on the other hand, the duty is placed on the Crown in general, then Section 21(2) would appear to prevent injunctive relief being granted, but as Professor William Wade has pointed out (*Injunctive Relief against the Crown and Ministers* [1991] 107 L.Q.R. 4, n 4–5) there are likely to be few situations when there will be statutory duties which place a duty on the Crown in general instead of on a named minister. In broad terms therefore the effect of the Act can be summarised by saying that it is only in those situations where prior to the Act no injunctive relief could be obtained that Section 21 prevents an injunction being granted. In other words it restricts the effect of the procedural reforms that it implemented so that they did not extend the power of the courts to grant injunctions. This is the least that can be expected from legislation intended to make it easier for proceedings to be brought against the Crown.

So this is the vital point: Section 21(2) was designed to ensure that the immunity of the Crown from injunctions should not be sidestepped by injuncting an officer of the Crown. For example, since an injunction could not be issued to prevent Her Majesty exceeding the speed limit down the Mall, neither could the keeper of the keys be ordered by injunction not to hand the car keys to Her Majesty! But it did not extend the immunity of the Crown to Ministers of the Crown. This conceptual recognition of the distinction between Ministers and the Crown has long been advanced and defended by Wade, being sensitive as he was to the consequences for the rule of law if this distinction was not upheld.

Perhaps the correct position can be summed up in the words of Wade:

> ... correctly understood, [Section 21(2)] applies only to protect the Crown's own immunity, and does not alter the personal liability of a minister or official who commits a wrong or who misuses a power conferred upon him in his own name. For example, take

---

[28] Wade and Forsyth, 11th ed 703.

the provision of the European Communities Act 1972 that 'Her Majesty may by Order in Council, and any designated minister or department may by regulations, make provision' for implementing Community obligations, subject to the restriction (among others) that no tax may thereby be imposed. If an Order in Council attempted to impose a tax, no injunction could be granted either against the Crown or against a tax-collecting official since to restrain the latter would stultify the immunity of the former. But if a designated minister made regulations to the same effect, he or his officials could be restrained by injunction since that would not be to give relief against the Crown. This is the vital distinction ... between the Crown, which is immune, and ministers and Crown servants, who are not.[29]

This passage from Wade corrects the interpretation of Section 21(2)—so setting 'Error Three' right—and then goes on to fit this proposition into the general distinction between Ministers of the Crown and the Crown—thus setting 'Error Two' right.

D. Merricks v Heathcote Amory

Now the error—'Error Three'—in *Merricks v Heathcote Amory*,[30] the case that commenced the confusion over Section 21(2), can be plainly seen. The case concerned a dispute over a proposed scheme to regulate the marketing of potatoes made under the Agricultural Marketing Acts, 1931 to 1949. The Acts required the scheme to be laid in draft before both Houses of Parliament for approval. The plaintiff (claimant) alleging that the draft scheme was ultra vires and void sought a mandatory injunction against the Minister both as an individual and as the Minister of Agriculture, Fisheries and Food restraining him, in either capacity, from seeking approval from either House.

The plaintiff from the outset accepted that, if the Minister was acting as 'a representative of the Crown' Section 21(2) precluded relief against him. But the plaintiff contended that he was not so acting but was acting as a person designated by Section 1 of the Act of 1931 to perform these duties, or alternatively, in a purely individual capacity. But it was held that 'the Minister in carrying out or proposing to carry out his functions under Section 1 of the Act of 1931 and in dealing with the scheme was acting as a representative or officer of the Crown, so that an injunction would not lie'.[31] This reasoning is clearly marred by 'Error Two'.

Once more it is Lord Woolf that corrects the error. He comments as follows on *Merricks*:

Upjohn J.'s approach appears to treat a duty placed upon a named Minister as being placed upon the Government as a whole ... [This approach] would mean that the Act of 1947 had the surprising effect of treating the wrongful act of a named Minister as being

---

[29] Wade and Forsyth, 704 (footnotes omitted).
[30] [1955] Ch 567.
[31] Wording drawn from the head note.

that of the Crown so that the Minister could no longer be sued personally in tort or for injunctive relief. Thus while the outcome of the *Merricks* case was correct, the reasoning of Upjohn J. was incorrect, if and in so far, by his remarks which have been cited, he was seeking to suggest that a Minister when acting in his official capacity could not be sued personally and an injunction granted. In any event his remarks could have no application to proceedings for the prerogative orders or judicial review which he was not considering.

Lord Woolf's judgment is a tour de force through the technicalities of Crown immunity. Vitally it restricts Section 21(2) to its proper role and recognises the importance for the rule of law of the distinction between Ministers of the Crown and the Crown. The injunction requiring the return of *M* had been properly made and it was a contempt of court for the Home Secretary not to procure his return. As already mentioned, Professor Wade remarked *M v The Home Office* 'put the rule of law back on the rails'.[32] But much remains to be said.

IV. Putting the Rule of Law 'back on the rails': Part Two Judicial Review and the Coercion of Ministers

M v The Home Office concerned proceedings for contempt and the finding that Ministers did not enjoy Crown Immunity and so might be answerable for contempt does not have a direct effect on the availability of coercive relief against Ministers in judicial review proceedings. This stance is strengthened by the fact that it is plain that the Crown Proceedings Act 1947 did not apply to proceedings for judicial review.[33] Thus the Section 21(2) argument considered above—whose rejection is crucial to the outcome in *M*—is simply not applicable in judicial review. None the less *M v Home Office* has had a profound effect on the development of the law of coercive relief against Ministers in judicial review. This was because in *Factortame Ltd. v Secretary of State for Transport*[34] the House of Lords had held that the courts had no jurisdiction to grant interim injunctions against

---

[32] (*The Times* 17 August 1993).

[33] As Lord Woolf explained: 'The language of Section 23 [of the 1947 Act] makes it clear that Part II of the Act does not generally apply to all proceedings which can take place in the High Court. In particular, it does not apply to the proceedings, which at that time would have been brought for prerogative orders. If there is any doubt about this, that doubt is removed by the general interpretation provisions of the Act contained in Section 38, Section 38(2) providing: 'In this Act, except in so far as the context otherwise requires or it is otherwise expressly provided, the following expressions have the meanings hereby respectively assigned to them, that is to say: 'Civil proceedings' includes proceedings in the High Court or the county court for the recovery of fines or penalties, but does not include proceedings on the Crown side of the [Queen's] Bench Division.' Proceedings for the prerogative orders were brought on the Crown side.'

[34] [1990] 2 AC 85.

the Crown in judicial review proceedings[35] and overruled two decisions to the contrary effect.[36]

The nub of the House of Lords reasoning in *Factortame* was that:

> injunctions had not been available in Crown side proceedings prior to 1947 and the effect of Sections 21(2) and 23(2)(b)[37] of the Crown Proceedings Act 1947 had been to preserve that position; that Parliament had not, by Section 31(2) of the Senior Courts Act 1981, intended to confer jurisdiction on the court to grant injunctions against the Crown in proceedings for judicial review and RSC, Ord 53, r 1(2) could not have extended the jurisdiction of the court in that respect; and that, accordingly, RSC, Ord 53, r 3(10)(b) did not enable an interim injunction to be granted in judicial review proceedings against the Crown.[38]

This reasoning needs to be unpacked a little. Clearly the House of Lords had fallen into the conceptual error of failing to recognise the distinction between the Crown and Ministers of the Crown, ie 'Error Two'. And while the former might be immune from coercive proceedings the latter were not. For the reasons given in *M* and described above it was simply wrong to suppose that prior to the 1947 Act 'injunctions had not been available in Crown side proceedings prior to 1947'.

Moreover, it seems also to be wrong to suppose 'that Parliament had not, by Section 31(2) of the Senior Courts Act 1981 intended to confer jurisdiction on the court to grant injunctions against the Crown in proceedings for judicial review'. As we shall see in Section 31(2) Parliament had in fact said just that.

> So where did *Factortame* go wrong? The starting point is Section 31(2) of the Senior Courts Act 1981 which provides that in an application for judicial review a declaration may be made or an injunction granted ... any case ... [where] the High Court considers that, having regard to—the nature of the matters in respect of which relief may be granted by orders of mandamus, prohibition or certiorari; the nature of the persons and bodies against whom relief may be granted by such orders: and all the circumstances of the case it would be just and convenient for the declaration to be made or the injunction to be granted ...

Having regard to the prerogative relief that can be granted against Ministers as we have seen, the availability of the declaration and injunction seems to follow. Moreover, as Lord Woolf remarked in *M*:

> In Section 31 the jurisdiction to grant declarations and injunctions is directly linked to that which already existed in relation to the prerogative orders .... It has never been

---

[35] As Bridge said in *Factortame*: 'the true position is that Parliament has not provided for the grant of interim relief against the Crown in judicial review' (at 124).

[36] *R v Licensing Authority* ex parte *Smith Kline & French Laboratories Ltd (No 2)* [1990] 1 QB 574 and *R v Governor of Pentonville Prison* ex parte *Herbage* [1987] QB 872.

[37] Section 23(2)(b) reads as follows: '... any reference in this Part of this Act to civil proceedings against the Crown shall be construed as a reference to the following proceedings only:—(b) proceedings for the enforcement or vindication of any right or the obtaining of any relief which, if this Act had not been passed, might have been enforced or vindicated or obtained by an action against the Attorney General, any Government department, or any officer of the Crown as such; ... and the expression 'civil proceedings by or against the Crown' shall be construed accordingly'.

[38] Westlaw head note.

suggested that a declaration is not available in proceedings against a Minister in his official capacity and if Order 53 and Section 31 apply to a Minister in the case of declarations then, applying ordinary rules of construction, one would expect the position to be precisely the same in the case of injunctions.

As an examination of the position prior to the introduction of judicial review indicates, because of the scope of the remedies of mandamus and prohibition the availability of injunctions against Ministers would only be of any significance in situations where it would be appropriate to grant interim relief ....

As Lord Woolf pointed out, Lord Bridge in *Factortame* acknowledged that 'the question at issue depends, first, on the true construction of Section 31' and that if Section 31 'were to be construed in isolation' there would be 'great force in the reasoning' that Section 31 did enable injunctions to be granted for the first time against Ministers of the Crown in judicial review proceedings.[39] Why then did Lord Bridge come to the conclusion that an injunction could not be granted against a Minister in proceedings for judicial review?

In Lord Woolf's view this was because Lord Bridge had not realised that permitting interim injunctions to be made against Ministers was not:

> a dramatic departure from what was the position prior to the introduction of judicial review for an injunction to be available against the Crown or a Minister of the Crown .... [Moreover, his] conclusion was not ... based on as comprehensive an argument of the history of both civil and prerogative proceedings as was available to your Lordships. In particular he did not have an account of the developments which had taken place in the granting of prerogative orders against Ministers, which meant that in practical terms the only consequence of treating Section 31 as enabling injunctions to be granted against Ministers acting in their official capacity would be to provide an alternative in name only to the orders of prohibition and mandamus which were already available and to allow interim relief other than a stay for the first time. A further reason was his reliance upon *Merricks*, which as we have seen "should be approached with caution".[40]

Lord Woolf concluded that Lord Bridge had put forward:

> a very closely and carefully argued justification for adopting a narrow approach to the effect of Section 31 of the Senior Courts Act 1981. It deserves very careful attention coming, as it does, from a judge who is acknowledged to have made an outstanding contribution to this area of the law. Nonetheless, I do not regard it as justifying limiting the natural interpretation of Section 31 so as to exclude the jurisdiction to grant injunctions, including interim injunctions, on applications for judicial review against

---

[39] 143–9.

[40] Lord Bridge was also influenced by the fact that the new Ord 53 was introduced following the Law Commission's Report on Remedies in Administrative Law (1976) (Law Com n 73) (Cmnd 6407), which drew attention to the problem created by the lack of jurisdiction to grant interim injunctions against the Crown and recommended that the problem should be remedied by amending s 21 of the 1947 Act. The report included a draft of the legislation proposed. This proposal of the Law Commission was never implemented. Instead the decision was taken following the Law Commission's Report to proceed by amendment of the Rules of the Supreme Court rather than by primary legislation.

Ministers of the Crown ... I am, therefore, of the opinion that, the language of Section 31 being unqualified in its terms, there is no warrant for restricting its application so that in respect of Ministers and other officers of the Crown alone the remedy of an injunction, including an interim injunction, is not available. In my view the history of prerogative proceedings against officers of the Crown supports such a conclusion. So far as interim relief is concerned, which is the practical change which has been made, there is no justification for adopting a different approach to officers of the Crown from that adopted in relation to other respondents in the absence of clear language such as that contained in Section 21(2) of the 1947 Act. The fact that in any event a stay could be granted against the Crown under Ord.53, r. 3(10), emphasises the limits of the change in the situation which is involved. It would be most regrettable if an approach, which is inconsistent with that which exists in Community Law should be allowed to persist if this is not strictly necessary. The restriction provided for in Section 21(2) of 1947 does, however, remain in relation to civil proceedings.

V. The Enforcement of Injunctions against Ministers: Why Have no Ministers Been Sent to Gaol?

We have seen above that it is now clear that interim relief, ie interim injunctions are available against Ministers. When an injunction is made—but not obeyed—then proceeding for contempt of court is the usual sanction. The contempt jurisdiction is thus of great importance.

But in the last analysis the House of Lords' judgment in *M v Home Office* contains an inconsistency about enforcement.[41] According to Lord Templeman, 'the courts are armed with coercive powers' against ministers and officials.[42] On the other hand, according to Lord Woolf, 'the Crown's relationship with the courts does not depend on coercion' and 'the object of the exercise is not so much to punish an individual as to vindicate the rule of law by a finding of contempt' leaving it to Parliament to determine the consequences.[43] But it was made clear that in the absence of personal wrongdoing Ministers would not be punished for contempt: 'The very fact of making such a finding would vindicate the requirements of justice' said Lord Woolf.

Lord Woolf is doubtless right that in most cases it will be sufficient to vindicate the rule of law to make the finding of contempt. But it is not clear why ministers should be treated differently from other officials who may undeniably be punished for contempt. As *M v Home Office* itself shows, ministers do not invariably respect

---

[41] The account in the next paragraph is drawn from that of Wade and Forsyth in *Administrative Law* (11th ed) at 703–6.
[42] At 705. Examples concerning ministers are *Bhatnager v Minister of Employment and Immigration* [1990] 71 DLR (4th) 84; *State of Victoria v Australian Building Federation* [1982] 152 CLR 25.
[43] *M. v Home Office* (above) at 425.

orders of the court, and just how coercive such orders really are in various situations may be in issue on future occasions. Ultimately it is the executive power, which has to enforce court orders, whose efficacy against the government thus depends in a sense upon the government's willingness to police itself.[44]

Some alternative modes of enforcement have been tried. When the Scottish Ministers were found to be in contempt[45] the First Division[46] ordered the attendance before it of two senior civil servants, one as a representative of the Scottish Ministers the other for his own failings in the events leading up to the contempt. The House of Lords held it would have been proper to make such orders (and even to order a minister to appear) had they been given proper notice and the reasons for the order and an opportunity to be heard.[47] But when civil servants in the Home Office deliberately failed to comply with an undertaking to release a detainee, the court simply made a finding of contempt against the Home Office[48] and remarked that 'apart from a finding of contempt there [is] … no other sanction potentially open to the court'.[49] No consideration was given it seems, to ordering the erring civil servants to attend court to account for their failings.

VI. The Scottish Dimension

In Scotland the law was, notwithstanding some doubts, that prior to the 1947 Act the courts had power 'to pronounce interdict and interim interdict against the Crown'.[50] In other words in Scottish Law the Crown was directly subject even to coercive remedies. That being the case there was little need in Scotland to draw the distinction sharply between the Crown and Ministers of the Crown that as we have seen is vital in England.[51] Much of the fuss and drama that attended *M v Home Office* would simply not arise in Scotland.

But Scotland had its own errors to make with a little help from the UK's Parliament in enacting the 1947 Act. That Act specifically provided (Section 42) that Section 21 was one of the sections of the Act that did apply in Scotland. Thus in Scotland, as in England, the court 'shall not in any civil proceedings grant any injunction or make any order against an officer of the Crown if the effect of

---

[44] As observed by Nolan, [1992] QB at 314.
[45] Prison authorities had interfered with prisoner's correspondence with legal representatives and the courts after undertaking not to do so.
[46] Of the Inner House of the Court of Session.
[47] *Beggs v Scottish Ministers* [2007] UKHL 3.
[48] *R (Lamari) v Home Secretary* [2012] EWHC 1895.
[49] Para 37 *Beggs* not referred to; exemplary damages and costs were for later consideration.
[50] Lord Justice Clerk (Ross) in *MacDonald v Secretary of State for Scotland* [1994] SC 234 at 238 and see Adam Tomkins, 'The Crown in Scots Law', 262ff at 272 in McHarg and Mullen (2006) (eds) *Public Law in Scotland*.
[51] But see *Beggs v The Scottish Ministers* [2005] SC 342.

granting the injunction or making the order would be to give any relief against the Crown which could not have been obtained in proceedings against the Crown'.

As we have seen Section 21(2) has no application in judicial review proceedings in England. This is because Section 38(2) defines 'Civil proceedings' as not including 'proceedings on the Crown side of the King's Bench Division'—what in modern jargon is the application for judicial review. But judicial review 'in Scotland is based on the supervisory jurisdiction of the Court of Session which has been exercised on a somewhat broader basis, to control not only public bodies but bodies which are private in nature'.[52] It has nothing to do with proceedings on the Crown side of the King's Bench Division and would naturally be thought of as a 'civil proceeding' and so within Section 21(2). It was held in *McDonald v Secretary of State for Scotland*[53] that an interdict would not issue against the Secretary to prevent the commission of a delict. Would the same apply to prevent coercive remedies against Ministers in Scottish judicial review proceedings? The answer given in *Davidson v Scottish Ministers* was no. The phrase 'civil proceedings' in Section 21(2) is read as not including 'proceedings invoking the supervisory jurisdiction of the Court of Session', ie judicial review proceedings.[54]

VII. Conclusion

Let us take stock. First 'Error One', viz, the failure to appreciate that because the High Court is a court of unlimited jurisdiction, it can never act outside its powers. Thus an order of the High Court, be it ever so unreasonable or even contrary to law, is never invalid. It is valid—and has to be obeyed—until it is set aside or overturned on appeal. This was the error made by the Home Secretary, albeit on advice from lawyers and civil servants, when he decided not to obey Garland J's Order. Here was the fundamental threat to the rule of law; officials decided that they might choose whether to obey the law or not. 'Error One' was not in terms set right but the finding of contempt against the Secretary of State makes it clear that it would now be an unwise counsel who advised a Secretary of State that he 'might reasonably stay his hand' as far as compliance with a court order was concerned.

Second, 'Error Two', viz, the failure to recognise the distinction between Ministers of the Crown who were liable to coercive remedies in respect of the exercise of their own legal powers and the Crown itself which remains, as it ever was, immune. This error too was a threat to the rule of law since the vast majority of the powers exercised by central government consist in powers entrusted by law

---

[52] Rodger in *Davidson v Scottish Ministers*, para 80.
[53] [1994] SC 234.
[54] *Davidson v Scottish Ministers* [2005] UKHL 74, para 33 (Nicholls) (prisoner held in allegedly non-Convention compliant conditions, seeking interim coercive relief).

to Ministers of the Crown. If these Ministers only obeyed the law 'as a matter of grace', the rule of law in truth did not reach into central government. But the acceptance by Lord Woolf of the long held views of Professor Wade that there was a 'vital distinction … between the Crown, which is immune, and ministers and Crown servants, who are not'[55] set this error right and constituted a triumph for the thought of Professor Wade.

Third there is 'Error Three', viz, the misinterpretation of Section 21(2) of the 1947 Act so that that section seemed to reinforce 'Error Two' by preventing coercive relief against Ministers even in the exercise of their own powers. Again it was the acceptance by Lord Woolf of the long held views of Professor Wade that ' …. correctly understood, [Section 21(2)] applies only to protect the Crown's own immunity, and does not alter the personal liability of a minister or official who commits a wrong or who misuses a power conferred upon him in his own name … '. This set this error right and constituted once more a triumph for the thought and analysis of Professor Wade.

Since Section 21(2) did not apply to the application for judicial review, 'Error Three' really had no significance for judicial review, the chief mechanism whereby the rule of law is imposed upon the executive. But this was to reckon without Lord Bridge in *Factortame*. Misled by *Merricks* and the brilliance of counsel; befuddled by 'Error Two' he interpreted Section 31 of the Senior Courts Act 1981 as influenced by Section 21(2). Once more Lord Woolf set all this right.

The saga of *M v Home Office* raises important questions. How could it come about that at such a late stage it could be thought—and so held by a judge—that Ministers only obeyed the law as a matter of grace? How could it come about that such a galaxy of legal talent could have made the errors detailed in what has been set out above? But it is not clear that these questions have crisp answers—other than at the abstract level that we are all prone to error and that errors made in the past (eg *Merricks* or *Factortame*) may cast long shadows that conceal injustice. But we can take some comfort from the fact that the errors identified above were, on the whole, set right. But not too much comfort for the threat to the rule of law came not only from a Minister who—on legal advice—decided not to obey a court order, but from judges who inadvertently, no doubt, fell into elementary constitutional error. The judiciary should be the reliable defender of the rule of law. In the end, with the decision of the House of Lords, it was. But before then the foundations rocked. The larger lesson surely is that the battle for the rule of law is never won but requires eternal vigilance.[56]

---

[55] Wade and Forsyth, 704 (footnotes omitted).
[56] *cf* 'eternal vigilance is the price we pay for liberty' attributed to Jefferson; see www.monticello.org/site/jefferson/eternal-vigilance-price-liberty-quotation.

8

A v Secretary of State for the Home Department [2005]: The *Belmarsh* Case

RICHARD CLAYTON

I. Introduction

The House of Lords' decision in *A v Secretary of State for the Home Department* is rightly regarded as a constitutional case of the highest importance.[1] The war on terror following the attack on the World Trade Centre in September 2001 created a febrile political backdrop to the case. In April 2004 the Home Secretary, David Blunkett, criticised the Special Immigration Appeal Commission's decision to release on bail one of the appellants in the case, who had been detained without trial because he was suspected of being a terrorist, as 'extraordinary', adding that others might call it 'bonkers'.[2] Against that background, a nine judge panel of the House of Lords addressed a number of difficult issues, demonstrating that the Human Rights Act 1998 (hereinafter HRA) had fundamentally recast basic public law principles. They examined the lawfulness of preventative detention without trial of non-nationals on national security grounds, a subject area where the English courts have traditionally been highly deferential to executive decision-making.[3] However, a challenge made under the HRA 1998 raised new legal possibilities, which went well beyond traditional administrative law principles, demonstrating that Parliament cannot insulate itself altogether from a legal challenge where Convention rights are, themselves, breached. As a result, Parliament decided to rewrite the legislation and to introduce a new regime to combat terrorists.

---

[1] [2005] 2 AC 68. Widely referred to as the *Belmarsh* case. Belmarsh being the prison in South East London in which the appellants were detained.
[2] *G v Secretary of State for the Home Department* S.C./2/2002, Bail Application SCB/10, 20 May 2004.
[3] See, eg, Simpson (1992) '*In the Highest Degree Odious: Wartime Detention without Trial*' Oxford University Press.

II. The Anti-Terrorism Crime and Security Act 2001

The immediate reaction of the British Government to terrorist destruction of the World Trade Centre on 11 September 2001 was a meeting of the Civil Contingencies Committee, a Cabinet committee chaired by the Home Secretary, which deals with major crises such as terrorism or natural disasters. After consulting with the two main opposition parties, Parliament was recalled on 14 September 2001. The Prime Minister, Tony Blair, then promised Parliament that there would be reviews of the extradition laws, the mechanisms of international justice, the link between terrorism and crime, and the sources of terrorist finance.[4] When Parliament was again recalled on 4 October 2001, the Prime Minister announced a legislative package addressing a variety of governmental concerns: extradition, the exclusion and removal of terrorist suspects, abuse of asylum and incitement to racial hatred.[5] On 15 October 2001 the Home Secretary told the Commons that, although the wholesale revision of existing anti-terrorism laws was not needed, specific and targeted measures required an emergency Bill.[6] The Prime Minister was eager to emphasise that the response was no 'knee-jerk' reaction,[7] and the Home Secretary said that he had thought 'long and hard ... [and] not rushed into these measures'.[8] The Home Secretary then announced he had taken every possible step to get the best legal advice before committing the Government to action.[9] He had begun reviewing extradition before 9 November,[10] and the Government decided to wait ten weeks before introducing its proposals to Parliament, wanting to get things right in terms of meeting the UK's international obligations.[11] The Chancellor of the Exchequer, Gordon Brown, next announced that financial measures against alleged terrorists reflected decisions by G7 finance ministers and central bank governors, as well as UN Security Council Resolutions.[12]

On 19 November 2001, two months after the terrorist attacks on New York, the Bill was put before Parliament. It was widely criticised being described as 'the most draconian legislation Parliament has passed in peacetime in over a century'.[13] Nevertheless, in opening the Second Reading debate, the Home Secretary thanked his advisers, officials and ministerial team for assistance, and indicated that the

---

[4] HC Debs, vol 372, col 606.
[5] ibid col 675.
[6] ibid col 923.
[7] ibid col 635.
[8] ibid col 928.
[9] ibid col 936.
[10] ibid col 923.
[11] ibid col 928.
[12] ibid cols 940–941.
[13] A Tomkins (2002) 'Legislating Against Terror: The Anti-Terrorism, Crime and Security Act 2001' Public Law pp 205–20.

decision-making process had been informed by the reports of the Joint Lords/Commons Select Committee on Human Rights, and the Home Affairs Committee.[14]

The 2001 Act covered a wide range of areas. Many of its measures were not specifically targeted at terrorism, and the Home Affairs Committee was critical of the swift timetable for such a long bill including non-emergency measures.[15] For example, the 2001 Act rewrote parts of the Terrorism Act 2000 relating to seizure of suspected terrorist assets,[16] gave new powers to Her Majesty's Customs and Excise and Inland Revenue to require the disclosure of information for law enforcement purposes,[17] substituted racially-aggravated with racially or religiously aggravated in some parts of the criminal law,[18] and made it illegal to deal in biological or chemical weapons, or set off a nuclear explosion, or to disclose information which might prejudice the security of any nuclear site or of any nuclear material.[19]

However, the key provisions in the 2001 Act, which the Court had, ultimately, to address in the case, were contained in Part 4 of the Act. Part 4 allowed the Home Secretary to certify any non-British citizen whom he suspected to be a terrorist and detain them indefinitely, pending deportation, even when such a deportation would otherwise be prohibited. Part 4 was enacted because of the impact of the European Court of Human Rights (ECtHR) decision in *Chahal v the United Kingdom* in 1996.[20] In *Chahal* the ECtHR decided that the absolute character of Article 3 of the European Convention of Human Rights (the prohibition of torture and inhuman treatment) meant that if deportation would lead to a risk of torture or inhuman treatment the deportation could not be justified, even when it was ordered to protect national security, Although the Immigration Act 1971 permits deportation of those who are a threat to national security for cases where there is insufficient admissible evidence for prosecution, the *Chahal* decision effectively meant that Article 3 prevented non nationals from being deported to another country—if the individual being deported could argue there were substantial grounds for believing that they would be subjected to torture or inhuman treatment in that country.

The British Government's opposition to the *Chahal* principle has been unremitting since it lost the case in 1996, but has consistently failed to shift the Strasbourg Court. In the important case of *Saadi v Italy*[21] in 2009 the Grand Chamber emphasised the absolute character of Article 3, despite the UK Government's intervention to challenge the decision in *Chahal*. Although the UK Government argument that *Chahal* caused many difficulties for the Contracting States by

---

[14] HC Debs, vol 375, cols 21–22.
[15] www.publications.parliament.uk/pa/cm200102/cmselect/cmhaff/351/35102.htm
[16] Pt 1 of the Act.
[17] Pt 2 of the Act.
[18] Pt 5 of the Act.
[19] Pts 6 to 8 of the Act.
[20] [1997] 23 EHRR 413.
[21] [2009] 49 EHRR 30.

preventing them from enforcing expulsion measures,[22] the Grand Chamber rejected this submission in robust terms,[23] stressing that:[24]

> As the prohibition of torture and of inhuman or degrading treatment or punishment is absolute, irrespective of the victim's conduct (see *Chahal v United Kingdom*), the nature of the offence allegedly committed by the applicant is therefore irrelevant for the purposes of Article 3 see *Indelicato v Italy*[25] and *Ramirez Sanchez v France*).[26]

The particular difficulty posed by *Chahal* for immigration detention purposes is that the common law power to detain individuals are limited to such time, as is reasonable, to enable the deportation process to be carried out.[27] On the face of it, therefore, the decision in *Chahal* prevented an individual from being returned to a country within a reasonable time where there was a substantial risk of Article 3 treatment. As a result, it is not possible under the Immigration Act 1971 to detain alleged terrorists on *Chahal* grounds even though they could not be removed from the UK. The Government recognised that continuing to detain an individual in these circumstances was incompatible with the right to liberty under Article 5 of the Convention.

Consequently, the Government decided to utilise the procedure under Article 15 ECHR to derogate from the Convention. Article 15 states:

> 1) In time of war or other public emergency threatening the life of the nation any High Contracting Party may take measures derogating from its obligations under this Convention to the extent strictly required by the exigencies of the situation, provided that such measures are not inconsistent with its other obligations under international law.
> 2) No derogation from Article 2, except in respect of deaths resulting from lawful acts of war, or from Articles 3, 4 (paragraph 1) and 7 shall be made under this provision.

The Government, therefore, proceeded to opt out of Article 5 altogether by derogating from the Convention on the ground that there was a 'state of emergency threatening the life of the nation' under Article 15 of the Convention.[28] This meant that the UK gave notice to the Secretary-General of the Council of Europe under Article 15 that, in the Government's view, Part 4 of the 2001 Act constituted a justified derogation from the rights of those detained under Article 5.

Nevertheless, individuals detained under Part 4 were entitled to challenge the lawfulness of this process—their detention, by appealing to the Special Immigration Appeals Commission (SIAC), the judicial body created in 1997 following the

---

[22] ibid paras 117–123.
[23] ibid paras 137–141.
[24] ibid para 127.
[25] Judgment, 18 October 2001 para 30.
[26] Judgment, 4 July 2006 paras 115–116 (GC).
[27] Under the principles set out in *Hardial Singh* [1984] 1 WLR 704 approved by the Supreme Court in *R Lumba v Secretary of State for the Home Department* [2012] 1 AC 245.
[28] Section 30(1) of the 2001 Act.

Chahal decision.²⁹ The SIAC is chaired by a High Court judge, who sits with two other members who have been vetted by the security services and who have experience of security matters. Because the SIAC has the same status as the High Court and is a 'superior court of record' it is not amenable to judicial review by the High Court, although an appeal lies on a point of law to the Court of Appeal (Civil Division) and, with leave, to the House of Lords and now the Supreme Court.

But the powers of the SIAC are limited. On an appeal, it could cancel a certificate if it considered that there were no reasonable grounds for believing a detainee to be a suspected international terrorist, or if it considered that, for some other reason, the certificate should not have been issued.³⁰ On a review, the SIAC could cancel the certificate only if it considered that there were no reasonable grounds for the relevant belief or suspicion.³¹ In proceedings before the SIAC, ordinary evidence is heard in the presence of the appellant and his or her legal advisers. 'Closed' evidence from sensitive security sources can be received without disclosure to the appellant or his or her legal team. A 'special advocate' may be appointed to represent the appellant's interests, but must not communicate with the appellant after receiving the closed evidence. In practice, the special advocate procedure makes it difficult if not impossible for the special advocate to take proper instructions from an appellant or to make adequate representations, and this procedure has been strongly criticised.³²

On 13 November 2001 the derogation order came into force,³³ the derogation order was renewed by Parliament on 3 March 2003 without a vote, and renewed on 3 March 2004 with a vote. The Order was eventually repealed on 8 April 2005.³⁴ Between November 2001 and April 2005 the Government claimed that there existed in the UK a state of public emergency threatening the life of the nation, within the meaning of Article 15(1) of the Convention.

---

²⁹ Under the Special Immigration Appeals Act 1997.
³⁰ Section 25(2)(3) 2001 Act.
³¹ Section 26(5) 2001 Act.
³² See, eg the House of Commons Constitutional Affairs Committee paper *The Operation of the Special Immigration Appeals Tribunal and the use of Special Advocates* [2005] HC 323-1. In June 2009 a nine judge panel of the Supreme Court in *Secretary of State for the Home Department v AF (No 3)* [2010] 2 AC 269 applied the judgment of the Grand Chamber in *A v United Kingdom*, the Strasbourg sequel to the *Belmarsh* case, [2009] 49 EHRR 625 (see below), and held that while it might be appropriate, in the interests of national security in the context of combating terrorism, not to disclose sources of evidence on which the grounds for suspecting a person's involvement in terrorism-related activity were based, a controlee had to be given sufficient information about the allegations against him to enable him to give effective instructions to his special advocate in relation to them. So long as that requirement was satisfied, there could be a fair hearing without the need for detailed disclosure of the sources of evidence on which the allegations were based. However, where the disclosed material consisted of only general assertions and the case against the controlee was based solely or to a decisive extent on undisclosed materials the requirements of a fair trial under Article 6 would not be satisfied. See, in particular, the submissions of the special advocates made n *AF (No 3)* at para 334–335 identifying the difficulties faced by special advocates.
³³ Under the Human Rights Act 1998 (Designated Derogation) Ord 2001 SI 2001 n 3644 and The Human Rights Act 1998 (Amendment n 2) Ord 2001 SI 2001/4032.
³⁴ The Human Rights Act 1998 (Amendment) Ord 2005 SI 2005/1071.

III. The Human Rights Act (HRA) 1998

Before looking at the *Belmarsh* case itself, it is important to sketch out the implications of the HRA 1998 for the challenge the detainees chose to make.

The standard administrative law principles to which public bodies must comply where a decision is attacked on its merits are not onerous to satisfy. Because of the principle of separation of powers, it is no part of the judicial review to substitute the opinion of the judiciary or of individual judges for that of the authority constituted by law to decide the matters in question.[35] The standard of irrationality that a claimant must overcome to win a *Wednesbury* challenge is a very high one, the decision maker must reach a decision which no reasonable decision maker could make.[36] In contrast, the HRA 1998 calls for a very different perspective. The HRA 1998 gives effect to rights under the European Convention on Human Rights (ECHR) and is widely recognised as a statute of constitutional significance: the Convention is effectively our Bill of Rights by giving effect to Convention rights expressed in positive terms,[37] so that a rational decision may, nevertheless, breach Convention rights.[38]

More particularly, the HRA 1998 provides a legal route for claimants to challenge legislation, including primary legislation, which is said to breach Convention rights. Under the strong rule of construction created by Section 3 of the HRA 1998, legislation must be interpreted so far as possible to give effect to Convention rights. If, however, a Section 3 construction is not possible, then a senior court[39] is entitled to make a declaration of incompatibility under Section 4. The Government may then use a fast track procedure to remove the incompatibility by laying a draft remedial order before Parliament, by way of delegated legislation under the affirmative resolution procedure. In practice, successive governments have addressed declarations of incompatibility by making remedial orders. The upshot is that under the HRA 1998 the detainees were able to mount a full blooded

---

[35] *Chief Constable of The North Wales Police v Evans* [1982] 1 WLR 1155, per Hailsham 1160.

[36] *Associated Provincial Picture Houses Ltd v Wednesbury Corp* [1948] 1 KB 223

[37] See, eg the dicta in *Brown v Stott* [2003] 1 AC 681 of Lord Bingham at p 703 and Lord Steyn at p 708 and those of Woolf in *R v Offen* [2001] 1 WLR 253, 275. Similarly, in *McCartan Turkington Breen v Times Newspapers* [2001] 2 AC 277, 297 Lord Steyn said that the HRA was a constitutional measure designed to buttress freedom of expression, fulfilling the function of a Bill of Rights in our legal system. In *R (Laporte) v Chief Constable of Gloucestershire Constabulary* [2007] 2 AC 105 para 34. Lord Bingham described the HRA 1998 in giving effect to Articles 10 and 11 as representing a 'constitutional shift'.

[38] As a result for example, in the gays in the military case, *Smith v United Kingdom* [2000] 29 EHRR 493 the ECtHR concluded in relation to the domestic proceedings at [1996] QB 517 at para 138 that 'the threshold at which the High Court and the Court of Appeal could find the Ministry of Defence policy irrational was placed so high that it effectively excluded any consideration by the domestic courts of the question of whether the interference with the applicants' rights answered a pressing social need or was proportionate to the national security and public order aims pursued, principles which lie at the heart of the court's analysis of complaints under Article 8 of the Convention'.

[39] As defined by Section 4(5) of the HRA.

challenge not only against a decision of the Home Secretary under Part 4 of the 2001 Act to certify that a non-British national was a suspected terrorist but also against Part 4 itself and the derogation order.

A. The Belmarsh Case

Between 2001 and 2003 16 foreign nationals had been detained and held using these powers at HM Prison Belmarsh in South-East London. Eight were detained in December 2001, one in February 2002, two in April 2002, one in October 2002, one in November 2002, two in January 2002 and one in October 2003. One further individual was certified but detained under other powers. Of the total detained, two have voluntarily left the UK. The other 14 remained in detention as of 18 November 2003.[40]

On 30 July 2002 the SIAC upheld a challenge by the detainees.[41] There were two issues for the SIAC to decide. First, assuming that the measures breached Article 5, was the derogation from Article 5 lawful? Secondly, did the measures discriminate unjustifiably against the detainees on the ground of their nationality or immigration status?

On the first point, the SIAC decided that the UK had been entitled to derogate from the Convention under Article 15. Although no other signatory to the Convention had derogated from any obligation in it because of terrorist activities by or linked to Al Qa'ida, the SIAC accepted that each State had to look to its own situation, and that the material disclosed showed that the UK was akin to the US as an appropriate target for terrorist acts. The SIAC, therefore, found that the material before it justified the Government's conclusion that there did exist a public emergency threatening the life of the nation within the terms of Article 15, and the closed material confirmed that view. The SIAC drew attention to the fact that the powers in the 2001 Act were focussed exclusively on foreign nationals. However, the Attorney-General contended that this was justified, because the evidence showed that foreign nationals constituted 'the predominant source of the threat', and the SIAC accepted that the elected government's conclusion as to how best to achieve its legitimate aim was entitled to a degree of deference.

Nevertheless, the SIAC went on to decide that the powers of the 2001 Act could only be properly confined to non nationals in the UK if the security threat came almost exclusively from them. However, the SIAC found that the evidence demonstrated, beyond argument, that the threat was not confined solely to aliens. There were many British nationals already identified—mostly in detention abroad—who fell within the definition of 'suspected international terrorists', and it was clear the Government believed many others at liberty in the UK were also suspected international terrorists. The SIAC therefore held that the derogation

---

[40] HC Deb, 18 November 2003, col 27.
[41] [2002] HRLR 45.

was discriminatory on the grounds of national origin, contrary to Article 14 of the Convention. The upshot was that the detentions breached the detainees' Convention rights under the HRA 1998, and the SIAC made a declaration of incompatibility under Section 4 of the HRA 1998. However, in its judgment The SIAC felt constrained to observe that its decision might be of little use to the detainees, should Parliament decide to deal with the discrimination by extending the power of detention to nationals.

On 25 October 2002 the Court of Appeal reversed the SIAC's decision.[42] The decision of the Court of Appeal is important for present purposes because of its highly deferential approach to the issues in the case. Thus, Lord Woolf expressed the view in relation to the complaint that it was discriminatory to treat nationals and aliens differently that:[43]

> Whether the Secretary of State was entitled to come to the conclusion that action was only necessary in relation to non-national suspected terrorists, who could not be deported, is an issue on which it is impossible for this court in this case to differ from the Secretary of State. Decisions as to what is required in the interest of national security are self-evidently within the category of decisions in relation to which the court is required to show considerable deference to the Secretary of State because he is better qualified to make an assessment as to what action is called for.

Furthermore, Lord Woolf concluded that the Home Secretary was detaining the claimants no longer than necessary—before they could be deported or until the emergency was resolved, or when they cease to be a threat to the safety of the country. Lord Woolf also found that the Home Secretary's conclusion could be objectively justified.[44]

Brooke LJ took a similar approach; and set out principles he derived from Lord Hoffmann's analysis in *R v Secretary of State for Home Department ex p Rehman*.[45] In *Rehman* Lord Hoffmann took the view that the question of whether something is in the interests of national security is not a question of law for the courts to review, but one of judgment and policy for the executive alone, and went on to say that the terrorist attacks in the US on 11 September 2001 underlined what he called 'the need for the judicial arm of government to respect the decisions of ministers of the Crown on the question of whether support for terrorist activities in another country constitutes a threat to national security'. Respect should be accorded to the executive for two reasons: first, because 'only the executive has access to special information and expertise in these matters' and, secondly, because such decisions 'require a legitimacy which can be conferred only ... through the democratic process'. As a result, Brooke LJ said:

> 1) When there is an appeal to the Commission it is the Home Secretary, not the Commission, who is the principal decision-maker. 2) It must be remembered that the Home

---

[42] [2004] QB 335.
[43] ibid para 40.
[44] ibid para 52.
[45] [2003] 1 AC 153 at paras 57–58 and 62.

Secretary has the advantage of a wide range of advice from people with day-to-day involvement in security matters which the Commission cannot match. 3) Because what is at issue is an evaluation of risk, an appellate body traditionally allows a considerable margin to the original decision-maker. It should not ordinarily interfere with a case in which the Home Secretary's view is one which could reasonably be entertained. 4) Even though a very different approach may be needed when determining whether an appellant's Article 3 rights are likely to be infringed, this deferential approach is certainly required in relation to the question whether a deportation is in the interests of national security. 5) Although the Commission has the express power to reverse the exercise of a discretion, they should exercise restraint by reason of a common-sense recognition of the nature of the issue and of the differences in the decision-making processes and responsibilities of the Home Secretary and the Commission. 6) The events of 11 September are a reminder that in matters of national security the cost of failure can be high. Decisions by ministers on such questions, with serious potential rights for the community, therefore require a legitimacy which can be conferred only by entrusting them to persons responsible to the community through the democratic process.

The detainees then appealed to the House of Lords, which eventually assembled a special nine judge panel—rather than the usual five—to hear the case on account of its constitutional importance. The sensitivity of the appeal to the House of Lords was obvious from the outset, and in September 2004 the Treasury Solicitors (on behalf of the Government) wrote to the Senior Law Lord, Lord Bingham, suggesting that Lord Steyn should be recused from hearing the appeal since (they alleged) he had expressed a view on the central issue in the appeal in his lecture, 'Guantanamo Bay: the Black Legal Hole'.[46] Lord Goldsmith, the Attorney-General continues to maintain that the Government was right to maintain the challenge in the light of the *Pinochet* case,[47] whereas Lord Steyn is quite adamant that it was inappropriate for the Government to make the application to recuse him.[48]

IV. The Issues before the House of Lords

The issues that were argued out before the House of Lords can be summarised as follows:

(1) whether the derogation from Article 5 made under Article 15 was lawful;
(2) whether there was a 'public emergency threatening the life of the nation';

---

[46] [2004] ICLQ 53 1 where Lord Steyn said 'In my view the suspension of Article 5 of the European convention on human rights—which prevents arbitrary detention—so that people can be locked up without trial when there is no evidence on which they could be prosecuted is not in present circumstances justified'.
[47] *R v Bow Street Metropolitan Stipendiary Magistrate ex p Pinochet* [2000] 1 AC 119.
[48] A Paterson (2013), *Final Judgment The last Law Lords and the Supreme Court* Hart Publishing, at 302.

(3) whether the measures were 'strictly required by the exigencies of the situation'; and
(4) whether Part 4 of the 2001 Act was compatible with the prohibition of discrimination in Article 14.

A. Whether the Derogation from Article 5 Made under Article 15 was Lawful

The Attorney-General conceded on behalf of the Government that the detention violated the right to liberty under Article 5, unless the right was interpreted restrictively in the light of a valid derogation and all the Law Lords accepted that this concession was rightly made.[49] The Attorney-General also conceded, and all the Law Lords (except Lord Scott) accepted, that the validity of the derogation order[50] depended on whether it could be shown that the Government met the substance of Article 15(1) of the Convention.

However, Lord Scott was probably correct to doubt that the Government's concession was rightly made.[51] He pointed out that Article 15 does not form part of domestic law in the UK, because it is not a 'Convention right' listed in Section 1 and Schedule 1 of the HRA 1998. He took the view that a derogation order had no legal effect domestically but merely shows that measures had been deliberately rather than inadvertently enacted in a form that was inconsistent with a Convention right.

The House of Lords then went on to consider Article 15(1), which required the Government to establish the following:

(1) the existence of a public emergency threatening the life of the nation;
(2) the measures being strictly required by the exigencies of the situation; and
(3) the measures being consistent with the UK's other international obligations.

B. Whether there was a 'Public Emergency Threatening the Life of the Nation'

The majority decided that, in the light of the ECtHR case law and the nature of the large-scale terrorist attacks which had occurred, the lack of any specific threat

---

[49] However, the A-G made the concession solely for the purposes of that litigation only, keeping open the possibility of arguing before the ECtHR, if necessary, that the 2001 Act was compatible with Art 5, even without reference to a derogation.

[50] Made under made under s 14 of the HRA 1998.

[51] Lord Scott was rightly distinguishing between Convention rights taking effect as (i) statutory rights under the HRA 1998 and as (ii) international rights under the Convention, a distinction which Lord Nicholls later emphasised in *In re McKerr* [2004] 1 WLR 807, para 25 and which played a prominent role in *In re G (Adoption: Unmarried Couple)* [2009] 1 AC 38 in the reasoning of Lord Hoffmann at para 33 and of Baroness Hale at para 117. But see Professor Feldman's case comment where he argues the contrary: ECL Review 2005, paras 531–552.

of an immediate attack did not invalidate the assessment that there was a risk of terrorist attack at some unspecified time. They took the view that, since such an assessment was pre-eminently political in character and had been made by the executive and Parliament, great weight was to be accorded by the courts to their judgement. They, therefore, held that the SIAC had examined full evidence, was not shown to have misdirected itself and had reached a view open to it. The SIAC's conclusion was, accordingly, unimpeachable.

However, Lord Hoffmann memorably dissented in an opinion which strongly contrasts with the views he expressed in *Rehman*, where he added a post script in the following terms:[52]

> I wrote this speech some three months before the recent events in New York and Washington. They are a reminder that in matters of national security, the cost of failure can be high. This seems to me to underline the need for the judicial arm of government to respect the decisions of ministers of the Crown on the question of whether support for terrorist activities in a foreign country constitutes a threat to national security. It is not only that the executive has access to special information and expertise in these matters. It is also that such decisions, with serious potential results for the community, require a legitimacy which can be conferred only by entrusting them to persons responsible to the community through the democratic process. If the people are to accept the consequences of such decisions, they must be made by persons whom the people have elected and whom they can remove.

By contrast, in the *Belmarsh* case Lord Hoffmann took a different approach:

> 95) The question is whether such a threat is a threat to the life of the nation. The Attorney-General's submissions and the judgment of the Special Immigration Appeals Commission treated a threat of serious physical damage and loss of life as necessarily involving a threat to the life of the nation. But in my opinion this shows a misunderstanding of what is meant by 'threatening the life of the nation'. Of course the Government has a duty to protect the lives and property of its citizens. But that is a duty which it owes all the time and which it must discharge without destroying our constitutional freedoms. There may be some nations too fragile or fissiparous to withstand a serious act of violence. But that is not the case in the United Kingdom. When Milton urged the government of his day not to censor the press even in time of civil war, he said: 'Lords and Commons of England, consider what nation it is whereof ye are, and whereof ye are the governours'
>
> 96) This is a nation which has been tested in adversity, which has survived physical destruction and catastrophic loss of life. I do not underestimate the ability of fanatical groups of terrorists to kill and destroy, but they do not threaten the life of the nation. Whether we would survive Hitler hung in the balance, but there is no doubt that we shall survive Al-Qaeda. The Spanish people have not said that what happened in Madrid, hideous crime as it was, threatened the life of their nation. Their legendary pride would not allow it. Terrorist violence, serious as it is, does not threaten our institutions of government or our existence as a civil community.

---

[52] [2003] 1 AC 153 at para 62.

97) For these reasons I think that the Special Immigration Appeals Commission made an error of law ...

However, Lord Hoffmann immediately went on to reach a conclusion, which was, equally, striking:

> Others of your Lordships who are also in favour of allowing the appeal would do so, not because there is no emergency threatening the life of the nation, but on the ground that a power of detention confined to foreigners is irrational and discriminatory. I would prefer not to express a view on this point. I said that the power of detention is at present confined to foreigners and I would not like to give the impression that all that was necessary was to extend the power to United Kingdom citizens as well. In my opinion, such a power in any form is not compatible with our Constitution. The real threat to the life of the nation, in the sense of a people living in accordance with its traditional laws and political values, comes not from terrorism but from laws such as these. That is the true measure of what terrorism may achieve. It is for Parliament to decide whether to give the terrorists such a victory.

C. Whether the Measures were 'Strictly Required by the Exigencies of the Situation'

The eight Law Lords who considered this question held that the burden was on the Secretary of State to convince the courts that the measures were strictly required. However, their approaches differed in other respects. Lord Bingham, with whom Lord Carswell agreed, equated strict necessity with proportionality.[53] Lord Walker, by contrast, said that irrationality and disproportionality were separate grounds of challenge from 'strictly required', although there was 'a considerable degree of overlap'.[54] The views expressed by the others were less clear.

Lord Bingham in his leading opinion applied a structured proportionality test, as it was then understood.[55] He asked (i) whether there was a legislative objective sufficiently important to justify limiting a fundamental right, (ii) whether the measures were rationally designed to meet the legislative objective, and (iii) whether the means used were no more intrusive on rights than necessary to achieve the legitimate objective. He pointed out that the detainees' argument contained seven propositions.[56]

---

[53] Above, para 30 and 240.
[54] ibid para 195.
[55] In *Huang v Secretary of State for the Home Department* [2007] 2 AC 1 at para 19 Lord Bingham added the fourth requirement to the earlier three he analysed in this case, that the Court must always involve the striking of a fair balance between the rights of the individual and the interests of the community which is inherent in the whole of the Convention. The severity and consequences of the interference will call for careful assessment at this stage.
[56] Above, para 31.

He first observed that Part 4 of the 2001 Act was designed to remove the problems posed by *Chahal* in relation to deporting and detaining foreign terrorists in the immigration system. Second, the public emergency said to justify the derogation was the Al-Qaeda threat. Third, that threat did not result solely from the activities of foreign nationals subject to UK immigration control. The SIAC had found this as fact, and its finding could not be contradicted in view of the public statements the Government made. Fourth, Sections 21–23 of the 2001 Act were not rationally related to the Al-Qaeda threat, because (i) the regime did not cover UK nationals who represented an Al-Qaeda threat, (ii) it allowed supposedly dangerous foreigners to go abroad freely (the 'prison with three walls'), and (iii) the measures were not expressed to be limited to Al-Qaeda. Although the Government contested this proposition, Lord Bingham found this was the correct position in point of fact. Furthermore, in relation to (iii) the Government had offered an undertaking that the powers would be used only against those suspected international terrorists who were suspected of having links with Al-Qaeda, but Lord Bingham held that the courts must not allow the protection of fundamental rights to be dependent on concessions, undertakings or implications in legislation.[57] Fifth, the Government had not shown why measures being used to contain the Al-Qaeda threat from suspected UK nationals could not have been used equally well against foreign nationals. Sixth, Lord Bingham held that the right to liberty is fundamental, and any restriction of it must attract strict scrutiny by the judges.

The Attorney-General responded to this strict scrutiny submission by asserting the orthodox position that the executive was entitled to a wide discretionary area of judgment in national security matters, and argued that there was a danger of judicial supremacy over democratic decision-makers if the judges applied a standard of strict scrutiny to such decision. Lord Bingham emphatically rejected this approach—in dicta, which firmly anchor the HRA 1998 in its constitutional setting:

> the appellants are in my opinion entitled to invite the courts to review, on proportionality grounds, the Derogation Order and the compatibility with the Convention of Section 23 and the courts are not effectively precluded by any doctrine of deference from scrutinising the issues raised. It also follows that I do not accept the full breadth of the Attorney-General's submissions. I do not in particular accept the distinction which he drew between democratic institutions and the courts. It is of course true that the judges in this country are not elected and are not answerable to Parliament. It is also of course true … that Parliament, the executive and the courts have different functions. But the function of independent judges charged to interpret and apply the law is universally recognised as a cardinal feature of the modern democratic state, a cornerstone of the rule of law itself. The Attorney-General is fully entitled to insist on the proper limits of judicial authority, but he is wrong to stigmatise judicial decision-making as in some way undemocratic. It is particularly inappropriate in a case such as the present in which Parliament has expressly legislated in Section 6 of the 1998 Act to render unlawful any act of a public authority, including a court, incompatible with a Convention right, has required courts

---

[57] ibid para 33.

(in Section 2) to take account of relevant Strasbourg jurisprudence, has (in Section 3) required courts, so far as possible, to give effect to Convention rights and has conferred a right of appeal on derogation issues. The effect is not, of course, to override the sovereign legislative authority of the Queen in Parliament, since if primary legislation is declared to be incompatible the validity of the legislation is unaffected (Section 4(6)) and the remedy lies with the appropriate minister (Section 10), who is answerable to Parliament. The 1998 Act gives the courts a very specific, wholly democratic, mandate. As Professor Jowell has put it 'The courts are charged by Parliament with delineating the boundaries of a rights-based democracy' ('Judicial Deference: servility, civility or institutional capacity?').[58] See also Clayton, 'Judicial deference and 'democratic dialogue': the legitimacy of judicial intervention under the Human Rights Act 1998'.[59]

This approach led Lord Bingham, finally, to conclude that in the light of such strict scrutiny, neither the Derogation Order nor Sections 21 and 23 of the 2001 Act could be justified since Part 4 of the Act could not withstand scrutiny under Article 15(1) of the Convention.

Lord Nicholls agreed that under the HRA 1998 Parliament had imposed responsibility on the courts to make these assessments. The right of aliens to liberty is just as important as that of UK nationals. Wholly exceptional circumstances would be required to justify the indefinite detention of either.[60] Lord Walker, on the other hand, dissented. Lord Hope agreed that the right to liberty is fundamental, and said that in cases affecting liberty the margin of discretion or discretionary area of judgment is narrower than in relation to other rights.[61] Lord Scott said that Section 23 of the 2001 Act derogated from rights in a very extreme way. As the Secretary of State had not shown that less extreme measures would not have sufficed, the measures taken had not be shown to be strictly required.[62] Lord Rodger took the view that the words 'strictly required' forced the judges to compare the treatment of foreign nationals with that of UK nationals.[63] He thought that the Court of Appeal had been wrong to consider that the SIAC had decided that the measures were strictly required. Lady Hale, agreed with Lords Bingham, Nicholls, Hope, Scott and Rodger;[64] she said that there was no sense in locking someone up then allowing him to go voluntarily to a foreign country where he was almost immediately released, as had happened to one of the detainees. In her view, this showed that it had not been necessary to lock up either foreign nationals or UK nationals for security reasons.[65]

---

[58] [2003] Public Law 592, 597.
[59] [2004] Public Law 33.
[60] ibid paras 81, 84.
[61] ibid para 106–108.
[62] ibid para 155.
[63] ibid para 168.
[64] ibid para 219.
[65] ibid paras 230–231.

D. Whether Part 4 of the 2001 Act was Compatible with Article 14

The UK could have derogated from prohibition against discrimination under Article 14 of the Convention, but had chosen not to do so when derogating from the Convention. The House of Lords, therefore, had to consider whether detention under the 2001 Act was compatible with Article 14, bearing in mind that, as Lord Bingham said, treating like cases alike is a basic principle of democratic constitutions and is also a general axiom of rational behaviour.[66]

The Law Lords expressed different views concerning whether the detainees had been subject to different treatment on an illegitimate ground under Article 14 which states:

> The enjoyment of the rights and freedoms set forth in this Convention shall be secured without discrimination on any ground such as sex, race, colour, language, religion, political or other opinion, national or social origin, association with a national minority, property, birth or other status.

Lord Bingham held that both nationality and immigration status fall within the words 'or other status' under Article 14. Weighty reasons would be needed to justify treating people differently on the ground of their nationality.[67] Lords Hope, Scott and Baroness Hale all rejected the Attorney-General's argument that the relevant comparators for foreign nationals who were suspected international terrorists were foreign nationals who were not suspected international terrorists, who were equally liable to be detained pending removal.

The House of Lords also decided that the difference of treatment was justified as having a rational and objective justification, that it had a legitimate state aim and was proportionate. Lord Bingham accepted that the aim was to prevent international terrorism. The justifiability of differential treatment caused by the measures had to be assessed in the light of that aim.[68] Different treatment on the basis of nationality or immigration status may be justified in the context of controlling immigration, but not where the aim is related to security, since the threat to security did not depend on a person's nationality or immigration status.[69] Lords Hope, Scott and Rodger took similar views.[70] Lord Bingham also rejected the argument that imprisoning UK nationals as well as foreign nationals would have been worse than just imprisoning foreign nationals. Any discriminatory measure affects one group more than another, but cannot be justified on the ground that it would have been worse to impose the measure on everybody.[71] On the other hand, Baroness Hale, instead of upholding a proportionality complaint, decided that the difference

---

[66] ibid para 46 quoting Lord Hoffmann in *Matadeen v Pointu* [1999] 1 AC 98, at p 109.
[67] *Gaygusuz v Austria* [2006] 23 EHRR 364.
[68] *Belgian Linguistic Case (No 2)* [1968] 1 EHRR 252, para 10.
[69] ibid para 54.
[70] ibid paras 138, 158 and 190 respectively.
[71] ibid para 68.

of treatment did not serve a legitimate aim: because it could not be said to be rationally related to the aim—of combating terrorism. A democracy values everyone equally, and it would not be right to lock up only gay, black, disabled or female suspected international terrorists; no more can it be right to lock up only foreign ones.[72]

V. The House of Lords' Decision

The House of Lords made a declaration of incompatibility under Section 4 of the HRA 1998 that Section 23 of the Anti-terrorism, Crime and Security Act 2001 was incompatible with Articles 5 and 14 of the Convention on Human Rights. However, the memory of one of the Counsel in the case, Alex Bailin, was that:

> personally, I will never forget the atmosphere in the Lords' Chamber when judgment was handed down in the Belmarsh case. The judgment had not been circulated in draft in advance and it did feel something like a legal penalty shoot-out. The nine-judge Court had not given the slightest indication of its view during the hearing and there was no doubting that Lord Bingham fully appreciated the significance of the moment when he cautiously gave the first summary of his Opinion.[73]

My own recollection is at the time I spoke to a number of the lawyers involved in the case, during the period between the conclusion of the argument in October 2004, and the decision announced on 16 December 2004. None of those lawyers predicted that the House of Lords would overturn the Court of Appeal's judgment. The factor which excited most comment from those to whom I spoke was the advocacy of David Pannick QC, who intervened in the appeal on behalf of Liberty. I was told that David Pannick's submissions had an immediate and powerful impact on the nine Law Lords hearing the appeal, so much so that he seized the opportunity to reply by making oral submissions—in response to the Government's arguments made by the A-G, Lord Goldsmith, an opportunity not generally afforded to an intervenor in an appeal.

Despite the House of Lords' decision, the detainees remained in detention, except for two who chose to leave the UK and another, who had been released on bail on conditions amounting to house arrest. None of the detainees were entitled, under domestic law, to compensation in respect of their detention, and they therefore lodged an application to the ECtHR on 21 January 2005.

A. The Response to the House of Lords' Decision

The House of Lords' decision created a major problem for Charles Clarke on his first day as Home Secretary, following David Blunkett's resignation on

---

[72] ibid paras 236–238.
[73] http://ukscblog.com/lord-bingham-a-tribute/.

15 December 2004 amidst allegations that he helped fast-track the renewal of a work permit for his ex-lover's nanny.[74] When he made his statement on the *Belmarsh* judgment on 20 December 2014 Mr Clarke said 'I was not particularly surprised at the Law Lords' judgment. In fact, it would be a surprise if there were not deep controversy about the ethical, philosophical and moral issues that are involved. These are difficult questions, and it is not surprising that people will come to difficult and complicated judgments on them ...' Mr Tony Baldry (Banbury) (Con) asked: 'Does not the Home Secretary accept that the Law Lords did not make what he described as an ethical, moral or philosophical judgment, but a legal judgment?'[75]

Mr Clarke, nevertheless, decided that the detainees would remain in Belmarsh Prison until the Government made its considered response. But he also decided to invite Lord Bingham to have a general discussion about the problems of terrorism, which Lord Bingham declined, presumably because of his personal belief in the separation of powers.[76]

It is worth pointing out that a study of the media's response to the HRA 1998 shows that their response to the *Belmarsh* case was, in fact, rather balanced.[77] The Daily Mail as a right leaning tabloid and a self-declared critic of the HRA 1998 took a much more nuanced view. However, Lord Rees-Mogg, the peer and veteran journalist harshly criticised the House of Lords, accusing them of using the HRA 1998 to establish their supremacy over Parliament. The left wing MP, George Galloway, said 'I saw friends of David Blunkett are complaining that he has faced "trial by media". That's better than the trial he gave to those entombed at Belmarsh'.

The *Belmarsh* case provoked other strong expressions of opinion. Shami Chakrabarti, the former Director of Liberty, argued that, by 'acting as judge, jury and jailer, the Government has flouted the very values it claims to defend. It must now act honourably and charge or release all those currently held'.[78] On the other hand, the Foreign Secretary, Jack Straw, said that the Law Lords were simply wrong to imply that 'this is a decision to detain these people on the whim of the Home Secretary'.[79] But Lord Steyn, thought that Lord Bingham's judgment in the *Belmarsh* case, had contained the 'most eloquent and magisterial rebuke' to an Attorney-General since Lord Denning quoted the words of Thomas Fuller: 'Be you ever so high, the law is above you.'[80]

---

[74] Clarity about the circumstances and events leading up to and surrounding Mr Blunkett's departure emerged in the phone hacking trial of 2013/14. On 24 June 2014 Andy Coulson, former editor of the News of the World was found guilty of a charge of conspiracy to intercept voicemails (phone-hacking). Blunkett's evidence proved central to the verdict.
[75] Hansard HC vol 428, cola 1915 and 1919 (20 December 2004)
[76] Nicholas Phillips 'Introductory Tribute: Bingham of Cornhill' at xlix in *Tom Bingham and the Transformation of the Law: a Liber Amicorium* ed Adenas and Fairgreive (OUP, 2009).
[77] Lieve Gries *Mediating Human Rights Media, Culture and Human Rights Law* (Routledge, 2015) pp 30–32.
[78] www.telegraph.co.uk/news/1479156/Terror-suspects-win-Lords-appeal-against-detention.html.
[79] www.theguardian.com/uk/2004/dec/17/terrorism.immigrationpolicy.
[80] www.theguardian.com/uk/2005/jun/11/terrorism.uksecurity.

B. The Government Response to the House of Lords' Decision

The Government immediately accepted the House of Lords' decision and announced it would legislate to meet a deadline. The Government did not want to ask Parliament to continue the Part 4 powers for a further year from March 2005 following the House of Lords' decision, and, therefore proposed the Prevention of Terrorism Act 2005, which received Royal Assent on 11 March 2005 and came into operation on 14 March 2005. On 16 March 2005 the Government informed the Secretary General of the Council of Europe that it was withdrawing its derogation from Article 5, and on 3 April 2005 the Lord Chancellor made the HRA 1998 (Amendment) Order 2005,[81] repealing the designated derogation that had been inserted into Schedule 3 to the HRA 1998 by a derogation order which the House of Lords had held to be unlawful.

The Prevention of Terrorism Act 2005 repealed Part 4 of the 2001 Act and replaced it with a temporary measure: the main provisions of the 2005 Act only lasted 12 months unless renewed by an order requiring it to be laid in draft before and approved by each House. Instead of a detention regime, the 2005 Act established 'control orders', which were of course also subject to controversy and considered in a number of further House of Lords' decisions. Control orders were executive preventative orders, which subjected suspected terrorists to house curfew, relocation, and prohibitions or restraints on the use of electronic communications and financial services.

The 2005 Act was piloted through both Houses of Parliament in 17 days. The Clerk of the Parliaments described it as 'a prime example of emergency legislation'.[82] Of particular notoriety was the 'prolonged ping-pong', involving a '36-hour sitting of both Houses to reconcile differences of view ... where each House considered the Bill on five occasions following Third Reading in the Lords'.[83] The First Parliamentary Counsel, Stephen Laws, suggested that the Bill was the toughest piece of legislative drafting that he had worked on during the course of his career.[84] The timetabling also adversely affected the Joint Committee on Human Rights from undertaking effective parliamentary scrutiny. It did succeed in producing two reports on the legislation,[85] but its second report said that 'the rapid progress of the Bill through Parliament has made it impossible for us to scrutinise

---

[81] [2005] SI 1071.

[82] House of Lords Constitution Committee, Fast-track Legislation: Constitutional Implications and Safeguards (2008–09) (2009), HL 116-II, p159

[83] House of Lords Constitution Committee, Fast-track Legislation: Constitutional Implications and Safeguards (2008–09) (2009), HL 116-I, para 82.

[84] Civil Service World, Interview: Stephen Laws, February 14, 2012. See further BBC Radio 4, The Work of the Parliamentary Draftsmen, December 10, 2008. The National Archives, http://webarchive.nationalarchives.gov.uk/+/http://www.cabinetoffice.gov.uk/media/210692/draftsmanscontract1.pdf.

[85] Joint Committee on Human Rights, Prevention of Terrorism Bill: Preliminary Report (2004–05) (London: TSO, 2005), HL 61 and Joint Committee on Human Rights, Prevention of Terrorism Bill (2004–05) (London: TSO, 2005), HL 68.

the Bill comprehensively for human rights compatibility in time to inform debate in Parliament'.[86]

VI. The Strasbourg Decision

Since a declaration of incompatibility under the HRA 1998 was not binding on the parties, the applicants lodged an application with the ECtHR. On 19 October 2009 the Grand Chamber gave its decision.[87] Many of the issues decided by the House of Lord were re-litigated and the Grand Chamber held that the derogating measures had been disproportionate in that they discriminated unjustifiably between nationals and non-nationals with the result that there was a breach of the right to liberty under Article 5(1). The Grand Chamber made numerous holdings on other issues, which were not canvassed before the House of Lords including, in particular, finding that the detention in some cases based on closed material breached the right under Article 5(4) to take proceedings by which the lawfulness of detention shall be decided speedily by a court.

A. The Implications of the House of Lords' Decision

When interviewed Lord Bingham selected the *Belmarsh* case as the most important he had decided in his career. He said, with characteristic understatement, that 'It was the first serious challenge under the Human Rights Act, and one felt the stakes were quite high'.[88] Keith Ewing describes the decision as being 'one of the most important public law decisions since *Entick v Carrington*'[89] David Feldman has claimed that the *Belmarsh* case is 'perhaps the most powerful judicial defence of liberties' since the 1770s and it 'will long remain a benchmark in public law'.[90] Lady Arden states that it is a 'landmark decision' that should be seen as a 'powerful statement by the highest courts of the land of what it means to live in society where the executive is subject to the rule of law'.[91] The Incorporated Council of Law Reporting includes the *Belmarsh* case as one of its five public law cases[92] in

---

[86] Joint Committee on Human Rights, Prevention of Terrorism Bill (2004–05) (2005), HL 68, para 1
[87] [2009] 49 EHRR 29.
[88] http://ukscblog.com/lord-bingham-a-tribute/.
[89] Ewing 'Bonfire of Liberties: New Labour Human Rights and the Rule of Law' Oxford University Press 2010 at 237.
[90] D Feldman (2005) 'Proportionality and Discrimination in Anti-Terrorist legislation' 64 CLJ 271 at n 273.
[91] Arden (2005) '*Human Rights in the Age of Terrorism*' 121 LQR 604 at 622 and 625.
[92] The other four public law cases celebrated are *Liversidge v Anderson* [1942] AC 206; *Associated Provincial Picture Houses v Wednesbury*; *Anisminic v Foreign Compensation Commission* [1969] 2 AC 147 and *Pepper v Hart* [1993] 2 AC 593.

its 15 top decisions celebrated in its 150th anniversary edition of the Law Reports (1865–2015).[93]

The House of Lords' ruling, inevitably, has its critics. Finnis has argued that the House of Lords failed to grasp a fundamental aspect of liberty, that while a community may expect some of its members to abuse their liberty and to cause harm to others, the community need not accept the same risk from non-members.[94] Tomkins has suggested that the result in the House of Lords was unsurprising.[95] He points out that the House of Lords decision did not secure the release of the detainees, most of whom remain incarcerated. It triggered a Government response which may have represented an increase, not decreased, in the scope and scale of the state's repressive counter-terrorist measures. Furthermore, despite the House of Lords' decision, the remainder of the Anti-terrorism, Crime and Security Act 2001 remained intact. He also argues that the *Belmarsh* case did not foreshadow a beacon of light on national security issues.[96]

However, the *Belmarsh* judgment deserves to be viewed as standing on its own merits. It is a towering decision, from at least four perspectives. First, the House of Lords reached an arresting conclusion in a most unpromising terrain, reviewing administrative detention of aliens, where traditionally the courts have taken a very deferential approach. Second, the political climate in which the decision was made was intense and problematic, as the application to recuse Lord Steyn indicated. Third, the structured proportionality analysis undertaken by Lord Bingham stands almost alone among HRA 1998 cases in terms of its analytical rigour.[97] Last, and, not least, Lord Bingham clearly and unequivocally spelt out the rationale for the HRA's 1998 constitutional character: under the HRA 1998 the courts are charged by Parliament with delineating the boundaries of a rights-based democracy.

---

[93] Incorporated Council of Law Reporting for England and Wales (2015).

[94] FInnis 'Nationality, Alienage and the Constitutional Principle' 20070 123 LQR 417; and see, the recent lecture of Finnis 'Judicial Power: Past, Present and Future' 21 Oct 2015. |

[95] See, eg A Tomkins (2005) 'Case Comment: Readings of *A v Secretary of State for the Home Department*' Public Law 259.

[96] Tomkins (2010) 'National Security and the role of the Court: a changed landscape? LQR 543.

[97] The approach taken by the courts to proportionality under the HRA was usefully analysed by a paper published by the Ministry of Justice in September 2007, which also looked at human rights cases at the Court of Human Rights and in Germany, France and Spain. The paper pointed out that proportionality (as it is most rigorously applied) requires the well-known four stage analysis discussed; and distinguished proportionality as a legal concept from the concept of balancing, a broad brush approach which does not operate from a presumption that public interest goals must be restricted by rights or that rights take precedence over public interest goals which are not suitable and necessary to their purpose. The paper concluded the various jurisdictions it examined varied considerably in the level of scrutiny it applied to Government assertions through the proportionality lens. In Germany and Spain proportionality almost always involved the rigorous four stage inquiry. The picture was less consistent at the ECtHR, France and the House of Lords, In the England the courts are more prone to adopt the broad brush balancing approach. Even where proportionality is applied, the English courts appear to be more forgiving of government assertions than in other countries except France: see Gould Lazerus and Swiney 'Public Protection, Proportionality, and the Search for Balance' Ministry of Justice Research Series 10/07, September 2007.

9

R v North and East Devon Health Authority [2001]: *Coughlan* and the Development of Public Law

KIRSTY HUGHES*

I. Introduction

Pamela Coughlan was rendered tetraplegic, doubly incontinent and partially paralysed in the respiratory tract following a road traffic accident; she required extensive daily assistance and care, which was provided at Mardon House, a care home run by the local health authority. Prior to moving into the home, she was promised by the local health authority that she would have a 'home for life' there. However, in the 1990s the local health authority decided that the home was no longer financially viable and sought to close it and transfer responsibility for the provision of her health care to the local authority. Coughlan applied for judicial review on the basis that the health authority was seeking to unlawfully default on its promise. She succeeded before Hidden J in the Administrative Court and the local health authority appealed to the Court of Appeal. In 1999 the Court of Appeal declared that it would be unlawful, unfair and an abuse of power to evict her from Mardon House.[1]

Coughlan is undeniably significant because it was the first time that a court required a public authority to abide by a substantive promise. The courts had previously required certain procedures to be followed when reneging on a substantive expectation, but had never enforced the expectation itself. The case is also significant because even after *Coughlan* the courts have very rarely enforced substantive legitimate expectations, and *Coughlan* arguably remains the strongest example of a court resolutely enforcing a substantive benefit over a viable competing public interest. Thus the case was not merely the first time that a court protected a substantive legitimate expectation, but is the pinnacle of the enforcement of substantive legitimate expectations.

---

* I am grateful to Mark Elliott, David Feldman, Christopher Forsyth, Richard Gordon QC and the editors for their kind and insightful comments on earlier drafts. Any remaining errors are, of course, my own.

[1] *R v North and East Devon Health Authority* [2001] QB 213.

From the perspective of Pamela Coughlan who faced losing her home the Court's decision was critical, yet for the health authority the prospect of being compelled to abide by an assurance that it now believed was financially unwise was daunting. In other words *Coughlan* pitted a vulnerable individual who had been promised something fundamental to her quality of life against the freedom and autonomy of the health authority to make financially robust decisions that would impact upon the provision of services to the broader public. In establishing that a balance must be struck between such interests *Coughlan* forms an important part of the development of fundamental principles such as fairness and abuse of power, and the proportionality standard of review as part of administrative law. It also brought the relationship between the judiciary and, in this case administration, although more broadly, the executive into sharp focus.[2] Should the judiciary enforce substantive promises and preclude the executive from defaulting, or should the judiciary defer to executive decision-making unless the decision is *Wednesbury* unreasonable? By electing in *Coughlan* to protect fairness and prevent abuse of power the Court afforded a greater role to the judiciary in holding the executive to account. Thus the judgment forms an important part of the development of substantive judicial review and the protection of the individual.

To fully appreciate how the Court of Appeal came to find in favour of Pamela Coughlan it is necessary to examine both the context in which the case arose and the cases that have followed. The timing of the case and the composition of the bench are an important part of the story behind *Coughlan*. The case did not come out of nowhere; it followed a series of cases in which two prominent lawyers (and later judges) Sir Stephen Sedley and John Laws sought to push or oppose the development of legitimate expectations. In a string of cases whilst they were still at the bar the two barristers went head-to-head on the question of whether authorities could be bound by their expectations, and if so whether this was limited to procedural expectations or whether it also extended to substantive legitimate expectations. Examining the arguments that they developed at the bar and when first appointed to the bench it is apparent that Stephen Sedley always advocated protection of substantive legitimate expectations, whereas John Laws initially opposed such a development.[3] Their different stances are readily explicable by the fact that Laws as Junior Treasury Counsel always advised and represented government departments and was usually instructed by the Treasury Solicitor, whereas Sedley

---

[2] In considering this complexity it is noteworthy in this regard that the Secretary of State for Health and the Royal College of Nursing were given permission to intervene. The Secretary of State was accepted as a party to the proceedings and made oral submissions at the Court of Appeal hearing. The Royal College of Nursing made written submissions and a more limited oral submission. During the proceedings it was found that the boundary between government policy, NHS national or regional policy, and council policy were not easy to draw, and it was difficult to identify the precise origins of the policies. The Court noted that such complexities and uncertainties are not unusual and that in these situations the Court of Appeal was willing to accept that the Council's policy had at least some basis in national NHS recommendations. See Woolf at paras 13–14, 32–49.

[3] See *Re Findlay* [1985] AC 318; *R v Home Secretary* ex parte *Ruddock* [1987] 1 WLR 1482; *R v Secretary of State for Transport*, ex parte *Richmond-upon-Thames London Borough Council* [1994] 1 WLR 74; *R v Ministry of Agriculture, Fisheries and Food* ex parte *Hamble* [1995] 2 All ER 714, all discussed below.

was a civil liberties and public law specialist who virtually always represented parties challenging governmental decisions. Those differences initially continued when both lawyers were first appointed to the bench. It is perhaps not surprising then that it was Sedley who was on the bench in *Coughlan* when the doctrine of substantive legitimate expectations was advanced. By looking at the case in context, however, we can also see that Laws's views evolved considerably such that he later became a prominent advocate of substantive legitimate expectations and he transformed from a position of opposition to a man at the *avant garde* of judicial developments. Thus both judges played a fundamental role in developing the doctrine, and *Coughlan* and the development of substantive legitimate expectations provides an important illustration of the significance of individual judges to the evolution of public law, the role of different constitutional visions and how they change over time.

Overall it is by examining the historical context of *Coughlan* and the developments that have followed that we are able to contextualise the importance of the decision, its legacy, and ultimately to determine whether it can be considered a landmark case. We must therefore begin by considering what is a landmark case?

II. What is a Landmark Case?

The word landmark is evocative. It brings to mind images such as a lighthouse beaming across the water, a red and white buoy bobbing along in the waves, and Neil Armstrong firmly staking the US flag on the moon. Such images are suggestive of two important features that one may associate with a landmark, namely guidance and territory. The word 'landmark' naturally implies that 'the land is marked' in some way, that in the process some structure and guidance is imposed, and that authority is staked over such territory.

As a word 'landmark' is both a verb and a noun. As a verb the Oxford English Dictionary offers the following—somewhat tautological definition: '[t]o be or act as a landmark to; to provide with a landmark'.[4] As a noun it offers the following four definitions:

(i) the boundary of a country, estate, etc.; an object set up to mark a boundary line; (ii) a district; (iii) an object in the landscape, which, by its conspicuousness, serves as a guide in the direction of one's course (*orig.* and *esp.* as a guide to sailors in navigation); hence, any conspicuous object which characterizes a neighbourhood or district; and (iv) an object which marks or is associated with some event or stage in a process; *esp.* a characteristic, a modification, etc., or an event, which marks a period or turning-point in the history of a thing.[5]

---

[4] www.oed.com/view/Entry/105500?rskey=xq3jDT&result=2&isAdvanced=false#eid (accessed November 2016).
[5] www.oed.com/view/Entry/105499?rskey=xq3jDT&result=1&isAdvanced=false#eid (accessed November 2016).

This suggests three notions of a landmark, something that identifies the boundaries of an area, something that offers guidance or direction, and finally something that identifies a period or turning point in history. Each of these definitions has a geographical or historical character.

Applying these insights to a case, one can infer that a landmark case (i) identifies the boundaries of an area or concept; (ii) sets out guidance which directs future cases; and/or (iii) provides a turning point in history. Each of these meanings offers a spatial or temporal perspective. The first delimits an area of law, the second examines the influence of the case on subsequent cases, and the third is retrospective, raising the question as to whether the case marked a change from past practices? Each of these modes of analysis will be used here to reflect upon the extent to which *Coughlan* may be regarded as a landmark case.

III. Was *Coughlan* a Turning Point? The Law of Legitimate Expectations prior to *Coughlan*

Let us begin then by looking retrospectively at how *Coughlan* marked a change from past practices, and how this change came about. As commentators acknowledged at the time 'it is impossible to appreciate the significance of *Coughlan* without some understanding of the pre-existing case law'.[6] Before we get to Sedley and Laws we should start with another well-known judicial figure, Lord Denning, since it was his reasoning in *Schmidt v Secretary of State for Home Affairs* that set the wheels in motion for holding authorities bound by the legitimate expectations that they had created.[7] The applicants in *Schmidt* were foreign nationals resident in the UK for the purposes of studying scientology, which had been refused a further extension of their residency permits. Their application to the Court was rejected, but Lord Denning took the opportunity to proclaim that in certain circumstances authorities may create a situation in which applicants have an expectation of making representations before a policy can be changed. Whether such an expectation arises on the facts will depend on fairness, a principle that he derived from *Ridge v Baldwin* [1964] AC 40.[8] Examining this in the context of immigration Lord Denning held that it is only where a permit is revoked before the time limit expires that applicants should be given the opportunity to make representations because in that case there would have had been a legitimate expectation that he or she could remain until the end date of the permit. In all other cases once the permit

---

[6] P Craig and S. Schonberg 'Substantive Legitimate Expectations after Coughlan' (2000) *Public Law* p 684, 684.
[7] [1969] 2 Ch 149 (CA). For discussion see C Forsyth 'The Provenance and Protection of Legitimate Expectations' (1988) Cambridge Law Journal 238.
[8] ibid at p 170.

expires there is no legitimate expectation of being allowed to stay, and therefore no obligation on the executive. Thus it was Lord Denning who invoked legitimate expectations and wedded it to the developing principle of fairness.[9] By tying the doctrine to the principle of fairness the doctrine was left free to develop independently of its use on the continent. We will return later to the relationship between fairness and legitimate expectations and the way it evolved in *Coughlan* and subsequent cases, it is worth noting at this juncture, however, that what Lord Denning anticipated was strictly limited to an expectation of making representations; it did not extend to an expectation that a substantive benefit would be conferred.

It was more than fifteen years later that the first substantive legitimate expectation argument was raised in *Re Findlay*, a case in which four prisoners claimed that a change of parole policy meant that they had lost an expectation of early parole.[10] This was the first occasion on which Sedley and Laws took to the floor to argue over the scope of legitimate expectations, with Sedley arguing that the prisoners had reasonable expectations of release in the near future and that 'those expectations had been shattered or seriously reduced by the new policy'.[11] He also claimed that '[n]o reasonable Home Secretary could have reached the decision that, given their good behaviour, they should not be released on parole'.[12] Taken alone that part of Sedley's argument may appear to be limited to the assertion that it would be *Wednesbury* unreasonable not to release the prisoners, however, as Sedley developed his argument it was apparent that he in fact intended a far more intensive ground of review under the remit of legitimate expectation. This is apparent in his assertion that '[t]he expectations gave rise to a duty on the part of the Home Secretary not, without absolutely compelling reasons, to frustrate those expectations'.[13] Thus Sedley sought to upturn the standard of review such that the applicant did not need to establish that it would be *Wednesbury* unreasonable to refuse parole, but rather that the Home Secretary could only refuse parole if there were 'absolutely compelling reasons' for doing so. Such a move would significantly curtail the discretion of the Home Secretary and would mark a shift from a procedural expectation of consideration to a substantive one of entitlement to release, with judicial presumption tipped in favour of the applicant, and not executive discretion. Laws represented the Government and strongly opposed this argument.[14] The Lords agreed with him. Lord Scarman giving the single judgment of the Lords, stated that although he did not rule out the possibility of substantive legitimate expectations he was unconvinced that Parliament could have intended

---

[9] He later commented that this notion of legitimate expectations 'came out of my own head and not from any continental or other source'. Comment made in a private letter from Denning to C. Forsyth, see 'The Provenance and Protection of Legitimate Expectations' (1988) Cambridge Law Journal 238, 241.
[10] [1985] AC 318.
[11] [1985] AC 318, 324.
[12] [1985] AC 318, 324.
[13] [1985] AC 318, 324–325.
[14] [1985] AC 318, 325.

the Home Secretary to be constrained in this way as it would hamper changes of policy.[15]

Two years later Sedley and Laws were again opponents in *R v Home Secretary ex parte Ruddock*.[16] The applicants were prominent Campaign of Nuclear Disarmament (CND) campaigners, and the background to the case was that a former intelligence officer had revealed in a television debate that one of the applicant's telephones had been tapped, and that this had not been in accordance with published criteria. Sedley, representing the CND campaigners, argued that the applicants had a legitimate expectation that tapping would only take place if it were in accordance with the published criteria. Laws, representing the Government, counter-argued that the doctrine of legitimate expectations only applies to an expectation of being consulted or making representations and does not extend further. Taylor J examined the authorities, and found that in many cases the legitimate expectation had been one of consultation. However, he considered the different ways in which the doctrine was explained in *GCHQ* and detected that whilst Lords Diplock and Roskill had focused upon a right to consultation, Lord Fraser had been prepared to put it on a more general footing.[17] He also noted that fairness had been the focus of cases such as *Re Findlay* and ex parte *Asif Mahmood Khan*.[18] Thus on the basis of these authorities he concluded 'that the doctrine of legitimate expectation in essence imposes a duty to act fairly'.[19] Taken alone this statement seemed to leave open the possibility of a broader approach, yet whilst Taylor J thought that fairness extended beyond a right to be heard he offered no indication that it encompassed a conferral of a substantive benefit. Instead what he appeared to envisage was that it would be fair to expect the authority to publish a new policy if they were purporting to change policy,[20] and until they did it is fair to expect that they are applying the published criteria. Moreover, as Elliott notes, Taylor J suggested that the giving of reasons for a change of policy would suffice as a defence in such cases.[21] He did not declare that fairness required anything more.

Thus far there had been some judicial recognition of the doctrine of legitimate expectations and its relationship to fairness, but despite Sedley's efforts judicial engagement had been limited and hesitant. There was no indication that proportionality would become a standard of review for these cases, nor that the doctrine would be tied to abuse of power. That changed when Laws J and Sedley were appointed to the bench and a number of cases followed in which one or both of them were sitting as judges. These cases contained far richer developments of the doctrine.

---

[15] [1985] AC 318, 338.
[16] [1987] 1 WLR 1482.
[17] [1987] 1 W.L.R. 1482, 1494.
[18] [1987] 1 W.L.R. 1482, 1495.
[19] [1987] 1 W.L.R. 1482, 1497.
[20] [1987] 1 W.L.R. 1482, 1497.
[21] M Elliott 'From Heresy to Orthodoxy: Substantive Legitimate Expectations in English Public Law' (forthcoming) in M Groves and G Weeks (eds), *Legitimate Expectations in the Common Law World* (Oxford, Hart Publishing, 2016). See *Ruddock* [1987] 1 WLR 1482, 1497.

In Laws's first judicial engagement with substantive legitimate expectations he remained opposed to the doctrine. This arose in *R v Secretary of State for Transport, ex parte Richmond-upon-Thames London Borough Council*.[22] The claimants sought to argue that a policy on night-time flying restrictions had given rise to a substantive legitimate expectation and that allowing the Government to change that policy would defeat that expectation. Looking at the previous cases Laws found that the courts had only gone as far as determining that there could be a legitimate expectation that claimants' arguments will be heard, and that where a published policy is in place that individuals will be given notice of any proposed changes and an opportunity to make representations. According to Laws it was the latter type of expectation that was at the heart of *Ruddock*.[23]

An important element of his judgment in *Richmond-upon-Thames* was his rejection of the distinction between procedural and substantive legitimate expectations.[24] This foreshadowed his approach in later cases where he supports substantive legitimate expectations, on the basis that there can be no distinction between procedural and substantive expectations. Thus taken alone the dictum in *Richmond-upon-Thames* might suggest that he was always open to the development of substantive legitimate expectations. Yet that would be a premature assumption because in *Richmond-upon-Thames* Laws went on to expressly reject the argument that there could be a substantive legitimate expectation that a policy will not be changed, not just in this particular case, but as a matter of principle. His reasoning was that a broader approach would 'impose an obvious and unacceptable fetter upon the power, and duty, of a responsible public authority to change its policy when it considered that that was required in fulfilment of its public responsibilities'.[25] Moreover, it would entail the courts determining what is in the public interest and hence the merits of the policy. Thus Laws was adamant that a court's role in examining the merits of a decision is strictly limited to *Wednesbury* and there can be no further judicial scrutiny through the doctrine of legitimate expectations. He therefore rejected entirely the idea of a substantive doctrine of legitimate expectations subject to proportionality analysis.

> Mr. Gordon's submission is that these references to "the overriding public interest" imply that where a public authority has effectively given an assurance that it would continue to apply a policy which it has adopted, there are two conditions which must be fulfilled before it may lawfully change tack: not only that a right to be heard must be accorded to those affected, but also that the change must be justified by reference to "the overriding public interest".
>
> But this latter condition would imply that the court is to be the judge of the public interest in such cases, and thus the judge of the merits of the proposed policy change. Thus

---

[22] [1994] 1 W.L.R. 74.
[23] [1994] 1 W.L.R. 74, 92–93.
[24] [1994] 1 W.L.R. 74, 92–93.
[25] [1994] 1 W.L.R. 74, 93.

understood, Mr Gordon's submission must be rejected. The Court is not the judge of the merits of the decision-maker's policy. In fact, Mr Gordon disavowed any such proposition; but if, as must be the case, the public authority in question is the judge of the issue whether 'the overriding public interest' justifies a change in policy, then the submission means no more than that a reasonable public authority, having regard only to relevant considerations, would not alter its policy unless it concludes that the public will be better served by the change. But this is no more than to assert that a change in policy, like any discretionary decision by a public authority, must not transgress Wednesbury principles. That, however, is elementary and carries Mr Gordon nowhere.[26]

A year later Sedley's first judicial engagement with substantive legitimate expectations arose in *R v Ministry of Agriculture, Fisheries and Food* ex parte *Hamble*, and he took the opportunity to respond to Laws's judicial rejection of substantive legitimate expectations.[27] The case concerned a complex fishing licensing system. Hamble had purchased a boat (*The Nellie*) and various other boats intending to collect enough points to transfer a licence to *The Nellie*. A change of policy in the interim meant that Hamble was no longer eligible for a licence and he sought to challenge this by arguing that he had a legitimate expectation of acquiring a licence. Sedley J dismissed this, finding that at best Hamble had a hope of acquiring a licence, and there was no legitimate expectation on the facts. Yet despite rejecting the claim Sedley J elaborated on the doctrine and its role vis-à-vis substantive expectations. He examined Laws's reasoning in *Richmond-upon-Thames* and declared that although he agreed with Laws's starting and finishing points he could not agree that the law did not extend beyond procedural legitimate expectations. Unlike Laws, Sedley J was of the view that *Ruddock* demonstrated that the law extended to substantive legitimate expectations, and that in any event, principle necessitated extending the doctrine. His reasoning was that as the doctrine is based on fairness there is nothing to suggest that it would be 'any less unfair to frustrate a legitimate expectation that something will or will not be done by the decision maker than it is to frustrate a legitimate expectation that the applicant will be listened to before the decision maker decides whether to take a particular step'.[28] This was a far broader notion of fairness than the conventional view of fairness that had developed at that time which was rooted in procedural considerations. Nevertheless in Sedley's eyes this more extensive notion of fairness governed both procedural and substantive expectations and neither constituted a complete fetter on the executive, as both would be governed by proportionality. He acknowledged that procedural expectations are more likely to be upheld on proportionality analysis, but held that this does not mean that the law is only concerned with procedural legitimate expectations.[29]

Thus there were important differences between the approaches taken by Sedley J and Laws J that are representative of fundamental divergences in constitutional

---

[26] [1994] 1 WLR 74, 94.
[27] [1995] 2 All ER 714.
[28] [1995] 2 All ER 714, [1995] 1 CMLR 533, at [25].
[29] [1995] 2 All ER 714, [1995] 1 CMLR 533, at para 25.

vision and the role of the courts in administrative law. Whereas Sedley regarded fairness as a central principle, which necessitates judicial engagement and enforcement, and places the courts at the heart of matters, Laws was deeply concerned with the separation of powers and the limits on judicial analysis of the merits. Interestingly the latter was a view that was to change considerably over the coming years, as Laws aligned particular forms of substantive legitimate expectations with his broader constitutional vision of the role of the courts.[30]

Sedley's J argument in *Hamble* was not universally and warmly received. Indeed two years later when the Court of Appeal (consisting of Pill LJ, Hirst LJ and Peter Gibson LJ) was asked to look at the doctrine in *R v Secretary of State for Home Dept* ex parte *Hargreaves* they robustly overruled Sedley's analysis.[31] *Hargreaves* concerned the eligibility of prisoners for home leave. It had been prison policy that prisoners would be eligible for leave after serving one third of their sentence, but this was subsequently changed to one half of the sentence. The prisoners sought to argue that the original policy had given rise to a legitimate expectation that they would be eligible after serving one third of their sentence. The Court of Appeal rejected that argument. Moreover, they vigorously rejected Sedley's suggestion in *Hamble* that the Court should engage in balancing to determine whether an expectation should be upheld. Hirst LJ flatly rejected it as 'heresy',[32] and Pill LJ held that it was 'wrong in principle'.[33]

Let us take stock of the position pre-*Coughlan*. It is evident that when the Court of Appeal heard *Coughlan* there was considerable uncertainty over the relevance of substantive legitimate expectations. Although Sedley LJ had argued for a collapse of the distinction between procedural and substantive expectations, the expansion of fairness, and the use of proportionality, other judges including Laws, Pill and Hirst were firmly opposed to the idea that anything other than *Wednesbury* could be applicable. On one level this meant that the disagreement over substantive legitimate expectations was connected to a broader dispute over whether the courts could, and should, engage in a more intensive standard of review than *Wednesbury*. In this sense the dispute can be seen as an early example of ongoing ambiguity within administrative law; as we will see later in this chapter, although the courts now engage in more intensive forms of review, the circumstances in which they should do so and the form that it should take remains unclear and the subject of judicial differences. There was also uncertainty prior to *Coughlan* as to whether substantive legitimate expectations could be relevant to anything other than an expectation that a particular procedure, for example consultation, would be offered prior to changing a policy. Consequently, although there had been some developments of the doctrine and reflections on its relationship to fairness, its scope and application had thus far been highly limited. What was clear was that

---

[30] C/f later discussion at p 197–201.
[31] [1997] 1 WLR 906; [1997] 1 All ER 397.
[32] [1997] 1 WLR 906, 921.
[33] [1997] 1 WLR 906, 924.

the courts had never upheld a substantive legitimate expectation by requiring an authority to confer the benefit. That changed in *Coughlan*. In this regard *Coughlan* marked a distinct change from previous cases and provided a turning point in judicial history, and in this sense it is clearly a landmark case. We will turn now to consider the decision in *Coughlan* and its legacy, and in particular whether it sets out the boundaries of the concept, the necessary guidance or has had the requisite influence to satisfy the other criteria for a landmark case.

IV. The Decision in *Coughlan*

In 1993 Pamela Coughlan and seven other disabled patients were moved from a hospital to Mardon House, a NHS facility for long-term disabled patients. Before moving they were assured that this would be their home for life. In 1996 the health authority published a set of criteria indicating that the NHS should provide 'specialist' nursing care, and that local authorities should purchase 'general' nursing care. The health authority concluded that Coughlan, and the other patients at Mardon House, should be provided for by the local authority. A public consultation followed and in 1998 the health authority decided to close Mardon House and transfer Coughlan and the other patients to the local authority. No alternative placement for Coughlan was identified, a fact that was to later undermine the position of the health authority in the judicial proceedings. Coughlan sought judicial review of the decision asserting that as she had been a promised a home for life she had a legitimate expectation that she would continue to be cared for at Mardon House.

This all took place against the backdrop of growing concerns over postcode lottery health care. Transferring Coughlan's care from the health authority to the local authority would have meant that not only would she have been moved from Mardon House, but also that her care would have been means-tested and she would have had to pay for her long-term care. At first instance Hidden J held that the NHS could not distinguish between general nursing care and specialist nursing care and that they were responsible for providing all care.[34] The Court of Appeal took a more nuanced view, and whilst rejecting the distinction between 'general' and 'specialist' nursing care held that the local authority could in some circumstances be responsible for providing care.[35] The Court was reluctant to draw a sharp line as each case would depend on an appraisal of the individual facts. However, a general indication could be derived from whether the care was ancillary or incidental to the provision of accommodation.[36] For Coughlan the provision of nursing care was not ancillary or incidental and therefore it remained the

---

[34] [1999] 2 CCL Rep 27.
[35] [2001] QB 213.
[36] [2001] QB 213, at para 30.

obligation of the health authority. *Coughlan* also established the criteria for a consultation process,[37] which have been followed in subsequent cases.[38]

Crucially the case also raised the spectre of enforcing a substantive promise directly against a public authority. At first instance Hidden J had agreed that Coughlan had a legitimate expectation and that the health authority had not established an overriding public interest that justified departing from that promise. Despite the importance of the matter Hidden offered no reasoning to support his conclusion, asserting simply that 'Miss Coughlan and the other patients had been given a clear promise that Mardon House would be their home for life, and the Health Authority had established no such overriding public interest as justified it in breaking the promise'.[39]

Lords Woolf, Mummery LJ and Sedley LJ heard the appeal, and Lord Woolf gave the single judgment of the Court. In determining the appeal the Court examined the judicial role in substantive legitimate expectations cases and identified three possibilities. First, a court may decide that the public authority is only required to bear in mind its previous promise, giving it the weight it thinks right and no more. Under that approach the court's role is limited to reviewing on *Wednesbury* rationality grounds only. Second, the Court may decide that the promise induces a legitimate expectation of being consulted before a decision is made. In that case the court will require the consultation to be held unless there is an overriding reason to resile from the expectation and the court would review on fairness grounds the reasons given for failing to consult. Third, in cases where a lawful promise has induced a legitimate expectation of a substantive benefit the court would decide whether frustrating the expectation would be so unfair that it would amount to abuse of power. Here the court will assess the requirements of fairness against any overriding interest.[40]

---

[37] The Court of Appeal in *Coughlan* confirmed the consultation criteria that Sedley had advocated as a barrister and had been accepted by the Court in *R v Brent LBC* ex parte *Gunning* [1986] 84 LGR 168. As the Court explained in *Coughlan* those criteria are that '[i]t is common ground that, whether or not consultation of interested parties and the public is a legal requirement, if it is embarked upon it must be carried out properly. To be proper, consultation must be undertaken at a time when proposals are still at a formative stage; it must include sufficient reasons for particular proposals to allow those consulted to give intelligent consideration and an intelligent response; adequate time must be given for this purpose; and the product of consultation must be conscientiously taken into account when the ultimate decision is taken (*R v Brent LBC* ex parte *Gunning* [1986] 84 LGR 168)', at para 108. These consultation criteria have more recently been confirmed by the Supreme Court in *Moseley* [2014] 1 WLR 3947, at [25], with the Court acknowledging that the criteria originally derived from Sedley's submissions in *Gunning*.

[38] *R v Sheffield City Council* [2013] EWHC 2953 (QB); *R. (on the application of D) v Worcestershire CC* [2013] EWHC 2490 (Admin); *R. (on the application of Wakil (t/a Orya Textiles)) v Hammersmith and Fulham LBC* [2012] EWHC 1411 (QB); *R. (on the application of East Midlands Care Ltd) v Leicestershire CC* [2011] EWHC 3096 (Admin); *R. (on the application of EasyJet Airline Co Ltd) v Civil Aviation Authority* [2009] EWCA Civ 1361.

[39] Reported in Court of Appeal judgment at para 4 and confirmed in private correspondence with Richard Gordon.

[40] ibid at para 57.

The Court noted that in most cases the difficult issue would be determining which of the three approaches is applicable. In examining the third type of case the Court accepted that the doctrine was still being developed and that 'the limits to its role have yet to be finally determined by the courts'.[41] However, they anticipated that substantive legitimate expectations cases are likely to be limited to cases 'where the expectation is confined to one person or a few people, giving the promise or representation the character of a contract'.[42] Applying this to *Coughlan* the Court emphasised 'the importance of what was promised to Miss Coughlan', 'the fact that [the] promise was limited to a few individuals', 'and the fact that the consequences to the health authority of requiring it to honour its promise are likely to be financial only'.[43] This dismissive characterisation of the consequences of upholding the promise as 'financial only' has been rightly criticised by scholars ever since on the basis that upholding the promise had potentially far-reaching consequences for the funding of other patients.[44]

Interestingly, although *Coughlan* is now well known in both English administrative law, and in other common law jurisdictions, it initially went unreported.[45] *Coughlan* has since emerged as a landmark case in three senses. First, it marked a significant change from the outcomes of previous cases. Second, the Court of Appeal sought to establish guidance as to when a substantive legitimate expectation should be enforced, thus providing directions for future cases. Third, it was the first time that the Court delved into a bold form of proportionality review, thus marking an important moment in the development of review in administrative law.

The remaining parts of this chapter will reflect further on the guidance offered by *Coughlan* and its relationship to the development of the principles and tools of administrative law. Before doing so, however, it is worth pausing to acknowledge the aforementioned relevance of the composition of the bench in *Coughlan*. As commentators noted at the time '[b]oth Lord Woolf['s] and Sedley's LJ support for the doctrine of substantive legitimate expectation was well known prior to this case'.[46] Of course it was only natural that Sedley would have been keen to respond to the way in which his judgment in *Hamble* had been bluntly rejected in *Hargreaves*. Indeed the Court of Appeal took the opportunity to respond to that by citing a 'number of learned commentators' who 'have questioned this

---

[41] ibid at para 71.
[42] ibid at para 59.
[43] ibid at para 60.
[44] See, for example, M Elliott 'From Heresy to Orthodoxy: Substantive Legitimate Expectations in English Public Law' (forthcoming) in M Groves and G Weeks (eds), *Legitimate Expectations in the Common Law World* (Oxford, Hart Publishing, 2016); Philip Sales and Karen Steyn, 'Legitimate expectations in English public law: an analysis' [2004] Public Law 564, 591.
[45] Confirmed in private correspondence with Richard Gordon.
[46] M Roberts 'Public Law Representations and Substantive Legitimate Expectations' (2001) 64(1) Modern Law Review 112, 116. Roberts highlights the decision of Sedley in *Hamble* and Woolf's analysis in de Smith, Woolf and Jowell, *Judicial Review of Administrative Action* (Sweet & Maxwell, 1995) 417, para 8.038.

conclusion'.[47] As *Hargreaves* bound the Court of Appeal on ordinary principles of stare decisis, they got round it by distinguishing the decision. The prisoners in *Hargreaves* were said to have a legitimate expectation only of consideration in the light of whatever policy was in force for the time being, an expectation which had been met, while Coughlan had a legitimate expectation of a substantive benefit, as fairness required that the policy should not be resiled from unless there was an overriding justification.[48] Scholars would differ as to whether this was a viable distinction.

Examining the composition of the bench, and the strong opposition that other judges had shown towards substantive legitimate expectations in earlier cases it is certainly arguable that a Court of Appeal comprised of a different panel of judges may have reached a rather different verdict in *Coughlan*. Such a view is perhaps given credence by the fact that although *Coughlan* remains binding and other judges have accepted *Coughlan* itself, substantive legitimate expectations have rarely been enforced in later cases.[49] Moreover, in subsequent cases we find refinements of the doctrine, which are perhaps indicative of judicial attempts to limit substantive legitimate expectations, there is of course, the possibility of courts getting round *Coughlan* in a similar fashion to the way in which the Court of Appeal *Coughlan* distinguished *Hargreaves*. By examining judicial reception of *Coughlan* and the outcomes of cases that have followed we have a further opportunity to examine its influence and significance.

V. Limited Enforcement of Substantive Legitimate Expectations Post-*Coughlan*

There are very few cases and in which substantive legitimate expectations have been enforced post-*Coughlan*, even fewer cases in which a comparable promise has been enforced. Convesely there are many cases in which substantive legitimate expectations have been argued but rejected. It is therefore worth examining the cases in which promises have been enforced post-*Coughlan* to illustrate how these cases indicate a more limited form of enforcement. One case in which a substantive expectation was enforced was *Paponette and others v Attorney-General of Trinidad and Tobago*.[50] The appellants were owners and operators of 'maxi-taxis'. They agreed to move their vehicles to a taxi stand on premises owned by a competitor as they had been assured that management of the premises would be transferred to the taxi-owners

---

[47] ibid at para 75.
[48] ibid at para 76.
[49] It is worth noting here the rather different outcome in *Cowl v Plymouth* [2001] EWHC Admin 734; [2001] EWCA civ 1935; [2002] 1 WLR 803 another home for life case litigated shortly after *Coughlan*.
[50] [2010] UKPC 32; [2012] 1 AC 1.

association. No transfer of ownership occurred, and the competitor subsequently imposed charges upon the appellants. The Privy Council held that there was a legitimate expectation and that there had been an unlawful default on that promise. However, the reason that it was enforced in *Paponette* was that the authority had not provided any evidence of an overriding public interest, and the Court was not prepared to infer that there was such an interest. Thus the applicants succeeded not because they convinced the Court that the promise should be upheld over and above a competing public interest, but because the authority failed to identify a competing public interest at all.

There are several other cases in which the defendant has failed to identify a competing public interest. For example, in *R (on the application of Simpson) v Chief Constable of Greater Manchester* it was held that the applicants had a substantive legitimate expectation that if they passed an assessment stage they would be promoted when an appropriate vacancy became available and it was found that the Defendant had not justified the frustration of that expectation.[51] Similarly in *R (on the application of B) v Nursing and Midwifery Council* it was held that the Nursing and Midwifery Council could not set aside its previous decision that there was no case to answer in respect of allegations made against the applicant.[52] Part of the Court's reasoning was that there had been no change of circumstances that justified re-opening the case; the Council therefore failed to demonstrate a public interest that could defeat the legitimate expectation that it had created in its original determination.

In only two cases post-*Coughlan* have the courts upheld a substantive legitimate expectation in the face of a competing public interest. The first was *R (on the application of HSMP Forum (UK) Ltd) v Sec of State for the Home Department*; this is arguably the case that is closest to *Coughlan*.[53] In *HSMP Forum* the applicants argued that they had a legitimate expectation of being granted indefinite leave to remain under a policy that applied when they entered the UK. In the interim the policy had been changed to extend the period of continuous residence before leave to remain would be granted. The Secretary of State sought to assure the Judge that these individuals would not be removed from the UK, however, Mrs Justice Cox, found that even if they were not removed, those affected would suffer great detriment as a result of that change. She received extensive accounts of the adverse impact that the change would have upon 'the practical realities of people's private and professional lives', matters which had not been considered by the Secretary of State'.[54] Consequently she found that she was:

> unable to identify *a sufficient public interest* which justifies a departure from the requirement of good administration and straight forward dealing with the public, or which

---

[51] [2013] EWHC 1858; [2014] ACD 20.
[52] [2012] EWHC 1264.
[53] [2009] EWHC 711.
[54] ibid at para 76. See also discussion of *HSMP Forum* in *Granovski v Secretary of State for the Home Department* [2015] EWHC 1478.

outweighs the unfairness that the increase in the qualifying period visits upon those already admitted under the scheme.[55] (emphasis added)

It is worth noting that although the nature of the public interest behind the change of policy was not discussed in detail in *HMSP Forum* the Judge's reference to the need for 'a sufficient public interest', albeit ambiguous may be read as suggesting that she accepted that there was a public interest in changing the policy, but that on these facts it was not sufficient to defeat the expectation. In this sense *HMSP Forum* would differ from other legitimate expectations cases in which the defendant was unable to pinpoint any public interest to evaluate against the legitimate expectation and brings it closer to *Coughlan* in which there was also a public interest in reneging on the promise, but not on the Court of Appeal's view a sufficient one. Moreover, *HMSP Forum* appears to have resulted in the Court precluding the Secretary of State from reneging on the original policy and requiring the application of the original policy to those who had entered the UK under that scheme, an outcome akin to that in *Coughlan*.[56]

The second case was *R (Patel) v General Medical Council*.[57] The applicant had sought to train as a doctor, as he would be unable to register as a doctor in the UK without an approved qualification he sought confirmation from the General Medical Council (GMC) that the course he selected would satisfy their requirements. The GMC confirmed that it would accept the qualification and the applicant enrolled, however, whilst he was studying the GMC changed its policy, and when he sought to register with the GMC he was informed that they no longer accepted this qualification. He sought judicial review on the ground that he had a legitimate expectation that his qualification would be accepted. The Court of Appeal held that the GMC had made an individual clear and unambiguous assurance and that Patel had relied upon that assurance to his detriment; there could therefore be no doubt that he had a legitimate expectation.[58] The Court also found that the GMC should have considered whether it was necessary to introduce new rules with immediate effect, and that they had failed to do so.[59] That failure in itself was sufficient to establish that the decision should be retaken and that the authority should take those matters into consideration when retaking the decision.[60] However, the Court did not stop there it went on to consider whether the legitimate expectation meant that the GMC could not simply retake the same decision. Bearing in mind the hardship that the decision would cause to the applicant and the lack of consideration that had been given to the matter the Court held

---

[55] ibid at para 77.
[56] The Judge reported that her 'provisional view is that the Claimant is entitled to the relief sought, but I shall invite submissions from counsel as to the appropriate relief in this case before deciding on the form of the Order' at para 81. There is, however, no reported record of what order was granted following submissions.
[57] [2013] EWCA civ 327; [2013] 1 WLR 2801.
[58] [2013] EWCA civ 327; [2013] 1 WLR 2801, 2815–2818.
[59] [2013] EWCA civ 327; [2013] 1 WLR 2801, at paras 59–81.
[60] [2013] EWCA civ 327; [2013] 1 WLR 2801, at para 81.

that the public interest in changing the policy immediately could not defeat the applicant's legitimate expectation and that the GMC was required to recognise the applicant's qualification.[61]

These few cases in which the courts have upheld substantive legitimate expectations are significant, but limited. In most cases the public authority has either failed to point to a public interest at all, or has failed to demonstrate that they considered other possibilities before making the determination. There are very few cases in which a court has definitively held that a plausible public interest argument is outweighed by the legitimate expectation. *Patel* and *HSMP Forum* come closest to such a decision, and in both cases the courts looked at the hardship that would be caused to the applicants. *HMSP* is the stronger of the two cases and offers robust protection to the individual akin to that provided in *Coughlan*. *Patel* is also significant, however, in *Patel* the Court was willing to consider the possibility that the public interest could justify a change of policy, but was struck in this case by the fact that the policy was changed swiftly without allowing for a transition period, and it was this failure to justify the immediacy of the change that meant that the defendant had failed to justify reneging on the expectation. There is no sense in *Patel* that the authority would be prohibited from changing the policy entirely. Moreover, in both cases the individuals affected had significantly changed their position as a result of the scheme or promise and would suffer serious adverse detriment if the expectation that had been generated were reneged upon. Conversely there have been many more cases in which the courts have declined to find that a legitimate expectation was established or have refused to enforce such an expectation.[62]

The fact that the courts have rarely enforced a substantive legitimate expectation, and where they have done so it has sometimes been in limited ways, could indicate that public authorities have heeded *Coughlan* and are now much more cautious about making such promises or reneging on promises. Alternatively it could suggest that *Coughlan*, although not entirely a one-off, was a rare case, which arose due to the particular composition of the bench, and stands apart from the case law marking out the outer boundaries of the concept. That alone may be sufficient to render it a landmark case as the high point of judicial enforcement of substantive legitimate expectations. Such a view is perhaps further supported by the fact that if *Coughlan* were brought today a court may well consider it rather differently as the case would (at least for the time being) fall under the remit of the HRA 1998, which was not in force at the time of *Coughlan* albeit that the Court did consider Article 8 ECHR.[63] However, to focus purely on outcomes is to neglect the broader influence of *Coughlan*. Indeed although the courts have not routinely

---

[61] [2013] EWCA civ 327; [2013] 1 WLR 2801, at paras 82–86.

[62] *R (on the application of Birks) v Commissioner of Police of the Metropolis* [2014] EWHC 3041; *R (on the application of Alansi) v Newham LBC* [2013] EWHC 3722.

[63] At paras 90–93. See *YL v Birmingham City Council* [2007] EWCA civ 27 and [2007] UKHL 27, and *R v Leonard Cheshire* [2002] EWCA civ 366—note that these cases were concerned with the question of whether Convention rights could be applied against private care homes, but the underlying issue was

enforced substantive benefits, they have adopted central aspects of the reasoning of *Coughlan*. In the remaining sections we would consider that influence in both substantive legitimate expectations cases and in wider administrative law.

VI. Setting out Guidance and Identifying the Boundaries of a Concept—The *Coughlan* Legacy

Since *Coughlan* the courts have accepted that authorities may act in such a way as to give rise to substantive legitimate expectations and that the courts may enforce such expectations. The courts have, however, sought to refine the rationale for this development and to provide more nuanced guidance. Thus, at this juncture it is fair to say that although *Coughlan* was a major turning point, it was certainly not the end point in the process of refining this area of law. If a landmark case sets out the boundaries (the outer limits) then it would be fair to regard *Coughlan* as a landmark case, however, if a landmark case sets out definitive guidance then *Coughlan* fails on that definition. Later cases have seen significant further refinement of the doctrine; and it is here that Sir John Laws has come to the fore.

Only a month after *Coughlan* the Court of Appeal returned to legitimate expectations in *R v Department of Education and Employment, ex parte Begbie*.[64] This time both Laws LJ and Sedley LJ were sitting on the bench, and Peter Gibson LJ handed down the lead judgment. The case concerned a pre-election promise that students in receipt of assisted places in independent schools would be able to retain those places when the scheme was scrapped. When it later emerged that the applicant would not be able to remain on the assisted place scheme for her entire school education she sought to argue that the pre-election statement amounted to a promise that had given rise to an enforceable legitimate expectation. However, all of the judges agreed that there was no legitimate expectation, in part because the statement had been made before the government was in power.[65] Moreover, even if there had been an enforceable promise there had been no reliance or detriment, as the applicant had not changed her position in any way.[66] Scholars have discussed at length the role of detriment and reliance—again indicating the limits of the guidance offered by *Coughlan*.[67]

Although the argument failed in *Begbie*, Laws offered some interesting further reflections. Perhaps surprisingly, given his earlier stance, he accepted without

whether Article 8 ECHR would then provide protection against removal from the home. Note also that in *Coughlan* it was noted that her removal would breach Article 8 ECHR at para 117.

[64] [2000] 1 WLR 1115.
[65] [2000] 1 WLR 1115, 1126–1127.
[66] [2000] 1 WLR 1115, 1126–1127.
[67] For discussion and arguments in favour of requiring detriment for substantive legitimate expectations see P Sales and K Steyn, 'Legitimate expectations in English public law: an analysis' [2004] Public Law 564.

discussion that the doctrine extends to substantive legitimate expectations, and did not question the result in *Coughlan*. He then went on to consider the standard of review that should apply and its role in administrative law. He famously found that the standard of review is a sliding scale from *Wednesbury* to proportionality.[68]

Although he readily accepted that substantive legitimate expectations could be enforceable subject to a test of overriding public interest, he indicated that this more intensive standard of review would only be applicable in cases affecting a small class of people with no wide-ranging policy matters, as these cases offer 'no offence to the claims of democratic power'.[69] By distinguishing general policy cases from individual promise cases he perhaps sought to reconcile his rejection of anything other than *Wednesbury* in *Richmond-upon-Thames* with his acceptance of *Coughlan*. This reading of *Coughlan* is in keeping with his broader constitutional vision of the legitimate role of the courts and the 'claims of democratic power'. Prior to *Begbie* Laws had already written extra-judicially advancing the importance of fundamental rights within a Constitution, the role of the courts in protecting such rights, and the prospects for developing proportionality as a means of offering such protection.[70] Between *Richmond-upon-Thames* and *Begbie*, Laws had himself been involved in determining ex parte *Witham*.[71] The case itself had nothing to do with legitimate expectations: it concerned the imposition of court fees and access to the courts; but it was a very important case in developing his vision of the Constitution. Indeed it was in *Witham* that he established that there are certain constitutional rights (such as access to the courts) that cannot be removed by executive action without clear parliamentary approval. His analysis in *Begbie* of the type of case that can give rise to an enforceable substantive legitimate expectation is arguably much more akin to the fundamental rights that Laws thought the courts should protect, than the night-time policy on flying that he rejected in *Richmond-upon-Thames*.

However, it is questionable whether when it comes to the public interest the cases can be reconciled in quite the way that Laws argues. In particular his suggestion that individual promises (like the ones that were made in *Coughlan*) raise no 'wide-ranging issues of general policy, or none with multi-layered effects, upon whose merits the court is asked to embark', is an unrealistic distinction. If one considers the facts of *Coughlan* it is evident that keeping a care home open will have repercussions for resource allocation to other areas of health care.[72] Moreover, there is nothing to suggest that the complexity of the issues at stake is

---

[68] ibid at paras 80–81.
[69] ibid at para 81.
[70] J Laws 'Is the High Court the Guardian of Fundamental Constitutional Rights' (1993) Public Law 59; John Laws 'Law and Democracy' (1995) Public Law 72.
[71] [1998] 2 WLR 849.
[72] See similar criticisms advanced by M Elliott 'From Heresy to Orthodoxy: Substantive Legitimate Expectations in English Public Law' (forthcoming) in M Groves and G Weeks (eds), *Legitimate Expectations in the Common Law World* (Oxford, Hart Publishing, 2016); P Sales and K Steyn, 'Legitimate expectations in English public law: an analysis' [2004] Public Law 564, 591.

necessarily any less significant than the policy concerning night-time flights that Laws considered in *Richmond-upon-Thames* or the policy on entitlement to home leave in *Hargreaves*. Nevertheless, Laws's dictum in *Begbie* was an attempt at a further refinement of *Coughlan* and development of further guidance.

By contrast Sedley was constrained in his discussion of legitimate expectation in *Begbie*, and simply acknowledged that Laws may be correct that the 'distinction drawn in *Coughlan* between the first and third categories of legitimate expectation deserves further examination'.[73]

Nearly two years later Sedley was again on the Court of Appeal when it considered substantive legitimate expectations in *R (Bibi) v Newham London Borough Council*.[74] This case concerned the obligations of a local authority to house homeless refugees. In *Bibi* the Court acknowledged that the test advocated in *Coughlan* was an uncertain one and that 'without refinement, the question whether reneging on a promise would be so unfair as to amount to an abuse of power is an uncertain guide'.[75] The Court considered that in *Bibi* the appropriate remedy was not to require the authority to provide permanent housing, but rather to declare that the authority was under a duty to take into account the promise in determining the applicant's request for accommodation. Thus *Bibi* marked a further refinement to *Coughlan* providing courts with the option of enforcing a substantive legitimate expectation via a procedural obligation; affording the individual weaker protection than that which was offered in *Coughlan* shifting the balance back towards the public interest and signaling a further roll back from *Coughlan*, leaving *Coughlan* as the high watermark of judicial protection. Again Sedley was silent on the matter whilst Schiemann handed down the sole judgment of the Court.

Conversely Laws was getting into his stride and offered further guidance in *Nadarajah v Secretary of State for the Home Department*.[76] After reviewing *Coughlan* Laws declared that it 'demonstrate[s] that an abiding principle which underpins the legitimate expectation cases is the court's insistence that public power should not be abused'.[77] However, he went on to consider that 'abuse of power' is not in itself a sufficient guiding principle 'as it goes no distance to tell you, case by case, what is lawful and what is not'.[78] Rather the doctrine is 'grounded in fairness', and 'more broadly as a requirement of good administration, by which public bodies ought to deal straightforwardly and consistently with the public'.[79] He then considered that:

> a public body's promise or practice as to future conduct may only be denied … where to do so is the public body's legal duty, or is otherwise, to use a now familiar vocabulary, a

---

[73] ibid at para 103.
[74] [2001] EWCA civ 607.
[75] ibid at para 34.
[76] [2005] EWCA civ 1363.
[77] ibid at para 52.
[78] ibid at para 67.
[79] ibid at para 68.

proportionate response (of which the court is the judge, or the last judge) having regard to a legitimate aim pursued by the public body in the public interest.[80]

He acknowledged that it may be easier to justify frustrating a substantive expectation, but this was not in itself a difference of principle.[81] This marked a shift from his earlier stance on the matter, bringing him to a similar (albeit certainly not identical) position to that advanced by Sedley in *Hamble* twenty years earlier. It also marked an attempt to reconcile these developments with broader developments in administrative law, a point that we will return to shortly.

It would be wrong, however, to suggest that Sedley and Laws now consider themselves to be on precisely the same page. Indeed a clear divergence of opinion over the approach taken in *Hamble* remained apparent in *Bhatt*, a case heard by the two judges a few years after *Nadarajah*. It was on this occasion that Sedley sought to revisit the condemnation of *Hamble* in *Hargreaves* and declared that the time has come to say that the description of heretical was mistaken.[82] Laws was not, however, willing to determine that *Hamble* was akin to *Coughlan*. Indeed he remained of the view that a legitimate expectation will only arise where there is 'a specific undertaking, directed at a particular individual or group, by which the relevant policy's continuance is assured',[83] that *Coughlan* is a particularly strong case, and that legitimate expectations 'are more elusive than they appear'.[84] Thus whilst Sedley was prepared to see *Coughlan* as part of a broader protection of expectations created by policies and statements, Laws limited it to situations akin to specific promises to particular individuals. The scope of the doctrine and whether the same doctrine applies to each of these circumstances continues to be contested by scholars.[85]

Cases such as *Begbie, Bibi, Nadrajah* and *Bhatt* saw further refinement to *Coughlan*. In some ways they narrowed its scope and application, in others they elaborated on the requisite criteria. What is apparent is that *Coughlan* alone did not provide the end point, nor the entire map of legitimate expectations. It is certainly arguable that there remains great uncertainty as to the scope and elements of the doctrine and whether the cases can be regarded as part of one coherent doctrine or rather several related doctrines.[86] Thus *Coughlan* does not provide definitive guidance, but what case does? All public law cases form part of the

---

[80] ibid at para 68.
[81] ibid at para 69.
[82] ibid at para 69.
[83] ibid at para 43.
[84] *R (on the application of Bhatt Murphy) v The Independent Assessor* [2008] EWCA civ 755, at para 27.
[85] See for example, A Perry and F Ahmed 'The Coherence of the Doctrine of Legitimate Expectations' (2014) 73(1) Cambridge Law Journal 61; M Elliott, 'Legitimate Expectations: Procedure, Substance, Policy and Proportionality' (2006) CLJ 254; R Clayton, 'Legitimate Expectations, Policy, and the Principle of Consistency' (2003) 62 CLJ 93; P Daly 'A Pluralist Account of Deference and Legitimate Expectations' (forthcoming).
[86] ibid.

development of the principles of administrative law, there are some that do more than others, but there is no one case that sets out definitive guidance. What is clear is that *Coughlan* appears (at least for now) to have marked out the outer edges of legitimate expectations, and established the broad reach of the doctrine. In the interim Laws has sought to explore the theoretical underpinnings of the doctrine, and although this has brought him closer to the position adopted by Sedley there remain considerable differences. Those differences are indicative of broader differences within public law as to the scope of developing grounds of review and the proper constitutional role of the courts.

VII. Establishing the Principles of Administrative Law

Finally it is worth noting that although *Coughlan* has not resulted in the enforcement of many substantive legitimate expectations, the principles that underpinned the case have formed part of the broader development of Administrative Law, in particular a move towards a more substantive form of review that affords a greater role to the courts in determining normative merits-based questions.[87] Here we examine three elements of this shift that arise from *Couglan* (i) abuse of power and fairness, (ii) proportionality as a standard of review, and (iii) the role of the individual and public interest in administrative law. Examining these principles and their place in Administrative law it is apparent that *Coughlan* is an important part of these broader developments. In this sense *Coughlan*, whether it amounts to a landmark case or not, is seen as part of the broader tapestry of public law.

A. Abuse of Power and Fairness

Whereas earlier legitimate expectation cases focused upon fairness,[88] *Coughlan* introduced the idea that fairness is connected to abuse of power. Prior to *Coughlan* abuse of power only appeared in Inland Revenue cases.[89] In fact it was in an Inland Revenue case that the seeds of the relationship between abuse of power and

---

[87] For further discussion of the developments underpinning *Coughlan* see M Groves 'Substantive Legitimate Expectations in Australian Administrative Law' [2008] Melbourne University Law Review 470; and M Elliott 'From Heresy to Orthodoxy: Substantive Legitimate Expectations in English Public Law' (forthcoming) in M Groves and G Weeks (eds), *Legitimate Expectations in the Common Law World* (Oxford, Hart Publishing, 2016).

[88] *Attroney General of Hong Kong* v *Ng Yuen Shiu* [1983] 2 AC 629, 638; *Council of Civil Service Unions* v *Minister for the Civil Service* [1985] AC 374, 415; *R.* v *Inland Revenue Commissioners*, ex parte *MFK Underwriting* [1990] 1 WLR 1545, 1570. For discussion of the role of fairness see T Allan 'Pragmatism and Theory in Public Law' [1998] Law Quarterly Review 422, 435.

[89] In the tax context abuse of power was of particular importance in *R v Inland Revenue Commissions* ex parte *Preston* [1985] AC 835 where it was held that reneging on a guarantee would amount to an abuse of power. For discussion see M Roberts 'Public Law Representations and Substantive Legitimate

fairness were sowed, namely in *R v Inland Revenue Commissioners*, ex parte *Unilever Plc* where the Court of Appeal held that 'to reject Unilever's claims in reliance on the time-limit, without clear and general advance notice, is so unfair as to amount to an abuse of power'.[90] Yet in *Unilever* the Court did not consider substantive legitimate expectations, nor that the courts should use proportionality. That changed in *Coughlan* when the Court declared that the courts must determine 'whether to frustrate the expectation is so unfair that to take a new and different course will amount to an abuse of power'.[91]

This twin relationship between fairness and abuse of power is interesting because taken individually the principles appear to pull in different directions. Fairness directs the court to consider the implications for the individual affected, whereas abuse of power would appear to centre upon the legitimacy of the actions and intentions of the decision-maker. Thus fairness and abuse of power, despite appearing together in *Coughlan*, seem naturally directed towards different questions, and indicate different premises for administrative law. Fairness suggests a concern for the dignitarian interests of the individual. Conversely, abuse of power indicates a preoccupation with the limits of executive action and perhaps good governance. Taken separately they suggest different points of intervention, fairness allowing for greater judicial intervention, and abuse of power setting a higher threshold for such intervention. To suggest, however, that frustrating a promise is so unfair as to amount to an abuse of power curtails the role of the decision-maker such that power is only conferred upon the decision-maker on the basis that he or she exercises it fairly. Fairness becomes not simply a principle of aspiration but a clear limit on executive action.

The twin abuse of power/fairness principle has been called upon to do further work beyond legitimate expectations. An example of this can be found in *Secretary of State for the Home Department v R (Rashid)* where the Court was clear that this principle of fairness giving rise to abuse of power is not limited to the law of expectations, but is a general principle of administrative law: the Court declaring that legitimate expectations is 'only one application' of the principle of 'unfairness amounting to an abuse of power'. Applying this in *Rashid* the principle was found to be relevant to 'an expectation that a general policy for dealing with asylum applications will be applied and will be applied uniformly'.[92]

Expectations' (2001) 64(1) Modern Law Review 112, 118; Paul Reynolds 'Legitimate Expectations and the Protection of Trust in Public Officials' [2011] Public Law 330, 331–332; M. Groves 'Substantive Legitimate Expectations in Australian Administrative Law' [2008] Melbourne University Law Review 470, 476.

[90] [1996] STC 681 Part IV.
[91] ibid at para 57. The same combination of the two principles has appeared in other cases, including *R (on the application of Bancoult) v Secretary of State for Foreign and Commonwealth Affairs* [2008] UKHL 61, [2009] 1 AC 453, Carswell at para 135. 'The basis of the jurisdiction is abuse of power and unfairness to the citizen on the part of a public authority'. For criticism of abuse of power see P Craig and S Schønberg 'Substantive Legitimate Expectations after Coughlan' [2000] Public Law 684.
[92] [2005] EWCA civ 744, at para 34. For discussion see M Elliott (2005) *Judicial Review* 281.

Thus *Coughlan* is part of a broader sense in which fairness has become part of judicial determination of the scope of legitimate executive action. By allowing fairness to define abuse of power and curtail the scope of power in this way the courts set limits upon the scope of executive power. This is a classic means of allowing greater judicial intervention, which depending upon one's constitutional vision, is achieved either through the process of developing the common law Constitution or under the guise of *modified* ultra vires style analysis.[93] In this sense *Coughlan* is part not only of the development of the scope and boundaries of administrative law, but in turn the broader constitutional framework.

B. Proportionality

A further important development in administrative law has been the use of proportionality as a standard of review. Although traditionally proportionality has been limited to cases involving EU law, qualified human rights and legitimate expectations cases, there have been suggestions that proportionality may be applicable in a broader range of cases and that the standard of review cannot be determined simply by examining the subject matter of the case at hand. This is a matter that has peaked judicial interest, but has not been determined by the courts.[94] Lord Carnwath's recent comments in *Youssef* are particularly illuminating as to the likely process for future developments: '... he noted that the matter needed to be considered by an enlarged Supreme Court and that 'such a review might aim for rather more structured guidance for the lower courts than such imprecise concepts as "anxious scrutiny" and "sliding scales"'.[95]

In one sense *Coughlan* could perhaps be seen retrospectively as part of the evolution of proportionality as a tool of administrative law. This is not to suggest that proportionality has become a standard tool in all administrative law cases, that this was the intention at the time of *Coughlan,* nor that proportionality is used in

---

[93] For a range of views see T Allan 'The Constitutional Foundations of Judicial Review: Conceptual Conundrum or Interpretative Enquiry?' [2002] 61 CLJ 87; P. Craig 'Ultra Vires and the Foundations of Judicial Review' [1998] CLJ 63; M Elliott, *The Constitutional Foundations of Judicial Review* (Hart, 2001) Chapters 3–4; M. Elliott, 'The Ultra Vires Doctrine in its Constitutional Setting: Still the Central Principle of Administrative Law' [1999] CLJ 129.

[94] For judicial engagement with these matters see: *Youssef v Secretary of State for Foreign and Commonwealth Affairs* [2016] UKSC 3; *Keyu v Secretary of State for Foreign and Commonwealth Affairs and Secretary of State for Defence* [2015] UKSC 69; and *Secretary of State for the Home Department v Pham* [2015] UKSC 19, *Kennedy v Charity Commission* [2014] UKSC 20. For discussion of *Pham* as indicative of a growing willingness of the courts to engage in proportionality analysis in other cases see M Elliott 'Beyond the European Convention: Human Rights and the Common Law' (2015) 68(1) Current Legal Problems 85; M Elliott 'From Heresy to Orthodoxy: Substantive Legitimate Expectations in English Public Law' (forthcoming) in M Groves and G Weeks (eds), *Legitimate Expectations in the Common Law World* (Oxford, Hart Publishing, 2016). See also H Wilberg and M Elliott (eds.) *The Scope and Intensity of Substantive Review: Traversing Taggart's Rainbow* (Hart, 2015).

[95] [2016] UKSC 3, at para 55.

the same way across different types of administrative law. Simply, that there has been a growing acceptance of more intensive standards of review across a broader range of cases than took place under *Wednesbury* review.[96] Indeed it is clear from Lord Carnwath's comments that there is some judicial dissatisfaction with the various proportionality tools than have been developed, including the sliding scale model developed by Laws in *Begbie*.

Moreover, despite the growth of proportionality there are important differences in the ways in which the courts use these standards of review vis-à-vis different grounds of review. In this regard the approach taken in *Coughlan* has been identified as a looser form of proportionality, which failed to develop the structured methodology and tools seen in other proportionality cases.[97] As M. Elliott explains 'the balancing test (in legitimate expectations) does not equate to proportionality review proper: there are, after all several stages within the proportionality test, of which the fair-balance test is only one'.[98] The stages to which he refers are those set out in *Huang* and *Bank Mellat (No 2)*.[99]

(1) Legitimate objective sufficiently important to justify limiting fundamental right.
(2) Measures designed to meet objective are rationally connected to it.
(3) Means used to impair the right are no more than necessary.
(4) Fair balance is struck between needs of the individual and interests of community as a whole.

It is this four-stage approach that the applicants in *Youssef* sought to argue should be applicable to all judicial review cases.[100] It is beyond the scope of this chapter to consider whether this test should be applicable to all judicial review cases, instead we will look at the narrower question of whether all four stages are applicable and appropriate in legitimate expectations cases, and use this to reflect upon the broader implications for the development of a common standard in administrative law and the insights that *Coughlan* offers as to any such process.

Although Elliott suggests that the approach adopted in *Coughlan* had much in common with one of those elements (namely stage (4) balancing) it is arguable

---

[96] For further discussion of the use of proportionality and a possible reformation of administrative law see T Poole 'The Reformation of English Administrative Law' (2009) 68 *Cambridge Law Journal* 142; P Craig 'Proportionality, Rationality and Review' [2010] *New Zealand Law Review* 265; Jeff King 'Proportionality: A Halfway House' [2010] *New Zealand Law Review* 327; Tom Hickman 'Problems for Proportionality' [2010] *New Zealand Law Review* 303; J Varuhas The Reformation of English Administrative Law? 'Rights', Rhetoric and Reality' (2013) 72 *Cambridge Law Journal* 369.

[97] M Elliott 'From Heresy to Orthodoxy: Substantive Legitimate Expectations in English Public Law' (forthcoming) in M. Groves and G. Weeks (eds), *Legitimate Expectations in the Common Law World* (Oxford, Hart Publishing, 2016).

[98] M Elliott 'From Heresy to Orthodoxy: Substantive Legitimate Expectations in English Public Law' (forthcoming) in M. Groves and G. Weeks (eds), *Legitimate Expectations in the Common Law World* (Oxford, Hart Publishing, 2016).

[99] *Huang v Secretary of State for the Home Department* [2007] UKH 11 [2007] 2 AC 167; *Bank Mellat v HM Treasury (No 2)* [2013] UKSC 39, [2014] AC 700.

[100] [2016] UKSC 3.

that at least some of the other elements would have applied in *Coughlan* even if this approach had been used. Indeed (1) and (2) would have been accepted by the Court—namely that there was a legitimate objective behind the decision to transfer Coughlan from the home, and that closing the home was rationally connected to that objective. The Court could legitimately be criticised for not giving sufficient weight to those factors, but even in other proportionality cases (ie qualified human rights cases) an evaluative assessment of those matters does not usually take place until stages (3) and (4).

This brings us to stage (3) where it is worth considering further the applicability of the requirement that the means used to impair the right are no more than necessary. First, it is highly doubtful whether even in human rights cases the courts routinely apply a least restrictive means test. Second, regardless of what happens in human rights cases, it is questionable whether a least restrictive means test should be applicable where the courts are faced with a substantive legitimate expectation as opposed to an interference with a fundamental right. In a human rights case under the HRA 1998 the right has been conferred upon the individual by Parliament, and the scenarios in which the right can be interfered with are also prescribed by Parliament (incidentally this raises interesting questions about how this should operate under common law constitutional rights, but that is for another day). Conversely in cases concerning substantive legitimate expectations, no such right has been conferred by Parliament; instead, the executive has acted in such a way as to give rise to an expectation, what is it therefore that mandates that the executive should only be able to renege on that expectation when it is the least restrictive means of achieving a legitimate aim? It may be entirely constitutionally appropriate for intervention to be justified on a lower standard such that the executive can renege on promises even if this is not the least restrictive means of achieving a goal, provided that there is an overriding public interest, thus rendering stage (3) inappropriate for legitimate expectations cases. Moreover, the fact that the courts may accept a process of consultation or a right to make representations as sufficient to satisfy the executive's duty suggests that there is no duty to use the least restrictive means of interfering with the right.

This reasoning is further supported by the fact that it seems somewhat illogical to speak of a least restrictive means of interference when one is considering substantive legitimate expectations. This is apparent if one considers the nature of human rights as opposed to legitimate expectations. Where a right is infringed the individual will still retain the right, it will continue to exist and the individual will be able to rely upon it in other contexts. Thus it makes sense to speak of an 'interference' with the right, as the right is not entirely displaced. The same cannot be said to apply to a substantive legitimate expectation, an expectation has a binary existence it is either enforced or it is rejected, it cannot continue to exist beyond the occasion in question and the individual cannot employ it in other contexts. Given this binary existence it becomes difficult to speak of a least intrusive way of defeating that expectation when the expectation is for a specific outcome. This is evident if we examine the difference between a human right and an expectation by applying it to the facts of *Coughlan*. If in 1999 the HRA 1998 had been in force then the Court would (in principle) have had to consider whether closing Mardon House was the least intrusive means of interfering with *Coughlan*'s right to respect for the home under Article 8 ECHR. Even if the Court determined that this was the case and that the interference was therefore justified *Coughlan* would have retained a right to respect for the home, which would be applicable in other contexts. Yes it would have been interfered with on this occasion, but she would still possess the right. Conversely if the Court determined that her expectation was trumped by the public interest, then the expectation would be extinguished, it would no longer continue to exist, she would be removed from Mardon House, and it would make little sense to speak of a least intrusive means of interfering with the expectation, as the expectation is defeated.

There are perhaps, some ways in which it could make sense to speak of the least intrusive means of interfering with the expectation eg through requiring the executive to go through a process of consultation, or by providing the applicant with an opportunity to make representations, or through the benevolent exercise of powers doctrine. The process of engaging in consultation or the opportunity to make representations arise as duties developed through the common law doctrine of legitimate expectations, in this sense they may impose some limits upon the executive which are similar to, but not the same as the obligation to use the least restrictive means. A fundamental difference, however, is that whilst consultation and representations are concerned with the process of reneging on a promise, the least restrictive means test does not focus purely upon process but looks at alternative ways of substantively interfering with a right, thus encompassing and necessitating judicial consideration of other possible outcomes. Moreover, the benevolent exercise of powers doctrine is generally thought of as alternative remedy rather than an obligation upon the executive to use the least restrictive means of interfering with the expectation.

The broader point that emerges here is that although *Coughlan* may be seen to be part of the development of proportionality, it is part of the development of a plurality of approaches to proportionality, as different grounds of review may necessitate diverse processes of reasoning that reflect differing duties and contexts. Whilst *Coughlan* clearly employed a form of proportionality that lacked the more sophisticated features of later judicial developments,[101] and there may be good reasons for developing a more refined tool for substantive legitimate expectations cases, *Coughlan* is perhaps not simply a less sophisticated form of proportionality, which needed to be refined, but rather a different form of this reasoning process. In this sense *Coughlan* and the cases that have followed form part of a

---

[101] M Elliott 'From Heresy to Orthodoxy: Substantive Legitimate Expectations in English Public Law' (forthcoming) in M Groves and Greg Weeks (eds), *Legitimate Expectations in the Common Law World* (Oxford, Hart Publishing, 2016).

broader elaboration of a range of approaches to proportionality, a process which is on-going, and where cross-fertilisation is beneficial, but we should perhaps not expect a uniform approach to emerge as there may be good reasons for differences, including the important point that proportionality is a standard and not a ground of review. Indeed even *within* the human rights context where proportionality is more firmly established we do not necessarily see a uniform approach to proportionality.[102]

C. The Individual and the Public Interest

Underpinning both the developing principles in public law and the standards of review is a concern for both the individual and the public interest in public law. Striking the balance between protecting the individual and protecting the public interest is ever at the backdrop in public law cases. It can be seen in decisions concerning standing, the development of grounds of review such as a right to make representations or duties to give reasons, and the standard of review that is used whether it is *Wednesbury*, correctness, super-*Wednesbury*, anxious scrutiny or proportionality. The development of further grounds of review based on natural justice principles, and of more intensive standards of review, is indicative of a broader concern with protecting the individual against administrative action. Again we need to be cautious not to overstate this, administrative law has certainly not given up its concern for the public interest, but it is perhaps fair to say that *Coughlan* is one of the clearest examples of a shift towards greater protection of the individual applicant that is before the court.

VIII. Conclusion

Let us reflect on the place of *Coughlan* in the broader patchwork of administrative law. If one is looking for cases that mark out the outer limits of judicial development and the pinnacle of judicial protection then *Coughlan* is evidently such a case. Testament to its significance is the fact that it has been acknowledged as such by scholars writing from perspectives across the field of administrative law. For example, Elliott refers to *Coughlan* as a 'turning-point' that it 'is widely regarded as the real landmark case' in substantive expectations.[103] Likewise, Wade

---

[102] For further discussion of the development and use of proportionality see T Hickman 'The Structure and Substance of Proportionality' [2008] Public Law 694; T Hickman *Public Law After the Human Rights Act 1998* (Hart, 2014).
[103] M Elliott 'From Heresy to Orthodoxy: Substantive Legitimate Expectations in English Public Law' (forthcoming) in M. Groves and G. Weeks (eds), *Legitimate Expectations in the Common Law World* (Oxford, Hart Publishing, 2016).

and Forsyth identify it as 'an outstanding example of a substantive right created by legitimate expectation',[104] and Paul Craig asserts that'[t]he law must now be seen in the light of *Coughlan*'.[105]

Another indication of its significance is its impact in other common law jurisdictions 'where it has received mixed responses'. The Australian High Court has refused to follow *Coughlan*,[106] declaring that 'the phrase "legitimate expectation" when used in the field of public law either adds nothing or poses more questions than it answers and thus is an unfortunate expression which should be disregarded'.[107] In New Zealand the courts have been more ambivalent.[108] The courts in South Africa have also been apprehensive, and have recently turned to other legal mechanisms based upon rationality, without entirely closing the door on the matter.[109] Whilst in Canada the courts have rejected substantive legitimate expectations, but have developed an approach based upon a form of public law estoppel.[110] Conversely, Hong Kong has long followed *Coughlan* in recognising substantive legitimate expectations,[111] and Singapore has relatively recently determined that substantive legitimate expectations exist as a stand-alone ground of judicial review.[112] Thus although *Coughlan* has not been universally adopted it has had a ripple effect across the common law world.

Coughlan is also important in illustrating a number of other important features of administrative law. The first is the way in which the principles and foundations

---

[104] W Wade and C. Forsyth *Administrative Law* (OUP, 2014) p 320.

[105] P Craig *Administrative Law* (Sweet & Maxwell, 7th ed.) at 22-012.

[106] *Re Minister for Immigration and Multicultural Affairs; ex parte Lam* [2003] HCA 6; (2003) 214 CLR 1.

[107] *Kaur v Minister for Immigration and Citizenship* [2012] HCA 31 at [61]. For discussion of the Australian response to substantive legitimate expectations see Matthew Groves 'Substantive Legitimate Expectations in Australian Law' [2008] Melbourne University Law Review 470; and Matthew Groves and Greg Weeks 'The Legitimacy of Expectations about Fairness: Can Process and Substance be Untangled?' in John Bell (*et al*) *Public Law Adjudication in Common Law Systems: Process and Substance* (Hart, 2015).

[108] See discussion in *Re Family First New Zealand* [2015] NZHC 1493, at paras 95–100.

[109] See discussion in M Murcott A Future for the Doctrine of Substantive Legitiation Expectation? The Implications of Kwazulu-Natal Joint Liaison Committee v MEC for Education, Kwazulu Natal' (2015) 18(1) Potchefstroom Electronic Law Journal 3133, available on SSRN.

[110] *Agraira v Canada (Minister of Public Safety and Emergency Prepraedness)* 2013 SCC 36; *Canada (Attorney-General) v Mavi* [2011] 2 SCR 504; *Mount Sinai Hospital Centre v Quebec (Minister of Health and Social Services)* [2001] 2 SCR 281. For discussion of substantive legitimate expectations and Canadian law see M. Liston 'Transubstantiation in Canadian Public Law; Processing Substance and Instantiating Process' in John Bell (*et al*) *Public Law Adjudication in Common Law Systems: Process and Substance* (Hart, 2016).

[111] *Ng Siu Tung v Director of Immigration* [2002] 1 HKLRD 561 (CA (HK)). For discussion see Kevin Yam and Benny Tai 'The Advent of Substantive Legitimate Expectations in Hong Kong: Two Competing Visions' [2002] Public Law 688; Teresa Martin, 'Hong Kong Right of Abode: Ng Siu Tung & Others v Director of Immigration—Constitutional and Human Rights at the Mercy of China' (2004) 5 San Diego International Law Journal 465.

[112] *Chiu Teng@Kallang Pte Ltd v Singapore Land Authority* [2013] SGHC 262. For discussion see Charles Tay Kuan Seng 'Substantive Legitimate Expectations: The Singapore Reaction' (2014) 26 Singapore Academy of Law Journal 609; Zhida Chen 'Substantive Legitimate Expectations in Singapore Administrative Law' (2014) 26 Singapore Academy of Law Journal 237; and Swati Jhaveri 'The Doctrine of Substantive Legitimate Expectations: the Significance of *Chiu Teng@Kallang Pted Ltd v Singapore Land Authority*' [2016] Public Law 1.

of administrative law can evolve significantly over a relatively short period of time. It was less then three years between the declaration that Sedley's judgment in *Hamble* was heretic and the enforcement of the substantive legitimate expectation in *Coughlan*. The second is the importance of individual judges to these developments, without the engagement of both Sedley and Laws the law of legitimate expectations, whilst by no means settled, would certainly be far more jejune. The third is the role of the lower courts, and particularly the Court of Appeal in the development of administrative law, although many recent proclamations on matters such as common law constitutional rights have come down from the Supreme Court, the entirety of substantive legitimate expectations has been developed from the lower courts. The House of Lords had the opportunity to get involved in *Bancoult*, but steered clear of seeking to establish any principles.[113] Compare this with the statements of Lord Neuberger (with whom Lord Hughes agreed) in *Keyu* and Lord Carnwath in *Youssef* that further development of proportionality should only be taken following consideration by an enlarged Supreme Court; a vastly different set-up from the three panel Court of Appeal that introduced proportionality and substantive legitimate expectations in *Coughlan*.[114] Given the differing constitutional views exhibited by the Justices of the Supreme Court in recent cases it is likely that there would be strong divergences within a nine-panel bench faced with such a task and the result would not be swung as easily as it perhaps was in *Coughlan*.[115] The fourth is the way in which principles of fairness, abuse of power, proportionality and concern for the individual have gained greater prominence in administrative law. This is not to suggest that these principles and standards of judicial review are used consistently, nor universally across all of administrative law, but it is certainly the case that there has been growing engagement with these matters beyond simply legitimate expectations, and in this sense *Coughlan* forms part of a broader transformation of administrative law. Thus returning to our understanding of what constitutes a landmark case and our iconic images, it is fair to say that *Coughlan* identified the boundaries of legitimate expectations, is part of the development of modern broader principles of administrative law, that it set out some guidance, which needed to be refined in subsequent cases (and will continue to be refined), and that it marked a clear turning point in history. Thus *Coughlan* can be seen to be a lighthouse beaming across the water—providing a level of protection not seen in other cases. It can also be seen to be a flag staking out unchartered territory. And finally it can be seen to be a red and white buoy bobbing along in the sea of administrative law, supporting its own weight, with its head firmly above the water, yet open to new currents and direction.

---

[113] *R (on the application of Bancoult) v Secretary of State for Foreign and Commonwealth Affairs* [2008] UKHL 61, [2009] 1 AC 453.
[114] *Youssef v Secretary of State for Foreign and Commonwealth Affairs* [2016] UKSC 3 at [55]; *Keyu v Secretary of State for Foreign and Commonwealth Affairs and Secretary of State for Defence* [2015] UKSC 69 at [132].
[115] See for example the differences which emerge from *R (on the application of Nicklinson) v Ministry of Justice* [2014] UKSC 38.

10

R (Jackson) v Attorney-General [2005]: Reviewing Legislation

ELIZABETH WICKS

I. Introduction: The Hunting Act 2004 and the Legal Challenge in *Jackson*

Jackson v Attorney-General[1] is a landmark case in British public law. It involves a challenge to the Hunting Act 2004 based on the argument that it is not a valid Act of Parliament due to its enactment by way of the procedure laid out in the Parliament Act 1949. The Hunting Act stemmed from a Labour party election manifesto promise in 2001 to ban foxhunting, an issue which engenders passionate feelings on both sides of the debate. After the election, there seemed less enthusiasm for the measure amongst Labour ministers but there remained pressure from Labour backbenchers as well as a widespread campaign.[2] When the Government's Hunting Bill finally found its way onto the floor of the House of Commons, it did not ban hunting completely but sought to regulate it by means of a licensing scheme. Amidst public protests, a backbench Labour MP, Tony Banks, introduced an amendment to ban hunting entirely. The amendment was passed by the House of Commons with a majority of 208 in a free vote, but the House of Lords then rejected it by a similarly large majority of 212. A sense of the reason for the rejection can be found in the manner in which the topic is later expressed by Lord Steyn in *Jackson*: 'The New Labour government decided that it would abolish the ancient liberty of the British people, regularly exercised by a great many individuals up and down the land, to take part in fox hunting. It was a deeply controversial measure.'[3]

With the two Houses unable to agree a compromise, in 2004, the Hunting Act became law through the procedure laid out in the Parliament Act 1949. It prohibits all hunting of wild mammals with dogs, except where an exemption applies. The Act soon faced a number of legal challenges. The most significant challenge in constitutional law terms, however, was that brought in *Jackson* in which it was

---

[1] *R (Jackson) v Attorney General* [2005] UKHL 56; [2006] 1 AC 262.
[2] T Mullen (2007), 'Reflections on *Jackson v Attorney General*: Questioning Sovereignty' 27 Legal Studies 1, at p 1.
[3] *Jackson*, n 1 above, para 72 *per* Steyn.

argued that the 2004 Act was not a valid Act of Parliament due to its reliance upon the amended 1949 Parliament Act procedure. The appellants were members of the Countryside Alliance, a prominent lobbying group on rural issues, although the proceedings were brought in their personal capacities. Mullen has queried whether the appellants had standing given that they had not been prosecuted or threatened with prosecution under the Act. This was not an issue challenged by the Attorney-General, however, and Mullen takes the view that, 'it suited the government to have the main issues in the case determined. ... it was more convenient to have it decided in advance of entry into force rather than prolong the uncertainty by waiting until the question was raised in defence to prosecutions'.[4] At the crux of the challenge was whether the amended procedure of the 1949 Act could be used by the House of Commons to create a valid Act of Parliament. As Plaxton succinctly expresses it: 'in using this revised process it employed neither the procedure required at common law nor that expressly approved by Parliament as a whole. It seems to have used a procedure expressly approved only by itself.'[5] The appellants sought a declaration that '1) The Parliament Act 1949 is not an Act of Parliament and is consequently of no legal effect. 2) Accordingly, the Hunting Act 2004 is not an Act of Parliament and is of no legal effect.'[6] Both the Queen's Bench Divisional Court[7] and the Court of Appeal[8] declined to make such a declaration. This chapter will focus upon the judgment of the House of Lords.

Jackson is a significant case, not only because of the decision on the validity of the Hunting Act 2004, but also for the musings of senior judges on the evolution of what arguably remains the key principle of the Constitution: parliamentary sovereignty. This chapter argues that *Jackson* is a legacy of two distinct periods of constitutional evolution. The first culminated in the early years of the twentieth century with a conflict between the elected liberal government and the hereditary second chamber that threatened the very stability of the UK's parliamentary executive system. The Parliament Act 1911 which resulted from this constitutional crisis ensured that the elected House of Commons would henceforth enjoy unchallenged superiority over the House of Lords. A more recent period of constitutional evolution characterised by post-Dicey constitutional thought has gone further in an attempt to ensure democratic values such as the rule of law dominate a contemporary theory of parliamentary sovereignty. This chapter analyses both steps in the ongoing democratisation of the Constitution and thereby place the landmark *Jackson* judgment in historical and political context. Therefore, it begins with a detailed discussion of the background to both Parliament Acts. Then, after an analysis of the main issues raised by the judgment itself, the case will be placed in the context of the two steps towards democratisation identified above.

---

[4] Mullen, n 2 above, p 4.
[5] M Plaxton, (2006) 'The Concept of Legislation: *Jackson v Her Majesty's Attorney General*' 69 Modern Law Review 249, at p 251.
[6] *Jackson*, n 1 above, para 2 Maurice Kay and Collins.
[7] [2005] EWHC 94 (Admin) (Kay and Collins).
[8] [2005] EWCA civ 126; [2005] QB 579 Lord Woolf, Phillips and May.

II. Background: The Parliament Acts

A. Constitutional Crisis and the Parliament Act 1911

The Parliament Act 1911 was described by Lord Bingham as 'the product of a constitutional crisis by some margin the most acute to afflict this country during the twentieth century'.[9] The crisis[10] arose due to the inevitable conflict between a Conservative-dominated House of Lords and a Liberal-dominated House of Commons following the landslide election victory of the Liberal Party in 1906.[11] Beginning with the Government's much-heralded Education Bill in 1906, over the next three parliamentary sessions every Bill which was opposed by Arthur Balfour, the Leader of the Opposition, in the House of Commons was subsequently rejected or amended out of all recognition by the House of Lords. As Lloyd George (the Chancellor of the Exchequer) was later famously to say, the House of Lords was not acting as the watchdog of the Constitution but as 'Mr Balfour's poodle. It fetches and carries for him. It barks for him. It bites anybody that he sets it on to.'[12] The conflict came to a head with the introduction of George's radical 1909 Budget. Facing large fiscal debts but needing to find money for the extensive social reforms for which the Liberals were elected, Lloyd George sought to raise revenue by increasing direct taxation.[13] In a striking, although not entirely unpredictable, move the House of Lords rejected Lloyd George's Budget by 350 votes to 75. Whether this was, as the government of the day argued,[14] a violation of a 200-year-old constitutional convention, is debatable. The very idea of a 'budget' in the sense of an omnibus Bill including all revenue measures for the year was a relatively new concept in 1909.[15] However, there is no doubt that by rejecting the budget, the House of Lords was issuing a direct challenge to the House of Commons' control

---

[9] *Jackson*, n 1 above, para 8 *per* Bingham.
[10] The discussion in this section is largely drawn from the more detailed exploration of these events of 1906–1911 in E Wicks, *The Evolution of a Constitution: Eight Key Moments in British Constitutional History* Oxford, Hart, 2006, Ch 5.
[11] There was a huge majority of 357 for the Government in the House of Commons. By contrast, the House of Lords contained a nominal Conservative majority of 391. R. Jenkins (1954), *Mr Balfour's Poodle* London, Collins, pp 19–24).
[12] Quoted in D Butler & G Butler (2000), *Twentieth Century British Political Facts 1900–2000* (London, Macmillan, 8th ed) at p 286.
[13] The 1909 budget included seven entirely new taxes, plus significant increases in tobacco and liquor duties, death duties, stamp duties, and income tax. It was extremely controversial and united a variety of powerful interests in opposition to it, including the land interest, tariff reformers and the licensed trade.
[14] See Asquith at Hansard, HC Debs 5th Series, Vol 13, col 552 (2 December 1909).
[15] Balfour made this very point in the House of Commons: 'How long has that unbroken tradition continued? It evidently could not go back before the period when all our provisions for taxation were embodied in one Bill, and that is within the memory of men living … It is quite true that the Budget embodying the taxes of the year was never rejected, because there never was a Budget Bill embodying them: it is an entirely modern invention …' (ibid at col 562).

over financial measures for the year, and this was certainly something unusual.[16] It had, in effect, refused supply.

The Government's response left no doubt that this was not merely an issue of one budget, but a matter of the relationship between the two Houses of Parliament. Prime Minister Asquith argued that in rejecting the budget, the Lords had 'opened out a wider and more far-reaching issue', which he described as 'whether when the Tory Party is in power the House of Commons shall be omnipotent, and whether when the Liberal Party is in power the House of Lords shall be omnipotent'.[17] It was, he claimed, 'a system of false balances and loaded dice'.[18] A general election was called, and subsequently held in January 1910.[19] The Liberals narrowly won, but lost their absolute majority and henceforth needed to rely upon Irish support. The so-called 'People's Budget', which had received somewhat muted support from the electorate (at a time, of course, when the majority of 'the people' remained disfranchised) was reintroduced and passed into law with little debate.[20] The conflict between the Houses had by then moved on. No longer an issue of the Government's financial policies, the battleground now was reform of the Lords.

Reform of the House of Lords had been contemplated by the Liberal party even before the budget crisis.[21] Now, in March 1910, a series of resolutions were introduced into the House of Commons to put this plan into action. In essence these resolutions comprised what was to become the Parliament Act: the House of Lords would not be able to amend or reject money Bills; it would only be able to delay other Bills for two sessions; and the maximum duration of Parliament would be reduced from seven years to five years.[22] Some peers, in a desperate effort to retain the veto of the Lords, made some efforts at this stage to introduce reform of the composition of the upper house in the hope that this would legitimise the exercise of its powers. Even within the Liberal Cabinet, there was disagreement about whether reform of powers or composition would be optimal. A compromise was eventually reached under which the absolute veto would be replaced by a suspensory veto but only as a means whereby composition reform could subsequently be

---

[16] Blewett suggests that the Lords had not attempted to challenge the House of Commons' control over the general financial provisions of the year since the seventeenth century. N. Blewett (1972), *The Peers, The Parties and the People: The General Elections of 1910* London, Macmillan, p 98.

[17] Hansard, n 14 above, col 558.

[18] ibid.

[19] The results of the election were as follows: Liberals 275; Unionists 273; Labour 40; Irish Nationalists 82. See Blewett, n 16 above, Ch 7 for analysis.

[20] It remains a budget of unprecedented significance. As Murray notes, the modernisation of the British system of taxation, the financing of the social service state, the defeat of tariff reform, the slide towards civil war in Ireland, as well as the destruction of the absolute veto of the Lords, all flowed from it. B. Murray (1980), *The People's Budget 1909–1910: Lloyd George and Liberal Politics* Oxford, Clarendon Press, p 290.

[21] As early as 1907 Campbell-Bannerman had proposed the replacement of the Lords' absolute veto with a suspensory veto.

[22] These principles were very similar to the Campbell-Bannerman scheme but with one significant exception. In 1907, it had not been thought necessary to legislate that the Lords had no power to amend or reject money Bills; by 1910, it was clear that this would have to be included at the core of the government's legislative plans.

pursued.[23] Therefore, a preamble was inserted into the newly drafted Parliament Act which infamously declared that 'it is intended to substitute for the House of Lords as it at present exists, a Second Chamber constituted on a popular instead of a hereditary basis'. Such further reform has been somewhat delayed.[24]

When King Edward VII died suddenly in May 1910, the two main parties agreed to participate in a constitutional conference in an attempt to reach a compromise solution, and thus protect the new monarch from being thrust into a constitutional crisis. The conference was doomed to failure, however, with the insurmountable stumbling-block of Irish home rule. The opposition insisted that 'constitutional legislation', including home rule, be submitted to a referendum of the people if both Houses failed to agree. The Government, fully intending to introduce home rule and knowing that the public would not support it in a referendum, refused this ultimatum and the conference stalled. Indeed, Norton argues that the impetus for the 1911 Act was not the people's budget, but rather Irish home rule.[25] He claims it is this topic that explains the stance taken by the different parties on the Lords' reform issue.[26] Norton correctly states that 'it was not so much a peers-versus-people debate as a home rule-versus-the union debate, with the House of Lords viewed primarily from the perspective of which side of the argument one took'.[27]

Another general election was called. The new king could be protected no longer and Asquith asked George V for a pre-election guarantee that he would create additional Liberal peers should the government be returned to power and make such a request. George V reluctantly agreed. The December 1910 election, despite a large number of seats changing hands, produced a very similar result to the previous one. The Parliament Bill was reintroduced into the Commons in February 1911. Again the Lords, including at this stage Lord Lansdowne, the Conservative Leader in the Lords, contemplated composition reform as a means of retaining their veto powers, but when the Government declared that the Parliament Bill scheme would still be pursued, and that even a reformed House of Lords would have its veto power removed, any appetite for composition reform amongst the peers evaporated. Once the Parliament Bill passed the Commons, the stage was set for a final showdown. The Lords proposed sweeping amendments during the committee stage and the Bill returned to the House of Commons amended out of all recognition. On 20 July, Asquith wrote to Lords Balfour and Lansdowne

---

[23] Blewett, n 16 above, p 152.
[24] The hereditary principle was finally reduced, if not entirely removed, in the House of Lords Act 1999; constitution on a popular basis remains unachieved over a century later.
[25] P Norton (2013), 'Parliament Act 1911 in its Historical Context' in D Feldman, *Law in Politics; Politics in Law* Hart Publishing, p 155.
[26] For example, the constitutional conference broke down on the issue as the Conservatives insisted on the exemption of a home rule bill, and eventually the Conservative leadership failed to oppose the Parliament Bill in order to avoid swamping the Lords with Liberal peers who were pro-home rule. (ibid pp 166–167).
[27] ibid p 167.

confirming that the Government would, if necessary, ask the King to use his prerogative to secure the Bill's passage and that he had agreed to act on that advice.[28] The revelation caused uproar amongst the opposition and it soon divided into two positions. On one side, Balfour and Lansdowne both now argued that, in light of the Government's threat to create peers, the Parliament Bill should be allowed to pass. Those who supported this argument were soon to be named the 'hedgers' in contrast with those on the other side of the argument who were called 'ditchers' as they would fight to the last ditch to oppose the Parliament Bill.[29] The King insisted that the Parliament Bill be returned to the House of Lords to give the Lords a last chance to pass the Bill without the need for him to use his prerogative to create new Liberal peers. When a division was called on 10 August, the result was 131 for the Government and 114 against. The 'hedges', guided by the leadership of Balfour and Lansdowne, abstained while the 'ditchers' voted against the Bill as they had promised. Crucially, however, Earl Curzon rallied 37 Conservative peers to vote with the Government and in favour of the Bill in order to cancel out the activities of the 'ditchers'. The Parliament Bill, which removed the legislative veto of the House of Lords, had passed. The threat of a mass creation of Liberal peers had worked and, in the words of Cross, 'the oldest legislative assembly in the world, had abdicated'.[30]

Unionist fears of the use to which the Parliament Act was to be put proved well-founded when, in the very next session of Parliament, the Government of Ireland Bill (introducing home rule) was placed before Parliament, together with a Welsh Church Bill (disestablishing the Welsh church). Both were rejected by the Unionist-dominated House of Lords and both nevertheless became law under the new Parliament Act procedure. However, the delay imposed on home rule by the Lords' rejection had serious implications because, with the intervention of the First World War and civil war in Ireland, it was a policy that never came into force. It might be said that this was a missed opportunity to address the Irish question and one, which led to a tragic legacy. For the next thirty years there was no reliance upon the Parliament Act as the Lords did not resort to the use of their final remaining power of a two-year suspensory veto. This is largely explainable by the fact that for most of this period either the Conservatives or a coalition government were in power. However, the post-war election of 1945 created a new stage for conflict between the two Houses when a strong Labour government was elected with a mandate for extensive social, economic and political change. The 1911 Act was not to be the last word on the relationship between the two Houses of Parliament.

---

[28] Jenkins, p 11 above, p 219.
[29] ibid p 220.
[30] C Cross *The Liberals in Power 1905–1914* (Westport, Greenwood Press, 1963), p 129.

B. Reneging on the Deal? The Parliament Act 1949

In the general election of 1945, a Labour government led by Clement Attlee was elected to power. At a time of international instability and while attempting to rejuvenate the UK after the war, the Attlee administration was committed to widespread domestic reforms, including an extensive programme of nationalisation and the creation of the national health service. Amongst these innovative policies, Labour's election manifesto had included an ominous sentence: 'We give clear notice that we will not tolerate obstruction of the people's will by the House of Lords'.[31] One explanation for this vigorous approach may be that Attlee's Labour government had the support of even fewer peers than Asquith's Liberal government had enjoyed in the early twentieth century. There were, in 1945, only 16 Labour peers out of a total House of Lords membership of 789.[32] Despite the establishment of a sensible convention (named after the Conservative leader in the House of Lords, Lord Salisbury) that the House of Lords would not reject nor even delay any government Bills implementing the Government's manifesto commitments, a government with such an insignificant presence in the upper house looked vulnerable, especially if seeking to introduce radical policies.

While the backdrop to the 1911 Act had been Irish home rule, the backdrop to the 1949 Act was nationalisation. In particular, the Government's plans to nationalise the iron and steel industries had not been specified in its 1945 manifesto and therefore were potentially vulnerable to rejection by the Lords (not being protected under the Salisbury convention). The immediate impetus for a further reduction in the powers of the House of Lords arose from some internal differences within the Labour Cabinet.[33] The more conservative elements in the Cabinet (such as Herbert Morrison) sought to delay the nationalisation of iron and steel, while more radical elements (such as Aneurin Bevan) worried that postponing this policy would facilitate its rejection by the Lords due to the two-year delaying power under the 1911 Act.[34] This concern highlights the inherent problem with the 1911 scheme. While the powers of the Lords are limited, they are not removed, nor is the issue of their legitimacy addressed at all. Thus, by the mid-twentieth century the upper house remained dominated by one political party and the playing–field remained blatantly uneven. The Labour government of 1945 recognised that while a Conservative government enjoys a full five years in power; a non-Conservative government is guaranteed only three years to implement its policies, after which the Lords can either prevent Bills becoming law or require a general election on

---

[31] 'Let us face the future', April 1945, p 3. Quoted in D Hitchner (1948), 'The Labour Government and the House of Lords' 1 The Western Political Quarterly 426, at p 426.
[32] C Ballinger, 'The Parliament Act 1949' in Feldman, n 25 above, p 173.
[33] Hitchner, n 31 above, p 427.
[34] ibid.

the issue. While the Salisbury convention, and the related doctrine of the mandate, might protect policies specified in sufficient detail in the Government's election manifesto, any other policies become difficult to implement. As Hitchner wrote in the late 1940s, 'however hallowed the concept of the election mandate may be as a principle, it is not easily transferred from pure to applied form. Parliamentary government is not government by referendum. A Cabinet and a parliamentary majority cannot be expected to renounce all controversy for the last two-fifths of their life.'[35] The Labour government thus sought to further reduce the powers of the Lords by legislating to enable a Bill to become law after a one-year delay rather than two years as required by the 1911 Act. The Conservative opposition was outraged, arguing that this change would destroy the constitutional safeguards of the 1911 Act. It is a view that seems to attract some sympathy from Lord Brown in *Jackson* when he notes that the 1911 Act may be viewed as a new constitutional settlement and thus 'a consensual arrangement which could not then be changed at the instance of one party alone'. Lord Brown recognises, therefore, that 'to do as the House of Commons did in 1949 must strike many as quite simply unfair, akin to reneging on a deal'.[36]

The perception that the 1911 Act represented a consensual constitutional safeguard rests upon the concept of the doctrine of the mandate. While the purpose of the 1911 Act was undoubtedly to limit the capacity of the unelected House of Lords to impede the legislative progress of government, the retention of a delaying power could be perceived as allowing enough time to consult the people when the two Houses disagree. Indeed this was explicitly recognised as the original purpose of the delaying power in an agreed statement of party leaders from 1948:

> It is an essential constitutional safeguard to ensure that, in the event of serious controversy between the two House of Parliament, on a measure on which the view of the electorate is doubtful, such a measure shall not pass into law until sufficient time has elapsed to enable the electorate to be properly informed of the issues involved and for public opinion to crystallise and express itself.[37]

However, this position is accorded too much weight by some writers. Weill claims, for example, that the 'fundamental contribution of the House of Lords to Britain's democracy' is 'in enabling the People to voice their opinions over constitutional change. The Lords' veto fulfilled a role that is parallel to that of a constitutional court exercising judicial review over primary legislation.[38]

---

[35] ibid p 438.
[36] *Jackson*, n 1 above, para 185 *per* Brown.
[37] Parliament Bill 1947: Agreed Statement on Conclusion of Conference of Party Leaders, Feb–Apr 1948, Cmnd 7380, para 9, quoted in R. Weill, 'Centennial to the Parliament Act 1911: the manner and form fallacy' [2012] Public Law 105, at p 118. This conference of party leaders actually reached agreement on composition reform for the Lords (which the Conservatives favoured) but the stumbling block for a complete agreement was the length of the delaying power (See Ballinger, n 32 above, pp 434–5).
[38] Weill, n 37 above, p 124.

Whatever the original purpose of the delaying power, it is absurd to regard the House of Lords as giving voice to the people (especially, although not exclusively, at a stage in history when the hereditary concept still dominated the House).

While the 1949 Act retains the concept of a delaying power, its main difference from the earlier reform represented 'a changed view as to the reasonableness of the amount of impediment that the Lords should be permitted to impose'.[39] However, the Labour government's arguments for further limitation of the powers of the upper house was rather undermined in the late 1940s by the unexpected good behaviour of the Lords. None of the Government's Bills were rejected by the Lords (and indeed even the Iron and Steel Bill eventually passed without problem). But there was one Bill that the Government knew with certainty would only be passed using the Parliament Act procedure and that was the Bill containing the controversial amendments to the Parliament Act itself. The passage of the Parliament Act 1949 nicely illustrates the hoops through which non-Conservative governments had (and indeed still have) to jump in order to be sure of making law. The Bill had to be introduced before the end of 1947 in order to provide time for the 1911 Act requirements to be met; an extra short session of Parliament was held specifically to allow the Bill to pass the Commons for a second time; and retrospectively was required in the terms of the Bill in order to ensure the nationalisation of the iron and steel industries (which was included in a Bill already before Parliament) could be passed before the next election if it was necessary to use this amended procedure. It might be argued that this is no fit way for an elected government to have to govern.

Did the use of the 1911 procedure to pass an amendment to that Act raise concerns of acting ultra vires at the time? It seems not. It was openly accepted by both the Government and the opposition that the 1949 Act could, and might have to, pass using the 1911 procedure. The only concern expressed about the constitutionality of the new law was on the specific question of its retrospective application.[40] While Salisbury did raise the question of ultra vires, he was apparently assured by lawyers that there is no problem in using the 1911 Act procedure to amend the Act itself. For example, Viscount Simon (formerly Lord Chancellor) wrote 'No English constitutional lawyer, and no court in this country would ever maintain [that a Bill passed by Commons with Royal Assent was not law]'.[41] Given the later challenge in *Jackson*, this is interesting and may support the view expressed in that case by many of the Law Lords that, as a matter of practical reality, the 1949 Act cannot be challenged on ultra vires grounds. For example, Lord Hope noted that the 'political reality is that of a general acceptance by all the main parties and by

---

[39] Ballinger, n 32 above, p 172.
[40] ibid p 179.
[41] Quoted ibid.

both Houses of the amended timetable which the 1949 Act introduced. I do not think that it is open to a court of law to ignore that reality'.[42]

Back in 1949, the Lords rejected the Parliament Bill for a third time after which the speaker issued a certificate under the Parliament Act 1911. Royal Assent was soon given and the Parliament Act 1949 became law in December 1949. By this time, the Iron and Steel Bill had already received assent, having passed both Houses without problem. In hindsight, the amendment to the 1911 Act was not needed in order for Labour to implement its desired policies during this administration, and for a further four decades the amended procedure was not used. But towards the end of the twentieth century, governments of both major political parties sought to enact controversial legislation without the consent of the House of Lords.[43] The heated opposition to the ban on foxhunting facilitated a legal challenge to one such piece of legislation and the scene was set for a judicial assessment of the validity of an Act of Parliament—a rare event indeed.

III. The Judgment

Jackson v AG provided a rare opportunity for nine Law Lords[44] to explain their views on a range of constitutional matters. The judgments are erudite and intriguing, encompassing political history, constitutional theory and a smattering of realpolitik. The case invited the judges of the highest domestic court to consider the validity of what purported to be an Act of Parliament. The significance of the case being heard was downplayed, but it is hard to view it as anything other than a deviation from the old enrolled Bill rule.[45] Some of the Law Lords viewed the matter as one of mere statutory interpretation; others saw it as a problem which could only be resolved by an accurate understanding of parliamentary sovereignty.[46]

---

[42] *Jackson*, n 1 above, para 124 *per* Hope. He continued by saying that 'It is no longer open to the courts, if it ever was, to say that that Act was not authorised by Section 2(1) of the 1911 Act' (para 128). See also Nicholls at para 69 and Carswell at para 171.

[43] Ironically it was the Conservative government of Margaret Thatcher that first used the amended Parliament Act procedure to enact the War Crimes Act 1991. Tony Blair's New Labour Government then resorted to its use for three pieces of legislation within five years: the European Parliamentary Elections Act 1999, the Sexual Offences (Amendment) Act 2000 and the Hunting Act 2004.

[44] Bingham, Nicholls, Steyn, Hope, Rodger, Walker, Carswell, Brown, and Hale. All but Walker give their own detailed judgments.

[45] *Edinburgh and Dalkeith Railway v Wauchope* [1842] 8 Cl & F 710; *Pickin v British Railway Board* [1974] AC 765 HL. In *Jackson*, Hope notes that Campbell in *Edinburgh* said only that if a measure appears to have passed both Houses and received the Royal Assent that is the end of the enquiry and then Hope points out that 'an Act passed under the 1911 Act does not measure up to that test' (*Jackson*, n 1 above, para 112).

[46] Hope seems to view the entire case as one about parliamentary sovereignty as it is the focus of his entire judgment and he even says explicitly that: 'What this case is about therefore is the place which the court occupies in our Constitution with regard to the legislative sovereignty of Parliament.' (*Jackson*, n 1 above, para 109).

Many elements of the law and politics of the Constitution are touched upon. For this reason, the discussion in this section cannot be comprehensive. Instead, the focus will be upon four major, and interrelated, questions considered by the Law Lords in this important case. First, whether the Parliament Act 1949 was delegated or primary legislation; second, whether Parliament has been redefined by this Act; third, whether there are any exceptions to the legislation that can be passed using the 1949 Act procedure; and finally, and underlying all of the other questions, the current status of the doctrine of parliamentary sovereignty.

A. Delegated or Primary Legislation?

At the crux of the challenge to the validity of the Hunting Act 2004 in *Jackson* was the delegation argument. This states that the legislation passed using the 1911 Parliament Act procedure has not been passed by the sovereign Parliament and therefore is not primary legislation but rather delegated legislation. Thus, under this argument, the 1949 Act was a futile attempt by a delegated body (the House of Commons and Monarch) to increase the scope of its delegated authority. There are, in effect, two strands to this argument: first, that legislation passed using the 1911 procedure is merely delegated, rather than primary, legislation; and secondly, that the 1949 Act represented an attempt by a delegated body to increase the scope of its delegated authority. The argument fell at the first hurdle. The House of Lords in *Jackson* rejected the argument that the legislation made under the 1911 Act procedure is not primary legislation, even though such legislation is required to state on its face that it is made by the authority of the 1911 Act and thus appears to depend for its validity on a prior enactment.[47] As Lord Bingham explained, the 1911 Act created a new way of enacting primary legislation.[48] Crucial to this conclusion was the fact that laws passed using the 1911 procedure are labelled 'Acts of Parliament' within the 1911 Act itself. That phrase, in Lord Bingham's view, is used only to denote primary legislation.[49] Also significant to this conclusion is the Court's reluctance to view the 1911 Act as involving a delegation of any kind. As Lord Bingham notes, the object of the Act was not to enlarge the powers of the Commons but to restrict those of the Lords.[50]

It might be countered, however, that the Act actually does both: the powers of the Lords are explicitly restricted and thus the powers of the Commons are implicitly increased. In the long story of the relationship between the two Houses of Parliament, of which the Parliament Acts are a crucial chapter, the powers of one House are inevitably measured against their influence over the sovereign body as a

---

[47] *Jackson*, n 1 above, para 22 *per* Bingham.
[48] ibid para 24. See also Lord Hope at para 111: it is primary legislation 'albeit enacted in a different way'.
[49] ibid.
[50] ibid para 25.

whole. For example, it is impossible to view the constitutional convention limiting the powers of the Monarch to veto legislation as not increasing the power of both Houses to produce legislation. In the UK's evolving Constitution, the limitation of one body inevitably elevates the power and significance of the other parts of the Constitution. Thus, even though the purpose of the 1911 Act was to restrict the powers of the Lords, this was expected, and indeed intended, to have the simultaneous effect of increasing the powers of the Commons. A stronger justification for the rejection of the view of the Commons and monarch as delegates is that 'they themselves constituted two of the delegators'.[51] On this basis, the Law Lords' rejection of the delegation view is hard to criticise. It leads on, however, to the more difficult question of how to define the body comprising Commons and monarch.

B. (Re)defining Parliament

Some of the judges took the view that the 1911 Act redefined Parliament; others found such a view to be unhelpful. Lord Hope, for example, explicitly rejects a redefinition view and states that he does not think it is helpful to describe the 1911 Act as having remodelled or redefined Parliament.[52] Nevertheless, even Lord Hope accepts that the Act has in practice altered the balance of power between the two Houses.[53] In this way, if no other, the internal dynamics of Parliament might be viewed as redefined. Lord Steyn has no qualms about describing Parliament as redefined[54] and holds that the 1911 Act 'simply provides for an alternative mode by which Parliament, as reconstituted for specific purposes, may make laws'.[55] On this view, the will of Parliament can be ascertained in more than one manner. Lord Steyn further explains his view that the word 'Parliament' involves 'both static and dynamic concepts. The static concept refers to the constituent elements that make up Parliament: the House of Commons, the House of Lords, and the Monarch. The dynamic concept involves the constituent elements functioning together as a law making body'.[56] On this view, the underlying issue is the question of which body is sovereign.

As will be discussed more fully below, a redefinition view is linked to a manner and form interpretation of parliamentary sovereignty. The question thus changes from whether or not Parliament is sovereign to become a question of which 'Parliament' is sovereign on any particular issue. While the tripartite body will always be sovereign, the newly created bipartite body is also sovereign

---

[51] ibid para 173 *per* Carswell.
[52] ibid para 113 *per* Hope.
[53] ibid.
[54] ibid para 86 *per* Steyn.
[55] ibid para 94 *per* Steyn.
[56] ibid para 81 *per* Steyn. It is perhaps in this sense that Brown refers to redefinition. By recognising that the 1911 Act has 'redefined the sovereign Parliament's legislative process', Brown focuses on redefinition in terms of process rather than institution (para 187).

for all matters, except that denied it within the terms of the 1911 Act—namely, extending the lifetime of Parliament. This idea of more than one body being the 'sovereign Parliament' requires us to first look at what the issue is, then ask who is the sovereign body on this particular issue. Such an approach is supported and explained by Forsyth: 'The clear definition of what "Parliament" means, in particular circumstances, provides the means whereby parliamentary sovereignty is preserved—there is nothing on which Parliament cannot legislate, yet constitutional guarantees (such as the prohibition upon extending the life of Parliament) remain effective.'[57] This interpretation is not universally accepted. Ekins, for example, rather than viewing different bodies as 'the sovereign Parliament' regards only 'Parliament' as sovereign and takes the view that it is always the tripartite Parliament that legislates, even in circumstances when unanimity of its constituent parts is not required under the Parliament Act procedure.[58] Under either view, the bipartite Parliament of Commons and Monarch cannot legislate to extend the lifetime of Parliament either because it is not the sovereign body on that issue (Forsyth) or because unanimity of all three bodies is required on that issue (Ekins). The question of whether this limitation is entrenched and/or joined by any other implicit limitations on the law-making power of the bipartite body is one that presented some challenges to the Law Lords.

C. Exceptions to the Use of the Parliament Act Procedure

The Court of Appeal judgment in *Jackson*, while accepting that both the Parliament Act 1949 and the Hunting Act 2004 were valid Acts of Parliament, had suggested that there were some limits to the use to which the Parliament Act procedure could be put. The Court claimed, obiter, that the 1911 Act could not be used 'so as to produce results that will constitute a different constitutional settlement'.[59] It gave examples such as an extension to the life of Parliament or the abolition of the House of Lords and held that these, unlike the reduction in the delaying power by one year in the 1949 Act, would be changes 'so fundamental, that they could only be enacted or expressly made possible by what is traditionally the sovereign Parliament. That is to say by the triumvirate of the Monarch, the Lords and the Commons.'[60] Even though expressed obiter, this was an aspect of the Court of Appeal's judgment that the Attorney-General at the time was very keen to see

---

[57] C Forsyth, 'The Definition of Parliament after *Jackson*: Can the Life of Parliament be Extended under the Parliament Acts 1911 and 1949?' (2011) 9 International Journal of Constitutional Law 132, at p 141.

[58] R Ekins, 'Acts of Parliament and the Parliament Acts' (2007) LQR 91, at p 98: 'I read the 1911 Act not to authorise Queen and Commons to legislate but instead to provide that Parliament may act even when the Lords do not assent.' Under this view, the Lords participate in legislating even when they do not assent to the Bill's passage.

[59] CA judgment, n 8 above, para 46.

[60] ibid para 48.

overruled by the House of Lords,[61] and such proved to be the case. Lord Bingham was critical of the Court of Appeal's approach, claiming that it was 'contradicted both by the language of the section and by the historical record'.[62] The latter point is worth some attention. A number of the judgments correctly point out that the primary purpose of the removal of the Lords veto power in the 1911 Act was in order to effect a major constitutional change, namely Irish home rule.[63] Indeed, as Lord Bingham remarks, if the liberal government had been willing to exclude major constitutional changes from the ambit of the Parliament Bill (as the Court of Appeal sought to do), the constitutional conference of 1910 may not have broken down and agreement on reform could have been reached at that stage.[64] The Law Lords are entirely correct to recognise that the bypassing of the Lords was intended to be effective even for major constitutional changes and the Court of Appeal's purported restriction is not only hard to define, but also fundamentally flawed.[65]

This is not the end of the matter, however, because despite this apparently strong rejection of the Court of Appeal's explicit exception approach, some of the Law Lords seem inclined to the view that there are exceptions, but that they are undefined ones. Thus Lord Hope considers the issue to be a broader one of whether even a sovereign Parliament is truly unlimited:

> a conclusion that there are no legal limits to what can be done under Section 2(1) does not mean that the power to legislate which it contains is without any limits whatever. Parliamentary sovereignty is an empty principle if legislation is passed which is so absurd or so unacceptable that the populace at large refuses to recognise it as law.[66]

A close reading of Lord Hope's judgment suggests that he views the entire case as an issue of the correct meaning of parliamentary sovereignty and central to his significant discussion of the meaning of this doctrine is this acceptance that there are constitutional limits to sovereignty. Lord Brown, who does not take such a radical view on sovereignty in his judgment, nevertheless also expresses doubts that there are no exceptions to the law-making powers of the bipartite body:

> I am not prepared to give such ruling as would sanction in advance the use of the 1911 Act for all purposes, for example to abolish the House of Lords, (rather than, say, alter its Constitution or method of selection) or to prolong the life of Parliament, two of the extreme ends to which theoretically this procedure could be put.[67]

---

[61] Goldsmith, the Attorney-General, was quoted as saying that the Court of Appeal's conclusion that the 1911 Act procedure has limits was 'unwarranted and unworkable' and would bring 'chaos to the government's legislative programme' by which he seemed to have in mind further reform of the composition of the House of Lords. C Dyer (2005), 'Goldsmith urges Law Lords not to risk 'chaos'' *The Guardian*, 15 July 2005.
[62] *Jackson*, n 1 above, para 30 *per* Bingham.
[63] See Rodger at para 131 and Hale at para 157.
[64] *Jackson*, n 1 above, para 31 (per Bingham).
[65] Steyn para 96 and Brown para 194, describing it succinctly as 'unwarranted in law and unworkable in practice') also explicitly reject the Court of Appeal's approach.
[66] *Jackson*, n 1 above, para 120 *per* Hope.
[67] ibid para 194 *per* Brown.

Extending the lifetime of Parliament raises specific issues, discussed below, due to its inclusion as an explicit exception in the 1911 Act, but the doubts expressed here about the use of the Parliament Act procedure to abolish the House of Lords are not founded upon the text but solely upon principle. And arguably, unlike the Court of Appeal's attempt to make explicit the principle, Lord Brown's suggested exception is ungrounded and implicit.

Only Lord Carswell seems to agree with the Court of Appeal on this issue, although his agreement is somewhat ambiguous. He notes the 'general lack of enthusiasm for the proposition espoused by the Court of Appeal', but nonetheless explains that he inclines 'very tentatively to the view that its instincts may be right, that there may be a limit somewhere to the powers contained in Section 2(1) of the 1911 Act, though the boundaries appear extremely difficult to define.'[68] When explained in such terms, it is hard to distinguish between Lord Carswell's approach—which inclines towards accepting the Court of Appeal's exception approach—and that of Lords Hope and Brown—who explicitly reject it and yet propose their own potential exceptions. When Lord Carswell expressly reserves his opinion on whether a legal challenge could succeed on the use of the 1911 Act for a 'fundamental disturbance of the building blocks of the Constitution',[69] he seems to be lending support to the enlightened view of a non-absolute sovereignty expressed variously by Lords Steyn, Hope and Baroness Hale.

To these reservations about the use to which the Parliament Act procedure can legitimately be put, must be added a more widespread concern about the need to protect the one statutory exception. The 1911 Act reserves an extension of the lifetime of Parliament to the tripartite Parliament—or, in other words, this is the one issue on which the House of Lords retains a veto. Such protection could theoretically be circumvented by a two-stage process. Such a removal would involve two Acts passed under the 1911 Act procedure: one to amend the terms of the 1911 Act and thus remove the exception; and then a second to extend the lifetime of Parliament. Lord Bingham accepts that such a two-stage removal of the lifetime of Parliament protection would be acceptable, but he is alone amongst the judges in doing so.[70] Lord Rodger specifically reserves his opinion on this question,[71] but for the other judges such an approach would not be permissible. For Lord Hope, for example, there is 'an implied prohibition' to prevent such a two-stage removal.[72] Even Lord Nicholls, for whom there is no other exception to the use of the Parliament Act procedure, agrees on this point, arguing that the express exclusion 'carries with it, by necessary implication, a like exclusion in

---

[68] ibid para 178 *per* Carswell.
[69] ibid. He pre-empts his point with recognition that it may well be that no government in the real political world would seek to use the 1911 Act for such a 'fundamental disturbance' of the Constitution.
[70] ibid para 32 *per* Bingham.
[71] ibid para 139 *per* Rodger.
[72] ibid para 122 *per* Hope.

respect of legislation aimed at achieving the same result by two steps rather than one. If this were not so the express legislative intention could readily be defeated.'[73]

In summary, while at first glance the House of Lords overrule the Court of Appeal on there being exceptions to the use of the Parliament Act procedure, on closer investigation, many of the judges envisage there being limits to the use to which this procedure can be put. Most notably a majority recognise a further implied limitation connected with the single explicit limitation in the 1911 Act. Some go further, however, and propose either specific or non-specific exceptions relating to major constitutional changes. While this might seem to be a significant step, it must be placed in the context of an evolving conceptualisation of the powers of a sovereign Parliament. It is not only the bipartite Parliament that some judges perceive as limited in law-making power, as will now be discussed.

D. The Evolution of Parliamentary Sovereignty

A number of the Law Lords took the opportunity offered in *Jackson* to comment upon their contemporary understanding of the doctrine of parliamentary sovereignty. In doing so, they provided grist for the mill of the debate over the doctrine's current status. Lords Steyn, Hope and Baroness Hale all expressed reservations about the traditional absolute conception of sovereignty provided by Dicey.[74] They were the first senior judges to do so in a judicial capacity since the nineteenth century. For all three judges, the key to their understanding of parliamentary sovereignty was the existence of a Constitution imposing limits upon the legislative powers of Parliament. Lord Steyn, for example, explicitly rejected the argument that the UK has an uncontrolled Constitution giving as evidence the case of *Factortame* in which the supremacy of European Union (EU) law was categorically established by means of the suspension of an Act of Parliament which conflicted with it.[75] He also mentioned the other usual suspects in any discussion of Parliament's sovereignty today when he noted that the Scotland Act 1998 points to 'a divided sovereignty' and that the ECHR as incorporated by the HRA 1998 created 'a new legal order'.[76] These developments led Lord Steyn to note that:

> The classic account given by Dicey of the doctrine of the supremacy of Parliament, pure and absolute as it was, can now be seen to be out of place in the modern United Kingdom.[77]

Similarly Lord Hope explained that 'Parliamentary sovereignty is no longer, if it ever was, absolute. It is not uncontrolled ... It is no longer right to say that its freedom to legislate admits of no qualification whatever. Step by step, gradually

---

[73] ibid para 59 *per* Nicholls.
[74] A Dicey, *Introduction to the Study of the Law of the Constitution* (1959) London, Macmillan, 10th ed., at pp 39–40.
[75] *R v Secretary of State for Transport ex parte Factortame (No. 2)* [1991] 1 AC 603.
[76] *Jackson*, n 1 above, para. 102 (per Steyn).
[77] ibid.

but surely, the English principle of the absolute legislative sovereignty of Parliament which Dicey derived from Coke and Blackstone is being qualified.[78]

Both of these senior judges, however, continued to regard parliamentary sovereignty as an important principle of the Constitution.[79] This is not, therefore, a debate about whether Parliament is still sovereign but rather, and so much more interestingly, about what that sovereignty actually means today.

So, while Lord Steyn had no doubt that the supremacy of Parliament is still the general principle of the Constitution, it is, in his view, 'a construct of the common law. The judges created this principle'.[80] This is an interesting development from his previous point because the examples given by Lord Steyn of limited legislative sovereignty are self-imposed by Parliament; they stem from Acts of Parliament. Without the European Communities Act 1972, Scotland Act 1998 and Human Rights Act 1998, the new legal order identified by Lord Steyn would not have developed. Indeed, Lord Hope explicitly notes that most of the qualifications on Parliament's sovereignty to which he has alluded are the product of measures by Parliament itself.[81] However, the point made by Lord Steyn in emphasising that the sovereignty of Parliament is a judge-made phenomenon enables these judges to go much further in their critique because, by implication, it could thus be unmade by judges also. Indeed, he expresses that 'it is not unthinkable that circumstances could arise where the courts may have to qualify a principle established on a different hypothesis of constitutionalism'.[82]

Lord Hope further explains this very point when he claims that, the principle of parliamentary sovereignty 'which in the absence of a higher authority, has been created by the common law is built upon the assumption that Parliament represents the people whom it exists to serve'.[83] Thus examples are given of the types of laws, which the courts might step in to oppose, even if passed by a sovereign Parliament. They include attempts to abolish judicial review or the ordinary role of courts. Even Baroness Hale who seems rather to support the traditional view of parliamentary sovereignty in her judgment, claiming that the constraints on what Parliament can do are generally political and diplomatic rather than constitutional, nevertheless agrees with Lords Steyn and Hope that the courts 'will treat with particular suspicion (and might even reject) any attempt to subvert the rule of law by removing governmental action affecting the rights of the individual from all judicial scrutiny'.[84] It is, then, the rule of law (and the judges' vital role in upholding that principle) that has the potential to impose external restraints upon Parliament's sovereignty to sit alongside the self-imposed restraints of European

---

[78] ibid para. 104 (per Hope).
[79] Hope, for example, claims the Constitution is 'dominated by the sovereignty of Parliament'. (ibid.)
[80] ibid para 102 *per* Steyn.
[81] ibid para 105 *per* Hope.
[82] ibid.
[83] ibid para 126 *per* Hope.
[84] ibid para 159 *per* Hale.

legal supremacy and (arguably) devolution and human rights. Where Dicey, writing in the nineteenth century, had seen parliamentary sovereignty as 'the very keystone of the law of the Constitution',[85] in *Jackson* three senior judges seem to agree that the 'rule of law enforced by the courts is the ultimate controlling factor on which our Constitution is based'.[86] The change is the result of constitutional evolution: a gradual move from the absolute power of the sovereign to a constitutional democracy.

IV. *Jackson* in Context: The Evolution of a Constitutional Democracy

In *Jackson*, Lord Carswell explicitly notes that the UK Constitution 'has for the last 200 years developed by evolution rather than revolution'.[87] He continues by noting the characteristics and vulnerabilities of its unwritten nature: 'An unwritten Constitution, even more than a written one, is a living organism and develops with changing times, but it is still a delicate plant and is capable of being damaged by over-vigorous treatment, which may have incalculable results'.[88] For this reason, Lord Carswell recognises the moderate steps by which radical change has been introduced.[89] On no issue is this more obvious than the nature of Parliament itself. Two significant, but incremental, changes have shaped recent evolution of the Constitution: the increasing supremacy of the House of Commons over the House of Lords and the Monarch; and the growing recognition of a new conception of Parliament's legislative supremacy which is less absolutist and more democratic in nature.

A. The Changing Relationship between the Two Houses of Parliament

The 1911 Parliament Act was a turning point in the relationship between the two Houses of Parliament. Once the House of Commons had taken the first steps on the road towards democratic representation under the Great Reform Act of 1832, it had started to move beyond the control of members of the House of Lords. Before long, a conflict was brewing. When it erupted during the liberal government's battle with the Conservative-dominated House of Lords in the early years of the twentieth century, it culminated in the removal of the veto power for the

---

[85] A Dicey, n 74 above.
[86] ibid para 107 *per* Hope.
[87] ibid para 176 *per* Carswell. This a point developed in some detail in Wicks, n 2 above.
[88] ibid.
[89] ibid.

Upper House, and with it the parity between the two Houses. The 1911 settlement cannot be considered in isolation from the other significant steps taken in the eighteenth and nineteenth centuries to establish the framework for a modern Parliament and executive. Walpole's influence over the executive in the period 1721–1742 has a convincing claim to represent the emergence of the office of Prime Minister, while successive Reform Acts, beginning with the ground-breaking First Reform Act of 1832, both increased the franchise and removed the most blatant corruption from the House of Commons, and when considered alongside the resolution of the constitutional crisis of 1911 form a three-pronged move towards a democratic governmental system.[90] All three developments were guided by an increased democratisation of the British Constitution, although the meaning of this concept was also evolving, and doing so gradually. By 1911, a Prime Minister (usually elected) had replaced the monarch at the head of government; a large proportion of the (male) people were able to vote for elected representatives; and those elected representatives could legislate ultimately unhampered by the primarily hereditary Upper House.[91] By this date, the real source of power in the Constitution was the executive-dominated House of Commons, much as it is today.[92] And while further moves towards greater democratisation would soon follow, including women winning the vote and the removal of most of the hereditary peers from the House of Lords, a trend had been established: a democratically elected government would legislate through the House of Commons, while the other two branches of the tripartite sovereign Parliament would advise and scrutinise, but never again challenge.

It is perhaps surprising that, with this developing trend towards democratisation, both the Upper House and the Monarchy have not only survived but also retained a formal role in Parliament's law-making function. It is, however, their other assets that have preserved these two entities: the scrutinising role of the Lords and the ceremonial role—and, to many, patriotic symbolism—of the Monarchy. Whether the House of Lords could be abolished by the House of Commons without its own acquiescence is an interesting constitutional question. Pannick has argued that the 1911 Act cannot be used to abolish the House of Lords because of the need for that House to consent to any Bill to extend the lifetime of Parliament.[93] That proviso certainly assumes the continued existence of a second chamber, although a substantial reform of the House of Lords would, in Pannick's view, be possible under the Parliament Act 1911.[94] Although at least one judge

---

[90] See Wicks, n 10 above, Chs 3–5 for discussion of these three developments.
[91] Hale in *Jackson* recognised that the purpose of the 1911 Act was one of democratisation: 'to ensure that the elected House could always get its way in the end. The United Kingdom would become a real democracy' (*Jackson*, n 1 above, para 156).
[92] Wicks, n 10 above, p 110.
[93] D Pannick, 'Securing Political Success by Repetition (F. Smith): Can the Parliament Act 1911 be used by the House of Commons to insist on Reform of the House of Lords?' [2012] Public Law 230, at p 235.
[94] ibid p 236.

in *Jackson* expressed reservations about the use of the Parliament Act procedure to abolish the Upper House, it is hard to find a sufficient constitutional justification for restricting the procedure in this way. It is, after all, a use that could have been specified as excluded from the Act at its origin if required. Of course, Lord Carswell's point that successive governments, even those with massive majorities, have recognised the delicacy of the unwritten Constitution and therefore exercised a degree of moderation when approaching radical changes such as this, is relevant to the likelihood of the Parliament Act's use to abolish the Upper House. Pannick also points out that even if an outright abolition of the House of Lords would not be effective under the Parliament Act procedure, a transformation of the House by means of composition, or a further restriction of its remaining delaying power would be possible. Indeed, a complete removal of all powers from the Lords other than to reject a Bill to extend the lifetime of Parliament, would be permissible even under Pannick's view.[95]

Reform of the composition of the House of Lords has barely been off the political agenda since the start of the twentieth century and the substantial reform that has taken place—including the introduction of life peers and removal of most of the hereditary peers—has resulted in a largely ineffectual institution. It could be argued that the perceived illegitimacy of the House of Lords throughout the twentieth century was a far more effective restraint upon its powers than the Parliament Act had ever sought to be.[96] If the House is to reclaim a core role in legislating for the UK, its composition must be further reformed in a way that finally restores legitimacy to the House. It is not surprising that successive governments have failed to achieve such reform because their dominance of the Lower House makes the increased legitimacy of the Upper House a potentially dangerous development. The trend towards democratisation has superficially enabled governments to emphasise the need for the people's elected representatives in the House of Commons to have the final say on legislation. But any informed understanding of democracy must go beyond an elected government and engage with issues of the constitutionally appropriate limitation of such a government. In *Jackson*, Lord Bingham recognised the concern that the Parliament Acts have eroded the checks and balances of the British Constitution, leaving entirely unconstrained a House of Commons now dominated by the executive. Lord Bingham notes in this context the 'willingness of successive governments of different political colours to invoke the 1949 Act not for the major constitutional purposes for which the 1911 Act was invoked ... but to achieve objects of more minor or no constitutional import. ...'[97] The principle of democracy supports the limitation of the House of Lords veto power (especially when it was a predominantly hereditary chamber) and the primacy of the elected government, but untrammelled legislative power exercisable

---

[95] ibid.
[96] Wicks, n 10 above, p 107.
[97] *Jackson*, n 1 above, para 41 *per* Bingham.

even by an elected government is a cause for concern. Democracy requires that an elected government can only do so much. The response of at least some senior judges to this concern is the focus, described above (and necessarily obiter in *Jackson*), on how the sovereignty of this Parliament dominated by the executive in the House of Commons, is now correctly conceived as limited.

B. The Evolving Conceptualisation of Parliamentary Sovereignty

In the *Jackson* context, and more broadly, it is hard not to agree with Barber's claim that parliamentary sovereignty 'did not provide a protection for Parliament or for the electorate; it provided a puzzle to entertain constitutional lawyers. ...'[98] While Dicey's traditional doctrine remains the starting point for any constitutional law lecture on parliamentary sovereignty, very quickly attention must now turn, not only to the myriad of challenges to his conception, but also to an increasing variety of alternate theories of parliamentary sovereignty. It is no longer as simple as a dichotomy between Dicey being right or the Westminster Parliament having lost its sovereignty to the EU. Now it is a question of what Parliament's sovereignty means today. This is the question that some of the judges in *Jackson* were keen to engage with, and contribute to. There are, broadly, two primary issues in contemporary analysis of parliamentary sovereignty. The first is the limit of parliamentary sovereignty by Parliament itself explained by means of a manner and form argument. The second is the limit of parliamentary sovereignty by the courts by means of the evolution of the rule of recognition to prioritise the rule of law. The latter approach falls within a legal constitutionalism approach. What is interesting about the discussion of parliamentary sovereignty in the *Jackson* case is that the challenge to the doctrine relevant to the case is the first one and yet the contributions most talked about are those that focus upon the second challenge. Indeed, Ekins notes that 'It is possible that *Jackson* will be remembered primarily for these assertions. This would be unfortunate for, with respect, the dicta in question are unargued and unsound, as well as less interesting than the live issues in the case.'[99] With some reservations about the criticisms of the contributions which, although under-developed are hardly lacking in support, it is certainly true that a greater focus on the issues relating to Parliament's legislative sovereignty which were pertinent to the interpretation of the Parliament Acts and thus to the resolution of the case would have been of great value and authority. It is perhaps significant, however, that while the first type of challenge outlined above retains the sovereignty paradigm, the second challenge does not necessarily do so. Despite the insistence by all judges in *Jackson* that Parliament remains sovereign, the focus of some judges on the prioritisation of the rule of law leads down a road travelling

---

[98] N Barber, 'The Afterlife of Parliamentary Sovereignty' (2011) 9 IJCL 144, at p 148.
[99] Ekins, n 58 above, p 103.

away from the sovereignty paradigm in a direction that the manner and form challenge never ventures.

V. Parliament Limiting its own Sovereignty: The Manner and Form Argument

A nice definition of the meaning of manner and form is provided by Zhou: 'the essence of manner and form conditions is found in the distinction between a formal (or procedural) requirement and a substantive requirement. To enact a valid law, Parliament must follow the relevant procedure in force at that time. However, the sovereign Parliament remains theoretically unrestrained from adopting any new procedural rules it can think of.'[100] This is an enlightening definition because it makes clear that manner and form does not necessarily mean entrenchment. Parliament must follow the procedure required at the time but can change that procedure for the future. Having originated with writers such as Jennings and Heuston in the mid-twentieth century,[101] to many it seemed as if this particular challenge to Dicey's absolutist doctrine was a relic of the past, with new trendier challenges taking the form of legal constitutionalism. However, the *Jackson* case has done much to resurrect manner and form as a meaningful rival to Dicey's continuing view of sovereignty. This is not at all surprising because the Parliament Act 1911 was always the prime exhibit of a 'manner and form' condition. It was a change in the procedure required to pass laws and it was created by Parliament itself, using the procedure required at the time (namely passage through both Houses of Parliament and royal assent).

Zhou argues that the House of Lords in *Jackson* accepted (explicitly or implicitly) the manner and form approach by reason of conceding that the Parliament Act 1911 created a new method of legislating.[102] This seems hard to deny. If the Parliament Act 1949 is a valid Act of Parliament, and the House of Lords in *Jackson* held that it was, then Parliament must have changed its procedure for making law because this 'Act' was not passed by the House of Lords. There is a far more challenging question raised by this, however. The Parliament Act procedure is an example of 'downward' redefinition. In other words, it was a change in procedure that made it easier for Parliament to legislate. *Jackson* accepts this as possible. Does it necessarily follow from this that Parliament could also make it harder for future Parliaments to legislate? Would the courts enforce that new, stricter, manner and form requirement? Baroness Hale thought so: 'If the sovereign Parliament can

---

[100] Han-Ru Zhou, 'Revisiting the 'Manner and Form' Theory of Parliamentary Sovereignty' [2013] LQR 610, at p 615. See also M Gordon, 'The Conceptual Foundations of Parliamentary Sovereignty: Reconsidering Jennings and Wade' [2009] Public Law 519.
[101] I Jennings, *The Law and the Constitution*. (1959) 5th ed. Hodder & Stoughton London; R Heuston, *Essays in Constitutional Law* (1964) 2nd ed Stevens, London.
[102] ibid.

redefine itself downwards, to remove or modify the requirement for the consent of the Upper House, it may very well be that it can also redefine itself upwards, to require a particular Parliamentary majority or a popular referendum for particular types of measure. In each case, the courts would be respecting the will of the sovereign Parliament as constituted when that will had been expressed.'[103] This is the real revelation of the *Jackson* judgment. It is not, of course, a view shared by all of the Law Lords as some express no view on the matter while others explicitly reject such an approach. But it is the most pressing and pertinent of all of the constitutional issues raised by *Jackson*. Does the court's acceptance of the Parliament Act procedure imply that it would also enforce 'upwards' redefinitions of Parliament in the future? Zhou argues that it would be illogical not to do so. He gives the interesting example of a repeal of the Parliament Acts. If these Acts represent a downwards redefinition, surely their repeal would make the law-making process more difficult and thus represent an upwards definition?[104] This is not an entirely convincing example, however, because it seems to confuse two different issues: whether Parliament can change its procedure to make legislating more difficult, and whether Parliament can prevent its successors from repealing the change in procedure. Repeal of the Parliament Acts must be possible but that is not the same as the creation of a new more restrictive means of legislating.

The real problem with the manner and form argument is that it is not just a procedural issue but could also potentially impose an indirect substantive limit. Barber gives the example of a requirement of unanimity in a referendum of the people.[105] On the surface that is an issue of the requisite procedure for law-making but in reality it excludes a matter from the legislative reach of Parliament. This has always been the vulnerability of the manner and form argument. It is perhaps the reason why reservations about Dicey's continuing view of sovereignty so often lead to a different line of attack: that of the explicit imposition of substantive limits. While reaching the same result, the latter at least has the merit of explicit justificatory support. It allows the courts to identify certain issues that are to be removed from Parliament's remit, rather than leaving it to the political will of a Parliament of the day. That, of course, is also its weakness.

VI. Legal Constitutionalism: The Rule of Law as the Ultimate Controlling Factor

In *Jackson*, Lords Steyn, Hope and Baroness Hale all seem to agree on certain constitutionally significant and controversial points. As Mullen explains, they 'appear to converge on the notions that the sovereignty of Parliament is an evolving doctrine,

---

[103] *Jackson*, n 1 above, para 163 *per* Hale.
[104] Zhou, n 100 above, p 626.
[105] Barber, n 98 above, p 148.

that it is ultimately in the keeping of the courts, and that it has now evolved to the point at which the Diceyian notion of unlimited legislative sovereignty no longer represents the true constitutional position'.[106] In their obiter comments, these three senior judges elevate the rule of law to the dominant position in the UK Constitution. For this reason, Mullen argues that *Jackson* 'may be seen as, if not a battle, at least an important skirmish, in the conflict between political and judicial constitutionalism'.[107] Mullen even suggests that certain judges are 'staking out their positions for future battles' because they fear the Government cannot be trusted on issues such as human rights, the rule of law, and the preservation of democracy and want to be in position to strike down certain legislation with some precedent for doing so.[108] While such an explicit motive is unsupported, there is no doubt that the obiter statements in *Jackson* would provide some tentative, non-binding, precedent for such a controversial move.

The key to understanding this elevation of the rule of law is an appreciation of the justification for parliamentary sovereignty. It is clear that Parliament acquired its sovereign legislative authority by gaining legitimacy over the centuries. Thus the developments discussed in the previous section such as the extension of the franchise, the positioning of the head of government within Parliament and, of course, the superiority of the elected House of Commons over the unelected House of Lords, has mirrored a recognition of sovereign legislative authority residing with Parliament. There are, of course, differing views on when Parliament first became sovereign (at least in the Diceyian sense of legally unlimited). The better, if controversial, view is that this is a relatively recent development, dating from the nineteenth century.[109] While there is no doubt that the 1689 constitutional settlement resulted in a Parliament that was legislatively supreme over the other branches of government, it did not necessarily require, or even suggest, that Parliament would be legally unlimited, let alone legally illimitable, much less did any previous constitutional development. Earlier in the seventeenth century, for example, it had been clear that certain fundamental principles of the common law imposed limits on Parliament.[110] However, as Parliament became more legitimate with the gradual democratisation of the House of Commons following the first three reform Acts, all three branches of government began to act as if Parliament's legislative supremacy was indeed a form of legally unlimited sovereignty. By the late nineteenth century, despite many enduring shortcomings and battles yet to be won (not least by the suffragette movement), the gradual democratisation of

---

[106] Mullen, n 2 above, p 14.
[107] ibid p 15.
[108] ibid.
[109] For a different view, see J Goldsworthy, *The Sovereignty of Parliament: History and Philosophy* (2001) Oxford, Oxford University Press and *Parliamentary Sovereignty: Contemporary Debates* Cambridge, (2010) Cambridge University Press.
[110] See the judgment of Coke in *Dr Bonham's Case*: 'When an Act of Parliament is against common right or reason, or repugnant, or impossible to be performed, the common law will control it, and adjudge such Act to be void.'(1610) [1614] 8 Co Rep 107a, at para 118. See also *Calvin's case* (7 Co Rep 1 at p 14); *Day v Savadge* Hob 85 at p 87; *Lord Sheffield v Ratcliffe* (Hob 334a at p 346)).

the Commons had significantly increased the legitimacy of the legislative branch of government. It was only at that time that the courts first began to categorically reject the idea, explicit in the seventeenth century Coke's doctrine, that some type of higher, fundamental constitutional principles imposed legal restraints upon legislative freedom.[111] By the time of Dicey's first edition of *The Law of the Constitution* in 1885, there was little reason to doubt his unambiguous description of parliamentary sovereignty as a cornerstone of the Constitution, nor his archetypal nineteenth century definition of that sovereignty in terms of legal illimitability.[112]

The apparent connection between the historical development of Parliament's democratic legitimacy and its acquisition of sovereign authority has often been relied upon in recent years to justify the superiority of Acts of Parliament and their protection from judicial interference.[113] However, if Parliament acquired its authority by accumulating legitimacy over the years, there are, as Jowell has argued,[114] possible justifications for limiting parliamentary sovereignty. The first of these is on the basis of legitimacy. The argument here is that Parliament cannot legislate to undermine its own legitimacy, as for example by abolishing elections. As Jowell explains, the legitimacy of parliamentary sovereignty 'rests upon Parliament's representative and accountable features. Such laws would degrade those features and therefore negate the basis of that legitimacy. They would undermine the very condition upon which Parliament's claim of supremacy rests.'[115] This is a convincing argument. There is a clear connection between Parliament's democratic legitimacy and its acquisition of sovereign legislative authority and, furthermore, this is a connection that successive governments have sought to rely upon in order to legislate on controversial topics including changing fundamentals of the Constitution (as with the European Communities Act 1972, and the HRA 1998). Parliament is sovereign because it is a democratically accountable body. If that precondition changed, it would become much more difficult to justify its lack of legal accountability. It is not clear, however, that the obiter comments in *Jackson* relied upon this reasoning. The types of laws identified as vulnerable to a judicial intervention were less focused on preserving the democratic character of Parliament and more focused on preserving the democratic function of the courts. This is where a second possible justification for limiting parliamentary sovereignty

---

[111] In *Lee v Bude & Torrington Junction Railway* [1871], for example, Willes said 'We sit here as servants of the Queen and the legislature. Are we to act as regents over what is done by Parliament with the consent of Queen, lords and commons? I deny that any such authority exists.' [1871] LR 6 CP 576, at p 582.

[112] A Dicey draws significantly upon Austin's positivist theory of the sovereign as a body which the bulk of society obeys and which does not habitually obey any other body. *The Province of Jurisprudence Determined* (1832) London, Weidenfeld & Nicolson, 1955.

[113] See, for example, Jack Straw's comments when introducing the Human Rights Act in 1998: 'In enacting legislation, Parliament is making decisions about important matters of public policy. The authority to make these decisions derives from a democratic mandate. Members of this place possess such a mandate because they are elected, accountable and representative.' HC Debs, vol 306, col 770, 16 Feb 1998.

[114] J Jowell, 'Parliamentary Sovereignty under the New Constitutional Hypothesis' [2006] Public Law 562, at p 565.

[115] ibid p 572.

identified by Jowell may be relevant. This relates to laws that purport to infringe the fundamentals of the Constitution, including concepts such as the rule of law and the protection of human rights. This seems to be more the focus of the judges in *Jackson* where the emphasis is on preserving the rule of law by preventing any attacks on judicial review or the ordinary role of the courts.

It is interesting to note that the rule of law plays a vital role in the decision in *Jackson* beyond being the focus of the obiter discussion of parliamentary sovereignty because it is the rule of law that is used to justify the courts' role in this challenge to the Hunting Act. As Lord Bingham, whose judgment is arguably the most sympathetic to the traditional view of parliamentary sovereignty, says: 'The appellants have raised a question of law which cannot, as such, be resolved by Parliament. But it would not be satisfactory, or consistent with the rule of law, if it could not be resolved at all.'[116] It is for this reason that any concerns about the enrolled Bill rule, and the appropriate limits of judicial enquiry into Acts of Parliament, are set aside. The fact that this reliance upon the rule of law is an implicit foundation for the very hearing of the case before it is then used by Lord Hope to substantiate his description of the principle as the 'ultimate controlling factor' of the Constitution. He notes that 'the fact that your Lordships have been willing to hear this appeal and to give judgment upon it is another indication that the courts have a part to play in defining the limits of Parliament's legislative sovereignty'.[117] Therefore, perhaps the strongest support for the radical and controversial nature of this elevation of the rule of law over and above Parliament's sovereign legislative authority, comes not from the obiter comments of three judges but from the willingness of all three branches of government, not to mention much of legal academia, to see the challenge to the Hunting Act 2004 as a legitimate issue for the courts. It was not enough that a sovereign Parliament had purported to pass this law, because the appellants had raised a question of law about it and it was vital that the courts be able to address that. Indeed, it is to enable the courts to continue to play such a role under the UK Constitution that the increasing calls for a rule of law boundary to parliamentary sovereignty have emerged. The *Jackson* judgment in both substance and rhetoric has undoubtedly strengthened the position of the rule of law in the constitutional structure of the UK. And just as the House of Commons' increase in powers inevitably led to a limitation on the powers of the House of Lords, so too will the elevation of the rule of law signal a more limited sovereign realm for the Westminster Parliament.

VII. Conclusion

The Parliament Act 1911 had a noble purpose, even if subsumed beneath party politics: it sought to ensure that the elected government could implement its

---

[116] *Jackson*, n 1 above, para 27 (per Bingham).
[117] ibid para 107 *per* Hope.

legislative policies. While the 1949 Act was both unnecessary and unnecessarily antagonistic, it further strengthened the dominance of the elected House over the unelected one. Today a political party with a majority in the House of Commons can be expected to make whatever laws it wishes, with only political restraints, moral qualms and non-binding scrutiny (from the media as well as the Lords) to influence its legislative direction. The traditional unique characteristic of the British Constitution—parliamentary sovereignty—then ensures that laws passed by the House of Commons (with or without the consent of the House of Lords and by convention invariably given Royal Assent) are unchallengeable by any other body. And that is the problem. An executive-dominated House of Commons, when coupled with the conventional limits on the powers of the Monarch and the Parliament Acts' restrictions on the powers of the House of Lords, means that parliamentary sovereignty is but a small step away from executive sovereignty. It is no surprise therefore that Dicey's traditional doctrine has been the subject of reconsideration in recent years. While of course the self-imposed restrictions on Parliament's legislative freedom, from statutes such as the European Communities Act 1972 and (albeit in a different and non-legal manner) the Scotland Act 1998 and Human Rights Act 1998, have contributed to this, they do not stand alone. Members of the senior judiciary in *Jackson* joined leading academics in recognising that another traditional constitutional principle may have a role to play in protecting our democratic Constitution. Indeed, the landmark status of *Jackson* is largely due to its role in underscoring the constitutional significance of the rule of law.

The rule of law has been championed as a protector of the British democratic Constitution. Over the last couple of centuries, parliamentary sovereignty served a vital role in cementing the democratic nature of the British Constitution. But given concerns about the future of democratic principles when residing solely in the hands of the executive branch of government, it may well be that the time is ripe for the rule of law to move to the front line of this defence against tyranny. There is no need for it to replace parliamentary sovereignty, however, because our understanding of that principle can, and must, evolve away from Dicey's nineteenth century absolutist form. The doctrine of parliamentary sovereignty is a legacy of the gradual democratisation of Parliament and still has much to commend it but it will be a stronger, and more meaningful, doctrine, not to mention a better guarantee of that democracy, if it encompasses some consideration of that original purpose. The rule of law is the means by which the judiciary may be able to ensure that the executive-dominated House of Commons is true to the democratic principle that justifies Parliament's sovereign authority, but a role must still be played by Parliament itself, including a revitalised and legitimate upper house. A truly democratic Parliament fit for the twenty first century would be entitled to regard its laws as sovereign but only under a constitutional framework that adheres to the rule of law.

11

Bancoult and the Royal Prerogative in Colonial Constitutional Law

SATVINDER S JUSS

I. Introduction

The *Chagos Islanders Case*—known also as *Bancoult*[1]—concerned the royal prerogative of colonial governance in the Crown's overseas territories. As a source of power, the royal prerogative has in modern times been described as, 'to all intents and purposes [a] government or even prime ministerial prerogative'.[2] It is not immune from judicial surveillance because as long ago as the *Case of Proclamations* in 1611[3] it was established that the English courts had jurisdiction to determine the existence and extent of the prerogative power. *Bancoult* challenges that proposition. How, why and to what extent it does so, is the subject-matter of this chapter. *Bancoult* turns out to be a landmark case. It is, however, not a straightforward, but a difficult case. It held that the primary exercise of the prerogative could be reviewable on the grounds that the power breaches the principle of certainty or fundamental rights.

Whereas in this respect it moves judicial control of the prerogative forwards, the ultimate decision of the House of Lords left the unhappy impression that when it comes to the exercise of its legal powers in the Colonies, the Crown can behave as an absolute monarch, notwithstanding the most basic axioms of the Rule of Law. It can moreover do so free from any constitutional constraints. The case is troubling because it implied an absence of constitutional limits on the exercise of prerogative powers in circumstances where the rights of British subjects were involved. Yet, if British subjects enjoy a right of abode in a British territory, can

---

[1] *Bancoult, R (On The Application of) v Secretary of State For Foreign and Commonwealth Affairs* [2008] UKHL 61 (*Bancoult (No 2)*) on 22 October 2008. Available at www.bailii.org/uk/cases/UKHL/2008/61.html This was preceded by the judgment in the Divisional Court in *R (Bancoult) v Secretary of State for Foreign and Commonwealth Affairs* [2001] QB 1067 (*Bancoult (No 1)*) in November 2000.
[2] B Markesinis, '*The Royal Prerogative Revisited*' (1973) 32 CLJ 287, at 288.
[3] *Case of Proclamations* (1611) 12 co rep 74; 77 ER 1352.

constitutional rights really be permanently removed by the primary exercise of prerogative powers? And, do the UK's international obligations to promote the well-being of the inhabitants of its territories, count for nothing when the courts are asked to interpret the constitutional limits of the prerogative power of colonial governance—especially given the decolonisation process of the last 50-years?

Historically, the Royal Prerogative has provided the Executive with the ability to sidestep, and even to ignore, the democratic role of Parliament in crucial matters of state policy, whether this be the signing of treaties, engaging in war, or the relentless pursuit of its own national interests over the interests of others. Yet, precisely because of its amplitude the power has long been regarded even by the Government as being anachronistic.[4] The House of Lords judgment in *Bancoult* takes insufficient account of this anachronism. It violates the fundamental constitutional principle of the rule of law by equating it with the interests of the Government quite simply because that interest is expressed through the exercise of the prerogative power. Unsurprisingly, there has been concern, and it has ranged from academics to eminent judges. In their seminal article, Professor Mark Elliott & Amanda Perreau-Saussine state that the House of Lords' judgment in *Bancoult* 'constitutes an important and disappointing statement of contemporary judicial attitudes to the prerogative'.[5] Sir Stephen Sedley too, in a learned article[6] had earlier perspicaciously raised as a serious unrealised possibility that State action, is not beyond the purview of the courts, so that it was high time that the State, in the name of the Crown, could sue and be sued in its own right. He asked rhetorically: '[h]ave we in fact reached a point at which, in the undemonstrative way of the common law, the State in the shape of the executive and in the name and right of the Crown can be recognized as an entity capable of being impleaded and subjected to the legal processes which alone makes the rule of law a reality?' In his

---

[4] Ministry of Justice, 'The Governance of Britain, (Cm 7170; 2007), at paras 15–17 where it is said that, 'The flow of power from the people to government should be balanced by the ability of Parliament to hold government to account. However, when the executive relies on the powers of the royal prerogative—powers where government acts upon the Monarch's authority—it is difficult for Parliament to scrutinise and challenge government's actions'.(at para 15). Furthermore, that, 'It is important that the key decisions that affect the whole country—such as the decision to send troops into armed conflict—are made in the right way, and with Parliament's consent. The same is true of treaties that the UK makes with its partners in Europe and across the world. Government's power to deploy troops and ratify treaties stems from the royal prerogative. In a modern 21st century parliamentary democracy, the Government considers that basing these powers on the prerogative is out of date.' (at para 17). Available at www.gov.uk/government/uploads/system/uploads/attachment_data/file/228834/7170.pdf.

[5] M Elliott & A Perreau-Saussine, '*Pyrrhic Public Law: Bancoult and the sources, status and content of common law limitations on prerogative power*', Public Law, (October, 2009), pp 697–722, at p 698.

[6] S Sedley, '*The Crown in its own Courts*' (pp 253–266) in C. Forsyth and I. Hare, The Golden Metawand & the Crooked Cord: Essays in Honour of W Wade (OUP, 1998) asked (at p 257). S Sedley was commenting on an earlier case involving the exercise of ministerial prerogative in *M v Home Office* where it was held that the Courts have jurisdiction to judicially review the actions of officers of the Crown, and that a minister exercising power on behalf of the Crown can be held in contempt of court (see, *M v Home Office* [1993] UKHL 5. Available at www.bailii.org/uk/cases/UKHL/1993/5.html.

critique of the tangled and tortuous *Bancoult* litigation Professor Tomkins,[7] in his invaluable book on the British Constitution, saw it as a realised possibility.

On 29 June 2016 the Supreme Court (which replaced the House of Lords in October 2009) rejected a challenge by *Bancoult* to set aside the 2008 judgment of the House of Lords.[8] In a majority ruling of 3/2 against, the justices said that a failure to disclose key Foreign Office documents in the form of a draft of a 2002 Feasibility Study would not have altered the outcome because Lord Mance in giving the leading judgment said there was 'no probability, likelihood or prospect'[9] that a court would have made a different decision if it had seen the documents. Yet, when the Government removed the Chagossians right to return to their homeland it had relied on this 2002 Feasibility Study which examined how they could be settled, but this had never been presented to the original hearing, and the Government had concluded that the costs of long-term inhabitation of the outer islands would be prohibitive and life there would be precarious.[10] A later Feasibility Study of 2014–15 was published by KPMG in March 2015, which in the words of Lord Mance, 'assesses the risks differently' such that it finds, 'that, at some cost and taking into account (for the first time) the possibility of resettlement on Diego Garcia itself' that, 'there would be scope for supported resettlement. Lord Mance inferred from this that "in practical terms, the background has shifted, and logically the constitutional ban needs to be revisited'.[11] The possibility of a favourable outcome for the Chagossians was thus raised. There are over 2,000 Chagossians in UK and 'a sizeable number settled in Crawley in Sussex, simply because it was near Gatwick airport where they landed'.[12] Newspaper reports wrongly suggest that most are unemployed and on benefits finding integration into British society difficult and long to return to their life as a fishing island community, but clearly they do want their right of return restored. The Government view after the latest

---

[7] A Tomkins, Our Republican Constitution, (at pp 123–4). This misquotes the material sentence of S Sedley's commentary on *M v Home Office* by omitting the question mark at the end, allowing the author to suggest that Stephen had stated as established law something, which he had in fact set out as a potential desirability. The result was that the omission of the question mark enabled the author of 'Our Republican Constitution' to contrast Stephen's commentary with what he had held to be the law in *Chagos Islanders v Attorney General Her Majesty's British Indian Ocean Territory Commissioner* [2003] EWHC 2222 (QB).

[8] Bancoult, *R (on the application of) v Secretary of State for Foreign and Commonwealth Affairs* (No 2) [2016] UKSC 35 (29 June 2016) Available at www.bailii.org/uk/cases/UKSC/2016/35.html

[9] Lord Mance at para 65 in Bancoult, R (on the application of) v Secretary of State for Foreign and Commonwealth Affairs (No 2) [2016] UKSC 35 (29 June 2016). Available at www.bailii.org/uk/cases/UKSC/2016/35.html.

[10] J Colley, 'Chagos Islands residents forcibly removed from homeland lose Supreme Court appeal', *The Independent*, 29 June 2016. Available at www.independent.co.uk/news/uk/home-news/chagos-islands-lose-supreme-court-appeal-home-diego-garcia-us-air-force-base-a7108741.html.

[11] Mance at para 72 in Bancoult, R (on the application of) v Secretary of State for Foreign and Commonwealth Affairs (No 2) [2016] UKSC 35 (29 June 2016) Available at www.bailii.org/uk/cases/UKSC/2016/35.html.

[12] J Doward, '*Chagos Islanders' fate to be decided by top cour*', The Guardian, 26 June 2016. Available at www.theguardian.com/world/2016/jun/25/verdict-chagos-islands-45-year-fight-home.

judgment was expressed in terms that: 'We remain committed to our current review of resettlement and will continue to keep Parliament, Chagossians and their supporters closely informed of progress on the issue.'[13]

The *Bancoult* saga is the longest Supreme Court case ever heard and other Supreme Court challenges are planned by the Chagossians in the future. The Supreme Court's split decision fully acknowledged that its earlier 2008 decision had moved the law forward and that, in the words of Lord Mance who gave the majority decision, the exercise of prerogative powers were 'susceptible to judicial review on ordinary principles of legality, rationality and procedural impropriety'.[14] Even if 'there has been a new 2014–2015 feasibility study, published by KPMG in March 2015, which assesses the risks differently' such that there is 'the possibility of resettlement on Diego Garcia itself'' so that 'in practical terms, the background has shifted, and logically the constitutional ban needs to be revisited', the fact is that, 'it is open to any Chagossian now or in the future to challenge' the Government's position, 'in the light of all the information now available'.[15] But it is the dissenting judgments of Lord Kerr and Lady Hale that most clearly demonstrate how the law has moved forwards, although the politics has yet to catch up. Lord Kerr reminds us how in 2008: 'Lord Hoffmann decided that there was a power of review and that the main point in the appeal was "the application of the ordinary principles of judicial review"'.[16] The other two members of the majority, Lords Rodger and Carswell had agreed also, 'that the courts had power to review' and could do so 'on the normal judicial review grounds'.[17] The other two judges, Lords Bingham and Mance, gave 'powerful dissenting speeches' and 'concluded that the government did not have power by Order in Council to exclude the Chagossians from their homeland'.[18] Baroness Hale was brisk in her statement that, 'Any doubts about whether it is legally possible for the imperial power to exile a people from their homeland have to be rigorously suppressed. That question of law has been finally resolved in these proceedings by the decision of the majority in *Bancoult (No 2)*'.[19] As David Snoxell has commented: '[t]he court's decision was a legal defeat, but a substantial moral and political victory for the Chagossians'.[20] It is open to the Government to conduct a review and ultimately settle the issue once and for all. The litigation here is a good example of the limits of public law because ultimately the issue is one of political will and courage.

---

[13] O Bowcott, '*Chagos islanders lose supreme court bid to return to homeland*' The Guardian, 29 June 2016. Available at www.theguardian.com/world/2016/jun/29/chagos-islanders-lose-supreme-court-bid-to-return-to-homeland.
[14] Mance *op cit* at para 14.
[15] Mance, *op cit* at para 17.
[16] Kerr, *op cit* at para 112 referring to Hoffmann's judgment at para 52.
[17] Kerr *op cit* at para 113 referring to Rodger's judgment at para 105 and Carswell's judgment at para 122.
[18] Kerr op cit at para 115 referring to Lord Bingham at para 71 and Mance at para 160.
[19] Hale, op cit at para 189.
[20] T Prayag, 'Passing the dossier to the next government will lead to more prolonged delay', La Sentinelle, 14–20 July 2016, pp 27–29) at p 27.

This chapter is an attempt to locate the *Bancoult* litigation in its proper political context and to suggest that the House of Lords in 2008 could—and indeed should—have taken a different decision. A decision that had already been made by Laws LJ in the Divisional Court in 2000 when the matter first arose, and affirmed resoundingly later by Sedley LJ in the Court of Appeal in 2007. Given the complexity and breadth of this chapter, it will be signposted as follows. Section II considers the colonial backdrop to the Chagos Islands dispute both with Mauritius and with the Islanders themselves, and describe how it was that Oliver Bancoult came to making his legal challenge. Section III focuses on how the Royal Prerogative came to be exercised in the Chagos Islands through the medium of two Orders on Council, one which exiled the Islanders by denying the right of abode, and the other when the British government had apparently raised the prospect of the Islanders return back to their homeland, only then to renege by reinstating their exile. Section IV considers the arguments of Finnis, which were influential in the House of Lords in reversing the Court of Appeal's decision in favour of the Chagos Islanders, that given how large and complex the Empire was there may be a loss of perspective inimical to the common good of the realm so that the makers of colonial laws may be immunised from judicial scrutiny. The difficulties with this doctrine, and the evidence to back it up, is analysed. Section V examines the House of Lords' decision itself in *Bancoult* and the unhappy impression it left of judicial feebleness with the decision being a split on some of the most fundamental issues even though it endorsed the principle of judicial control of the prerogative power. Finally, section VI makes for the author's own arguments, namely, that the modern exercise of the prerogative of colonial governance is anachronistic and should only have been exercised in the interests of the inhabitants of the Chagos Islanders. The Supreme Court's judgment in 2016 now shows that a different decision was possible back in 2008 by the House of Lords. In this way, it is to be hoped that readers of this chapter get a sense of what is going to be covered here.

II. Judicial Scrutiny of Colonial Law[21]

The Chagos Archipelago used to be part of the British colonial entity of Mauritius. In 1965 this provincial entity enclave was dismembered from Mauritius after the 'agreement' at the Constitutional Conference at the Lancaster House in London,[22] on the forthcoming Independence of Mauritius. However, where the Chagos Islanders were concerned, '[t]here had been no debate in the House of Commons,

---

[21] The phrase used by Finnis: see, Finnis, Common Law Constraints: Whose Common Good Counts, Oxford Legal Studies Research Paper No: 10/2008, (available at www.worldlii.org/int/journals/lsn/abstracts/1100628.html).

[22] An account of the discussions appears at https://en.wikipedia.org/wiki/Chagos_Archipelago_sovereignty_dispute.

no serious debate within government departments, and certainly no enquiry as to the welfare and needs, let alone the status, of the population'.²³ The Mauritian representative to the colonial government could hardly not 'agree' with what was decided at Lancaster House, because as Stephen Allen has explained in his recent book, 'in relation to the detachment of the Chagos Islands, the elected representatives of the Mauritian government had no meaningful choice but to give their consent to the course of action proposed by the UK Government given the threat that Chagos Islands would be unilaterally excised from the colony of Mauritius, if they resisted'.²⁴

The outcome was the creation of the British Indian Overseas Territories (BIOT) a colonial administrative entity of 55 islands removed some 1,200 miles from Mauritius, which as Marc Wesley explains was '[t]he result of an intentional act at the height of the decolonisation movement' but one which 'has had lasting repercussions for these former residents'.²⁵ This is because what quietly escaped attention at the time of the creation of this first British Colony, since World War I, was a sinister agreement, which followed two years later between the UK and the US. Under this, the island of Diego Garcia was granted to the US on a 50-year lease, with an option of renewal. The US could establish a strategically located military facility as it had always wanted. More, however, was to come. As Marc Wesley notes, '[s]trikingly juxtaposed to this territorial transference was an agreement to "covertly transfer" the population of the BIOT islands, prior to the USA taking possession of the territory' and the result was that between 1965 and 1973 the Chagossians were relocated, predominantly, to Mauritius.²⁶ In short, the island population was sent into exile.

All of this would never have been known were it not for the fact that in 1999 Louis Oliver Bancoult brought his legal action in London against the removal of his people from their homeland. *Bancoult* was then aged 36 years. But as a three-year old in 1967 he had travelled with his Ilois parents, from the Island of Peros Banhos in Chagos Archipelago, to Mauritius. There they had sought medical treatment for his infant sister who had become badly injured when a cartwheel ran over her leg. *Bancoult* was never able to return to Peros Banhos because, as he claimed, he was prevented from doing so by the British authorities, who had systematically removed the last inhabitants of the Chagos Archipelago: first, from Diego Garcia in 1971; then from Salomon Island in 1972; and finally, from Peros Banhos in 1973.²⁷ In the intervening years—and before *Bancoult* launched his court action, and as the noteworthy voice of Mr David Snoxell reminds us—a small number of British MPs in the form of Tam Dalyell, Eric Avebury and Jeremy Corbyn, had

---

²³ See, Submission of Richard Gifford, Legal Representative, Chagos Refugees Group, Select Committee on Foreign Affairs, 6 July 2008. (at para 6) Available at www.publications.parliament.uk/pa/cm200708/cmselect/cmfaff/147/147we94.htm.
²⁴ S Allen, *The Chagos Islanders and International Law* (Hart Publishing, 2014) at p 128.
²⁵ M Wesley, Human Rights Law Review, vol 16 issue 2, p 11.
²⁶ M Wesley, Human Rights Law Review, vol 16 issue 2, p 2.
²⁷ Laws at para 6 in 2000.

in the mid-seventies harboured suspicions that something was afoot. They had raised questions in Parliament, but '[t]he international community remained largely oblivious until 1999'.[28] To that extent the *Bancoult* case is a salient example of the exercise of imperial power in modern colonial governance.

From the beginning, the FCO officials in London had two major concerns. First, a concern over UN scrutiny of the way in which the BIOT territory had been excised from Mauritius. This was highlighted when in 2013, the Foreign Office acknowledged that a secret Archive of boxes of files existed going back to 1968, and it was reported that: '[t]he Mauritius papers could be particularly sensitive as they could shed light on Britain's decision to expel about 1,500 Chagos Islanders a few years later, having agreed to lease Diego Garcia to the United States for use as a military base'.[29] Thus it was that when in 2011 fundamental questions were raised about who has sovereignty over the Indian Ocean territory, and the Mauritian government officials asserted that this could lead to the unravelling of Britain's disputed claim and the eventual return of the islanders, a decision was made in January 2013 by the Permanent Court of Arbitration at the Hague[30] that it would hear a challenge to the UK's unilateral declaration in 2010 of a *Marine Protected Area* (known as the 'MPA') around the Chagos Islands.

In March 2015 an arbitral tribunal, constituted under the United Nations Convention on the Law of the Sea under the auspices of the Permanent Court of Arbitration, made the Chagos Arbitration Award. Colson and Vohrer have written well on this,[31] noting that 'the Tribunal chose not to parse its words'. It undertook 'a thorough review of the record'[32] and held that in 1965 'the under-takings provided by the United Kingdom at Lancaster House formed part of the quid pro quo through which Mauritian agreement to the detachment of the Chagos Archipelago from Mauritius was procured'.[33] This conclusion did not resolve the matter because the Lancaster House meeting 'preceded independence by three years and the legal basis for those undertakings was British constitutional law'.[34] This led

---

[28] D Snoxell, 'The role of Parliament and litigation in resolving the Chagos tragedy' at Greenwich University Conference on Chagos Litigation: A Socio-Legal Dialogue (29 June 2015). See, www.gre.ac.uk/ach/services/events/the-chagos-litigation-a-socio-legal-dialogue/important-dates.

[29] I Cobain and R. Norton-Taylor, '*Files that may shed light on colonial crimes still kept secret by UK.*' *The Guardian*, 26 April 2013. What was discovered was 1.5 tons of paper, from about 37 countries, some of which related to a proposed royal visit by Prince Philip to Mauritius in 1968. Available at www.theguardian.com/uk/2013/apr/26/national-archives-colonial-documents-secret.

[30] O Bowcott & J Vidal, '*Britain faces UN tribunal over Chagos Islands marine reserve.*' *The Guardian*, 28 January 2013. This is because decisions by the tribunal, which arbitrates in disputes over the United Nations law of the sea, are binding on the UK. At the preliminary hearing the UK's attempt to challenge the court's jurisdiction was defeated. Britain is now obliged to explain highly sensitive political decisions dating back to 1965. Available at www.theguardian.com/world/2013/jan/28/britain-tribunal-chagos-islands-marine-area.

[31] D Colson and B. Vohrer, '*In re Chagos Marine Protected Area (Mauritius v United Kingdom)*', The American Journal of International Law [Vol 109, n 4 (October 2015)], pp 845–851 at p 847.

[32] ibid at p 849.

[33] *Chagos Marine Protected Area Arbitration (Mauritius v United Kingdom)* at p 421. Available at www.pcacases.com/pcadocs/MU-UK%2020150318%20Award.pdf.

[34] D. Colson and B Vohrer, *op.cit* at para 849.

the tribunal to circumvent the problem by concluding that '[t]he independence of Mauritius in 1968 ... had the effect of elevating the package deal reached with the Mauritian Ministers to the international plane and of transforming the commitments made in 1965 into an international agreement'.[35] Indeed, the Tribunal had little doubt that the UK, 'is estopped from denying the binding effect of these commitments ... in view of their repeated reaffirmation after 1968'.[36] However, whereas it is the case that, 'Mauritius clearly succeeded in achieving a determination that the Lancaster House Undertakings are legally binding and that the establishment of the MPA did not take Mauritian interests into account',[37] nevertheless, the arbitral tribunal did not 'address and decide major and long-standing territorial sovereignty questions',[38] quite simply because it could not have. This is because '[m]any states parties to the Convention, [ie the United Nations Convention on the Law of the Sea] including major powers, are embroiled in such politically sensitive, not to say explosive, disputes', and it is hard to imagine that that they would, 'knowingly, and without comment in their approval of the Convention', have determined that 'these long standing territorial sovereignty disputes would henceforth be subject to the dispute settlement regime of the Convention'.[39] The result may be legally satisfying but it is not entirely untroublesome from the Chagos Islanders point of view. As Colson and Vohrer conclude, 'it is open to question whether the award advances the interests of the exiled Chagos Islanders', because, '[i]f anything, by finding that the Lancaster House Undertakings are legally binding, the award would seem to have only reinforced the status quo'.[40]

This started a process which could lead to the return of the islands' exiled inhabitants, because the result of the decision is that Britain's colonial-era decision to sever an Indian Ocean archipelago from Mauritius and turn it into a US military base will have to be justified before an international tribunal.[41] In the House of Lords decision of 2008, Lord Mance, without developing the point any further, had referred to Article 73 of the United Nations Charter to the effect that Member States which 'assume responsibilities for the administration of territories whose peoples have not yet attained a full measure of self-government recognize' have to abide by 'the principle that the interests of the inhabitants of these territories are paramount'. Indeed, they have to 'accept as a sacred trust the obligation to promote to the utmost, the well-being of the inhabitants of these territories'.[42]

But, Lord Mance, despite stating this provision, had not gone further to develop its implications. Yet, one only has to look at the relevant public international law provisions to note how a colonial power's sovereign claim is now diminished.

---

[35] ibid at para 425.
[36] ibid at para 448.
[37] ibid at para 850.
[38] ibid at para 851.
[39] ibid at para 85.
[40] ibid at para 85.
[41] ibid.
[42] *Bancoult* (no 2) [2008] UKHL 61; [2009] 1 AC 453 at para 145.

Thus, when Article 73 of the UN Charter[43] enjoins a colonial power to develop self-government, it is on condition that it has 'to take due account of the political aspirations of the peoples, and to assist them in the progressive development of their free political institutions'. Colonialism has had its day. This is clear from the 1960 Colonial Declaration[44] which now, 'Solemnly proclaims the necessity of bringing to a speedy and unconditional end colonialism in all its forms and manifestations', and further declares that the, 'subjection of peoples to alien subjugation, domination and exploitation constitutes a denial of fundamental human rights, is contrary to the Charter of the United Nations and is an impediment to the promotion of world peace and co-operation'. The General Assembly Resolution 1541 (XV) of 15 December 1960, affirms that, 'Non-Self-Governing Territories' are 'in a dynamic state of evolution and progress towards a "full measure of self-government"' and that until such time that a territory and its peoples attain a full measure of self-government, colonial powers have 'the obligation to transmit information under Article 73e'.[45] Article 73e itself is one which requires a colonial power 'to transmit regularly to the Secretary-General for information purposes ... statistical and other information of a technical nature relating to economic, social, and educational conditions in the territories for which they are respectively responsible ...' The combined effect of all these provisions is to markedly qualify a colonial power's

---

[43] Article 73 reads as follows:

> Members of the United Nations which have or assume responsibilities for the administration of territories whose peoples have not yet attained a full measure of self-government recognize the principle that the interests of the inhabitants of these territories are paramount, and accept as a sacred trust the obligation to promote to the utmost, within the system of international peace and security established by the present Charter, the well-being of the inhabitants of these territories, and, to this end:
>
> (a) to ensure, with due respect for the culture of the peoples concerned, their political, economic, social, and educational advancement, their just treatment, and their protection against abuses;
> (b) to develop self-government, to take due account of the political aspirations of the peoples, and to assist them in the progressive development of their free political institutions, according to the particular circumstances of each territory and its peoples and their varying stages of advancement;
> (c) to further international peace and security;
> (d) to promote constructive measures of development, to encourage research, and to co-operate with one another and, when and where appropriate, with specialized international bodies with a view to the practical achievement of the social, economic, and scientific purposes set forth in this Article; and
> (e) to transmit regularly to the Secretary-General for information purposes, subject to such limitation as security and constitutional considerations may require, statistical and other information of a technical nature relating to economic, social, and educational conditions in the territories for which they are respectively responsible other than those territories to which Chapters XII and XIII apply.

Available at www.un.org/en/sections/un-charter/chapter-xi/

[44] See, the *Declaration on the Granting of Independence to Colonial Countries and Peoples Adopted by General Assembly* resolution 1514 (XV) of 14 December 1960. Available at www.un.org/en/decolonization/declaration.shtml.

[45] Available at www.un.org/en/decolonization/ga_resolutions.shtml.

sovereign authority over a given colonial territory on a temporal basis. Sovereignty then, was only valid until the imperative of decolonisation was achieved. Colonial powers are under a public international law obligation to make this happen. A recent book by Stephen Allen,[46] makes this clear. He makes the suggestion that the label 'BIOT' does not make a territory a UK colony. It constitutes it as a 'Non-Self-Governing Territory' pursuant to the provisions of Chapter XI of the UN Charter. Allen argues that the UK claim that it possesses a valid sovereign authority over BIOT is questionable, and that is why it is disputed by Mauritius. Consequently, the Mauritian claim threatens to compromise the entitlements of the Chagos Islanders in respect of BIOT as a matter of international law. What is required according to Allen to resolve the competing claims to the Chagos Islands is a more nuanced approach to the resolution of sovereignty disputes. In fact, the distinction between a Colony and a 'Non-Self-Governing Territory' no longer serves any useful purpose because nearly every Colony now is either a Mandate/Trust Territory or a 'Non-Self-Governing Territory'.

Second, there was a concern amongst Foreign Office officials over the depopulation or 'ethnic cleansing'[47] of the Chagos Archipelago. David Vine's book, *Island of Shame*, has already chronicled how London and Washington colluded in a scheme of population removal more redolent of the eighteenth or nineteenth century than the closing decades of the twentieth,[48] but the evidence suggests, that contrary to what is popularly believed, it was more London's doing than Washington's. In fact, it was engineered by a handful of FCO officials in London themselves. The creation of the MPA by HM Commissioner for the British Indian Ocean Territory made commercial fishing impossible and the Chagos Islanders relied on fishing rights, so when the basis of the MPA was challenged in court Stanley Burnton LJ in 2012 observed how, '[t]he MPA, if maintained, renders commercial fishing unlawful, and would make it more difficult for the Islanders to sustain themselves if they were to succeed in returning to the Islands'.[49]

The fact is that the MPA was deliberately designed to force the Chagos Islanders off their lands. When a WikiLeaks disclosure took place in 2010,[50] this confirmed the existence of a cable from Colin Roberts, the Director of the Foreign &

---

[46] S Allen, *The Chagos Islanders and International Law*, (Hart Publishing, 2014).

[47] P Monaghan, 'Britain's shame: the ethnic cleansing of the Chagos Islands' Politics First, 23rd April 2015. Available at www.politicsfirst.org.uk/2016/britains-shame-the-ethnic-cleansing-of-the-chagos-islands/.

[48] D Vine, *Island of Shame: The Secret History of the U.S. Military Base on Diego Garcia*, (Princeton University Press, Paperback, 2011). The book has been described by J. Freedland as a 'meticulously researched, coldly furious book that details precisely ... [O]ne likes to think that if Barack Obama were somehow to stumble across a copy of David Vine's fine book, he would instantly realize that a great injustice has been done--one that could easily be put right.' (see, Jonathan Freedland, '*A Black and Disgraceful Site*' (28 May 2009, New York Review of Books www.nybooks.com/articles/archives/2009/may/28/a-black-and-disgraceful-site/).

[49] *Bancoult, R (on the application of) v Secretary of State for Foreign & Commonwealth Affairs* [2012] EWHC 2115 at para 3. Available at www.bailii.org/ew/cases/EWHC/Admin/2012/2115.html.

[50] Reliance upon this information was rejected by the High Court in *Bancoult, R (on the application of) v Secretary of State for Foreign & Commonwealth Affairs* [2013] EWHC 1502 (Admin) (11 June 2013). Available at www.bailii.org/ew/cases/EWHC/Admin/2013/1502.html. Bancoult alleged

Commonwealth Office Overseas Territories, sent out to the US State Department in May 2009, reporting what Colin Roberts had told them, namely, that there would be no 'Man Fridays' left on the islands following the establishment of the MPA.[51] Once the MPA park was established this would, 'in effect, put paid to resettlement claims of the archipelago's former residents'.[52] Colin Roberts added: 'We do not regret the removal of the population.' In March 2015, the Permanent Court of Arbitration (PCA) unanimously ruled that the UK's establishment of a Marine Protected Area (MPA) around the Chagos Archipelago contravened its obligations under the UN Convention on the Law of the Sea.[53] That not only

the decision was flawed by an improper motive (to prevent the return of Chagossians) said to be evidenced by a copy of a US cable from its London Embassy recording a meeting with BIOT officials in 2009 published by WikiLeaks, failure to reveal in the public consultation that the Foreign Secretary's own consultants had advised in 2002 that resettlement of the population was feasible, failure to disclose in the consultation that the MPA proposal would adversely affect the historical or traditional fishing rights of Chagossians and fishing rights of Mauritius under public international law and, breached the UK's obligations under Article 198 of the Treaty on the Functioning of the European Union. But the High Court made a preliminary ruling that the WikiLeaks' document was inadmissible as a copy of an authentic US Embassy cable under the Vienna Convention on Diplomatic Relations 1961. (see statement by Junior Government Counsel, Penelope Nevill at www.20essexst.com/case/r-appn-bancoult-v-ss-foreign-commonwealth-affairs).

[51] The Cable was disclosed in *The Guardian*: see, '*US embassy cables: Foreign Office does not regret evicting Chagos islanders*' The Guardian, 2nd December 2010. Available at www.theguardian.com/world/us-embassy-cables-documents/207149. This is as follows:

'7. (C/NF) Roberts acknowledged that 'we need to find a way to get through the various Chagossian lobbies.' He admitted that HMG is 'under pressure' from the Chagossians and their advocates to permit resettlement of the 'outer islands' of the BIOT. He noted, without providing details, that 'there are proposals (for a marine park) that could provide the Chagossians warden jobs' within the BIOT. However, Roberts stated that, according to the HGM,s current thinking on a reserve, there would be 'no human footprints' or 'Man Fridays' on the BIOT's uninhabited islands. *He asserted that establishing a marine park would, in effect, put paid to resettlement claims of the archipelago's former residents*. Responding to Polcouns' observation that the advocates of Chagossian resettlement continue to vigorously press their case, Roberts opined that the UK's 'environmental lobby is far more powerful than the Chagossians' advocates.' (Note: One group of Chagossian litigants is appealing to the European Court of Human Rights (ECHR) the decision of Britain's highest court to deny 'resettlement rights' to the islands' former inhabitants. See below at paragraph 13 and reftel. End Note.) Je Ne Regrette Rien'

[52] Friday, 15 May 2009, 07:00am, confidential London 001156, NOFORN SIPDIS EO 12958 DECL: 05/13/2029, TAGS MARR, MOPS, SENV, UK, IO, MP, EFIS, EWWT, PGOV, PREL, Subject: HMG floats proposal for marine reserve covering the Chagos Archipelago (British Indian Ocean Territory). REF: 08 LONDON 2667 (NOTAL). Classified By: Political Counselor Richard Mills for reasons 1.4 b and d1. (C/NF) Summary. HMG would like to establish a 'marine park' or 'reserve' providing comprehensive environmental protection to the reefs and waters of the British Indian Ocean Territory (BIOT), a senior Foreign and Commonwealth Office (FCO) official informed Polcouns on May 12. The official insisted that the establishment of a marine park—the world's largest—would in no way impinge on USG use of the BIOT, including Diego Garcia, for military purposes. 'He agreed that the UK and U.S. should carefully negotiate the details of the marine reserve to assure that U.S. interests were safeguarded and the strategic value of BIOT was upheld. He said that the BIOT's former inhabitants would find it difficult, if not impossible, to pursue their claim for resettlement on the islands if the entire Chagos Archipelago were a marine reserve'. End Summary.

[53] See, *In the Matter of the Chagos Marine Protected Area Arbitration (Mauritius v UK)*. Available at https://pca-cpa.org/en/home/. But also see, www.ejiltalk.org/mauritius-v-uk-chagos-marine-protected-area-unlawful/.

raised fundamental questions of national sovereignty, but also transformed the dispute into an inter-state matter, akin to the Anglo-Argentinian dispute regarding the Falklands.[54] It also gave hope of individual redress given that the European Court of Human Rights had just decided in December 2012 that, the Chagossians having renounced their rights because they already received compensation in the 1980s, could not now call on the Court to assume jurisdiction to examine the Islanders' claims to resettlement.[55]

These recent disclosures support the suggestions of David Snoxell, Britain's former Mauritius High Commissioner, made in a Conference in London in 2015 on the Chagos litigation. First, that from the beginning, 'the UK intention was that this new colony should be uninhabited (in an attempt to avoid UN scrutiny)'.[56] This was despite the case that 'the US was asking only for the population to be removed from Diego Garcia, not from the other islands in the Archipelago'. Contrary to popular myth therefore, '[i]t was the FCO alone that decided on the clean sweep of all the islands, not the US'.[57] In 1966 the US had agreed that, 'situations might arise when it was feasible to make use of islands without either partial or total removal of inhabitants' and that, '[t]hese cases should be decided on their merits at the time'.[58] A secret minute from 1968 confirms, however, that the decision to depopulate the islands was a British decision. It confirms that there was 'no reason to relocate the population prior to an island coming into use to meet a requirement. This would apply to other islands of the Chagos Archipelago as long as our activity was confined to Diego Garcia'.[59]

As for Mr Louis Oliver Bancoult he should have faced even less of an impediment in his quest to return because the US position was that it 'would interpose no objection to use of Peros Banhos and Salomon for resettlement … the

---

[54] This required the application of the *United Nations Conventions on the Law of the Sea*.
[55] *Chagos Islanders v The United Kingdom*—35622/04 [2012] ECHR 2094. Available at www.bailii.org/eu/cases/ECHR/2012/2094.html.
[56] Snoxell writes, that 'The half-hearted offer to Mauritius to discuss environmental protection of the islands comes nowhere near what Mauritius has consistently advocated since 2000—discussions about the future of BIOT to include sovereignty, resettlement and the MPA. Although our standard right of reply in the UN used to state 'We remain open to discussions regarding arrangements governing BIOT and the future of the Territory' *we have in fact strung Mauritius along for years.*'
[57] Paper given by David Snoxell, '*The role of Parliament and the Courts in resolving the Chagos tragedy*' (on file with author) at Greenwich University conference on Chagos litigation: A socio-legal dialogue, 29 June 2015 (See, www.gre.ac.uk/ach/services/events/the-chagos-litigation-a-socio-legal-dialogue/important-dates).
[58] See Folio 1 para 29, 15/16 November 1966 in Secret PIOD File 1968/9 HPN 10/6 (FCO 32/484) 'BIOT Defence: Chronological Summary of events relating to the Establishment of the BIOT in November 1965'. (see, the List the List of papers and other publications relating to the Chagos Archipelago and the Chagossians.' (Updated April 2015). https://sites.google.com/site/thechagosarchipelagofacts/papers-publications.
[59] Folio 1 Secret Minute dated 10 December 1968 from Heathcote—Smith (Temporary Grade 4 Officer in Pacific and Indian Ocean Department (PIOD) doing research on BIOT establishment) to TCD Jerrom, PIOD, entitled BIOT: Reversion of Islands. (see, the List the List of papers and other publications relating to the Chagos Archipelago and the Chagossians' (Updated April 2015). https://sites.google.com/site/thechagosarchipelagofacts/papers-publications.

US has no current plans for the use of these two islands' because, 'currently our planning is limited to a most austere facility on Diego Garcia'.[60] But by 1970 the FCO officials in London were beginning to formulate their own position as is clear from a letter to a BIOT Administrator: 'You should know that view is beginning to emerge here in the FCO that we should begin to relocate all the workers in the Chagos Archipelago (and maybe Farquhar and Des Roches) now, regardless of whether or not the Diego Garcia project goes through this year or later. The US Administration has no inkling yet of the way our thoughts are going.'[61]

Second, and leading on from this, according to Mr Snoxell, in order to achieve the depopulation of the archipelago, 'Parliament and the UN were deceived into believing that the population were contract workers from Mauritius and the Seychelles' but that, 'some of them went back five generations on Chagos'. This is clear from a secret and personal letter of 13 November 1970 from Miss M.J. Emery, the Head of PIOD, to Bruce Greatbatch, the BIOT Commissioner, to the effect that: 'We would not wish it to become general knowledge that some of the inhabitants have lived on Diego Garcia for at least two generations and could, therefore, be regarded as "belongers". ....'[62] The difficulty for the Chagossians now, according to Snoxell, is that the, 'FCO, constrained as it is, by bureaucratic instincts of covering up past mistakes, revolving personnel and FCO Ministers', has been acting in a way where, '[t]here is an almost reckless determination that whatever the costs (probably well over £5m) litigation must be pursued to the bitter end, rather than as the ECHR twice suggested, through an out of court settlement'. Significantly, Snoxell does add however, that, '[t]hat said I believe that current officials are doing what they can to bring about a resolution of the issues'.

But the point is, all of this was recognised by the courts. The pressing demands of the US, as Britain's foremost ally, were expressly noted by Lord Hoffmann. He had referred to this 'group of coral atolls known as the Chagos Archipelago',[63] having 'a very small community (less than 1,000 on the three islands) who called themselves Ilois' and whose people's 'main economic activity was gathering coconuts and extracting and selling the copra or kernels'[64] such that they 'lived an extremely simple life'.[65] But according to Lord Hoffmann, '[i]nto this innocent

---

[60] Folio 1 para 105, 22 November 1968. (see, the List the List of papers and other publications relating to the Chagos Archipelago and the Chagossians' (Updated April 2015). https://sites.google.com/site/thechagosarchipelagofacts/papers-publications.

[61] Folio 4 of HPN 18/1 Part C (FCO 32/725), which has a letter entitled 'Resettlement of Inhabitants of BIOT' from ACW Lee, PIOD, of 16/1/70 to John Todd, BIOT Administrator. (see, the List the List of papers and other publications relating to the Chagos Archipelago and the Chagossians' (Updated April 2015). https://sites.google.com/site/thechagosarchipelagofacts/papers-publications.

[62] Folio 75 Secret and personal letter of 1/11/70 from Miss M. Emery, Had of PIOD, to Bruce Greatbatch, BIOT Commision, copied to Port Louis, New York and Washington. (see, the List the List of papers and other publications relating to the Chagos Archipelago and the Chagossians' (Updated April 2015). https://sites.google.com/site/thechagosarchipelagofacts/papers-publications.

[63] Hoffmann at para 3.

[64] ibid at para 4.

[65] ibid at para 5.

world there intruded, in the 1960s, the brutal realities of global politics. In the aftermath of the Cuban missile crisis and the early stages of the Vietnam War, the United States felt vulnerable without a land based military presence in the Indian Ocean'.[66] The shabby treatment of a defenceless primitive indigenous island population by UK government officials was also remarked upon by Lord Rodger who had lamented in the opening remarks of his speech how, '[t]he unhappy—indeed, in many respects, disgraceful—events of forty years ago …. have ultimately led to this appeal. ….'.[67]

Even the myth-making, of the sort that the islands carried no native population fooled no-one. Lord Hoffmann noted how, 'it is accepted by the Secretary of State that the removal and resettlement of the Chagossians was accomplished with a callous disregard of their interests', and the reason was, 'very largely the government's refusal to acknowledge that there was any indigenous population for which the United Kingdom had a responsibility. The Immigration Ordinance, denying that anyone was entitled to enter or live in the islands, was part of the legal façade constructed to defend this claim.'

But what prevailed upon the House of Lords ultimately was the recognition of the Cold-War anxieties of the 1970s when the US and Britain were locked in a bitter ideological struggle with Communist Russia. As Lord Hoffmann explained, '[t]he government adopted this position because of a fear (which may well have been justified) that the Soviet Union and its "non-aligned" supporters would use the Chagossians and the United Kingdom's obligations to the people of a non-self-governing territory under Article 73 of the United Nations Charter to prevent the construction of a military base in the Indian Ocean.'[68]

Yet, even if this was true in the 1970s it was not true forty years later in 2008 when the House of Lords came to giving its final decision. Given that there are legal obligations of trusteeship under Chapter XI of the UN Charter, and given that international law is an accepted source of English law, it is difficult to see how judicial review of the prerogative could have been carried out devoid of the consideration that a trustee administering a colonial territory, could abandon the interests of its colonial subjects in the single-minded pursuit of interests of its own.

III. The Chagos Islanders

The *Chagos Islanders Case* will be remembered for its abandonment of the common law's affirmation of a Subject's right to be free from exile. Yet paradoxically,

---

[66] ibid at para 6.
[67] ibid at para 75.
[68] *Bancoult* (No 2) [2008] UKHL 61; [2009] 1 AC 453 at para 10.

freedom from exile was a right celebrated by the UK only too recently in the 800th Anniversary of Magna Carta in 2015.[69] Whilst, Lord Dyson, Master of the Rolls and chairman of the Magna Carta Trust, explained how Magna Carta was 'a symbol of democracy, justice, human rights and perhaps above all the rule of law for the whole world',[70] a letter to *The Times* by David Snoxell, who served as the British High Commissioner to the Republic of Mauritius from September 2000–2004, to which many of the Islanders were exiled, took a less prosaic view of the continuing role of the Rule of Law in the major constitutional law cases of the day in modern times.

One could almost be forgiven for thinking that the Rule of Law—which together with its sister precept, the Separation of Powers—was one of two major bulwarks of the English Constitution in AV Dicey's Introduction to the Study of the Law of the Constitution in 1885,[71] was perhaps never meant to be less rhapsodic in its application outside mainland Britain. For David Snoxell, who is currently the Coordinator of the Chagos Islands British Indian Overseas Territories (BIOT) All-Party Parliamentary Group (APPG), which in its staunch defence of the right of the Chagossians to return to their homeland, has been a thorn in the side of the British Government,[72] the:

> 800th anniversary on June 15 is a fitting occasion on which to recall that while we celebrate the liberties enshrined in Magna Carta there is a prima facie breach of Clause 39 ("No man shall be ... exiled ... except by the lawful judgment of his equals or by the law of the land"). The Chagos Islander, British nationals, were exiled from their homeland, *British Indian Ocean Territory*, under Royal Prerogative, between 1968 and 1973, and dumped in Mauritius and Seychelles. Many have since died.

There was, he argued, no legal or climatic reason why the Chagos islanders shouldn't return home—so why will the UK government not act?[73] Earlier at a

---

[69] At an event at Runnymede, where King John sealed the original accord in 1215, the British Prime Minister, David Cameron, at the time had offered lyrical praise that, 'Magna Carta went onto change the world': See, 'Magna Carta changed the world, David Cameron tells anniversary event'. www.bbc.co.uk/news/uk-33126723.

[70] ibid.

[71] www.constitution.org/cmt/avd/law_con.htm.

[72] In one judgment reference is made in Court to how government came under pressure from the APPG: 'The pressure being mounted by the APPG and Bancoult, Gifford etc. to try to get HMG to change its policy on resettlement is gaining in intensity. They are also trying to engage the US separately. Jeremy Corbyn and Oliver Bancoult have written to President Obama ... and three officials from the US Embassy were invited and attended the fourth APPG meeting. The focus of questions was on defence/security with the APPG questioning the need to keep islands 150 miles away from Diego Garcia clear for defence purposes. Is this keenness to get a political solution sorted out an indication of their concern about their prospects at the ECHR? If they do lose then any legal means of resettlement, other than a complete change of policy by HMG, is at an end'. (per Richards in *Bancoult, R (on the application of) v Secretary of State for Foreign & Commonwealth Affairs* [2013] EWHC 1502. Available at www.bailii.org/ew/cases/EWHC/Admin/2013/1502.html.

[73] *The Times*, 9 June 2015. Available at www.thetimes.co.uk/tto/opinion/letters/article4465230.ece. This was the first time where in the letter to The Times David Snoxell revealed the role he played in the Order in Council at the High Commission.

conference, he had expressed sadness at how: '[i]ronically the UK was one of the main architects of the international legal system and we remain a strident champion of international law, though not when the UK is found in breach. It is hard to think of another British example of a wholesale denial of fundamental human rights which is still on-going and unresolved.'[74]

Where is the British Indian Ocean Territory (BIOT), and who are the Chagos Islanders? How indeed did the Royal Prerogative come to be exercised in such a pitifully dismal manner and in such a far-off place? In June 2004 British Government ministers had placed two Orders in Council before Her Majesty for approval,[75] the first of which declared that no person has the right of abode in BIOT nor the right without authorisation to enter and remain there, with the result that, '[t]he Chagossians were thus effectively exiled'.[76] Although the well known *GCHQ*[77] case had four decades earlier established that delegated prerogative powers were amenable to judicial review this was the first time that its direct exercise was challenged,[78] so that, in the words of Elliot and Perreau-Saussine, 'Bancoult is the first English decision to establish clearly that the prerogative itself—as distinct from secondary powers derived from exercises of the prerogative—exists in the shadow of the rule of law'.[79] But why 'shadow of the rule of law'? Why not the rule of law itself? The remark is tantalising but there are reasons for such a tepid embrace of the decision.

The two Orders in Council were challenged on the grounds that the office of Commissioner of BIOT[80] only had power to 'make laws for the peace, order and good of the Territory'.[81] Exiling the Chagossians from their homeland was,

---

[74] D Snoxell, '*The role of Parliament and litigation in resolving the Chagos tragedy*' at Greenwich University Conference on Chagos Litigation: A Socio-Legal Dialogue (29 June 2015). See, www.gre.ac.uk/ach/services/events/the-chagos-litigation-a-socio-legal-dialogue/important-dates.

[75] The British Indian Ocean Territory (Constitution) Order 2004 ('the Constitution Order') and the British Indian Ocean Territory (Immigration) Order 2004 ('the Immigration Order').

[76] Sedley at para 11 referring to the Divisional Court's words. See, *Secretary of State for the Foreign & Commonwealth Affairs v Bancoult, R* (on the application of) [2007] EWCA civ 498. Available at www.bailii.org/ew/cases/EWCA/Civ/2007/498.html.

[77] *Council of Civil Service Unions v Minister for the Civil Service* [1984] UKHL 9. Available at www.bailii.org/uk/cases/UKHL/1984/9.html.

[78] See the seminal study of M Elliott & A Perreau-Saussine, '*Pyrrhic Public Law: Bancoult and the sources, status and content of common law limitations on prerogative power*', Public Law, (October, 2009), pp 697–722, at p 699.

[79] M Elliott & A Perreau-Saussine, '*Pyrrhic Public Law: Bancoult and the sources, status and content of common law limitations on prerogative power*', Public Law, (October, 2009), pp 697–722, at p 716.

[80] An office created under powers contained in the Colonial Boundaries Act 1895 which detached the Chagos Archipelago, and some other islands, from the colony of Mauritius and constituted them a separate colony known as BIOT.

[81] Section 15 of the Constitution Order goes on to reserve to Her Majesty full power to make laws for the peace, good order and good government of the BIOT; to limit any challenges to those permitted by the 1865 Act; and to include in the lawmaking power the making of provision 'for the purposes for which the Territory was constituted and is set aside', including the punishment and removal of unauthorised entrants. (See Sedley at para 18 at *Secretary of State for the Foreign & Commonwealth Affairs v Bancoult, R* (on the application of) [2007] EWCA civ 498. Available at www.bailii.org/ew/cases/EWCA/Civ/2007/498.html).

one would have thought, hardly 'good governance' if there was no population to govern. A number of fundamental questions, therefore, arose before the courts. Did Her Majesty in Council act ultra vires, because the legislation was not 'for the peace, order and good of the Territory'?[82] Or, was there authority for the proposition that, within the limits of the grant, a power to make laws for the peace, order and good of the Territory is as ample and plenary as the power possessed by the Imperial Parliament itself? If the latter, then the words for 'the peace, order and good government of the Territory' are not words of limitation, and this would mean that they did not confer on the courts of a colony, (just as they do not confer on the courts of a State) jurisdiction to strike down legislation on the ground that, in the opinion of a court, the legislation does not promote or secure the peace, order and good government of the colony.

After all, the courts of the UK cannot invalidate laws made by the Parliament of the UK on the ground that they do not secure the general welfare and public interest of its people. So, the same logic would apply to the exercise of its legislative power by the Commissioner of BIOT. It too would not be susceptible to judicial review on that score.[83] This indeed was the Government position. It argued that the provisions of the Orders in Council were not for the peace, order and good of the Chagos Islands, in the case, which has been termed *Bancoult 1* when it was heard by Sedley LJ in the Court of Appeal. This, they maintained, is because the Orders in Council, 'were made in right of the United Kingdom, not in right of the BIOT'.[84]

In what came to be known as *Bancoult (No 2)*[85] the House of Lords considered the validity of Section 9 of the British Indian Ocean Territory (Constitution) Order 2004 under which, 'no person has the right of abode in the Territory'.[86]

---

[82] As Sedley LJ explained, said at para 46: 'one can readily accept that the colonial use of the peace, good order and good government of the prerogative power is for the most part beyond the reach of judicial review, but not that it is always or necessarily so' because as Sedley LJ (at para 46) said, 'even if its subject-matter is incontestably the colony, it is capable of being rendered invalid by jurisdictional error or malpractice. ... In the second place, it must also be open to challenge if its subject-matter, on examination, is manifestly not the peace, good order and good government of the colony.' He went on to add (at para 48) that, 'the use of the prerogative power of colonial governance enjoys no generic immunity from judicial review. What are immune, in my judgment, are prerogative measures lawfully enacted and rationally capable of addressing the peace, good order and good government of the colony.' (See, *Secretary of State for the Foreign & Commonwealth Affairs v Bancoult, R* (on the application of) [2007] EWCA civ 498. Available at www.bailii.org/ew/cases/EWCA/Civ/2007/498.html).

[83] Lord Rodger at para 108 which referred to 'the classical case law' as 'summarised by the High Court of Australia in a unanimous judgment in *Union Steamship Company of Australia Pty Ltd v King* [1988] 166 CLR 1' where 'Their Honours were considering the scope of the power conferred by Section 5 of the Constitution Act 1902 (NSW) to make laws 'for the peace, welfare, and good government of New South Wales.'

[84] Carswell at para 127.

[85] *Bancoult, R (On The Application of) v Secretary of State For Foreign and Commonwealth Affairs* [2008] UKHL 61 (Bancoult No. 2) on 22 October 2008.

[86] Section 9 of the British Indian Ocean Territory (Constitution) Order 2004 states: '(1) Whereas the Territory was constituted and is set aside to be available for the defence purposes of the Government

At issue was the Colonial Laws Validity Act 1865. The background to that Act was a statement made by Lord Mansfield in *Campbell v Hall* (1774) 1 Cowp 204, 209 that, 'although the King had power to introduce new laws into a conquered country, he could not make "any new change contrary to fundamental principles"'. This meant that, '[i]f the King's power did not extend to making laws contrary to fundamental principles (presumably, of English law) in conquered colonies', then as Lord Hoffmann explained, it was arguable, 'that the same limitation applied to the legislatures of settled colonies'. Lord Hoffmann regarded this to be a, 'rather more arcane argument'.[87]

What was interesting, however, was that, '[i]t was never altogether clear what counted as fundamental principles', and this is why, 'the Colonial Laws Validity Act was intended to put the question to rest by providing that no colonial laws should be invalid by reason of repugnancy to any rule of English law except a statute extending to the colony', according to Lord Hoffmann. A 'colonial law' was described 'as a law made for a colony by its legislature or by Order in Council', and a 'colony' as 'all of Her Majesty's possessions abroad in which there shall exist a legislature'.[88]

Two aspects were notable about such laws. First, only a colonial law which is in any respect 'repugnant to ... any Act of Parliament extending to the Colony ... shall, to the Extent of such Repugnancy, but not otherwise, be and remain absolutely void and inoperative'.[89] Second, and on the other hand, 'No Colonial Law shall be ... void or inoperative on the Ground of Repugnancy .... *unless the same shall be repugnant to the Provisions of some such Act of Parliament*, Order, or Regulation as aforesaid' (emphases added).[90] Accordingly, the Government argued that since BIOT is a colony with a legislature, namely, the Commissioner, and since the Constitution Order is a law made for the Colony by Order in Council and therefore

---

of the United Kingdom and the Government of the United States of America, no person has the right of abode in the Territory. (2) Accordingly, no person is entitled to enter or be present in the Territory except as authorised by or under this Order or any other law for the time being in force in the Territory.'

[87] Hoffmann at para 36.

[88] Section 1 of the Colonial Laws Validity Act 1865. Available at www.legislation.gov.uk/ukpga/Vict/28-29/63/section/1.

[89] Section 2 provides: '*Any Colonial Law which is or shall be in any respect repugnant to the Provisions of any Act of Parliament extending to the Colony to which such Law may relate*', or repugnant to any Order or Regulation made under Authority of such Act of Parliament, or having in the Colony the Force and Effect of such Act, shall be read subject such Act, Order, or Regulation, and *shall, to the Extent of such Repugnancy, but not otherwise, be and remain absolutely void and inoperative.*(emphases added in Judgment). Per Hoffmann at para 36 (see, *Bancoult, R (On The Application of) v Secretary of State For Foreign and Commonwealth Affairs* [2008] UKHL 61 at para 38. Available at www.bailii.org/uk/cases/UKHL/2008/61.html).

[90] Section 3 provides that: 'No Colonial Law shall be or be deemed to have been void or inoperative on the Ground of Repugnancy to the Law of *England, unless the same shall be repugnant to the Provisions of some such Act of Parliament*, Order, or Regulation as aforesaid'. (emphases added in Judgment). Per Lord Hoffmann at para 36 (see, *Bancoult, R (On The Application of) v Secretary of State For Foreign and Commonwealth Affairs* [2008] UKHL 61 at para 38. Available at www.bailii.org/uk/cases/UKHL/2008/61.html).

a 'colonial law', it 'cannot be void or inoperative by reason of its repugnancy to English common law doctrines of judicial review'.[91] The Court of Appeal, however, had already rejected this archaic argument. It had held in 2007 that the 1865 Act was concerned with the repugnancy of otherwise valid colonial laws to the law of England, but that was not to say that the principles of judicial review could *not* be used to determine whether the Order in Council was valid in the first place. If the Order in Council was beyond the powers of Her Majesty in Council to make, then 'no question of repugnancy arose, as there was no colonial law which could be repugnant to anything'.[92]

In the House of Lords, however, Lord Hoffmann took a different view, and he did so on the basis of a paper by Finnis[93] where he had, 'persuasively argued that this is a slippery argument because repugnancy to English law (or fundamental principles of English law) can be regarded, and was regarded in the first half of the nineteenth century, as limiting the *powers* of colonial legislatures rather than as being an independent ground for invalidating laws otherwise validly made'. For Lord Hoffmann that, 'a distinction between initial invalidity for lack of compliance with doctrines of English public law and invalidity for repugnancy to English law is too fine to be serviceable'.[94] If the effect of this, however, is to suggest that the rule of law is what the State says it is then this cannot be right not least because forty years after the *GCHQ* case this is not where we would expect to be today. Sedley LJ in the Court of Appeal had made precisely this point when referring to the *GCHQ* case[95] as, '[t]he modern locus classicus' in the memorable 'speech of Lord Scarman'[96] who had left no doubt that:

> .... that the law relating to judicial review has now reached the stage where it can be said with confidence that, if the subject matter in respect of which prerogative power is exercised is justiciable, that is to say if it is a matter upon which the court can adjudicate, the exercise of the power is subject to review in accordance with the principles developed in respect of the review of the exercise of statutory power.

Indeed, the law had gone onto being developed further in this respect to fully 'recognise the amenability in principle of prerogative power to judicial review',

---

[91] Hoffmann, at para 37 (see, *Bancoult, R (On The Application of) v Secretary of State For Foreign and Commonwealth Affairs* [2008] UKHL 61 at para 38. Available at www.bailii.org/uk/cases/UKHL/2008/61.html).

[92] *Bancoult, R (On The Application of) v Secretary of State For Foreign and Commonwealth Affairs* [2008] UKHL 61 at para 38. Available at www.bailii.org/uk/cases/UKHL/2008/61.html.

[93] The Paper was written for the Oxford Law Faculty (*Common Law Constraints: Whose Common Good Counts?* (http://papers.ssrn.com/sol3/papers.cfm?abstract_id=1100628).

[94] Hoffmann at para 39 (see, *Bancoult, R (On The Application of) v Secretary of State For Foreign and Commonwealth Affairs* [2008] UKHL 61 at para 38. Available at www.bailii.org/uk/cases/UKHL/2008/61.html).

[95] *Council of Civil Service Unions v Minister for the Civil Service* [1985] AC 374, 40.

[96] *Secretary of State for the Foreign & Commonwealth Affairs v Bancoult, R (on the application of)* [2007] EWCA Civ 498 (23 May 2007) at para 40.
Available at www.bailii.org/ew/cases/EWCA/Civ/2007/498.html.

as Sedley LJ made clear[97] the case of *Abbasi* had already held that, '[i]t is not an answer to a claim for judicial review to say that the source of the power of the Foreign Office is the prerogative. It is the subject-matter that is determinative'.[98] It is therefore all the more troubling that we should today be talking about the prerogative of colonial governance falling under the, 'shadow of the rule of law', as Mark Elliott & Amanda Perreau-Saussine state, rather than the rule of law itself, though it is manifestly understandable why such a view would be expressed. That this has come to pass is entirely on account of the position taken by the House of Lords. This followed from its adoption of the arcane constitutional theory of Professor Finnis to which we must now turn.

IV. Colonial Legislatures and The Rule of Law

Professor John Finnis, a renowned legal and constitutional theorist, has propounded a view on the legal and political responsibilities of UK ministers when acting to affect the law of a British Overseas Territory. His views played a pivotal role in the decision of the House of Lords to reverse the Court of Appeal's interpretation of the Colonial Laws Validity Act 1865 (CVLA),[99] in the courts below. The Court of Appeal had held that UK ministers *could not* properly legislate in the interests of the UK as a whole (including its dependent territories), but only in the interests of the particular territory itself. Before that, Laws LJ,[100] had concluded in the High Court that, 'the colonial legislature's authority is not wholly unrestrained; peace, order and good government may be a very large tapestry, but every tapestry has a border'.[101] That premise was modified by the House of Lords on the basis of Finnis's arguments. So much so, the House of Lords even expressed doubts about its own earlier decision over how ministers may act in legislating in dependent territories.[102]

The House of Lords was faced with the UK Government argument that, BIOT is a colony with a legislature, namely, the Commissioner, and that the Constitution Order is a law made for the Colony by Order in Council and therefore a 'colonial law'. The logical implication of this was that it, therefore, cannot be void or inoperative by reason of its repugnancy to English common law doctrines of judicial review.[103] Lord Hoffmann observed how the Court of Appeal had rejected this

---

[97] At para 41.
[98] *R (Abbasi) v Secretary of State for Foreign and Commonwealth Affairs* [2002] EWCA 1598, at para106.
[99] J Finnis in *Halsbury's Statutes* (4th edn 1973) vol VI, para 1074 and fn 29.
[100] *Bancoult* (No 1) [2001] QB 1067 at para 43.
[101] ibid at para 55.
[102] See, *Common Law Constraints: Whose Common Good Counts*, Oxford Legal Studies Research Paper No: 10/2008. Available at http://impact.ref.ac.uk/CaseStudies/CaseStudy.aspx?Id=14595.
[103] See, *Bancoult, R (On The Application of) v Secretary of State For Foreign and Commonwealth Affairs* [2008] UKHL 61 (22 October 2008): www.bailii.org/uk/cases/UKHL/2008/61.html. at para 37.

argument on the ground that the 1865 Act was concerned with the repugnancy of otherwise valid colonial laws to the law of England, and how '[the principles of judicial review, on the other hand, determined whether the Order in Council was valid in the first place. No question of repugnancy arose because, if the Order in Council was beyond the powers of Her Majesty in Council, there was no colonial law which could be repugnant to anything]'.[104]

To resolve this question, Lord Hoffmann had regard to a paper written for the Oxford Law Faculty by Professor Finnis,[105] who, in the words of Lord Hoffmann, 'has persuasively argued that this is a slippery argument because repugnancy to English law (or fundamental principles of English law) can be regarded, and was regarded in the first half of the nineteenth century, as limiting the "powers" of colonial legislatures rather than as being an independent ground for invalidating laws otherwise validly made'. Lord Hoffmann went onto agree with this and to add that 'a distinction between initial invalidity for lack of compliance with doctrines of English public law and invalidity for repugnancy to English law is too fine to be serviceable'.[106] As Lord Hoffmann explained:

> the courts were not to concern themselves with the law of England, although they might well apply local principles of judicial review identical with those existing in English law. But these proceedings are concerned with the validity of the Order, not simply as part of the local law of BIOT but, as Professor Finnis says, as imperial legislation made by Her Majesty in Council in the interests of the undivided realm of the United Kingdom and its non-self-governing territories.[107]

Finnis' views, however, are a contradiction in terms. On the one hand he had accepted that, 'the judicial protection of rights and the rule of law are indispensable elements of the common good', but on the other he had asserted that where judges are invited 'to consider directly whether "overriding and sufficient reasons" exist for some legislative act' that this 'can involve a loss of perspective inimical to the common good of a realm so large and complex as the empire was and even the United Kingdom with its dependent territories. ....'.[108] Size and complexity, however, are surely no bar to the judicial protection of rights and the enforcement of the rule of law. Where bad things happen are they any less condemnable simply because they happen in the outer reaches of the realm? Surely not. To suggest there would be a loss of perspective inimical to the common good in such a case would be to suggest an absence of constitutionalism which is more in keeping with the business of government in the nineteenth century.

---

[104] At para 38.
[105] The Paper was *Common Law Constraints: Whose Common Good Counts?* (http://papers.ssrn.com/sol3/papers.cfm?abstract_id=1100628).
[106] ibid at para 39.
[107] ibid at para 40.
[108] ibid at para 24.

In formulating his thesis, Finnis placed reliance on the Jamaican case of *Phillips v Eyre*[109] and the Privy Council decision in *Liyange*[110] for the proposition that the dependent legislature may make laws 'which are repugnant.... to any principles or rules of natural justice'. It is difficult to see how this can realistically be maintained today given the development of international law standards on the application of human rights norms.[111] If Finnis is right than there ought in principle to be nothing wrong with the removal of 'Man Fridays' from the Chagos Archipelago—as the cable from the US State Department in May 2009 reporting what Colin Roberts, the Director of the Foreign & Commonwealth Office Overseas Territories, had apparently promised to do. This is to say nothing of the emergence of the idea of imperial trusteeship,[112] which arose after the loss of the 13 American Colonies under George III. Frost and Murray have recently referred to the unresolvable antinomies here of, 'how the imperial common good is riven by competing theoretical justifications for empire: one, based in liberal imperialism, emphasises the civilising nature of empire and focuses on the good governance of colonies; the other, based in a utilitarian imperialism, instead focuses on how best to appropriate colonial possessions for the benefit of the imperial power'.[113] In 2016, when the appeal against the House of Lords decision was determined by the UK Supreme Court Lady Hale had ruefully remarked how, '[t]hus far, it is the latter which has not only driven the actions of government but has also triumphed in the courts'.[114]

In the opinion of Finnis the CVLA had the effect of 'liberating the makers of colonial laws—immunizing their laws—from judicial scrutiny' and that this was true even in relation to allowing slavery, polygamy, prohibition of Christianity,

---

[109] *Phillips v Eyre* [1869] LR 4 QB 225 and (1870) LR 6 QB.

[110] *Liyange v R* [1967] 1 AC 259 PC (Cey) See also fn 15 of Elliott & Perreau-Saussine.

[111] But, it has been argued conversely that the CVLA can realistically be 'interpreted as conferring unlimited powers of colonial despotism on the Crown' is wholly untenable and not least because it 'confuses history with adjudication. See, Elliott & Perreau-Saussine at p 701–702.

[112] G Mellor & J. Simmons, *British Imperial Trusteeship, 1783–1850*, especially the review by Robert Livingston Schuyler in *Political Science Quarterly*, vol 68, No 1 (Mar., 1953), pp 132–134. The notion of imperial trusteeship has been a contested one, however: see, the skeptical article by John Gallagher and Ronald Robinson, 'The Imperialism of Free Trade', *Economic History Review*, 2nd. Ser, (1953) pp 1–15. But the better view is in Andrew Porter, '*Trusteeship, Anti-Slavery, and Humanitarianism*' in A. Porter & WM R. Louis, The Oxford History of British Empire,: Volume III, The Nineteenth Century, (OUP, 1999) where it is argued that throughout the nineteenth century, territorial conquest, white settlement, commercial growth, economic development, and above all issues of slavery and the slave trade, raised questions about the ethics of economic exchange, the politics of equal rights or racial differences, and the purpose of Imperial power. The two conceptions of 'trusteeship' differed substantially. There are implications for the relationship of humanitarian activity and Britain's Imperial experience. Humanitarians' dependence on the Imperial government took many forms. In mid-century, the humanitarian movement became temporarily but essentially the creature of habit. There were signs of changing emphases and new directions in the development of Britain's humanitarian tradition before 1914.

[113] T Frost and C Murray, '*The Chagos Island cases: the empire strikes back*' (2015) 66 NILQ 263 at 266. Referred to also by Lady Hale in her dissenting judgment in *Bancoult, R (on the application of) v Secretary of State for Foreign and Commonwealth Affairs* (No 2) [2016] UKSC 35, at para 188.

[114] ibid at para 72.

authorisation of punishment without trial, and the uncontrolled destruction of indigenous peoples, and he drew upon the 'fundamental principles' in the advice given by the Law Officers in the build up to the passage of the CVLA.[115] Such a thesis is unconvincing being based on a reliance on the traditional colonial cases of revolt and rebellion against an Imperial government. These are not cases that demonstrate the colonial government duties when it is seeking to exercise power for 'peace, order, and good government' in the twentieth century long after the process of decolonisation has begun. Quite simply, the Chagos Islanders case of *Bancoult* was not a case of insurrection and insurgency seeking to impose order over chaos! The logic is wholly introverted.

The reliance on the nineteenth-century case of *Phillip v Eyre* was misconceived. The case was one of compensation to the Jamaican Governor, by the passage of an Act of Indemnity by the colonial legislature, after his merciless obliteration of a revolt that came hot on the heels of his proclamation of martial law. The issue there was whether a colonial legislature could remove a right of action against the Governor in England. Lord Cockburn held that it could. The private international law principle of comity or respect for foreign legislation, could be extended to the colonies with their own colonial legislature, with respect to Acts occurring within that foreign jurisdiction. There was no need to invoke the CVLA and no need for an English court to interfere with colonial legislation.

The reliance on the mid-twentieth century case of *Liyange* was equally misconceived because it also involved the leaders of a failed coup where the realm itself was threatened. The charges against them were that, 'first that they conspired to wage war against the Queen', and did so 'by means of criminal force' such as to 'overthrow otherwise than by lawful means the Government of Ceylon by law established'.[116] The case concerned the review of the validity of colonial legislation which made the coup leaders subject to prosecution before three judges directed by a Minister without a jury.[117] The Privy Council held that there was no power to review. To do so would be to transgress the fundamental principle of the separation of powers which was central to the colonial Constitution of Ceylon. In both these types of cases, the 'common good of a realm so large and complex as the

---

[115] see, Finnis, *Common Law Constraints: Whose Common Good Counts*, Oxford Legal Studies Research Paper No: 10/2008, (available at www.worldlii.org/int/journals/lsn/abstracts/1100628.html).

[116] Pearce in his opening remarks in *Liyange*.

[117] As Pearce explained, 'Under Section 440A of the Criminal Procedure Code the Minister of Justice could direct that the defendant be tried by three judges without a jury in the case of the offence of sedition and any other offence in which such a mode of trial would be appropriate by reason of civil commotion, disturbance of public feeling or any other similar cause. That clause was amended so as to apply expressly not only to sedition but to any other offence under Part VI of the Penal Code, the part which dealt with offences against the State, the offences with which the appellants were charged. Thus the Minister could direct that the appellants should be tried by three judges without a jury. With this section one may conveniently read Section 9 of the first Act whereby in cases in which the Minister directs a trial by three judges without a jury, the three judges should be nominated by the Minister of Justice, and Section 17 which provided for the addition of two more judges to the Supreme Court, such provision to come into operation on such date as the Minister might appoint.'

empire' may well have a completely different connotation to the outright exiling of an entire population of an island which has to be administered through laws made for the peace, order and good government of the territory.[118] Accordingly, liberating the makers of colonial law,[119] so as to immunise their laws from judicial scrutiny, was the last thing that the courts should have entertained here.[120] The three cases used to justify this outcome amount to nothing more than an up-side down logic and amount to a false basis for the removal of the Chagossian Islanders. The irony is that 'peace and order' already existed in the lives of this simple population of coconut gatherers. Into this 'innocent world' intruded, as Lord Hoffmann had rightly observed, 'the brutal realities of the cold war.'[121] Another judge might well have said—as Lord Atkin once did in what has since come to be seen as the greatest judicial dissent in English history—that:

> I know of only one authority which might justify the suggested method of construction. "When I use a word," Humpty Dumpty said in rather a scornful tone," it means just what I choose it to mean, neither more nor less." "The question is," said Alice, "whether you can make words mean different things." "The question is," said Humpty Dumpty, "which is to be master—that's all." (*Looking Glass*, c. vi.) After all this long discussion the question is whether the words "If a man has" can mean "If a man thinks he has." I am of opinion that they cannot, and that the case should be decided accordingly.[122]

V. Confusion in the House of Lords

By deciding to adopt the thesis advocated by Professor Finnis, the House of Lords took a regressive step back from cherished time-honoured common law values that helped develop the Rule of Law. The House of Lords found itself going down a confused and confusing line of judicial reasoning. At the outset of this chapter, it was suggested that the decision moves judicial control of the prerogative forwards, but that it still leaves the unhappy impression of judicial feebleness.

---

[118] For Elliott & Perreau-Saussine, '*Liyange* is best interpreted as reiterating that the CVLA limits the sources of law for colonial review of colonial legislation to those (including Imperial legislation) that form part of the colonial constitution. ...' See, Elliott & Perreau-Saussine at p 703.

[119] As Elliott & Perreau-Saussine suggest the basis of the argument by Finnis amounts to no more than 'inferences drawn from the Colonial Secretary's apparent dissatisfaction with advice given to his predecessor to the effect that colonial legislation would be invalid if inconsistent with fundamental principles of English law'. See, Elliott & Perreau-Saussine at fn 19.

[120] Elliott & Perreau-Saussine add that, 'it is far from clear that this satisfies the stipulation in *Pepper v Hart* [1993] AC 593 HL that ministerial statements may be taken into account only when "clear"'. (at fn 19).

[121] Hoffmann at para 6.

[122] Lord Atkin in *Liversidge v Anderson* [1941] UKHL 1.
(Available at www.bailii.org/uk/cases/UKHL/1941/1.html). The judgment is all the more remarkable given that it was given in war-time emergency during the Second World War.

Although, three of the five judges, Lords Hoffmann, Bingham and Mance, held that the Crown cannot without parliamentary consent lawfully abrogate or override a British subject's constitutional rights, there are troubling ambiguities. Lords Bingham and Mance considered there to be a constitutional right of abode (with Lord Mance even describing it as 'fundamental' and 'constitutional')[123] such that the constitutional right operates to legally constrain prerogative power. But Lord Hoffmann held that there was no such right. He added obiter that a right not to be tortured could operate as a limit on the scope of prerogative powers of colonial governance, such that an Order in Council could not legally authorise the use of torture.[124] The remaining two judges were even more dissonant. Lord Carswell did not think there were any 'fundamental principles' at stake here, but if this is so His Lordship's description of 'how near' a right of abode is to 'being an inalienable constitutional right'[125] is more than a little curious.[126] Lord Rodger held that it is 'certainly arguable' that there was a 'fundamental principle' of English law that no citizen should be exiled or banished from a British colony'.[127] Paradoxically, however, he then held that in a colonial territory the rights of British subjects are always subject to abrogation by the Crown, before proceeding to hold that even torture could be permitted by virtue of an Order in Council in a colony as the 'law of the land',[128] because the prohibition in Magna Carta of banishment only held so long as it was not in accordance with the law of the land.

Bancoult argued nevertheless that the power of colonial governance prevented the enactment of legislation that violated a constitutional right of abode. Sydney Kentridge on his behalf submitted that, the Orders in Council were invalid because 'Her Majesty had no power to legislate by Order in Council "contrary to fundamental principles" of English common law'.[129] Sydney Kentridge also submitted: 'the right of a "belonger" not to be excluded from the territory to which he belonged was just such a fundamental principle'. For support of this principle he relied on 'Chapter 29 of Magna Carta', but he also 'cited the statement of Blackstone, *Commentaries on the Laws of England* (15th edition, 1809) vol 1, p 137, that "no power on earth, except the authority of Parliament, can send any subject of England out of the land against his will; no, not even a criminal"' Lord Rodger in response ruled: 'I accept that both of these point to the existence of such a principle'.[130] Kentridge also argued that the only legitimate purpose for which the power may be used is for the purposes of 'peace, order and good government'

---

[123] *Bancoult* (no.2) [2008] UKHL 61; [2009] 1 AC 453 at para 151.
[124] *Bancoult* (no 2) [2008] UKHL 61; [2009] 1 AC 453 at para 35.
[125] *Bancoult* (no 2) [2008] UKHL 61; [2009] 1 AC 453 at para 123.
[126] As M Elliott & A Perreau-Saussine observe 'that is senseless if there exists no such things.' See, M Elliott & A Perreau-Saussine, '*Pyrrhic Public Law: Bancoult and the sources, status and content of common law limitations on prerogative power*', Public Law, (October, 2009), pp 697–722, at p 706.
[127] *Bancoult* (no 2) [2008] UKHL 61; [2009] 1 AC 453 at para 89.
[128] *Bancoult* (no 2) [2008] UKHL 61; [2009] 1 AC 453 at para 86.
[129] In this he relied on the words of Lord Mansfield in *Campbell v Hall*, 1 Cowp 204, 209.
[130] *Bancoult* (No 2) [2008] UKHL 61; [2009] 1 AC 453 at para 87.

of the Colony. Sanctioning the banishment of the entire population from the colony by Section 9 of the Constitution Order did not comport with this power. Therefore, its exercise was invalid and unlawful.

Yet, Lords Hoffmann, Rodger and Carswell nevertheless found against *Bancoult*. Whilst accepting that the historical use of the prerogative power was indeed to secure and promote 'peace, order and good government' in the ceded territories, the established legal authorities[131] suggested the existence of a plenary law-making power.[132] This being so the courts 'will not inquire into whether legislation within the territorial scope of the power was in fact for the "peace, order and good government", or otherwise for the benefit of the inhabitants of territory'.[133] In the words of Lord Rodger the exercise of power here 'is equal in scope to the legislative power of Parliament'.[134] This is difficult to understand given that the reference to the power is for purposes of 'peace, order and good government'. The power cannot be used to wage war, to create disorder, or to banish into exile the entire population of the Island. Even an Act of Parliament is subject to review on this basis. A Minister's irrational exercise of power is reviewable in the same way as the Governor's in a colony. This surely, is an abnegation of judicial power.

But an even more troubling question was the deployment of Orders in Council raising questions before the courts of their constitutional status. Whilst prerogative orders enacted under original authority, as distinct from conferred authority, can be treated as primary legislation,[135] Orders in Council are better conceived as a form of secondary legislation.[136] Prerogative legislation still, however, remains different from primary legislation in vital respects. First, whereas full parliamentary scrutiny is applied to Acts of Parliament it is markedly absent in cases of prerogative legislation thereby robbing it of the seal of democratic approval. In the absence of parliamentary oversight it is constitutional heresy to immunise prerogative legislation from judicial review.[137] In *Huang* in 2007 the House of Lords implied that rules that 'are not the product of active debate in Parliament' have less of 'the imprimatur of democratic approval'[138] so that they are not necessarily entitled to 'due deference'[139] in the way that primary legislation is. In prerogative

---

[131] See, *Union Steamship Co. of Australia Pty Ltd. V King* (1988) 166 CLR 1 referred to at para 108.
[132] *Bancoult* (No 2) [2008] UKHL 61; [2009] 1 AC 453 at para 44, and per Hoffmann at para 108; per Rodger at para 124, per Lord Carswell.
[133] *Bancoult* (No 2) [2008] UKHL 61; [2009] 1 AC 453 at para 50.
[134] *Bancoult* (No 2) [2008] UKHL 61; [2009] 1 AC 453 at para 109.
[135] A McHarg, 'What is Delegated Legislation?' [2006] Public Law 539, 541.
[136] B Pontin and P Billings, '*Prerogative Powers and the Human Rights Act: Elevating the Status of Orders in Council*' [2011] Public Law 21. For another view see also, M Cohn, '*Judicial Review of Non-Statutory Executive Powers after Bancoult: a Unified Anxious Model*' [2009] Public Law 260, at 269 who expresses the questionable view that it is 'little short of revolutionary' to suggest that the Status of an Order in Council is 'no higher than statute-based secondary legislation.'
[137] As M Elliott & A Perreau-Saussine put it 'the protective effect of the sovereignty of Parliament is removed.' See, M Elliott & A Perreau-Saussine at p 707.
[138] *Huang v Secretary of State for the Home Department* [2007] UKHL 11 at para 17. Available at www.bailii.org/uk/cases/UKHL/2007/11.html.
[139] ibid at para 14.

legislation it is the Crown in Council, rather than the Crown in Parliament, and the doctrine of parliamentary supremacy cannot be used to preclude judicial intervention. Second, constitutional principle has long been clear that the powers of the Crown in Council are not limitless.[140] Judicial review of prerogative legislation operates only because such powers are subject to constitutional constraint. It is all the more remarkable then that Lords Carswell and Rodger conceived the prerogative power of colonial governance in absolute terms. Lord Rodger's categorisation of it as a plenary power led to his suggestion that, 'prerogative legislation made for these colonies is in the same position as legislation made by Parliament for this country'.[141] The chief attribute of subordinate legislation is that it has limited purposes. If the exercise of statutory powers cannot be purposeless than neither can the exercise of prerogative powers.[142] The power is subject to the proper purposes doctrine. This is precisely why Laws LJ conceived the power accurately when declaring in *Bancoult (No 1)* that even if this is a very large tapestry it still has a border.[143]

It is worth recalling that the British Indian Ocean Order 1965 was passed, as a Statutory Instrument, under the Colonial Boundaries Act 1895. It created the Office of the Commissioner of BIOT, which had the authority to 'make laws for the peace, order and good government of the territory'.[144] The Commissioner of BIOT in turn enacted the Immigration Ordinance 1971. This stipulated that no one without permission would be allowed to enter or remain in the territory of BIOT. The suggestion by Elliott & Perreau-Saussine that, it provided 'a legal basis for exiling the whole of the Chagossian population in consultation with the US government',[145] is only half true—as we now know—because the policy of population exile was driven by the FCO officials in London and not the US. When Louis Oliver Bancoult first brought his challenge Lord Justice Laws in the Divisional Court in 2000[146] held that, given that the evacuation and deportation of the colony's civilian population could not be in the interests of peace, order and good government of the territory, the Immigration Ordinance 1971, was ultra vires the BIOT Order of 1965, although those affected were unable to claim damages

---

[140] *Case of Proclamations* (1611) 12 co rep 74; 77 ER 1352.

[141] This is tantamount to what M Elliott & A Perreau-Saussine have rightly described as an analysis which 'goes a considerable distance towards conferring upon the Crown in Council in de facto terms precisely the sovereign law-making power that lacks in the de jure sense.' See also, M. Elliott & A. Perreau-Saussine at p 708 where they draw attention to the fact that all save Lord Hoffmann assume that constitutional rights can be alienated by clear parliamentary legislation, by presupposing a traditional view of parliamentary sovereignty, but which is now no longer universally accepted: see *Jackson* [2006] 1 AC 262, per Lord Steyn at 102, Lord Hope at 104–107 and Baroness Hale at para 159.

[142] *R v Somersett CC* ex parte *Fewings* [1995] 1 All ER 513 (per Laws at 525).

[143] As Laws explained, 'peace, order and good government may be a very large tapestry, but every tapestry has a border; see, *Bancoult (No 1)* [2001] 1067 at 1103.

[144] BIOT Order 1965 Article 11(1).

[145] Elliott & Perreau-Saussine at p 698.

[146] The challenge was upheld by the Divisional Court in *R (Bancoult) v Secretary of State for Foreign and Commonwealth Affairs* [2001] QB 1067 ('*Bancoult' (No 1)*') in November 2000. Available at www.bailii.org/ew/cases/EWHC/Admin/2000/413.html.

for their illegal treatment.[147] This case, which came to be known as *Bancoult (No 1)*, saw the Chagossians now being permitted to return to the outer islands—although not to Diego Garcia.[148] When the full picture is considered it is clear that *Bancoult (No 1)* was the right decision. *Bancoult (No 2)* was the wrong decision.

VI. Conclusion

The starting point to the modern exercise of the prerogative of colonial governance is that the power is anachronistic, and that if it is to be exercised at all today then the legal obligations of trusteeship under Chapter XI of the UN Charter must be observed given that international law is an accepted source of English law. None of the judgments in the House of Lords fully developed this premise. The use of a 'colonial law' to affect purposes which a democratically elected Parliament would not otherwise endorse is also something not to be easily ignored by the Courts. Some of the judges in the *Bancoult* litigation took cognisance of this limitation. Sedley LJ considered that it was only in the specific context of the allocation and assignment of authority to colonial legislatures that the formula of 'peace, order and good government' acquired the status of plenary power, but that the Crown's remaining powers of colonial governance were still subject to a limitation through these very words.

This meant that, 'the permanent exclusion of an entire population from its homeland for reasons unconnected with their collective well-being cannot have [the] character [of governance] and accordingly cannot be lawfully accomplished by the use of prerogative powers'.[149] Given that the Crown has to exercise governance over the Colonies as a Crown function the territory interests are not coterminous with interests of the UK state and its allies. As a result, '[t]he governance of each colonial territory is in constitutional principle a discrete function of the Crown' such that '[t]hat territory's interests will not necessarily be the interests of the United Kingdom or of its allies'.[150] This is a different constitutional theory from that of Professor Finnis, but all the more apposite given that we are in the twenty-first century now, and not in the heyday of the Empire in the nineteenth.

Lord Bingham had little doubt that Section 9 of the Constitution Order could not be enacted,[151] and Lord Mance said that only the proper governance of the

---

[147] Sedley held in *Chagos Islanders v Attorney General & Anor* [2004] EWCA civ 997 (22 July 2004) that, though the position may have been different in a civil law system, no liability in damages arose by this unlawful conduct. Available at www.bailii.org/ew/cases/EWCA/Civ/2004/997.html.

[148] For anyone who was a British Dependent Territories Citizen the *Immigration Ordinance 2000* removed, except in the case of Diego Garcia, the entry and residence restrictions if he/she had a connection with BIOT.

[149] *Bancoult* (No 2) [2007] EWCA civ 498; [2008] QB 365 at para 67.

[150] ibid at para 67.

[151] *Bancoult* (No 2) [2008] UKHL 61; [2009] 1 AC 453 at para 71.

territory could be countenanced.[152] Lord Hoffmann believed the prerogative's exercise by the Crown to be, 'in the interests of her undivided realm, including both the United Kingdom and the colony'.[153] Whilst Lords Rodger[154] and Carswell[155] took a markedly different approach, suggesting that it was a matter for the Crown and not the Court, on grounds that was non-justiciable question, that position is difficult to sustain given that they also held that the question whether the power was exercised rationally was a justiciable question.[156] In *Shergill*[157] recently the Supreme Court explained how under the doctrine of the Separation of Powers, an issue is treated beyond the constitutional competence of the courts if, for example, it involves certain transactions of foreign states, 'although the boundaries of the category of "transactions" of states which will engage the doctrine now are a good deal less clear today than they seemed to be forty years ago'. The constitutional limits of the court's competence are 'as against that of the executive in matters directly affecting the United Kingdom's relations with foreign states'.[158] Here there was no question of relations with foreign states. Accordingly, the matter could not be said, 'to be inherently unsuitable for judicial determination by reason only of its subject-matter'.[159]

In the light of this Lord Carswell's reservations that the courts should not make judgments of this sort because, 'they could very easily get into the area of challenging what is essentially a political judgment, which is not for courts of law',[160] are untenable. One is inclined to agree with Mark Elliott and Amanda Perreau-Saussine that: '[i]t is difficult to resist the conclusion that a measure of unnecessary deference lives on in relation to the prerogative merely because it *is*

---

[152] ibid at para 157.
[153] ibid at para 47.
[154] ibid at para 109.
[155] ibid at para 130.
[156] ibid at para 109 and 131 (where Lord Rodger did not accept the contention that, 'that judicial review of an order in council would trespass against the rule that prerogative orders are regularly made against Ministers in their official capacity, but never against the Crown" and where Carswell noted that, "It must be borne in mind that it is the *Wednesbury* standard which must be applied to the Secretary of State's decision to have the Orders in Council enacted'.
[157] *Shergill & Ors v Khaira & Ors* [2014] UKSC 33 (11 June 2014): www.bailii.org/uk/cases/UKSC/2014/33.html. For a discussion, see S. Juss 'Back to the future: justiciability, religion, and the figment of 'judicial no-man's land' (2016) Public Law, April pp 198–206.
[158] ibid at para 42.
[159] As the Supreme Court explained, 'There is a number of rules of English law which may result in an English court being unable to decide a disputed issue on its merits. Some of them, such as state immunity, confer immunity from jurisdiction. Some, such as the act of state doctrine, confer immunity from liability on certain persons in respect of certain acts. Some, such as the rule against the enforcement of foreign penal, revenue or public laws, or the much-criticised rule against the determination by an English court of title to foreign land (now circumscribed by statute and by the Brussels Regulation and the Lugano Convention) are probably best regarded as depending on the territorial limits of the competence of the English courts or of the competence which they will recognise in foreign states. Properly speaking, the term non-justifiability refers to something different. It refers to a case where an issue is said to be inherently unsuitable for judicial determination by reason only of its subject-matter.' (at para 41).
[160] *Bancoult* (No 2) [2008] UKHL 61; [2009] 1 AC 453 at para 130.

the prerogative' and that 'our highest court remains in thrall to what Lord Roskill referred to "as the clanking of medieval chains of the ghosts of the past".[161] All the more reason then why this landmark case falls outside the rule of law. A different view was possible. Sedley LJ had already held that although a court may not substitute its view for that of the Executive, it may decide whether prerogative legislation is 'rationally and legally capable of providing for a territory's wellbeing'.[162] This was echoed by Lord Mance that: '[a] Constitution which exiles a territory's population is a contradiction in terms'.[163] Frost and Murray had in 2015 referred to the competing forces of 'liberal imperialism' and 'utilitarian imperialism' and in her dissenting judgment in 2016 Lady Hale had quoted their words in her judgment that in 2008, 'Lord Hoffmann acknowledged that a choice between the liberal and utilitarian faces of imperialism did rest with the court, and decisively affirmed the utilitarian importance of the imperial interests at stake …'[164] Yet, there is every reason to doubt now whether this 'utilitarian' view of imperialism, about 'how best to appropriate colonial possessions for the benefit of the imperial power' will prevail over the 'liberal' view of imperialism, about 'the civilising nature of empire and focuses on the good governance of colonies'.[165] Even the majority in 2016 accepted that given that, in the words of Lord Clarke, 'there is a critical factor which is in any event conclusive', namely, '2014–2015 feasibility study' which considers, among other things, 'the possibility of resettlement on Diego Garcia' then 'that is not the end of the road' because this 'new factor' is such that it 'concludes that there would be scope for supported resettlement', so that quite simply 'the background has now shifted and logically the constitutional ban needs to be revisited'.[166] This view was shared by Lord Mance.[167] The result in 2016 is likely to be a pyrhic victory for the Government.

The question, of course, is whether a different view was possible back in 2008. It is now clear from the 2016 decision that it was. The dissenting judgment of Lord Kerr was unequivocal that, 'a decision to remove the Chagossians from their homeland with little or no provision for their future would indeed be a

---

[161] M Elliott & A Perreau-Saussine at pp 710–711 referring to *GCHQ* [1985] AC 374 at p 417–418 reminding us that Roskill was quoting from Atkin's speech, rendered in a different context, in *United Australia Ltd v Barclays Bank Ltd* [1941] AC 1 HL at p 29.

[162] *Bancoult* (No 2) [2007] EWHC civ 498; [2008] QB 365 at para 51.

[163] *Bancoult* (No 2) [2008] UKHL 61; [2009] 1 AC 453 at para 157.

[164] T Frost and C Murray, '*The Chagos Island cases: the empire strikes back*' (2015) 66 NILQ 263 at 287. Referred to by Lady Hale in her dissenting judgment in *Bancoult, R (on the application of) v Secretary of State for Foreign and Commonwealth Affairs* (No 2) [2016] UKSC 35, at para 188.

[165] T Frost and C Murray, '*The Chagos Island cases: the empire strikes back*' (2015) 66 NILQ 263 at 266.

[166] *Bancoult, R (on the application of) v Secretary of State for Foreign and Commonwealth Affairs* (No 2) [2016] UKSC 35, at para 78.

[167] *Bancoult, R (on the application of) v Secretary of State for Foreign and Commonwealth Affairs* (No 2) [2016] UKSC 35, at para 72.

profoundly intrusive measure and one for which compelling justification would be required'.[168] So much so that:

> [i]n accordance with the standard set by Lord Hoffmann, the decision to remove the Chagossians without making adequate provision for them and their subsequent actual removal when that provision was not in place must therefore have been irrational when those events occurred. The fact that their removal, when it in fact occurred, was unreasonable cannot, … be left out of account in assessing whether the subsequent decision to perpetuate the Chagossians' exile was rational.[169]

Lady Hale in her dissenting judgment helpfully reminded us of the elementary principles at play, namely, that 'Courts have … to do justice according to law' and that 'the decision to exile a people has to be taken in accordance with the law; and the people to whom it is of such momentous importance are entitled to expect the highest standards of decision-making and the most scrupulous standards of fairness from the institutions of imperial government'. Yet, here the earlier feasibility study of 2002 relied upon by the Government 'showed that the government had made it plain to the consultants what it wanted the conclusions to be' and that 'important changes had been made to the conclusion' so that 'the central findings about climate change had been changed' when it was clear that 'the islands were not in a cyclone belt'. In a rare judicial statement, highlighting the central role played by judicial personalities in hard cases arising before the courts, Lady Hale also added for good measure that: '[t]he question whether this might have made a difference has to be answered objectively rather than by reference to the particular judges who were then sitting on the case'.[170]

In fact, there are other reasons why a different view was entirely possible in 2008, whatever the judicial personalities. It is one that fully exposes the internal incoherence and confusion of thought in the majority's collective judgment back in 2008. In a bizarre three-page letter—allegedly written by Rose Likins, the acting Assistant Secretary of State at the US State Department, to Denise Holt of the UK Foreign Commonwealth Office[171] a case against resettlement of Chagossians in their homelands is made out on the grounds that, 'the United States is seriously concerned that repopulating the outer islands would provide terrorists the cover and concealment to establish permanent operating bases from which they could monitor island operations with minimum risk of counter detection.'[172] This was a risk which could not be run because, 'Diego Garcia is an important forward operating base from which the United States can conduct rapid and tailored air,

---

[168] *Bancoult, R (on the application of) v Secretary of State for Foreign and Commonwealth Affairs* (No 2) [2016] UKSC 35, at para 117.
[169] Hale, *op.cit* at para 118.
[170] Hale, *op cit* at para 193.
[171] Letter on File with the Author.
[172] ibid at para 2.

sea, land operations in four of the seven continents of the world' and that '[f]rom a defense position, the repopulation of the outer islands presents an unacceptable risk to military operations. ....'.[173]

This letter was not the creation of the US State Department, but written after consultation with the FCO officials in London who ventriloquised it so that it could be used in the legal proceedings.[174] Even more than that, it was roundly castigated by the House of Lords when in his judgment Lord Hoffmann said that '[s]ome of these scenarios might be regarded as fanciful speculations'. It is all the more reason therefore why Lord Hoffmann should not then have proceeded to conclude that, 'but, in the current state of uncertainty, the government is entitled to take the concerns of its ally into account'.[175] It was surely little more than lame to suggest that:

> [i]t is true that the Chagossians will now require immigration consent even to visit the islands. But the government have made it clear that such visits, to tend graves and so forth, will be allowed, and since in practice they are funded by the BIOT administration, immigration consent will be no more than an additional formality. Furthermore, there is no reason why, if at some time in the future, circumstances should change, the controls should not be lifted.[176]

The judgment of Laws LJ, on the other hand, was much more to be preferred in *Bancoult (No 1)* namely, that a rationality review was entirely possible in the proper circumstances of this case because a reference to, 'the peace, order and good government' of any territory means nothing, surely save by reference to the territory's population. They are to be *governed* not removed'.[177] It may confidently be asserted that, that view of the predominance and pre-eminence of the rule of law in public law proceedings, is now likely to prevail over considerations of political expediency in any future legal action.

---

[173] ibid at paras 2–3.
[174] See, D Snoxell, 'Anglo-American Complicity in the Removal of the Inhabitants of the Chagos Islands, 1964–73', Journal of Imperial & Commonwealth History (vol 73, March 2009, 2009, pp 127–134), who sets out earlier correspondence and Memoranda from 1964–1972 designed to shore up the Government case. He makes it clear that that the FCO in London was under no pressure from the Americans to remove the population from all the Islands. The policy to do so was driven entirely by the FCO officials themselves. If the Americans had objected the policy would not have been implemented. As long ago as April 1969 the UK Prime Minister, on the recommendation of the Foreign Secretary had given authority for the wholesale removal of the Chagossian population from their homeland, but the FCO only affected that policy form 1971–73. This is clear from a 1980 letter to the British High Commission in Mauritius: 'I am sure the Americans do not want to get mixed up in this. They look to us to sort it out and I should think they consider that we made a hash of the Diego Garcia clearance. Our agreement with them leading to the 1966 Exchange of Notes required only Diego Garcia to be empty. They had no objections to the other Chagos Islands remain populated; it was our decision to clear the lot and resettle in Mauritius.' (see, *Folio 119 of FCO File 31/2770. M. Hewitt, EAD to W.A. ward, High Commissioner of Mauritius, dated 4 December 1980.*)
[175] Hoffmann at para 56.
[176] ibid at para 55.
[177] *Bancoult* (No 1) [2011] QB 1104.

12

AXA General Insurance Ltd v HM Advocate and Others [2012]: The Nature of Devolved Legislation and the Role of the Courts

THE HONOURABLE MR JUSTICE LEWIS

I. Introduction

The process of devolution represents one of the major constitutional developments within the UK in recent decades. The decision in *AXA General Insurance Ltd. v HM Advocate and Others* ('*Axa*')[1] is a landmark decision examining the current constitutional arrangements in relation to the devolved legislatures within the UK. The decision considers the nature of devolved legislation and the role of courts in relation to judicial review of that legislation.

Devolution has led to the creation of elected legislatures for Scotland, Wales and Northern Ireland. Those devolved legislatures have competence to make laws within certain defined limits for their respective polities. The constitutional structure of the UK has moved from there being a single, sovereign source of legislative power within a unitary state to there being a sovereign UK Parliament but also other elected legislature enacting legislation for the differing constituent parts of the UK. Something along the lines of a federal, or quasi-federal division of powers has emerged. Inevitably, when power is shared between different institutions within the state, the courts undertake the task of policing the constitutional settlement to determine the scope of the powers of the new legislatures, the nature of the laws made by those legislatures and the proper role of the courts in arbitrating on such questions. Those issues all arose for consideration in *Axa*.

---

[1] [2012] 1 AC 868.

II. The *AXA* Case

The case concerned a challenge to legislation enacted by the Scottish Parliament, namely the Damages (Asbestos-related Conditions) (Scotland) Act 2009. The Act concerned employees who had been exposed to asbestos. Such exposure could result in individuals developing asymptomatic pleural plaques, that is physical changes in the lining, or pleura, of the lung. The plaques had no discernible effect on the individual's physical health or wellbeing. Their presence did, however, indicate that there had been exposure to a level of asbestos at which there was an increased risk of other, asbestos-related medical conditions. From about the mid-1990s, former employees with pleural plaques began to bring proceedings in negligence claiming damages for the anxiety associated with the development of pleural plaques. In 2008, however, in litigation concerning employees in England the House of Lords in *Rothwell v Chemical & Insulating Co Ltd.*[2] held that such plaques did not constitute an injury and could not give rise to a claim for damages.

Exposure to asbestos, and the development of pleural plaques, was a particular problem in relation to certain areas such as Clydebank where industries that exposed their employees to asbestos were located. The Scottish Parliament, therefore, enacted legislation providing that asymptomatic pleural plaques did constitute actionable harm for the purposes of an action for damages for personal injury. This had the practical effect of reversing the decision of the House of Lords in *Rothwell* so far as Scotland was concerned. The practical effect of the Scottish legislation was that employees in Scotland would be able to bring a claim against, and recover damages from, their employers if they had been diagnosed as having pleural plaques which had been caused by negligent exposure to asbestos. That, in turn, would expose insurance companies to claims by employers on their indemnity insurance policies.

Insurance companies, therefore, brought a claim in Scotland for judicial review challenging the lawfulness of the Scottish legislation on two grounds. First, they contended that the legislation contravened their rights to property under Article 1 of the First Protocol to the ECHR and so was outside the competence of the Scottish Parliament by virtue of Section 29(2)(d) of the Scotland Act 1998. Second, they contended that the legislation was open to judicial review on common law grounds as an unreasonable, irrational and arbitrary exercise of statutory power conferred on the Scottish Parliament by the Scotland Act 1998. Those two challenges provided the opportunity for the UK Supreme Court to consider the role of the courts in reviewing the vires or lawfulness of legislation enacted by the devolved legislatures and the nature of that devolved legislation itself.

---

[2] [2008] AC 281.

III. The Structure of the Devolution Settlements

Each devolution settlement is different, reflecting the different histories and political realities of the three constituent parts of the UK to which they relate. In essence, the structure has similar features.[3] Each involves the creation (or re-establishment) of a democratically elected legislature. Each settlement confers the power on the devolved legislature to 'make laws known as Acts'[4] within defined areas and subject to ensuring that the legislation is compatible with the obligations imposed by EU law and is compatible with Convention rights, that is the rights guaranteed by the ECHR which have been incorporated into domestic law by the HRA 1998. Any provision of legislation which is not within the legislative competence of the devolved legislature or which contravene EU law or are incompatible with Convention rights 'is not law'.[5]

The way in which the devolved legislation defines the scope of the legislative competence of each devolved legislature differs. In Scotland, the Scottish Parliament is given general legislative power to make laws save in relation to reserved matters which are those matters defined in Schedule 5 to the Scotland Act 1998.[6] By contrast, the National Assembly for Wales is not given a general power to legislative from which certain exceptions are carved. Rather, the Assembly is given power to make laws in relation to the specific subjects listed in Schedule 7 to the Government of Wales Act 2006 which range from agriculture, through housing, education, local government, town and country planning and the Welsh language.

The Wales Bill, being considered by Parliament in 2017, will mark the latest stage in devolution in Wales with the adoption of a reserved powers model, whereby the Assembly will have power to legislate save in those areas reserved for the UK Parliament.

---

[3] The original Welsh settlement in the Government of Wales 1998 Act created an executive not a legislative body. The Government of Wales Act 2006 provided for the National Assembly for Wales to acquire the power to enact legislation in defined areas following a referendum and the National Assembly acquired such powers on 3 May 2011.

[4] Section 28(1) of the Scotland Act 1998; s 107(1) of the Government of Wales Act 2006; and s 5 of the Northern Ireland Act 1998.

[5] Section 29(2) of the Scotland Act 1998; s 108(2) of the Government of Wales Act 2006; and s 6 of the Northern Ireland Act 1998.

[6] By virtue of the combination of ss 28 and 29(2)(b) of the Scotland Act and see subject to certain specific restrictions on the legislative competence of the Scottish Parliament: see s 29(2)(c) of the Scotland Act 1998. See also and s 6 of the Northern Ireland Act 1998, which adopts a similar, but not identical, model.

IV. The First Issue—Determining The Scope of Legislative Competence

In relation to the first ground of challenge in *AXA*, the courts were performing the role of enforcing the specific limitations on the scope of the legislative competence of the Scottish Parliament. The Scotland Act 1998 itself expressly says that a provision of an Act of the Scottish Parliament is not law if it is incompatible with a Convention right. In considering the scope of the rights of the claimant insurance companies under Article 1 of the First Protocol of the ECHR, and in determining if the Scottish legislation violated those rights, the courts were undertaking a role traditionally undertaken by a court of law, including a court in a quasi-federal structure where legislative power is allocated, shared or divided between different institutions within the state. The courts were identifying and enforcing the specific legal limits on the powers of the legislature, those limits being laid down in the constitutional document itself.

Similarly, the court undertakes the same task when considering whether legislation is within the specific areas that are within the legislative competence of the devolved legislature. In the context of Wales, for example, the Supreme Court had to consider whether an Act of the Assembly creating an agricultural wages board fell within the legislative competence of the Assembly to make laws relating to the subject of agriculture. The Supreme Court observed that the question of whether the question of whether a provision is outside the competence of the Assembly must be determined by applying the particular rules contained in the constitutional document itself, in this case Section 108 of, and Schedule 7 to, the Government of Wales Act 2006.[7] This role is usual in quasi-federal or federal structures, although it represents a new, explicitly constitutional role for the courts in the UK. The judge operates as a constitutional border guard policing the boundaries of the legislative competence of the devolved legislature and casting a judicial search light upon its actions to ensure that it has not encroached or trespassed upon areas outside its borders and, in the UK context, ensuring that devolved legislatures do not extend their powers into areas not devolved to them by the Parliament.

V. The Second Issue—The Nature of Devolved Legislation and the Role of the Courts

The second issue in *Axa* did raise new, and far-reaching questions about the nature of devolved legislation and the role of the courts in reviewing that legislation.

---

[7] *Re Agricultural Sector (Wales) Bill* [2014] 1 WLR 2622 at para 6. See also *Attorney General v National Assembly for Wales Commission* [2013] 1 AC 792 at para 80. On the application of the test for determining whether provisions of an Assembly Act are within legislative competence, see Lewis (2015) (eds) *Judicial Remedies in Public Law* para 4-069.

AXA General Insurance Ltd v HM Advocate and Others

The basis of the challenge was that the Scottish legislation was invalid, as it was outside the legislature's powers, applying the conventional common law grounds of challenge used to review the lawfulness of action by statutory bodies. The claim was that the Scottish legislation was an unreasonable, irrational and arbitrary exercise of the legislative authority conferred upon the Scottish Parliament. The basis of the substantive argument was that it was unreasonable to require pleural plaques to be treated as a compensatable injury when, in fact, the plaques did not cause any harm and it would not be reasonable to require large sums of money to be paid out to persons who had not in fact suffered any injury for which compensation was needed.

That challenge raised in stark terms the question of whether and to what extent the legislative acts of the devolved legislatures were subject to judicial review on ordinary common law grounds, unconnected with enforcing the specific limits on their competence contained in the constitutional settlement itself. Three broad strands of contention emerged. First, one contention was that the Scottish Parliament was a body created by statute and had statutory powers conferred upon it. The court should exercise its inherent supervisory jurisdiction in respect of the exercise of such statutory powers, as it would with any such body and so should subject the exercise of statutory power to judicial review on traditional public law grounds, to ensure that the body has not acted unlawfully. The second contention was that the constitutional context, involving as it did the exercise of powers by a democratically elected legislature, indicated that judicial review of devolved legislation on conventional public law grounds was not intended by Parliament to be subject to such review. The third, and more radical argument, presented in response to the insurance company's claim was that devolved legislation within a devolved legislature's competence was primary legislation and, like primary legislation enacted by the UK Parliament, was not subject to common law review. The constitutional settlement provided that primary legislation may now be made either by the UK Parliament or, within its area of legislative competence by a devolved legislature. The ability to make law in an area of legislative competence had therefore been shared between the devolved legislature and the UK Parliament. Any legislation that emerged from that process was primary legislation and was not subject to judicial review on common law grounds.

A. The Choice Between the First and Second Approaches

There was general acceptance that devolved legislation was amenable to judicial review. That, in fact, follows from the premise that judicial review would be one means by which the courts could determine if provisions of devolved legislation were within the legislative competence of the devolved legislature. The real issue was the grounds upon which the court could conduct that review. For the claimant insurers, the position of the Scottish Parliament was no different from any other statutory body exercising statutory powers. The courts would review the exercise of those powers, on well-established public law grounds such as rationality or reasonableness. Exercises of statutory power by the statutorily created Scottish Parliament were, according to the claimant insurers no different. They relied upon the observation in *West v Secretary of State for Scotland*[8] that:

> The Court of Session has power, in the exercise of its supervisory jurisdiction, to regulate the process by which decisions are taken by any person or body to whom a jurisdiction, power or authority has been delegated or entrusted by statute, agreement or any other instrument.

There were essentially two views put forward for rejecting this approach to judicial review of devolved legislation. First, there is the reasoning essentially set out by Lord Hope. In essence, regard had to be had to the constitutional context in which devolved legislation came to be enacted.[9] The Scotland Act 1998 created a self-standing, democratically elected legislature. It had a democratic mandate to make laws for the people of Scotland. Acts of the Scottish Parliament enjoyed the highest legal authority. Given those features, it was the elected devolved legislature, which was best placed, and had the constitutional authority, to determine what laws should be enacted for the polity. Consequently, it would be 'wrong for the judges to substitute their views on these issues for the considered judgment of a democratically elected legislature'. In those circumstances, Acts of the Scottish Parliament were not subject to judicial review at common law on the grounds of irrationality, unreasonableness or arbitrariness.

Lord Reed considered that the extent of judicial review in relation to a particular exercise of power by a public authority depended upon the circumstances, including the nature of the public body in question, the type of power being exercised, the process by which it is exercised and the extent to which the powers of the body have limits or purposes which the courts identify and upon which they can adjudicate. In the case of the Scottish Parliament, that was a democratic legislature making laws subject to a process, which involved democratic scrutiny. In that context, the Scotland Act 1998 left it to the Scottish Parliament itself to determine its own policy goals and to decide for which purposes its legislative power should be used, and the political and other considerations relevant to the exercise of those powers. The traditional grounds of review at common law were, by contrast, developed in relation to administrative bodies given limited powers to be used for identifiable purposes and were designed to prevent the use of such powers being exceed, or used for an improper purpose. In those circumstances, the traditional grounds of review did not apply to the exercise of plenary powers by the Scottish legislature that decides how, and for what purpose, its powers should be used and which required no justification beyond the will of the legislature.

---

[8] [1992] SC 385.
[9] Hope dealt specifically with the Scottish Parliament but made it clear that the Welsh and Northern Irish devolved legislatures had the same essential nature: see [2012] 1 AC 868 at para 43. See also *Attorney General v National Assembly for Wales Commission* [2013] 1 AC 792 at para 81.

The approach of Lord Reed depended in part, therefore, upon the constitutional context but ultimately relied more upon the fact that the powers conferred by the legislation in question, the Scotland Act 1998, were not, by their terms, amenable to review on traditional common law grounds. Lord Mance doubted whether the reasons for the limitations on judicial review of acts of devolved legislatures were confined so closely to purpose, and the ability to identify limits on the purpose, as Lord Reed had indicated.

The preferable view is that the constitutional context is one where judicial review on common law grounds is inappropriate. If necessary, it can be expressed in conventional terms on the grounds that the UK Parliament did not intend when enacting the various constitutional devolution acts that the devolved legislatures were to be subject to judicial review on traditional common law grounds. The reality is, as Lord Hope identified, that such review is constitutionally inappropriate. The devolved legislatures are democratically elected bodies and exercising powers to make primary legislation. It is constitutional inappropriate for courts, with no such mandate, and without possessing the necessary expertise of the area in which competing needs and arguments are being considered, to be subjecting devolved legislation to traditional common law review on grounds such as reasonableness.

Lord Reed is correct in identifying the practical limits that would lie in the way of a court adjudicating on such matters in the context of devolved legislation.[10] But those practical considerations reinforce, rather than provide the motivating force, for the recognition that traditional judicial review is constitutionally inapposite in relation to devolved legislation.

One further consideration arises. The Supreme Court in *AXA* did not have to deal with any questions of judicial review on common law grounds relating to procedural failures. There is little or no prospect of such grounds being available in relation to devolved legislation. Concepts of procedural fairness or natural justice are not applicable to the enactment of legislation,[11] fairness is provided through the means to influence the legislative process. The courts are unlikely to accept that individuals have any procedural rights derived from legitimate expectations, including even express promises—such a resolution of the devolved legislature itself—as to what devolved legislation will or will not contain, or how legislation will be enacted. It is extremely unlikely that such statements will be seen as capable of binding a devolved legislature in the exercise of its legislative powers. The devolution statutes themselves provide that legislation is not to be vitiated by any failure to comply with the relevant statutory procedures governing the enactment of legislation.[12]

---

[10] The same is true of exercises of the prerogative power, where the executive determines whether and how to exercise the power: see *R (Sandiford) v Secretary of State for Foreign and Commonwealth Affairs* [2014] 1 WLR 2697 at para 60–66 and 78 to 83. There may still be residual cases, where some of the traditional grounds of judicial review may be applicable: see Lewis *Judicial Remedies in Public Law* (5th ed.) at para 2-023-024.

[11] *Bates v Lord Hailsham of St Marylebone* [1972] 1 WLR 1373.

[12] See s 28 of the Scotland Act 1998 and s 107 of the Government of Wales Act 2006; and s 5(5) of the Northern Ireland Act 1998.

B. The Third Choice

The third argument, not accepted by the Supreme Court was, in many ways, the most constitutionally radical. The argument was that legislative competence in defined areas was now shared between the UK Parliament and the devolved legislatures. The constitutional statutes creating the devolved legislature provided another way in which primary legislation may be made for the relevant constituent part of the UK. Primary legislation could be made either by the UK Parliament—which retained its sovereignty and, hence, its legal power to make any laws it wished, including laws for a constituent part of the UK—or a devolved legislature, following prescribed procedures, designed to secure democratic scrutiny and accountability, and with Royal Assent. The courts did not review primary legislation enacted by the UK Parliament and such legislation was not subject to judicial review on traditional common law grounds. There was no inherent difference in the nature of the devolved legislation. Each was the expression of democratic will and each was primary legislation.

In that regard, the situation was argued to be analogous to that brought about by the Parliament Act 1911. Prior to that Act, primary legislation had to be enacted by the Queen in Parliament that is by the Commons and the Lords with Royal Assent. Following that Act, primary legislation could be enacted by the Queen and Commons alone, without the assent of the Lords. As the Judicial Committee of the House of Lords recognised in *R (Jackson) v Attorney-General*,[13] the Parliament Act 1911 was not 'authorising a new form of sub-primary parliamentary legislation but creating a new way of enacting primary legislation'[14] and that the Parliament Act 1911 created a 'second parallel route'[15] by which primary legislation could be enacted.

One further comment needs to be made about this third argument. The argument drew a distinction between the sovereignty of Parliament and legislative competence. The UK remained sovereign in the sense that it could make, or unmake any law, including the provisions of the Scotland Act 1998 or any other legislation. The devolved legislatures were not sovereign in this sense for two reasons. First, they only had power to make primary legislation within their areas of legislative competence. They are not free to make laws outside that area of legislative competence. Second, they are still subordinate to the UK Parliament in the sense that that Parliament can legislate for the devolved legislature and, as a matter of law,[16] may also remove or limit the legislative competence of a devolved legislature.

---

[13] [2006] 1 AC 262.
[14] ibid *per* Bingham at para 24.
[15] ibid *per* Nicholls at para 64. See also per Steyn at para 86, Hale at para 160 and Brown at para 187.
[16] As a matter of political agreement, and possibly as a matter of emerging constitutional convention, the UK Parliament does not legislate within a devolved legislature's area of legislative competence without the agreement of that devolved legislature.

The Supreme Court in *AXA* did not accept this third constitutional argument about the nature of devolved legislation and did not accept that this was the basis upon which judicial review of devolved legislation was limited. The reasons were variously expressed. The fundamental reason, however, was the Supreme Court's view of the need to preserve the opportunity for the maintenance of the rule of law.

In the context of primary legislation of the UK, the Supreme Court recognised that the ability of the courts to review legislation and reject it is, to say the least, highly problematic. The constitutionally orthodox view is that the courts cannot declare any enacted law, made by the UK Parliament, to be invalid.[17] That approach has had to be aligned with the UK's membership of the European Union where laws, which conflict with European Union law are inapplicable to that extent.[18] Even here, the Supreme Court has, recently, left open the question of the position under domestic constitutional law if the requirements of EU law conflicted with what was perceived to be a fundamental principle of British constitutional law.[19] The precise reasons underlying the basic principle of the sovereignty of Parliament are not always clear and may not have remained the same over time. It reflects, in part, the recognition that the UK Parliament is the democratically elected legislature and it, not the courts, has ultimate democratic legitimacy within the state. The courts have consistently recognised the importance of the separation of powers between the legislature, the executive, the judiciary and the importance of respect for the proceedings and decisions of the legislature.[20] In part, it seems, it reflects the political reality. In the event that the courts did consider that legislation enacted by the UK Parliament, and given Royal Assent, ought not to be recognised as valid, it is by no means clear how the courts could enforce obedience to such a decision. If an Act of the Parliament authorised the executive to undertake a course of action, and the courts contemplated declaring the legislation invalid, it is not clear how the courts could realistically continue to enforce its view should the elected legislature take a different view. In reality, it is difficult to imagine such a clash of views occurring other than in a situation where the traditional values underlying the Constitution were already under great strain, and there was already a constitutional crisis and the steps taken by the courts would be one aspect of that wider constitutional crisis within the state.

Nonetheless, the courts have exhibited a concern that there may come a time when there was a clash between the rule of law and the sovereignty of Parliament. Thus the courts have left open the question of whether there are circumstances in which the courts may, legitimately, rule that duly enacted legislation is not to be

---

[17] *R (Jackson) v Attorney General* [2006] 1 AC 262 at para 9.
[18] *R v Secretary of State for Transport* ex parte.*Factortame (No 2)* [1991] AC 603.
[19] *R (Buckinghamshire County Council) v Secretary of State for Transport* [2014] 2 WLR 324 at paras 202–11.
[20] See, most recently, *Wheeler v Office of the Prime Minister* [2014] EWHC 3815 (Admin) and the cases cited there.

recognised as valid law. The circumstances in which such an eventuality may arise has, theoretically, been restricted to extreme cases such as where legislation was being used to usurp recognised principles underlying the foundation of a modern democracy committed to the rule of law, such as legislation enacted by a parliamentary authority intended to restrict the franchise in order to retain power,[21] or to remove the ability of the courts to undertake judicial review of the legality of administrative action[22] or, more generally, to protect the fundamental rights of individuals.[23] The motive force underlying the refusal of the Supreme Court in *AXA* to recognise that devolved legislation was not immune from judicial review in all circumstances was the desire to preserve the possibility of judicial review of devolved legislation which violated such basic constitutional norms.

How this aim would be achieved is less clear. The Supreme Court referred to devolved legislation as delegated. That indicates the possibility that the legislation conferring legislative competence could impliedly be read as limiting the powers of the devolved legislature. It is not clear that 'delegated' is, in fact, an appropriate word to describe the nature of legislation enacted by a devolved legislature. 'Shared' may be a more acceptable way of describing the relationship between the UK Parliament and the devolved legislatures. Even then, it could be argued that competence was shared on the basis that the devolved legislature would not violate the fundamental constitutional principles underlying the Constitution as a whole. In reality, however, the willingness (and ability) of the courts to prevent a devolved legislature from violating constitutional norms is likely to depend on a view of the appropriate relationship between the courts and a democratically elected legislature rather than any formulaic description of the relationship between devolved legislation and legislation enacted by the UK Parliament or by a perception of the relationship between one legislature and another.

Similarly, there is a suggestion that the immunity of legislation enacted by the UK Parliament may rest upon the conceptual foundation that it is sovereign whereas devolved legislatures are not. The precise relationship between concepts of sovereignty and immunity of legislation from judicial review is unclear. In many ways, they are both concepts, which encapsulate the idea that the legislature, as the democratic body within the state, must, ultimately, be free to achieve its aims. It is not so much that sovereignty dictates immunity from review as that both concepts describe the political reality that, in the absence of a more fundamental constitutional norm, the latest expression of the will of the political sovereign will be given effect to by the courts. Viewed in that light, the fact that the United Kingdom Parliament is sovereign in that it can, in theory, legislate on any topic—and could repeal legislation enacted by a devolved legislature—does not of itself explain why primary legislation enacted by the UK Parliament is immune from judicial

---

[21] See dicta of Hodge in *Moohan v Lord Advocate* [2015] 2 WLR 141 at para 35.
[22] See, eg, dicta of Steyn in *R (Jackson) v Attorney General* [2006] 1 AC 262 at para 102; and Hope in *AXA* [2012] 1 AC 868 at para 51.
[23] See, eg Hope at para 49 and Mance at para 97 of *AXA* [2012] 1 AC 262.

review but primary legislation enacted by the devolved legislature is not. If primary legislation enacted by a democratically elected, devolved legislature is within its legislative competence—and if the legislation has not been repealed by the UK Parliament—that legislation could similarly be seen as the latest expression of the will of an elected legislature with constitutional responsibility for enacting legislation within a particular area.

Ultimately, therefore, the rejection of the third approach is based upon a judicial assessment of the constitutional fundamentals underlying the modern state and the proper role of the courts and the elected legislature. The twin principles underlying a modern Constitution in a democratic state are respect for the rule of law and respect for the expression of the democratic will. The courts will give recognition to legislation enacted by a democratically elected and accountable legislature within its area of legislative competence. That reflects the democratic legitimacy of the elected legislature. It also reflects the modern constitutional understanding that a democratic state requires more than giving effect to the latest expression of the will of the legislature but also requires proper respect for the fundamental rights of individuals and the principles underlying the Constitution such as the requirements of the rule of law.

C. Further Observations on The Scope of the Constitutional Limitations on the Devolved Legislature

Three further observations may be made on the scope of the constitutional limitations on the devolved legislatures. First, the precise scope of any common law constitutional limitations on the legislative competence on devolved legislatures remains unclear. As indicated above, the concern of the courts so far has been that legislation may seek to remove the ability of the courts to review the legality of executive action or may seek to entrench the powers of a parliamentary majority party. Legislation of that nature would be seen as undermining the rule of law or the basis of democracy itself. The courts need, however, to be circumspect in imposing additional restrictions on the powers of devolved legislatures. The precise scope of the constitutional limitations should respect the fundamental democratic legitimacy of the devolved legislature. They should also respect the fact that there are specific limitations already included within the constitutional settlement and those settlements were the subject of popular referenda in the relevant constituent part of the UK. In those circumstances, the courts should generally be wary of imposing further judicial-made restrictions on the legislative competence of devolved legislatures. The courts have recognised, in relation to the UK Parliament, that it will only be in truly exceptional circumstances that the courts should contemplate questioning the validity of an act of the UK Parliament. Similar considerations call for similar constitutional caution in dealing with legislation enacted by a democratically accountable devolved legislature, acting within the specific limits of its legislative competence. It is, in practice, difficult to envisage any such situations arising.

Furthermore, one other feature needs to be considered in the context of devolved legislatures and the protection of constitutional values should a grave set of circumstances arise, the courts would not be the only constitutional actors involved in the drama. There will be three potential constitutional actors. There will be the devolved legislature, the courts and the UK Parliament. That latter Parliament still retains ultimate legal sovereignty. The UK Parliament retains the power to legislate for any part of the UK and to restrict the powers of a devolved legislature. It has the ability to prevent a devolved legislature from acting in a way that violates fundamental constitutional values. Any clash of constitutional values is unlikely simply to involve the courts and the devolved legislature. In the event of a constitutional crisis of such gravity occurring as to necessitate the courts considering the validity of the acts of a devolved legislature, it is difficult to imagine that the situation would not also involve a response on the part of the UK Parliament. The situation would not be the straightforward clash between the rule of the law on the one hand and the acts of a sovereign legislature on the other as envisaged in *Jackson*. There would in reality be a tripartite situation involving the courts concern to protect the rule of law, the constitutional role of a devolved legislature and the powers of a sovereign Parliament.

Second, and less theoretically, there is also reference in the *AXA* judgment to the need to protect fundamental human rights.[24] In that regard, it is relevant to bear in mind that the legislation creating the devolved legislatures already recognises and provides for the protection of fundamental human rights in that provisions of devolved legislation will not be law in so far as they are incompatible with Convention rights. There has recently been a renewed emphasis on the development or recognition of rights at common law rather than relying upon the provisions of the HRA 1998.[25] The precise reasons underlying the recent emphasis on the development of common law rights are unclear as is the extent to which, in fact, the common law has the necessary ability in many instances to provide additional significant protection to individuals.[26]

There may well be no difficulty in recognising the development of common law rights as a means of controlling administrative action. There may also be no difficulty in courts interpreting devolved legislation in a way that ensures respect for fundamental rights, as for example, interpreting an act of the Scottish Parliament in such a way as to ensure that administrative power is exercised in accordance with principles of procedural fairness. There would, however, be far greater

---

[24] See per Hope at para 49, Mance at para 97 and Reed at para 149 in *AXA* [2012] 1 AC 262.
[25] See, eg, *Kennedy v Charity Commission* [2014] 2 WLR 808; and *Osborne v Parole Board* [2013] UKSC 61. The question of whether repeal of the Human Rights Act 1998 would be consistent with the principles underlying the current devolution settlements is considered below.
[26] See the analysis by R Clayton in (2015) *The Empire Strikes Back: Common Law Rights and the Human Rights Act* Public Law 3.

difficulty in recognising additional common law principles and then seeking to review devolved legislation itself on the grounds that the legislation violated those principles' rights. Given that the constitutional settlement, enacted by the UK Parliament and subjected to popular referenda, expressly provides for the protection of individual rights and already reflects a balance between those rights and the needs and powers of society generally, there is likely to be less constitutional justification for developing additional common law rights in a way which would upset that constitutional balance.

The third observation is this. One of the issues under political debate is the continuation in its present form of the HRA 1998. It may be that ultimately no change emerges to that Act. However, the constitutional settlement expressly includes the Convention rights incorporated by that Act as a definition of the limits on the legislative competence of the devolved legislatures. If there are to be changes to the HRA 1998, and in particular if the Convention rights are to be changed in content, then it seems inevitable that consideration will need to be given at the political level as to whether there needs to be corresponding changes to the constitutional settlement.

VI. Conclusion

The UK has undergone fundamental constitutional changes in terms of the creation of devolved legislatures with legislative competence to enact primary legislation. The UK has, in reality, moved from being a unitary state with a single, sovereign legislature to a quasi-federal structure with legislative competence shared between the UK Parliament and the devolved legislatures. That change required the courts to consider the nature of the devolution settlement, the nature of devolved legislation and the relationship between the courts and the devolved legislatures. The *AXA* case is the defining authority charting the waters of the new constitutional settlement. The courts have the traditional role of policing the boundaries of the constitutional settlement to ensure that devolved legislation is within the specific limits imposed by the constitutional settlement itself. In addition, the UK Supreme Court in *AXA* had to determine which of three constitutional models to adopt. The courts could have treated the exercise of legislative power by the devolved legislature as akin to the exercise of any statutory power by any statutory body and subject to the same degree of judicial review on the same traditional common law grounds of judicial review. The courts could have adopted an approach whereby legislative competence was now shared between the UK Parliament and the devolved legislatures within the areas of devolved legislative competence. Legislation enacted within those areas, whether by the UK Parliament or the devolved legislature, would be seen as primary legislation immune from review by the court. Alternatively, the court could have taken a middle way which recognised the constitutional context in which devolved legislation was enacted, that the challenged legislation had been enacted by a democratically elected and accounted legislature, by a procedure which itself involved democratic scrutiny. Given the democratic mandate of the devolved legislature, the courts opted for that middle way and recognised that judicial review on traditional common law grounds such as rationality, reasonableness or arbitrariness was inappropriate. Those matters were matters of judgment for the legislators. The courts may, however, have a deeper constitutional role, in addition to that of enforcing the specific limits on the legislative competence of the devolved legislature. The UKSC recognised that it has a fundamental constitutional obligation to protect the rule of law. Should a time come when legislative competence was being exercised in a way which undermined the proper observance of the rule of law in a modern democratic state, the UK Supreme Court reserved the possibility of the common law qualifying and restricting the power of the devolved legislature in order to prevent it subverting the constitutional values that it was created to serve.

13

Evans v Attorney General [2015]: The Underlying Normativity of Constitutional Disagreement

THOMAS FAIRCLOUGH

I. Introduction

R (oao Evans) v Attorney General[1] is a fascinating constitutional case well worth being considered a landmark Supreme Court decision. Sometimes judicial decisions represent a turn in the road from which we can trace a major shift in our understanding of an area of law. These are the cases that we would usually term as 'landmark'[2] because we can source major doctrinal development to the particular decision. These decisions often become the centerpiece for whichever area of law they develop. There is, however, a second (as opposed to secondary) sense in which a case can be worthy of being called a landmark decision; unlike landmark cases in the sense identified above *Evans* is not one that marked a major shift in a particular doctrinal area of judicial review.[3] Instead, *Evans* is a striking case in terms of the range of judicial opinion; indeed, it is hard to think of a case where the

---

[1] [2015] UKSC 21; [2015] 2 WLR 813. I will focus only on the domestic argument and ignore the European Union dimension.

[2] One can think of the development in *R v North East Devon Health Authority, ex p Coughlan* [2001] QB 213 (CA) (legitimate expectations) considered in Ch 9 of this volume; Lord Greene MR's decision in *Associated Provincial Picture Houses v Wednesbury Corporation* [1948] 1 KB 223 (CA) (substantive review); *Council of Service Unions v Minister for the Civil Service* [1985] AC 374 (HL) (development of judicial review and, specifically, review of non-statutory powers); and *Ridge v Baldwin* [1964] AC 40 (HL) (procedural fairness).

[3] It may be that since *Evans* is about the strength of the common law principle of legality in relation to common law principles/values it could be termed a landmark decision in our first sense. In this way *Evans* may follow *R v Secretary of State for the Home Department, ex p Simms* [1999] 2 AC 115 (HL) and *R v Secretary of State for the Home Department, ex p Pierson* [1998] AC 539 (HL) as the major marks in the line of the principle's jurisprudential development. However, it is too early to know whether *Evans* can be treated as a landmark case in this way. Indeed, at the time of writing this Chapter *Evans* has only been mentioned in five subsequent decisions and none of these would have been decided any differently on the jurisprudence pre-*Evans*.

Supreme Court has diverged so much on how to answer legal questions and the role of constitutional principles within the process of adjudication. It is not the existence of disagreement per se that makes *Evans* such an important case; rather, it is the range of disagreement and the starkness of the differing constitutional orders proposed by each Justice that make *Evans* an extraordinary decision. Examining such disagreement gives us an insight into judicial reasoning and the different constitutional visions each Justice holds. In this way *Evans* follows cases such as *Anisminic*[4] and *Jackson*[5] in constitutional importance. In the second sense identified *Evans* is an incredibly important decision the full ramifications of which have yet to be felt.

Reflecting on the differing decisions and rationales offered by the Supreme Court Justices enables us to recognise how normative concerns underlying different constitutional approaches can lead us to resolve many seemingly irreconcilable polarising doctrinal debates that continue to vex public lawyers in the UK. This chapter argues that *Evans* helps to remove opaque doctrine from public lawyers' eyes, revealing with clarity the role of normative arguments in litigation that, in turn, help to shape the principles of constitutional and administrative law (and by extension shape the doctrine thereof). The aim of this chapter, to that extent, is not to provide support for any single Justice in *Evans* nor the vision of constitutionality that he may furnish; the aspiration is more modest in that this piece merely seeks to recognise that *Evans* reveals the strong normative discourse behind doctrinal quandaries. It is in this revealing nature that *Evans* is a case worthy of being called a landmark decision and why it will exert influence in a wide-range of public law cases for many years to come. It is the aim of this chapter to explore the insight and possible implications of the reasoning in *Evans*.

II. Entangled in a Factual Web: History of the Black Spider Memos Litigation

Evans revolved around the fact that Prince Charles had sent letters to Government Ministers giving his views on political issues. Mr Robert Evans, at the relevant time a *Guardian* journalist, used the Freedom of Information Act 2000 (FoIA) in an attempt to gain access to the so called 'black spider memos'.[6] Evans' efforts resulted in a ten-year legal battle that reached its zenith in the judgment of the Supreme

---

[4] *Anisminic Ltd v Foreign Compensation Commission and Another* [1969] 2 AC 147 (HL). *Anisminic* is a landmark decision in both senses I identify but it is similar to *Evans* in the second sense. See further Ch 4.

[5] *R (Jackson and others) v Attorney General* [2005] UKHL 56; [2006] 1 AC 262.

[6] Named after the style of Prince Charles's handwriting.

Court that this chapter examines. However, to fully appreciate the Supreme Court's decision one has to understand the complicated facts and litigation that form the context of the Justices' conclusions.

Prince Charles has a long history of communicating with Government Ministers on political issues. What follows is just an overview of the breadth of his policy-orientated concerns. As far back as September 1969, at the age of only 20, letters released under the 30-year rule show that he wrote to the then Prime Minister, Harold Wilson, giving his views about the conservation and depletion in numbers of wild salmon. Wilson later responded in November 1969 and May 1970 keeping Charles updated on developments in the protection of Atlantic salmon fishing. In the following years, Charles often spoke out publically regarding, as he saw it, important social, environmental, and political issues. In 1981 he wrote in the *Observer* lauding the objectives of a development group aiming to provide technology to third world countries. On 14 December 1982 he used a speech at the 150 anniversary of the British Medical Association's foundation to urge a renewed focus on 'healing' and to warn of the 'frightening' dependence on pharmaceutical drugs. Likewise, he spoke out in favour of organic food production on the 8 January 1983 and in November 1986 about the wasted talent in socio-economically deprived parts of the UK. Further in 1987 Prince Charles had over ten meetings with Ministers and wrote letters to them about government policy in relation to the disabled, South Africa, and Romania. In 1989 he wrote to the Secretary of State for Energy reproaching him for the Government's inaction on the greenhouse effect. If one moves ahead over a decade this practice continues; on the 27 September 2002 the *Guardian* published letters Charles had written to the then Lord Chancellor bemoaning the 'absurd degree of politically correct interference' and the potential effects of the Human Rights Act 1998. Such was the influence of the Prince of Wales in political life that his letters were put 'effectively at the top of the file and are treated with great reverence'[7] and amounted to a 'form of lobbying'.[8] Indeed, the unusualness of Charles's interference led Adam Tomkins to go as far as to say that communication to such a degree as that between the Prince of Wales and the Government was an 'innovation' that he had himself assumed rather than inherited by virtue of his position; in this sense the correspondence was a new constitutional development.[9]

This political activity by the Prince of Wales did not go unnoticed and led many to seek to determine his real influence on political actors in the UK. On the 8 and 11 of April 2005 Evans made the freedom of information requests that gave rise to the Supreme Court's determination almost ten years later. He sent requests to

---

[7] Evidence of Paul Richards, a former special advisor to Hazel Blears and Patricia Hewitt, found in the Third Appendix to the Upper Tribunal's decision in *Evans v Information Commissioner* [2012] UKUT 313 (AAC), [125].
[8] Evidence of Professor Adam Tomkins to the Upper Tribunal: ibid [54].
[9] ibid [56] and [58].

seven departments and offices (which I will refer to collectively as departments for ease)[10] concerning the period between 1 September 2004 and 1 April 2005 and asked for:

(1) A list of all correspondence sent by Prince Charles to each minister, including the identity of the recipient, sender, and date for each piece of correspondence;
(2) A similar list sent by each minister to Prince Charles;
(3) Complete copies of each piece of correspondence listed; and
(4) A schedule giving a brief description of each document relevant to the request.

The Department for Environment, Food and Rural Affairs (DEFRA) informed Evans that it would not be disclosing the information requested in line with regulatory provisions concerning environmental information. The other six departments neither confirmed nor denied holding the requested information; after an internal review of their answer (which Evans had requested) each department maintained their initial response. Evans then complained to the Information Commissioner, who began an investigation under FoIA. Despite later confirming that the information sought was held each department still refused to produce it to Evans; the Commissioner, issuing separate decision notices for each department, confirmed that each department had been entitled to refuse to produce the documents. On the 13 January 2010 Evans appealed to the Information Tribunal, which transferred to the First-tier Tribunal and then the Upper Tribunal on the 13 September 2010, where the case occupied the parties for some two years. The Upper Tribunal[11] examined whether, as Section 2(1)(b) FoIA puts it, the 'public interest in maintaining the exclusion of the [Section 1(1) FoIA] duty to confirm or deny [outweighed] the public interest in disclosing'. If the public interest fell in favour of exclusion then the Commissioner and departments would be justified in refusing to disclose the information sought. Whilst the arguments clearly cut both ways for the Upper Tribunal they found for Evans, holding that governmental accountability and transparency together with increased and informed understanding (and therefore debate) about the Crown and its relationship with the Executive outweighed the factors against disclosure such as its effect on undermining certain constitutional conventions and the perceived neutrality of the Crown.[12] As a result, the relevant departments were ordered to disclose the information to Evans.

---

[10] Evans wrote to seven departments requesting disclosure: the Department for Business, Innovation, and Skills (DBIS); the Department of Health (DH); Department for Children, Schools, and Families (DCSF); Department for Environmental, Food, and Rural Affairs (DEFRA); Department for Culture, Media, and Sport (DCMS); the Northern Ireland Office (NIO); and the Cabinet Office (CO).
[11] *Evans v Information Commissioner* [2012] UKUT 313 (AAC).
[12] The precise reasoning is outside of the scope of this chapter; however, the Upper Tribunal gives a superb elongated analysis at [123]–[214] of its judgment.

Usually, pending an appeal or (exceptionally) legislation overturning a judicial determination, litigation comes to a close after judgment. However the Attorney General, on behalf of the Government, invoked the power in Section 53 FoIA, which provides that:

> A decision notice or enforcement notice to which this section applies shall cease to have effect if ... the accountable person in relation to that authority gives the Commissioner a certificate signed by him stating that he has on *reasonable grounds* formed the opinion that ... *there was no failure* [to comply with statutory duties].[13] (emphasis added)

This is an executive override power,[14] whereby the Government sought to neutralise the Upper Tribunal's order and thus prevent Charles's letters reaching the public domain without the effort, risk, and extended publicity that taking the case to the Court of Appeal would entail. This is a unique power in the UK, as the Lord Chief Justice Lord Judge noted, 'It is an understatement to describe the situation as unusual. Indeed the researches of counsel suggest that is a unique situation and that similar statutory arrangements cannot be found elsewhere in this jurisdiction'.[15]

Rather than allow the saga to end here, Evans sought to judicially review the Attorney General's use of Section 53(2); he argued that the Attorney General did not have reasonable grounds to form the opinion that there was no failure to comply with the relevant statutory duties and therefore his purported veto was no veto at all because it fell outside of the scope of Section 53(2). The case in the Supreme Court was the final stage of the judicial review of the veto.[16] The question for the court was simple: did the Attorney General have the legal power to veto the Upper Tribunal given the facts of the case?

III. The Justices' Judgments

The Attorney General argued that, within the salient facts, it could not be said that his views were unreasonable as they reflected the views of the Commissioner and, in addition, the Upper Tribunal had acknowledged that there were 'cogent arguments for non-disclosure'.[17] However, despite there being arguments that cut both ways, on the question of whether the Attorney General was legally entitled to set aside a judicial order with which he disagreed, the majority of the Supreme Court answered in the negative. Examining the judgments (and disagreement between them) proves illuminating for any student of British constitutional law.

---

[13] s 53(2) FoIA.
[14] So described by the Lord Chief Justice Lord Judge: 'Notwithstanding the unchallenged judgment of the Upper Tribunal. ... a member of the executive is empowered to set aside or nullify the decision' *R (oao Evans) v Attorney General* [2013] EWHC 1960 (Admin).
[15] ibid [10].
[16] Evans having lost in the High Court but won on appeal in the Court of Appeal previously.
[17] *Evans* (n 1) [49] (Lord Neuberger).

Lord Neuberger, with whom Lords Kerr and Reed agreed, spoke for the majority within the majority and held a:

> [s]tatutory provision which entitles a member of the executive ... to overrule a decision of the judiciary merely because he does not agree with it ... would cut across two constitutional principles which are also fundamental components of the rule of law. First ... a decision of a court is binding as between the parties and cannot be ignored or set aside by anyone ... Secondly, it is also fundamental to the rule of law that decisions and actions of the executive are ... reviewable by the court at the suit of an interested citizen. Section 53, as interpreted by the Attorney General's argument in this case, flouts the first principle and stands the second principle on its head.[18]

As such, Lord Neuberger argued that Section 53 could not be 'invoked effectively to overrule that judgment merely because a member of the executive ... takes a different view'. Thus, Lord Neuberger, whilst careful to pay lip service to the orthodox view that Parliament could always legislate to make its meaning 'crystal clear',[19] concluded that the two principles he identified shaped the law (and as such the Attorney General's power)[20] such that, in the end, Section 53 could only be used if there was a material change in circumstance since the tribunal's decision or said decision was demonstrably flawed.[21]

Lord Mance, with whom Lady Hale agreed, also held that the Attorney General's exercise of the veto power was unlawful. Instead of using constitutional principles directly to understand the law, Lord Mance focused on the standard of review that would apply when assessing the Attorney General's action. Any test must be 'context-specific' for Lord Mance, 'in the sense that it must depend upon the particular legislation ... and upon the basis on which the Attorney General was departing from the decision'.[22] Further, it was clear that the Attorney General had to show he had reasonable grounds for refusing disclosure, which was higher than mere rationality.[23] In considering what is reasonable one must consider the factual investigation by the Tribunal and the extent to which the Attorney General can replicate that; effectively, if a Tribunal is better equipped to make a decision then a relevant person would need cogently argued grounds for issuing a certificate vetoing the Tribunal's decision.[24] Lord Mance was clearly alive to the

---

[18] ibid [51]–[52] (Lord Neuberger).
[19] ibid [58] (Neuberger).
[20] This is acknowledged at [68]–[69] (Neuberger).
[21] *Evans* (n 1) [71] (Neuberger). This was something Lord Neuberger accepted would result in a 'narrow range of potential application' of s 53: ibid [86].
[22] ibid [128] (Mance).
[23] ibid [129] (Mance).
[24] ibid [130] (Mance). *Cf* the former Lord Chief Justice Lord Judge's views in the High Court: 'It is fundamental to the constitutional separation of powers, the independence of the judiciary, and the rule of law itself that ... ministers are bound by and cannot override judicial legislation ... that is the context in which the constraints on the power granted to ministers by the terms of the legislative provisions must be examined' *Evans* (n 14) [12]–[13]. As a result, Lord Judge, whilst not going as far as Lord Neuberger in the Supreme Court, said that 'the principle of constitutionality requires the minister to address the decision of the Upper Tribunal ... head on, and explain in clear and unequivocal terms

separation of powers issues in the case; he makes clear that 'section 53 must have been intended by Parliament to have, and can and should be read as having, a wider potential effect than that which Lord Neuberger has attributed to it'.[25] For Lord Mance whilst the words of the statute have a (large) part to play, context is key, and his understanding of that context will shape the words. This differentiates him from Lord Neuberger because it 'reflects the differing extents to which Lords Neuberger and Mance were prepared to permit fundamental constitutional principles to operate'.[26] More specifically, whilst using similar constitutional principles the weight attached to them differed between Lords Neuberger and Mance; a different formula for testing propositions of law was used by Lords Neuberger and Mance respectively.

Lord Hughes dissented, stating that the section 'can mean nothing other than that the accountable person ... is given the statutory power to override the decision'.[27] To arrive at such a radically different conclusion Lord Hughes, like the others, said that he was applying Parliamentary intention. However, this intention was found in the '*plain words of the statute* ... If Parliament had wished to limit the power to issue a certificate to these two situations [i.e. the two situations that, for Lord Neuberger, represented the only scenarios in which the power would be legally exercisable] that is undoubtedly what the subsection would have said'.[28] It appears that for Lord Hughes the literal meaning of the statute (and that alone) is what constitutes the law.

Lord Wilson also dissented. He stated that the answer Lord Neuberger provided 'did not ... interpret section 53 ... It re-wrote it. It invoked precious constitutional principles but among the most precious is that of parliamentary sovereignty, emblematic of our democracy'.[29] Lord Wilson found it 'helpful to notice the circumstances in which section 53' came into being;[30] Parliament had decided that there needed to be a power to override the evaluation of public interests of the Commissioner, tribunals, or courts when it decided to give a right to information (as opposed to a discretion).[31] His Lordship also stated that since the veto power could only be used in narrow circumstances anyway Parliament had clearly recognised the difficulties of executive override.[32] For Lord Wilson, then, it is fair to summarise that what Parliament had done and intended was all that mattered

---

the reasons why, notwithstanding the decision of the court, the executive override has been exercised on public interest grounds': *Evans* (n 14) [14]. It is worth nothing that though Lord Judge agreed with Mance on the test he disagreed with him on the application of it and found for the Attorney General.

[25] *Evans* (n 1) [124] (Lord Mance).
[26] M Elliott, 'A tangled constitutional web: the black-spider memos and the British constitution's relational architecture' [2015] PL 539, 546.
[27] *Evans* (n 1) [153] (Lord Hughes).
[28] ibid [155] (Hughes) (emphasis added).
[29] ibid [168] (Wilson).
[30] ibid [170] (Wilson).
[31] ibid.
[32] ibid [172] (Wilson).

and this was discovered by a historical analysis of the provision in question. Whilst this may lead to undesirable consequences in the circumstances of the case,[33] the judiciary must follow the words of the statute understood in the context of their enactment, which constitute the law, and which had therefore expressly conferred a power of override in the circumstances.[34]

IV. Disagreement in the Supreme Court

There are, then, four distinct methods of determining the validity of propositions of law at play in *Evans*: for Lord Neuberger, we determine the law by reference to what the statute says combined with constitutional principles (which weighed heavily). This is a strong constitutionalist approach. Conversely, Lord Mance seems to suggest the law is whatever the statute says it is, understood in its wider constitutional context, which is a weaker constitutionalist approach (at least relative to Lord Neuberger's very strong method). Lord Hughes argues that the law is whatever the 'plain words of the statute' mean (thereby seemingly advocating a literalist interpretation); and, for Lord Wilson, the law is whatever the statute says, understood by the historical Parliamentary context in which it was passed, supporting an intent-based originalist method. What sense can be made out of these different approaches? If we approach public law by focusing solely on the doctrinal elements of the decisions then such disagreement becomes highly problematic for public law as a practice.

Each of the Justices' approaches is different because each uses different criteria for determining the content of the law. Whilst they may have similarities (Lord Hughes and Wilsons' use of related criteria, for example, is why the differences are not always noticed) they are distinct and would give rise to differing results depending on the factual matrices in a given case. The problem with this disagreement goes deeper than may initially be noticed. If the four Justices are following different criteria in their identification of legality, that is, using different criteria to decide on whether a postulated legal proposition is true or false, then 'each must mean something different from the other when he says what the law is'.[35] It is clear that Lord Neuberger means something different to Lord Mance, who means something different again to Lord Wilson, who is talking past Lord Hughes when discussing the answer of the legal question brought before the Supreme Court for determination.

---

[33] 'Without in any way agreeing with the Attorney General that the public interest in maintaining the exemption did outweigh the public interest in disclosure ... there were reasonable grounds for him to hold that opinion [within the context of the Act]': ibid [183] (Wilson).
[34] ibid [179] (Wilson).
[35] R Dworkin, *Law's Empire* (Hart 1998) 43.

So then what is the significance of the disagreement in the case?[36] If they use different criteria in assessing legality then on a surface level they are 'talking past one another'.[37] The ensuing (inevitable) disagreement would be, at least superficially, pointless; it would not be genuine debate since they are not all talking about the same thing. Likewise, any convergence (such as between Lords Neuberger and Mance or Lords Wilson and Hughes) is also futile; it would be sheer luck that there was convergence. On a doctrinal reading the divergent judicial attitudes towards legality not only reflect differing approaches to how we answer legal questions but also seem to make any real debate difficult.

Indeed, this difficulty vis-à-vis disagreement goes beyond just the judiciary. Such theoretical disagreement initially seems prevalent in the academic community too. *Evans* has prompted a substantial amount of academic literature. I wish to, briefly, look at two sides; each supported by prominent public law academics yet startlingly different in view point. The first is a piece by T R S Allan;[38] a constitutional lawyer known for his strong commitment to a substantive version of the rule of law and common law constitutionalism. He starts by telling us that the Justices in *Evans* were examining principles and understood them differently from one another.[39] After examining the approach of each Justice he comes to the conclusion that Lord Neuberger's technique is right since it 'is the most candid and convincing ... Provided that some possible future application (as regards Tribunal decisions) could be envisaged there was no violence to the statutory language ... it is also *true* that the idea of parliamentary sovereignty *must* be explained in the context of our commitment to the rule of law'.[40] In a later piece Allan somewhat tempers his robust defence of Neuberger but comes to similar conclusions. He states that the dissenters' view would 'sanction the *unconstitutional* overriding of a judicial decision by a member of the executive' and that Lord Hughes' literalist approach should be treated with caution since Acts cannot be seen as self-contained codes.[41] Allan seems to hold that statutory interpretation *must* take place with a nexus to a substantive version of the rule of law. Anything else, for Allan, is wrong.[42]

---

[36] *Evans*: they all explicitly refer and debate to and with each others' speeches.
[37] Dworkin, (n 35) 44.
[38] T R S Allan, 'The Rule of Law, Parliamentary Sovereignty, and a Ministerial Veto Over Judicial Decisions' (2015) 74(3) CLJ 385.
[39] ibid.
[40] ibid 388 (emphasis added).
[41] T R S Allan, 'Law, Democracy, and Constitutionalism: Reflections on *Evans v Attorney General*' (2016) 75(1) CLJ 38, 44–5 (emphasis added).
[42] Whilst Allan argues he is fully engaging in the interpretivist method to be discussed below there is an ambiguity in Allan's work that suggests that he does in fact think that a substantive version of the rule of law *must* be correct, thereby denouncing all other versions of the grounds of law as *wrong* in a similar sense to how I have portrayed a superficial view of *Evans* (that is, *in fact* wrong as opposed to *normatively* wrong). Suffice to say that Allan's self-characterisation of his work as interpretivist does not mean that he engages with the interpretivist approach to its full extent. In this regard, I agree with Stuart Lakin's analysis of T R S Allan, *The Sovereignty of Law* (OUP 2013)): S Lakin, 'Defending and Contesting the Sovereignty of Law: The Public Lawyer as Interpretivist' (2015) 78(3) MLR 549.

The second piece is by Richard Ekins and Christopher Forsyth;[43] both of these authors are known to focus on parliamentary intention as the foundation of judicial review and, as might therefore be expected, provide a very different take on *Evans* to Allan. They start by stating that Parliament's decision (in enacting Section 53 FoIA) was ignored by 'the misinterpretation of legislation, in which courts impose on a statute an artificial reading that departs from Parliament's intention'.[44] That is to say that the majority in *Evans* acted wrongfully. Indeed, they state that 'whatever one thinks of [the FoIA's] merits, it should have been- but was not- faithfully applied by the Supreme Court'.[45] Further, when discussing Lord Neuberger's two factual matrices that would legitimate Section 53's use they say 'there is not a hint in the statutory language or in the context in which that language was chosen to suggest the qualification that the judgment imposes'.[46] So statutory language and context (Lords Hughes and Mances' views respectively) are heavily involved in the criterion of legal validity; indeed, 'Parliament simply did not enact the proviso that Lord Neuberger contemplates'.[47] This is relevant since 'the [judgment of Lord Neuberger] does not attend properly to the reasoning and choice of the enacting Parliament, which in our *constitution has authority to make the law it chooses to make*'.[48] This analysis reaches its peak when they state:

> Lord Neuberger is not much moved by the evident disconnect between the meaning he imposes on the statute and any meaning that there is reason to think Parliament intended ... Yet the fundamental aim of statutory interpretation is to find and give effect to the intention of Parliament in enacting the statute, reading the statutory language in the context of enactment to determine how Parliament chose to change the law.[49]

This is because 'the *controlling question* ... is what rule did *Parliament choose to promulgate?*'.[50] The grounds of law for Ekins and Forsyth can be taken to be 'whatever Parliament chose to promulgate' or something similar.[51]

What do we make of the difference between Allan on the one hand and Ekins and Forsyth on the other? It has to be noticed, once again, that the disagreement is deep-seated and, on a superficial level, irreconcilable. If law is about the criteria used to recognise a given proposition as a legal proposition then it must be that the Justices in *Evans* and the academics examined above are simply talking past one another. Once this conclusion takes hold deep despair sets in about legal practice.

---

[43] R Ekins and C Forsyth, 'Judging the Public Interest: The rule of law vs. the rule of courts' (2015) Judicial Power Project.
[44] ibid 4–5.
[45] ibid 5.
[46] ibid 12.
[47] ibid.
[48] ibid 14 (emphasis added).
[49] ibid.
[50] ibid (emphasis added).
[51] I leave aside here the difficulties in endorsing *both* Lord Hughes and Lord Mances' differing approaches; as pointed out above, their grounds of law would lead to divergent conclusions in differing factual scenarios.

It must be incorrect to say that when the judiciary disagrees about the answer to a case they are having a fruitless disagreement. Further, it seems startling to say that Allan and Ekins and Forsyth are not having meaningful debate

If the reader (like myself) is troubled by such fundamental theoretical disagreement about how to approach legal questions then how can we characterise the disagreement so as to rescue the judiciary and academic community at large from talking past one another and thus rendering their debates otiose? Further, depending on our recasting of theoretical disagreement, what are the consequences for our grounds of law and the wider doctrinal questions in the Constitution?

V. Interpreting *Evans*

Law, I argue after Dworkin, is an interpretive concept[52] and seeing it this way resolves the difficulties I outlined above. In short, instead of seeing the disagreement in *Evans* as a surface level, doctrinal debate (which, I have argued above, when viewed in isolation is not a real discussion in any meaningful sense) it is better to see the disagreement as revolving around the normative values that the Justices find underlying legal practice. They may disagree about which values should be upheld or the weight to attach to them but the point is that they are having a normative debate rather than a factual one about the correct shared criteria of legality, which, for each Justice, actually shapes their view of doctrinal public law.

To illustrate what I mean by an interpretive practice it will be helpful to imagine a social practice on a smaller scale. Let us imagine the rules of vegetarianism and follow the stages in their development. The first stage is that the vegetarians of our imagined community follow shared rules. They will say that vegetarianism prohibits consumption of animal meat and the purchase of products which animals have died to produce (leather goods, for example). This works for a time but, eventually, the vegetarians of our imagined society will start to question the purpose of vegetarianism, which exists quite independently and logically prior to their rule(s). This is the second stage. Imagine, upon reflection, some vegetarians argue that, because the point of vegetarianism is the protection of sentient beings, it is equally wrong to buy any animal produce at all. Other vegetarians may say although vegetarianism is about the protection of animals as long as the food is free-range and organic then buying animal produce conforms with vegetarianism. A third group may argue that if vegetarianism is about the protection of sentient beings then being a vegetarian logically entails political activism. All groups insist they are following what vegetarianism requires yet are using different factual criteria to one another in their determination. This changing of the social practice is the third (and final) stage of interpretivism.

---

[52] Dworkin's views are expounded throughout multiple volumes; the most succinct are Chs 2 and 3 of Dworkin (n 35).

It is clear then that, after reflection, the three different groups are using different sets of criteria in identifying the meaning of the word 'vegetarian', which, at a surface level, is similar to our Justices in *Evans*. However, despite coming to differing criteria all camps have engaged in interpretive practice, which renders their disagreement real. The uniting link between vegetarianism and the point of the practice (in our hypothesis: respect for animals) acts 'as a kind of plateau on which further thought and argument are built',[53] whilst people may argue over differing *conceptions* of vegetarianism they are united in the abstract *concept* of it. This renders their disagreement real, in the sense that they are arguing for the best understanding or conception of vegetarianism. In this way, normative discourse enters into the meaning of a practice; a social practice's meaning is sensitive to its point's best understanding, which is normative. What this tells us is that disagreement makes perfect sense in the context of an interpretive methodology.

So then, social practices are understood in light of their best interpretation. This involves seeking the purpose of the practice upon which we can mostly agree. You then understand the social practice in light of this purpose and the values it has. The shape of the practice is moulded not by agreement but normative understanding of the point of the practice (whether that be vegetarianism or law or other social practices). Any disagreement is seen as revolving around the value underlying the point of the practice. This makes disagreement real but only when one looks past the surface disagreement at the dynamic normative reality.

It is important here to note that the *practice* is understood by reference to the best normative reading of its point. There is a distinction between interpretation and invention. An interpreter must achieve a considered balance between the salient features of a given legal system and the normative elements that best justify these features; in Stuart Lakin's words 'moral theory partly determines the content of the practice, and the standing features of the practice constrain the available range of moral theories'.[54] In this way, an interpreter of the British Constitution will need to examine features such as the relevance of legislation and Parliament, whereas an inventor of a constitution will 'have no genuine regard for the standing features of British constitutional practice'.[55] Essentially, the work of interpretivism is to help explain the constitution as it actually is which necessarily, in an interpretivist framework, requires normative evaluation; however, whilst values play their part in determining constitutional requirements one should not use one's own view of the ideal constitution and say it is constitutive of the *actual* constitution without a level of 'fit' between the standing features and the values underlying legal practice.[56]

---

[53] ibid 71.
[54] Lakin (n 42) 566.
[55] ibid.
[56] Dworkin (n 35) 342: 'no principle can count as a justification of institutional history unless it provides a certain threshold adequacy of fit' however 'amongst those principles that meet [this threshold] the morally soundest must be preferred'. Where exactly this threshold is is contentious and not examined, by reason constraints on space, in this paper. *Cf* T R S Allan, 'Interpretation, Injustice, and Integrity' (2016) 36(1) OJLS 58, 68–74.

So, the first thing that we must do is identify the point of legal practice. Why do we have law? The answer to this would have to be sufficiently abstract so as to be largely agreeable (thereby putting everyone on the same 'plateau') but concrete enough to have meaning. Dworkin suggests that law's purpose is 'to guide and constrain the power of government ... law insists that force not be used or withheld ... except as licensed or required by individual rights and responsibilities flowing from past political decisions about when collective force is justified'[57] and I do not take issue with this definition here.

To summarise, law is to be understood by reference to its point. The point of law is to regulate coercion and make sure that legal rights and responsibilities flow from standards established prior to their realisation. The effect this has on our thinking will depend largely on what value(s) we see as underlying the practice and is neutral between the different Justices' approaches in *Evans*; each judgment and its approach is equally viable with the other speeches in the case yet which we think is correct will depend on normative argument. Interpreting legal practice requires one to understand the practice in light of its point and one's understanding of the point will be conditioned by the values served by the point. In this way, understanding legal practice is an inherently normative exercise. Understanding legal practice is about one's understanding of the value(s) of having state action legitimated by prior authorisation. These values are used to understand the standing features of the Constitution. This is broadly the same as suggesting that legal practice can only be understood by the rule of law and the values underlying it,[58] which gains explicit judicial support in *Jackson*, where Lord Hope said, 'the rule of law ... is the ultimate controlling factor on which our constitution is based'[59] and, more broadly, 'it is of the essence of supremacy of the law that the courts shall disregard as unauthorised and void the acts of any organ of government, whether legislative or administrative, which exceed the limits of the power that organ derives from the law'.[60] This, of course, tells us nothing about which values underpin legal practice or what their repercussions are.

What does this mean for our constitutional landscape? This depends on the values we identify. To illustrate how this works in *Evans* let us return to some of

---

[57] Dworkin (n 35) 93. It is important to note that whilst Dworkin utilises this point he does not think that this *has* to be the point. He could, he acknowledges, be wrong. Some take issue with this. John Gardner argues that this reduces law's unifying purpose to a matter of coercion, which he argues is implausible and far from uncontroversial: J Gardner, 'Law's Aims in *Law's Empire*' in S Hershovitz (ed), *Exploring Law's Empire: The Jurisprudence of Ronald Dworkin* (OUP 2006) 208. I do not intend to engage in this debate here but merely point to Dworkin's response to these arguments: R Dworkin, 'Response' in S Hershovitz (ed), *Exploring Law's Empire: The Jurisprudence of Ronald Dworkin* (OUP 2006) 310. Further, N Stavropoulos, 'The Relevance of Coercion: Some Preliminaries' (2009) 22(3) Ratio Juris 339 is an excellent piece in this debate.

[58] For an overview of the debate see P Craig, 'Formal and Substantive Conceptions of the Rule of Law: An Analytical Framework' [1997] PL 467. Dworkin took the purpose of law as being the rule of law.

[59] *Jackson* (n 5) 304 (Lord Hope).

[60] ibid.

the Justices' speeches.[61] By doing so we can see how Lords Neuberger, Hughes and Wilson hold widely different views but how these outlooks map onto different values that could viably underpin the purpose of law as controlling state coercion; the values that they give most weight to shapes their respective approaches in stark and illuminating ways. First, can see how Lord Hughes's judgment reflects the idea that having state power used only in pre-authorised circumstances is useful because this promotes certainty, predictability, and generally facilitates people being able to organise their own lives knowing when the state will and will not intervene.[62] Whether a proposition of law is valid for him will depend on how these values are served and so he argues that one should just look at the words of the statute in isolation; their plain meaning is enough to identify the legal rights and duties involved. This would arguably make what the law is (and is not) clear and more understandable to the layman since he would not have to understand the law in context of various rights and principles that take a degree of learning to understand. Lord Hughes is, in this way, most clearly the Razian[63] in the Supreme Court

Further, Lord Wilson relies heavily on an orthodox majoritarian form of democracy in his reasoning. We can see his judgment as a suggestion that the reason Parliament has ultimate authority to decide legal norms and standards is because they represent the supreme democratic body and they are best placed, therefore, to represent the will of the people in establishing standards which authorise state coercion.[64] Indeed, Lord Wilson specifically challenges Lord Neuberger by saying he 'invoked precious constitutional principles but among the *most precious* is that of parliamentary sovereignty, emblematic of our democracy', which is surely a normative principle served through his parliamentary contextualist approach.[65]

On an interpretivist view these positivistic plain fact approaches to law could prevail as the type of tests for determining the validity of propositions of law. However, crucially, they do not do so because of some empirical consensus.[66] Instead, a positivist approach would be the best interpretation (if it is) because of the normative force of such a theory in explaining the standing features of our

---

[61] The Justices in *Evans* do not exhaust the range of interpretations available but they do illustrate the point to a high degree. For further examples see Dworkin (n 35) Chs 3–6 and S Lakin, 'Debunking the Idea of Parliamentary Sovereignty: The Controlling Factor of Legality in the British Constitution' (2008) 28(4) OJLS 709, 732.

[62] This is similar to the normative value(s) found in Raz's authority theory of law: J Raz, *The Authority of Law* (OUP 1979) 210.

[63] ibid.

[64] Whilst there are problems with Parliamentary democracy it is more democratic an institution than the judiciary.

[65] *Evans* (n 1) [168] (Lord Wilson) (emphasis added). I agree with Allan's analysis of Lord Wilson's speech; Allan makes clear that by invoking democracy it should be a *morally defensible* form of democracy, which is more nuanced than majoritarian rule: Allan (n 41).

[66] In this way I take issue with H L A Hart's rule of recognition approach in H L A Hart, *The Concept of Law* (OUP 1997) used in J Goldsworthy, *The Sovereignty of Parliament* (OUP 1999) to legitimate a positivist approach. Allan (41) and Lakin (n 61) are both erudite works criticising such an approach in the British setting. R Dworkin, *Taking Rights Seriously* (HUP 1977) is incredibly useful in the more detached, theoretical setting.

constitution. Positivism is not, as Allan strongly argues, 'simply confused and misguided'[67] nor necessarily 'dogmatic'[68] but is instead a viable interpretation of the British Constitution built on normative foundations.[69]

Lord Neuberger may believe that the reason we insist on coercive power being authorised before use is because this represents due process and a lack of arbitrariness. It captures, for him, the idea that everyone is an equal in society. These values underpin the purpose of the legal system and so the standing features of that system are explained by these values. Lord Neuberger's approach seems to encapsulate this normative understanding; he takes the statute and interprets it to its best meaning through the lens of due process and non-arbitrariness, both values served by his interpretation.

The aim of viewing the debate between the Justices in this way is to show that the disagreement is about the *value* found in the (broadly tacitly accepted) *purpose* of law. It is not to say that the judiciary consciously act in such an analytical way, it is merely to suggest that this way of thinking about law helps to make the disagreement real. It re-orientates judicial and academic disagreement from non-sense to sense. They agree on the concept of law (that law's purpose is to ensure state coercion flows from standards established prior to its use) but disagree about conceptions of law (different concrete iterations of what the concept *means* when one looks at the values underlying the concept). Like our vegetarian example, this acts 'as a kind of plateau on which further thought and argument are built'.[70] By recognising the consequences of this argument we can see *Evans* as a major case in terms of its clarity vis-à-vis normative divergence.

VI. Normative Reasoning and Doctrinal Change

The aim of this chapter has mainly been to show that the doctrine one accepts in public law as the correct one depends, in part, on the value(s) we find underlying the legal system as a whole. Others have done this in various contexts[71] but this chapter seeks to add to that by evaluating *Evans*, a Supreme Court decision where normative disagreement is at its most apparent. It illuminates a working approach for discussing doctrinal public law issues in the UK. In short, the doctrinal architecture of public law is built on normative foundations; if and when the latter

---

[67] Allan (n 42) 340.
[68] ibid 50.
[69] This argument re positivism and Allan's purported use of interpretivist methodology builds on the critique Lakin has made of Allan: see Lakin (n 42).
[70] Dworkin (n 35) 71.
[71] For example, George Letsas has applied Dworkinian jurisprudence to the European Convention on Human Rights in G Letsas, *A Theory of Interpretation of the European Convention on Human Rights* (OUP 2009) and Lakin has done so when questioning Parliamentary sovereignty: Lakin (n 61).

moves or shifts the former does so too. Depending on which interpretation is best, there are numerous possibilities for solving doctrinal problems that have vexed public lawyers for decades. Given what has been said we can speculate as to the real legacy of *Evans*.

The most obvious (and alluded to above) is the *ultra vires*/common law constitutionalism debate[72]; that is, which provides the basis of judicial review, the common law or Parliament's intent? This depends on which we think best serves our constitution when properly interpreted. It could be the former if we are minded to accept the values that underlie Lord Neuberger's speech; that is, if we think that the values law serves include non-arbitrariness and good governance. Likewise, it is *equally* valid to argue that Parliamentary intention is the basis of judicial review since, like Lord Hughes, we think that law is about certainty and consistency, values best served by Parliament being the ultimate authority of law.

Likewise the debate about whether the courts could strike down legislation can be reconciled on an interpretivist approach. If one thinks roughly along the lines of Lord Neuberger one may be tempted to think that legislation that does not, and, crucially, cannot be interpreted, as complying with the values that underlie the law cannot *count as law* and therefore a statute is only a *purported statute*; the courts would be right to refuse to apply it because it is *not law in the first place*.[73] On the other hand, we may say that law is communicative in the way Lord Hughes's speech envisages; the value of insisting state power is used in accordance with prior established rules is that they provide authoritative guidance. In this way, law is understood as a functional method by which the state communicates reasons for action. Since we cannot have authoritative reasons if we question that authority by reference to controversial criteria (eg moral debate) law *cannot* be about moral concerns and you *cannot* question the validity of legislation on those grounds (as opposed to procedural grounds).[74] Similarly, we may, if we think law is largely predicated on the value of democracy, in a way reminiscent of Lord Wilson, think that the courts should not challenge statutes since the judiciary does not hold a democratic mandate in the same way Parliament does.[75]

Further, the questions over whether, and if so how, *Wednesbury* should be replaced with proportionality[76] is one that can be answered within an interpretive framework. The traditional approach has been to reserve *Wednesbury* for

---

[72] For an overview see an excellent collection of essays in C Forsyth, *Judicial Review and the Constitution* (Hart 2000).

[73] This is an outline of Allan's views: Allan (n 42) 139–142. Likewise, Lakin develops this in the jurisprudential sphere by using *Jackson* (n 5): Lakin (n 61).

[74] This is a rough account of Raz's work in an interpretative framework; see J Raz, *Ethics in the Public Domain: Essays in the Morality of Law and Politics* (OUP 1994) Chs 9–10. For a fuller account, see R Dworkin, *Justice in Robes* (HUP 2008) 198–212, 227–331.

[75] Whilst this is arguable it is problematic; I agree with Allan (n 42) and Lakin (n 61) that democracy is more nuanced than majoritarian rule. In this way certain acts, although mandated by the people at large, cannot be justified by reference to democratic values.

[76] For an overview see the well-rounded collection of essays in H Wilberg and M Elliott, *The Scope and Intensity of Substantive Review: Traversing Taggart's Rainbow* (Hart 2015).

common law claims and proportionality for claims under the Human Rights Act 1998. Generally the distinction given is that 'weight and balancing form no part of reasonableness review',[77] which is appropriate in the common law context but not in the framework of statutory human rights. Again, the values underlying the Justices' speeches in *Evans* prove useful. They all agree that Executive action can only be done if legal but disagree about how we assess legality. It may be that someone following Lord Hughes's approach would say that, unless otherwise directed (eg, albeit indirectly, by the Human Rights Act 1998), you should take a very light touch approach to substantive review because the questioning of the substantive legality of state action (especially if done pursuant to statute) is, in most cases, wrong.[78] He may say that this fails to serve the values of law, that is, certainty, predictability, and so on. He might say that it is *morally* wrong for state actors to abuse their power or act in a way that we find uncomfortable but there is little that the *courts* should do to rectify the actors' actions.

Again, the opposing view of Lord Neuberger is illuminating. He may argue that since the law is about due process and a lack of arbitrariness that action has to be objectively justified; he may suggest that a decision taken, even under a literally interpreted wide statute, must conform with these standards and, as a result, such action must not do more than is necessary to achieve a legitimate aim depending on the circumstances. In this way, he may favour proportionality over *Wednesbury*, even at common law. More interestingly, he does not even have to phrase it in this fashion.[79] There has been an emergence of late of 'a flexible approach to the principles of judicial review'[80] whereby categorisation is not as important as the principles at play.[81] These principles come from the *value* one finds in the law; thus, rather than relying on strict categorisation and trying to apply that consistently the standard of review is reflective of the principles that one finds.

---

[77] P Craig, 'The Nature of Reasonableness Review' [2013] CLP 1.
[78] This is a plausible interpretivist reading of Philip Sales's argument that the traditional *ultra vires* doctrine makes it improper for courts to engage in proportionality review (which he sees as a more stringent form of review than *Wednesbury*) unless such an approach has been sanctioned by Parliament (eg by the HRA): P Sales, 'Rationality, Proportionality, and the Development of the Law' [2013] 129 LQR 223.
[79] This is similar, though not the same as, Mark Elliott's approach when he argues 'against approaches that promise neat, bright-line distinctions but which do so by mistaking underlying normative or constitutional complexity through the application of a formalist doctrinal veneer': M Elliot, 'From Bifurcation to Calibration' in H Wilberg and M Elliott (eds), *The Scope and Intensity of Substantive Review: Traversing Taggart's Rainbow* (Hart 2015) 62.
[80] *Pham v Secretary of State for the Home Department* [2015] UKSC 19; [2015] WLR 1591[60] (Lord Carnwath). It is interesting to note that Lord Neuberger agreed with Lord Carnwath. Here, Carnwath was endorsing *Kennedy v The Charity Commission* [2014] UKSC 20; [2014] 2 WLR 808 where, at [51], Mance held 'The common law no longer insists on the uniform application of the rigid test of irrationality once thought applicable under the so-called *Wednesbury* principle. ... The nature of judicial review in every case depends on the context'.
[81] See *Kennedy* [54] (Lord Mance), citing Craig (n 77) with approval stating 'both reasonableness review and proportionality involve considerations of weight and balance, with the intensity of the scrutiny and the weight to be given to any primary decision maker's view depending on the context'.

As such, the proportionality/*Wednesbury* debate is an obfuscation of a deeper debate: the focus on form neglects the importance of substance; what matters is intensity of review and that will be shaped by our best interpretation of law in a given context.[82]

Whilst *Evans* does not directly touch on these issues in so many words it does, I argue, illuminate and accentuate the role that normative discourse already has (albeit often beneath the doctrinal surface) in public law adjudication. Once this is appreciated one can see almost endless possibilities, only a tiny portion of which I have identified and explained above. The doctrine a lawyer prefers is just that: one that she *prefers*. Preference, as I suggest *Evans* helps to demonstrate, is a normative condition relating to one's understanding of legal practice. Seemingly irreconcilable doctrinal divergences are only surface deep; instead, *Evans* helps throw light on debates that have plagued public law for too long. These debates are essentially an exercise of normative discourse; shedding the doctrinal veneer, as I suggest *Evans* comes most starkly to doing, renders the normative underlay of constitutional adjudication bare.

VII. Conclusion

As stated throughout, the purpose of this chapter has been to show how *Evans* illuminates the way in which arguments over the values that underpin legal practice shape our understanding of that practice. That is not to suggest that such a values-based approach to the understanding of cases and public law doctrine is new; quite the reverse. My suggestion is much more modest: public law discourse is often affected by normative concerns hiding beneath the surface. Landmark cases, in the first sense I described at the beginning of this chapter, often come about due to one side winning the moral argument. *Evans*, however, is a rarity in public law because it is a case where the normative disagreements are not hidden but instead explained and debated in open sight. Broadly, we openly see Lord Neuberger arguing strongly for the substantive rule of law, Lord Mance for separation of powers, Lord Hughes for clarity and Lord Wilson for Parliamentary democracy.

None of this is to say that law is solely a normative exercise and we can rid ourselves of doctrine; it is only to say that one can only understand a social practice and its features by reference to the value(s) that are served by the point of that practice. We understand law by reference to a dialogue between its features and values. This can give rise to a positivistic or a strong constitutionalist view of law[83]

---

[82] This is not to say that there are no normative benefits to the clearer structure one generally finds in proportionality as compared to *Wednesbury*. It is merely to state that, via the internal perspective in a case in front of a judge, the intensity of review is central.

[83] As well as every other viable interpretation.

but, the essential argument is, it does so *because* the values and features support such a conclusion. In this way, we can see the disagreement found in *Evans* as an interpretive exercise; this moves us from an impasse to substantive debate. It is hoped that this piece will further the cause taken up by others of removing an otiose and opaque barrier to legal reasoning; by recognising that when the judiciary and academics argue over traditionally 'doctrinal' issues like Parliamentary sovereignty or *Wednesbury* and proportionality they are really normatively disagreeing over the *values* underpinning legal practice we remove such a barrier. We then see that the stark doctrinal disunity in public law reveals a deeper unity and shared debate. In this way, the doctrinal becomes the theoretical; and the theoretical becomes the doctrinal.

Epilogue: *Miller*, the Legislature and the Executive

PAUL CRAIG

The Supreme Court in *Miller*[1] upheld the Divisional Court,[2] and decided that the government could not trigger Article 50 TEU to begin withdrawing from the EU without statutory authorisation from Parliament. The case concerned structural constitutional review, in which the Supreme Court demarcated the ambit of legislative and executive power, the latter being exercised through the prerogative. *Miller* is of enduring constitutional importance, and fully deserves its place within this book. This is so for three reasons.

First, it forced courts and commentators alike to confront ambiguities in the well-known constitutional precepts through which limits to prerogative power are commonly expressed: the prerogative cannot be used to alter the law of land or affect rights, and that it cannot be deployed so as to circumvent statute that covers the same ground. It was contestation as to the meaning of these precepts that divided the majority and the dissent in *Miller*, and disagreement in this regard also underpinned academic discourse.

Secondly, the case is of lasting importance for its more general methodological lessons as to how we resolve the ambiguities adverted to above. The twin lessons in this respect are in some ways remarkably simple. The boundaries of particular doctrinal precepts can only be resolved if we articulate the background values that inform them, and use these as the touchstone to help us determine contested issues as to the reach of doctrine. The other lesson is that when determining the doctrinal issue, we ensure that the answer, whatsoever it might be, coheres with related constitutional principles.

Thirdly, *Miller* is a landmark constitutional case because of what it tells us about the relationship between the 'legal' and the 'political'. Underlying every significant constitutional case there is always a political story. It takes two to tango. It takes two sides to engage in litigation. Ms Miller brought the case because the government was determined to trigger Article 50 without securing statutory approval. Why it chose to be intransigent in this respect is one dimension of the 'political' that informs this story; the consequence of its losing is yet another.

---

[1] *R (on the application of Miller) v Secretary of State for Exiting the European Union* [2017] UKSC 5.
[2] *R (on the application of Miller) v The Secretary of State for Exiting the European Union* [2016] EWHC 2768 (Admin).

I. Limits on Prerogative Power: The Ambiguities

There are, as is well-known, three dimensions to legal control over the prerogative: the first is as to whether it exists; the second is as to its extent; the third concerns the manner of exercise. *Miller* turned on contestation as to the second of these issues. The word 'extent' in this context captures the limits or constraints placed on an admitted prerogative. It is a matter for the courts to decide, and the decision is normative in nature. The courts will determine the types of constraint they believe should, as a matter of principle, be placed on prerogative power. Thus the courts have fashioned constraints that the prerogative cannot alter the law of the land or effect rights, and that it cannot be used where it would place statute law in abeyance or frustrate statutory rules.[3] The precise meaning of these constraints can be contestable, so too can their application in a particular case. There are, therefore, always two related, but distinct, issues when we consider the extent of the prerogative: what types of constraint should, as a matter of principle, be placed on prerogative power; and how does a constraint apply to the facts of a particular case.

A. Constraints on Prerogative Power: Altering the Law of the Land and Rights

The first limit to prerogative power is that it cannot alter the law of the land, a proposition derived from the *Case of Proclamations*. It concerned the legality of two proclamations made by the King: one prohibited new buildings in London, the other the making of starch from wheat. The court held that the King cannot by his proclamation change 'any part of the common law, or statute law or customs of the realm'.[4] Nor could the King create any new offence by way of proclamation, for that would be to change the law. It was for the courts to determine the existence and extent of prerogative powers. The principal beneficiary was Parliament, since the case concerned the extent of monarchical regulatory power independent from the legislature. The denial of such power meant that if the King wished to attain these ends he must do so through statute.

The principles embodied in the *Case of Proclamations* were reinforced by the Bill of Rights 1688, which provided that 'the pretended power of suspending of laws or the execution of laws by regall authority without consent of Parlyament is illegall'[5] and that 'the pretended power of dispensing with laws or the execution of laws by regall authoritie as it hath beene assumed and exercised of late is illegall'.[6]

---

[3] The argument concerning the last of these constraints is developed below.
[4] (1611) 12 Co. Rep. 74 at 75.
[5] Bill of Rights 1688, 1 Will. and Mar. Sess.2, c. 2, Article 1.
[6] Bill of Rights 1688, 1 Will. and Mar. Sess.2, c. 2, Article 2; Sir Stephen Sedley, 'The Judges' Verdicts', www.lrb.co.uk/2017/01/30/stephen-sedley-the-judges-verdicts.

The application of the principle from *Proclamations* in *Miller* raised difficult issues concerning the meaning of 'the law' that could not be changed through the prerogative, and the nature of the rights that could not be affected by use of the prerogative. The Supreme Court's reasoning was as follows.

The majority regarded EU law as a novel source of law within the UK legal order.[7] It, and the rights emanating from it, was therefore part of the law of the land that could not be altered through recourse to the prerogative. The majority acknowledged that the EU rights brought into UK law through the European Communities Act 1972 (ECA 1972) could vary from time to time, and that this would cease when the UK withdrew from the EU. This did not, however, mean that withdrawal, with the consequential impact on rights, could be done through the prerogative without Parliamentary authorisation. There was, said the majority, no indication that Parliament had intended this. There was a vital difference between changes in domestic law resulting from variations in EU law arising from new EU legislation, and changes in domestic law resulting from withdrawal by the UK from the EU.[8]

The principal dissent was given by Lord Reed, who held that the prerogative over the making and unmaking of treaties was a fundamental part of the UK constitutional order, which could only be curtailed expressly or by necessary implication. The ECA 1972 contained no express limitation on the Crown's prerogative power, nor were there any words through which to infer that this was the necessary implication of the statute.[9] Lord Reed denied that triggering Article 50 TEU would impact on rights. Parliament had, he said, recognised in the ECA 1972, section 2(1), that rights given effect under the ECA could be altered or revoked from time to time without the need for a statute, and he rejected the distinction drawn by the majority between such changes in rights and that resulting from withdrawal from the EU.

B. Constraints on Prerogative Power: Statute Covering the Area of the Prerogative

The second constraint on prerogative power is that it cannot be exercised if statute covers the same area. The seminal case was *Attorney General v De Keyser's Royal Hotel*,[10] which arose out of the Crown's decision, acting under the Defence of the Realm Regulations, to take possession of a hotel to accommodate personnel of the Royal Flying Corps. The Crown contended that the hotel owners had no legal right to compensation. The Defence Act 1842 gave broad powers to the Crown

---

[7] *Miller* (n 1) [65].
[8] ibid at [76]-[78], [83].
[9] ibid at [160], [177], [194], [197].
[10] *Attorney General v De Keyser's Royal Hotel* [1920] AC 508.

to take possession of land, subject to compensation. The Crown maintained that the taking was, however, justified by the prerogative, which was said to warrant temporary seizure of property in time of emergency, without any legal right to compensation.

Their Lordships were unpersuaded by the argument. Lord Atkinson held that it would be absurd to construe a statute so as to enable the executive to disregard limits contained in it by reliance on the prerogative. Lord Parmoor was equally clear in this respect: when executive power had been directly regulated by statute, the executive could no longer use the prerogative, but had to observe the restrictions which Parliament imposed in favour of the subject.[11]

The decision in *Miller* did not turn on application of the *De Keyser* principle as such, but the Supreme Court nonetheless said some important things about it. The majority accepted the principle from *De Keyser*, and its application in subsequent cases. It held, moreover, that it was highly improbable that Parliament had the intention that ministers could subsequently take the UK out of the EU without the approval of the constitutionally senior partner, which was Parliament.[12] If that had been the intent it was, in accord with the principle of legality, incumbent on Parliament to have made this clear, and thus pay the political cost of the choice. There was, said the majority, no evidence that the ECA 1972 was intended to clothe the executive with that far-reaching choice.[13]

Lord Reed also accepted the principle in *De Keyser*, but did not believe that it was applicable to this case. It was central to *De Keyser* that Parliament had regulated the area in relation to which the executive sought to exercise the prerogative. This was not so here. The 1972 Act did not regulate withdrawal from the EU. It merely recognised the existence of Article 50 TEU, but said nothing as to who should take the decision to invoke Article 50.[14]

II. Limits on Prerogative Power: Values and the Resolution of Ambiguities

The preceding analysis is but a bare summation of the contending views of the majority and the dissent in *Miller*. The contrasting arguments were considerably more complex. Resolution of these intricate arguments is equally difficult, and cannot be undertaken here. My own views in this regard can be found elsewhere.[15]

---

[11] ibid at 575.
[12] *Miller* (n 1) [85]–[90].
[13] ibid at [87]–[88].
[14] ibid at [233].
[15] Paul Craig, '*Miller*, Structural Constitutional Review and the Limits of Prerogative Power', forthcoming.

The present focus is rather on methodology, which in this context connotes the importance of identifying the background values that inform doctrinal precepts, and the need to ensure that decisions made in one doctrinal area cohere with those made elsewhere.

The value that underlies the twin constraints on prerogative power in *Proclamations* and *De Keyser* is the sovereignty of Parliament. It is Parliament that is the legitimate legislator within the UK and the limits protect that authority from being undermined. If the executive could change the law of its own volition, it could thereby bypass legislation without the need for amendment and repeal, hence the principle in *Proclamations*. If the executive could use the prerogative where Parliament had already addressed the issue in a statute it could then avoid the legislation crafted by Parliament, hence the principle in *De Keyser*, and its extension to cases where the prerogative would frustrate the legislation. *Proclamations* protects Parliamentary sovereignty directly, by preventing recourse to the prerogative where it would change the law; *De Keyser* protects sovereignty indirectly, by precluding use of the prerogative where the formal law is left intact, but the executive seeks to circumvent it by use of the prerogative.

The value underlying recognition of a prerogative power to manage international relations, including the making and unmaking of treaties was identified by William Blackstone.[16]

> This is wisely placed in a single hand by the British constitution, for the sake of unanimity, strength, and despatch. Were it placed in many hands, it would be subject to many wills, if disunited and drawing different ways, create weakness in a government; and to unite those several wills, and reduce them to one, is a work of more time and delay than the exigencies of state will afford.

For Lord Reed, 'the value of unanimity, strength and dispatch in the conduct of foreign affairs are as evident in the 21st century as they were in the 18th',[17] and Timothy Endicott voiced strong views to the same effect.[18] It can be readily acknowledged that unanimity, strength and dispatch are important values in the conduct of international relations. We accept that the executive has the primary responsibility for negotiation of treaties, which cannot be done in a collective.

The argument is nonetheless difficult when applied to the issue in *Miller*, which was whether Parliament should have to give statutory approval before the triggering of Article 50 TEU. It is not self-evident that unanimity, strength or dispatch should be regarded as the principal values in this determination; it is not self-evident that the executive has advantages in making this decision over Parliament; and it is not self-evident that the executive values would be placed in jeopardy by requiring a vote in Parliament. Consider these issues in turn.

---

[16] Sir W. Blackstone, *Commentaries on the Laws of England* (1765–1769), Book I, Ch 7, 'Of the King's Prerogative'.
[17] *Miller* (n 1) [160].
[18] T. Endicott, '"This Ancient, Secretive Royal Prerogative"', UK Const. L. Blog, 11 Nov 2016, https://ukconstitutionallaw.org/.

The decision to trigger Article 50 and leave the EU ranks among the most significant peace time treaty determinations ever made by the UK. It is an issue on which the country was fiercely divided, notwithstanding the referendum. The UK constitutional tradition is one of parliamentary as opposed to popular sovereignty, which is why the referendum was not legally binding, although it was clearly important in political terms. The values that matter here are those that are fundamental to a parliamentary democracy, viz that major decisions are not made without approval by Parliament.

It is not self-evident that the executive would have any advantages over Parliament when making this determination. The executive may claim epistemic advantages and experience in relation to some aspects of foreign policy. The reality is that such advantages were not relevant to the current determination, or to analogous decisions of this nature. MPs knew the issues concerning EU membership as well as the executive.

Nor is it self-evident that requiring a vote in Parliament placed the executive's strategy for triggering Article 50 TEU in jeopardy. To the contrary, the date chosen by the executive, the end of March, had no especial magic; it was not jeopardised by the parliamentary vote, which was accomplished in a matter of weeks; and if the government had not contested the issue in litigation parliamentary approval would have been secured earlier.

Consideration of the values underlying constraints on prerogative power and the values that underpin a particular prerogative can therefore assist us in resolving the issues that arise in a case such as *Miller*. They serve to explain why for many people the intuitive answer was that the decision to leave the EU should not rest with the executive acting alone, but should rather be dependent on statutory approval by Parliament. Respect for parliamentary sovereignty underpinned the constraints on prerogative power as expressed in *Proclamations* and *De Keyser*, while the rationale for according the executive prerogative power over treaty making had scant if any relevance to the issue in *Miller*.

It is, as noted above, equally important to ensure that the constitutional principles that inform decisions in one area cohere with those in another. This can be exemplified as follows. In *HS2* the Supreme Court affirmed that there was a category of constitutional statutes, which included the ECA 1972.[19] It will not readily be accepted that a constitutional statute can be impliedly repealed. While this possibility cannot be ruled out entirely, it is generally accepted that the burden of justification should be set very high, such that in the absence of express repeal the inference would have to be irresistible.[20] The normative justification is that a statute of such importance should not be repealed or amended other than through specific decision by the sovereign Parliament.

---

[19] *R (on the application of HS2 Action Alliance Ltd) v Secretary of State for Transport* [2014] UKSC 3 at [207]; *H v Lord Advocate* [2012] UKSC 24.
[20] *Thoburn v Sunderland City Council* [2003] QB 151 at [63].

The reasoning in *Miller* is a natural corollary of that in *HS2*. A statute worthy of the denomination constitutional should not be rendered devoid of effect through recourse to the prerogative. Thus, while the triggering of Article 50 TEU would not in itself repeal the ECA 1972, withdrawal would deprive it of substance, since we would no longer be party to the EU. The majority in *Miller* believed that this consequence should not ensue without parliamentary authorisation, or to put the same point in a different way, recourse to the prerogative could only be countenanced if the executive could show specific authority for this course of action, thereby ensuring, in accord with the principle of legality, that Parliament had thought through the consequences of its action.

The requirement that triggering exit via prerogative power was dependent on proof of specific statutory authorisation coheres with the reasoning in *HS2* and is sound in terms of normative principle. If statutes of such importance should not generally be susceptible to implied repeal, in order thereby to safeguard the sovereign Parliament, then it follows that they should not be capable of being deprived of effect by the executive, without specific authorisation from the sovereign Parliament. The range of statutes, over and beyond constitutional statutes, that should be treated in this manner remains to be seen. This argument is reinforced by the point made earlier to the effect that the triggering of Article 50 does not involve the values commonly associated with prerogative power in relation to treaty making, and that by contrast it is the very kind of determination that should be made by Parliament.

III. Limits on Prerogative Power: The 'Legal' and the 'Political'

There is a political dimension to every leading constitutional case. It may be readily apparent, it may not, but it is always there. Truth to tell, it would be more accurate to speak of political dimensions, since this better captures the heterogeneity that represents reality.

The most obvious political dimension to *Miller* is why the case ever went to the courts. The salient issue is why the government fought the action, not why Ms Miller initiated it. There are various possible answers, but none is terribly satisfactory. It might be contended that the government truly believed that it should be able to trigger Article 50, through recourse to the prerogative. It might alternatively have felt worried by the prospect of backbench revolt if a Bill to authorise withdrawal were to be placed before Parliament.

The former rationale is, however, pretty weak, since the government lawyers would have told the Prime Minister that this was not an open and shut case. This is more especially so because they would have to fight the case with one hand tied behind their backs, since they could not argue that Article 50 was revocable and thus could not easily rebut the claimant's argument that triggering of Article 50 would terminate rights derived from EU law. The government lawyers would, moreover, have known, and duly advised the Prime Minister, that you simply do not know what will happen when you get into court. The only thing that you know is that the matter is now no longer in your control. All of which was borne out by the litigation, since not only did the government lose, but the judgment elaborated constraints on the prerogative relating to constitutional statutes that had not been articulated hitherto.

The latter rationale is also pretty weak, given that the government did not encounter any real difficulty in securing passage of the legislation authorising the triggering of Article 50. Barely a day after the *Miller* judgment the Prime Minister introduced the European Union (Notification of Withdrawal) Bill 2017, which had undoubtedly been drafted considerably earlier. The House of Commons duly passed the Bill by a large majority. There were attempts to impose substantive and procedural constraints on how the government conducts the negotiations, but they were not successful, and the Bill secured its majority without any amendment. There were some rocky moments in the House of Lords, but there was never any likelihood that it would block the legislation.

We return then to the inquiry posed above, as to why the Prime Minister chose to fight the case. It might be contended that she did not wish to show weakness in her early days in the job. Yet the reality is that she could have secured her aims without doing so, and without resort to litigation. It would have been perfectly possible for the Prime Minister to have said in October 2016 that while she did not accept that she had, as a matter of law, to secure parliamentary authorisation before triggering Article 50, she would nonetheless place the appropriate Bill before Parliament. The statute would have been duly enacted well before Christmas without litigation, thereby avoiding the costs and avoiding also being told what to do by the courts.

There is a second and very different political dimension to *Miller*. We should be wary of a story whereby lawyers are seen, and perhaps see themselves, as the saviour of the Constitution, riding valiantly to the rescue of the stricken maiden, Parliament, thereby saving it from the clutches of the wicked dragon, viz the all-powerful executive. There is a real danger of constitutional solecism here. Sovereignty resides with Parliament, and has done so for circa 400 years. It does not reside with the executive. It is therefore unarguable that Parliament could, at any time since 23 June 2016, have enacted a statute requiring the government to seek its approval before triggering Article 50. If it had done so it would have been game over. The specific statute would have trumped the prerogative. Parliament did not therefore need to await rescue by the bold legal prince on its white charger.

This begs the question as to why Parliament was quiescent in this respect, to which the answer is eclectic. Some MPs might genuinely have felt that the issue should, for reasons of principle, be left to the executive; others, particularly, hard Brexiteers, were committed functionally to the prerogative, since they were concerned in the aftermath of the referendum at attempts to undo their victory on the floor of the House. The principal explanation as to why most MPs were not clamouring for voice through enactment of a statute was in reality rather different. They were fearful of backlash from their constituents who had voted to leave, who would be angered if they felt that their victory was in danger of being undermined by demands for such a statute, a fear made all the more real by the fact that it would be whipped up by certain sections of the media. Much easier for MPs to remain largely silent on this, such that demands for Parliamentary voice rarely rose to susurration let alone clamour, and rely instead on the courts through the instrumentality of the *Miller* judgment to give Parliament voice without the attendant political dangers of actively seeking it.

INDEX

Note: Alphabetical arrangement is word-by-word, where a group of letters followed by a space is filed before the same group of letters followed by a letter, eg 'legal practice' will appear before 'legality'. In determining alphabetical arrangement, initial articles and prepositions are ignored.

A v Secretary of State for the Home Department, see *Belmarsh* case
abolition of House of Lords, 224–25, 229–30
abuse of power, 201–203, 209
academics:
   Evans v Attorney General, 293–95
   Padfield v Ministry of Agriculture Fisheries and Food decision criticism, 51
   Ridge v Baldwin decision reception, 33–6
   scholarship, EU membership, 132–33
accountability:
   democratic, *see* democratic accountability
   government ministers, *see* government ministers
   to parliament, 55–56
Acker QC, Desmond, 22–23, 87
Act of Settlement 1701, 4, 6
Act of Union 1707, 4
adjudication, public law, 302
administrative action:
   illegality, 103
   irrationality, 103
   judicial reviews of, 11, 40, 103
   procedural impropriety, 103
administrative acts:
   dismissal not under police discipline regulations, 21–2
administrative bodies, 40
administrative decisions:
   natural justice, 37
administrative functions, 40
administrative justice, 51, 55
administrative law:
   adumbration of general principles of, 100, 102
   Coughlan case establishing principles, 201–207
   judicial reviews, 40
   modern, *Council of Civil Service Unions v Minister for the Civil Service* judgement place in development of, 100–105
   principles, establishing, 201
      abuse of power and fairness, 201–203
      individuals and public interest, 207
      proportionality, 203–207
   principles to which public bodies must comply, 166
   void/voidable distinction, 34–35
Administrative Law (William Wade), 12, 23
adumbration of general principles of administrative law, 100, 102
Agricultural Marketing Act 1958, 46–52, 54, 57, 61
Al-Qaeda, 173
Alexander, Robert, 110
aliens, natural justice, 37
Allan, TRS, 133, 136, 293, 294, 295, 299
Allen, Stephen, 244, 248
Anisminic v Foreign Compensation Commission, 49, 50, 60–61, 286
Anisminic:
   application to Foreign Compensation Commission, 68–70
   challenge to determination seeking declarations, 70–71
   demise, 91–92
   Israeli military action damage claim, 69
   merits of claim, 91–92
   name change from Sinai Mining, 65
   The Economic Development Organisation (TEDO) as successor in title to, 69–70, 74, 80–81, 84
   costs, 75–6
   Court of Appeal judgment, 76–78
   Egypt Fund established by UK Government, 66–68, 71, 75, 83, 91
   first-instance judgment, 72–74
   Foreign Compensation Commission:
      admission of claims, 81–82
      Anisminic's application to, 67, 68–70
      Court of Appeal, 77–78
      determination a nullity, 72–74, 78–79, 80
      errors of fact, 79, 82
      errors of law, 72, 74, 79, 80, 82
      and Foreign Office, deciding whether to appeal, 74–76

judicial reviews of determinations, 72
jurisdiction, 79, 82, 87, 88
redetermination of Anisminic's
 claim, 90–91
response to judgment, legislation, 83–90
High Court:
 first-instance judgment, 72–74
 jurisdiction, 76
House of Lords:
 appeal to, 78–80
 obiter dicta, 92–93
 ratio, 80–82
 reception of judgment, redetermination of
  Anisminic's claim, 90–91
 response to judgment,
  legislation, 83–90
long-term significance, 92–95
Sinai Mining's dealing with
 Egyptians, 64–6
Suez Crisis and consequences, 63–64
Anti-Terrorism Crime and Security Act 2001,
 162–65, 170, 173, 174, 176, 178, 180
anti-terrorism laws, 162
APPG (Chagos Islands British Indian Overseas
 Territories (BIOT) All-Party Parliamentary
 Group), 253
armed forces combat immunity, 7
Armstrong, Robert, 97–98, 99, 109
Arthian Davies LJ, 21
asbestos, 272
Ashworth J:
 R v Criminal Injuries Compensation Board,
  ex parte *Lain*, 108
Asif Mahmoud Khan, ex parte, 186
Asquith, HH, 214
*Associated Provincial Picture Houses
 v Wednesbury Corporation*, 103, 110
asylum, abuse of, 162
Atkin LJ, 29
Atkin, Lord, 262
Attlee, Clement, 217
audi alteram partem rule, *see* natural justice
Austin, R, 51
Australia:
 legitimate expectations and, 208
authorisation before use of coercive
 power, 299
'authority' and individuals:
 natural justice as essential element
  between, 41
Avebury MP, Eric, 244
*AXA General Insurance Ltd v HM Advocate and
 Others*, 271–72
 conclusion, 283–84
 legislative competence, determining
  scope, 274
 nature of devolved legislation and role of
  courts, 274–83

Bagehot, W, 4
Baker, J, 95
Baldry MP, Tony, 177
Balfour, Arthur, 213
Balfour, Lord, 215–16
Bancoult, 7, 209
 Chagos Islanders, 252–8
 colonial legislatures and rule of law, 258–62
 conclusion, 266
 House of Lords, confusion in, 262–6
 introduction, 239–43
 judicial scrutiny of colonial law, 243–52
Bank Mellat v HM Treasury (No 2), 204
Bankes LJ, 29
Banks MP, Tony, 211
Barber, N, 233
Bellamy, R, 59
Bellson, Samuel, 18, 19
Belmarsh case, 161, 163, 167
 Court of Appeal, 168–69
 House of Lords, 169–70
  Anti-Terrorism Crime and Security
   Act 2001 compatibility with Convention,
   175–76
  decision, 176–79
  derogation, whether lawful, 170
  implications of decision, 179–80
  measures strictly required, whether, 172–74
  public emergency threatening life of nation,
   whether, 170–72
  response to decision, 176–79
  Special Immigrations Appeal Commission,
   detainees' challenge upheld, 167–68
  Strasbourg decision, 179–80
Bennett, Alan, 17, 19
Berlins, Marcel, 41
Bevan, Aneurin, 217
Bill of Rights 1688, 4, 6
Bingham, Lord, 7, 120, 136
 Bancoult, 242, 263, 266
 Belmarsh case, 169, 172–77, 179, 180
 Jackson v Attorney General, 221, 225, 230, 236
 Parliament Act 1911, 213
biological weapons, 163
BIOT, *see* British Indian Ocean Territory
bipartite Parliament, 222–24
black spider memos litigation history, 286–89
Blackstone, W, 227
Blain J, 37
Blair, Tony, 162
Blunkett, David, 161, 176–77
Board of Education v Rice, 13
'the books', law recorded in, 3–4
borough police forces, 15–16
Bourne, Wilfred, 84
Brabazon, Lord, 126
Bradlaugh, ex parte, 73
Bradley, A, 132

Bradley, AW, 33–35
breach of natural justice, 29, 34
Brexit, 138–41
Bridge, Lord, 127
   Factortame litigation, 136, 156–57, 160
Bridge, Nigel, 71, 78, 107–108
Brightman, Lord:
   Council of Civil Service Unions v Minister for the Civil Service, 110
Brighton conspiracy trial, *see Ridge v Baldwin*
British Constitution, *see* Constitution
British Indian Ocean Territory (BIOT), 244, 248, 254–58, 258
British Indian Ocean Order 1965, 265
British Indian Overseas Territory (Constitution) Order 2004, 255–57, 258, 266
British Nationality Act 1981, 125
British Overseas Territories, 258
British-owned property in Egypt, sale and liquidation, 64
Brooke LJ:
   Belmarsh case, 168–69
Brown, Gordon, 162
Brown, Lord:
   Jackson v Attorney General, 218, 225
Brown, Simon, 99
Browne J:
   Anisminic v Foreign Compensation Commission, 65, 71, 72–74, 76, 78, 79, 81, 87, 91, 92
Burgess, David, 147
Burmah Oil v Lord Advocate, 86
Burnton LJ:
   Bancoult, 248

Camden, Lord, 3–10
Campbell v Hall, 256
Canada:
   legitimate expectations and, 208
   public law estoppel, 208
CAP (Common Agricultural Policy), EU, 121
Carnwath, Lord:
   Walton v The Scottish Ministers, 140
   Youssef v Secretary of State for Foreign and Commonwealth Affairs, 203–204, 209
Carr v Upper Tribunal, 78
Carswell, Lord:
   Bancoult, 242, 263–64, 265, 267
   Belmarsh case, 172
   Jackson v Attorney General, 225, 228, 230
Case of Proclamations 1611, 4, 6, 239
cause, dismissal for, 13, 27, 30
certiorari, 13–14, 28, 29, 70, 72, 82, 90, 93, 108
CFP (Common Fisheries Policy), *see* European Union
Chagos Arbitration Award, 245–46
Chagos Archipelago, 243–52
Chagos Islanders, 252–8

Chagos Islanders Case, *see Bancoult*
Chagos Islands British Indian Overseas Territories (BIOT) All-Party Parliamentary Group (APPG), 253
Chahal v United Kingdom, 163–65, 173
Chakrabarti, Shami, 177
Chalfont, Lord, 88
Chalmers, Damian, 130
characterisation, 13
Charles, Prince of Wales, 287–89
Charlton, Noel, 75, 84
Charter, United Nations, 247–48
checks and balances:
   Constitution, 230
chemical weapons, 163
Chief Constables, 15, 16, 33
   see also Ridge v Baldwin
City of London Police, 16
Civil Contingencies Committee, 162
civil law systems:
   common law and, contrasting styles, 116
   teleological interpretation, 116
Civil Service Order in Council 1982, 97, 104, 110
CJEC (Court of Justice of the European Community), *see* European Court of Justice
claims:
   admission, Foreign Compensation Commission in *Anisminic*, 81–82
clarity, 302
Clarke, Charles, 176–77
Clarke, Lord, 268
Cockburn, Lord:
   Phillips v Eyre, 261
coercion, 143
   regulation, 297, 298
coercive power:
   authorisation before use, 299
coercive relief against government ministers, *see* government ministers
coercive remedies:
   Scotland, 159
Cohen, Lord:
   Anisminic v Foreign Compensation Commission, 71
Coke, E, 227, 235
collective memory, 1
Colley, Linda, 2
Colonial Boundaries Act 1895, 265
colonial constitutional law:
   royal prerogative in, *see Bancoult*
Colonial Declaration, United Nations, 247
colonial governance, power of:
   use for purpose of peace, order and good governance, 263–64, 266
colonial laws, 256–59, 262, 266
Colonial Laws Validity Act 1865, 256–62
colonial legislatures:
   rule of law and, *Bancoult*, 258–62

colonial powers, 248
Colson, D, 245–46
combat immunity, armed forces, 7
Commentaries on the Law of England (Blackstone), 263
Commissioner of BIOT, 254–56, 258, 265
committal, warrants for, *see* warrants
committees of investigation, 46–48, 51, 53–54, 57
Common Agricultural Policy (CAP), EU, 121
Common Council of the City of London, 16
Common Fisheries Policy (CFP), *see* European Union
common law, 2
   civil law systems and, contrasting styles, 116
   claims, *Wednesbury* for, 300–301
   constitutional limitations on legislative competence of devolved legislatures, 281–82
   constitutionalism/*ultra vires* constitutionalism debate, 300
   EU:
      law interpretation approach, 132
      UK relationship and, 134
   interests willing to protect, government ministers' decisions affecting, 55
   as judicial reviews basis, 300
   legality principle, *see* legality
   limits on Parliament, 234
   Parliamentary sovereignty as construct of, 227
   principles:
      application reinforcing rule of law and furthering political Constitution, 45
      underpinning judicial review of executive power, 44
   protection of interests important to, 51
   rights at, 282–83
   furthering, 61
Commonwealth Shipping Agreement 1931, 125
compensation:
   Egyptian nationalised property of British nationals, 66
   R v Criminal Injuries Compensation Board, ex parte Lain, 98, 100, 106–109
   Sinai Mining Co Ltd, 64–65
competition law, 130
complaints:
   government ministers duties to refer, 51–52
   procedures, 50–51
conceptual approach to EU law, 116
conditions of service, police, 16
Congreve v Home Office, 6
Constitution, 2, 140
   checks and balances, 230
   democratisation, 212, 229
   development by evolution, 228
   interpretation, 299
   Parliament as general principle of, 227
   Parliamentary sovereignty as cornerstone of, 235, 237
   rule of law:
      as dominant position, 234
      as fundamental principle of, 144
      protector of, 237
      ultimate controlling factor, 228, 236
      values, 6
   unwritten:
      rule of law values embedding into, 6
      delicacy, 230
constitutional architecture:
   Padfield, *see Padfield v Ministry of Agriculture Fisheries and Food*
constitutional change, 140
constitutional crisis:
   Parliament Act 1911 and, 213–16
constitutional democracy evolution, 228–32
constitutional disagreement:
   underlying normativity of, 285–303
constitutional doctrine:
   narratives role in analysis of, 6
   Parliamentary sovereignty as, 5
   rule of law as, 5
Constitutional Fundamentals (Wade), 136
constitutional fundamentals unalterable by EU law, 135
constitutional law:
   colonial, royal prerogative in, *see Bancoult*
constitutional limits:
   absence on exercise of prerogative powers, 239
   on devolved legislatures, 281–83
constitutional narratives, 1
constitutional revolution, 116
constitutional rights, 263
   of abode, 263
   operating to constrain prerogative powers, 263
constitutional statutes, 134–35
constitutional structure of UK:
   rule of law position in, 236
constitutional supremacy, 2
constitutionalism, 130
   absence, 259
   judicial, 234
   legal, 55, 231, 232, 233–36
   political, 234
   ultra vires/common law debate, 300
construction approach, EU law, 136
consultation:
   absence of, *Council of Civil Service Unions v Minister for the Civil Service*, 97–99
   legitimate expectations, 206
contempt of court:
   government ministers, 144
   M v The Home Office, *see M v The Home Office*
control orders, 178
Convention Rights, 51

Cooper, Cecil, 75–76
Cooper v Wandsworth Board of Works, 27
Cooper v Wilson, 17
Corby MP, Jeremy, 244
Costa v ENEL, 131
costs:
  Anisminic v Foreign Compensation Commission, 75–6
Coughlan case, 181–83
  administrative law, establishing principles, 201–207
  conclusion, 207–209
  decision, 190–93
  as landmark case, 183–84
  law of legitimate expectations prior to, 184–90
  law of legitimate expectations, limited enforcement after, 193–97
  legacy, guidance and boundaries, 197–201
Council of Civil Service Unions v Minister for the Civil Service, 6, 97–100, 112, 186, 254, 257
  conclusion, 113
  consultation, absence of, 97–99
  judgement place in development of modern administrative law, 100–105
  national security, 97–99, 110–11
  prerogative powers, 97
    House of Lords, 109–11
  reviewability, 105–109, 113
Countryside Alliance, 212
county police forces, 15
Court of Justice of the European Community (CJEC), *see* European Court of Justice
Court of Session:
  supervisory jurisdiction of, 159
courts:
  Anisminic, *see Anisminic v Foreign Compensation Commission*
  Belmarsh case, *see Belmarsh* case
  Crown and, relationship between, 3
    constitutional, 4
  decisions binding as between parties, including executive, 5
  devolved legislation and, 271, 274–83
  government ministers' accountability to, 60, 61
  jurisdiction:
    giving effect to will of Parliament, 134
  legislation:
    reviewing and rejecting, 279–82
    striking down debate, 300
  limiting Parliamentary sovereignty, 231
  Padfield v Ministry of Agriculture Fisheries and Food decisions, 47–52
  policy not necessarily 'no go' area for, 55
  reception of judgment, *Anisminic*, 90–91
  response to judgment, legislation, *Anisminic*, 83–90
  Ridge v Baldwin, reception of decision, 36–9

Craig, Paul, 132, 133, 136, 137, 208
crime:
  terrorism and, links between, 162
Criminal Injuries Compensation Board, 106–9
Crown:
  in Council, 265
  courts and, relationship between, 3
    constitutional, 4
  immunity, 150–54
  Parliament and:
    constitutional relationship between, 4
Crown Proceedings Act 1947, 158–59
Curzon, Earl, 216
CVLA (Colonial Laws Validity Act 1865), 256–62

Dalyell MP, Tam, 105, 244
Damages (Asbestos-related Conditions) (Scotland) Act 2009, 272
Datafin, *see R v Takeover Panel*, ex parte *Datafin Plc*
Davidson v Scottish Ministers, 159
Davis, Glyn, 33
Davis, KC, 15
de Freitas v Benny, 106
de Smith, Stanley, 12–15, 26, 35, 40, 99, 105, 106, 110, 138
De Verteuil v Knaggy, 22
decision-making:
  majority, unfairness flowing from, 59
decisions:
  government ministers, *see* government ministers
  nullity, 93–94
declarations, 72
decolonisation, 248
Defra (Department for Environment, Food and Rural Affairs), 288
democracy:
  legislation undermining basis of, 281
  Parliamentary, 302
democratic accountability, 56
  Parliament, 235
democratic legitimacy of devolved legislatures, 281
democratic principle:
  unconvincing as rationale for sovereignty, 138
democratic values:
  ensuring, 61
democratically elected legislatures:
  devolution, 273
  Parliament, 279
  Scottish Parliament, 275, 276–77
democratisation:
  Constitution, 212, 229
  House of Commons, 234–35
  Parliament, 237

denial of privileges, 14
Denning, Lord:
  Anisminic v Foreign Compensation Commission, 71, 88–89, 90
  Laker Airways, 106
  Macarthy's Ltd v Smith, 120, 131
  Padfield v Ministry of Agriculture Fisheries and Food, 37, 48, 51
  Ridge v Baldwin, 36, 37, 184
  Schmidt v Secretary of State for Home Affairs, 184
Department for Environment, Food and Rural Affairs (Defra), 288
depletion in fish stocks, 123
deportation, 163
derogation from European Convention on Human Rights, 164–65, 167–68, 170, 178
determinations:
  nullity, Foreign Compensation Commission in Anisminic, 72–74, 78–79, 80
  void, 79
  voidable, 79
development aspects, public law, 100
Devlin, Lord:
  Ridge v Baldwin, 24, 25, 31, 32
devolution, 271
  democratically elected legislatures, 273
  lawfulness of legislation enacted by devolved legislatures, 272
  Northern Ireland, 271, 140
  Scotland, 140, 271
  structure of settlements, 273
  Wales, 140, 271
devolved legislation:
  constitutional caution in dealing with, 281–2
  courts reviewing and rejecting, 281–82
  human rights protection, 282–83
  judicial review, 275–77
  lawfulness, 272
  nature of and role of courts, 274–83
  as primary legislation, 275, 277, 278
  role of courts and, 271
  Scotland, 274
  Wales, 274
devolved legislatures:
  constitutional limitations on, 281–83
  democratic legitimacy, 281
  lawfulness of legislation enacted by, 272
  legislative competence:
    common law constitutional limitations of, 281–82
    determining scope, 274
  Parliament and, legislative competence shared between, 278
  UK Parliament ultimate legal sovereignty, 282
Dicey, AV, 2, 6, 132, 143, 227, 228, 231, 234, 235, 237, 253
Dilhorne, Viscount, 88, 89, 90

Diplock LJ:
  Padfield v Ministry of Agriculture Fisheries and Food, 47–48
Diplock, Lord:
  adumbration of general principles of administrative law, 100, 102
  Anisminic v Foreign Compensation Commission, 71, 76–77, 78, 94
  Council of Civil Service Unions v Minister for the Civil Service, 106, 110
  Garland v British Rail Engineering Ltd, 120, 131
  IRC v National Federation of the Self-Employed, 105
  judicial review, 103, 113
  ex parte Lain, 102
  O'Reilly v Mackman, 38, 101–102
  R v Criminal Injuries Compensation Board, ex parte Lain, 108, 109
  R v Home Secretary ex parte Ruddock, 186
  rules on standing, 100–101
disapplication of statutes, implied, 133
disapplication principle, 140
disciplinary regulations, police, 16–17, 20–26, 33
discretion:
  government ministers, see government ministers
discretionary powers, 13–14, 49
dismissal:
  for cause, 13, 27, 30
  police, see police
disobeying the law:
  government ministers, 144
disregarding parts of statutes, 140
doctrinal change, 299–302
Donaldson, Lord:
  Datafin, 102, 112
Donovan, J, 18–20
downward redefinition, 232
Durayappah v Fernando, 38
duty to act fairly, 36, 37
Dworkin, R, 295, 297
Dyson, Lord, 253

ECHR, see European Convention on Human Rights
ECJ, see European Court of Justice
economic complexity surrounding EU membership, 117, 133
The Economic Development Organisation (TEDO), Egypt, see Egypt
ECtHR, see European Court of Human Rights
Edwards v Barstow, 104
EEZ (Exclusive Economic Zones), 123, 139
Egypt:
  British-owned property, sale and liquidation, 64

compensation for nationalised property of British nationals, 66
The Economic Development Organisation (TEDO), 64
  sale of Sinai Mining Co Ltd to, 64–65, 66, 67
  as successor in title to Anisminic, 69–70, 74, 80–81, 84
Sinai Manganese Co, 64–65
Suez Crisis, 63–66
Egypt Fund established by UK Government, 66–68, 71, 75, 83, 91
Ekins, R, 223, 231, 294, 295
Elliott, Mark, 204, 207, 240, 254, 265, 267–68
Ellis v Earl Grey, 150
embellishment of narratives, 8
Emery, MJ, 251
Employment Protection (Consolidation) Act 1978, 133
enforcement:
  rule of law, 259
Entick v Carrington, 2, 179
  facts and issues, 2–4
  reasons for being landmark, 4–10
Equal Pay Act 1970, 132
Equal Pay Directive, 133
Equal Treatment Directive, 132, 133
errors:
  of fact:
    Foreign Compensation Commission in *Anisminic*, 79, 82
  of law:
    decisions, 93–94
    Foreign Compensation Commission in *Anisminic*, 72, 74, 79, 80, 82
ESC (European Scrutiny Committee), 139–40
establishment, freedom of, 128
EU, *see* European Union
European Communities Act 1972, 115, 117, 131, 133–37, 141, 227, 237
European Convention on Human Rights (ECHR), 140
  AXA case, 272, 274
  Chahal v United Kingdom, 163
  Coughlan case, 196
  devolution and, 273, 274
  legislation incompatible with, 166, 176
  prohibition of torture and inhuman treatment, 163–64
  rights under, 166
  UK derogation from, 164–65, 167–68, 170
  withdrawal of, 178
European Court of Human Rights (ECtHR), 163, 179
  Chagos Islanders, 250
European Court of Justice (ECJ), 131, 132
  national courts and, competing competences, 133, 135–6

teleological approach to interpretation, 136
European Maritime and Fisheries Fund, 129
European Scrutiny Committee (ESC), 139–40
European Union (EU):
  Brexit, 138–39
  Common Agricultural Policy (CAP), 121
  Common Fisheries Policy (CFP), 116–17, 139
    legal basis, 122
    national sovereignty conflicts, 125
    reform, 129
  constitutionalism, 130
  Integrated Maritime Policy (IMP), 129
  law:
    conceptual approach to, 116
    constitutional fundamentals unalterable by, 135
    construction approach, 136
    impact on sovereignty, 115–16
    precedence over UK law, 115–16, 118, 226
    primacy, 133, 141
    UK compatibility, 120
  membership:
    academic scholarship, 132–33
    political and economic complexity surrounding, 117, 133
    public opinion, 132–33
    quotas, fishing, 117
    UK leaving, 138–39
European Union Act 2011, 135, 137
Evans v Attorney General, 5, 55, 285–86
  academic commentary, 293–95
  black spider memos litigation history, 286–89
  conclusion, 302–303
  interpretation, 295–99
  normative reasoning and doctrinal change, 299–302
  Supreme Court:
    disagreement in, 292–95
    justices' judgments, 289–92
Evans, Vincent, 83
Evershed, Lord:
  Ridge v Baldwin, 24, 25, 31–32
Ewing, Keith, 179
Exclusive Economic Zones (EEZ), 123, 139
executive:
  action if legal, 301
  court decisions binding as between parties, including, 5
  decisions on matters of policy, 48
  domination of Parliamentary sovereignty, 231
  House of Commons domination, 230, 237
  national security, entitled to wide discretionary area of judgment in, 173
  override:
    Evans v Attorney General, see Evans v Attorney General
    unconstitutional, of judicial decisions, 293
  Parliament and, relationship between, 60

power:
  checking, 55–56
  judicial review of, common law principles underpinning, 44
  subject to judicial reviews, 6
preventative orders, 178
public law jurisdiction of, 9
seeking to diminish power of judges, 4–5
sovereignty, 237
extending lifetime of Parliament, 223, 225
extradition, 162

Factortame litigation, 115–17, 149, 154–55, 156–57, 226
  aftermath, 129
  Common Fisheries Policy, 121–6, 139
  conclusion, 138–41
  facts of case in context of Britain's maritime history, 117–21
  impact on UK legal system, 129–30
  litigation, 127–8
  sovereignty in question, 131–8
failings of judicial reviews, 56–57
fair procedures, 34
fairness, 184–85, 186, 201–203, 209
  enactment of legislation, 277
  failure to observe requirements of, 38–39
  of processes, 57
farmers and the Milk Marketing Scheme, *see Padfield v Ministry of Agriculture Fisheries and Food*
Faulks, N, 19–21, 23
Feldman, David, 179
fettered discretionary powers, 49
Findlay, Re, 185–86
Finnis, John, 180, 258–61, 266
fishing:
  companies, 118
  depletion in fish stocks, 123
  EU quotas, 117
  industry sustainability, 121
  local, vulnerability to foreign vessels, 119
  over-fishing, 123, 124
  ownership of vessels, 126
  policy and negotiation, 125
  policy vacuum, 116
  quota hopping, 126, 127, 128, 139
  quotas, 129
  registration of vessels, 118, 119, 125
  Scottish vessels dominance, 139
  Spanish vessels, 127
  Total Allowable Catches (TAC), 124
flags of convenience, 125
FoIA (Freedom of Information Act 2000), 286, 289
Foreign Compensation Act 1950, 66–67, 70–72, 75–79, 82, 83–84, 86, 93

Foreign Compensation Act 1962, 75, 92
Foreign Compensation Act 1969, 83–90
Foreign Compensation Commission, 66–68
  Anisminic, see *Anisminic v Foreign Compensation Commission*
  determinations:
    Court of Appeal, 77–78
    judicial reviews of, 72
    nullity, 72–4
Foreign Compensation (Egypt) (Determination and Registration of Claims) Order 1962, 68–69, 72, 77–85
formal rules:
  rule of law compliance, 9
formalist version of rule of law, 9
Forsyth, C, 208, 223, 294, 295
Foster MP, Sir John, 86
France:
  Suez Crisis, 63–65
Fraser, Lord:
  Council of Civil Service Unions v Minister for the Civil Service, 99, 110
  R v Home Secretary ex parte Ruddock, 186
freedom of establishment, 128
Freedom of Information Act 2000, 286, 289
Frost, T, 260, 268
fundamental rights:
  protection, 9

Galloway, George, 177
Gardiner, Lord, 88, 95
Gardiner QC, Gerald, 20
Garland J:
  M v Home Office, 146–48, 149
  Garland v British Rail Engineering Ltd, 120, 131
Gaskell, N, 128
GCHQ case, *see Council of Civil Service Unions v Minister for the Civil Service*
Geneva Convention on the High Seas, 126
George V, King, 215–16
Gibson, Peter LJ:
  R v Department of Education and Employment, ex parte Begbie, 197
  R v Secretary of State for Home Dept ex parte Hargreaves, 189
Gillick v West Norfolk and Wisbech AHA, 102
Glidewell J, 97, 104–105, 106
Goldsmith, Lord:
  Belmarsh case, 169, 176
Gordon, Richard, 147
Gouriet v Union of Post Office Workers, 106
government:
  interests, rule of law equating with, 240
  law purpose to guide and constrain power of, 297

government ministers:
  accountability:
    to courts, 60, 61
    legal, 45
    to Parliament, 60, 61
    political, 45
  coercive relief against, 150, 151, 152, 154, 157–58
    Scotland, 159
  contempt of court, 144
  decisions:
    affecting interests that common law willing to protect, 55
    final powers, 57
    judicial interference with, 60
    natural justice application to, 27
  discretion, 47, 49, 51, 53
    unlawful exercise of discretionary power conferred by parliament, 43–44, 48
  disobeying the law, 144
  distinction between the Crown and its ministers, 150–54, 155, 159–60
  duties to refer complaints, 51–52
  enforcement of injunctions against, 157–58
  interim injunctions against, 144, 150
  legal accountability, 45
  political accountability, 45
  prevention of pursuit of justice, parliament's ability to allow, 50
  reasons given by, 52
  unlawful exercise of discretionary power conferred by parliament, 43–44, 48
Government of Wales Act 2006, 273, 274
Greatbatch, Bruce, 251
Greer LJ, 17
Griffiths, Lord, 10

Hale, Baroness, 8
  Bancoult, 242, 260, 268, 269
  Belmarsh case, 174, 175–76
  Evans v Attorney General, 290
  Jackson v Attorney General, 225, 226, 227, 232–34
Halifax, Earl of, 2
Hammersley, DI, 17–19
Harlow, C, 56
Harman LJ, 21–22
  Anisminic v Foreign Compensation Commission, 71
Haynes-Smith, ex parte, 29
hearings:
  rights to, 12
Heath, DS, 17–19
Her Majesty's Treasury v Ahmed and Others, 7
Heuston, R, 132, 232
Hewart, Lord, 30
Hidden J:
  Coughlan case, 181

High Court:
  Order status, failure to recognise, *M v The Home Office* Error One, 148, 159
high treason:
  warrants for arrest and committal for, 3
Hirst LJ:
  R v Secretary of State for Home Dept ex parte Hargreaves, 189
Hitcher, D, 218
HK, Re (An Infant), 36
Hodson, Lord:
  Padfield v Ministry of Agriculture Fisheries and Food, 48
  Ridge v Baldwin, 23, 25, 31, 32
Hoffmann, Lord:
  Bancoult, 242, 251–52, 256–59, 262–64, 267, 268, 270
  Belmarsh case, 171–72
  R v Secretary of State for Home Department ex p Rehman, 168, 171
Holroyd LJ, 21
Home Affairs Committee, 163
Home Secretary:
  Metropolitan Police Force overseen by, 16
Hong Kong:
  legitimate expectations and, 208
Hope, Lord, 7, 134, 219
  AXA case, 276, 277
  Belmarsh case, 174, 175
  Jackson v Attorney General, 222, 225–27, 233–34, 236, 297
House of Commons:
  democratisation, 234–35
  executive domination, 230, 237
  bipartite Parliament, 222–24
  House of Lords and, changing relationship between, 228–31
  laws passed unchallengeable, 237
  Parliament Act 1911 and, 213–15
  Parliament Act 1949 procedure, 211–12, 218
  supremacy over House of Lords, 228, 234, 237
  Transport Committee, 119
  tripartite Parliament, 222–23, 225, 229
House of Lords:
  abolition, 224–25, 229–30
  composition, reform, 230
  House of Commons and, changing relationship between, 228–31
  House of Commons supremacy over, 228, 234, 237
  legislative veto removed, 216, 228–9, 230
  reform, 214–16, 229, 230
  tripartite Parliament, 222–23, 225, 229
Howe, Geoffrey, 108
HRA, *see* Human Rights Act 1998
Huang v Secretary of State for the Home Department, 204

Hughes, Lord:
  Evans v Attorney General, 291–94, 298, 300, 301, 302
  Keyu v Secretary of State for Foreign and Commonwealth Affairs and Secretary of State for Defence, 209
human rights:
  cases, 205
  expectations and, difference between, 206
  protection, devolved legislation, 282–83
  Select Committee on Human Rights, 163
Human Rights Act 1998, 99, 140, 161, 196, 227, 237
  claimants challenging legislation, 166–67
  claims, proportionality for, 301
  devolution and, 273, 283
  incompatibility declarations, 166, 176, 179
  media response, 177
Human Rights Act 1998 (Amendment) Order 2005, 178
Hunting Act 2004, 211–12, 221, 236

illegality:
  judicial reviews of, 103, 111
Immigration Act 1971, 163, 164
Immigration Ordinance 1971, 252, 265
IMP (Integrated Maritime Policy), EU, 129
imperialism, 260, 268
imprecision of rule of law, 5, 6
impropriety, procedural, *see* procedural impropriety
Incorporated Council of Law Reporting:
  Belmarsh case, 179–80
Indelicate v Italy, 164
independence, Scotland, 139, 140
individuals:
  'authority' and, natural justice as essential element between, 41
  concern for, 209
  public interest, 207
inhuman treatment, prohibition of, 163–64
insurance companies' claims for judicial review, 272
Integrated Maritime Policy (IMP), EU, 129
interdict and interim interdict against the Crown, Scotland, 158–59
interests of justice, *see* justice, interests of
interference with rights, 14
interim injunctions against government ministers, 144, 150
interim interdict against the Crown, Scotland, 158–59
international justice mechanisms, 162
Internationale Handelsgesellschaft, 131
interpretation:
  invention and, distinction between, 296
interpretive concept, law as, 295
interpretivism, 295–96, 298

invention:
  interpretation and, distinction between, 296
investigation committees, *see* committees of investigation
IRC v National Federation of the Self-Employed, 100–101, 103, 105
Ireland:
  home rule, 215
  Sea Fisheries (Conservation and Rational Exploitation) Order 1977, 123–24
irrationality:
  judicial reviews of, 103, 104, 111
Island of Shame (Vine), 148
Israel:
  Suez Crisis, 63–65

Jackson v Attorney General, 134, 278, 286, 297
  background: the Parliament Acts, 213–20
  conclusion, 236–37
  constitutional democracy evolution, 228
    changing relationship between the two Houses of Parliament, 228–31
    Parliamentary sovereignty conceptualisation evolution, 231–32
  in context, 228–32
  Hunting Act 2004, 211–12
  judgment, 220–21
    delegated or primary legislation, 221–22
    Parliament Act procedure, exceptions to use of, 223–26
    Parliamentary sovereignty evolution, 226–28
    (re)defining Parliament, 222–23
  legal challenge, 211–12
  legal constitutionalism, 233–36
  Parliament Acts:
    constitutional crisis and the Parliament Act 1911, 213–16
    procedure, exceptions to use of, 223–26
    reneging on the deal: Parliament Act 1949, 217–20
  Parliament:
    changing relationship between the two Houses of Parliament, 228–31
    limiting own sovereignty, manner and form argument, 232–33
    (re)defining, 222–23
  Parliamentary sovereignty:
    conceptualisation evolution, 231–32
    evolution, 212, 226–28
    Parliament limiting own sovereignty, manner and form argument, 232–33
    rule of law as ultimate controlling factor, 233–36
Jacob, F, 138
Jennings, I, 132, 232
Jowell, J, 235–36
JOYS (*The Judge Over Your Shoulder*), 104

Judge, Lord, 289
The Judge Over Your Shoulder (JOYS), 104
judges:
    executive seeking to diminish power of, 4–5
judicial activism, 56, 61
judicial bodies or functions, 40
judicial confidence to depart from literal
    wording of legislation, 50
judicial constitutionalism:
    political constitutionalism and, conflict
        between, 234
judicial elements, 30
judicial interference:
    with government ministers' decisions, 60
judicial power:
    assertion of, 4
judicial protection of rights, 259
Judicial Review of Administrative Action
    (Stanley de Smith), 12–15, 99, 105, 110
judicial reviews, 2
    of administrative action, 11, 40, 103
    administrative law, 40
    basic grounds for, 103, 111, 113
    basis, common law or Parliament's
        intent as, 300
    boundaries by reference to principle, 100
    colonial laws, 258–59
    contribution to political process,
        59–61
    of determinations, Foreign Compensation
        Commission in *Anisminic*, 72
    devolved legislation, 275–77
    Entick v Carrington as, 5
    Evans v Attorney General, 289
    executive power:
        common law principles underpinning, 44
        subject to, 6
    failings, 56–57
    foundational principle, 10
    of illegality, 103, 111
    importance, 55
    insurance companies' claims for, 272
    of irrationality, 103, 104, 111
    legitimacy in democratic age, 61
    limits as remedy, 56
    M v The Home Office, 145–47, 154–7
    Padfield, see *Padfield v Ministry of Agriculture
        Fisheries and Food*
    parliamentary democracy, reinforcing and
        sustaining, 61
    of powers and discretions derived from
        prerogative powers, 100
    prerogative legislation, 264
    prerogative powers amenable to, 257–58
    principles, 26
    of procedural impropriety, 103, 111
    process-oriented focus, 56–57
    public law challenges by way of, 101
    rule of law encompassed, 9
    scepticism about, 56
    Scotland, 159
    undermining parliamentary democracy,
        57–58
judicial scrutiny of colonial law, 243–52
jurisdiction:
    courts, see courts
    Foreign Compensation Commission in
        Anisminic, 79, 82, 87, 88
    High Court in *Anisminic*, 76
    obiter dicta to *Anisminic*, 92
justice:
    interests of, 48
        judicial rather than executive, 55
    parliament's ability to allow government
        ministers' prevention of pursuit of, 50

Kentridge, Sydney:
    Bancoult, 263
Kerr, Lord:
    Bancoult, 242, 268–69
    Evans v Attorney General, 290
*Keyu v Secretary of State for Foreign and
    Commonwealth Affairs and Secretary of State
    for Defence*, 209
Kinnock, Neil, 104–105

Lain, see *R v Criminal Injuries Compensation
    Board*, ex parte *Lain*
Laker Airways, 106
Lansdowne, Marquess of, 88, 89, 215–16
law:
    coercion regulation, 297, 298
    disapplication principle, 140
    disobeying, government ministers, 144
    English:
        choice between EU law and UK
            statute, 132
    EU, see European Union
    Factortame litigation impact on UK legal
        system, 129–30
    as interpretive concept, 295
    police, relating to, 16
    private, 9
    public bodies empowerment to act within, 10
    purpose: to guide and constrain power of
        government, 297
    recorded in 'the books', 3–4
    supremacy decisions based on normative
        arguments, 136–7
    see also colonial laws, common law; public
        law; rule of law
The Law of the Constitution (Dicey), 235
Law of the Sea Convention, see UN Convention
    on the Law of the Sea
Lawrence QC, Geoffrey, 18
Laws, John, 148–49, 182–83, 185–87

Laws LJ, 134, 209
  Bancoult, 242, 258, 265, 270
  Nadarajah v Secretary of State for the Home Department, 199–200
  R v Department of Education and Employment, ex parte Begbie, 197–98
  R v Secretary of State for Transport, ex parte Richmond-upon-Thames London Borough Council, 199
  R (on the application of Bhatt Murphy) v The Independent Assessor, 200
Laws, Stephen, 178
Lawson, Neil, 21, 22
Leach, Harry, 18–19
Leach, John, 18
least restrictive means of interfering, 206
least restrictive means tests, 205–206
legal accountability:
  government ministers, 45
legal constitutionalism, 55, 231, 232, 233–36
legal illimitability:
  Parliamentary sovereignty, 234–35
legal practice, understanding, 297
legality, 6, 7–8
  assessing, 301
  identification of, 292–95
legislation:
  courts reviewing and rejecting, 279–81
  courts striking down debate, 300
  devolved, see devolved legislation
  incompatible with European Convention on Human Rights, 166, 176
  judicial confidence to depart from literal wording of, 50
  primary, see primary legislation
  undermining basis of democracy, 281
  undermining rule of law, 281
legislative competence:
  Parliamentary sovereignty and, distinction between, 278
legislative Parliamentary sovereignty, 236
legitimate expectations:
  abuse of power and fairness, 201–203
  Australia, 208
  Canada, 208
  consultations, 206
  Coughlan case, see Coughlan case
  doctrine, 98, 100, 101–102, 186
  Hong Kong, 208
  individuals and public interest, 207
  New Zealand, 208
  procedural, 187
  proportionality, 203–207
  representations, 206
  Singapore, 208
  South Africa, 208
  substantive, 185–86, 187–90
    enforcement, 181–83, 193–97, 209

libel, seditious, 3
liberal imperialism, 260, 268
liberty, USA, 8
limiting Parliamentary sovereignty, see Parliamentary sovereignty
limits to discretionary powers, 49
Liversidge v Anderson, 28
Liyange, 260, 261
Lloyd George, David, 213
local fishing, vulnerability to foreign vessels, 119
Local Government Board v Arlidge, 28
Loreburn LC, Lord, 13
Lyons, Anthony John, 17–18, 19

M v The Home Office, 4, 129–30, 143–5
  conclusion, 159–60
  contempt of court proceedings, 149, 159
    Crown Proceedings Act 1947, Section 21, 151–54
    Merricks v Heathcote Amory, 153–54
    simple solution, 150–51
  enforcement of injunctions against ministers, 157–58
  Error One: failure to recognise High Court Order status, 148, 159
  Error Two: failure to recognise the distinction between Ministers of the Crown and the Crown, 150, 153, 155, 159–60
  Error Three: interpretation of Section 21(2) to prevent injunctions or other coercive relief against Ministers exercising powers entrusted by law, 152–53, 160
  Home Secretary agrees to disobey order for return of M, 147–8
  judicial review and coercion of ministers, 154–7
  order set aside, 149
  refusal of asylum and judicial review of decision, 145–46
  return of M ordered, 147
  Scottish dimension, 158–59
  second application for judicial review and removal of M, 146–47
Macarthy's Ltd v Smith, 131
Magna Carta, 6, 253, 263
maintenance of rule of law, devolved legislation and, 279
majority decision-making:
  unfairness flowing from, 59
Mance, Lord:
  AXA case, 277
  Bancoult, 241–42, 246, 263, 266–67, 268
  Evans v Attorney General, 290–91, 292, 293, 294, 302
mandamus, orders of, 47, 53
mandate:
  doctrine, 218
  terms of, 110, 111

manner and form argument:
    Parliament limiting own sovereignty, 232–33
Mansfield, Lord:
    Campbell v Hall, 256
Marine Protected Area (MPA) around Chagos Islands, 245, 249
maritime history of Britain:
    Factortame litigation in context of, 117–21
Marshall, G, 132
master and servant, 27
Mauritius, 243–52
Maxwell-Hyssop MP, Robin, 86
McCarthy & Stone (Developments) Ltd v Richmond-upon-Thames London Borough Council, 10
McDonald v Secretary of State for Scotland, 159
Medical Foundation for the Care of Victims of Torture, 145
memory, collective, *see* collective memory
merchant fleet, 119
    see also fishing
Merchant Shipping Act 1894, 115, 118
Merchant Shipping Act 1988, 115–17, 118–20, 125–28, 134, 139
Merchant Shipping Act 1995, 139
Merricks v Heathcote Amory, 153–54
Metropolitan Police Force, 16
Milk Marketing Board, 45–47, 50, 53–54, 57, 58–59
Milk Marketing Scheme, 45–46
ministers, *see* government ministers
minority protection, 58–59
monopolies, 58
Morley, Sir Alexander, 84
Morris of Borth y Gest, Lord:
    Anisminic v Foreign Compensation Commission, 78, 79, 82
    Padfield v Ministry of Agriculture Fisheries and Food, 48, 51, 52–53, 55
    Ridge v Baldwin, 23–26, 30, 32
Morrison, Herbert, 217
Morton, J, 17
MPA (Marine Protected Area) around Chagos Islands, 245, 249
Mullen, T, 212, 233–34
Mummery LJ:
    Coughlan case, 191
Municipal Corporation Act 1882, 20–21
Murray, C, 260, 268
Mustill, Lord, 39
myths, 1

Nadarajah v Secretary of State for the Home Department, 199–200
Nakkuda Ali v Jayaratne, 14, 22, 23, 29, 30, 36, 38
narratives, 6
    constitutional, 1
    embellishment, 8

role in constitutional doctrine analysis, 6
strengthening Parliamentary sovereignty, 6
strengthening rule of law, 6
Nasser, Gamal Abdel, 63
National Assembly for Wales, 273
national courts and ECJ:
    competing competences, 133, 135–6
national security:
    Council of Civil Service Unions v Minister for the Civil Service, 97–99, 110–11
    deportation, 163
    executive entitled to wide discretionary area of judgment, 173
    preventative detention without trial of non-nationals, 161
nationalisation, 217–20
natural justice:
    in 1950s, 11–15
    administrative decisions, 37
    aliens, 37
    applicability, 31
    audi alteram partem rule, 11, 12–14, 26, 32, 35, 36, 38
    breach, 29, 34
    circumstances of cases, 37
    dismissal under police discipline regulations, 21–25
    enactment of legislation, 277
    as essential element between individuals and 'authority', 41
    exclusion in wartime, 28, 30
    failure to observe requirements of, 38–39
    ministers' decisions, application to, 27
    nemo judex rule, 35
    Ridge v Baldwin, 11–15, 21–24, 26–32
    statutory bodies, observance by, 37–8
neglect of duty, 30
Neill, Patrick QC, 76, 78
nemo judex rule, *see* natural justice
Neuberger, Lord, 5, 8
    Evans v Attorney General, 290–94, 298–302
    Keyu v Secretary of State for Foreign and Commonwealth Affairs and Secretary of State for Defence, 209
New Zealand:
    legitimate expectations and, 208
N'g Yuen Shiu, 98, 102, 113
Nicholls, Lord:
    Belmarsh case, 174
    Jackson v Attorney General, 225–26
Nield LJ:
    Padfield v Ministry of Agriculture Fisheries and Food, 47
Non-Self-Governing Territories, 247, 248
normative arguments, supremacy decisions based on, 136–7
normative discourse, 295–296
normative reasoning, 299–302

normativity of constitutional disagreement, 285–303
Northern Ireland, 139
  devolution, 140, 271
Norton, P, 215
nuclear explosions, 163

objective tests, 28
observer effect, 6
office terminable at pleasure, 27
Oliver, Dawn, 137–8
O'Neill, Con, 122–23, 125, 141
Orders in Council, 264
O'Reilly v Mackman, 38, 70, 98, 101–102, 112
ouster clauses, 72, 94, 105
over-fishing, 123, 124
overriding public interest, 187
Owen, Dr David, 105
ownership of fishing vessels, 126

Padfield v Ministry of Agriculture Fisheries and Food, 43–45, 106, 150
  aftermath, 53–54
  background, 45–46
  conclusions, 61
  constitutional architecture and, 54–55
    checking executive power while increasing accountability to parliament, 55–56
    judicial review, *see* judicial review *in this entry below*
    minority protection, 58–59
    policy not necessarily 'no go' area for courts, 55
  court decisions, 47–49
    Agricultural Marketing Act 1958 objects and policy, 50–52
    reasons, 52
  dissent by Lord Morris, 52–53
  issues, 46–47
  judicial review:
    contribution to political process, 59–61
    failings, 56–57
    undermining parliamentary democracy, 57–58
Panel on Take-overs and Mergers, 111–12
Pannick, David, 176, 229, 230
Paponette and others v Attorney-General of Trinidad and Tobago, 193–94
Parker, ex parte, 30, 32
Parker, Lord:
  Council of Civil Service Unions v Minister for the Civil Service, 110
  Padfield v Ministry of Agriculture Fisheries and Food, 47
  Ridge v Baldwin, 36, 37
  R v Criminal Injuries Compensation Board, ex parte *Lain*, 106, 108, 109

R v The Commissioners of Customs and Excise, ex parte *Cook*, 150
Parker QC, Roger, 72, 76, 78
Parliament:
  ability to allow government ministers' prevention of pursuit of justice, 50
  accountability to, increasing, 55–56
  bipartite, 222–24
  changing relationship between the two Houses of Parliament, 228–31
  common law limits on, 234
  court jurisdiction giving effect to will of, 134
  Crown and, constitutional relationship between, 4
  democratic role, royal prerogative sidestepping or ignoring, 240
  democratically accountable body, 235
  democratically elected legislature, 279
  democratisation, 237
  devolved legislatures and, legislative competence shared between, 278
  dynamic concept, 222
  executive and, relationship between, 60
  extending lifetime of, 223, 225
  as general principle of the Constitution, 227
  government ministers' accountability to, 60, 61
  intent as judicial reviews basis, 300
  limiting own sovereignty, manner and form argument, 232–33
  limiting Parliamentary sovereignty, 231
  (re)defining, 222–23
  sovereign, 222–23
  static concept, 222
  tripartite, 222–23, 225, 229
  ultimate legal sovereignty over devolved legislatures, 282
Parliament Act 1911, 212–20, 223–26, 228–30, 232–33, 236–37, 278
Parliament Act 1949, 211–12, 217–20, 230, 232–33, 237
Parliamentary authority:
  sovereignty, 131
parliamentary democracy, 59, 302
  judicial reviews reinforcing and sustaining, 61
  judicial reviews undermining, 57–58
Parliamentary sovereignty, 1–2, 222–23
  basic principle of, 279
  common law construct, 227
  conceptualisation evolution, 231–32
  as constitutional doctrine, 5
  as cornerstone of the Constitution, 235, 237
  evolution, 212, 226–28
  executive domination, 231
  justification for, 234
  legal illimitability, 234–35

legislative, 236
legislative competence and, distinction
  between, 278
limiting:
  by courts, 231
  justifications for, 235
  by Parliament, 231
  by Parliament, manner and form argument, 232–33
narrative strengthening, 6
as political doctrine, 5
rule of law and, 212, 231
  clash between, 279–80
rule of law, explained in commitment to, 293
peace, order and good governance, 263–64, 266
Pearce LJ, 21
Pearce, Lord:
  Anisminic v Foreign Compensation Commission, 78, 80, 82, 92
  Padfield v Ministry of Agriculture Fisheries and Food, 48, 58–59, 60
Pearson, Lord:
  Anisminic v Foreign Compensation Commission, 78, 79–80, 82
Peres, Shimon, 64
Permanent Court of Arbitration, 245, 249
Perreau-Saussine, Amanda, 240, 254, 265, 267–68
Phillips v Eyre, 260, 261
Pill LJ:
  R v Secretary of State for Home Dept ex parte Hargreaves, 189
Pinochet case, 169
Plaxton, M, 212
pleural plaques, 272
police:
  borough police forces, 15–16
  Brighton conspiracy trial, *see Ridge v Baldwin*
  Chief Constables, 15, 16, 33
    see also Ridge v Baldwin
  City of London Police, 16
  conditions of service, 16
  county police forces, 15
  disciplinary regulations, 16–17, 20–26, 33
  dismissal, 17
    void, 23–24, 26, 29, 30
    voidable, 23, 29, 30, 31
  law relating to, 16
  Metropolitan Police Force, 16
  suspension from duty, 18
Police Act 1919, 16
policy:
  executive decisions on matters of, 48
  fishing:
    negotiation and, 125
    vacuum, 116
  matters, 47, 48–49, 55, 81
  not necessarily 'no go' area for courts, 55

political accountability:
  government ministers, 45
political complexity surrounding EU membership, 117, 133
political constitutionalism:
  judicial constitutionalism and, conflict between, 234
political doctrine:
  Parliamentary sovereignty as, 5
  rule of law as, 5
political process:
  judicial reviews contributing to, 59–61
Portugal, fishing, 124
positivism, 298–299
powers:
  abuse of, 201–203, 209
  of colonial governance, *see* colonial governance, power of
  division on devolution, 271
  executive override, *see* executive
  prerogative, *see* prerogative powers
  separation, *see* separation of powers
precedence of EU law over UK law, 115–16, 118
prerogative legislation, 264–65
prerogative powers:
  amenability to judicial review, 257–58
  constitutional right operating to constrain, 263
  Council of Civil Service Unions v Minister for the Civil Service, see Council of Civil Service Unions v Minister for the Civil Service
  exercise, absence of constitutional limits on, 239
  judicial review of powers and discretions derived from, 100
  see also royal prerogative
prerogative relief, 135
preventative detention without trial of non-nationals, 161
Prevention of Terrorism Act 2005, 178
primacy of EU law, 133, 141
primary legislation:
  devolved legislation as, 275, 277, 278
principle:
  judicial review boundaries by reference to, 100
prioritisation, rule of law, 231–32
privacy, USA, 8
private law, 9
privileges, denial of, 14
procedural impropriety:
  judicial reviews, 103, 111
procedural legitimate expectations, 187
process-oriented focus, judicial reviews, 56–57
processes, fairness, 57
professional bodies:
  deprivation of membership, 27

prohibition, 28
Prohibitions del Roy, 6
property, deprival of, 27
proportionality, 198, 203–207, 300–302
  analysis, 187
  legitimate expectations, 203–207
  plurality of approaches to, 206–207
  principle, 103
protection of fundamental rights, 9
public bodies:
  administrative law principles to which must comply, 166
  empowerment to act within the law, 10
  justification of legality of actions, 51–52
  presumption of acting within powers, 52
public interest, 28, 50
  individuals, 207
  overriding, 187
public international law:
  decolonisation obligations, 248
public law:
  adjudication, 302
  challenges by way of judicial review, 101
  development aspects, 100
  doctrinal, 295
  executive, jurisdiction of, 9
  implied, 10
  standing, rules on, 100–101
public opinion:
  EU membership, 132–33

quasi-judicial bodies or functions, 40
quotas, fishing:
  quota hopping, 126, 127, 128, 139

R (oao Evans) v Attorney General, see Evans v Attorney General
R (Jackson) v Attorney General, see Jackson v Attorney General
R v Bolton, 73
R v Budimir, 134
R (on the application of Simpson) v Chief Constable of Greater Manchester, 194
R v Commissioners of Woods, Forests, Land, Works and Buildings, ex parte Budge, 150
R v Criminal Injuries Compensation Board, ex parte Lain, 98, 100, 106–109, 110–11, 112, 113
R v Department of Education and Employment, ex parte Begbie, 197–98, 200, 204
R v Electricity Commissioners, ex parte London Electricity Joint Committee Co, 27, 28–30, 38, 107
R (Patel) v General Medical Council, 195–96
R v Home Secretary ex parte Ruddock, 186, 187, 188
R v Horseferry Road Magistrates' Court, ex parte Bennett, 10
R v Inland Revenue Commissioners, ex parte Unilever Plc, 202
R v Lord Chancellor ex parte Witham, 55, 198
R v Ministry of Agriculture, Fisheries and Food ex parte Hamble, 188–89, 192, 200, 205
R (Bibi) v Newham London Borough Council, 199, 200
R v North and East Devon Health Authority, ex parte Coughlan, see Coughlan case
R (on the application of B) v Nursing and Midwifery Council, 194
R v Secretary of State for Employment ex parte Equal Opportunities Commission, 133
R v Secretary of State for Foreign Affairs, ex parte World Development Movement (Pergau dam case), 101
R (Abbasi) v Secretary of State for Foreign and Commonwealth Affairs, 258
R (Bancoult) v Secretary of State for Foreign and Commonwealth Affairs, see Bancoult
R (on the application of HSMP Forum (UK) Ltd) v Sec of State for the Home Department, 194–95, 196
R v Secretary of State for the Home Department, ex parte Doody, 39
R v Secretary of State for Home Dept ex parte Hargreaves, 189, 192–93
R v Secretary of State for Home Department ex p Rehman, 168
R v Secretary of State for the Home Department, ex parte Simms, 8
R (HS2 Action Alliance Ltd) and others v Secretary of State for Transport, 135
R v Secretary of State for Transport, ex parte Factortame, see Factortame litigation
R v Secretary of State for Transport, ex parte Richmond-upon-Thames London Borough Council, 187–8, 198
R v Takeover Panel, ex parte Datafin Plc, 102, 111–12, 113
R v The Commissioners of Customs and Excise, ex parte Cook, 150
R (on the application of Bhatt Murphy) v The Independent Assessor, 200
racial hatred, incitement to, 162
Radcliffe, Lord:
  Anisminic v Foreign Compensation Commission, 71
  Edwards v Barstow, 104
Ramirez Sanchez v France, 164
Raz, J, 298
recognition, rule of, *see* rule of recognition
Reed, Lord:
  AXA case, 276–77
  Evans v Attorney General, 290
  R (HS2 Action Alliance Ltd) and others v Secretary of State for Transport, 135
Rees, Stanley, 21

Rees-Mogg, Lord, 177
referendums, 137
　Brexit, 138–41
　Scotland, 140
registration of fishing vessels, 118, 119, 125
Reid, Lord:
　Anisminic v Foreign Compensation Commission, 78–80, 83, 92–94
　Padfield v Ministry of Agriculture Fisheries and Food, 43, 49, 50–51, 52, 54, 58–59
　Ridge v Baldwin, 15, 23–24, 25, 26–30, 32, 40–41
　Smith v East Elloe Rural District Council, 73
remedial orders:
　legislation incompatible with European Convention on Human Rights, 166
repeal of statutes, implied, 133, 134
representations, 14
　legitimate expectations, 206
repugnancy to any rule of English law, 256–57, 258–60
reviewability:
　prerogative powers, 105–109, 113
　see also judicial reviews
Ridge v Baldwin, 11, 184
　aftermath, 33
　conclusion, 39–41
　context:
　　Brighton conspiracy trial, 17–33
　　natural justice in the 1950s, 11–15
　　policing, 15–17
　decisions of High Court and Court of Appeal, 21–22
　in House of Lords, 22–4
　natural justice, 11–15, 21–24, 26–32
　non-compliance with police discipline regulations, 24–26
　reception of decision:
　　academics, 33–6
　　courts, 36–9
rights:
　at common law, 282–83
　constitutional, 263
　fundamental, *see* fundamental rights
　to hearings, 12
　human, *see* European Convention on Human Rights; human rights; Human Rights Act 1998
　interference with, 14
　judicial protection of, 259
　substantive, rule of law recognition, 9
Roberts, Colin, 248–49, 260
Rochdale Report on Shipping (1970), 119
Rodger, Lord:
　Bancoult, 242, 252, 263–64, 265, 267
　Belmarsh case, 174, 175
　Jackson v Attorney General, 225
Roskill, Lord, 268

Council of Civil Service Unions v Minister for the Civil Service, 110
R v Home Secretary ex parte *Ruddock*, 186
Rothwell v Chemical & Insulating Co Ltd, 272
Royal Commission on the Police, 33
royal prerogative, 7, 8
　in colonial constitutional law, *see* Bancoult
　democratic role of Parliament, sidestepping or ignoring through, 240
　existence in shadow of rule of law, 254
rule of law, 2
　colonial legislatures and, *Bancoult*, 258–62
　as constitutional doctrine, 5
　dominant position on the Constitution, 234
　enforcement, 259
　equating with government interests, 240
　formal rules compliance, 9
　formalist version, 9
　as fundamental principle of the Constitution, 144
　imprecision, 5, 6
　ingrained fidelity to, 143
　judicial reviews encompassing, 9
　legislation undermining, 281
　maintenance, devolved legislation and, 279
　narrative strengthening, 6
　outside mainland Britain, 253
　Parliamentary sovereignty and, 212, 231
　　clash between, 279–80
　Parliamentary sovereignty explained in commitment to, 293
　as political doctrine, 5
　position in constitutional structure of UK, 236
　prioritisation, 231–32
　as protector of the Constitution, 237
　royal prerogative existence in shadow of, 254
　substantive, 302
　as substantive concept, 6–7
　substantive rights recognition, 9
　substantive version, 9
　'thick' version, 9
　'thin' version, 9
　threat to, 159–60
　ultimate controlling factor of the Constitution, 233–36, 297
　values, embedding into unwritten constitution, 6
Rule of Law (Bingham), 136
rule of recognition:
　Parliamentary sovereignty and, 231
rules on standing, 100–101
Russell LJ:
　Anisminic v Foreign Compensation Commission, 76, 78, 91–92
　Padfield v Ministry of Agriculture Fisheries and Food, 47

Saadi v Italy, 163
Sachs LJ:
   Padfield v Ministry of Agriculture Fisheries and Food, 47
Salisbury convention, 217–18
Salisbury, Lord, 217, 219
Salmon LJ, 37
Sargant, Edmund, 87
Scarman, Lord, 102
   Council of Civil Service Unions v Minister for the Civil Service, 110, 257
   Re Findlay, 185–86
Schmidt v Secretary of State for Home Affairs, 37
Scotland:
   AXA case, *see AXA General Insurance Ltd v HM Advocate and Others*
   coercive remedies, 159
   Crown Proceedings Act 1947, 158–59
   devolution, 140, 271
   devolved legislation, 274
   fishing vessels, 139
   independence debate, 139
   independence referendum, 140
   insurance companies' claims for judicial review, 272
   interdict and interim interdict against the Crown, 158–59
   judicial reviews, 159
   parliament, *see* Scottish Parliament
   supervisory jurisdiction of Court of Session, 159
Scotland Act 1998, 226, 227, 237, 272, 273, 274, 276
Scott, Lord:
   Belmarsh case, 170, 174, 175
Scottish Parliament:
   democratically elected legislature, 275, 276–77
   statutory powers, 275
Sea Fisheries (Conservation and Rational Exploitation) Order 1977, Ireland, 123–24
search and seizure:
   warrants for, *see* warrants
Secretary of State:
   warrants issued by, 3
Secretary of State for the Home Department v R (Rashid), 202
seditious libel, 3
Sedley J:
   R v Ministry of Agriculture, Fisheries and Food ex parte Hamble, 188–89, 192
Sedley LJ:
   Bancoult, 242, 255, 257, 266, 268
   Coughlan case, 191, 192
   R v Ministry of Agriculture, Fisheries and Food ex parte Hamble, 209
   R (Bibi) v Newham London Borough Council, 199

R (on the application of Bhatt Murphy) v The Independent Assessor, 200
Sedley, Sir Stephen, 182–83, 185–86, 240
Select Committee on Human Rights, 163
self-regulation, 112, 118
Sellers LJ:
   Anisminic v Foreign Compensation Commission, 76
Senior Courts Act 1981, 156, 160
separation of powers, 253, 261, 267, 279, 302
servant, master and, 27
Shergill & Ors v Khaira & Ors, 267
SIAC, *see* Special Immigration Appeals Commission
Simmenthal Case, 131
Simon, Viscount, 219
Sinai Manganese Co, Egypt, 64–65
Sinai Mining Co Ltd, 63
   compensation, 64–65
   name change to Anisminic, 65
   sale to The Economic Development Organisation (TEDO), *see* Egypt
   see also Anisminic v Foreign Compensation Commission
Sinai Peninsula, 64
Singapore:
   legitimate expectations and, 208
Skemp, Terena, 83–85, 88
Slynn, Gordon, 78
Smith v East Elloe Rural District Council, 73–74
Smith and others (FC) v The Ministry of Defence, 7
Snoxell, David, 242, 244, 250, 251, 253–54
social bodies:
   deprivation of membership, 27
South Africa:
   legitimate expectations and, 208
south-eastern farmers and the Milk Marketing Scheme, *see Padfield v Ministry of Agriculture Fisheries and Food*
sovereign Parliament, 222–23
sovereignty:
   changing nature of, 134
   Common Fisheries Policy conflicts, 125
   democratic principle unconvincing as rationale for, 138
   EU law impact, 115–16
   executive, 237
   limitation, 136
   Parliamentary, *see* Parliamentary sovereignty
   parliamentary authority, 131
   in question, *Factortame* litigation, 131–8
   timeless quality, 138
Spain, fishing, 124, 127
Special Immigration Appeals Commission (SIAC), 100, 161, 164–65, 167
specific performance, 27
Standing Joint Committees, 15–16

standing, rules on, 100–101
static concept, Parliament, 222
statutes:
   constitutional, 134–35
   disapplication, implied, 133
   disregarding parts, 140
   repeal, implied, 133, 134
statutory bodies:
   natural justice observance by, 37–8
statutory interpretation:
   purposive approach, 48–49
statutory powers, Scottish Parliament, 275
Stewart MP, Michael, 84
Steyn, Lord:
   Belmarsh case, 169, 177, 180
   Jackson v Attorney General, 211, 222, 225, 226, 227, 233–34
Straw, Jack, 177
Streatfeild J, 21–22
structured proportionality, 172, 180
substantive concept:
   rule of law, 6–7
substantive legitimate expectations, 185–86, 187–90
   enforcement, 181–83, 193–97, 209
substantive rights:
   rule of law recognition, 9
substantive rule of law, 302
substantive version of rule of law, 9
Suez Crisis, 63–66
   see also *Anisminic v Foreign Compensation Commission*
supervisory jurisdiction of Court of Session, 159
supremacy, constitutional, 2
supremacy decisions based on normative arguments, 136–7
Supreme Court Act 1981, 155–56
suspension from duty, police, 18
sustainability, fishing industry, 121

TAC (Total Allowable Catches), fishing, 124
Taverne MP, Dick, 84
Taylor J:
   R v Home Secretary ex parte Ruddock, 186
TEDO (The Economic Development Organisation), Egypt, *see* Egypt
teleological approach to interpretation, ECJ, 136
teleological construction, 116
Templeman, Lord, 4
   M v Home Office, 144, 157
Templeman, Sydney QC, 76, 78
terrorism:
   crime and, links between, 162
   detention of suspected terrorists indefinitely pending deportation, 163
   financial measures against alleged terrorists, 162
   finance sources, 162
   seizure of suspected terrorists; assets, 163
   suspects, exclusion and removal, 162
Terrorism Act 2000, 163
Thatcher, Margaret, 97, 104–105, 111
The Economic Development Organisation (TEDO), Egypt, *see* Egypt
Thesiger, Frederick, 150
'thick' version of rule of law, 9
'thin' version of rule of law, 9
Thoburn v Sunderland City Council, 134
Tomkins, Adam, 180, 240, 287
torture, prohibition of, 163–64
Total Allowable Catches (TAC), fishing, 124
treason, *see* high treason
Treaty of Rome:
   Common Fisheries Policy, 122, 124
   freedom of establishment, 128
trespass, 5, 9, 10
Tribunals and Inquiries Act 1958, 67
tripartite Parliament, 222–23, 225, 229
trusteeship, United Nations, 266
Tushnet, M, 59

UK leaving EU, 138–39
ultra vires/common law constitutionalism debate, 300
UN Convention on the Law of the Sea (UNCLOS), 123, 126
   Chagos Arbitration Award, 245–46
   Marine Protected Area (MPA) around Chagos Islands, contravention of UK obligations, 249
underlying normativity of constitutional disagreement, 285–303
unfairness:
   flowing from majority decision-making, 59
unfettered discretionary powers, 49
United Nations:
   Charter, 247–48
   Colonial Declaration, 247
   trusteeship, 266
unreasonableness, 103–104
unreviewable discretionary powers, 49
Upjohn, Lord:
   Anisminic v Foreign Compensation Commission, 71
   Durayappah v Fernando, 38
   Padfield v Ministry of Agriculture Fisheries and Food, 48, 49, 60, 61
upward redefinition, 232–33
US Supreme Court:
   Entick v Carrington reference, 8
utilitarian imperialism, 260, 268

vegetarianism, 295–96
Video Recording Acts 1984 and 2010, 134
Vine, David, 248
Vohrer, B, 245–46

void determinations, 79
void dismissal, 23–24, 26, 29, 30
void/voidable distinction:
  administrative law, 34–35
voidable determinations, 79
voidable dismissal, 23, 29, 30, 31

Wade, HWR, 12, 15, 22–3, 26, 35, 36, 40, 43, 87, 88, 116, 132, 136, 144, 152–54, 160, 207–208
Wales:
  devolution, 140, 271
  devolved legislation, 274
  National Assembly for Wales, 273
Wales Bill, 273
Walker, Lord:
  Belmarsh case, 172, 174
Walton v The Scottish Ministers, 140
Wandsworth v Winder (No 1), 101
warrants:
  for committal:
    high treason, 3
    search and seizure distinguished, 8
  high treason, arrest and committal for, 3
  for search and seizure, 3
    committal distinguished, 8
  Secretary of State, issued by, 3
  seditious libel, arrest and committal for, 3
wartime:
  natural justice exclusion in, 28, 30
Watch Committees, 16, 17
  Ridge v Baldwin, see Ridge v Baldwin
Watts, Ronald, 84

Wednesbury, 103, 185, 187–88, 189, 191, 198, 204, 207, 300–302
Weights and Measures Act 1985, 134
Weill, R, 218
Wesley, Marc, 244
West v Secretary of State for Scotland, 276
White, Montgomery, 71, 83
Whitlock, William, 85–87, 88
Wilberforce:
  Anisminic v Foreign Compensation Commission, 78, 80, 81, 89, 90
William Baird & Co, 66, 71, 91
Willink, Sir Henry, 33
Wilson, Lord:
  Evans v Attorney General, 291–92, 293, 298, 300, 302
Wood MP, Richard, 86
Wood v Woad, 34
Woolf, Lord:
  Belmarsh case, 168
  Coughlan case, 191, 192
  M v Home Office, 129–30, 144, 155–57, 160
  Merricks v Heathcote Amory, 153–54
  R v Department of Education and Employment, ex parte Begbie, 197
World Trade Centre, 161, 162

Youssef v Secretary of State for Foreign and Commonwealth Affairs, 203–204, 209

Zebrugge disaster, 119
Zhou, Han-Ru, 232–33

Lightning Source UK Ltd.
Milton Keynes UK
UKHW021322030221
378171UK00004B/212